CultureGrams™

World Edition 2006

Volume 1: The Americas

This volume contains 37 country reports featuring 25 categories:

Land and Climate
History
Population
Language
Religion
General Attitudes
Personal Appearance
Greetings
Gestures
Visiting
Eating
Family
Dating and Marriage
Diet
Recreation
The Arts
Holidays
Commerce
Government
Economy
Transportation and Communications
Education
Health
Events and Trends
Contact Information

In partnership with the David M. Kennedy Center for International Studies at Brigham Young University

This book (Volume I) includes CultureGrams™ 2006 World Edition cultural reports for The Americas.

Related CultureGrams™ 2006 World Edition volumes (Volumes II, III, and IV) include cultural reports for Europe, Africa, and Asia and Oceania, respectively.

This book was printed using the following fonts: Helvetica Neue, Swiss 721, Times New Roman.

The CultureGrams™ series is published in Provo, Utah, U.S.A.

ISBN-13: 978-1-931694-93-3 (v.1)
ISBN-10: 1-931694-93-1 (v.1)

ISBN-13: 978-1-931694-97-1 (4 vol. set)
ISBN-10: 1-931694-97-4 (4 vol. set)

© 2005 ProQuest Information and Learning Company and Brigham Young University. It is against the law to copy, reprint, store, or transmit any part of this publication in any form by any means without written permission from ProQuest.

Contents

VOLUME I

Introduction v
North America vii
South America ix
CultureGrams™
    Antigua and Barbuda 1
    Argentina 5
    Bahamas 9
    Barbados 13
    Belize 17
    Bolivia 21
    Brazil 25
    Canada 29
    Chile 33
    Colombia 37
    Costa Rica 41
    Cuba 45
    Dominican Republic 49
    Ecuador 53
    El Salvador 57
    Grenada 61
    Guatemala 65
    Guyana 69
    Haiti 73
    Honduras 77
    Jamaica 81
    Mexico 85
    Montserrat 89
    Nicaragua 93
    Panama 97
    Paraguay 101
    Peru 105
    Puerto Rico 109
    Saint Kitts and Nevis 113
    Saint Lucia 117
    Saint Vincent and the Grenadines . 121
    Suriname 125
    Trinidad and Tobago 129
    United States of America 133
    Uruguay 137
    U.S. Virgin Islands 141
    Venezuela 145
Country Data Tables
    Capitals A-2
    Population and Area A-4
    Development Data A-6
Concepts and Terminology A-11
Glossary of Cultural Terms A-15

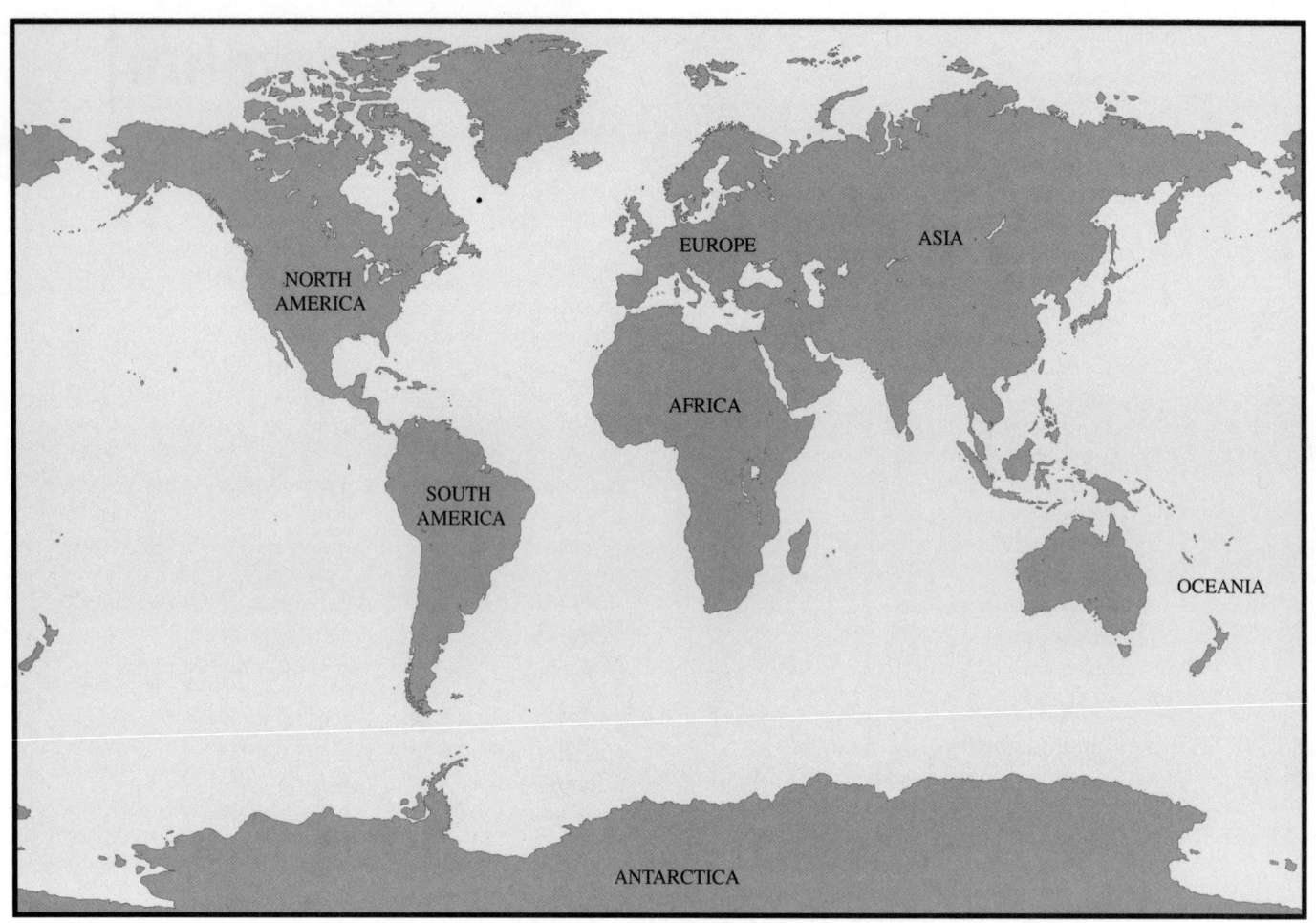

Introduction

Because learning about other countries and cultures makes a difference—to you, your community, and the world at large—we have created CultureGrams. Our reports give you a framework for understanding and appreciating how other people live and think. In a small way, they let you stand in someone else's shoes, an experience which becomes the basis for tolerance, respect, mutual understanding, and communication. CultureGrams helps you take each culture on its own terms and appreciate it for the gifts it brings to the world table: its religions and worldviews, arts and traditions, peoples and languages.

What Is a Culture?
Broadly, a culture can be said to be those beliefs, traditions, and institutions that create and mediate individual, community, and national identity. History and geography are defining elements, but they are not the only elements. Ethnicity, economics, religion, and other factors all shape, and are shaped by, a culture. This is why each CultureGram has 25 different categories: we want you to see each culture's many facets and draw connections between them.

Why Are CultureGrams Unique?
The CultureGrams World Edition is a concise reference tool created by natives and long-time residents to give you an insider's perspective. Its information ranges from mile-high views of a nation, its society, and institutions to close-up views of communities, families, and individuals. Each report seeks a balance between generality and breadth, on one hand, and detail and depth on the other. This tension lets us create multidimensional and realistic portraits of a place and its peoples. Moreover, CultureGrams are updated annually and reviewed by natives and experts periodically to ensure that the reports reflect changes in the culture.

For the Teacher
If you teach history, geography, a foreign language, ESL, or current events—among other subjects—you can use CultureGrams as the basis for in-class discussions, debates, presentations, research papers, reports, and reading and writing exercises. Use CultureGrams to help students make connections and form hypotheses about how various aspects of a culture are related. Compare and contrast the cultures of countries as diverse as Niue and Ghana. For example, you could compare family structure, look at the correlation between economy and religion, or see how the language of instruction affects education. Make your own UN or national parliament and debate social, political, and economic issues. Or have a culture fair and ask students to act as a citizen of the country they have been assigned. No matter how you use CultureGrams, you will find that your students learn more about themselves and the world than you ever thought possible.

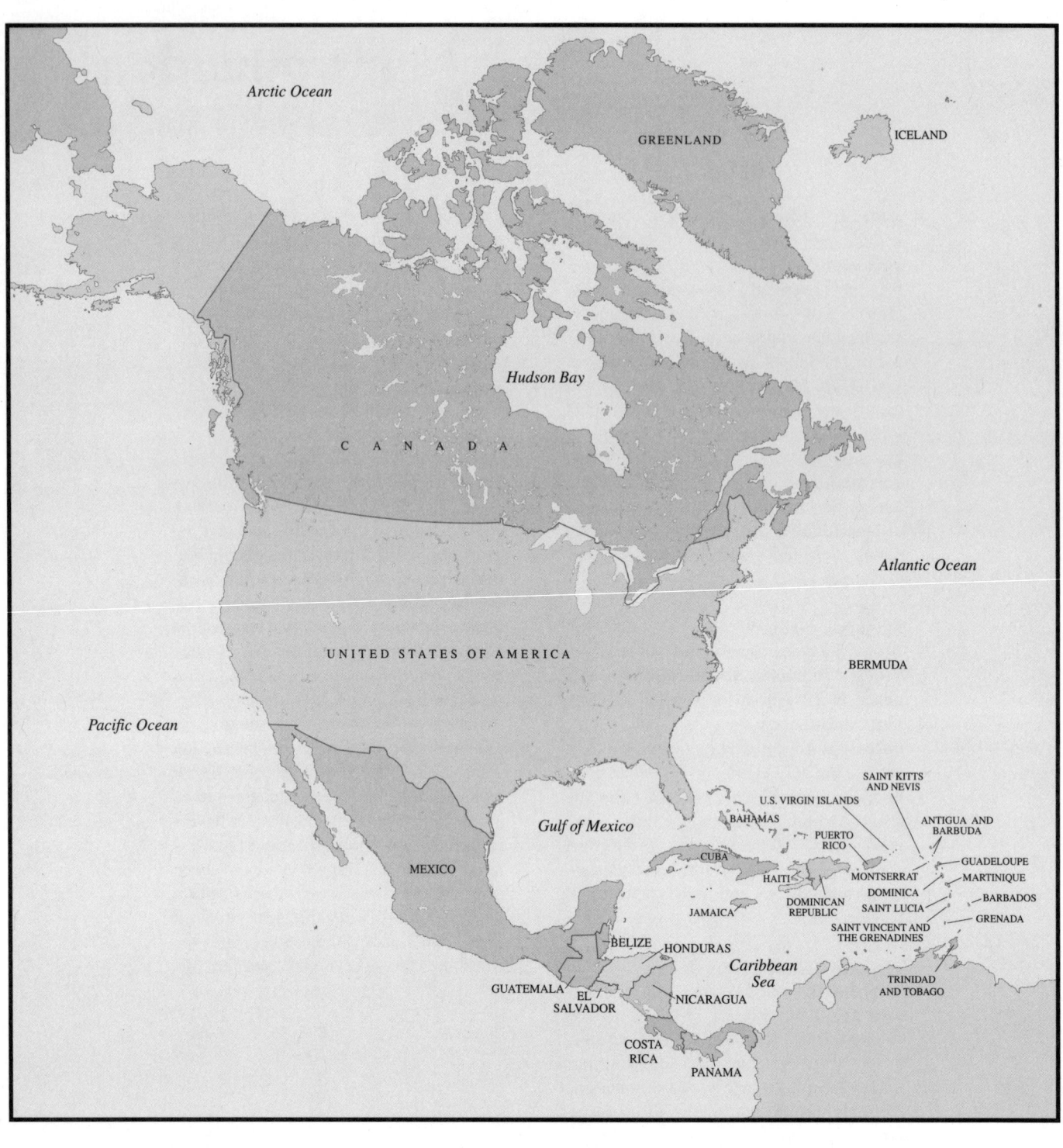

North America

AN OVERVIEW

North America, the world's third largest continent, extends from the Arctic Ocean to South America and includes just more than 17 million square miles (44 million square kilometers) of land. Major political divisions include Canada in the north, the United States of America in the central portion of the continent, Central America in the south, and the islands of the Caribbean, located between the Atlantic Ocean to the north and the Caribbean Sea to the south. The Caribbean Islands are characterized by a number of small island countries. Greenland and Iceland are part of North America geographically, but belong to Europe politically.

North America is surrounded by the Pacific, Atlantic, and Arctic Oceans to the west, east, and north, respectively. The Gulf of Mexico and Caribbean Sea, functional parts of the Atlantic Ocean, are located to the east of Central America and to the southeast of the United States of America. Major water bodies in the interior of North America include Hudson Bay in northeastern Canada and the Great Lakes, which border the United States and Canada.

The physical geography of North America includes coastal plains, hills and high mountains, and vast plains in the central portion, particularly in the United States. To the west, the Rocky Mountains extend north from Central America to Canada, making them the longest mountain range in the world. Land cover varies from tropical forests in Central America, to subtropical, temperate, desert, and montane environments in the central portion of the continent. Boreal forests, tundra, and permanent ice are found farther north. Elevation extremes range from -282 feet (-86 meters) in Death Valley, California, to 20,320 feet (6,194 meters) at the top of Mount McKinley in Alaska.

Demographically, some 458 million people populate the North American continent. These individuals belong to a rich variety of ethnic groups that are predominantly white, Hispanic, or African-American. Hundreds of Amerindian groups also exist. The primary religions are Roman Catholic, Protestant, and Jewish. Official languages include English, Spanish, and French, but immigration into Canada and the United States has brought great linguistic diversity. Most people live along major coastlines and tend to gravitate toward large urban centers. The United States of America and Canada boast some of the highest qualities of living and the strongest economies in the world. No other continent produces more consumer goods or consumes more resources than North America. The United States of America has the highest agricultural production in the world. In addition to abundant renewable and nonrenewable natural resources, this region is home to most high-technology firms and is a major influence in worldwide technological innovation.

Douglas Ramsey, Ph.D.
Department of Geography
and Earth Resources,
Utah State University

South America

AN OVERVIEW

South America, the world's fourth largest continent, encompasses an area of 6,880,700 square miles (17,820,000 square kilometers). The equator passes through the region's north, while the region's southernmost tip extends to the Antarctic. The continent's two most prominent geographic features are the Amazon River Basin and the Andes mountain range. The Amazon River is 4,080 miles (6,566 kilometers) long and has more than one thousand tributaries; its basin occupies the entire northern half of Brazil. Within the basin is found a large variety of plant and animal life, including more than one thousand bird species. The Andes, the second highest mountain range in the world, extend down the entire western part of the continent. Dry deserts, temperate pampas (grassland plains), tropical rain forests, high plateaus, and active volcanoes are other geographical features of the region.

South America's climates range from temperate to tropical. Elevation rather than location is often the determining factor in average temperature. The climate of the tropics is characterized by heavy rainfall, high humidity, and unchanging warm temperatures. Areas outside of the tropics are more arid and temperate. The variety of climates makes the region rich in natural resources. Agricultural products grown in tropical regions include sugar, nuts, cacao, tropical fruits, rubber, tobacco, and coffee. Livestock—sold for beef, meat, and leather—flourish in the pampas of the south. Many countries are also rich in minerals such as oil, copper, silver, and gold.

The combination of European, Asian, African, and indigenous cultures has created a diverse South American population. More than 80 percent of South Americans are Roman Catholic. However, Protestant and non-Christian religions have been growing significantly. While Spanish is the national language of the majority of countries, Portuguese is the continent's most spoken language due to the population size of Brazil, whose official language is Portuguese. Other official languages include English, French, and Dutch. Indigenous languages, such as Aymara, Guaraní, and Quechua, are primarily spoken among the populations of the western Andean mountain regions. Throughout the region, indigenous and other rural inhabitants are leaving their small rural villages for urban life. Of the 50 most populous cities in the world, 7 are found in South America. Large differences in standards of living are part of the social makeup of the region. South Americans are generally positive about life and express themselves creatively through music and dance. The literary talent of the region is an important influence worldwide and has resulted in several Nobel Prizes in literature being awarded to South American writers. The natural and human variety of the region make South America rich in culture and beauty.

Mark L. Grover, Ph.D.
Department of Humanities/Religion,
Harold B. Lee Library
Brigham Young University

CultureGrams World Edition 2006

Antigua and Barbuda

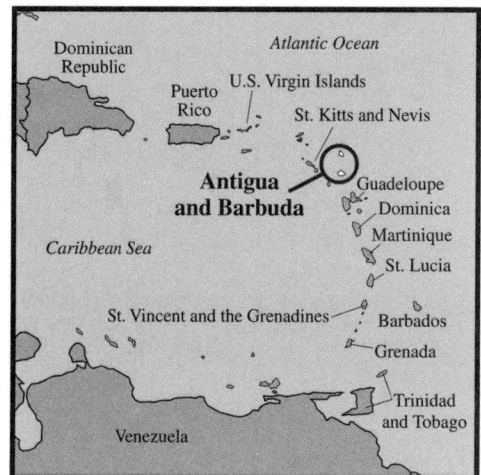

Boundary representations are not necessarily authoritative.

BACKGROUND

Land and Climate. Located 250 miles (400 kilometers) southeast of Puerto Rico, Antigua is relatively low and flat and has a dry, sunny, desert-like climate most months of the year. Boggy Peak, the island's highest elevation, at 1,319 feet (402 meters), is located near a small tropical rain forest.

Located across shallow water 30 miles (48 kilometers) north of Antigua, Barbuda is even flatter; its highest elevation is only 207 feet (63 meters). Barbuda is covered by shrubs and brush. It features beaches with pink sand, a seabird sanctuary, abundant wild deer, and plentiful lobster. Including small uninhabited islands, the country covers 170 square miles (440 square kilometers). Hurricanes periodically afflict the islands.

History. Called Wadadli by the indigenous people who maintained a vibrant culture through the 17th century, Antigua was renamed by Christopher Columbus in 1493 for the Santa María de la Antigua Cathedral in Spain. (*Antigua* is pronounced without the *u*.) A lack of water and a thriving indigenous population discouraged European settlement for many years, but English settlers crossed over from Saint Kitts in 1632. Despite attempts by the local tribes to dislodge them, the settlers persisted, cultivating tobacco, indigo, and ginger.

In 1674, Christopher Codrington came from Barbados and established the first large sugar plantation, called Betty's Hope. His success prompted other settlers to turn to sugar, and during the next one hundred years, the landscape was cleared of all vegetation to grow this highly demanded cash crop. More than 150 wind-powered sugar mills (the ruins of many are still standing) soon dotted the island. Antigua was divided into parishes, whose boundaries still remain.

The plantation economy thrived on the labor of thousands of slaves the British had imported from Africa. Colonists even used Barbuda as a slave-breeding center. When emancipation finally came in 1834, many of the freed Africans began new lives in villages that bear names like Freetown, Liberta, and Freeman's Village. But landowners continued exploitation by charging former slaves for hoe rentals and other services; this kept them working for minimal compensation into the 1930s. Reduced profitability of sugar and growing labor unrest in the 1940s led to the demise of the island's sugar industry, and by 1970, the last sugar refinery on the island had closed. Most light industries were replaced by the tourism industry.

When Britain began granting greater autonomy to its colonies following World War II, Antigua's Vere Cornwall Bird was named chief minister. Antigua joined the West Indies Federation in 1958, but that body dissolved in 1962. In 1967, Antigua and Barbuda became a West Indies Associated State. This status granted internal autonomy, with Bird as premier. In 1981, with Barbuda as a dependency, Antigua achieved full independence under the leadership of Bird's Antigua Labour Party (ALP). Barbuda attempted to remain a British colony, but the request was denied. The ALP consistently won elections, and Bird remained prime minister until he retired in 1994. His son Lester B. Bird continued the tradition by winning elections in 1994 and 1999. But Bird was defeated in 2004, ushering in a new era of politics. The nation is heavily dependent on tourism, and the government is seeking ways to diversify the economy.

THE PEOPLE

Population. The country's population is nearly 68,500 (about 1,600 live on Barbuda) and is growing slightly. Nearly half of all Antiguans live in the area surrounding the capital, Saint

Antigua and Barbuda

John's. Barbuda is sparsely populated; most people live in Codrington. Despite the island's small size, Antigua's regions are identified with distinct population groups. For example, Old Road prides itself on connections to certain family and West African lines that Freetown may not share.

Barbuda's population consists almost entirely of African descendants. Most Barbudans go to Antigua to shop, work, or live, but many Antiguans have never been to Barbuda. Antigua's population is 96 percent black and 3 percent white. One percent consists of Portuguese, Syrian, Lebanese, and other immigrants. Most white residents are foreigners engaged in business and tourism.

A crossroads in the Caribbean, Antigua historically has attracted seafaring peoples, so Spanish and French peoples have mixed with the African population. The island is also home to more recent immigrants from countries in the region. Although racial disputes are virtually unheard of, the racial groups do not mix socially. Likewise, while tourism brings thousands of people to the island (especially in winter), contact between tourists and locals is limited mostly to professional services.

Language. Most Antiguans speak English. But they also speak a dialect similar to others in the region; it is a mixture of English and various African and European languages. Commonly used words such as *nyam* (to eat) have African origins. Forms of speech vary among areas and classes. Many upper-class Antiguans look down on those who speak the dialect, but most people appreciate it for its color and expressiveness. Traditional sayings are still popular, such as *No tro way you belly and tek trash tuff um* (Don't lose the substance for the shadow) and *Wah eye no see heart no grieve* (What you don't know won't hurt you). The dialect is used often in casual, friendly situations. *T'all* means "Not at all," and *How!* means "But of course!" *You lie* can mean "You are kidding." Barbudans have their own accent.

Religion. Antiguans are religious people. Women and children attend church regularly, while men go less frequently. Most people belong to various Protestant groups. The Anglican Church, with the island's largest cathedral (St. John's), is the nation's state religion. The Methodist Church also has a long tradition in the country, and there are many Catholics among the non-black population. Various other Christian groups have facilities and churches on the island, and there are some followers of Islam, the Baha'i Faith, and Rastafarianism.

General Attitudes. The people of Antigua and Barbuda are relaxed, friendly, and warm. They take a casual approach to life, sometimes expressed in the phrase *Soon come*. This idiom reflects the general feeling that life takes care of itself—that it is in God's hands and not necessarily in humankind's. Time is also viewed on a casual basis. People are more important than schedules. It is rarely a problem if someone is late to an event or appointment.

Antiguans are extremely proud of their families, homes, and nation. This pride is manifest in the community spirit that surrounds school and church events and the displays of local talent. People are especially proud of their international cricket reputation. A number of star players for championship West Indies teams are from Antigua. National pride also emerges during the annual Carnival arts festival, when performers compete in various events.

Personal Appearance. Public dress is neat, sharply pressed, and stylish. Funerals, weddings, and other special events bring out the most elegant and formal clothes in one's wardrobe. Sunday, particularly, is a day for dressing up. At parties or recreational events, Antiguans combine vivid Caribbean colors with international fashions.

Men wear lightweight trousers and pressed shirts with colorful designs to work. Some men wear ties, and a few wear suits. The combination *shirt-jacket* (formal, embroidered, cotton shirt, cut square and worn like a jacket) is common in offices. Laborers wear work pants or uniforms. Women wear stylish dresses, high-heeled shoes, and jewelry in offices; for some occupations, they wear dress uniforms.

Around the home, men and women dress in shorts, T-shirts, and athletic shoes or sandals. Women also wear comfortable dresses. In this modest society, people wear bathing suits at the beach but cover up in town.

CUSTOMS AND COURTESIES

Greetings. Antiguans and Barbudans generally greet one another informally. *How are you?* or *Hi* is common, but friends also use variations like *What's up?*, *How you do?*, or *Alright?* The response to *Alright?* is *Okay, Okay*. The greetings *Good morning*, *Good day*, *Good evening*, and *Good night* are used at specific times; for example, *Good evening* is inappropriate after dark.

Most Antiguans address friends by first name, but they address a boss by title (*Mr.*, *Mrs.*, *Miss*). Titles are also used during professional exchanges (e.g., between a customer and a shopkeeper). Children and young people address their elders and relatives with *aunt*, *uncle*, or an appropriate familial title.

Male friends use various hand-slapping, fist-touching, and thumb-locking handshakes as well as long handshakes. An entire brief conversation might be conducted with hands clasped together. A man waits for a woman to extend her hand before shaking it.

Gestures. Although modest and reserved in appropriate circumstances, Antiguans generally are lively and expressive among friends. A conversation may include a person acting out or demonstrating something with body gestures. People usually point with the index finger, but some situations call for pointing with the hands, arms, or even the head, eyes, or shoulders. Hand and facial gestures punctuate conversation and often express something better than words can. Raising the hand, palm out, and wagging an extended index finger from side to side indicates disagreement. It is usually accompanied with *No, no, no*. A hearty "thumbs up" means things are going well. Sucking air through the teeth is called *chups* or *choops* and expresses exasperation or annoyance (at a flat tire or the store being out of bread, for example). Often, a mild *chups* provokes laughter and is a good release of tension. However, when directed at an individual, the noise is very rude. People do not like to hear their names called out in public, so a discreet "pssst" is often used to get someone's attention. A quick *Hey!* or *Yo!* is also common between friends.

Visiting. Antiguans enjoy socializing with relatives, neighbors, and friends. They use the term *lime* or *liming* for the time spent relaxing and chatting with each other. Most visits occur on weekends or after work. Appointments or plans are rarely made; people sitting in the yard or on the porch are usually willing to chat. Friendly encounters elsewhere can turn into a social visit. For example, much socializing occurs in public, whether among men meeting to repair a fishing net or among women shopping or washing clothes in public areas. Neighbors socialize while preparing meals.

When visiting someone who is inside a home, a person often

approaches the gate and shouts *Inside!* The occupant then comes out to greet the person, and the two may spend the entire visit on the porch. Friends or relatives often will be invited inside. It is polite to offer light refreshments such as fruit juice or herbal tea. Visitors often *walk with* (carry) fresh fruit from trees in their yards to share with hosts. Visits can be of any length, and hosts rarely ask guests to leave. Whole families may visit, especially among relatives. Conversation topics are seasonal (cricket or calypso dominate), but people also might sit for extended periods without talking. At more formal invitational events (birthdays, graduations, and holidays), hosts provide food and drink, and guests bring appropriate gifts.

Eating. During the workweek, people start the day with a simple breakfast of fruit, porridge, or eggs. Most workers stop for a full meal at midday, either in the workplace, at restaurants, or at home. Boys and girls usually help with cooking at home. Food is often cooked in *coal pots* (clay ovens) placed outside the kitchen. Saturday is a busy day for chores and errands, so people might buy barbecued chicken or fried fish at the market for the main meal. Evening meals are light if the main meal is eaten at midday.

On Sundays, the family has a large breakfast. Later, grand preparations precede an extended-family evening meal featuring roast pork, leg of lamb, or beef. So much food is served that plates are generally sent home with relatives for those who could not come. When fishermen bring in a good catch, a pot of *fish water* (fish stew) is usually cooked up and shared. Church picnics or celebrations bring out many cooks cooperating on a large scale, serving dishes like *goat water*, a spicy stew made with goat meat.

LIFESTYLE

Family. The extended family forms the heart of Antiguan society. Grandparents and aunts and uncles often raise children for parents who live out of the country for economic reasons. Families are large, and living space is often shared among nuclear units. No matter what the living arrangements, families maintain strong ties and gather frequently. In Antigua, people like to joke that everybody is really related to each other if one traces the line back far enough.

Bearing or fathering children is highly valued. The traditional two-parent family is the norm, but it is not uncommon for a young unmarried woman to have children and live with her parents. In such cases, the baby's father provides financial support and is encouraged by both families to be involved in the child's life. Half siblings live with their mother, and women are not uncommon as heads of households. Men may have children with different women and never marry, and some women choose to remain single parents.

Dating and Marriage. Boys and girls have many opportunities to socialize and interact, including school parties and dances, church functions, and holiday events. Couples are affectionate, but not in public. At some point in a courtship, the young woman brings the young man home for her family's approval. Parents and churches encourage marriage over other types of relationships. Weddings are lavish, with a decorated church service, formal attire, and plenty of food and dance music.

Diet. People keep small gardens in their yards, but most food is imported. Antigua is subject to drought and supports little agriculture or livestock raising. Tropical fruits (coconuts and mangoes) and vegetables (pumpkins, yams, and potatoes) grow well. There is some fishing, but hotels are expanding increasingly into spawning areas of the mangrove wetlands, threatening future catches.

The basic diet revolves around rice, *peas* (usually red beans or white pigeon peas), meat (chicken, pork, beef, goat) and fish, plus fruits and vegetables in season. During mango season, when mangoes ripen on trees by the thousands, people commonly *turn their pots down* (cook less) and eat large amounts of the fruit. At Christmastime, the bright red sorrel fruit is mixed with sugar and spices in a delicious tea. Antiguans boast that their local pineapple (Antigua black) is the sweetest in the world.

A popular dish is seasoned rice (rice, peas, vegetables, and meat chunks with seasonings). *Fungee* is a soft bread made with cornmeal and okra that is baked in a bowl. *Doucana* is made of coconut, sweet potatoes, flour, sugar, and spices, served with spicy *saltfish* (dried cod). *Pepperpot*, a spicy vegetable stew, varies from home to home. Specialties include *Johnnycakes* (sweet fried dumplings), *souse* (pickled pigs' feet), and blood sausage (called *rice pudding* or *black pudding*). Fast food is making its way into the national diet. Sidewalk vendors sell roasted corn or peanuts as snacks.

Recreation. Antiguans are passionate about sports. Cricket is most popular; games are played during a November-to-May season. Soccer dominates the rest of the year, and basketball is almost as popular. Girls are not as involved in athletics as boys are, but they do compete in netball (similar to basketball) leagues. Other social activities for women usually center on household duties or their children's activities. Dominoes and *draughts* (a form of checkers) are popular with men and boys, who play on tables set up on porches under trees. A direct link to the nation's African heritage is the strategy game *warri*. Complicated stratagems are required to capture the opponent's 24 seeds (4 in each of 6 cups). Water sports remain the domain of tourists and some in the upper class. Most Antiguans do not swim; at beach parties, they *sea bathe* in shallow water.

The Arts. Antiguans love music and dancing; anyone with a speaker system can get a party going at a restaurant or picnic. Church choirs (mostly consisting of women) are numerous and practice regularly. Calypso developed during slavery as an improvisational style for soloists and is now the most popular musical form in Antigua. Calypso music competitions are especially prominent and are long-anticipated. Aspiring musicians perform original songs. Calypsos usually carry comical, political, or social messages. Steel-drum music appeared when traditional bamboo percussion instruments were replaced by steel pans cut from oil drums. Other popular styles include reggae and *soca* (a mixture of soul music from the United States and calypso music). The Antiguan Jazz Festival attracts many West Indians every year in October.

Antiguan crafts developed around traditions brought by slaves from Africa. Folk pottery is still produced, especially in Sea View Farm Village. Harmony Hall in Brown's Bay is a center for the Antiguan arts community, and annual displays include the Artists' Exhibition and Craft Fair in November. The architectural heritage of the British is evident in the famous St. John's Cathedral, which boasts figurines of John the Baptist and St. John the Divine taken from one of Napoleon's ships.

Holidays. Old Year's Night (31 Dec.) and New Year's Day (1 Jan.) cap off the important Christmas season, which is marked by religious and secular celebrations. Easter (Friday–Monday) is as significant as Christmas. Labour Day (technically 1 May, but observed the first Monday in May) is important because of the role labor unions had in gaining national independence.

Antigua and Barbuda

Pentecost (50 days after Easter) is a time of spiritual renewal and also coincides with Barbuda's *Caribana* (Carnival). CARICOM Day (4 July) celebrates Caribbean unity. During Antigua's Carnival and national arts festival, emancipation from slavery (1 Aug.) is celebrated. This is an important time for Antiguans and Barbudans living abroad to return home. Parades, dancing, and music fill the streets for a week. The climax of Carnival is the Calypso King competition. Street dancing at dawn the next day celebrates the first morning of freedom from slavery. Christmas is celebrated on 25 and 26 December. The 26th is Boxing Day, which comes from the old British tradition of giving servants a holiday and boxed gifts. It is now a day to relax and visit.

Commerce. Major shops and businesses are located in St. John's. Most are open from 8 a.m. to 5 p.m. St. John's also has a large open-air market featuring fresh produce. Supermarkets offer a full variety of food.

SOCIETY

Government. As a parliamentary democracy within the Commonwealth, Antigua recognizes Britain's queen Elizabeth II as head of state. She is represented by a governor-general, currently James Carlisle, who also acts as head of government after elections before a prime minister is named. Baldwin Spencer currently serves as prime minister. Parliament has two houses, the Senate and the House of Representatives, each with 17 seats. The senators are appointed and the representatives are elected. The ruling party can amend the constitution. The major parties are the ALP and the United Progressive Party (UPP). The voting age is 18.

Economy. Tourism is the primary industry. St. John's is also home to a commercial deepwater harbor. While most revenues from tourism go to foreign developers, Antiguans benefit from jobs and taxes on the industry. The government employs one-third of the labor force, and tourism employs most of the rest. Some manufacturing exists, often related to the tourist industry (beds, towels, etc.). While poverty persists among some segments of the population, opportunities for advancement have expanded in recent years. Antigua is a member of the Caribbean Community (CARICOM) and the Organization of Eastern Caribbean States (OECS) and uses the East Caribbean dollar (XCD) as its currency.

Transportation and Communications. A number of buses serve the island, although private cars are common and a fleet of taxis cater to tourists. Following the British tradition, traffic moves on the left. Buses leave the station when full and do not follow schedules; they stop on request. All locations in St. John's are accessible by foot, but people avoid long walks in the hot afternoon. Telecommunications systems are modern and extensive. One broadcast television station is supplemented by satellite and cable services. There are two radio stations, and daily and weekly newspapers remain active. Internet access is readily available.

Education. Most Antiguans have had some secondary schooling. The system is modeled after Britain's. Public schools are free; more expensive private schools exist and are often church-affiliated. Schoolchildren are required to wear uniforms; parents purchase textbooks. Mandatory schooling lasts to age 16. Antigua State College provides post-secondary vocational training and college preparatory classes. Qualified students attend universities abroad; many never return home due to the lack of advanced career opportunities. Figures for functional literacy may be much lower than the adult literacy rate.

Health. The country's one hospital is adequate for minor treatment and surgeries, but serious cases may be flown to Puerto Rico. Most people have health insurance, and the government provides medical benefits. Parishes generally have a clinic with a doctor who provides basic care free of charge. Nurse practitioners and nurse midwives play an important role.

DEVELOPMENT DATA
Human Dev. Index* rank .... 55 of 177 countries
Adjusted for women.........................NA
Real GDP per capita $10,920
Adult literacy rate .... 86 percent
Infant mortality rate .... 20 per 1,000 births
Life expectancy................. 69 (male); 74 (female)

AT A GLANCE
Events and Trends.
- Former Prime Minister Bird's party, the ALP, dominated parliament from 1976 until 2004. In the 2004 national elections, the ALP won just 4 of 17 House of Representatives seats. Bird was replaced by Baldwin Spencer, who promised to help clean up corruption in the government.
- Upon taking office in 2004, Baldwin Spencer said his party had found the economy was in even worse shape than had been expected. Spencer noted that he and the UPP were trying to introduce a new, more transparent political culture that would stop fiscal corruption in the future.
- In June 2003 the U.S. House of Representatives voted to ban credit-card payments to internet casinos. The bill prompted Antigua and Barbuda to file a complaint at the World Trade Organization, saying the ban would threaten its economy. However, the U.S. Senate did not vote on the bill in 2004, leaving the law unpassed.
- By signing a 2002 initiative of the Organization for Economic Co-operation and Development (OECD), Antigua and Barbuda agreed to increase the accountability of the nation's important offshore financial services industry.
- Hurricanes are a major threat to Antigua and Barbuda's economy and infrastructure. In the past decade, Lenny (1999), José (1999), and Georges (1998) have hit the islands, as did Hurricane Luis (1995), which damaged three-fourths of the nation's homes.

Contact Information. The Embassy of Antigua and Barbuda, 3216 New Mexico Avenue NW, Washington, DC 20016; phone (202) 362-5122. Antigua and Barbuda Department of Tourism, 610 Fifth Avenue, Suite 311, New York, NY 10020; phone (888) 268-4227; web site www.antigua-barbuda.org. Consulate General, 25 SE Second Avenue, Suite 300, Miami, FL 33131; phone (305) 381-6762.

ProQuest Information and Learning Company
300 North Zeeb Road, P.O. Box 1346
Ann Arbor, Michigan 48106 USA
Toll Free: 1.800.528.6279
Fax: 1.800.864.0019
www.culturegrams.com

© 2005 ProQuest Information and Learning Company and Brigham Young University. It is against the law to copy, reprint, store, or transmit any part of this publication in any form by any means without written permission from ProQuest. This document contains native commentary and original analysis, as well as estimated statistics. The content should not be considered strictly factual, and it may not apply to all groups in a nation. *UN Development Programme, Human Development Report 2004 (New York: Oxford University Press, 2004).

CultureGrams™ World Edition 2006

Argentina
(Argentine Republic)

Boundary representations are not necessarily authoritative.

BACKGROUND

Land and Climate. With an area of 1,068,296 square miles (2,766,874 square kilometers), Argentina is the eighth largest country in the world; it is one-third the size of the United States. Its name comes from the Latin word *argentum*, which means "silver." Laced with rivers, Argentina is a large plain rising from the Atlantic Ocean in the east to the towering Andes Mountains in the west along the Chilean border. The Chaco region in the northeast is dry except during the summer rainy season. Las Pampas, the central plains, are famous for wheat and cattle production. Patagonia, to the south, consists of lakes and rolling hills and is known for its sheep. Approximately one-half of the land is used for agriculture; another 19 percent is forested.

The nation has a varied landscape, containing such wonders as the Iguazú Falls (1.5 times higher than Niagara Falls) in the north and the Perito Moreno Glacier of Santa Cruz to the south. Argentina's climate is generally temperate, though hot in the subtropical north and cold in the subantarctic region of southern Patagonia. Cool ocean breezes help keep Buenos Aires relatively smog-free. The seasons are opposite those in the Northern Hemisphere: the warmest month is January and the coolest is July.

History. Before the Spanish began to colonize Argentina in the 1500s, the area was populated by indigenous groups, some of whom belonged to the Incan Empire. However, most groups were nomadic or autonomous. Colonization began slowly, but in the 1700s the Spanish became well established, and indigenous peoples became increasingly marginalized. The British tried to capture Buenos Aires in 1806 but were defeated. The British attempt to conquer the land, coupled with friction with Spain, led to calls for independence. At the time, the colony included Paraguay and Uruguay as well as Argentina.

A revolution erupted in 1810 and lasted six years before independence was finally declared. *Porteños* (coastal inhabitants favoring a centrist government based in Buenos Aires) then fought with those who favored a federal form of government. The actual fighting did not last long, but there was no clear winner and tensions remained. Argentina finally became a unified nation in 1862. (Paraguay and Uruguay had long since become independent.)

Civilian rule was enhanced in 1912 by a law that gave all males the right to vote. The government was generally peaceful but weak and vulnerable to coups. After a military coup in 1943, Juan Domingo Perón (a key figure in the coup) emerged as the country's leader. He was elected president in 1946. He and his wife Evita gained a kind of hero status during that time. Perón ruled until he was overthrown in 1955. After a series of military and elected governments, Perón returned to power in 1973 but died in 1974, leaving his third wife, Isabel, to rule. She was ousted in 1976 by the military, which then waged a seven-year-long "dirty war" against armed and unarmed civilians in its efforts to reconstruct the Argentine nation. Between 10,000 and 30,000 civilians were killed or "disappeared" with the government's approval.

Argentina

In 1982, Argentina went to war with Great Britain over las Islas Malvinas (the Falkland Islands). The military's defeat in the war led to 1983 elections that ended military rule and brought Raúl Alfonsín to power. Carlos Saúl Menem (of the Partido Justicialista, also known as the Peronist Party) was voted president in 1989, becoming the first democratically elected Argentine president to peacefully replace another president who had been elected. Menem worked toward containing runaway inflation, privatizing state-held enterprises, and stabilizing democratic institutions.

A new constitution that lifted the ban on reelections and reduced the presidential term to four years enabled Menem to be reelected in 1995. He pursued an agenda of economic reform, but the economy worsened. A quick succession of presidents followed as several left office over the economy. In May 2002, Eduardo Duhalde became the fifth president in two weeks. He was replaced in 2003 by Nestor Kirchner. The economy has improved under Kirchner, but the country still faces major challenges, including unemployment, social and political unrest, and the large deficit.

THE PEOPLE

Population. The population of Argentina is just over 39 million (the second largest in South America) and is growing annually at about 1 percent. Roughly 90 percent of the residents live in urban areas. With more than 13 million people in its metropolitan area, the capital city of Buenos Aires is one of the most populated cities in the world. As much as 97 percent of the population descends from European immigrants (Italian, Spanish, German, Welsh, English, French, and Russian). Mestizos (people of mixed Spanish and indigenous heritage), along with indigenous people, and others comprise the remaining percentage.

Language. While Spanish is the official language of Argentina, accents vary by region. Perhaps the most distinctive is the *porteño* (Buenos Aires) accent, which has been influenced by Italian. The *porteño* pronunciation of *y* and *ll* as "sh" is particularly distinctive. For example, *llamar* (to call) is pronounced more like "shah-MAHR" than the typical "yah-MAHR." People throughout Argentina also commonly use *vos* rather than the *tú* or *usted* forms of address. Italian, German, French, and English are spoken by members of the older generation and by some of their descendants. Quechua, Guaraní, and Mapuche are languages spoken by indigenous peoples.

Religion. Roughly 85 percent of the people belong to the Roman Catholic Church, which exercises great influence over many social customs and celebrations. For example, the Argentine Constitution requires that a candidate for the office of president or vice president be Roman Catholic. Most weddings and funerals follow traditional Catholic norms. In spite of this influence, the majority of Catholics are not actively involved with their church, and Argentine society is somewhat more secularized than other Latin American countries.

Non-Catholic Christian churches are gaining popularity. Approximately 7 percent of the people are members of various Protestant churches, another 2 percent are Jewish, and the remaining 6 percent belong to other religious organizations. Religious freedom is guaranteed, and church and state are officially separate.

General Attitudes. Argentines are proud of their nation, which has risen above difficult times to become a modern and democratic state. The days of the "dirty war" are past, and today political problems are solved through democratic institutions rather than coups. People want to improve their economic and social status and provide a better future for their children, but many are worried that because of the economic decline, prosperity is becoming elusive and perhaps unattainable. Financial security, home ownership, and strong personal and family relationships are important to Argentines. Having political or social power or being close to someone who has power is an indicator of social status. Higher education has a long history in Argentina and is also considered a mark of social status and refinement.

Urban Argentines tend to be cosmopolitan, progressive, and outgoing. Proud of their educational institutions and European heritage, they consider themselves somewhat superior to their rural countrymen and to residents of other Latin American countries. Rural Argentines are more conservative.

Personal Appearance. While dress may differ considerably from region to region, it generally is conservative. People desire to be well dressed in public. In Buenos Aires, European and North American fashions are popular. Argentine women consider European designs to be more fashionable than styles from North America. Older women usually wear skirts, but the younger generation prefers dressing more casually. In other areas, dress may reflect regional culture. For example, the *gauchos* (cowboys) of the Pampas region wear traditional clothing, including a wide-brimmed hat, neckerchief, *bombachas* (wide-legged pants), and boots.

CUSTOMS AND COURTESIES

Greetings. When greeting formally or for the first time, Argentines shake hands and nod slightly to show respect. In urban areas, a brief embrace with a kiss on the cheek is common. Both men and women will greet friends, whether male or female, with a kiss on the cheek. A person might wave and smile at an acquaintance who is too distant to greet verbally; it is impolite to call out a greeting. *¡Buenos días!* (Good morning—*¡Buen día!* in Buenos Aires) or *¡Buenas tardes!* (Good afternoon) are commonly used when people pass on the street or greet friends and acquaintances. When one approaches a stranger or an official for information, it is polite to greet the person before asking questions.

When first introduced or in formal situations, Argentines customarily address people by title (*Señor*, *Señora*, etc.) followed by the surname, if known. Friends and relatives use given names. Older, respected persons are addressed by first name, preceded by the title *Don* (for men) or *Doña* (for women).

Gestures. Argentines often use hand gestures in daily conversation to supplement verbal communication. They may also use gestures to communicate with others from a distance. For example, to order a cup of coffee from a distant server, Argentines hold up an extended thumb and index finger separated slightly, with the other fingers folded in a fist.

During conversation, personal space tends to be limited, and individuals might touch each other or stand close; eye contact is considered important. Passing between conversing individuals is considered rude; if it is necessary, one excuses the action by saying *Con permiso* (With your permission). Yawning without covering one's mouth is impolite, as is placing one's hands on the hips. Pointing with the index finger is considered rude. It is improper for a man and woman to show affection in public. Men remove hats in buildings, elevators, and in the presence of women. Opening doors for and forfeiting seats to women and the elderly are common practices.

Argentines generally do not consider it rude to comment on a person's physical characteristics. For example, *negrito* (little dark one) and *gordita* (little fat one) are typical terms of endearment.

Visiting. Argentines often visit friends and relatives without prior arrangement. People enjoy having guests in the home and usually offer them refreshments, such as espresso-style coffee. In some regions, friends and relatives commonly share a ritualistic round of *mate* (MAH-tay), an herbal tea drunk from a communal cup with a *bombilla* (metal straw). Sharing a round of *mate* is a sign of friendship and acceptance.

Invited guests are not expected to arrive on time, as the individual person is considered to be more important than punctuality. Guests may arrive 30 minutes late or later without offending the hosts. Visitors greet each person in the group individually; a group greeting is inappropriate. Dinner guests often bring a small gift, such as flowers, candy, or pastries, to their hosts. Guests do not take a seat until the hosts direct them to do so. Compliments about the home, meal, or hosts' family are appreciated. When leaving, guests again address every person present, using such common parting phrases as ¡Chau! (bye!) or *Hasta luego* (until later). The hosts usually open the door for guests when they leave.

Eating. Argentines typically eat three meals each day. The main meal traditionally is served at midday. However, because of work schedules, urban families may be able to gather together only for supper, which often is served after 9 p.m. Many Argentines also enjoy an afternoon teatime, which includes a cup of tea and a snack.

Diners eat in the continental style, with the fork in the left hand and the knife in the right. It is considered polite to keep both hands (but not elbows) above the table, not in the lap. Using a toothpick in public is considered bad manners, as is blowing one's nose, talking with one's mouth full, or clearing one's throat at the table. Eating in the street or on public transportation is inappropriate. Tipping is not required but is becoming customary in many restaurants.

LIFESTYLE

Family. Urban families tend to be rather small, averaging two children, but rural families are larger. The responsibility of raising children and managing household finances falls heavily on the mother, who, in turn, exerts great influence on family decisions. More women are working outside the home, but they still comprise only about one-third of the workforce. Men tend to work long hours, often not coming home before 9 p.m. Children are central to the family and receive a great deal of attention. Families will sacrifice much to give their children a good education. Until 1987, divorce was illegal in Argentina, but it is now legal and on the rise.

As in most Latin American countries, Argentines have two family names. The last name is the mother's family name. The second-to-last name is the father's family name and acts as a surname. For example, Joaquín Martínez Goyena would be called Joaquín Martínez.

Dating and Marriage. Group activities between boys and girls begin at about age 15, when girls celebrate their most important birthday (*cumpleaños de quince*), which ends their childhood. A favorite activity of young couples is dancing. Young people also play sports, dine out, and go to movies. Serious relationships develop slowly over several years; most couples marry between 23 and 27 years of age. Weddings are often elaborate, containing three events: a civil ceremony, a church wedding, and a large reception with dinner and dancing.

Diet. Italian food, especially pasta, is the primary cuisine of most Argentines. French foods are widely available. Argentines traditionally have eaten more beef per capita than any other people in the world. Because the country is a major beef producer, domestic prices are usually low enough for most people to eat beef every day. Road and construction companies are known to provide workers access to portable grills for use at lunchtime. A favorite way to entertain is the weekend *asado* (barbecue). Other common foods include *empanadas* (meat or vegetable turnovers) and baked, stuffed beef. Lamb, in addition to beef, is common fare in Patagonia. In northern provinces, a preferred winter stew is *locro* (made of meat, corn, and potatoes). In the summer, particularly in the north, people drink *tereré*, a cold version of *mate* mixed with lemonade. Local wines and soft drinks are also popular. Ice cream is a year-round favorite, and *Heladerías* (ice cream shops) generally offer more than 60 flavors. The average diet also includes chicken and a wide variety of fruits and vegetables.

Recreation. *El pato* (the duck) is a national sport in which players on horseback compete to toss a six-handled ball into a high basket. The game originated in Las Pampas, where it was initially a violent sport played with a leather-stuffed duck instead of a ball. Children and adults alike enjoy *fútbol* (soccer). A typical weekend *asado* often includes a game of *fútbol*. Other popular sports include basketball, volleyball, and rugby. Horse racing, field hockey, tennis, and polo are enjoyed by the upper class. In their leisure time, Argentines also enjoy watching television, reading, playing cards, relaxing with friends, and going to movies. Older men often play chess or *bochas* (lawn bowling) in public squares.

The Arts. European culture has strongly influenced Argentine art and music, particularly symphonic music and operas. Buenos Aires is home to a fine opera house (the *Colón*). Native American influence is evident in folk arts, including horn-carving, silver work, leather work, ceramics, and weaving. The National Foundation for the Arts is leading a movement to preserve these crafts.

The tango (the music and the dance) originated in Argentina. For years it has been more popular outside of Argentina than among Argentines, who prefer dancing and listening to salsa and other types of music from the United States, Argentina, or Central America. However, the tango is enjoying a revival among some young adults. The guitar, the violin, and the *bandoneón* (similar to an accordion) accompany the dancers.

Representing bravery, freedom, and self-sufficiency, the *gaucho* (cowboy) is an important Argentine symbol and a frequent subject in painting and literature. *El gaucho Martín Fierro* (1872), the national epic poem, describes *gaucho* life. *Gaucho* themes were also incorporated into classical music by composers in the early 20th century.

Holidays. Argentines celebrate religious holidays more festively than national holidays, using the latter for leisure time or to do household repairs. On Christmas Eve, the extended family gathers at 9 p.m. for dinner, music, and often dancing. Candies are served just before midnight, when fireworks displays begin. The evening also includes opening gifts from *Papá Noel* (Father Christmas). New Year's Day is marked with fireworks as well. Other holidays include Good Friday and Easter; Labor Day (1 May); Anniversary of the May Revolution (25 May); Malvinas Day (10 June); Flag Day (20 June); Independence Day (9 July); Death of General José de San Martín, who is known as "the liberator" of Peru, Chile,

Argentina

and Argentina for his defeat of the Spanish in 1812 (17 Aug.); Student Day (21 September—first day of spring, marked by students gathering in parks for picnics and soccer); and Columbus Day (12 Oct.).

Commerce. In Buenos Aires, stores generally open at 9 a.m. and close at 8 p.m. In other cities, they open weekdays at 8 a.m., close for lunch between noon and 3 or 4 p.m., and remain open until 8 p.m. On Saturday, stores close around 1 p.m. Offices typically are open between 9 a.m. and 6 p.m. Banks generally open from 10 a.m. to 3 p.m. Restaurants open their doors for dinner around 9 p.m.

Supermarkets and malls are becoming more common in urban areas. However, most Argentines still buy many basic items at neighborhood shops (*almacenes* or smaller *kioskos*).

SOCIETY

Government. The Argentine Republic has 23 provinces and 1 federal district (Buenos Aires). The executive branch consists of a president, vice president, and cabinet. The president (currently Nestor Kirchner) is both chief of state and head of government. The National Congress has two houses: a 72-seat Senate and a 257-seat Chamber of Deputies. Members of the independent Supreme Court are appointed by the president. The voting age is 18.

Economy. Agriculture has always been the mainstay of the Argentine economy, although it employs a decreasing percentage of the population. Argentina is famous for its livestock and is one of the world's largest exporters of beef, hides, and wool. The country also exports large amounts of wheat, corn, and flaxseed, as well as soybean and cotton. Important industries include food processing, meat packing, motor vehicles, consumer goods, textiles, chemicals, printing, and metallurgy.

Former president Menem's reforms stimulated economic growth throughout the 1990s. Inflation decreased from 3,000 percent to less than 1 percent, and foreign investment increased. However, an economic recession began in tandem with the global emerging markets crisis in 1998. Conditions worsened as Brazil, Argentina's largest trading partner, devalued its currency by more than 40 percent in January 1999. The loss of exports and foreign capital plunged Argentina into recession. In 2002, the government defaulted on its loans; the currency board (in which the *peso* was pegged to the U.S. dollar) collapsed, and the *peso* rapidly devalued; unemployment skyrocketed; and more than half the population slipped into poverty. Although the economy has since become more stable, leaders must still manage the nation's huge foreign debts.

Transportation and Communications. Transportation and communications systems are well developed. While Argentines have access to private cars, taxis, subways, and trains, buses generally are the favored form of intra-city transportation. A few people ride motorcycles, but bicycles are reserved for recreation. Airlines link major cities in Argentina and neighboring countries. Buenos Aires is the most important seaport. Televisions and telephones are increasingly common, and service is improving. Postal service is extensive but not always reliable. Newspapers are widely available and often represent a defined ideological perspective. Internet use is growing rapidly; many households have internet access.

© 2005 ProQuest Information and Learning Company and Brigham Young University. It is against the law to copy, reprint, store, or transmit any part of this publication in any form by any means without written permission from ProQuest. This document contains native commentary and original analysis, as well as estimated statistics. The content should not be considered strictly factual, and it may not apply to all groups in a nation. *UN Development Programme, Human Development Report 2004 (New York: Oxford University Press, 2004).

DEVELOPMENT DATA
Human Dev. Index* rank . . . . 34 of 177 countries
　Adjusted for women . . . . 36 of 144 countries
Real GDP per capita $10,880
Adult literacy rate . . . . 97 percent (male); 97 (female)
Infant mortality rate . . . . 16 per 1,000 births
Life expectancy . . . . 71 (male); 78 (female)

Education. School is compulsory and free from ages six through fourteen. Secondary and higher education are also free but require an entrance examination. Nearly three-fourths of all eligible students are enrolled in secondary schools. Argentines may seek higher education at many national and private universities, as well as at teacher-training colleges, vocational schools, and other institutions. Argentina's adult literacy rate is one of the highest in Latin America. Most middle-class Argentines are educated in state-subsidized parochial schools.

Health. Argentines enjoy relatively good health and have access to both public and private healthcare facilities. Public hospitals provide care for citizens free of charge. The most modern facilities are found in Buenos Aires. Care is less reliable and less available in rural areas. Trade unions often provide health services for their members. Access to safe water and sanitation is still lacking in some rural areas and in suburban shantytowns.

AT A GLANCE
Events and Trends.
- Argentina's economy was looking comparatively healthy in December 2004. The economy had grown by about 9 percent in the previous year, and unemployment had dropped to about 13 percent. However, the biggest challenge was still reaching an agreement on how to pay about US$100 billion in foreign debts.
- In April 2004, an arrest warrant was issued for former president Carlos Menem, who had been living in Chile for more than a year. He returned to Argentina in December, after promising that he would not flee from Argentine charges of fraud and embezzlement that may have occurred during his presidency.
- In December 2004, the stock market in Argentina hit its highest ever level since opening in 1986. Argentine stocks had already gained more than 70 percent in 2003, following the economic collapse of 2002.
- In May 2003, Nestor Kirchner was sworn in as president after a close race with former president Carlos Menem. Since taking office, Kirchner has made drastic changes, including attempting to restructure the national debt and pushing to prosecute military officers accused of human-rights abuses during the "dirty war."

Contact Information. Embassy of Argentina, 1600 New Hampshire Avenue NW, Washington, DC 20009; phone (202) 238-6400. Tourist Information, 12 West 56th Street, Fifth Floor, New York, NY 10019; phone (212) 603-0443; web site www.turismo.gov.ar/eng/menu.htm.

ProQuest Information and Learning Company
300 North Zeeb Road, P.O. Box 1346
Ann Arbor, Michigan 48106 USA
Toll Free: 1.800.528.6279
Fax: 1.800.864.0019
www.culturegrams.com

CultureGrams™ World Edition 2006

Commonwealth of the Bahamas

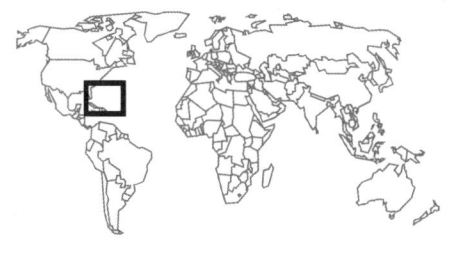

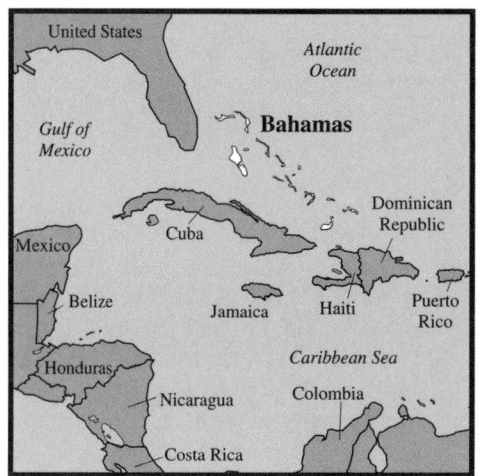

Boundary representations are not necessarily authoritative.

BACKGROUND

Land and Climate. The Commonwealth of the Bahamas consists of roughly 700 islands and 2,500 cays spread across more than 100,000 square miles (259,000 square kilometers) of the western Atlantic Ocean. The nation's total land area is 5,353 square miles (13,860 square kilometers), a little larger than the state of Connecticut. Only about 30 islands are inhabited. New Providence Island, just 21 miles long (34 kilometers) and 7 miles wide (11 kilometers), is home to the capital, Nassau, and a majority of the nation's population. All other islands besides New Providence are collectively known as the Family (or Out) Islands.

Most islands are flat with low rocky ridges; the nation's highest point, Mount Alvernia on Cat Island, is only 206 feet (63 meters) above sea level. The islands are surrounded by coral reefs and clear, shallow water. The sea floor near the islands can be seen from the surface of the water, a feature that gave the islands their name (from *baja mar*, Spanish for "shallow sea"). The islands' wildlife includes flamingos, parrots, iguanas, and a variety of exotic underwater animals.

Situated in the trade wind belt, the Bahamas experiences warm temperatures year-round. From June to September, the hottest months, the average daily high temperature in Nassau is 88°F (31°C). During the coldest months of January and February, the average is 77°F (25°C). Summer is the rainy season, when daily rainfall averages nearly 7 inches (18 cm) in Nassau. Climate is fairly uniform throughout the islands, although northern islands receive more rainfall and are sometimes subject to winter cold fronts from North America.

History. The Lucayans (the word means "island people"), a branch of the Arawak tribe, settled the islands now known as the Bahamas between A.D. 600 and 800. Columbus met them on his first landing in the New World in 1492. The Lucayans soon became victims of Spanish slave raids, and they had no resistance to the influenza and measles the Spaniards brought. The entire Lucayan population was wiped out by 1515.

The islands remained uninhabited until 1647, when English religious dissidents from Bermuda settled on Eleuthera. Britain established the Bahamas as a colony after a larger settlement was founded on New Providence Island during the mid-1660s. Pirates flocked to Nassau because of its proximity to the routes of Spanish treasure ships. When Britain restored control in 1718, many pirates accepted the amnesty that was offered and became citizens of the fledgling colony.

The Bahamas remained loyal to Britain during the American Revolution, after which many loyalists moved to the Bahamas to stay under the British flag. The new colonists brought their slaves with them, increasing the number of people of African ancestry from one-half of the total population in 1770 to three-fourths by 1800. In 1834, Bahamian slaves were emancipated along with slaves throughout the British Empire. However, with no land provided to the newly-freed population, and without political rights or access to education, they continued to work for whites and lived in a form of pseudo-slavery after their emancipation.

The colony prospered only during times when political and economic conditions in the United States allowed it to use its location to engage in the smuggling of illegal goods (such as Confederate cotton during the U.S. Civil War and liquor during the Prohibition). Experiments with tourism were only moderately successful until after World War II, when greater accessibility from the U.S. mainland led to the rapid growth of the industry. Hotels were built, new jobs became available, and

Bahamas

U.S. dollars flowed to the islands. However, the minority white population—which controlled the government and the hotels, restaurants, and stores—received most of the new prosperity. The Progressive Liberal Party (PLP), formed in the 1950s to champion the cause of the black majority, gained control of the government in 1967. Under the leadership of Prime Minister Lynden Pindling, the new government improved educational and economic opportunities for the black majority. The PLP also began working to secure the colony's independence, which Britain granted in 1973.

As tourism continued to grow—and an increasing number of people shared in the new nation's wealth—a black middle class gradually emerged. During the 1990s, the government encouraged greater foreign investment, spurring further development of the tourism infrastructure. Now, with more than 3.5 million visitors spending nearly $2 billion in the Bahamas each year, tourism remains the dominant sector of the nation's economy and a powerful influence on Bahamian society.

THE PEOPLE

Population. The population of the Bahamas is about 300,000, growing at an annual rate of slightly less than 1 percent. Some sources estimate that 85 percent of the population is of African descent, 12 percent is of European descent, and the remainder is of Asian and Hispanic descent. However, the Bahamian government does not track this information because many Bahamians do not view themselves in terms of one ethnic category. Immigration from Caribbean nations, particularly Haiti, has swelled in recent years. Roughly 70 percent of Bahamians live on New Providence Island, with the balance scattered throughout the roughly 30 other inhabited islands of the archipelago. Following Nassau, the largest urban center is Freeport on Grand Bahama Island.

Because of the nation's small size and population—as well as a socio-economic homogeneity brought about by a large middle class—many Bahamians know each other. People meeting for the first time often share mutual acquaintances. This creates a small-community atmosphere throughout the entire nation.

Language. Bahamians speak English, often with distinctive Bahamian accents or dialects that include unique idioms or expressions such as *He done reach* to mean "he has arrived." The Bahamas's proximity to the United States has resulted in a significant influence of American English phrases. Upper class urban Bahamians sometimes speak with a British accent. Immigrants from Haiti speak Haitian Creole, a Haitian version of French.

Religion. Most Bahamians are Protestants. Evangelical denominations, such as the Baptists and the Church of God, are growing the fastest. The Catholic Church has also grown in recent years due in part to the influx of Haitian migrants. Today, 32 percent of Bahamians are Baptist, 20 percent are Anglican, 19 percent are Roman Catholic, 6 percent are Methodist, 6 percent belong to the Church of God, and 12 percent are adherents of other Protestant religions. The remaining 5 percent belong to other religions or have no declared religion.

Most Bahamians are serious about their religious beliefs, and the churches play an important role in their members' lives, with several services each week and frequent social activities, such as picnics at the beach on Sunday afternoons. Church leaders regularly comment on, and often influence, government decisions.

General Attitudes. Bahamians are generally happy people who enjoy the simple pleasures of social contact. The atmosphere of the islands is laid-back, and people take time to talk to friends and strangers, even if doing so diverts them from their schedule. People love to throw parties and are typically gregarious and spontaneous. Bahamians value a good sense of humor, are not easily upset, accept both adversity and good fortune calmly, and do not get overly anxious about circumstances over which they have little control.

Bahamians, particularly younger people, value education and hard work. The desire to improve one's financial circumstances through education and employment is sometimes countered by pressure from others not to act above one's station in life. This tension is often described by the phrase *Crab in a crab bucket*, meaning "like a crab trying to escape from a bucket being pulled down by the other crabs."

Personal Appearance. Bahamians wear Western-style clothing appropriate for the warm climate of the islands. Styles are casual and shorts predominate on the Family Islands, but clothing is typically more formal in Nassau. Men who work at Nassau's banks, businesses, and government offices wear business suits; women wear dresses, stockings, and high heels. School children wear uniforms, which typically include pants for boys, skirts for girls, and white shirts for both. On Sundays, everyone wears their best clothing, including suits for men and elaborate hats and brightly colored dresses for women.

CUSTOMS AND COURTESIES

Greetings. Exchanges of greetings are often casual and informal, but can also mimic more formal British and American patterns for those in the middle or upper classes. A typical casual black Bahamian greeting is *OK*, meaning "Hello, I'm OK, how are you?" *Hey man, what's happ'n* is another common greeting, and is used informally by both black and white Bahamians. To show respect, one uses the greetings *Good morning*, *Good day*, and *Good afternoon*, accompanied by the proper form of address and surname, as in "Good day, Mr. Thompson." On some of the Family Islands, it is more common to use the proper form of address with the given name rather than the surname, as in "Good day, Miss Mariah."

Gestures. Bahamians are generally unreserved when greeting or talking. They expect enthusiastic smiles and warm body language, including hugs, handshakes, and pats on the back. People frequently gesture when engaged in conversation, and facial expressions are animated. Those who cross their arms, avoid physical contact, or look too serious generally give a negative impression. A common gesture is to *suck teeth* (making a sucking noise with parted lips) to express contempt or disgust. To add emphasis, one will tip the head back slightly once or twice while making the noise.

Visiting. Bahamians tend to arrive late to scheduled visits, often an hour or two, and will stay as late as possible. Conversation is usually jovial. Bahamians love to discuss religion and politics, especially during election years.

Sunday is an important day for visiting family. Extended families often get together, generally after church, to eat a large meal. Many Bahamians enjoy a leisurely Sunday afternoon drive, which offers an opportunity to drop in at friends' homes. Arranging the visit beforehand is rarely expected. Guests who visit enjoy the custom of taking leftover food home after a meal.

Eating. Although mealtime is an important occasion for family interaction, traditional sit-down family meals are reserved mainly for Sundays. Home cooking is still generally preferred, but U.S. influence has brought fast food into the average household at least twice a week. Bahamian food is generally high in cholesterol and calories; more than half of the population may be considered overweight. International fare is available at restaurants in Nassau and Freeport. Tipping is customary and a 15 percent gratuity is generally automatically added.

LIFESTYLE

Family. The Bahamian family has traditionally been large (averaging between 6 and 10 children), but in recent years the trend has been toward smaller families. Today, most women have only two or three children. More than half of all households are headed by single mothers, due primarily to the practice of *sweethearting*, in which a man fathers children with multiple women. It is common for men to cheat on their spouses, and as many as 70 percent of all births are out of wedlock. These children are referred to as *outside children*, though there is no stigma associated with the title. Men often fail to provide financial support for them after the relationship with the mother has ended, and women frequently have *sweetheart* relationships to secure financial support for children from previous relationships. Because so many women raise their families alone, grandparents usually play an active role in caring for children.

Dating and Marriage. Relationships between young Bahamians often develop through school interaction. Most Bahamians espouse conservative religious values. In practice, however, society is much less rigid, and teenage pregnancy is common. The practice of *sweethearting* is less widespread among upper-class couples, who typically court between one and three years before marrying.

Marriage ceremonies are held in churches. Those attending the wedding wear tuxedos or elaborate gowns. The event is usually preceded by a bridal shower, in which the bride receives gifts to set up the new household. Because most couples today marry later in life than people of previous generations, couples tend to make all wedding decisions and finance the event themselves, rather than rely on family members.

Diet. The Bahamian diet is rich in flavor and calories. For breakfast, Bahamians often eat grits with a main dish of fish, corned beef, or sausage. Lunch and dinner are typically heavy meals consisting of steamed or fried meat served with *peas n' rice* (rice combined with *pigeon peas*, a type of bean), coleslaw, potato salad, or baked macaroni and cheese.

The local delicacy is conch (a large mollusk; pronounced "konk"), which is eaten fresh but called scorched conch (partially diced and marinated with limejuice). Conch can also be used to make conch salad (diced and marinated with sour orange or lime juice, and mixed with chopped tomatoes, peppers, and onions), cracked conch (tenderized by a mallet and fried), or a spicy chowder. A wide variety of local fish (including snapper, grouper, and wahoo) are baked, fried, broiled, grilled, or stewed. Bahamians of all income brackets enjoy these local foods. Chicken, the most popular meat, is fried, grilled, or used to make a spicy soup or stew called *chicken souse*.

Favorite desserts include potato bread, coconut and pineapple tarts, guava and coconut *duff* (pudding), and fresh coconut pie. *Peanut cake* (a form of peanut brittle) and poached peanuts are common snacks.

Recreation. The sailing of workboats is the national sport. In the past, these boats were used primarily for fishing, and races were held as a means of raising money for their upkeep. Now the boats are maintained only for racing. Although most people do not participate directly in the sport, races are popular spectator events. Food, music, and dancing accompany the races, and large crowds flock to beaches for weekend competitions and several major annual regattas. For many of the Family Islands, an annual regatta is the year's premier social and economic event. The Family Island Regatta, the nation's largest competition, is held in Exuma around Easter. Soccer, basketball, track-and-field, volleyball, golf, cricket, and baseball are other popular sports.

The islands' beautiful beaches and clear water make water sports and beach picnics favorite activities. People also enjoy listening to music and dancing. Going to the movies is popular in Nassau. Movie theaters do not exist on many of the Family Islands, so people rely on satellite dishes or videotapes to enjoy films. Dominoes, often enjoyed outdoors under a shade tree, is a popular game among men of all ages.

The Arts. Although pop music from the United States is listened to most frequently, traditional Bahamian music is still popular. Goatskin drums, saws, and maracas provide a blend of island rhythms known as *goombay* music or *rake n' scrape*. Caribbean calypso and steel drum music is also common. *Soca* music—which combines calypso with U.S. soul music—and *meringue* from the Dominican Republic are the most popular styles of dance music. Music played during the New Year's Junkanoo festival has a heavy beat and utilizes percussion instruments such as the goatskin drum, maracas, and the tambourine, punctuated by blasts on the whistle and horn. Many Bahamians enjoy singing in evangelical church choirs.

Holidays. Public holidays include New Year's Day; Good Friday; Easter Monday; Whitmonday (seventh Monday after Easter); Labour Day (first Friday in June); Independence Day (10 July); Emancipation Day (often called August Monday, celebrated the first Monday in August), which commemorates the end of slavery; Discovery Day or National Heroes Day (12 Oct.); Christmas, and Boxing Day (26 Dec.), a traditional British holiday.

One of the nation's most important cultural events is the festival of Junkanoo. Originated by slaves as a New Year's celebration, Junkanoo was discouraged—and sometimes banned—by the white colonial governments. Since the advent of black majority rule in 1967, Junkanoo has been promoted as a manifestation of black Bahamian culture. The holiday is celebrated with music and Mardi Gras-style parades on Boxing Day and New Year's Day. Parade participants walk along Nassau's Bay Street dressed in colorful and elaborate costumes.

Commerce. Nassau and Freeport are urban centers with well developed retail business. Large supermarkets are common, but the fish and produce market at Potter's Cay in Nassau is still an active place where locally grown vegetables and fresh grouper and conch can be purchased in stalls or directly from the boats. Almost all foods sold at supermarkets are imported, making most items about 50 percent more expensive than in the United States. On the Family Islands, retail distribution is not as well developed and smaller grocery stores predominate. Selection is more limited than in Nassau, prices are generally higher, and stores may be closed for an hour for lunch. Most stores throughout the islands are closed on Sundays.

SOCIETY

Government. The Bahamas, a constitutional monarchy with Queen Elizabeth II as its nominal head of state, is an indepen-

Bahamas

dent member of the Commonwealth of Nations. The governor-general (currently Dame Ivy Dumont) acts as the official representative of the Queen. The prime minister (currently Perry Christie), appoints the governor-general and must command a majority in the House of Assembly. The 40 members of the House are elected to five-year terms. General elections are called by the prime minister and must be held at least once every five years. Members of the 16-seat Senate are appointed to five-year terms by the governor-general in consultation with the prime minister and the opposition party leader.

Economy. Tourism is the engine of the Bahamian economy. The sector employs half of the workforce, produces three-fourths of foreign exchange earnings, and supports a per capita GDP typically exceeded in the Western Hemisphere only by the United States and Canada. Most tourist infrastructure is located in Nassau, but tourism is also strong in the Family Islands, where smaller hotels and resorts predominate. This has brought good jobs and middle-class lifestyles to remote parts of the nation. Because the industry is dependent on U.S. visitors, it sometimes suffers during slumps in the U.S. economy. Financial services comprise the second largest economic sector. Fishing is also important, particularly on the Family Islands.

The Bahamian dollar (BSD) is pegged to the value of the U.S. dollar. This simplifies currency exchange for U.S. tourists as well as for Bahamians, who make frequent shopping trips to the United States to buy goods unavailable in the Bahamas or to buy items that are cheaper in the United States, such as clothing, household goods, and automobiles.

Transportation and Communications. Residents of Nassau commute to work by car, so most main thoroughfares have bumper-to-bumper traffic during rush hours. A system of *jitneys* (privately-owned, small buses holding up to 25 passengers) is reliable but has not alleviated the congestion. Outside of Nassau, traffic jams are rare. A system of mail boats provides transportation for mail, freight, and people between Nassau and the other islands on a weekly, bi-weekly, or (for the distant and less-developed islands) monthly basis. The national airline links all major islands. As with mail boats, air routes radiate from Nassau, making it necessary to change planes in Nassau when traveling from one Family Island to another.

The postal system is efficient, with post offices in almost every small settlement throughout the islands. There is no delivery to homes or businesses; mail is picked up at the post offices. The national telephone company provides phone service to all major islands. The government-owned radio and television stations can be received on many of the islands. Recently, privately operated radio and television stations have been permitted to operate. The two principal Nassau newspapers circulate primarily in Nassau, but copies do find their way to the other islands. A relatively recent development is the circulation of regional newspapers on Abaco, Eleuthera, Exuma, and several other islands.

Education. Bahamians have access to free public education at the elementary and secondary level, as well as subsidized tuition at the College of the Bahamas. Students are required to attend school through age 16. Churches run private schools,

DEVELOPMENT DATA
Human Dev. Index* rank . . . . 51 of 177 countries
   Adjusted for women. . . . . 46 of 144 countries
Real GDP per capita $17,280
Adult literacy rate . . . . 95 percent (male); 96 (female)
Infant mortality rate . . . . 17 per 1,000 births
Life expectancy . . . . 64 (male); 70 (female)

many of which offer scholarships to underprivileged children. Students from private schools attend colleges and universities at a higher rate; many go abroad to the United States, Canada, and the United Kingdom. Teachers are often imported to compensate for a shortage of qualified local teachers; many come from other Commonwealth countries in the Caribbean, such as Jamaica and Guyana.

Increasing numbers of young Bahamians seek higher education and have ambitious personal goals. A university degree is now a prerequisite for high-income jobs, giving educational achievement greater importance. Bahamian women tend to be more willing than men to pursue higher education. The College of the Bahamas's current transition to full university status is designed to accommodate students who are unable to travel abroad for their education because of economic or other limitations.

Health. The Bahamas has two major public hospitals, in Nassau and Freeport. There is also a private hospital in Nassau with state-of-the-art facilities. Government health clinics are located in many communities throughout the nation. Health care professionals provide home care for specific needs. Residents of the Family Islands who require hospitalization are transported to Nassau by air. Lack of medicine and modern equipment are the most significant deficiencies in the public sector. The Bahamas has one of the region's highest rates of AIDS per capita. AIDS awareness programs have been implemented, with education beginning in high school. Many chronic health problems—including high blood pressure, heart disease, and diabetes—also result from the rich Bahamian diet.

AT A GLANCE
Events and Trends.
- In 2004, the islands were battered by two major hurricanes, Frances and Jeanne. Although the Bahamas was not as severely damaged as other countries in the Caribbean, hundreds of homes were harmed, and several people died.
- In July 2004, the Bahamas was unsure to what extent it would participate in the Caribbean Community's (CARICOM) Single Market Community. The Bahamanian government was debating if joining would be a boon to the country's economy and what the terms of joining would be.

Contact Information. Embassy of the Bahamas, 2220 Massachusetts Avenue NW, Washington, DC 20008; phone (202) 319-2660. Bahamas Ministry of Tourism, P.O. Box N-3701, Market Plaza, Bay Street, Nassau, Bahamas; phone (242) 302-2098; web site www.bahamas.com.

ProQuest Information and Learning Company
300 North Zeeb Road, P.O. Box 1346
Ann Arbor, Michigan 48106 USA
Toll Free: 1.800.528.6279
Fax: 1.800.864.0019
www.culturegrams.com

© 2005 ProQuest Information and Learning Company and Brigham Young University. It is against the law to copy, reprint, store, or transmit any part of this publication in any form by any means without written permission from ProQuest. This document contains native commentary and original analysis, as well as estimated statistics. The content should not be considered strictly factual, and it may not apply to all groups in a nation. *UN Development Programme, Human Development Report 2004 (New York: Oxford University Press, 2004).

Barbados

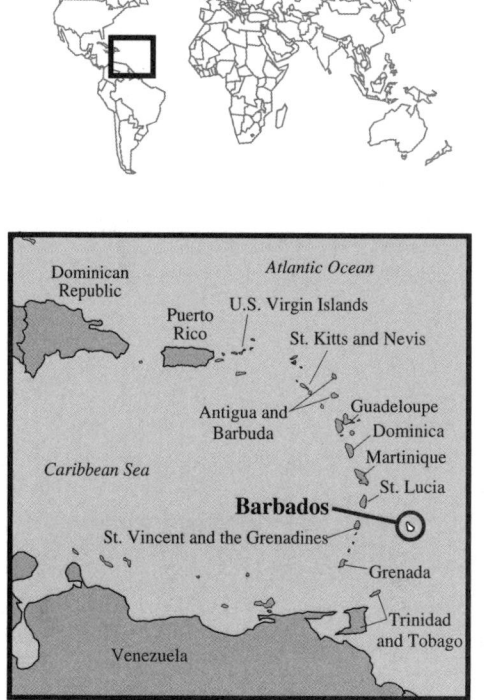

Boundary representations are not necessarily authoritative.

BACKGROUND

Land and Climate. Often called "Little England" or "Island in the Sun," Barbados is the easternmost island in the Caribbean archipelago. It belongs to a chain of islands known as the Lesser Antilles. The island is 166 square miles (430 square kilometers) in size—nearly 2.5 times the size of Washington, D.C. From the central highland area, the terrain slopes gradually to the sea and is interrupted by only a few hilly areas. Moderated by the ocean and by trade winds, the tropical climate provides an average year-round temperature of 85°F (29°C). The rainy season is from June to October. Barbados has no rivers; instead, rainwater percolates through the soil to form underground wells, which are used for drinking water. The rainwater also forms channels that run to the ocean. A thin layer of topsoil covers the thick layer of coral that underlies most of the island. The soil is very fertile, making the island lush with flowering trees, shrubs, and tropical flowers. Three-fourths of Barbados is suitable for cultivation. Barrier reefs that surround the island make it particularly rich in marine life. Natural resources include fish, sugarcane, tropical fruits, cotton, crude oil, and natural gas.

History. The original inhabitants of Barbados were Arawak Indians. They disappeared for unknown reasons before European explorers arrived in the 1500s. Portuguese explorers found an abundance of bearded fig trees when they arrived on the island; hence, it was named *Barbados*, which originated from the Portuguese term *os barbudos* (bearded ones). The British came to the island in 1625, when Captain John Powell claimed it in the name of King James I. Two years later, Captain Powell brought the first colonists and settled Holetown. As the population grew, sugarcane was introduced, and slave labor was brought in from Africa. Independence-minded colonists were forced to surrender to England's forces in 1652 by signing the Articles of Capitulation, which later became the Charter of Barbados.

Barbados freed its slaves between 1834 and 1838, allowed women to vote in 1944, and provided voting rights to all citizens in 1951. A leader of a growing independence movement, Sir Grantley Adams, became the first premier under home rule in 1954. On 30 November 1966, Barbados gained full independence from Great Britain. Errol Barrow was the first prime minister of an independent Barbados. The country maintains ties to Britain as a member of the Commonwealth of Nations.

Since independence, Barbados has enjoyed a high degree of political stability. The island capitalized on its natural strengths and by the 1980s had developed a successful tourist industry. With economic and political stability, the nation was able to provide a high standard of living for its inhabitants.

During the global recession of the early 1990s, the economy suffered various setbacks. After his election in 1991, Prime Minister Erskine Lloyd Sandiford (of the Democratic Labour Party) introduced an austerity package to improve economic conditions. Reforms stabilized the economy but were unpopular among voters. Leaders in parliament also became disillusioned with Sandiford's leadership, forcing him to call for early elections in 1994. A strong voter turnout brought economist Owen Arthur, leader of the Barbados Labour Party, to power as prime minister. Boosted by a strong economy and considerably lower unemployment, Arthur's Barbados Labour Party was reelected overwhelmingly in January 1999, winning 26 of 28 seats. The government continues to seek greater economic growth and reduced unemployment.

Barbados

THE PEOPLE

Population. The population of Barbados is approximately 278,000 and is growing only slightly. Although the birthrate is steady, emigration holds net growth to less than 1 percent. With about 1,670 persons per square mile (645 per square kilometer), Barbados's high population density makes it seem like a city-country. Around 60 percent of the population lives in urban centers stretching along the western side of the island, which is more sheltered from storms. The capital city of Bridgetown is the largest urban area and serves as a "downtown" for the entire island. Urban, commercial areas are referred to as *town* areas rather than cities. An estimated 90 percent of the population is black, mostly of African origin. An additional 6 percent is of mixed heritage and 4 percent is white. East Indian and Middle Eastern groups comprise a small percentage. The people of Barbados are called Barbadians, but they are often referred to as Bajans.

Language. The official language is English. Bajans also speak a dialect that descends from the English spoken by early colonists, indentured servants, and slaves. Referred to as *speaking Bajan* or *broken English*, the dialect is used informally between family and friends. In speaking Bajan, "What are you all doing tonight?" becomes *Whuh wunna doin' tonight?* Numerous proverbs are also expressed in the dialect, including *Day does run 'til night catch it* (Whatever you do will catch up with you in the end).

Religion. Although more than 100 religions are practiced in Barbados, the majority (67 percent) of Barbadians are Protestant Christians. About 40 percent belong to the Anglican Church, 8 percent to Pentecostal churches, and 7 percent to the Methodist Church. The Roman Catholic Church also has a strong presence. Nearly 30 percent of the people belong to smaller Christian and non-Christian organizations or to no church at all. There are also small Hindu, Muslim, and Jewish communities. The first Jewish synagogue was built on the island in 1654.

For many Bajans, religion plays an important role in daily life. The school day begins with an assembly that includes a Bible reading, hymn, and prayer. Many families pray before meals, and most official public functions open with prayer. Regardless of one's religious affiliation, funeral attendance is considered important. Bajans make a special effort to attend services of even distant relatives and acquaintances. The number of attendees at a funeral often indicates the deceased's standing in the community.

General Attitudes. Bajans are warm, happy, friendly, and generous. However, they may seem reserved around strangers and are considered somewhat more restrained than their Caribbean neighbors. The success of the country's tourist industry is partly due to Bajan hospitality. A generally peaceful atmosphere in the country allows the police to patrol unarmed. Social unity is important to Barbadians. Their view of life is evident in their carefully kept, pastel-colored homes and in lively festivals that reflect past and present culture. Such festivals often celebrate Bajan's dual African-British heritage.

Bajans find arrogant, aggressive, and ostentatious behavior distasteful. Their independence—their ability as a nation to dictate their own affairs—is important to them. They take great pride in the country's accomplishments in music, sports, education, politics, and economics. The successes of Bajan athletes in cricket, track-and-field, and other sports are celebrated in Calypso songs, national holidays, and gifts from the business community. The people value honesty, humor, and education. Parents generally stress a good education as a means to a better future for their children. A car and a plot of land are other desired possessions.

Personal Appearance. North American fashions are popular in Barbados, and many Barbadians shop overseas for clothing. Women usually wear tailored dresses or blouses and skirts to work, and they get very dressed up for parties and other social events. They wear their finest dresses and hats to church meetings. For casual events, women usually dress in colorful, long skirts with sandals. Sometimes they wear their hair in small braids with colorful beads at the ends. Jeans and T-shirts are popular casual wear for both sexes.

Many (particularly older) men wear lightweight pants with a casual shirt of white, pastel, or flowered fabric. This *shirt-jac* suit generally is accepted everywhere (parties, offices, and churches), but a more formal suit is required for certain events. Younger men may wear tailored pants and a dress shirt in the workplace. Swimwear is limited to the beach and is not worn in the city or other public places.

CUSTOMS AND COURTESIES

Greetings. Bajans generally greet each other with a handshake and a smile. Friends often embrace upon meeting and sometimes give a kiss on the cheek. Similar gestures are exchanged when parting. Young men may greet by bumping with a fist the top of the other's extended fist. A common greeting is *Hello! How are you?* An answer such as *Not bad* is a friendly response. Less formal greetings used by younger people include *Yo, what's up?, Wuh you sayin'?* (How are things?), and *How ya gine?* (How are you doing?). Particularly in rural areas, it is considered polite to greet strangers in passing with a *Hello* or a nod. An evening telephone call begins with *Hello, good night.*

Coworkers typically address one another by first name, while a superior generally is addressed by title (*Mr., Mrs., Ms., Miss*) and surname. A superior might also be addressed as *Skipper, Admiral, Boss-man,* or *Doc.* Friends and relatives may call one another by nickname. Children respectfully address older family friends as *aunt(ie)* or *uncle.*

Gestures. Barbadians often use their hands when conversing to emphasize or communicate a point. However, personal space is respected. They call taxis and buses by waving the hand. They often express disgust by clenching the teeth and sucking in air (sounding something like "chupse"); the level of annoyance or contempt can be measured by the loudness of the *chupse*. People may show defiance, anger, or frustration by standing *akimbo* (placing their hands on their hips) while arguing a point. Bajans frequently will fold their arms as a sign that they are paying attention, but such a gesture can also signal defiance. Raising an arm above the head with the palm facing out and waving side-to-side signals good-bye, but a similar gesture with the palm at eye level and a quicker side-to-side motion can indicate disapproval.

It is considered polite to forfeit seats to pregnant women or the elderly on public buses. Seated bus passengers may show courtesy by holding a standing passenger's parcel or child. If one must pass between people who are talking, one should wait for a break in the conversation to ask for permission to pass by saying *Excuse me please?* Occasional (not constant) eye contact during conversation is appropriate. Pointing at people with the index finger is considered rude.

Visiting. Friends and relatives may visit at home unannounced, usually on weekend afternoons. A favorite time for men to get together is Sunday morning, when topics of conversation range from politics to cricket. Visits often take place on the patio or front porch. Otherwise, a visitor is invited into the parlor or living room and offered a drink (juice, soda, beer, or rum) along with sandwiches and biscuits.

Visiting also occurs at cricket matches and other sporting events when old friends see each other. Shops in the country districts and barber salons in the town are important places for lively discussion, especially around election time.

Eating. Bajans eat three meals a day. Families usually try to gather for breakfast and dinner, although this is subject to varying schedules. Sunday lunch is a traditional family meal. For most people, the traditional *teatime* has been replaced with midmorning and midafternoon snacks, which may include tea, coffee, juice, fruit (mangoes, cherries, tamarinds, bananas, or oranges), cheese, chocolate, peanuts, or sweet bread (usually made with coconut). Barbadians eat in the continental style; the fork is in the left hand, and the knife remains in the right. They keep the elbows off the table.

LIFESTYLE

Family. The extended family is important in Barbados, and parents, children, grandparents, and cousins enjoy substantial interaction. This pattern is changing somewhat with modernization, but it is still important. Extended families may live together or near one another.

A high percentage of children are born out of wedlock. Teenage pregnancies continue to be a problem. Divorce is increasing. Single-parent families (usually with only the mother) are common. In homes where the father is present, he is the leader. Economic circumstances have caused many women to seek employment outside the home, leaving the care of children to grandparents. Nearly half of the workforce is female. People who have emigrated to the United States, the United Kingdom, or Canada for work still maintain extended family ties through monetary support and visits.

Many families live in traditional *chattel houses*. These look like wooden mobile homes, set on coral stone 3 or 4 feet above ground for better air circulation. They are designed for easy assembly and disassembly, as plantation workers in the past often were required to move from one working area to another. They are so well built that they may be passed from one generation to the next. Other permanent homes are made of brick or concrete, and many are painted with pastel colors. Families commonly paint their homes before Christmas in preparation for holiday visitors.

Dating and Marriage. Dating usually begins in the early teens. Young Bajans socialize at school, church, *fetes* (parties), the beach, the cinema, sporting events, and each other's homes. Public displays of affection between couples (beyond holding hands) are uncommon. Many people do not marry. Even in two-parent homes, some couples are not married. Couples who have lived together for years are protected by common-law legislation. Many young people wait to marry until after they have established themselves financially or have begun their careers. Weddings traditionally are held in a church, followed by a gala reception in a local hall, hotel, or restaurant. The reception typically features an elaborate wedding cake and music by a Bajan steel band.

Diet. Bajan food is a unique combination of African and English traditions. Staples include rice, *peas* (legumes), potatoes, chicken, and fish. The national dish is flying fish and *cou cou* (made of okra and cornmeal). Also popular are lobster, shrimp, red snapper, turtle, tuna, kingfish, and *dorado*, a local fish. Sea urchin eggs are a delicacy. Goats and black-belly sheep provide meat. The tropical soil yields mangoes, papayas, bananas, cucumbers, tomatoes, guavas, avocados, coconuts, squash, eggplant, breadfruit, and numerous other vegetables. Popular local dishes include *jug-jug* (sorghum and green pigeon peas), *pepperpot* (a spicy stew), *macaroni pie* (made with cheese or mincemeat), and *conkies* (cornmeal, coconut, pumpkin, raisins, sweet potatoes, and spices steamed in a banana leaf). Favorite pastries include *jam puffs* (jam-filled sourdough pastry) and turnovers (filled with coconut and sugar). Fast foods such as pizza, hamburgers, fried chicken, and hot dogs are popular.

Both cow and goat milk are popular. *Tea* is the term used for any breakfast drink (tea, Milo, Ovaltine). Barbados is well-known for its rum.

Recreation. Cricket is the national sport. Bajans also enjoy soccer, cycling, basketball, rugby, and volleyball. With excellent wind and water conditions, surfing and windsurfing are favorites. Scuba and skin diving are popular because the area has extensive coral reefs, clear water, and interesting dive sites, some of which feature the wrecks of sunken ships. People enjoy swimming, particularly on the more sheltered south and west coasts. Other sporting activities include horse racing, squash, tennis, and table tennis. Favorite games are bridge, chess, dominoes, and *draughts* (checkers), the national game. Sunday and holiday picnics at the beach are popular. Young people enjoy *liming* (hanging out) in town on weekends. Vacationing Barbadians may visit another English-speaking island or relatives in the United States, Canada, or England.

The Arts. Music and dance are intrinsic parts of Bajan culture. Calypso, reggae, *dancehall* (of Jamaican origin), *soca* (a mixture of soul music from the United States and calypso music), and North American pop styles are favored. Musicians compete in annual competitions. *Wukking up*, a uniquely Bajan dance style, features rhythmic waist-winding movements. It is usually performed to calypso. Popular folk songs are thought to originate from West African slave songs dating back to the 1600s.

Barbados's arts are intertwined with the island's natural surroundings, especially the ocean, flora, and fauna. Weavers incorporate plants and natural materials into baskets and mats. Jewelry made from shells, feathers, and wood set in copper or silver is common. Potters make use of red clay, which is an abundant resource, creating an array of pots, tiles, and domestic items. Many painters and sculptors have found success in Barbados's prosperous art market, and several galleries and museums display artists' work.

Holidays. Four annual festivals celebrate important events in Barbados. The Holetown Festival (three days in February) celebrates the arrival of the first settlers; the Oistins Fish Festival, held on Easter weekend, is a tribute to the fishing industry; the Crop Over Festival (June–early August) celebrates the end of the sugarcane harvest; and the National Independence Festival of the Creative Arts (Nov.) is an opportunity for people to display various talents. Other holidays include New Year's Day, Errol Barrow Day (21 Jan.), Easter (Friday–Monday), May Day (1 May), Whitmonday, Kadooment Day (first Monday in August), Emancipation Day (3 Aug.), United Nations Day (first Monday in October), Independence Day (30 Nov.), Christmas, and Boxing Day (26 Dec.). Kadooment Day is the culmination of the Crop Over Festival. On this day, trucks broadcasting calypso and other music follow *bands* (groups of

Barbados

people in brightly colored costumes) parading and dancing through the streets. The festivities include costume and music contests, street vendors, and craft displays.

Commerce. Most businesses are open on weekdays from 8 a.m. to 4:30 p.m. and until noon on Saturday. Grocery and convenience stores are open somewhat later. Banking hours are generally shorter. Most businesses close on Sunday, although large stores remain open when cruise ships are in port. Standard government office hours are 8:30 a.m. to 4:30 p.m. Supermarkets are becoming more prevalent in Barbados. People also buy basic goods at small neighborhood shops. Outdoor markets feature fresh fruits, vegetables, spices, and fish.

SOCIETY

Government. Barbados is a parliamentary democracy. The country is divided into 11 parishes and the capital city, Bridgetown. As a sovereign member of the Commonwealth of Nations, Barbados recognizes Queen Elizabeth II as the head of state. She is represented in-country by a governor-general (Clifford Husbands).

The prime minister is leader of the majority party in the House of Assembly, which has 30 seats. The current prime minister is Owen Arthur. Parliament also has a Senate, whose 21 members are appointed. National elections are held at least every five years. The major political parties are the Barbados Labour Party and the Democratic Labour Party. All citizens may vote at age 18.

Economy. Barbados has one of the highest standards of living in the Caribbean. Women earn a comparable share of the nation's income. Tourism, light manufacturing, and the sugar industry are primary sources of foreign exchange. Tourism has been the largest industry and employer in Barbados for more than 20 years. The country exports sugar, rum, and textiles. It trades with the United States, other Caribbean nations, the United Kingdom, and Canada. Barbados is an active member of the Caribbean Community and Common Market (CARICOM). The currency is the Barbadian dollar (BBD), which is pegged to the U.S. dollar at a fixed 2-1 ratio.

Transportation and Communications. The majority of Barbadian households have at least one car. However, most people make use of the island's efficient network of public buses, minibuses, and taxis. The island has a central paved highway and an adequate network of roads. Following the British tradition, cars travel on the left side of the road. Barbados has one international airport.

One government-owned television station and a satellite-subscription television service serve the island; there are many radio stations. In addition to two daily newspapers, foreign-language papers are available. Telecommunications links to other nations are well established, and internet use is growing.

Education. Barbados boasts one of the finest public education systems in the Caribbean. More than 85 percent of pupils complete primary schooling and attend secondary school. Attendance is compulsory until age 16. Private schools have less than 5 percent of the total enrollment. Primary and secondary schools, patterned after British schools, generally require uniforms. The government pays for qualified students to study at the University of the West Indies, a regional college with campuses in Barbados, Trinidad, and Jamaica. Technical-training schools, as well as schools for physically and mentally handicapped children, are also available.

Health. The government-operated National Health Service includes the Queen Elizabeth Hospital and a network of *polyclinics*, which provide free medical and dental care to all Barbadians. A private hospital also offers services. Home to the largest desalination facility in the Caribbean, Barbados offers its inhabitants a secure and reliable source of water, despite frequent droughts. Tap water is safe to drink, and most homes have running water.

DEVELOPMENT DATA
Human Dev. Index* rank . . . . 29 of 177 countries
    Adjusted for women . . . . 27 of 144 countries
Real GDP per capita $15,290
Adult literacy rate . . . . 99 percent (male); 99 (female)
Infant mortality rate . . . . 13 per 1,000 births
Life expectancy . . . . 74 (male); 79 (female)

AT A GLANCE
Events and Trends.
- In September 2004, the government of Barbados announced that it would donate $1 million to help fund disaster relief and humanitarian services in Haiti, which was dealing with the damage left by major tropical storms as well as political instability.
- Throughout 2004, leaders in Barbados discussed the possible effects of joining the Caribbean Community (CARICOM) Single Market and Economy (CSME). In short, this economic union between Caribbean nations would allow free movement of labor, goods, and services across the region. Some Barbadians were concerned that larger nations with industrial economies and many skilled laborers would overrun Barbados's smaller economy. The CSME was scheduled to take effect in 2005.
- In early 2004, Barbados appealed to the United Nations to settle a longstanding dispute with Trinidad and Tobago regarding fishing and maritime boundaries. The disagreement has been going on for more than ten years and is largely concerned with where each country's ships are allowed to fish.
- In September 2003, Barbados lifted all taxes on computer hardware and software in an attempt to spur the nation's use of new technologies. Leaders hope the move will draw investment to the country.
- Barbados's offshore financial services industry has developed in recent years into one of the most important sectors of the economy. In 2002, Barbados was removed from an international list of countries considered uncooperative tax havens.

Contact Information. Embassy of Barbados, 2144 Wyoming Avenue NW, Washington, DC 20008; phone (202) 939-9200. Barbados Tourism Authority, 3440 Wilshire Boulevard, Suite 1215, Los Angeles, CA 90010; phone (800) 221-9831; web site www.barbados.org.

ProQuest Information and Learning Company
300 North Zeeb Road, P.O. Box 1346
Ann Arbor, Michigan 48106 USA
Toll Free: 1.800.528.6279
Fax: 1.800.864.0019
www.culturegrams.com

© 2005 ProQuest Information and Learning Company and Brigham Young University. It is against the law to copy, reprint, store, or transmit any part of this publication in any form by any means without written permission from ProQuest. This document contains native commentary and original analysis, as well as estimated statistics. The content should not be considered strictly factual, and it may not apply to all groups in a nation. *UN Development Programme, Human Development Report 2004 (New York: Oxford University Press, 2004).

Belize

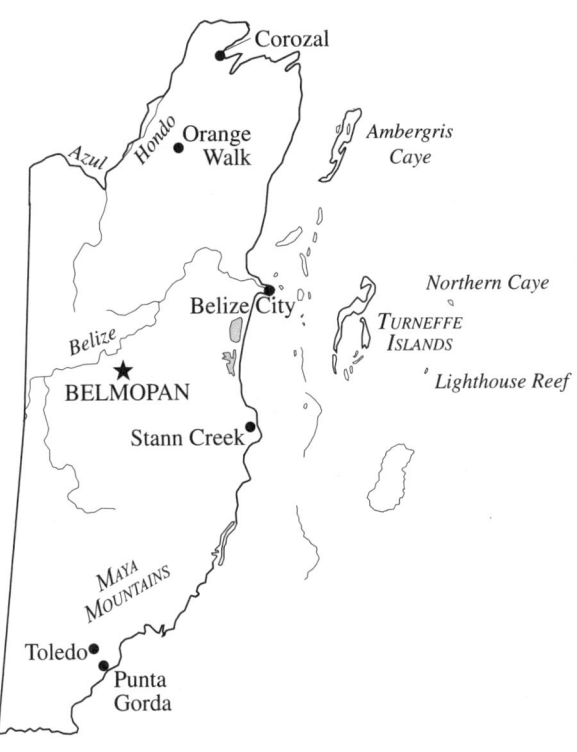

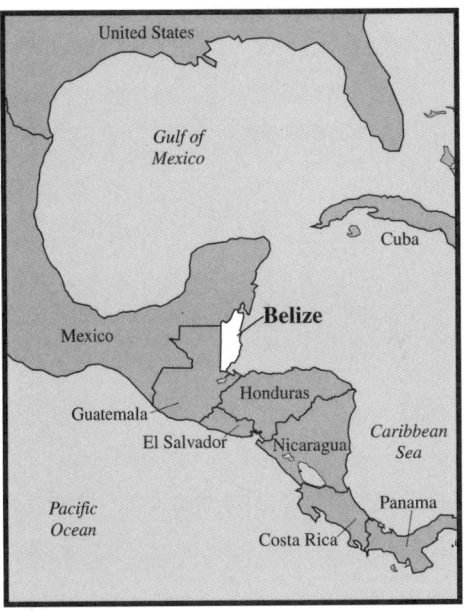

Boundary representations are not necessarily authoritative.

BACKGROUND

Land and Climate. Covering 8,866 square miles (22,963 square kilometers), Belize is about the size of Massachusetts. Located in Central America, it is bordered by Mexico, Guatemala, and the Caribbean Sea. The landscape is diverse for such a small area. The northern half of Belize is flat with marshes and lagoons, while coastal areas are covered by mangrove swamps. The land rises to the south and west, reaching an elevation of 3,688 feet (915 meters) in the Maya Mountains. More than 60 percent of the country is forested. Belize has the world's second largest barrier reef with hundreds of small islands called *cayes* (pronounced "KEYS"). Beautiful rivers, forests, reefs, and *cayes* are home to thousands of plant and animal species, from giant, fast-growing *guanacasta* trees to crocodiles and manatees.

Belize has two seasons: dry (February–July) and wet (August–January). Humidity is high year-round. The south receives the most rain. Temperatures average between 80 and 85°F (27–29°C), although it is cooler in the mountains. In Belmopan, the capital, days are hot and nights are cool. Belize is subject to coastal flooding and hurricanes between June and October.

History. The Maya thrived in the area between the third and ninth centuries A.D. as part of a civilization that covered Guatemala, Honduras, Southern Mexico, and El Salvador. Numerous city-states existed throughout Mayan lands, and these were often at odds with each other. Mayan ruins are still evident all over Belize. Little is known of the period after the decline of the Mayan people until the arrival of the first Europeans in the 16th century. The Spanish came in search of gold but found none. British pirates arrived during the 17th century and took advantage of the islands and reefs to lure ships onto the rocks for looting. British woodcutters soon followed and brought slaves to help in logging the huge forests. The pirates also turned to woodcutting. The logwood and later the mahogany trade became very lucrative for these British, who were known as the Baymen.

The Spanish tried to claim the region, but at the decisive Battle of St. George's Caye in 1798, the Baymen and their slaves fought back Spanish invaders. With the Spanish Empire all around them, the Baymen asked Britain for protection. Spain and Britain signed a treaty to allow Belize to become a crown colony in 1862. England had promised to build a road between Belize City and Guatemala City as part of that treaty. The fact that the road was never built led to a long-term dispute between the two neighbors. Guatemala claimed all of Belize as its own territory because of the treaty's failure.

The British granted internal self-rule in 1964, but Belize was called British Honduras until 1973. In 1981, with support from the United Nations and a strong independence movement, Belize became a sovereign country within the Commonwealth of Nations. British troops remained to protect the borders, but after a 1991 agreement in which Guatemala recognized Belize's sovereignty, Britain decided (in 1993) to withdraw most of its troops. However, Guatemala still lays claim to a large

Belize

portion of Belize. Negotiations between the two countries are continuing.

THE PEOPLE

Population. The population of Belize is roughly 273,000 and is growing at about 2.5 percent. About one-fourth of the population lives in Belize City. Orange Walk is the next largest city. Each of the country's six districts has a main town where the bulk of that district's population lives. Many Belizeans live and work abroad, especially in the United States.

Belize has a diverse blend of peoples. Mestizos, or people with mixed European and indigenous ancestry, represent 49 percent of the population. Creoles, people with some degree of African ancestry, account for about 25 percent. People of full Mayan blood comprise 10.5 percent of the population. The Garinagu, people who share a Caribbean and African background, comprise 6 percent.

Mestizos are primarily descendants of 19th-century immigrants from Mexico, although the group includes immigrants from other Latin American countries. Refugees from neighboring countries (mainly El Salvador and Guatemala) have added significantly to the mestizo population. Creoles dominate in Belize City. Many are descendants of early European (mostly English or Scottish) settlers and African slaves. Creoles were once the largest group but now loses many people to emigration. Most rural villages are comprised of mestizos, Mayas (Kek'chi, Mopan, and Yucatan), or Garinagu—who live mostly in the south. A small minority of East Indians have been in Belize for generations and are joined by other groups, including Mennonites, Chinese, Arabs, and North Americans.

Language. English is the country's official language, and with the exception of people in remote areas, everyone speaks it. Most people also speak Creole, and everyday speech is often a combination of Creole and English. Creole is a melodic English-based language with roots in the days of slavery. Although it is traditionally an oral language, efforts are under way to establish grammar and spelling standards for a written form. Spanish is spoken by mestizos throughout the country (especially in the Cayo, Corozal, and Orange Walk districts) but not necessarily by all mestizos. Still, it has overtaken English as the first language of many Belizeans. While school instruction must be in English, Creole or Spanish may be used in the first few years to clarify instruction for children who do not speak English. Mayan groups speak their native languages. The Garinagu usually speak both Garífuna and English.

Religion. Freedom of religion is valued and respected in Belize. Most major Western Christian denominations are represented, but the Roman Catholic (62 percent) and Anglican (12 percent) Churches dominate. Most mestizos and Maya are Catholic. Creoles generally belong to Protestant churches, but many are Catholic. A number of other Christian faiths are practiced. Schools generally are run by churches, so most people are affiliated with a religion. Some indigenous religious practices are found among the Maya and Garinagu.

General Attitudes. Belizeans are fun-loving, friendly, and generally laid-back. They appreciate honesty and value a sense of humor. The pace of life is not regulated by the clock so much as by events or people. Punctuality may be admired but generally is not expected. Men commonly practice *machismo*, demonstrating their manhood through overtly masculine acts or sexually oriented language. Women usually ignore such behavior and accept it as part of life. More egalitarian relationships are also developing as women move into the workforce.

Although Belize is located in Central America, its history, culture, and government structure are closely linked to the Caribbean, which gives Belizeans great pride. Belizeans value their diverse ancestries and linguistic abilities. But for a small nation of so many ethnic groups and cultures, Belize is relatively free of racial tension. Equality and coexistence are important concepts. Prejudices exist but do not usually extend to hatred. A neighborhood in Belize City might consist of every possible ethnic group and have few racial problems. One reason is that the people do not often mix; they coexist. But another more powerful reason is that most ethnic groups subscribe in some degree to Creole cultural practices, and Belizean Creoles have adopted aspects of the cultures around them. Most people can speak Belizean Creole, which further enhances harmony.

Personal Appearance. In Belize, the way a person is dressed is considered a mark of taste and status. Even those who cannot afford new or expensive fashions take pride in wearing clean, pressed clothing, particularly in the workplace and on weekend outings. Office, bank, hotel, and school employees commonly wear uniforms. Many men, especially professionals, wear *guayaberas*, loosely worn cotton shirts that are sometimes embroidered. While women traditionally wear dresses or skirts at work, pants are becoming more common. Agricultural workers generally wear older clothing, with rubber boots or flip-flops.

U.S. fashions are popular almost everywhere in Belize. Casual wear is the norm for leisure activities, while evening and religious events generally call for best dress. In rural areas, clothing tends to be casual.

The Maya often wear traditional clothing. This might include long, heavy, brightly colored skirts with white, embroidered blouses for women, and work clothes and straw hats for men. Garinagu women also commonly wear traditional clothing, which could consist of a simple, colorful blouse, a matching knee-length skirt, and a head scarf. The Mennonites, a group originally from Germany, maintain conservative, simple clothing and do not follow modern fashions.

CUSTOMS AND COURTESIES

Greetings. Belizeans are informal and friendly in *hailing* (greeting) one another. It is rude not to *hail* even a slight acquaintance or not to return a *hail*. *Hailing* strangers is not uncommon in Belize City or in the districts. When entering a place of business, one also *hails* the clerk or receptionist. When strangers pass on the street, a simple nod or wave is acceptable; acquaintances might add *Hey, how?* or *Y'aright?*

When greetings precede conversation, a handshake is common. Friends (particularly men) might shake by clasping the palms and locking thumbs or all fingers, or by exchanging a *knock-it* (lightly touching closed fists). Men often pat each other on the back when they shake hands. Women generally reserve hugs for close friends and relatives. Spanish speakers greet by saying ¡*Buenos días!* (Good morning), ¡*Buenas tardes!* (Good afternoon), ¡*Buenas noches!* (Good evening), or just ¡*Buenas!* any time of day. In Creole, one might use *Wa di gwan?* (What's happening?) or a number of other phrases.

In formal settings, people address others by title. Children usually address their elders by adding *Miss* or *Mister* before the name, and they often answer questions by saying *Yes, ma'am* or *No, sir*.

Gestures. Creoles and Garinagu are especially animated. Mestizos are very reserved among people unfamiliar to them. Nonverbal communication is prevalent; hand and facial gestures can be varied and complicated. Belizeans might indicate direction with the head or lips. Staring or pointing at someone is rude. Sucking air through the teeth can mean "Give me a break." People might hiss to get one's attention, but this is offensive to many (especially women). To hail a taxi or bus, people move the hand up and down before the vehicle passes.

Visiting. Belizeans are very hospitable. Unannounced visitors are welcomed and made to feel at home. Arranged visits most often occur on weekends. Before television was introduced in 1980, visiting was an integral part of everyday life. It has since diminished in cities but is still important in villages. When one visits a home, it is polite to *hail* the occupants from the gate or street until they come out. A lengthy conversation might take place over the fence before one is invited into the yard or home. Offering a guest refreshments, usually at least a drink, is considered good manners. In areas without refrigeration, people might offer fresh coconut. Though not expected, it is also polite for the guest to bring the host a small gift, such as sweets.

Eating. Families generally spend mealtime together, although women may eat after or separately from the men in some Mayan and mestizo families. Conversation is usually limited and mainly carried out between adults. For most, the main meal of the day is *dinner*, which is eaten at midday. Schools and businesses close so people can eat at home. In cities, people also frequent restaurants. The evening meal, called *supper* or *tea*, is lighter than *dinner*. For some groups (such as the Kek'chi Maya), the main meal is in the evening.

Meals in rural areas usually are less varied than in cities; rice, beans, tortillas, fresh fruit, and chicken are often the only available foods. Urban people might eat these foods in addition to burgers, *tamales*, fish, and a variety of other dishes.

LIFESTYLE

Family. Families tend to be large and often include the extended family. It is common for grandparents to raise grandchildren after their own children have left Belize for economic or other reasons. Leaving children behind has created problems in Belize, as minors now form a majority of the population in Belize City. Adult children usually remain at home until they marry or have a child. Single-parent families are abundant among the Creole population, and women have become the leading family figure in that group. In a Creole village, it is common for households to have a female head and several generations living together without any adult men.

In most other homes, the father takes the leading role. Younger mothers are more inclined to work outside the home than older women, but women are generally expected to take care of the home and family.

Apartment living is not popular. Most families own or rent homes. Rural homes may be simple thatched huts. In coastal towns and villages, houses are built of wood or cement and rest on stilts because of the threat of hurricane flooding. As elevation increases, stilts become less common. Because of the small population, the government can allot land to Belizeans who apply for it, making land and home ownership feasible.

Dating and Marriage. Urban dating follows a similar pattern as in North America. However, schools may prohibit their students from going to popular dating destinations, such as discos, so private parties and school dances are the primary way young people meet. Village dating revolves around church activities. Among the Maya and some mestizos, boys may only be allowed to meet with a girl in her home.

Many Belizean young women become single mothers early and never marry. Likewise, many young men father a number of children by several women and never formally marry. Some couples enter into common-law marriage relationships. For those who do marry formally, a church ceremony is usually followed by a lively reception that includes food, music, and dancing.

Diet. The most common staple is white rice and kidney beans. This dish may be accompanied by stewed chicken, beef, or fish. A staple among the Maya is corn, which is usually present in some form (such as tortillas) at every meal. Fish and seafood are common on the coast. Other popular foods include *tamales* (cornmeal dough stuffed with filling and steamed in banana leaves), *panades* (fried corn shells with beans or fish), meat pies, *escabeche* (onion soup), *chirmole* (soup), and *garnaches* (fried tortillas with beans, cheese, and sauce). Fruits (such as bananas, oranges, mangoes, papaya, and limes) are abundant and part of the daily diet. Vegetables are more limited and often imported.

Recreation. The most popular sports are *football* (soccer) and basketball. Organized leagues receive great local support. Softball is popular with men and women. National championships are held for both men's and women's teams. Volleyball, track-and-field, cricket, and boxing are enjoyed in many areas. Cycling is popular; the largest athletic event is the annual cross-country race held Easter weekend. It is a source of pride and a national tradition that attracts an international group of cyclists. Urban people like to go to the *cayes* for recreation. Belizeans also enjoy attending concerts and school fairs or watching the latest movies at home on cable and video.

The Arts. Native arts include a wide variety of wood and stone carving, textiles, baskets, and pottery. These are produced for tourists, used in many homes, and given as gifts.

Belizeans appreciate many kinds of music: reggae, calypso, *soca* (a mixture of U.S. soul and calypso), and various types of music from the United States. A local favorite is *punta-rock*, music with fast rhythms that is a mixture of synthesized sounds and traditional Garífuna drumming. The *punta-rock* dance style is among the most popular forms and is thought of as a Belizean creation. Traditional drums made of hollow tree trunks are often used in performances.

Holidays. The largest and most celebrated national holidays occur in September. A street parade/party takes place on St. George's Caye Day (10 Sept.) and on Independence Day (21 Sept.). Various "September celebrations" take place between these two holidays. Baron Bliss Day (9 Mar.) honors a Portuguese noble who donated his fortune to the country and its people. Garífuna Settlement Day (19 Nov.) marks the arrival of the Garinagu to Belize. They originally came from Saint Vincent and settled in Honduras before migrating to Belize.

Belizeans celebrate Christmas with religious parades and services as well as with feasts, visits to friends and relatives, and lively parties. Easter weekend is popular for vacations; religious ceremonies are limited. Belize also celebrates Labor Day (1 May) and a number of other holidays.

Commerce. Weekday business hours are 8 a.m. to 5 p.m. Stores generally open again in the evening for two hours. Most businesses close for lunch. Bank hours vary. Most close at 1 or 2:30 p.m., Monday through Thursday, with longer hours Friday. Larger grocery stores are open all day Saturday and on Sunday morning. Small shops have varying hours and usually are operated out of private homes.

Belize

SOCIETY

Government. Belize is a parliamentary democracy. Queen Elizabeth II of Britain is head of state but is represented in Belize by a governor-general (currently Sir Colville Young). The head of government is the prime minister (currently Said Musa), who is the leader of the National Assembly's dominant party. The country has a bicameral legislature. The House of Representatives has 29 members, and the Senate has 12 members. Representatives are directly elected and senators are appointed. The nation is divided into six districts. Belize has two political parties—the People's United Party (PUP) and the United Democratic Party (UDP). General elections are held at least every five years. The voting age is 18.

Economy. Belize's economy has been expanding since independence. Large amounts of foreign aid have contributed greatly to the economy's success. Belize is a member of the Caribbean Community and Common Market (CARICOM), a regional economic association. Nearly 40 percent of the labor force is employed in agricultural production. The country's main exports are sugar, citrus fruits, molasses, bananas, wood and wood products, and clothing. Sugar traditionally has been the primary cash crop, but citrus fruits are now nearly as strong. The United States, the United Kingdom, and Mexico are Belize's major trading partners. Tourism is a fast-growing source of income; ecotourism and adventure tours are very popular. Construction is also becoming increasingly important to the economy. Like many other Caribbean countries, Belize has established an offshore financial sector.

Inflation is low, but unemployment remains a problem, especially among the youth. Although the country has experienced economic progress, that progress has not yet benefited the majority of the population. Poverty affects roughly one-third of the total population and around two-thirds of all rural people. The currency is the Belizean dollar (BZD), which is pegged to the U.S. dollar using a 2-1 ratio.

Transportation and Communications. The Northern, Western, and Hummingbird Highways are paved and link most cities. Roads leading to remote areas are rough. The national network of private bus systems is widely used, but a monopoly has allowed for sharp increases in fares. In cities and towns, most people get around by walking or riding bikes. The number of private cars is growing. Several small private domestic airlines provide commuter and tourist travel.

In major towns, most people have telephones; villages usually have at least one phone. Radio and television broadcasts together reach nearly all Belizeans, who remain well-informed on local, regional, and international news.

Education. The majority of primary and secondary schools are church operated but receive large government subsidies. Students pay fees, buy their own books and supplies, and usually must wear uniforms. A few government schools exist for children of families that cannot afford these costs, but generally there are not enough spaces to accommodate all. Children are required to attend school until the equivalent of the eighth grade in the United States, but secondary schooling is not required. Many students are unable to complete their primary education due to cost, family obligation, or other factors.

Space in secondary schools is limited, and acceptance depends on one's passing the Belize National Selection Exam. Those who complete a secondary education can attend junior college, teacher's college, or the University College of Belize. The government is focusing reform efforts on standardizing curriculum in all schools, dealing with educational inequities, and providing more vocational education in each district.

Health. Health care is accessible to many citizens, particularly those in the towns and in Belize City. Each district has a small hospital, and there is a large hospital in Belize City. A health worker is assigned to each village but might not always be present. Clinics and private doctors serve those who can afford to pay. Preventable diseases still afflict the country. Many Belizeans seek treatment from local "bush" doctors knowledgeable about natural and herbal remedies. Rainwater tanks and municipal water systems are used widely although some concern for water safety exists.

DEVELOPMENT DATA

Human Dev. Index* rank . . . . 99 of 177 countries
Adjusted for women. . . . . 80 of 144 countries
Real GDP per capita $6,080
Adult literacy rate . . . . 77 percent (male); 77 (female)
Infant mortality rate . . . . 26 per 1,000 births
Life expectancy . . . . 70 (male); 73 (female)

AT A GLANCE

Events and Trends.

- In October 2004, Belize passed a law aimed at fighting child abduction. The law mandates that if a child comes to Belize with only one parent, the travelers will be denied entrance unless the parent can show written permission from the other parent or a court.
- In January 2004, a London court refused to stop the construction of a government-approved hydroelectric dam. Opponents say the US$30 million project would threaten one of the most ecologically diverse rainforests in the world and raise electricity costs. Supporters insist that without the dam, Belize would continue to depend on Mexico for much of its energy.
- In 2002 Belize and Guatemala announced plans to resolve their territorial disputes. However, a planned referendum on the resolution had yet to go before voters in 2004.
- Some progress is being made between Belize and Guatemala. In 2004, the two countries set up a joint health commission to deal with health issues such as malaria, dengue fever, and rabies along their mutual border. The commission has successfully reduced the occurrences of the diseases as well as promoted solidarity between the countries.

Contact Information. Embassy of Belize, 2535 Massachusetts Avenue NW, Washington, DC 20008; phone (202) 332-9636; web site www.embassyofbelize.org. Belize Tourist Board, New Central Bank Building, Level 2, Gabourel Lane, PO Box 325, Belize City, Belize; phone (800) 624-0686; web site www.travelbelize.org.

ProQuest Information and Learning Company
300 North Zeeb Road, P.O. Box 1346
Ann Arbor, Michigan 48106 USA
Toll Free: 1.800.528.6279
Fax: 1.800.864.0019
www.culturegrams.com

© 2005 ProQuest Information and Learning Company and Brigham Young University. It is against the law to copy, reprint, store, or transmit any part of this publication in any form by any means without written permission from ProQuest. This document contains native commentary and original analysis, as well as estimated statistics. The content should not be considered strictly factual, and it may not apply to all groups in a nation. *UN Development Programme, Human Development Report 2004 (New York: Oxford University Press, 2004).

CultureGrams 2006 World Edition

Republic of Bolivia

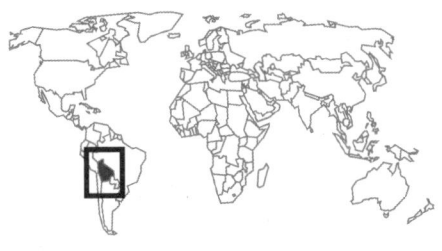

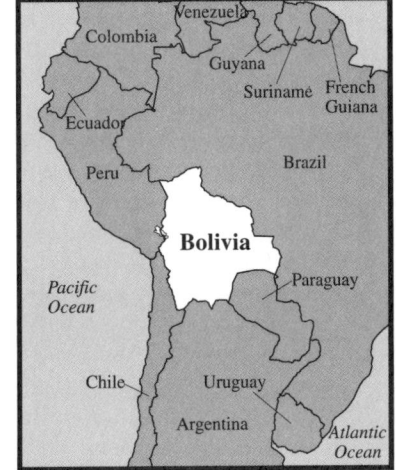

Boundary representations are not necessarily authoritative.

BACKGROUND

Land and Climate. Located in the heart of South America, Bolivia is a landlocked country of 424,165 square miles (1,098,582 square kilometers); it is almost three times the size of Montana. There are five distinct geographical areas: the high, cold, and dry mountain-rimmed Altiplano to the west; Las Yungas, a region of medium-elevation valleys northeast of La Paz and Cochabamba; the agricultural highland valleys in the center of the country; the Gran Chaco, a vast subtropical plain shared with Paraguay and Argentina; and the *llanos* or *el trópico*—wet, hot, forested lowlands in the east and northeast. Grasslands are common on these lands, which makes the area good for cattle ranching. Forests cover about half of Bolivia.

The Andes Mountains, which run north-south through the country, climb to more than 21,000 feet (6,401 meters). They are permanently covered with snow above 16,000 feet (4,800 meters). The famous Lake Titicaca, the highest navigable body of water in the world (12,500 feet, or 3,810 meters), lies on the north end of the Altiplano. The country has two main seasons. Summer (November–April) is the rainy season. Winter is from June to September. In La Paz, the average annual temperature is 65°F (18°C).

Unlike most countries, Bolivia has two capital cities: La Paz is the main capital, where the president and legislature are located; Sucre is home to the country's highest courts. When Bolivians refer to the capital, they are talking about La Paz.

History. The Tiahuanaco civilization inhabited the area near Lake Titicaca between 1500 B.C. and A.D. 1200. Aymara and other groups were conquered in the 1400s by Incan armies, bringing the area into the Inca Empire. The Incas introduced the Quechua language and a new social system. The Spanish began their conquest in 1532, and by 1538 all of present-day Bolivia was under Spanish control. Countless indigenous people died in forced labor. Known as Upper Peru during Spanish rule, Bolivia was one of the first colonies to rebel. Political uprisings occurred frequently in the 1700s but were always crushed. It was not until the independence movement of 1809 that Upper Peru began to see success. After the 16-year War of Independence, the area gained autonomy on 6 August 1825 and was named after its liberator, Simón Bolívar.

Bolivia's first president was overthrown in 1828, and the country experienced decades of factional strife, revolutions, and military dictatorships. Much of its original territory was lost between 1879 and 1935 in wars with Chile, Brazil, and Paraguay. The War of the Pacific (1879–84) was most significant because Bolivia lost its access to the sea. The lack of sea access has restricted Bolivia's economic growth. Bolivians have regularly appealed to Chile for the return of the territory. In 1992, Peru granted Bolivia access to the sea via the Ilo port in southern Peru. With this access, Bolivia hopes to increase foreign trade.

The government attempted to improve conditions and stabilize the country during the 1950s, but a military coup ended the reforms in 1964. A series of coups brought various dictatorships to power, each of them oppressive to the indigenous majority's population. From 1971 to 1978, Hugo Banzer Suárez led an authoritarian military regime that was credited with creating economic growth but criticized for human-rights abuses. Economic conditions worsened through the 1980s, characterized by spiraling inflation that peaked at 11,700 percent in 1985.

After other leaders stepped down, a representative democracy was finally established in August 1985 with the election

Bolivia

of President Víctor Paz Estenssoro. He reduced inflation to less than 20 percent and stabilized the economy. His term ended peacefully in 1989, when Jaime Paz Zamora was elected.

Gonzalo Sanchez de Lozada became president in 1993. Significantly, his vice president, Victor Hugo Cárdenas, was Aymara—the first indigenous person to rise to such a high office in Latin America. Sanchez de Lozada worked to integrate indigenous groups into society, but his plans to export Bolivias vast stores of natural gas drew public protests, which eventually forced him to resign.

The country continues to struggle to end the cycle of poverty, curb the practice among poor farmers of growing coca plants (cocaine base) as a cash crop, and reduce injustice against indigenous peoples.

THE PEOPLE

Population. Bolivia's population of 8.7 million is growing at about 1.6 percent annually. About one-third of the population lives in rural areas. La Paz has more than one million people and Santa Cruz has about the same number. Nearly 70 percent of the total population is of indigenous ancestry, including Quechua (30 percent), Aymara (25 percent), Guaraní, Mojeño, Chimane, and smaller groups. Some 25 percent of the people are *criollo* (or mestizo), who are of mixed indigenous and European heritage. Another 15 percent are of European descent. Quechua Indians are prevalent throughout the country, but are especially concentrated near Cochabamba and Sucre; the Aymara are concentrated in the Altiplano.

Language. *Castellano* (Spanish), Quechua, and Aymara are all official languages. Spanish is used in government, schooling, and business and is the native tongue of about 40 percent of the population. Most people speak some Quechua. Indigenous groups speak their own languages, especially in rural areas. However, Quechua and Aymara are often liberally peppered with Spanish words. Many indigenous people from rural areas who move to cities speak Spanish with their families to avoid stigma. Many young indigenous-language speakers also speak Spanish.

Religion. Approximately 95 percent of the people are Roman Catholic. Some indigenous belief systems and an active Protestant minority (*evangélicos*) are also present. Bolivians of the Altiplano mix Aymaran and Quechuan traditions with their Catholic beliefs. For instance, reverence for *Pachamama*, or goddess Mother Earth, is popular. People toast to her or bless things in her name. A *ch'alla* is the blessing of any material possession or event by offering symbolic articles and alcohol to *Pachamama* and *Achachila*, gods of the mountains. Homes in rural areas may be given a *ch'alla-* every year at *Carnaval*.

General Attitudes. In Bolivia, time is viewed differently than in North America. People enjoy getting as much pleasure out of an experience as possible, with less regard to how much time they spend. Scheduled events begin late, as all understand that arriving on time is not expected. The Aymara view the past as something they can see in front of them but the future as unseen and therefore behind them.

Bolivians admire honesty and frown upon those who are too proud and who flaunt or talk excessively about their wealth. They do not like confrontation and avoid disagreement. Kindness, gentleness, and concern for another's welfare are keys to friendship in Bolivia. Bolivians like to remind others that they are also "Americans" because they live in South America. They call people from the United States *norteamericanos*.

Divisions exist between societ's upper classes—Europeans and mestizos—and indigenous groups, who have often been barred from participating in society because of their race. Those who have wanted to assimilate into society have had to speak Spanish and change their way of dress. Many also adopt Spanish names. The indigenous movement is working to ensure that all the benefits of a democratic society are extended to all citizens without forcing them to abandon their traditions. People of European and mestizo ancestry tend to believe that other groups should assimilate into society by leaving tradition behind and adopting a more Westernized culture.

Personal Appearance. How Bolivians dress depends on where they live and their social class. Generally, urban residents wear Western-style clothing. Children dress neatly for school. Having clean shoes is very important. Many women wear a *pollera* (a full, colorful skirt). Rural women (called *cholitas*) wear a *pollera* with a *manta* (shawl). They often wear their hair in braids and may wear bowler derby hats, bonnets, or stovepipe hats, depending on where they are from.

Some indigenous people make their clothing out of wool. Common colors include red, black, and off-white. Native men might wear shin-length pants, a shirt, and a thick leather belt. They often wear a *poncho* and a hat. Women wear a long, dark-colored dress tied at the waist with a colorful belt. They also may wear a small shoulder cape and oval hat. Women carry babies on their backs in an *aguayo* (a woven square cloth).

CUSTOMS AND COURTESIES

Greetings. Spanish-speaking Bolivians greet friends and acquaintances with a cheerful *¡Buenos días!* (Good morning), *¡Buenas tardes!* (Good afternoon), or *¡Buenas noches!* (Good evening). To say How are you? you could say *¿Cómo estás?* in Spanish, *Imaynalla kanki* in Quechua, or *Kamisaki* in Aymara.

In Spanish, one adds the title *Señor* (Mr.), *Señora* (Mrs.), or *Señorita* (Miss) for first-time introductions or when greeting strangers. *Señorita* is used for any woman, unless she is older or the speaker knows she is married. Bolivians show respect for a person by using the title *Don* (for men) or *Doña* (for women) before his or her first name. Rural people (*campesinos*) even use these titles with close friends. Strangers do not call each other by first name.

Greetings are accompanied by a handshake. However, if a person's hand is wet or dirty, he or she may offer an arm or elbow. It is important to greet everyone in a home. In cities, greetings for both men and women are always accompanied by a kiss on or near the cheek. Bolivians maintain little personal space and stand close during conversation. Close friends and relatives frequently greet with an *abrazo*. It consists of a hug, a handshake, two or three pats on the shoulder, and another handshake. Female friends often embrace and kiss each other on the cheek. They commonly walk arm in arm. Spanish farewells include *Hasta luego* (Until later) or the casual *Chau*. *Adiós* implies good-bye for a long time. In southern areas, *Adiós* is also used as a quick greeting when people pass on the street. In both Quechua and Aymaran *Q'ayaqama* means See you tomorrow.

Gestures. Bolivians often use hands, eyes, and facial expressions to communicate. To beckon children, one waves the fingers with the palm down. Patting someone on the shoulder signifies friendship. A raised hand, palm outward and fingers extended, twisting quickly from side to side, states "There isn't any" or "no"—a gesture often used by taxi and bus drivers when their vehicles are full. Waving the index finger indicates a strong "no." One covers the mouth when yawning or coughing. Eye contact in conversation is essential. Avoiding another's eyes shows suspicion, lack of trust, or shyness.

Visiting. Bolivians enjoy visiting one another. Both arranged and unannounced visits are common. Urban visitors generally give flowers or small gifts to the host upon arrival. Hosts might also present visitors with gifts, which are not opened in front of the giver. Hosts make their guests as comfortable as possible. Compliments given during the meal instead of after will bring a second helping.

Upon arrival, visitors are invited inside and offered a drink or light refreshments; refusing them is impolite. It is also impolite to start a conversation on the doorstep. Visitors staying a few days are welcomed with a hug and kiss on the cheek. Hosts provide special meals as a welcoming gesture, and if possible, all family members are present to greet the guests. Guests are not asked how long they will stay, as this is interpreted as a desire to have them leave soon.

Eating. Bolivian families eat most meals together. They typically have one large and two small meals per day. Rural families might eat four meals. Upon entering a room where people are eating, Bolivians often say *Buen provecho* (similar to *Bon appétit*). Everyone (including guests) is expected to eat everything on the plate. People eat meat with utensils, not hands. Generally, one is not excused from the table until all are finished eating. It is polite to say *Gracias* (Thank you) to all at the table when one finishes eating and to wish them *Buen provecho* upon leaving. Dining out is most common at lunch. In restaurants, the host typically pays for the meal. A tip is usually left when in large groups or in a nice restaurant in the city. *Chicharias*, bars indicated by a white flag hanging outside the establishment, serve *chicha*, a home-brewed alcoholic drink made from corn. *Chicharias* are an important meeting place, especially in the highland valley areas.

LIFESTYLE

Family. The family is central to Bolivian society. Middle- and upper-class families have one or two children. Poorer families traditionally are much larger, but children often die in infancy. While many rural couples live together in common-law arrangements, formal marriages are more common in cities. Children almost always live with their parents until they are married, and sometimes even after marriage.

Most women work in the home. Without modern conveniences, their work is difficult and time consuming. This situation can prevent women from pursuing work in the formal labor force, but many run small businesses (sewing, cutting hair, selling soda and other small items etc.) from their homes. Families in the upper- and middle-classes often have maids. While the father makes most family decisions, the mother exerts much influence on household affairs. Although children are taught the importance of education, illiteracy is high among the poor. Children generally are well disciplined and share in family responsibilities. The elderly live with their children's families.

Dating and Marriage. Chaperoned dating begins at about age 15. Dating is preceded by flirting. In many towns on Sunday (and other) evenings, young men and young women like to *dar vueltas* (take walks), where they walk in groups around the central plaza to make eye contact and flirt. The process of getting acquainted, dating seriously, and being engaged can take as long as three years. Men marry between the ages of 20 and 25, while women marry between ages 19 and 23. People usually do not marry until they have some financial security or property. For a marriage to be legal, a civil ceremony must be performed. However, most couples also have a religious ceremony, followed by a dance and reception. In rural areas, the celebration can last as long as a week. Because weddings are expensive, many rural people choose common-law marriages instead. Bolivians wear their wedding rings on the right hand.

Diet. Potatoes, rice, milk products, fruits, and soups (which often include *quinoa*, a protein-rich grain), are common staples in the Bolivian diet. Starches vary by region: yucca is eaten in the lowlands; corn is plentiful in the valleys; and potatoes are eaten daily in the Altiplano. Bolivia has hundreds of varieties of potatoes prepared in different ways. *Chuños* are freeze-dried potatoes that are used in soups or side dishes when rehydrated. Most foods are fried and seasoned with *llajua* (a spicy salsa). Peanuts may be used in soups (*sopa de maní*) and sauces. Chicken is the most common meat. Southern Bolivians eat a lot of beef and enjoy barbecues. Breakfast usually consists of tea or coffee, bread, and perhaps cheese. In rural areas, it might be a hot drink called *api* made of corn spiced with sugar and cinnamon. Lunch, the main meal, consists of soup and a main dish. In cities, people enjoy *salteñas* (meat or chicken pies made with potatoes, olives, and raisins) as a mid-morning snack.

Recreation. *Fútbol* (soccer) is the national sport. Other popular leisure activities include watching television (in urban areas), visiting with friends, and attending festivals. In the Chaco region, people get together to drink several rounds of *yerba mate*, an herbal tea. Dancing and singing are popular at various events.

The Arts. Many of Bolivia's cultural traditions have their roots in pre-Inca civilizations. Textiles have changed little from those roots, often incorporating the same dyes and patterns that have been used for hundreds of years. Since colonial times, Bolivians have been using gold and silver to ornament architecture, jewelry, and other objects. Basket weaving and wood carving are common crafts in the Guaraní region.

Music is an integral part of Bolivian culture. Played and promoted throughout the world, it can be divided into three types: fast, happy rhythms from the east and northeast; slow, romantic, and melancholic rhythms from the Andes Mountains; and happy, romantic rhythms from the central valleys. Much of the music is characterized by distinctive instruments: panpipes (*zampoña*), vertical flutes, various percussion instruments, and the *charango*, a 12-string, guitar-like instrument made from an armadillo shell. The *cueca*, *tinku*, and *saya* are traditional dances.

Holidays. Holidays include New Year's Day, *Carnaval* (Saturday before Ash Wednesday), *Día del Mar*, or Sea Day (23 March, when Bolivians remember the war with Chile in which Bolivia lost ocean access), Holy Week before Easter, Father's Day (19 Mar.), Labor Day (1 May), Mother's Day (27 May), Independence Day (6 Aug.), All Saints' Day (1 November, a day for the family to clean and decorate ancestral graves and enjoy a picnic), and Christmas. On Christmas Eve, some children place their old shoes in a window for *Papá Noel* (Santa Claus) to take them in exchange for new gifts. Children also receive gifts on Three Kings' Day (6 Jan.).

Dancing, wearing costumes, and pouring water on people are common during *Carnaval*. The city of Oruro holds one of the biggest *Carnaval* celebrations in the region. Almost every *pueblo* (village) has its unique *fiestas* in honor of its patron

Bolivia

saint or the Virgin Mary. These local events are noted for their music and colorful costumes.

Commerce. On weekdays, business is generally conducted from 8 a.m. to noon and 2 to 6 p.m. The midday break, or *descanso*, allows people to have lunch and relax. Government offices often close without warning. Strikes, known as *paros cívicos*, occasionally interfere with business hours.

SOCIETY

Government. The president (currently Carlos Mesa), the vice president, and the cabinet form the executive branch based at La Paz. *El Congreso Nacional* (National Congress), also in La Paz, consists of a 27-seat Chamber of Senators and a 130-seat Chamber of Deputies. The Supreme Court sits at Sucre, the legal capital. The president, vice president, and congressional representatives serve five-year terms. The constitution prohibits presidents from serving consecutive terms. Voting is mandatory at age 18.

Economy. With natural resources such as tin, natural gas, crude oil, zinc, silver, gold, lead, and tungsten, Bolivia's major industry is mining. Others include coffee and food production, textiles, and timber. Roughly half of the labor force is engaged in agriculture. Coca (used in making cocaine) has been the largest (illicit) cash crop; however, a government plan to eradicate production has resulted in decreased coca exports. Government efforts to stop coca trafficking are complicated by the drug's lucrative profits and centuries-old status as a traditional crop. It has many legitimate uses in society, including medicinal and dietary, and is a fundamental part of the culture.

Bolivia is one of the poorest and least developed Latin American countries. Limited access to adequate health care, education, and economic opportunities affects the quality of life for most Bolivians, particularly those in rural areas. About two-thirds of the population lives in poverty. Improving conditions for poor and indigenous populations remains a long-term goal. Unemployment is high, and underemployment affects almost half of the economically active population.

Massive debt forgiveness by foreign creditors of more than 80 percent of Bolivia's external debt has given a boost to the country's economic potential. The economy is growing, albeit slowly, and inflation is decreasing as the government continues to cut expenditures. The currency is the *boliviano* (BOB).

Transportation and Communications. Throughout its modern history, Bolivia has been handicapped by its landlocked location and lack of internal transportation and communications. Only a few major highways are paved. Airlines connect major cities and allow travelers to avoid rugged terrain. But buses, taxis, and trains are the most common forms of transportation. Buses are often crowded. More expensive minivans are faster and less crowded. Taxis often stop to pick up additional passengers going the same way. Several radio and television stations are in operation.

Education. Schooling is free and compulsory for ages 5 to 18. However, school conditions are poor. Those with money send their children to parochial or private schools. Though illiteracy is declining, problems still exist. Less than half of all children complete their primary education, and less than one-third go on to secondary school. Strikes, long distances to schools, and family labor needs contribute to this problem. In the past, indigenous children could not receive instruction in their own language because Spanish was the language used in all schools. Recent reforms require bilingual education. There are about 15 universities in Bolivia. One must pass two entrance exams to be admitted to a university.

Health. Sanitation facilities are poor. Contaminated water is the most serious health threat. Tap water must be boiled, but wood is hard to find and gas is expensive. Many rural areas lack running water and electricity. Local nurses and doctors have been training *responsables populares de salud* (community healthcare workers) in basic skills. These trainees help serve the needs of the rural population. The infant mortality rate is high because of disease and widespread poverty.

Only about half the population has adequate access to medical care. Traditional medicine is used in many rural areas. Many illnesses affect the populace, including hepatitis, cholera, and Chagas, a parasitic disease that causes intestinal problems and early death by heart attacks. The AIDS threat is growing.

DEVELOPMENT DATA

Human Dev. Index* rank . . . . 114 of 177 countries
  Adjusted for women . . . . 92 of 144 countries
Real GDP per capita $2,460
Adult literacy rate . . . . 93 percent (male); 81 (female)
Infant mortality rate . . . . 55 per 1,000 births
Life expectancy . . . . 62 (male); 66 (female)

AT A GLANCE

Events and Trends.

- In October 2003, violent protests forced President Gonzalo Sanchez de Lozada to resign. More than 50,000 Bolivians protested his plans to export natural gas so that Bolivia could reduce its national debt and gain international aid. Many people believed the exports would be used to help the wealthy, while the poor would still be ignored. Up to 80 people died in the protests. A year later, the Bolivian congress voted to bring Sanchez de Lozada back from exile in the United States and try him for failing to quell the protests and stop the deaths.

- However, a July 2004 referendum showed that more Bolivians favored exporting the natural gas. So the new president, Carlos Mesa, signed a deal to begin exports. Then, in March 2005, he resigned, saying more protests had made his position impossible. But he later agreed to stay on after Congress refused his resignation and would not allow early elections.

- In June 2003, Bolivia announced the discovery of seven new species of frogs, lizards, and snakes in a remote forest valley. The government declared the area protected, but it is still threatened by logging and agriculture.

Contact Information. Embassy of the Republic of Bolivia, 3014 Massachusetts Avenue NW, Washington, DC 20008; phone (202) 483-4410. Web site www.boliviaweb.com.

CultureGrams™
People. The World. You.

ProQuest Information and Learning Company
300 North Zeeb Road, P.O. Box 1346
Ann Arbor, Michigan 48106 USA
Toll Free: 1.800.528.6279
Fax: 1.800.864.0019
www.culturegrams.com

© 2005 ProQuest Information and Learning Company and Brigham Young University. It is against the law to copy, reprint, store, or transmit any part of this publication in any form by any means without written permission from ProQuest. This document contains native commentary and original analysis, as well as estimated statistics. The content should not be considered strictly factual, and it may not apply to all groups in a nation. *UN Development Programme, Human Development Report 2004 (New York: Oxford University Press, 2004).

CultureGrams™ World Edition 2006

Federative Republic of Brazil

Boundary representations are not necessarily authoritative.

BACKGROUND

Land and Climate. Brazil is the fifth largest country in the world and the fifth most populous. At 3,286,488 square miles (8,511,965 square kilometers), it is larger than the continental United States and comprises half of South America. Forests cover slightly more than half of Brazil's territory and include the world's largest tropical rain forest in the Amazon River Basin. Concerns over the destruction of the rain forests have prompted a global conservation effort. However, illegal logging and slash-and-burn clearing continue and may increase because of government plans to develop the area.

Brazil has five distinct regions: north, northeast, southeast, south, and central-west. The *Amazonas* (Amazon River) is the longest in South America, and it traverses lush rain forests in northern Brazil. Tropical grasslands and savannas extend across the sparsely populated central-west region. The northeast's vast stretches of land are commonly subject to droughts. The southeast, which is the most populated and industrialized region, is rich in minerals and natural resources. Agriculture and manufacturing are common in the south, which boasts one of the world's largest hydroelectric dams, near Iguaçu Falls.

Less than 5 percent of Brazil lies above 3,000 feet (914 meters). The country is south of the equator and has a mostly tropical climate. Humidity is high in coastal and forest regions, but the highlands (such as those around São Paulo) have a more moderate climate. The warmest month is January; the coolest is July. The south is more temperate than the north. Temperatures in the far south sometimes drop below freezing.

History. Brazil does not have a written history prior to the arrival of Europeans, but various groups inhabited the area when Pedro Álvarez Cabral arrived in 1500 and claimed the region for Portugal. The Portuguese colonized Brazil; French and Dutch groups both attempted to establish colonies but eventually were driven out by the Portuguese. After Spain conquered Portugal, it controlled Brazil from 1580 to 1640. Colonization took several decades, and expansion into the interior of the country did not really begin until after 1650.

When Napoleon captured Spain and Portugal (1808), the South American colonies were initially liberated from European control. However, the Portuguese royal family soon fled to Brazil and established Rio de Janeiro as the seat of the Portuguese Empire. Brazil then ceased to be a colony and became part of the Portuguese kingdom. The royal family returned to Portugal in 1821, leaving Dom Pedro I to govern. He declared Brazil's independence in 1822 after people in Portugal demanded that Brazil be returned to colonial status. His son, Dom Pedro II, was deposed in an 1889 military coup.

The military would eventually seize control five more times, although with relatively little violence. With military support, the dictator Getúlio Vargas ruled from 1930 to 1945, followed by elected presidents. A 1964 coup gave the military control until a return to civilian rule in 1985. A new constitution was ratified in 1988.

Elections in 1989 brought Fernando Collor de Mello, a conservative, to office as the first directly elected president in 29

Brazil

years. Collor's economic austerity campaign and corrupt activities crippled the economy. In a historic test of democracy, Brazil succeeded in removing the president from office by legal, constitutional means. Before impeachment proceedings could be carried out, however, Collor resigned in December 1992.

Vice President Itamar Franco assumed the presidency until elections in October 1994. Franco's finance minister, Fernando Cardoso, introduced an anti-inflation plan so successful that the economy began to boom in 1994. Cardoso, who had spent years in exile after the 1964 military coup, eventually upset the front-running presidential candidate and later became the first Brazilian president to be elected to a second consecutive term.

In 2002, the first left-wing president in 40 years came to power. Luiz Inacio Lula da Silva promised to reform the economy and to eradicate hunger. Although Lula has implemented several social programs, the nation still faces stark inequality of wealth and a weak economy.

THE PEOPLE

Population. The population of Brazil is approximately 184 million and is growing annually at a rate of about 1.1 percent. More than 80 percent of the people live in cities. Along with their greater municipal areas, São Paulo and Rio de Janeiro hold some 30 million people. Brasília, the new capital, was completed in 1960 after having almost every detail of the city planned by the government; its population now numbers more than two million.

About 45 percent of the population is younger than age 20. Brazilians of European (mostly Portuguese) descent comprise 55 percent of the population, while 38 percent is of mixed heritage and 6 percent is of African descent. The indigenous population numbers only about 300,000. Many of these peoples inhabit the Amazon region (a few groups have never been contacted by modern society). Among those of mixed heritage, many have some indigenous blood through intermarriage. Groups of German, Italian, Lebanese, and Japanese immigrants who settled in the south maintain ethnic communities. In fact, Brazil is home to the largest cohesive community of Japanese outside of Japan. The black population descended from African slaves brought to Brazil before the 1880s; they live mostly in northeastern states like Bahia.

Language. Portuguese is Brazil's official language. It differs slightly in pronunciation from the Portuguese spoken in Portugal. English and French are popular as second languages. Spanish is also becoming more popular in some circles as Brazil establishes stronger trade ties with its neighbors. (Although Portuguese speakers generally understand Spanish, some Brazilians are offended when deliberately spoken to in Spanish.) In southern cities, some descendants of European immigrants also speak German or Italian. Indigenous peoples may speak any one of more than a hundred local languages.

Religion. Brazil traditionally has been a strong Roman Catholic country. At one time, nearly 95 percent of the population claimed membership in the Catholic Church. However, membership has dropped to less than 70 percent, and other Christian churches are growing rapidly. Since the founding of the republic in 1889, there has been a separation of church and state, and religious freedom has been guaranteed. Although Brazilians consider themselves quite religious, most attend church only on special occasions. Some in the northeast and in urban areas countrywide practice Afro-Brazilian religions that combine various indigenous African beliefs with Catholicism. These Afro-Brazilian religions, such as Candomblé, Macumba, and Xangô, share many similarities.

General Attitudes. Brazilians are warm, fun-loving, and free-spirited. They are also outgoing and enjoy being around others. At the same time, they are hardworking. Brazilians are proud of the Portuguese heritage that sets them apart from other Latin American peoples. One point of pride is the "Brazilian way"—their ability to find creative ways around seemingly insurmountable problems. Brazilians often are opinionated and will argue for their convictions with vigor. In spite of economic difficulties, most Brazilians are hopeful about their country's future.

Social status commonly is measured by one's power to acquire possessions. People tend to view time more as a sequence of events than as a matter of hours and minutes. Therefore, people in most regions (except São Paulo) appear to have an extremely casual attitude about time. Brazilians in the north and northeast regions and small inland towns are traditionally more conservative. Folklore is stronger in these areas; traditional religious and military celebrations are also more common.

Personal Appearance. In general, Brazilians are fashionable and like to dress according to the latest styles. People in urban areas like to wear European (particularly Italian) fashions. People in the warmest and most humid regions dress more casually, and colors are lighter and brighter year-round. In São Paulo and parts of the southern region, people often dress in black, white, and other neutral colors. Stylish suits or skirts with jackets are common business attire.

Both men and women pay careful attention to their appearance. Shoes are well kept and polished. Manicures and pedicures are popular. People like to dress up for special occasions and parties. In rural regions, more traditional clothing is common, especially among the native peoples.

CUSTOMS AND COURTESIES

Greetings. In formal situations, Brazilians greet each other with a handshake. A common greeting among friends, except from one male to another, is to embrace and kiss on alternating cheeks or touch cheeks and "kiss the air." In some regions, three kisses are exchanged. Common verbal greetings include *Olá. Tudo bem?* (Hello. Is everything fine?) and *Como vai?* (How are you?). Young friends greet each other with a simple *Oi* (Hi). When one joins or leaves a small group, it is polite to shake hands with all who are present. Common parting terms include *Tcháu* (Good-bye) and *Até logo* (See you soon).

Superiors and authorities are often addressed formally with the titles *Senhor* (Mr.) or *Senhora* (Mrs.), followed by their surname. In less formal situations, first names are commonly used, sometimes preceded by *Seu* (for men) or *Sua/Dona* (for women).

Gestures. Brazilians often use gestures to communicate and express feelings. Gestures often accompany greetings. One beckons by waving all fingers of the hand with the palm facing either up or down. Pulling down the lower eyelid with an index finger signifies disbelief or caution. One may tap the fingers horizontally under the chin to indicate that another person does not know what he or she is talking about. The "OK" sign used in the United States, with the thumb and index finger forming a circle, is an offensive gesture.

Brazilians tend to stand close and touch each other often during conversation. Eye contact is important. Passing between conversing individuals is rude. Men tend to stare at and make comments about women passing by. This is not considered rude and generally is ignored by the women.

Visiting. Brazilians enjoy visiting. The tropical climate allows for much time outdoors, including chatting outside late into the evening. If a meal or snack is in progress, it is considered impolite not to ask visitors to join in eating. Most people will politely decline the invitation *Está servido?* (Will you join me?) with *Bom apetite* (Enjoy). Hosts generally also offer coffee or other refreshment toward the end of a visit. In rural areas, not accepting refreshments may be considered rude. If invited to dinner, one might take candy, wine, or a small gift to the hosts. Invited guests commonly arrive up to a half hour late, except perhaps in São Paulo. Guests are generally expected to stay at least two hours. While Brazilians enjoy conversation, they avoid controversial subjects (like politics and religion) at social gatherings. Asking personal questions about one's age, salary, etc., is considered inappropriate.

Eating. Brazilians value mealtime with family and friends. Extended family members often gather together for lunch on Sundays. Brazilians eat in the continental style, with the knife in the right hand and the fork in the left. One wipes the mouth frequently throughout a meal before drinking. After-meal conversation often takes place over a cup of strong *cafézinho* (black coffee). In restaurants, diners call the server by holding up the index finger or by softly saying *Garçom* (waiter). While the bill usually includes the tip, one may leave extra change. If the tip is not included, leaving 10 to 15 percent is customary.

LIFESTYLE

Family. Families traditionally are large and may include the extended family. However, smaller nuclear families, with one to three children, are becoming more common. The family is led by the father, but the mother influences decisions, especially those affecting the home. Women, including those who work outside the home, are responsible for household duties. Middle- and higher-income families often hire domestic help. Children rarely leave home before they marry. Unmarried men may leave early for employment reasons, but they usually live at home until they are 30. The elderly who cannot care for themselves live with their children because it is considered improper to send them to a nursing home.

Family ties are strong, and members rely on each other for assistance and enjoy being together. Among the urban youth, however, some of these values are becoming less important. While middle-income families live in modest homes or apartments, the poor commonly lack the basic necessities of life, including food, sanitation, and shelter. Women and children often work to help support their families.

Dating and Marriage. Group dating starts around age 14; couples gradually emerge from the group. Traditional families expect the young man to ask the girl's father for permission to be her boyfriend. Serious dating and engagements may last two or three years. Brazilians tend to marry young. Weddings often include two ceremonies: a civil ceremony and a religious one. Wedding parties are lavish and elegant, with much food, drink, and music.

Diet. Staple foods in the Brazilian diet include meat, bread, rice, beans, cheese, and eggs. Breakfast usually consists of *café com leite* (coffee with milk), fruit, and bread with marmalade. Lunch is the main meal and often includes beans, rice, meat, salad, potatoes, bread, and fruit. Dinner is lighter and may include a bowl of soup with bread, followed by coffee or milk with a piece of cake. Pastries are typical snacks. Favorite foods vary by region. In Bahia and other states, foods may be spiced with *dendê* (palm oil). In Rio de Janeiro, the favorite is *feijoada* (black beans with beef, pork, sausage, and sometimes a pig's ears, feet, and tail). *Churrasco*, which originated in the south, is a barbecue with a variety of meats. *Bife à cavalo com fritas* (meat with egg and french fries) is popular in many areas. Common drinks include lemonade, milk, fruit juices and shakes, soft drinks, coffee, and *mate* (MAH-tay), an herbal tea enjoyed in southern states.

Recreation. The national sport and passion is *futebol* (soccer). Businesses and schools may even close during the World Cup or important national competitions. Basketball and volleyball are also popular. People enjoy boating, fishing, swimming, and visiting the country's many fine beaches. Brazilians are avid fans of auto racing. During leisure hours, people commonly visit friends or watch television, particularly *telenovelas* (nighttime soap operas). Traditional dances and festivals are popular and vary by region. Brazilians will celebrate any occasion, and get-togethers often include singing and samba dancing. Weekend and holiday barbecues are common.

The Arts. All cultures within Brazil have influenced its music, dance, and festivals. For example, Samba is the most popular music and dance, ant it uses African rhythms blended with European-style singing. Pottery, often made by hand and painted with religious or domestic scenes, is popular. Weaving is also a common art.

European movements have influenced Brazilian art and literature, and artists and writers often combine traditional and modern styles in their work. Brazilian folklore features different mythical characters, such as *Cobra-Grande*, a huge snake living in the Amazon that frightens people by changing shape.

Holidays. *Carnaval*, a five-day festival preceding Ash Wednesday, is the most famous holiday in Brazil. It is marked by street parades, samba and *bloco* (group) dancing, parties, drinking, costumes, conga drums, and music. Some people spend months preparing costumes and saving for *Carnaval*. During this week, crime and car accident rates are unusually high.

Tiradentes Day (21 Apr.) celebrates the death of Joaquim José da Silva Xavier (known as Tiradentes); he was a dentist and nationalist who died in the struggle for independence. *The Festas Juninas* (June Festivals) coincide with the feasts of St. John and St. Peter and are celebrated with local fair-type activities. Other holidays include Easter, Labor Day (1 May), Independence Day (7 Sept.), Memorial Day (2 Nov.), and Republic Day (15 Nov.).

On Christmas Eve, people eat a big meal (turkey or ham) and exchange gifts. Only those gifts from *Papai Noel* (Father Noel) arrive on Christmas Day; all other gifts are exchanged the day before. New Year's Eve is a time for large parties. In some areas, Candomblé believers dress in white and blue to honor the sea goddess Iemanjá and gain energy for the new year. People place flowers and candles on beaches as part of the celebration.

Commerce. *Padarias* (neighborhood shops that sell bread and basic food items) open as early as 5 a.m. Most other stores are open weekdays from 8 a.m. to 6 p.m. and until noon on Saturday. However, business hours are regulated by local business associations; so shops may have longer weekend hours in some areas. Supermarkets are open every day of the week. Some offices and stores close from noon to 2 p.m. for the afternoon meal. Bank hours vary by state. Events are scheduled

Brazil

according to the 24-hour clock; for example, 3 p.m. is referred to as 15:00 (Fifteen hours).

SOCIETY

Government. Brazil is a federative republic consisting of 26 states and one federal district (Brasília). Technically, each state is autonomous with a legislative body and elected governor, but the federal government reserves all rights not delegated to the state. President Luiz Inacio Lula da Silva is head of state and government. A 1997 constitutional amendment allows presidents, governors, and mayors to run for two consecutive terms. The National Congress has an 81-seat Federal Senate and a 513-seat Chamber of Deputies. Voting is universal and compulsory for ages 18 to 70. It is optional for 16- and 17-year-olds and those older than 70.

Economy. Brazil has the largest economy in South America and the eighth largest in the world. However, income distribution is highly unequal, and poverty affects roughly 20 percent of the total population. Inequitable land distribution is a contributing factor: nearly half of all private lands are owned by only 1 percent of the people. Many of the landless live in *favelas* (shantytowns) on the outskirts of urban centers.

Hyperinflation and low growth marked the 1980s and early 1990s. The introduction of the new currency, the *real* (BRL), in 1994, helped to dramatically cut inflation.

Despite an economic crisis caused by weakened investor confidence and a subsequent currency devaluation, the Brazilian economy has remained relatively stable, spurred on by government spending cuts, tax increases and other emergency measures. Unemployment is moderate in some areas but high in larger cities such as São Paulo.

Brazil is largely self-sufficient in food and consumer goods. Agriculture employs about 20 percent of the population. Brazil is one of the world's largest producers of coffee, oranges, and bananas. Much of Brazil's sugarcane is used to produce ethyl alcohol, a fuel used in approximately one-third of Brazilian cars. The industrial sector exports automobiles and parts, textiles, minerals, and metals; other industries include cement and chemicals. Despite large reserves, Brazil lacks the capacity to refine the oil it mines on its own soil. Consequently, the country must import a fourth of the 1.8 billion barrels of oil it uses daily. Much of Brazil's natural gas is also imported. Brazil is a member of Mercosur, a regional free-trade pact that includes Argentina, Paraguay, and Uruguay.

Transportation and Communications. Domestic air travel is well developed between hundreds of local airports. Travel by intercity bus is more common, although buses tend to be crowded. São Paulo and Rio de Janeiro have rapid transit systems. City buses do not stop automatically; people must hail them with the wave of a hand. Readily available in large cities, taxis with red license plates have fixed meter rates.

Brazil's media are highly developed and include one of the world's largest television networks. Televisions are found in even the poorest areas. The country also enjoys a large film and music industry. Urban telephone service is good. Pay phones are operated by tokens or phone cards, not coins.

Education. Education consists of eight years of compulsory elementary education (to age 14) and three years of secondary education. About 40 percent of those who enter school proceed to the secondary level. Entrance to Brazil's top universities is difficult and is preceded by a special college-preparation course and entrance exams. About half of secondary school graduates go on to trade schools. Brazil has many fine libraries and research centers. There are hundreds of higher education institutions. A national adult literacy program has raised the literacy rate substantially.

Health. Brazil's healthcare system provides universal coverage. However, rural areas rarely have adequate facilities. Excellent private care is available in large cities to those who can afford it. Water often is not potable. Sanitation in some areas is insufficient. Yellow fever and malaria are found in some areas. More than 10 percent of the population suffers from malnutrition. A grassroots effort is dispatching mobile healthcare workers to rural areas to fight infant mortality through education and basic care. AIDS is a growing problem.

DEVELOPMENT DATA
Human Dev. Index* rank . . . . 72 of 177 countries
Adjusted for women . . . . 60 of 144 countries
Real GDP per capita $7,770
Adult literacy rate . . . . 86 percent (male); 87 (female)
Infant mortality rate . . . . 30 per 1,000 births
Life expectancy . . . . 64 (male); 73 (female)

AT A GLANCE

Events and Trends.

- In December 2004, Brazil announced it would break drug patents to provide AIDS drugs to its citizens for free. The country's controversial program has become a model for other developing countries, having lowered the rate of HIV infection and AIDS-related deaths.
- In October 2004, Brazil successfully launched its first rocket into space. The success was important because another rocket had exploded before launch in August 2003. That explosion had killed 21 people and deeply hurt the country's space program.
- In September 2004, Brazil, Germany, India, and Japan began campaigning for permanent seats on the United Nations Security Council. Right now only Russia, China, France, Britain, and the United States have permanent seats. Brazil and the other new applicants feel the system is outdated and needs reform to better represent more people around the world.
- In March and April 2004, groups of landless peasants invaded more than 50 properties. The peasants were trying to pressure President Lula to speed land redistribution. Currently, about 50 percent of private lands are owned by 1 percent of the population.

Contact Information. Embassy of Brazil, 3006 Massachusetts Avenue NW, Washington, DC 20008; phone (202) 238-2828; web site www.brasilemb.org. Brazilian Tourism Office, 2141 Wisconsin Avenue NW, Suite E-2, Washington, DC 20007; phone (800) 727-2945; web site www.braziltourism.org.

CultureGrams
People. The World. You.

ProQuest Information and Learning Company
300 North Zeeb Road, P.O. Box 1346
Ann Arbor, Michigan 48106 USA
Toll Free: 1.800.528.6279
Fax: 1.800.864.0019
www.culturegrams.com

© 2005 ProQuest Information and Learning Company and Brigham Young University. It is against the law to copy, reprint, store, or transmit any part of this publication in any form by any means without written permission from ProQuest. This document contains native commentary and original analysis, as well as estimated statistics. The content should not be considered strictly factual, and it may not apply to all groups in a nation. *UN Development Programme, Human Development Report 2004 (New York: Oxford University Press, 2004).

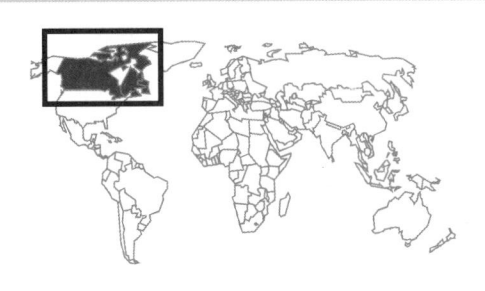

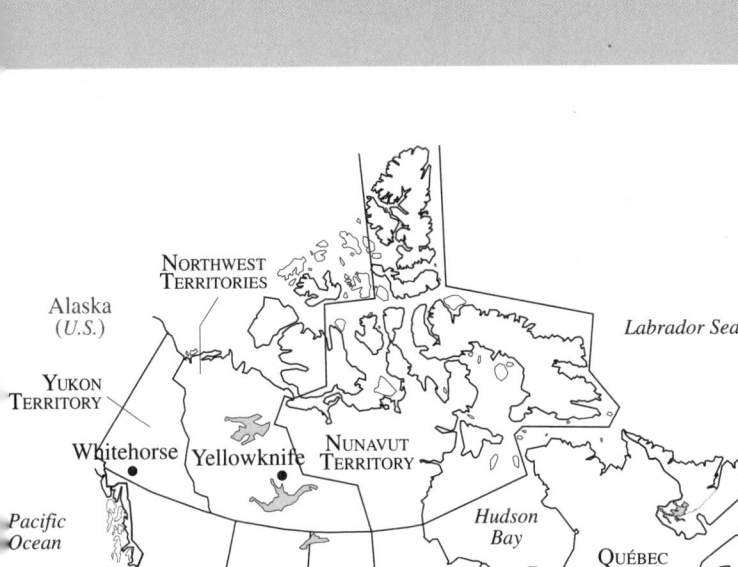

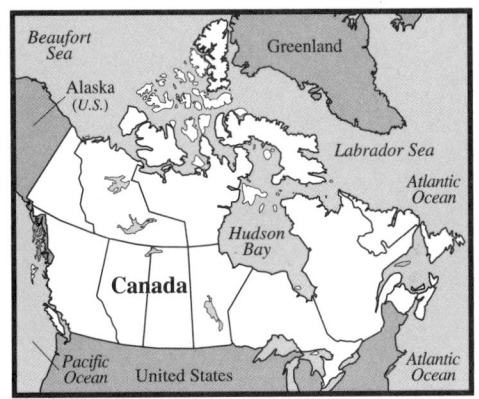

CultureGrams 2006 World Edition — Canada

BACKGROUND

Land and Climate. Canada is the second largest country in the world, after Russia. Due to its vast area of 3,851,788 square miles (9,976,085 square kilometers), Canada features a variety of climates and terrains. British Columbia has a wet climate on its Pacific coastline, near-desert conditions in the interior, and cooler temperatures in the high elevations of the Rocky Mountains and related ranges. Further inland, the provinces of Alberta, Saskatchewan, and Manitoba are dominated by southern prairies and northern forests and tundra.

Much of northern Canada—including parts of the Yukon, Nunavut (a new territory created in 1999), and Northwest Territories—is uninhabited because of the arctic climate and permanently frozen ground. The Great Lakes moderate the climate of southern Ontario, where summers are hot and humid but winters bring snow and freezing temperatures. East of Ontario is Québec, Canada's largest province. Roughly one-sixth the size of the United States, it is more than 1,000 miles (1,600 kilometers) east to west and north to south. The Canadian Shield—a huge, U-shaped, rocky expanse surrounding the Hudson Bay—covers most of Québec and includes thousands of miles of coniferous forest. Much of the province's timber, mining, and hydroelectric wealth is found there. Although the Appalachian Mountains extend into northern New Brunswick, most of the Atlantic provinces' interior terrain is fairly low and flat. This landscape gives way to plateaus, valleys, and rocky terrain along the coast.

History. Early native peoples included the Inuit, Inn, Beothuk, Micmac, and Malecite groups. The first Europeans were likely Vikings from Greenland who settled briefly in Newfoundland around A.D. 1000. English, French, and Basque fishermen came to Canada's Atlantic coast in the 1500s.

French colonists arrived in the 1600s, settling along the Saint Lawrence River in the territory they called New France. Throughout the 1600s, Britain fought with France for the territory. In 1763, the Treaty of Paris gave Britain control over New France, which was renamed Québec. At about the same time, British Loyalists who had left the 13 colonies after the American Revolution also began settling in the area.

In 1791, Québec was divided into Upper and Lower Canada. The two areas became the provinces of Québec and Ontario in 1867. That same year, Québec and Ontario joined with New Brunswick and Nova Scotia to establish a confederation called the Dominion of Canada. In the 1870s, Canada purchased the vast northwestern area called Rupert's Land from the Hudson's Bay Company (a British trading company). This land became part of Canada and was divided into the provinces of Manitoba, Saskatchewan, Alberta, and the northern territories (now known as the Yukon, the Northwest Territories, and Nunavut). Prince Edward Island joined the nation in 1873, but Newfoundland remained a separate colony until 1949.

Canada has retained both formal and informal ties with Britain since becoming a confederation. Although Queen Elizabeth II is the official head of state, Britain has had no control over Canada since constitutional changes made in 1982. A Charter of Rights and Freedoms was also established in 1982, guaranteeing fundamental human rights to all Canadians.

Each region in Canada has a unique history and each has faced its own challenges in recent years. Along the Atlantic coast, fishing resources are dwindling and unemployment is high. Some people from that area feel the federal government should do more to stimulate their economy. In the west, self-government for the many indigenous peoples in the region has

Canada

been an important political topic. Some western provinces also have traditionally been at odds with the more liberal political establishment centered in Ontario and Québec. Meanwhile, Québec has dealt with a movement toward secession or receiving special status among provinces. The most recent attempt at independence came in 1995 but was rejected by a slim margin of voters. Since then, support for sovereignty has declined and the province has opted to remain in the union and take advantage of Canada's strong economy.

THE PEOPLE

Population. About 32.5 million people live in Canada, and the population is growing by 0.92 percent annually. Roughly 38 percent of all Canadians reside in Ontario, 25 percent in Québec, 30 percent in the Western Provinces, and 8 percent in the Atlantic region. Most of the population lives within 100 miles (161 kilometers) of the U.S. border.

Canada has traditionally had a high immigration rate, which has helped it become culturally diverse. The nation is populated not only by those of British, French, and indigenous descent, but also by sizable Chinese, Italian, German, Portuguese, and Polish communities.

The largest cities are Toronto, with 4.7 million people; Montreal, with 3.4 million; Vancouver, with 2 million; and Ottawa, with 1 million.

Language. English and French are official languages in Canada. English dominates in most of the Atlantic region and in the Western Provinces. However, French is the first language of nearly 80 percent of residents of Québec and is used almost exclusively in some areas. It is also spoken by about a third of the population of New Brunswick. The nationwide demand for people who speak both official languages has prompted many school districts to offer French-immersion programs for English-speaking students.

Nearly one in five Canadians speaks a language other than English or French as their native tongue. In the 1990s, Chinese surpassed Italian as the third most common language in the country. Among indigenous groups, more than 50 languages are spoken.

Canadian spelling of English words follows U.S. standards in some cases (e.g., *organize* rather than *organise*) but British standards in others (*centre*, not *center*), and Canadians call the last letter of the alphabet *zed*, not *zee*. Some Canadians (especially in rural areas) use the word *eh* (pronounced "AY"), in much the same way as "Ya know?" or "Isn't it?" would be used in the United States.

Religion. About 77 percent of Canadians are Christians, but the beliefs of the different denominations are diverse, and society is highly secularized. The majority of the people are either Catholic (43.6 percent) or Protestant (29.2 percent). In urban centers, Islam (1.9 percent), Judaism (1.1 percent), Buddhism (1 percent), Hinduism (1 percent), and Sikhism (1 percent) are growing because of immigrant populations. Vancouver has the largest Sikh community outside of the Punjab province of India. A growing portion of the population (16.5 percent) claims no religion.

General Attitudes. Most Canadians are proud of their shared cultural heritage, which includes French, British, and other European influences. They are also proud of their multiculturalism; ethnic groups and immigrants are encouraged to maintain their distinct cultures.

Atlantic Canadians are considered conservative and traditional. Regional and provincial allegiances are strong among Atlantic Canadians and are often placed before national allegiance. To the west, the people of Ontario are considered fairly reserved and formal, while those in the Western Provinces are thought of as more open and friendly. Life in large urban areas is fast-paced, whereas the pace of life in the rest of Canada is more relaxed. The French people of Québec—who are known as *Québécois* or *Québeckers*—are particularly proud of their language and French heritage. They insist that they are different from the rest of Canada and that they should protect their unique cultural institutions.

Canadians take great pride in their nationality. Despite close ties and many similarities between their nation and the United States, Canadians emphasize that they are not just U.S.-type people living in Canada. Indeed, Canadians often dislike U.S. foreign policy and the prevalence of U.S. culture. Despite a close relationship with the United States, Canadians often see people from the United States as more aggressive and materialistic than themselves. Canadians also feel they are more tolerant, community-oriented, and polite. In general, Canadians admire people who are educated, skilled, modest, and polite. In relation to the rest of the world, Canadians see themselves as associated with humanitarianism and fairness.

Personal Appearance. Although dress habits are similar to those in the United States, Canadians are generally more conservative and somewhat more formal in their dress, especially when at work. This is particularly true in Ontario and Québec. When not at work, people often dress casually in jeans and a comfortable shirt. It is polite to remove sunglasses when speaking to someone and to remove hats in buildings.

CUSTOMS AND COURTESIES

Greetings. A firm handshake and *Hello, how are you?* are the most common greetings when one meets new people. Otherwise, a wave of the hand or nod of the head is an acceptable gesture when saying *Hello*. French-speaking people might greet friends and relatives with a light kiss on the cheek. Common French greetings include *Bonjour* (Good day) and *Ça va?* (How's it going?). Friends and young people often prefer to say *Salut* (Hi). When one passes a stranger on the street, a smile and a nod are appropriate. People use first names when addressing others in informal situations or when the more senior person requests it. Titles are used with new acquaintances and on formal occasions. The French term for "Good-bye" is *Au revoir*.

Gestures. Most gestures, positive and negative, are the same in Canada as in the United States. However, some gestures common in the United States might be offensive to a specific cultural group or in a particular area. Pointing at someone with the index finger is rude; using the entire hand to motion to someone is more polite. The "thumbs down" gesture used in the United States to mean "no" is offensive in Québec.

Eye contact is important during conversation, and smiles are always welcome. However, Canadian reserve dictates that a generous amount of personal space be allowed when conversing with others. French speakers tend to use hand gestures while talking somewhat more often than do English speakers.

Visiting. Although Canadians get together often, unannounced visits are not common. Dropping by during regular mealtimes is impolite. During wintertime, visitors nearly always remove their shoes, hats, and coats at the door. Hosts generally offer guests refreshments, including at least a drink and often a small snack. It is appropriate for guests to bring a gift, such as wine, chocolate, or flowers, to the hosts. House parties with alcoholic drinks and impromptu music are popular in both rural and urban areas. Houseguests staying for longer than a day usually write a thank-you note and give a thank-you gift. Promptness in showing gratitude is important.

Eating. The standard three meals per day are often complemented by afternoon tea and coffee breaks or snacks at work. Tea is popular among those of English heritage. Many people eat in the continental style, with the fork in the left hand and the knife in the right. Utensils are placed together on the plate after finishing a meal. One keeps both hands above the table during a meal. Women rest their wrists on the table, men their forearms; elbows may be placed on the table after the meal is finished. However, these formal manners are practiced less often as casual dining becomes more common. Eating on the streets is improper unless one is sitting at an outdoor café or standing at a food stand. At restaurants, tipping about 15 percent is expected.

LIFESTYLE

Family. While the family unit is the center of society, both parents commonly work outside the home. Traditional norms are still valued, particularly in rural areas, but nontraditional households have increased considerably over the last 30 years. About one-third of marriages are expected to end in divorce. A high proportion of children are now born out of wedlock, and there are many single-parent families. The average family has one or two children. Children often live with their parents until they go to college, marry, or get a full-time job.

Dating and Marriage. Dating usually begins between the ages of 13 and 16. Most young people enjoy dancing, going to movies, dining out, going to the beach, and attending sporting events such as hockey games. Casual sexual relationships are common. Fewer young people desire to marry, and if they do, they expect to marry at a later age (at 30 or so). Likewise, couples often wait longer to have children. Many people choose to live together before or instead of marrying. Weddings are usually celebrated with family and friends, but elaborate events are somewhat less common than in the United States.

Diet. In the Atlantic area, where fishing is common, seafood is a dietary staple. Dairy products also are consumed in fairly large quantities. A popular Atlantic region dish is *rappée* pie (made with grated potato and ground meat).

Québec regional cuisine displays a definite French influence and includes such foods as pea soup, French pastries, breads, crêpes, special cheeses, lamb, and veal. Potatoes and red meats are common with evening suppers. A favorite fast food is *poutine* (french fries covered with spicy gravy and cheese curds). Maple syrup is produced in Québec and is a favorite in desserts.

In western cities, hundreds of immigrant communities have made the urban Canadian palate increasingly diverse. Throughout the prairies, one can find wild rice, smoked fish, beef, ethnic (especially Asian) dishes, and a variety of foods similar to those in the United States.

People from indigenous tribes eat common North American foods like hamburgers as well as traditional items like *muktaaq* (whale skin), salmon, caribou, berries, and roots.

Recreation. Canada has two national sports: ice hockey during the winter and lacrosse during the summer. Canadians also enjoy fishing, hunting, golf, soccer, cycling, baseball, and bowling. Popular spectator sports include college football, basketball, and curling. Curling gets more international attention during the Olympics. It involves two four-person teams sliding a large stone with a gooseneck handle over ice toward a target.

Other favorite activities include cookouts and beach parties, gardening, hiking, and spending weekends at summer cottages. People also like to visit with friends, shop, watch television, and read. Local festivals and fairs, parks, and museums also offer recreational opportunities.

The Arts. Art galleries and museums are numerous, as are local art groups. After World War I, artists began to develop uniquely Canadian art by focusing on the nation's landscape. Immigrants who have moved to big cities have diversified the arts. Popular crafts include pottery and quilting.

The ocean greatly influences Atlantic Canadian songs, art, poetry, and prose as well as folk festivals and other community events. Prince Edward Island, birthplace of Lucy Maud Montgomery (author of *Anne of Green Gables*), is a popular destination for those interested in seeing sites associated with her books.

Montréal's annual jazz, comedy, and film festivals are popular attractions. The Canadian filmmaking industry is known for its innovation. Contemporary dance and traditional ballet companies enjoy wide audiences and critical acclaim.

Native American tribes are reviving traditional arts, many of which began before European settlers arrived. These include clothing decorated with paint, beads, and porcupine quills; jewelry; leatherwork; woodwork; and featherwork.

Holidays. Official Canadian holidays include New Year's Day, Easter, Victoria Day (which celebrates the birthday of British Queen Victoria on the third Monday in May), Canada Day (1 July), Labour Day (first Monday in September), Thanksgiving Day (second Monday in October), Remembrance Day (11 Nov.), Christmas, and Boxing Day (26 Dec.). Boxing Day comes from the old British tradition of presenting small, boxed gifts to servants. It is now a day to visit friends and relatives or to go shopping. In addition to public holidays, annual local festivals throughout the nation commemorate everything from military battles to cultural heritage. Most cities and towns also have a civic holiday, usually in August.

Holidays unique to Québec include the *Carnaval de Québec*, a two-week period in February filled with activities (although normal working hours prevail), and Québec's national holiday, which is distinct from Canada Day, called St. Jean-Baptiste Day (24 June). Also, French-speakers spend Victoria Day celebrating *Dollard Des Ormeaux*, a provincial battle hero in Québec. During the autumn maple-syrup season, maple farms known as *cabanes à sucre* (sugar cabins) serve as party centers and restaurants, serving food along with the latest maple harvest.

Commerce. Most government and business offices are open weekdays between 8 or 9 a.m. and 5 p.m. Most stores open at 9 a.m. and close between 6 and 9 p.m. Most retail shopping occurs in supermarkets and suburban shopping malls. Some shops also are open on Saturdays and Sundays. For example, stores generally are open on Sundays in Newfoundland and New Brunswick. However, in Prince Edward Island and Nova Scotia, Sunday shopping is an option only during the holiday season. Canadians usually begin working full time between the ages of 18 and 23.

SOCIETY

Government. Canada is a confederation with a parliamentary democracy; its government is patterned partly after the United Kingdom's but also has a federal system like the United States.

Canada

The federal government is responsible for national defense, international relations, the banking system, the criminal code, and the indigenous populations. The provinces are responsible for education, health care, and welfare. The greater resources of the federal government have led to its involvement in matters originally provincial (e.g., employment, insurance, and medicare). Each province has a unicameral legislature.

Ceremonial duties of the head of state are performed by the governor-general (currently Adrienne Clarkson), who represents Queen Elizabeth II. Canada's federal Parliament is made up of a Senate with as many as 105 senators appointed by the governor-general upon the prime minister's recommendation. The Senate rarely exercises its full powers, whereas the 301-member, elected House of Commons is the real legislative power. The prime minister (currently Paul Martin) heads the government and is the de facto chief executive. The leader of the party that gains the most seats in the House of Commons becomes the prime minister. Parliamentary elections are held at least every five years. The voting age is 18.

Five parties are currently represented in Canada's Parliament: the Liberal Party, the Progressive Conservative Party, the Canadian Alliance, the Bloc Québécois, and the New Democratic Party.

Economy. Canada has one of the strongest economies in the world. It is a leader in the production of gold, silver, copper, uranium, oil, natural gas, agriculture, wood pulp, and timber-related products. In 1993, Canada signed the North American Free Trade Agreement (NAFTA) with Mexico and the United States. NAFTA provides for freer movement of capital and goods, more cross-national investment, and a large market for many goods from each NAFTA country. Canada's currency is the Canadian dollar (CAD). Canadians refer to the one-dollar coin as the *loonie*, after the image of the waterbird (the loon) minted on the coin. Likewise, the two-dollar coin is called the *twoonie*.

Although most Canadians benefit from the country's general economic prosperity, more than 14 percent of the population lives in poverty. In addition, the Canadian dollar is usually somewhat weaker than the U.S. dollar and can be affected by variations in the U.S. dollar's value.

Transportation and Communications. In the Atlantic Provinces, ferries are a common way to travel between islands. In sparsely populated areas, private cars are important. In large cities like Montreal, public transportation is well developed and includes subways and buses. Domestic flights and trains are common in all parts of the country.

Communications systems are highly developed. The vast majority of Canadians have telephones and televisions. Numerous cable-television systems provide service to all segments of the population. Television is often dominated by U.S.-made programs, but the federal government actively supports the development of Canadian films and television shows. Major cities all have daily newspapers, and use of the internet is common.

Education. Each province is responsible for its educational system. In all provinces, education is compulsory and free for at least eight years, beginning at age six or seven. Each province also administers its own colleges and universities. While colleges are subsidized by the federal and provincial governments, students must pay tuition. Many students choose to complete a two-year technical training program and enter the workforce. About 40 percent of students seek some form of education beyond high school.

Until fairly recently, religious leaders had a role in directing schools' curricula. Now English or French school boards are in charge, but students in some areas may still choose to have Catholic, Protestant, or general moral education in addition to secular studies.

Health. Canadians generally enjoy good health. However, lung and heart disease from smoking and sedentary lifestyles affect many Canadians, and more than half are overweight. Hospitals and quality of care are excellent, although facilities and personnel are less available in rural and isolated regions. Canada has universal, compulsory national health insurance, which is funded by fairly high taxes. The insurance covers doctors' fees and most hospital costs. While patients must sometimes wait months for elective surgery and certain expensive procedures, all citizens have access to basic health care at public clinics.

DEVELOPMENT DATA
Human Dev. Index* rank . . . . 4 of 177 countries
   Adjusted for women. . . . . 4 of 144 countries
Real GDP per capita $29,480
Adult literacy rate . . . . 99 percent (male); 99 (female)
Infant mortality rate . . . . 5 per 1,000 births
Life expectancy . . . . 77 (male); 82 (female)

AT A GLANCE

Events and Trends.

- For the second time in two months, Canada announced in January 2005 that it had discovered a case of mad cow disease among its herds. It was the third case in Canada's history. The United States had recently reopened its border to Canadian meat but was considering whether to close the border again.

- In December 2004, Canada's highest court ruled that allowing civil unions between homosexuals did not violate the constitution. Prime Minister Paul Martin said legislation legalizing such unions throughout all of Canada would be discussed in 2005. More than half of Canada's provinces and territories already allowed homosexual unions.

- In July 2003, the Canadian government decided to begin providing marijuana for medical treatment. The United States and other nations panned the move as being soft on illegal drug usage. However, the Canadian government has expanded the ability of private growers to supply the medical marijuana.

Contact Information. Embassy of Canada, 501 Pennsylvania Avenue NW, Washington, DC 20001; phone (202) 682-1740; web site www.canadianembassy.org. Canadian Consulate General, 1251 Avenue of the Americas, New York, NY 10020; phone (212) 596-1628; web site www.canada-ny.org.

CultureGrams
People. The World. You.

ProQuest Information and Learning Company
300 North Zeeb Road, P.O. Box 1346
Ann Arbor, Michigan 48106 USA
Toll Free: 1.800.528.6279
Fax: 1.800.864.0019
www.culturegrams.com

© 2005 ProQuest Information and Learning Company and Brigham Young University. It is against the law to copy, reprint, store, or transmit any part of this publication in any form by any means without written permission from ProQuest. This document contains native commentary and original analysis, as well as estimated statistics. The content should not be considered strictly factual, and it may not apply to all groups in a nation. *UN Development Programme, Human Development Report 2004 (New York: Oxford University Press, 2004).

CultureGrams World Edition 2006

Republic of Chile

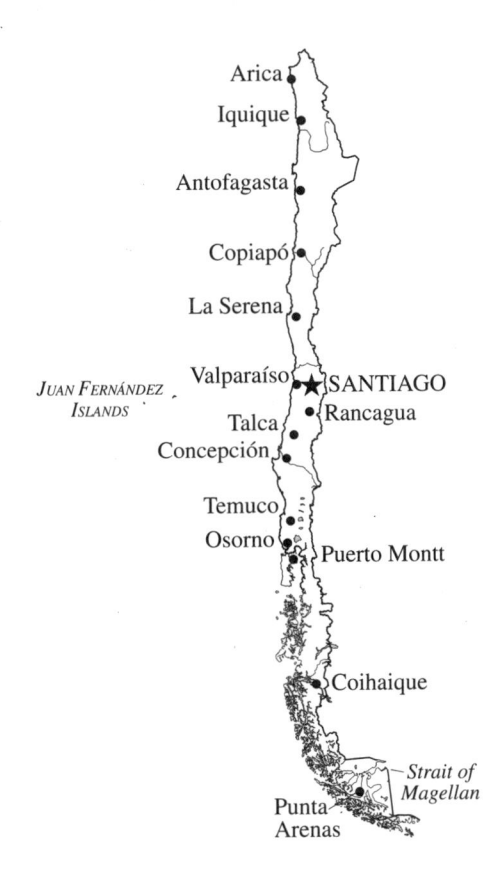

Boundary representations are not necessarily authoritative.

BACKGROUND

Land and Climate. Because it is so narrow, Chile may seem smaller than it actually is. Although its average width is about 112 miles (180 kilometers), the country's total area is 292,260 square miles (756,950 square kilometers)—making it slightly larger than Texas. Chile's territory includes 2,672 miles (4,300 kilometers) of South America's western coast and several islands: Isla de Pascua ("Easter Island"), Isla Sala y Gómez ("Sala and Gómez Island"), and Islas Juan Fernández ("Juan Fernández Islands"). Chile also lays claim to a 480,000-square-mile (1.24 million-square-kilometer) disputed section of Antarctica, claimed by Britain as well.

Because of its north-to-south length, Chile has many different climates and landscapes. The climate ranges from arid desert in the north to temperate in the central region and subarctic in the south. The landscape includes deserts, swamps, forests, the Andes Mountains, beautiful lakes, beaches, rich agricultural regions, volcanoes, and a wide variety of plants and animals. Chile has been called the "Switzerland of South America" for its natural beauty. The country is subject to relatively frequent earthquakes and resulting tidal waves. Because Chile lies in the Southern Hemisphere, its seasons are opposite those in North America: summer is between December and March.

History. The Incas from Peru were the first "explorers" of Chile, arriving in the north by the mid-15th century. They encountered the native Atacameño, Diaguita, Araucanian, and Mapuche cultures. The Portuguese sailor Ferdinand Magellan became the first European to sight Chilean shores in 1520, after successfully navigating around the southern tip of the American continent. Diego de Almagro claimed Chile as part of the Spanish Empire for Francisco Pizarro in 1536, and in 1541 Pedro de Valdivia commenced the Spanish conquest despite strong resistance by Araucanians. Chileans now revere many early indigenous warriors, like Caupolicán and Lautaro, as national heroes.

Chile began fighting for independence from Spain in 1810. Although initial revolts were suppressed, Chilean patriots eventually joined with the armies of José de San Martín in Argentina. In 1817, San Martín's forces invaded Chile by crossing the Andes Mountains. The Spanish were quickly defeated, and one of the revolution's heroes, Bernardo O'Higgins, became supreme dictator of the new republic. Opposed in land reform and other reform efforts, O'Higgins left the country in 1823 and Chilean politics remained unstable for several years. After 1830, however, stability and periodic reform allowed Chile to make progress. From 1879 to 1884, Chile fought the War of the Pacific against Peru and Bolivia. When Chile won the war, it annexed the provinces of Tarapaca and Antofagasta in the north, leaving Bolivia landlocked.

A civil war in 1891 was followed by less stable governments and military interventions. Chile returned to constitutional rule in 1932 with the reelection of President Arturo Alessandri. During most of the 20th century, Chile focused on promoting economic growth and addressing social problems.

Chile

By 1970, many people believed socialism could solve some of those problems without hindering growth, and soon Salvador Allende became the first freely elected Marxist president in South America. But the country soon faced economic disaster, and in 1973, General Augusto Pinochet Ugarte led a military coup, covertly aided by the United States, that ended Allende's government.

Backed by the military, Pinochet ruled by decree until, in 1988, he subjected himself to a plebiscite to determine if he should continue in power. Upon losing, he called for elections in December 1989. Pinochet's choice for president was defeated by the centrist-left candidate, Patricio Aylwin Azocar. Aylwin took office in 1990 as the first elected president since 1970. While Pinochet's rule was characterized by a dictatorial government and human-rights abuses—including the deaths or disappearances of at least 3,150 dissidents—Pinochet is credited for building a successful and productive economy. Aylwin built on that foundation, facilitating Chile's development as one of the most prosperous Latin American countries. He is credited with implementing successful antipoverty programs and maintaining a delicate balance between opposing political forces.

Later leaders emphasized more social spending for education and antipoverty measures. They also pursued closer economic ties with North and South America and constitutional reforms to reduce the military's political influence. Under these reforms, Chilean presidents are no longer permitted to serve two consecutive terms. The government remains focused on building the nation's economy and social services in the face of economic challenges, implementing constitutional reforms, and exposing the fate of those who disappeared during the Pinochet regime.

THE PEOPLE

Population. Chile's population of around 15.8 million is growing annually at about 1 percent, one of the lowest growth rates among South American countries. Less than 15 percent of the population lives in rural areas. More than one out of every three Chileans lives in the Santiago metropolitan region. About 95 percent of the people have either a European heritage or are of mixed European-indigenous descent. Many groups descend from Middle Eastern immigrants. Only 3 percent are purely indigenous (mostly Mapuche), and 2 percent have other ethnic origins. Many Chileans have ancestry from Spain, France, Germany, Switzerland, Croatia, Russia, Syria, or Lebanon, among other countries.

Language. Spanish, called *Castellano*, is the official language. But as in all South American countries, some terms common to Chile do not have the same meaning elsewhere. Chileans commonly add a suffix (*-ito*) to words and names to form diminutives and to show affection. For example, *Chaoito* is a "small good-bye," while *Carlitos* means "little Carlos" or "dear Carlos." English is taught in many schools and is understood by some Chileans with more formal education. Small minority groups also speak German (in southern Chile) and Mapuche.

Religion. Most Chileans profess a Christian faith. It is estimated that more than 80 percent of the population belongs to the Roman Catholic Church. Most other people belong to various Protestant groups or other Christian churches. There is a small Jewish minority, and many indigenous peoples follow traditional religious beliefs. Church and state are separate, and religious freedom is guaranteed.

General Attitudes. Although naturally friendly and warm, Chileans may be shy and reserved when first meeting someone. They are known for their sharp, witty, and somewhat cynical sense of humor. For this and their cultural and educational refinements, they are sometimes called the "British of South America." Chileans are very patriotic and take pride in their nation's cultural, educational, and economic achievements. When asked how they view Chile and its future, people commonly express confidence and optimism. However, their cynicism might express itself in a slight reservation or a biting remark about the country, its politics, or its inhabitants. Chileans consider themselves Americans. Thus, to avoid confusion, Chileans refer to people from the United States as *norteamericanos* and Canadians as *canadienses*.

The country has a large middle class, and education enables many poorer people to excel and build a better life. Chileans are a pragmatic people who believe in progress. Years of human-rights abuses under dictatorships have created a strong desire for social justice among the citizens. At the same time, Chile has a relatively rigid class structure in which European descendants are granted higher social status than those of indigenous heritage.

Personal Appearance. Fashions follow European styles and are quite sophisticated in urban areas. North American fashions are also popular, particularly among the youth. Many commercial entities (banks, department stores, etc.) require their employees to wear uniforms, usually a stylish suit or dress. Individuals take considerable pride in their appearance. Even in rural areas, where people are not as wealthy, it is important to be bathed and neatly dressed in ironed clothes. Although lower-income people may wear secondhand clothing from the United States, sloppy or tattered clothing is considered to be in poor taste.

CUSTOMS AND COURTESIES

Greetings. Greetings in Chile are important because they stress that one is welcome and recognized. The *abrazo* is the most common greeting among friends and relatives. It consists of a handshake and hug, supplemented with a kiss to the right cheek for women and family members. A handshake is appropriate when meeting someone for the first time. Eye contact is considered essential when greeting. Traditional verbal greetings include *¿Cómo estai?* (informal "How are you?") and *¡Gusto de verte!* (Nice to see you). Chileans show significant outward affection to friends and relatives. The *abrazo* is repeated with each individual when one leaves a small social gathering of friends or family. *Chao* (bye) is a common parting phrase.

Chileans usually use titles when addressing people. *Señor* (Mr.), *Señora* (Mrs.), and *Señorita* (Miss) are common for strangers and acquaintances, as are professional titles, such as *Doctor/a, Director/a, Profesor/a*. When speaking with the elderly or other respected people, one uses *Don* and *Doña* with their first name to show special respect and familiarity. Chileans, more than other Latin Americans, address others with the formal *usted* (you) more often than with the familiar *tú*.

Gestures. Respect and courtesy are important to Chileans. Eye contact and correct posture are important during conversation, while excessive hand gestures are avoided. Yawns are suppressed or politely concealed with the hand. Items, including money, are handed, not tossed, to other people. Chileans point with puckered lips rather than with the index finger. An upturned palm with the index finger or all fingers motioning toward oneself (the gesture used in the United States for beckoning) is the gesture to pick a fight in Chile.

Visiting. Chileans generally consider people to be more important than schedules, and punctuality is not stressed. People may arrive 30 minutes late or even later to a dinner appointment or scheduled visit. Punctuality is more closely observed in the workplace.

Guests wait outside the door of a home until invited inside. Hosts usually offer something to eat or drink; refusing is offensive. Dinner guests may bring a gift of flowers, chocolates, good wine, or (in lower-income areas) bread for the host family. Guests invited to lunch might offer to bring a dessert, such as cookies or ice cream. Chileans appreciate guests who show genuine interest in their family, especially their children.

Eating. Chileans eat the main meal at midday and a lighter meal between 8 and 10 p.m. Afternoon teatime (*onces*) is customarily taken around 5 or 6 p.m. At teatime, beverages, small sandwiches, and cookies or cakes are served. Chileans converse freely at the table. The hostess is often complimented on the meal. People eat in the continental style, with the fork in the left hand and the knife in the right. They keep both hands above the table at all times. It is impolite to leave directly after eating; instead, guests stay for conversation.

In a restaurant, a server can be summoned with a raised finger; meal checks are not brought to the table until requested. It is traditionally considered bad manners to eat food, except ice cream, while walking in public. However, as fast food increases in popularity, this habit is changing.

LIFESTYLE

Family. The family unit in Chile encompasses the extended family. While men have tended to dominate private and public life in the past, recent years have seen a change in attitudes about women in the home and professional world. Many women hold key political and business positions. And while the father takes the lead in families where a father is present, the mother has considerable influence on decisions. Reciprocity characterizes the relationship between the husband and wife. Both the man and the woman perform courtesies for each other.

It is customary for a person to bear two family names; the last name is the mother's family name and the second-to-last name is the father's family name. People either use their full name or go by their father's family name, which is the official surname. Therefore, a person named José Felipe Correa Péres could use his full name or be addressed as *Señor Correa*. As in other Latin American countries, married women retain their father's family name rather than use that of their husband's.

Dating and Marriage. Young people begin dating by the time they are 16. Group dating is emphasized early on. Men marry at about age 22 and women marry between ages 18 and 23. Couples often date from one to three years before getting engaged. Many consider it important to finish one's education before marrying. A civil wedding ceremony often is followed by a traditional Christian ceremony. Receptions commonly are held at the home of the bride. Divorce is not legal in Chile, nor is it recognized by the Catholic Church. Legal means of annulling a marriage are available but expensive.

Diet. Many national dishes are prepared with fish, seafood, chicken, beef, beans, eggs, and corn. Different regions feature different foods and dishes, but some favorites include *empanadas de horno* (meat turnovers with beef, hard-boiled eggs, onions, olives, and raisins), *pastel de choclo* (a baked meal of beef, chicken, onions, corn, eggs, and spices), *cazuela de ave* (chicken soup), *ensalada chilena* (cold tomato-and-onion salad), and seafood casseroles and stews. On rainy days, children enjoy eating *sopaipillas*, which are made from a deep-fried pumpkin dough sprinkled with sugar. *Manjar*, made by boiling an unopened can of sweetened condensed milk for hours, is a favorite bread spread and baking ingredient. Beverages usually are served at room temperature. Chile is well known for its wines; *pisco* (grape brandy) is the national drink.

Recreation. Popular activities include sports, theater, and music. *Fútbol* (soccer) is the most popular sport, and basketball is gaining in popularity. Chileans also enjoy swimming, going to parks, and watching videos at home. During the summer, vacations to the coast or the countryside are common. Taking advantage of the country's long coastline, Chileans enjoy fishing and, in some areas, surfing. Weekend or holiday barbecues are frequent social gatherings. Rodeos are popular in some areas. Cowboys (*huasos*) wear handwoven capes and straw hats. The main event consists of a pair of *huasos* skillfully guiding their horses to trap a steer against a padded arena wall. Points are earned for the portion of the steer that is pinned.

The Arts. Of its cultural arts, Chile is best known for poetry. Two poets received the Nobel Prize for literature, Gabriela Mistral (1945) and Pablo Neruda (1971). Contemporary Chilean authors, such as Isabel Allende, are known internationally.

European music and art are popular. Performing groups and museums enjoy patronage in larger cities. Traditional arts are a source of inspiration to contemporary artists and musicians. Textile and pottery designs of indigenous peoples are frequently integrated into modern designs. Chilean music and dance reflect both Spanish and native heritage. The *cueca*, a rhythmic dance of courtship, is the national dance. Chilean folk music (*tonadas*) has been influential in political and social reform. European and native instruments, such as the accordion, guitar, *guitarrón* (a 25-string guitar), piano, harp, and *rabel* (similar to a fiddle), are used to create a unique sound.

Holidays. Chile's holidays include New Year's Day, Easter, Labor Day (1 May), Naval Battle of Iquique (21 May), Day of National Unity (11 Sept.), Independence Day (18 Sept.), Armed Forces Day (19 Sept.), *Día de la Raza* or Day of the Race (12 Oct.), All Saints' Day (1 Nov.), and Christmas. People celebrate Independence Day at parks, where they eat *empanadas*, drink *chicha* (a sweet drink made with fermented grapes), and dance the *cueca* to guitar music. In many ways, Christmas is celebrated just like in North America, but some activities are different because Christmas takes place during summer in Chile. Families often hold outdoor barbecues the day before and open their gifts at midnight. Although Christmas is a family holiday, Chileans consider New Year's the most important time for family gatherings.

Commerce. In Santiago and other large cities, people usually work from 9 a.m. to 6 p.m., five or six days a week. In smaller cities and rural areas, midday meal breaks (*siestas*) are still observed, and shops and offices may close for up to two hours. Standard banking hours are from 9 a.m. to 2 p.m. Large supermarkets are found in major cities. Traveling markets (*ferias*) provide fresh fruits, vegetables, meat, fish, and flowers to smaller cities and towns.

SOCIETY

Government. The Republic of Chile is a multiparty democracy. The country is divided into 13 numbered regions, Region

Chile

I being the most northern. President Ricardo Lagos Escobar is chief of state and head of government. The National Congress has two houses: the Senate (49 members) and the Chamber of Deputies (120 members). Legislative politics revolve around two bloc coalitions: the center-right and the center-left. The legislature is located in the city of Valparaíso. The voting age is 18. All eligible citizens who have registered to vote are required by law to do so.

Economy. Chile's economy is one of the strongest in Latin America. The nation's foreign debt has decreased steadily, and the country enjoys considerable foreign investment. Chileans enjoy fairly good access to the health care, education, and economic resources necessary for a decent standard of living; however, women's wages are substantially lower than men's. The country's innovative pension system has generated substantial savings, and general inflation has remained low. However, fluctuating copper prices, regional and global economic difficulties, and droughts have caused unemployment to rise. Economic growth continues, but at a slower pace.

The government has instituted a program to help the poor by extending special small-business loans, investing in the poorest schools, and building permanent homes for low-income families. The income of the poorest Chileans has subsequently risen by 20 percent, and the population living below the poverty line has fallen.

Chile is one of the world's largest producers of copper, which accounts for nearly 40 percent of all exports. Fresh fruit has become another chief export. Agriculture, fish products, wood products, and mining are all important to the diverse economy. Chile has actively sought to expand its export market through international free-trade agreements. The currency is the Chilean *peso* (CLP).

Transportation and Communications. Public transportation in Chile is efficient, although many roads remain unpaved. Traffic in Santiago is heavy and can be hazardous. Smog and other pollution problems sometimes result in school and business closures as cars are restricted. The government is working to implement stricter emissions test requirements and reduce industrial pollution. Santiago has a subway, and elsewhere, private bus systems provide inexpensive travel in and between cities. Private cars are becoming more common. Trucks, motorcycles, and bicycles are used in rural areas to travel longer distances. Several airports serve domestic and international travelers.

A satellite system, cable television, and other technological advances have helped Chile increase communications and improve radio and television service throughout the country. The mail system is modern and efficient.

Education. Chile has one of the best-educated populations in Latin America; more than 80 percent of children graduate from secondary schools. Schooling is free and compulsory between ages five and seventeen. Parents may choose which school their child will attend. However, most parents send their children to the closest schools because they lack information about the schools and the cost of transportation is prohibitive.

Educational reforms that were implemented after the return to democracy have substantially increased government spending on education and turned over the operation of some state-sponsored schools to private companies. In addition to public schools, there are many private, commercial, and industrial educational institutions. Chileans value education, viewing it as the way to a better life. There are eight universities in Santiago alone; other universities and technical institutes are located throughout the country.

Health. Currently, health care is nationalized. However, the system is undergoing decentralization, and private insurance institutions are taking over a portion of care payment. Citizens have a choice as to whether they use the private or public healthcare system. Chileans have enjoyed increasingly good health over the past few years; infant mortality rates have dropped substantially. Water is potable in most areas. Typhoid fever and air pollution, particularly in Santiago, remain public health threats.

DEVELOPMENT DATA
Human Dev. Index* rank .... 43 of 177 countries
 Adjusted for women........... 40 of 144 countries
Real GDP per capita $9,820
Adult literacy rate .... 96 percent (male); 96 (female)
Infant mortality rate .... 9 per 1,000 births
Life expectancy .... 73 (male); 79 (female)

AT A GLANCE
Events and Trends.
- In December 2004, the Chilean government voted overwhelmingly to compensate roughly 28,000 people who were tortured under the regime of General Augusto Pinochet. Although most Chileans welcomed the move, some felt that the US$2,500 annual pension did not go far enough. Others felt that keeping the names of torturers secret for another 50 years was unfair.
- In November 2004, a new law for the first time allowed Chileans the right to divorce. Although the Catholic Church opposed the law, saying it would undermine society, the public widely favored the change. Divorce is now legal in every country around the world except Malta and the Philippines.
- In June 2003, Chile signed a free-trade agreement with the United States that will cut tariffs on goods traded between the two countries by up to 85 percent.
- After first being arrested in 1998, General Pinochet was found mentally unfit for trial in 2002. However, his immunity was stripped by Chile's Supreme Court in 2004, and he was put under house arrest in 2005 while awaiting trial.

Contact Information. Embassy of Chile, 1732 Massachusetts Avenue NW, Washington, DC 20036; phone (202) 785-1746; web site www.chile-usa.org.

© 2005 ProQuest Information and Learning Company and Brigham Young University. It is against the law to copy, reprint, store, or transmit any part of this publication in any form by any means without written permission from ProQuest. This document contains native commentary and original analysis, as well as estimated statistics. The content should not be considered strictly factual, and it may not apply to all groups in a nation. *UN Development Programme, Human Development Report 2004 (New York: Oxford University Press, 2004).

CultureGrams
People. The World. You.

ProQuest Information and Learning Company
300 North Zeeb Road, P.O. Box 1346
Ann Arbor, Michigan 48106 USA
Toll Free: 1.800.528.6279
Fax: 1.800.864.0019
www.culturegrams.com

CultureGrams™ World Edition 2006

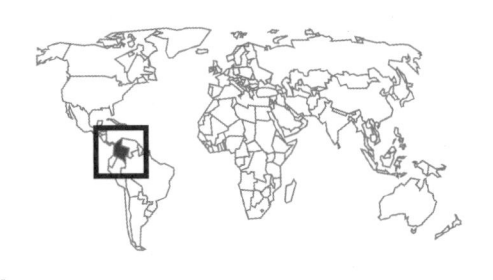

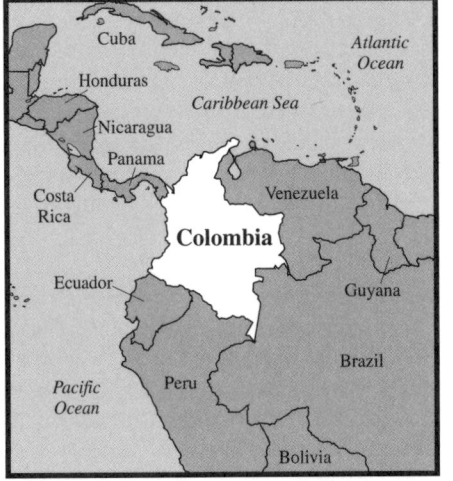

Republic of Colombia

BACKGROUND

Land and Climate. With 439,736 square miles (1,138,910 square kilometers), Colombia is about the size of California and Texas combined. It is located at the juncture between Central and South America and features an extremely diverse landscape. Divided by three branches of the Andes Mountains, Colombia has low coastal plains on the Caribbean Sea and the Pacific Ocean; cool mountain plateaus, valleys, and active volcanoes in the central Región Andina; and an eastern region with plains in the north and tropical jungle in the south. The country also includes several islands. While minor earthquakes are fairly common in Colombia, more serious tremors have periodically taken their toll.

There are no distinct seasons in Colombia, but differing elevations experience a variety of temperatures. Medellín, at 5,000 feet (1,524 meters) above sea level, averages 70°F (21°C), while Bogotá, the capital, at 8,000 feet (2,438 meters) averages 55°F (13°C). The coast is hot and humid. With such diversity in temperature, altitude, and rainfall, Colombia produces an incredible variety and abundance of vegetation and animal life. Coffee seeds brought to Colombia by Spanish missionaries found a perfect climate in Colombia. Coffee is one of the country's most important export crops.

History. The history of Colombia before the arrival of Europeans is uncertain, but many groups thrived in the area, producing sophisticated art, stone, and gold work. Chibcha, Carib, Arawak, Tairona, and Muisca peoples were present when the Spanish began settling the region in the 1500s.

The area was soon part of New Granada, which also encompassed present-day Venezuela, Ecuador, and Panama. Resentment against Spanish rule grew from the late 1700s until 1810, when nationalists claimed independence. However, independence was not really achieved until Simón Bolívar assembled an army to defeat Spanish troops at the Battle of Boyacá in 1819. He established the new *Gran Colombia* republic, from which Venezuela and Ecuador withdrew in 1830. With U.S. support, Panama declared itself independent in 1903 to make way for construction of the Panama Canal.

Colombia's name, originally the State of New Granada, changed several times before it became the Republic of Colombia. Civil war (*La Violencia*) between conservatives and liberals from 1948 to 1957 led to a constitutional amendment requiring the presidency to alternate between the Liberal and Conservative parties until 1974. Fully competitive elections have been held since that time.

The Medellín and Cali drug cartels and various guerrilla movements, such as the Revolutionary Armed Forces of Colombia (FARC), and National Liberation Army (ELN), began in the 1980s to cause unrest and violence. Some guerrilla factions eventually joined the democratic process in the 1990 presidential elections. Although drug traffickers killed several presidential candidates and committed violent acts to dissuade Colombians from voting, elections were held and César Gaviria Trujillo was elected president.

Gaviria took a solid stand against drug trafficking and violence. However, to encourage peace, he offered guerrilla groups the right to participate in a constitutional convention if they would disarm and renounce violence. Most groups accepted the offer and began participating in the political process. Gaviria also offered drug traffickers leniency and certain rights if they would confess and renounce their crimes. Not all guerrillas and drug traffickers cooperated with the government, but the violence did diminish for a short time.

Colombia

In 1990, a national assembly—including indigenous groups, guerrilla organizations, and nontraditional political parties—was formed to rewrite the 1886 constitution. The country's new constitution, which encourages political pluralism, the rule of law, and special rights for the long-ignored indigenous and black populations, took effect on 4 July 1991.

However, the rebel uprising has continued. Thousands of people—many of them civilians—have died by violence from these groups. Much of the killing, kidnapping, and extortion involves drug-related lands and moneys. In 1998, the government withdrew thousands of troops and police from the southeast, a FARC stronghold, to meet FARC's precondition for peace talks. Nevertheless, the peace talks faltered, bombings and attacks by guerrilla groups continued, and the government repealed FARC's safe haven.

Elected in 2002 on a promise to use the military to disable rebel groups, Alvaro Uribe has armed peasants, granted security forces new powers, and set up a civilian spy system that includes hefty financial rewards for informants. The violence continues to escalate and in many areas has reached the level of all-out war.

THE PEOPLE

Population. Colombia's population of about 42.3 million is growing at 1.53 percent annually. The majority of Colombians live in the west; much of the southeast is covered by jungle. The growth rate has been decreasing as Colombians flee the drugs and violence. People of mixed Spanish, indigenous, and black origins compose 58 percent of the population. Caucasians account for 20 percent. Others include a black-Caucasian mix (14 percent), black (4 percent), an indigenous-black mix (3 percent), and indigenous (1 percent). The black population descends from African slaves imported during the colonial era. Many Africans mixed with other peoples, especially after slavery was abolished in 1851. Black Colombians generally live along the coasts, comprising the majority of some cities, including Quibdó.

Approximately 75 percent of the population lives in urban areas. Some of the largest metropolitan areas are Bogotá, Medellín, Baranquilla, and Cali. Colombia also has a fairly young population; about one-third of Colombians are younger than age 15.

Language. The majority of Colombians speak Spanish, the country's official language. Most indigenous ethnic groups have their own languages. Among 80 groups, 40 languages are spoken. Dialects spoken by some black groups reflect their African roots. Many people from the San Andrés and Providencia Islands in the Caribbean speak Creole. Ethnic languages and dialects share official status with Spanish in certain areas, where formal education must be bilingual.

Religion. While Colombia's constitution guarantees freedom of religion, nearly 90 percent of the people belong to the Roman Catholic Church. Protestant and other Christian organizations have small but growing memberships. Many indigenous and black peoples retain beliefs from non-Christian, traditional worship systems. Although society is becoming more secularized, Catholicism remains an important cultural influence. For example, Catholic religious instruction, though no longer mandatory, still takes place in most public schools. Colombians commonly express their faith with phrases like *Si Dios quiere* (God willing) and *Que sea lo que Dios quiera* (Whatever God wills).

General Attitudes. Colombians take pride in their rich and diverse culture. The country's various geographic regions, climates, and subcultures enrich its food, music, dance, and art. Colombians are also proud of their *rumbero* spirit—their ability to both work and play hard. The family is a great source of pride, and family solidarity and mutual support are important. The individual is also important and takes precedence over timetables and punctuality. Most people value honesty, loyalty, a good sense of humor, and education. They find selfishness, arrogance, and dishonesty distasteful.

Colombians may seem rather cautious around outsiders. However, an initial lack of trust is more a survival skill than a lack of courtesy. Gaining someone's trust may require guarantees and manifestations of good faith. Citizens are proud of their history of democracy and independence. They may be critical of their own social problems but do not appreciate outside interference or criticism.

While minorities traditionally have been marginalized, the new constitution embodies hopes for equal treatment and opportunity for all. Most people are forward-looking and confident they can overcome their challenges. They take pride in the fact that, despite violence and political turmoil, Colombia's human and natural resources have allowed the country to reach high levels of economic development.

Personal Appearance. In Colombia, clothing is conservative, clean, and well kept. Appropriate attire for each occasion is essential. In urban areas, men wear suits, white shirts, and ties. In cities nearer the coast, suits generally are lighter in color. Women often wear comfortable dresses, and young people in urban areas dress casually. Dress in rural areas is less fashionable, but the people wear neat, clean clothing. Indigenous peoples often wear traditional clothing, which can include wrap-around dresses, bowler hats, and *ponchos*.

CUSTOMS AND COURTESIES

Greetings. Men commonly shake hands (not too vigorously) with everyone when entering a home, greeting a group, or leaving. Women kiss each other on the cheek if they are acquainted but offer a verbal greeting or handshake otherwise. Close friends or relatives may greet each other with an *abrazo* (hug), sometimes accompanied by a kiss on the cheek. Young females or young people of the opposite sex will also kiss each other on the cheek. In introductions, it is customary to address people by title (*Señor, Señora, Doctor*, etc.) rather than first name. Common greetings include *¡Buenos días!* (Good morning), *¡Buenas tardes!* (Good afternoon), *¡Buenas noches!* (Good evening), and *¿Cómo está?* (How are you?). *¡Hasta luego!* and, less formally, *¡Chao!* and *¡Nos vemos!* are popular parting phrases. Colombians commonly have two family names: the second-to-last name is the father's family name, and the last name is the mother's family name. The father's family name is the official surname. Therefore, a person named José Muñoz Gómez would be called *Señor Muñoz*.

Gestures. During conversation, Colombians tend to be expressive with their hands and face, particularly if the discussion becomes animated or heated. Maintaining eye contact and standing close are important; interrupting or backing away from the other person is considered rude. People beckon others with the palm down, waving the fingers or the whole hand. Smiling is an important gesture of goodwill. Colombian males may show deference and respect to women and the elderly by forfeiting seats, opening doors, or offering other assistance.

Visiting. While visiting is an important part of Colombian culture, customs vary with ethnic group and region. For example, in smaller towns with warm climates, people often sit on their porches and converse with passersby. Friends and relatives may visit unannounced, especially in rural areas where telephones are not widely available, but otherwise it is polite to make arrangements in advance. Colombian hosts are gracious and attempt to make guests feel comfortable, usually offering refreshments such as coffee, fruit juice, or soft drinks. Dinner guests generally arrive at least a few minutes late, and often much later. They may bring a small gift to the hosts, but this is not expected. Hosts commonly offer dinner guests an alcoholic beverage (rum, beer, etc.) before and after dinner. Politeness and etiquette are emphasized in Colombia. During formal visits, guests wait to sit until the hosts direct them to a seat. It is improper to put one's feet on furniture when visiting. Hosts often accompany departing guests out the door and even down the street.

Eating. Good manners and courtesy when eating are important to Colombians. Pleasant conversation is welcome at the table, as it stimulates a feeling of goodwill. Overeating is impolite; a host may offer more helpings, but these can be politely refused. Many consider it important to keep hands above the table. In a group, it is impolite to take anything to eat without first offering it to others. Eating on the street is improper. Tipping is not mandatory in restaurants, but some people leave a tip of about 10 percent.

LIFESTYLE

Family. Family unity and support are important to Colombians, and family members share their good fortunes with one another. Traditional values still strongly influence family relations. Divorce is relatively uncommon, due largely to the influence of the Roman Catholic Church. The typical family unit consists of a mother, father, and two to four children. The father usually provides for his family, and the mother is responsible for most domestic duties. However, an increasing number of women also work outside the home; more than one-third of the labor force is female.

Children traditionally live with their parents until they marry, but more university students and young businesspeople are leaving home earlier. Adult children often care for a widowed parent. Upper-class families enjoy many modern conveniences, but most Colombians don't have these luxuries. More than half of the population lives below the poverty line. As Colombia becomes more urbanized, apartments are becoming more popular than single-family dwellings.

Dating and Marriage. Depending on family custom, dating begins around age 14 or 15. Urban adolescents may begin dating at a younger age. Popular activities include going to parties, restaurants, movies, and discos; shopping at the mall; and participating in sports. On the night before a wedding, the groom may hire a small band to serenade the bride. Marriage ceremonies generally follow Catholic traditions, including a Mass. A reception with music and dancing follows at a club, restaurant, or home. Common-law marriages are gaining acceptance in Colombia.

Diet. Breakfast foods vary by region and may include juice, coffee, hot chocolate, fruit, eggs, bread, or *changua* (potato-and-egg soup). A small midmorning *merienda* (snack) may consist of *empanadas* (meat turnovers) or bread and a drink. Lunch, usually between noon and 2 p.m., is the main meal of the day. In smaller cities and towns, the family may gather (many businesses close) for the meal. Eating the main meal in the evenings is a trend in urban areas. Supper is usually at 7 or 8 p.m. Staple foods include soup, rice, meat, potatoes, salad, and beans. *Arroz con pollo* (chicken with rice), *frijoles con chicharrón* (pork and beans), and *sancocho* (stew with chicken, fish or meat and vegetables) are popular national dishes. *Arepa* is a cornmeal pancake. Coffee is the favorite drink of many. Sugar and milk are primary ingredients in popular sweets and desserts like *arequipe* (caramel sauce) and *arroz de coco* (rice pudding with coconut and rum). Ice cream is a common Sunday treat.

Recreation. *Fútbol* (soccer) is the most popular sport in Colombia, particularly among men. Other favorite sports include cycle racing, swimming, track-and-field, volleyball, basketball, and baseball. Attending bullfights is also popular. Colombians enjoy participating in the country's many festivals and joining with friends and family there to talk, dance, and laugh. Visiting is another favorite pastime. People socialize in their homes, in restaurants, or while strolling down city streets.

The Arts. Music and dance are central to Colombian culture. Much music is influenced by African or indigenous styles. Tropical rhythms are popular, including salsa, merengue, and *vallenato*. The *cumbia*, of African-Colombian roots, is a favorite style of music that began along the Atlantic Coast. The *bambuco*, from the Andes, is the national song and dance. Classical music is appreciated as well, and many people frequent the orchestras scattered throughout the country. Literature is important to Colombians, and many people take great pride in Gabriel García Márquez, who won the Nobel Prize in Literature in 1982.

Elaborate gold work is a legacy of the early indigenous peoples. Today's Colombian artists weave hammocks, sashes, bags, and blue and red *ruanas* (wool shawls). They also produce ceramics and decorative trim, called *passementerie*, for clothing or furniture.

Holidays. Holidays in Colombia include New Year's Day; Epiphany (6 Jan.); St. Joseph's Day (19 Mar.); Easter; Labor Day (1 May); Feast of St. Peter and St. Paul (29 June); Independence Day (20 July); Battle of Boyacá (7 Aug.); Assumption Day (15 Aug.); *Día de la Raza* (12 Oct.), which celebrates the discovery of the Americas and the resulting mix of ethnicities; All Saints' Day (1 Nov.); Independence of Cartagena (11 Nov.); and Christmas. Cities and towns also sponsor annual local festivals.

The nine days before Christmas (*la novena*) are marked by religious observances and parties. On Christmas Eve, families eat a large dinner, pray around *el pesebre* (the nativity), sing Christmas carols, and exchange gifts. Children receive gifts from the baby Jesus on Christmas Day.

Commerce. The Colombian workweek is basically 8 a.m. to 6 p.m., Monday through Friday. Shops are open from 9 a.m. to 6:30 p.m., Monday through Saturday, with some closing early on Saturday. Shops in larger cities may stay open later. Many people who live in urban areas buy basic goods at supermarkets. Open-air and farmers' markets also sell fresh produce at cheaper prices. Banks generally close at 4 p.m., but some stay open later.

SOCIETY

Government. The Republic of Colombia has a bicameral Congress; the Senate has 102 seats and the Chamber of Representatives has 166 seats. Senators are elected in a national vote, while representatives are elected regionally. President Alvaro Uribe is chief of state and head of government. The president and cabinet form the executive branch. The judicial branch is

Colombia

independent. The major political parties are the Liberal Party and the Conservative Party, although increasing frustration with escalating violence has opened political possibilities for independent candidates. All citizens may vote at age 18. Colombia has 32 states (*departamentos*).

Economy. Agriculture plays a key role in Colombia's economy. Coffee accounts for a little less than one-third of all export earnings; freshly cut flowers and bananas are also important exports. Other agricultural products include sugarcane, cotton, rice, tobacco, and corn. Oil is surpassing coffee as the country's main legal export. Natural gas, coal, iron ore, nickel, gold, copper, textiles, and chemicals all contribute to the economy. More than 90 percent of the world's emeralds are mined in Colombia. With about half of the country covered by forests and woodlands, the timber industry is becoming important. Colombia produces 80 percent of the world's cocaine and 60 percent of the heroin sold in the United States, but drug earnings remain in the hands of relatively few. The currency is the Colombian *peso* (COP).

Free-market policies during the past decades have led to high rates of foreign investment and solid growth for Colombia. Its people are proud of the fact that they are current on all foreign debt payments and have never defaulted. While the country has had a reputation for sound economic management, it is challenged by decaying infrastructure, illegal drug trade, and violence. Unemployment remains high—currently about 14 percent. The economy has struggled with periodic downturns. However, inflation has decreased to its lowest levels in 30 years. Rural poverty and an unequal distribution of income remain serious problems. Economic opportunities are more accessible to the ruling class.

Transportation and Communications. People in urban areas generally use public transportation, including buses, minibuses (*colectivos*), and taxis. A minority of people own cars; some use bicycles and motorcycles. Bus service is the most common link between cities, but travel by airplane is on the rise. While road construction has increased, only about 25 percent of all highways are paved and many are in poor condition; irregular terrain makes construction and maintenance costly. Coasts on two oceans provide shipping access to world markets. Colombia's television and radio infrastructure is owned by the government, but stations are privately operated. The country's free press has played a role in investigating and protesting corruption and terrorist violence.

Education. Primary education is compulsory and is free in public schools; many schools are private. Colombia's literacy rate has risen substantially as the number of rural schools increased; unfortunately, the literacy rate remains much lower among the indigenous and black populations. Approximately 75 percent of all students complete primary education (five years) and continue to the secondary level (six years). Secondary schools are found in most municipalities and offer either technical or academic tracks; many are private. Vocational schools and universities are located in major cities. Bogotá has 15 major universities. Scholarly achievement has been important throughout Colombia's history.

Health. Colombia's healthcare system is changing from a public to a mixed system that includes public and private options.

DEVELOPMENT DATA
Human Dev. Index* rank . . . . 73 of 177 countries
 Adjusted for women . . . . 59 of 144 countries
Real GDP per capita $6,370
Adult literacy rate . . . . 92 percent (male); 92 (female)
Infant mortality rate . . . . 22 per 1,000 births
Life expectancy . . . . 69 (male); 75 (female)

Individuals who can afford it usually seek private care. Private clinics and public or charity hospitals are available in cities but are lacking in rural areas. Urban facilities are better equipped. As many tropical diseases have been eradicated, life expectancy has risen; however, malaria and yellow fever still affect rural and tropical regions, and tap water is often not safe for drinking. Sanitation remains a problem in rural areas. Infant mortality is significantly higher and life expectancy is lower among black and indigenous peoples. Violence remains the leading cause of death in Colombia.

AT A GLANCE
Events and Trends.
- In November 2004, U.S. president George Bush visited and pledged to continue aiding Colombia in the fight against its rebels and illegal drug trade. The United States had already contributed US$3 billion to Colombia's anti-narcotics struggle since 1999. A 2003 deployment of U.S. forces into Colombia was the first direct U.S. involvement in Colombia's civil war. U.S. forces trained Colombian troops and protected a key oil pipeline.
- In July 2004, the government began formal peace talks with the right-wing United Self-Defense Forces of Colombia, known as the AUC. By November, the paramilitaries had demobilized and disarmed more than 1,000 of 13,000 fighters as a step toward peace. The group also promised to completely disarm by the end of 2005.
- In May 2004, FARC leader Ricardo Palmera was captured. He was the most senior Colombian rebel ever captured by the government. He was tried and sentenced to 35 years in jail, after which he was extradited to the United States for another trial.
- In February 2003, FARC rebels captured three U.S. contractors and executed two others who had been conducting anti-drug operations in Colombia. The rebel group held the survivors in hopes of negotiating the release of FARC prisoners held by the government, but no agreement had been reached by December 2004, even though President Uribe promised to block the extradition of FARC's Ricardo Palmera in exchange for the hostages' release. Colombia has the world's highest abduction rate, with about 3,000 people kidnapped per year.

Contact Information. Embassy of Colombia, Consular Section, 2118 Leroy Place NW, Washington, DC 20008; phone (202) 387-8338; web site www.colombiaemb.org.

© 2005 ProQuest Information and Learning Company and Brigham Young University. It is against the law to copy, reprint, store, or transmit any part of this publication in any form by any means without written permission from ProQuest. This document contains native commentary and original analysis, as well as estimated statistics. The content should not be considered strictly factual, and it may not apply to all groups in a nation. *UN Development Programme, Human Development Report 2004 (New York: Oxford University Press, 2004).

CultureGrams
People. The World. You.

ProQuest Information and Learning Company
300 North Zeeb Road, P.O. Box 1346
Ann Arbor, Michigan 48106 USA
Toll Free: 1.800.528.6279
Fax: 1.800.864.0019
www.culturegrams.com

CultureGrams World Edition 2006

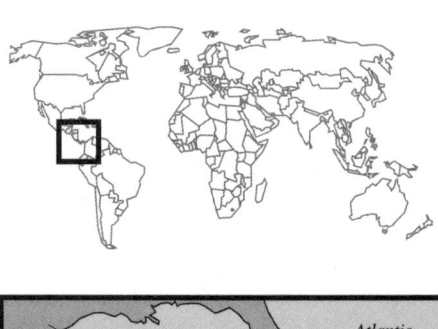

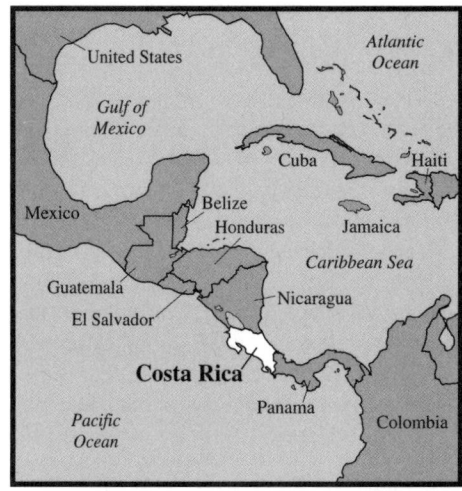

Republic of Costa Rica

BACKGROUND

Land and Climate. Costa Rica covers 19,730 square miles (51,100 square kilometers) and is just smaller than West Virginia. About 60 percent of Costa Rica is covered by different types of forests. More than 11 percent of the total territory is reserved as national parks. This small nation has a diverse landscape of tropical rain forests, mountain cloud forests, volcanoes, coastal lowlands, and beautiful rivers. Although the country lies entirely in the tropical climate zone, elevation changes allow for cooler temperatures in the central highlands. The coastal lowlands are hot and humid; temperatures average 81°F (27°C) year-round. Most people live at elevations where the climate is generally mild. In San José and other parts of the central valley highlands, temperatures average 67°F (19°C) year-round. Rainfall varies between the wet season (May–November) and the dry season (December–April). The land is subject to frequent earthquakes, hurricanes, and occasional volcanic eruptions.

History. A variety of native peoples lived in present-day Costa Rica before Columbus arrived in 1502. In the north, the indigenous cultures were influenced by Mayan civilization. Southern groups were more closely related to the indigenous peoples of South America. Spain eventually colonized the Costa Rican area along with most of Central America. Because minerals were scarce, the area was ignored by the Spanish crown and remained isolated. In 1821, Costa Rica joined other Central American nations in declaring independence from Spain during a nonviolent revolution. In 1824, it became a state of the Federal Republic of Central America. After the republic collapsed in 1838, Costa Rica became a sovereign nation.

Costa Rica has a long tradition of changes in government via democratic means. This tradition has been interrupted by military coups only three times in 150 years. Consequently, Costa Rica has one of the most stable democratic governments in Central America. Civil war erupted for six weeks in 1948 after a dispute over elections. José Figueres Ferrer led an interim government until 1949, when the election dispute was settled. Figueres (who was elected president in 1953 and again in 1970) abolished the army in 1948, and a new constitution was introduced in 1949. Costa Rica has enjoyed peace and democracy ever since.

The nation practices a philosophy of nonintervention in the affairs of foreign governments. Former president Oscar Arias Sánchez (who left office in 1990) was an avid supporter of the Central American Peace Plan. Arias won the Nobel Peace Prize for his efforts to bring peace to the region. The award is a great source of pride for all Costa Ricans; they believe it emphasizes their distinct heritage.

Weary of rising prices and falling incomes, voters elected businessman Miguel Ángel Rodríguez as president in February 1998. Promising to revitalize the economy, Rodríguez took office in May 1998, replacing José María Figueres. The election marked Costa Rica's 12th peaceful transfer of power since 1948. Government plans to privatize some state-owned industries led to the country's worst strikes, demonstrations, and unrest in many years. However, a court ruled the proposals unconstitutional in April 2000. The government is now pursuing other avenues to modernize the country's industries.

THE PEOPLE

Population. The population of Costa Rica is nearly 4 million and is growing at about 1.5 percent annually. The majority of people (87 percent) have a European heritage. About 7 percent

Costa Rica

are of mixed heritage (European and indigenous), although many of these are immigrants from other Latin American countries. Three percent of the population is black and lives mostly on the Atlantic Coast. These people are descendants of laborers brought from the Caribbean to build a railroad. They later worked on banana plantations and developed a distinct culture in the region around Puerto Limón. One percent of Costa Ricans are indigenous peoples. Another 1 percent are ethnic Chinese. About half a million Nicaraguans living in Costa Rica are illegal immigrants; Costa Rica deports thousands yearly. The general population is relatively young, with about 30 percent younger than age 15. Most people live in the central valley highlands.

Language. Spanish is the official language of Costa Rica. English is widely understood. Patua (creole English) is spoken by the black population. Bribri, spoken by some indigenous groups, is the most common indigenous language. Ten other native groups speak Spanish or a native tongue.

Costa Ricans call themselves *ticos* (the female form is *tica*) and are known by that name throughout Central America. The nickname comes from the Costa Rican custom of ending words with the suffix *-tico* (instead of the more common Spanish diminutive *-tito*). So instead of saying *chico* (small) or *chiquitito* (very small), Costa Ricans say *chiquitico*.

Religion. The Roman Catholic Church claims membership of about 80 percent of the population. Until the mid-1980s, it was the nation's official church, but it lost that status when the government decreed that a democratic nation should not support any particular religion. Although the Catholic Church continues to be very influential, the constitution guarantees religious freedom to the people. As is the trend elsewhere, secularization in Costa Rica is leading some people away from organized religion. At the same time, a growing number of religious people are joining other Christian churches, and religion still plays an important role in society.

General Attitudes. Costa Rica is a land of courtesy, domestic enterprise, hospitality, and gentleness. Militarism is despised by nearly all. Children are taught in school that armies are created to oppress rather than protect people. Aggressiveness, brusqueness, and violence are also shunned. *Ticos* say they are lovers of peace and conciliation. They avoid confrontation when possible; they may even say they will do something when they really don't intend to do it, just so they won't have to disagree.

People value privacy and quiet behavior but will vigorously defend personal honor. A strong work ethic is prevalent among most segments of society, and rural people especially accept hard labor as a necessary part of life. Individuality is an important characteristic, expressed in Costa Rica's relations with other nations and, to a lesser extent, on a personal level. The attitude is due partly to Costa Rican isolation during the colonial period; because *ticos* had little contact with colonial rulers, they developed greater independence. Still, group conformity in values, interests, and thought is important in society. Individuals are recognized as such, and all people are given respect, regardless of their social class.

There is little resentment among the classes because of the traditional respect for all people and a belief that some things are determined by God. The belief that Deity controls some aspects of life, such as one's health or success, is evident in daily speech. People often attribute their achievements to and place hope in God. This tradition is changing with greater education and people's desire for material progress.

Personal Appearance. Western dress is common throughout the country. Women try to dress fashionably; they generally pay more attention to their appearance than do men. Still, all *ticos* consider it necessary to be well groomed in public. Clothing is neat, clean, and generally modest, although women sometimes wear short skirts or tight clothes. People bathe every day and place great emphasis on personal cleanliness.

CUSTOMS AND COURTESIES

Greetings. Polite and respectful greetings are a social norm. Female friends or relatives greet each other with a light kiss on the cheek. If women are not yet acquainted, they may pat each other on the arm. Men shake hands. It is an insult not to shake every man's hand in a small group. Common terms for greeting include ¡*Buenos días!* (Good day), ¡*Buenas tardes!* (Good afternoon), and ¡*Buenas noches!* (Good evening). *Ticos* often respond to the greeting ¿*Cómo está?* (How are you?) with the expression *Pura vida* (Pure life). Also used as a way to say "OK," *Pura vida* has many uses. ¡*Hola!* (Hi) is a casual greeting popular among the youth; older people consider it disrespectful if used to greet them.

In rural areas, people greet each other when passing on the street, even if they are not acquainted. One might simply say ¡*Adiós!* or ¡*Buenas!* or more formally ¡*Adiós, señora!* or ¡*Buenos días!* This tradition is less common in urban areas. Rural people often bow their heads slightly and touch their hats in greeting. Greetings between strangers or acquaintances are brief, but people who know each other usually take a few minutes to talk about family, work, or health.

One addresses others by professional title either with or without a surname, depending on the situation. *Señor* (Mr.) and *Señora* (Mrs.) are also used, especially for people with whom one is not well acquainted. *Ticos* address friends, children, coworkers, and subordinates by first name. They use the title *Don* with the first name of an older man, or *Doña* for a woman, to show special respect for and familiarity with the person. For example, a child might call the mother of his best friend *Doña María*.

Gestures. Hand gestures are common and important to everyday conversation. In fact, Costa Ricans often use their hands to express an idea, either with or without verbal communication. To indicate "no," one vigorously waves the index finger (palm out, finger up). When expressing shock or when faced with a serious situation, *ticos* will shake the hand vigorously enough to snap (slap) the fingers together three or four times. There are many different hand greetings in addition to the handshake or wave. For instance, young people slap hands together in a greeting similar to a "high five." Eye contact is important, especially when one is discussing a serious issue or talking to a superior. It traditionally is understood that the lack of eye contact means one cannot be trusted. Chewing gum while speaking is impolite.

Visiting. Costa Ricans enjoy socializing but do not visit as often as people in other Latin American or Caribbean countries. Urban Costa Ricans generally prefer that visits be arranged in advance. Only close friends or relatives drop by unannounced, and then mostly in the afternoon after household chores have been done. Otherwise, uninvited visitors may not be asked into the home. In rural areas, people visit unannounced more often and rarely are turned away. Hosts usually offer visitors something to drink (like coffee) and refreshments (pastries, bread, or crackers). It is impolite to refuse such an offer. Invited guests generally are expected to arrive a few minutes late (later in rural areas). Punctuality is not customary, but being very late is also not appreciated.

Dinner guests usually bring a small gift to their hosts, such as flowers, wine, a plant, or something to share or mark the occasion. Close friends often bring more personal gifts. Gifts are also exchanged on special occasions. Hosts usually serve dinner guests refreshments and drinks while they socialize for an hour or so before the meal is served. After dinner, coffee and dessert accompany more conversation. Guests generally leave shortly thereafter.

If a Costa Rican invites someone to dinner or to spend a few days at his or her home, the potential guest must determine whether the invitation is sincere or whether the host is just trying to be polite. Polite invitations often are extended as a gesture of goodwill rather than as an expectation that guests will actually come.

Eating. Most people eat three meals a day, with midmorning and afternoon coffee breaks or snacks. Breakfast and dinner are the most important meals, as lunch is becoming more rushed and is more often eaten away from home. Business professionals make lunch dates, but dinner is otherwise the meal for entertaining guests. Mealtime is to be enjoyed and is extended by conversation. Costa Ricans enjoy conversation on a variety of subjects.

Table manners vary from family to family, but as a general rule, one keeps both hands above the table rather than in the lap. In restaurants, the bill customarily includes a tip of 10 percent. Further tipping is not expected.

LIFESTYLE

Family. Costa Ricans value family tradition and heritage. Immediate families have an average of three to five children; rural families are usually larger. Rural extended families often either share a dwelling or live as neighbors. While the husband makes most final decisions in the home, he shares many responsibilities with his wife. Most women do not work outside the home, but a growing number are entering the labor force. Close to one-third of the workforce is female. Women retain their maiden names when they marry. Children carry the surnames of both parents. The second-to-last name in a full name is the family surname.

Many families, even many of the poor, own their own homes, which are either wood-frame or cement-block structures. Some houses have a combination of materials, with blocks halfway up the wall and wood to the roof.

Dating and Marriage. Young Costa Ricans begin socializing in groups at young ages. Pairing off is rare, except in rural areas where there are fewer people. Movies, dances, picnics, the December bullfights, and a yearly civic carnival are favorite dating activities.

Girls generally are more restricted in dating than boys. They seldom can have visitors past 10 p.m., unless courtship is close to marriage. A boy sometimes asks a girl's parents for permission to date her, but this custom is disappearing and no longer occurs in urban areas. When a young couple is dating, the boy commonly is allowed a certain schedule for sitting with the girl on the porch or taking short neighborhood walks. This may be for two hours during a few evenings each week.

Marriage is a valued institution; Costa Rica has one of the highest marriage rates in Latin America. Families visit each other to show formal agreement on their children's marriage. Women generally marry in their early twenties, while men tend to marry somewhat later. Unmarried adults usually live with their parents, especially in rural areas. The exception is that university students sometimes live on their own if they are not yet married.

Diet. Costa Ricans eat rice and beans in various combinations for nearly every meal. Typical at breakfast is *gallo pinto* (mixture of rice and black beans). A common lunchtime meal is called *casado* and consists of beans, salad or eggs, meat, and plantains. Favorite dishes include *olla de carne*, a beef stew with potatoes, onions, and many vegetables. *Tamales* (meat, vegetables, and cornmeal wrapped in plantain leaves and boiled) are served for Easter and Christmas. Also common are *lengua en salsa* (beef tongue served in a sauce), *mondongo* (intestine soup), *empanadas* (turnovers), *arroz con pollo* (rice with chicken), and *gallos* (tortillas with meat and vegetable fillings). Bread, tortillas, and fruits are also staple items. *Ticos* of all ages enjoy coffee. Adults may take two or three coffee breaks each day.

Recreation. *Fútbol* (soccer) is the most popular spectator and participant sport. Basketball, baseball, volleyball, surfing, auto racing, swimming, cycling, running, and tennis are also popular. Fishing is good in many parts of the country. The wealthy enjoy golf and polo. Beaches are crowded between January and April. Local carnivals, festivals, and bullfights are popular attractions at various times throughout the year. Media broadcasts from the United States are common and have a significant impact on urban trends.

The Arts. Dancing is a favorite activity among *ticos* of all ages. Typical Latin dances such as salsa, merengue, and *cumbia*, as well as the Costa Rican swing, are popular. Folk dances include the national dance, the *Punto Guanacaste*, the *cambute*, and maypole dances. Typical musical instruments include the *chirimía* (oboe), guitar, xylophone, accordion, and the *quijongo* (a stringed instrument). People enjoy *soca* (a mixture of soul music from the United States and calypso music), calypso, reggae, and other music popular throughout the Caribbean, Central America, and North America.

Museums offer a glimpse of pre-Columbian life. Brightly painted *carretas* (oxcarts) are well known throughout the world. Other arts include pottery, *molas* (appliqué for clothing or textiles), and carved wooden masks.

Holidays. Costa Rican holidays include New Year's Day; Feast of St. Joseph (19 Mar.); Anniversary of the Battle of Rivas (11 Apr.), during which a Costa Rican army defeated the forces of a U.S. conqueror and in which the national hero, a drummer boy named Juan Santa María, lost his life; *Semana Santa* (Holy Week) and Easter; Labor Day (1 May); Feast of St. Peter and St. Paul (29 June); Annexation of Guanacaste to Costa Rica (25 July); Feast of Our Lady of the Angels (2 Aug.); Central American Independence Day (15 Sept.); *Día de la Raza*, recognizing the indigenous roots of Latin America (12 Oct.); Feast of Immaculate Conception (8 Dec.); and Christmas.

Christmas is generally celebrated with family, whereas New Year's is generally thought of as a time for friends, parties, drinking, and dancing. However, many Costa Ricans will interrupt festivities before midnight on New Year's Eve to go home and eat a small, quiet meal with family before returning to their party after midnight.

Commerce. Most businesses are open on weekdays from 8 a.m. to 6 p.m., although some shops close for a midday break. Stores may open on Saturday, but most are closed on Sunday. Government offices close weekdays at 4 p.m. Few business meetings are strictly formal, and socializing is an important part of a business relationship.

Costa Rica

SOCIETY

Government. Costa Rica is a democratic republic. Its executive branch has an elected president (currently Abel Pacheco) and two vice presidents. The unicameral Legislative Assembly is comprised of 57 legislators, who are elected to four-year terms. The judicial branch is separate. Costa Rica has seven provinces. Most Costa Ricans are affiliated with one of two major parties: the ruling Social Christian Unity Party (PUSC) and the National Liberation Party (PLN).

All citizens age 18 and older are required to vote in national elections. Election day is always a national holiday; people travel to their town of birth to vote and enjoy grand celebrations. Voter turnout traditionally has been high but dropped significantly in the last election.

Economy. Despite a relative lack of minerals and other traditional natural resources, Costa Rica has a fairly prosperous economy. Real gross domestic product per capita has more than doubled in the last generation. This is due in part to Costa Rica's stability; successful tourism, timber, and agricultural industries; and a generally egalitarian society. The country experienced steady growth in the early 1990s. In the mid-1990s the economy slowed because of low world prices for agricultural products, adverse weather conditions, and government measures to control inflation. Unemployment is low, but underemployment remains a problem. Poverty affects about one-fifth of the population.

Exports include coffee, bananas, beef, sugar, cocoa, and fertilizer. Costa Rica is one of the largest banana producers in the world. Ornamental flowers are becoming an increasingly important export. Cattle raising is concentrated in the Guanacaste province but is expanding to other areas. Manufacturing and tourism now contribute more to the economy than agriculture. Other industries include food processing, textiles, and construction materials. Costa Rica has excellent potential for hydroelectric power: nearly all of its electricity comes from hydroelectric power plants. Tourism facilities are well developed, so the industry is prosperous and important to the economy. Tourists are particularly drawn to Costa Rica's protected areas, and ecotourism has grown in popularity in recent years. Costa Rica has been a major recipient of foreign aid, and foreign investment in the country is increasing. The monetary unit is the Costa Rican *colón* (CRC), or plural, *colones*.

Transportation and Communications. Although cars are available, the most common form of transportation within and between cities is the bus. Fares are inexpensive and the system is efficient. Almost every town and tourist destination can be reached by paved roads. Taxis are commonly available; legal taxis are red. Telephones are located throughout the country, although remote areas still lack service. Rural homes usually do not have phones, but each town has at least one public phone. Satellite systems are used for international communications. Radio stations transmit throughout the country. There are also a number of television stations in Costa Rica. Several national newspapers have wide circulation. The postal system is efficient. Mobile phone and internet use are increasing.

Education. Costa Rica has one of the finest urban public education systems in the Americas. Nearly half of federal government spending goes toward education and health care. Primary education is compulsory and free for six years, beginning at age seven. Where facilities exist, children also attend kindergarten at age five and a preparatory year at age six. Enrollment in secondary schools is not mandatory, but more than 40 percent of all pupils advance to that level. Secondary schooling is also free. Both public and private universities serve the population. Evening schools educate the older generation as well as young people who cannot attend secondary school during the day. A high school diploma is considered very important. Costa Rica is home to four international education centers.

Health. A national healthcare system serves all citizens, and medical care is considered very good. Life expectancy has risen in recent years. Infant malnutrition and inadequate prenatal care remain problems in rural areas. Malaria is common along the Nicaraguan border and at lower elevations, and dengue fever (also spread by mosquitoes) has been reported on both coasts since 1993.

DEVELOPMENT DATA

Human Dev. Index* rank . . . . 45 of 177 countries
Adjusted for women . . . . 44 of 144 countries
Real GDP per capita $8,840
Adult literacy rate . . . . 96 percent (male); 96 (female)
Infant mortality rate . . . . 10 per 1,000 births
Life expectancy . . . . 76 (male); 81 (female)

AT A GLANCE

Events and Trends.

- Costa Rica faced two natural disasters within months of each other in late 2004 and early 2005. In November 2004, an earthquake measuring 6.2 on the Richter scale occurred about 30 miles south of the capital. Hundreds of houses and several major highways sustained damages. Then, in January 2005, floods forced 7,000 people out of their homes.
- During 2004, three former presidents of Costa Rica were accused of accepting money from companies in exchange for helping them do business in the country. Presidents José María Figueres (1994–8), Rafael Ángel Calderón (1990–4), and Miguel Ángel Rodríguez (1998–2002) were blamed. Figueres and Rodríguez allegedly accepted money from a French telecom company, while Calderón is accused of illegally taking money during a multi-million dollar purchase of medical equipment.
- In July 2004 the head of security at the Chilean embassy in Costa Rica took three Chilean diplomats hostage. The guard held the men during a seven-hour standoff before shooting them and finally himself. He reportedly may have been upset about a possible job transfer. The Chilean and Costa Rican president declared several days of mourning.

Contact Information. Embassy of Costa Rica, 2114 S Street NW, Washington, DC 20008; phone (202) 234-2945; web site www.costarica-embassy.org. Tourist Board; phone (800) 343-6332; web site www.visitcostarica.com.

Republic of Cuba

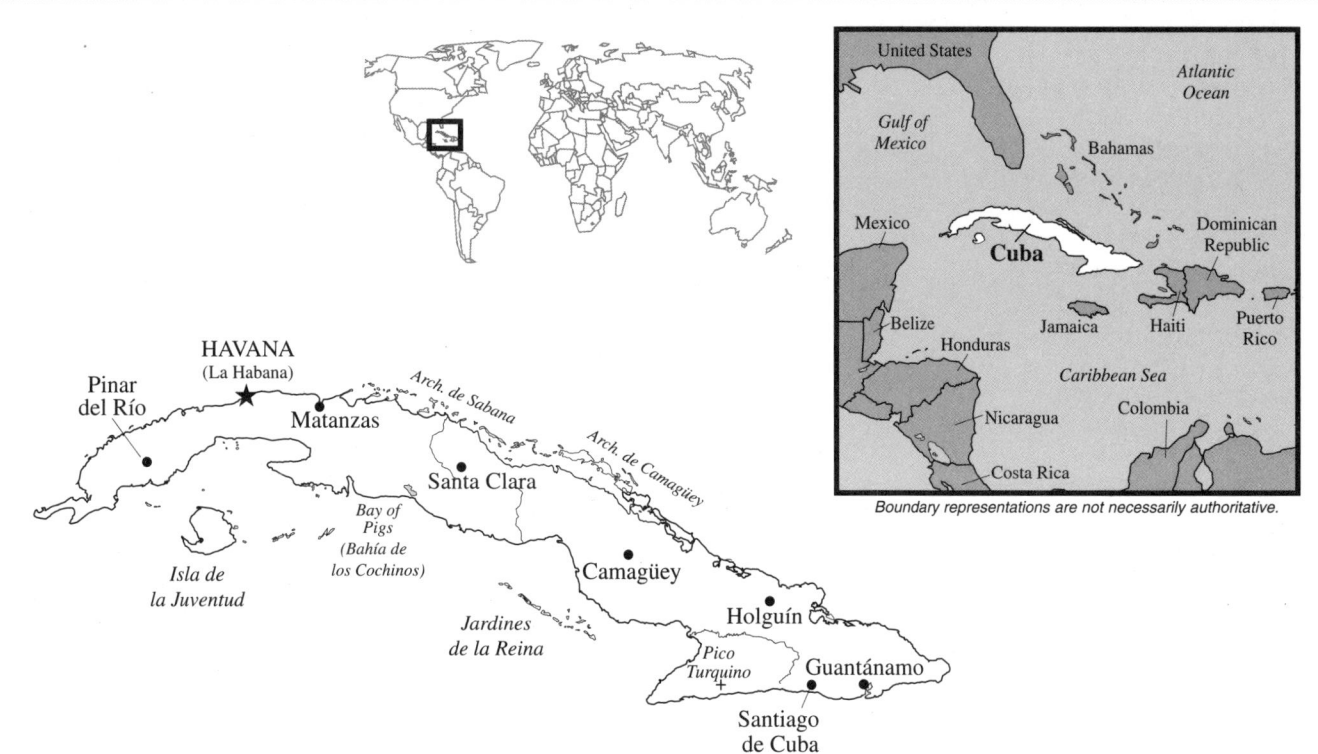

BACKGROUND

Land and Climate. Cuba is an archipelago of two main islands, Cuba and Isla de la Juventud ("Isle of Youth"), and about 1,600 keys and islets. With a total area of 42,803 square miles (110,860 square kilometers), Cuba is nearly as large as Pennsylvania. Cuba lies about 90 miles (145 kilometers) south of the United States. Low hills and fertile valleys cover more than half the country. Mountain ranges divide the country into three regions: the west, the center, and the east. Pico Turquino, the highest mountain peak, rises to 8,320 feet (1,974 meters). Tropical forests in the east contrast with central prairies and western hills and valleys, where the royal palm is the dominant tree.

Cuba's subtropical climate is warm and humid. The average annual temperature is 75°F (24°C). Cuba experiences a dry season from November to April and a hotter wet season from May to October. About two-thirds of all precipitation falls in this latter season, when hurricanes are also frequent.

History. Prior to the 1492 arrival of Christopher Columbus, Cuba was inhabited by three indigenous groups, the largest and most advanced being the Taíno. In 1511, a Spanish colony was firmly established; by 1535, the enslaved native population had been wiped out. Havana, founded in the early 1500s, became the capital and a gathering point for Spanish treasure fleets. In 1762, Havana fell into British hands for a short period until it was returned to Spain in exchange for Florida the following year. Beginning in the 18th century, African slaves were brought to Cuba to work on plantations. In the 19th century, sugar production became the basis of the economy. Despite numerous rebellions, and unlike much of Latin America, Cuba remained in Spanish hands. The various uprisings culminated in the Ten Years' War (1868–78), which ended after the loss of 200,000 lives but did not bring independence to the island.

José Martí, Cuba's national hero, led another revolt in 1895 but died early in the struggle. International protests over Spain's treatment of Cuba led to U.S. involvement and the 1898 Spanish-American War. Cuba gained independence, but it was not official until the end of U.S. occupation in 1902. Other occupations (1906–9, 1912) were based on the Platt Amendment to Cuba's constitution, which allowed U.S. intervention to maintain stability. In 1934, the United States canceled the amendment, receiving a 99-year lease on Guantánamo Bay—territory still held by the U.S. military.

U.S. investment was crucial to the Cuban economy through the 1950s, and sugar remained the chief export. In 1952, a military coup, led by Fulgencio Batista, established a dictatorship that increased corruption and turmoil. Popular opposition was organized into a rebel movement under the leadership of Fidel Castro. After a two-year guerrilla war, Castro overthrew Batista, who left the country in 1959.

Extensive economic and social change took place after the revolution. Agrarian reform, nationalization of industry and banking, creation of rural cooperatives, and other reforms were part of Castro's socialist-oriented path of development. These measures clashed with U.S. interests, and Washington responded by breaking off relations and imposing a trade embargo that is still in effect.

Cuba enjoyed support from communist governments throughout the 1970s and 1980s. Economic growth was steady, and important advancements were made in education, public health, and social security. However, the dissolution of the socialist bloc in the early 1990s seriously harmed Cuba's

Cuba

economy and standard of living. The government responded by promoting tourism, slowly building diplomatic relations with other countries, liberalizing some economic policies, and welcoming more international investment.

THE PEOPLE

Population. Cuba's population of 11.3 million is growing annually at about 0.35 percent. Three-fourths of the people live in urban areas; Havana has more than 2 million residents. Cubans of white Spanish descent comprise about 37 percent of the population, while 11 percent is of African ancestry. Another 51 percent is of mixed heritage. The remaining 1 percent is of Asian origin. The Cuban culture is highly integrated because each ethnic group influences society in a variety of ways. Approximately a fifth of all Cubans are younger than age 15. Nearly a million Cuban Americans live in Florida.

Language. Spanish is Cuba's official language. Slight accent and pronunciation differences exist among Cuba's three main regions. Many words, expressions, and idioms are unique to Cuban society and are not used in other Spanish-speaking countries. Some examples are *pelotear* (to pass the buck), *amarillo* (traffic official), and *rebambaramba* (a free-for-all). English is a required course in secondary schools and is popular among people interested in the tourist industry (many tourists speak English even if they are not from an English-speaking country).

Religion. Largely because of its history of Communism, Cuba has been among the least religious of all Latin American countries. Society is highly secularized, and most people show no preference for organized religion. While nearly half of the people have been baptized in the Catholic Church, very few practice the religion. However, recent years have seen growth in most congregations and a revival of religious devotion. The change began with a 1991 amendment to a policy that had excluded persons with religious beliefs from the Communist Party. Economic struggles have also contributed to the renewed interest in religion. The pope's 1998 visit encouraged many young people to explore religious issues and improved communication between religious leaders and the government. However, Catholic administrators continue to face many governmental restrictions.

Tenets of Catholicism are often combined with ideas from African religions to form a belief system known as *Santería*. Cuba also hosts a number of Protestant churches, including the Baptist, Methodist, and Presbyterian churches. Spiritualism, emphasizing communication with the dead, and *brujería* (witchcraft) are practiced by small groups. To operate in Cuba, churches must register with the government and satisfy rules of association. The division between church and state is strictly maintained.

General Attitudes. Cubans are friendly, warm, communicative, enthusiastic, and hospitable. It is uncommon to meet a Cuban who is not outgoing and fond of festivals, music, and dancing. The Cuban sense of humor allows residents to joke about almost anything, even hardships. This does not mean that Cubans are shallow or cavalier, but that they generally face difficulties with a positive attitude. In hard times, they look to friends and family for support. While many Cubans love their country, the difficulties of building a life in relative poverty breed complex emotions. Young people are increasingly confused by contradictions between what they are taught about their society and their daily experiences.

Despite troubles, Cubans are patriotic and value their national dignity. They are often impassioned in their opinions and will argue their convictions with energy. Men especially like to debate the economy, international politics, and baseball. Cubans have a casual view of time. Punctuality and schedules are not stressed. The joy of an event is considered more important than its duration.

Personal Appearance. Most people prefer lightweight, casual clothing. Cleanliness is important. Women of all ages wear slacks, jeans, short skirts, blouses, and canvas shoes or sandals. Dresses are worn at more formal events. Men wear long pants, jeans, and shirts or T-shirts in everyday situations. More formally, they may wear a *guayabera*, a traditional square-cut shirt. Shorts are popular in urban areas and at the beach, especially among younger people. Primary and secondary school students wear uniforms, as do students in medical colleges.

CUSTOMS AND COURTESIES

Greetings. Men greet with a handshake and ¿*Qué tal?* (How are you?). They often shake hands with everyone when entering a home or greeting a group. Most women kiss each other once on the cheek and offer a verbal greeting. Kissing on the cheek is also common between friends of the opposite sex, especially among younger people. Greetings between strangers are brief; friends spend a short time talking about their families or health. Common verbal greetings include ¡*Buenos días!* (Good morning), ¡*Buenas tardes!* (Good afternoon), and ¡*Buenas noches!* (Good evening). ¡*Adiós!* (Good-bye) is also a typical greeting when people pass on the street. When parting, people may say ¡*Hasta luego!* (So long).

People usually address others by first name, or they may use a professional title without a surname. Strangers frequently use *Compañero/Compañera* (Comrade), *Señor* (Mr.), and *Señora* (Mrs.). Nicknames are common among friends, acquaintances, and coworkers.

Gestures. Cubans use hand gestures while talking to reinforce ideas and emotions, which makes conversation rather lively. It is not considered rude to interrupt a friend or acquaintance during conversation. Maintaining eye contact while talking is important, especially in a formal situation. Lack of eye contact may be considered a sign of insincerity or spite. People stand close when talking, often touching or tapping each other when making a point. One beckons by waving fingers inward with the palm down. Beckoning people with the palm up is a hostile gesture.

Visiting. Cubans are extremely social, and visiting in the home is common. Friends also socialize on the street, while waiting in lines, and at gatherings in neighborhoods and work centers. Daytime visits are often unannounced but welcome. They may be long or short, without too much concern for schedules. Weekends and holidays are the most popular times to visit. Hosts usually offer guests something to drink, such as black coffee, wine, or a soft drink. Declining such offers is not impolite. If visitors arrive at mealtime, hosts politely offer to share the meal, but guests respectfully decline and leave. When rural people visit urban friends, they may take a gift of food; urbanites visiting in rural areas may offer money to help pay expenses related to their stay.

While Cubans enjoy inviting friends over for an evening meal or party, the practice has become less common because of evening energy blackouts and shortages of food and other supplies. Such socializing is casual, and guests often bring small gifts of rum, wine, or food to be consumed during the evening.

Eating. A light *desayuno* (breakfast) usually includes a cup of black coffee. Most workers and students eat *almuerzo* (lunch) at work or school. The family gets together for *comida* (dinner), the most important meal. Table manners vary from home to home. Generally, however, diners keep hands above the table, and pleasant conversation accompanies meals. Hosts expect to offer guests second helpings, but guests may decline. Except for expensive restaurants operated out of private homes, all restaurants are state owned. Ordinary citizens rarely eat at restaurants because of their price. People do enjoy snacks sold by street vendors.

LIFESTYLE

Family. Cubans maintain strong family ties. The nuclear family is standard, but many households include grandparents as well. Extended family members often build homes near one another to remain close. When adult children marry, they usually live with a parent until they can obtain housing, which is in short supply. Because of shortages in construction materials, the country is able to build only half of the 100,000 new homes needed each year. The government strictly controls all property; Cubans are allowed to buy new houses from the government or exchange homes of similar sizes with each other, but the traditional buying and selling of homes is prohibited. The average family owns a small house or apartment with all major utilities available. However, while about 85 percent of Cubans are homeowners, 40 percent of homes are in average or poor condition. A home that has undergone unauthorized modifications or is deemed too large for its occupants can be seized or its occupants fined.

Cuban women are active participants in the workforce. They represent the majority of the country's specialists and hold leading government and administrative posts. However, traditional values strongly influence family roles, so women are also responsible for most household chores and child care. Younger couples are beginning to share more responsibilities in the home.

As in most Latin American countries, a person bears two family names. The last name is the mother's family name; the second-to-last name is the father's family name and the person's surname.

Dating and Marriage. Young people have many opportunities to socialize. Couples usually meet at school, parks, youth parties, dances, music festivals, beach outings, and movies. Most people marry in their twenties. A civil ceremony is held in an urban "wedding palace" and is followed by a small family party. An increasing number of couples are also having church ceremonies. Common-law marriages are becoming more prevalent because of changes in social conventions and the high cost of weddings.

Diet. At present, the Cuban diet is based on foods grown locally. *Arroz y frijoles* (rice and beans) is the traditional staple meal. Indeed, rice is served at most meals, along with a dish such as potatoes, *boniatos* (sweet potatoes), *yuca* (cassava), *plátanos* (plantains), or tomatoes. Eggs are eaten boiled, fried, or cooked as an omelette (called a *tortilla*). Corn is the basis of many foods, including *harina de maíz* (cornmeal).

Roast pork, currently a luxury, is the favorite meat and is eaten on special occasions. Seafood is eaten in coastal areas. Tila pia, a freshwater fish found in Cuba's numerous reservoirs, is also popular. Favorite tropical fruits—mangoes, avocados, guavas, oranges, lemons, pineapples, and papayas—are eaten in season. Sweets (often homemade) usually are eaten as desserts or snacks; ice cream is popular but is in short supply.

Recreation. Sports are highly developed in Cuba. The most popular sport is baseball. Boys begin playing in leagues by age seven. Adult, college, and professional competition is well organized. Boxing, basketball, swimming, volleyball, and cycling are widely enjoyed. Girls enjoy sports in school, but women usually do not play sports. Dominoes is a national pastime, played by males of all ages (especially the retired) in front of homes and practically everywhere else. Cubans dance at discos, go to music festivals or movies, watch videos or television, and converse with each other.

The Arts. Music and dance are essential to Cuban culture. The people's Spanish and African heritage creates unique rhythms and sounds. Cuban jazz and salsa have spread throughout the world. Maracas, guitars, bongos, trumpets, and the *tres* (a small instrument similar to a guitar) are used to play the *son*, a genre of music that gave birth to the mambo. The cha-cha, which originated in Cuba, and *bolero* are still popular dances.

In the past, art and literature were outlets for political commentary. Late–19th-century writer and revolutionary José Martí promoted independence from Spain in his works. Now the arts are largely controlled to prevent antigovernment sentiment. However, the number of independent libraries that contain previously censored books is on the rise.

Holidays. Liberation Day (1 Jan.) commemorates the revolution of 1958 and 1959; it is preceded by New Year's Eve (31 Dec.) festivities. Other holidays are Labor Day (1 May), Anniversary of the Attack on the Moncada Garrison in Santiago de Cuba in 1953 (26 July), and Beginning of the War of Independence from Spain (10 Oct.). Mother's Day (second Sunday in May) is also popular.

Generally, religious holidays are not officially recognized but may be celebrated with feasts and religious services. Christmas Day is an exception; it became a national holiday in 1998. Christians attend special services during the Christmas season, Holy Week, and Easter. A holiday may honor both Catholicism and *Santería*. For instance, St. Lazarus's Day (17 Dec.) honors both that Catholic saint and the African god Babalú Ayé. A chapel near Havana dedicated to St. Lazarus and Babalú Ayé draws tens of thousands of pilgrims annually. St. Barbara's Day (4 Dec.) venerates a Catholic martyr and the African goddess Changó. And *Virgen de la Caridad del Cobre* (8 Sept.) honors Cuba's patron saint and the African goddess Ochún.

Commerce. Most establishments are open from 9 a.m. until 5 p.m. Many stores close on Sunday. Basic foods are rationed and sold in state-owned *bodegas* (neighborhood grocery stores). A much wider variety of items is available in stores that accept only foreign currency, primarily U.S. dollars. Cubans with access to dollars are far more able to provide for their families than those without. Various markets sell artisans' goods, prepared foods, and private agricultural produce. Bargaining is common in these private markets. Street vendors sell anything from rice to candles to flowers.

SOCIETY

Government. Cuba is a socialist state, and its constitution regards the Communist Party as the leading force of society. The country has 14 provinces and 1 special municipality (Isle of Youth). Legislative authority is vested in the National Assembly of People's Power. Special commissions nominate approved candidates to run for the Assembly, which has 609 seats. Opposition parties are illegal. The National Assembly

Cuba

elects from its membership the Council of State as the sitting legislature. Its president is both chief of state and head of government. President Fidel Castro Ruiz has governed since 1959. Executive authority is vested in the Council of Ministers, whose members are appointed by the National Assembly upon the proposal of the chief of state. Municipal and provincial assemblies deal with local affairs. The voting age is 16.

Economy. After trade links with the Soviet bloc dissolved in the early 1990s, declining living standards and a large wave of attempted emigration led the Cuban government to liberalize some economic policies. It opened free markets for produce and crafts; promoted some self-employment; reorganized some state enterprises; granted 2.6 million hectares of state land to farming cooperatives; increased soybean production to boost protein consumption; and established joint ventures with foreign firms in tourism, mining, communications, and construction. Mexico and Canada are Cuba's most important trading partners. Economic growth has been modest, hampered by natural disasters, the global economic downturn, and the continued U.S. embargo on goods.

Agriculture employs about 20 percent of the labor force. The main crops are sugarcane, tobacco, coffee, rice, grain, vegetables, and citrus fruits. Sugar is the most important export, but others include nickel, tobacco, cement, and fruit. Tourism is eclipsing sugar production as the largest source of revenue. The labor force is mostly skilled: three-fourths of all workers have a secondary or higher education. However, people lack opportunities and resources to fully achieve personal goals. Cubans cannot employ other Cubans in private businesses. The official currency is the Cuban *peso* (CUP). Until 2004, the U.S. dollar was not only legal but also the preferred currency for most Cubans. The U.S. government still prohibits all but Cuban Americans from sending dollars to Cuba. Cuban Americans often send money and gifts to family members remaining in Cuba. These remittances allow about half of all Cubans to access goods not otherwise available.

Transportation and Communications. In cities, people travel by bicycle or on crowded buses. Taxis are scarcely used. In the countryside, horse-drawn carts are widely used. Trains and buses travel between cities. An extensive highway system connects all parts of the country, but many roads are in disrepair. Motorcycles are more common than cars, and fuel is rationed. Strict laws prohibit moving from one province to another.

The telephone system is undergoing modernization; few homes outside Havana have phones. Media operations, including a well-developed film industry, are owned and controlled by the state. Most homes have televisions. There are more than 50 radio stations and 2 television stations. Several weekly newspapers are published, but a paper shortage restricts circulation. A lack of freedom of press is another hardship faced by Cuban journalists. Postal and telegraph services cover the entire country.

Education. Education is a priority in Cuban society, and the state provides free primary, secondary, technical, and higher education to all citizens. Education is mandatory between ages five and twelve (kindergarten through the primary level). More than 90 percent of all children continue with secondary education. Most teenagers attend boarding schools; exemptions are made for those accepted to art school. Secondary graduates may take college entrance exams or go to a technical training institute. Cuba averages 1 teacher for every 45 inhabitants. Preschool is available in urban areas. Special schools educate the mentally or physically challenged, and there are schools for students gifted in sports and the arts. Cuba has about 50 centers of higher education. Despite a shortage of basic supplies such as textbooks and paper, no child is without schooling.

Health. Cuba's healthcare system is a government priority; the country has some three hundred hospitals. A similar number of clinics provide various services, including maternity and infant care. Family doctors are assigned to serve each community, large and small. Despite a shortage of medicines and other supplies, Cuba's average life expectancy and infant mortality rates are the best in Latin America. Many childhood diseases have been eradicated through massive vaccination campaigns. More than 20 medical schools and other institutions train healthcare workers.

DEVELOPMENT DATA
Human Dev. Index* rank . . . . 52 of 177 countries
    Adjusted for women . . . . NA
Real GDP per capita $5,259
Adult literacy rate . . . . 97 percent (male); 97 (female)
Infant mortality rate . . . . 6 per 1,000 births
Life expectancy . . . . 75 (male); 79 (female)

AT A GLANCE
Events and Trends.
- By the end of 2004, about 500 people who the United States suspected of being Taliban or al-Qaeda members were sill being held at Cuba's Guantánamo Bay. The United States has been criticized by the international community for holding the detainees without trial since shortly after the terrorist attacks of 11 September 2001.
- The United States and Cuba have recently taken economic stabs at each other. In May 2004, U.S. rules changed such that Cuban Americans could visit Cuba only once every three years and were only allowed to send money to immediate family. Then in November, Cuba made buying and selling in dollars illegal and forced people to pay a 10 percent tax on dollars exchanged into pesos.
- In April 2004, the UN Human Rights Commission criticized Cuba's human rights record. The UN resolution was a response to the Cuban government's crackdown on dissidents in 2003, in which 75 people were jailed for terms of up to 28 years.

Contact Information. Cuban Interests Section of the Embassy of Switzerland, 2630 16th Street NW, Washington, DC 20009; phone (202) 797-8518; web site http://www.eda.admin.ch/washington_emb/e/home/cuban.html. Office of Foreign Assets Control, U.S. Department of Treasury, 1500 Pennsylvania Avenue NW, Washington, DC 20220; phone (202) 622-2520.

CultureGrams
People. The World. You.

ProQuest Information and Learning Company
300 North Zeeb Road, P.O. Box 1346
Ann Arbor, Michigan 48106 USA
Toll Free: 1.800.528.6279
Fax: 1.800.864.0019
www.culturegrams.com

© 2005 ProQuest Information and Learning Company and Brigham Young University. It is against the law to copy, reprint, store, or transmit any part of this publication in any form by any means without written permission from ProQuest. This document contains native commentary and original analysis, as well as estimated statistics. The content should not be considered strictly factual, and it may not apply to all groups in a nation. *UN Development Programme, Human Development Report 2004 (New York: Oxford University Press, 2004).

CultureGrams World Edition 2006

Dominican Republic

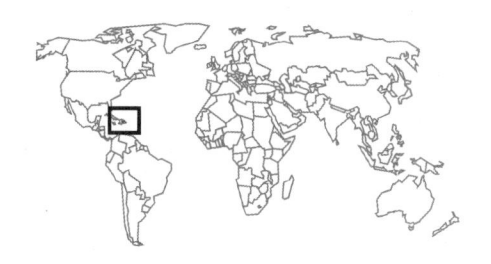

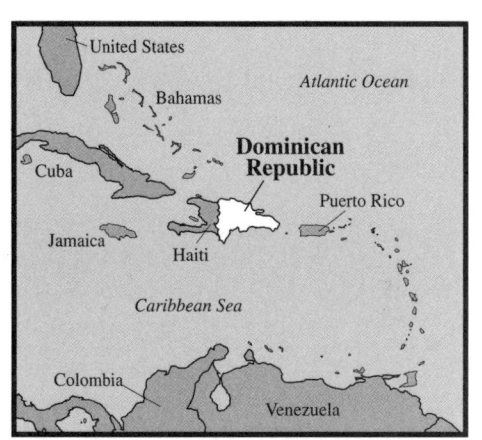

BACKGROUND

Land and Climate. The Dominican Republic occupies the eastern two-thirds of the island of Hispaniola, which it shares with Haiti. Covering 18,815 square miles (48,731 square kilometers), it is about twice the size of New Hampshire. The central mountain range, Cordillera Central, boasts the highest point in the Caribbean, Pico Duarte, at a little more than 10,000 feet (3,048 meters). The Cibao Valley lies in the heart of the country and is the major agricultural area.

The Dominican Republic has a variety of landscapes, from deserts in the southwest to alpine forests in the central mountains. Sugarcane fields spread over coastal plains in the north and east, and coconut plantations cover most of the tropical peninsula of Samaná. Pebble beaches under rocky cliffs afford spectacular views on the southern coast. Elsewhere the coasts are dominated by white sandy beaches and warm waters.

Weather generally is tropical, hot, and humid, especially in summer months and along southern and eastern coasts. A dry, desert-like climate, due to deforestation and little rainfall, prevails in western and southwestern regions. Rainy seasons may vary in different parts of the country, but they generally are in the late spring and early fall.

History. In pre-Columbian times, Arawak and Taíno Indians occupied the island. The arrival of Christopher Columbus in 1492 brought colonization, slavery, and disease, decimating the native population within decades. With the decrease in the indigenous workforce came the increased importation of West Africans to provide cheap labor for mines, sugar plantations, and cattle farms.

The capital, Santo Domingo, was the first permanent European settlement in the New World and was established by Spain in 1496. Santo Domingo's Colonial Zone is one of the great treasures of Spanish America today, with many original buildings still intact and newly restored.

In 1697, the western portion (now Haiti) of Hispaniola was given to France. In 1795, the entire island was ceded. Rebellious slaves seized Santo Domingo in 1801 and established Haiti as the first independent country in Latin America. The resulting Haitian domination of the Dominicans (1822–44) left a legacy of mistrust and strained relations that still endures. The Dominicans declared independence in 1844. Spain returned intermittently between local attempts at government. After an occupation by U.S. Marines (1918–24), a constitutional government was established.

Military dictator Rafael Leonidas Trujillo gained the presidency in 1930 and ruled for three decades until he was assassinated in 1961. His merciless persecution of Haitians in the late 1930s added to the list of grievances between the two countries. His death brought civilian unrest, political revolt, and division within the army. In 1965, U.S. Marines and an inter-American peacekeeping force stepped in. With stability restored, elections were held, and in 1966 the constitutional government was reestablished. Continuing under this system, today's Dominican Republic is the largest and most populous democracy in the Caribbean region.

An ally of Trujillo, Joaquín Balaguer, was nominally appointed president in 1961 but did not take office until 1966. For the next three decades, power rested in either his hands or those of his rival, Juan Bosch of the Dominican Liberation Party (PLD). As head of the Social Christian Reformist Party (PRSC), Balaguer narrowly won the 1994 elections and began his seventh term in office. Constitutional reforms required elections two years later and did not permit Balaguer to run for

Dominican Republic

a successive eighth term. The government has now embarked on a plan of economic reform and greater political openness. However, frequent power outages, high food prices, poverty, and high unemployment continue to fuel public discontent.

THE PEOPLE

Population. The Dominican Republic's population of roughly 8.8 million is growing at a rate of about 1.3 percent. More than one-third of the population is younger than age 16. The rural population is steadily decreasing through migration to cities. Mixed-race people account for 73 percent of the total population while 16 percent is Caucasian and 11 percent is black. The mixed-race group is a combination of descendents of Spaniards and other Europeans, West African slaves, and perhaps some indigenous peoples. A Haitian minority is included in the black population. Additionally, more than one million Dominicans live full- or part-time in New York City, U.S.A.

Language. The official language is Spanish, but Caribbean phrases, accents, and regional expressions give it a distinct personality. For example, when eating, people request *un chin* instead of the Spanish *un poquito* (a little bit) of something. Many people drop the *s* at the end of words, turning *dos* (two) into *do'*. Cibao Valley residents, or *Cibaeños*, may pronounce the *r, l*, and *i* differently. The formal Spanish form of address for "you" (*usted*) is used, but most people prefer the more familiar *tú*. Some creole is spoken near the Haitian border and in the *bateys* (sugarcane villages), where many Haitian workers live.

Religion. Dominicans are 95 percent Catholic by record, but a much smaller number regularly attends church or strictly follows doctrine. Especially in rural areas, Catholic traditions are sometimes combined with local practices and beliefs. Although Dominicans are fairly secular, Catholic traditions are evident in daily life. Some children are taught to "ask blessings" of their parents and other relatives upon seeing them. They might say *Bendición, tía* (Bless me, aunt), and the response is *Dios te bendiga* (May God bless you). Evangelical Christian churches, The Church of Jesus Christ of Latter-day Saints, the Seventh-day Adventist Church, and other denominations are also present throughout the country.

General Attitudes. Dominicans are warm, friendly, and gregarious. They are very curious about others and forthright in asking personal questions. Children are rarely shy. *Machismo*—the desire of men to prove their manliness or superiority—permeates society, especially among rural and low-income groups. A proud and aggressive attitude is admired in sports, games, and business. Many people have a sharp entrepreneurial sense, but this does not mean that business etiquette is aggressive.

The common expression *Si Dios quiere* (If God wishes) may make Dominicans appear fatalistic or indifferent. However, it more fully expresses the attitude that personal power is intertwined with one's place in the family, community, and grand design of Deity. Relationships are more important than schedules, so being late for appointments or spending time socializing instead of working is socially acceptable.

Confianza (trust) is highly valued and not quickly or easily gained by outsiders. Borrowing is common, and although an item may be forgotten and never returned, most people are generous and helpful. Economic, social, and political class divisions, most evident in cities, favor historically prominent families. Light skin and smooth hair are preferred over strong African features. Despite government efforts to build ties with Haiti, tension between Dominicans and Haitians continues.

Personal Appearance. Dominicans are clean and well groomed. They take pride in their personal appearance and place importance on dressing well. Dominicans draw on New York fashions, wearing the latest dresses, jeans, and athletic shoes. Clothes tend to be dressy and are always clean and well pressed. The people often prefer bright colors, shiny fabrics, and a lot of jewelry. Jeans and short skirts are acceptable for women in urban areas, but dresses or skirts and blouses are more common in the countryside. A special event, such as a town meeting, always requires dressing up. Men wear long pants and stylish shirts, except at the beach or when doing manual labor. Professional men wear business suits or the traditional *chacabana*, a white shirt worn over dark trousers. Children are also dressed up, especially for church or visiting.

CUSTOMS AND COURTESIES

Greetings. Men shake hands firmly when they greet. One offers a wrist or elbow if one's hand is dirty. Friends may also embrace. Most women will kiss each other once on the right cheek. A man with the *confianza* of a woman will kiss her on the cheek in greeting. A handshake and *¿Cómo está usted?* (How are you?) is a common formal greeting. Informally, one may say *¿Cómo tú e'tá'?* (note the removal of the *s*'s) or *¡Hola!* (Hi). After greeting, it is polite to ask about a person's family. Adults, particularly in the *campo* (countryside), often address each other as *compadre* (for men) or *comadre* (for women); both terms mean "friend." One might not greet a stranger on the street, but one would never enter a room without greeting each person. Nor would a person leave without saying goodbye to everyone.

Formal introductions are rare, but professional titles are used to address respected persons. Older and more prominent people may be addressed as *Don* (for men) or *Doña* (for women), with or without their first names.

Gestures. Dominicans are animated in conversation and often make gestures. They point with puckered lips instead of a finger. Wrinkling one's nose indicates one does not understand, rubbing one's fingers and thumb together signifies money, and an upright wagging forefinger means "No." To express disapproval, one points (with lips) at the object and rolls the eyes. "Come here" is indicated with the palm down and fingers together waving inward. One says "pssst" to get another's attention. To hail a taxi or bus, one wags a finger or fingers (depending on the number of passengers needing a ride) in the direction one is going. Numbers are often expressed with one's fingers instead of words.

Sitting with legs apart is unladylike, and most women ride sidesaddle on the backs of motorcycles. Personal space is limited; touching is normal and crowding is common.

Visiting. Visiting is an important form of social recreation, especially in rural areas and poor *barrios* (neighborhoods). Visits in the home are common, but much socializing also takes place in public (while shopping, washing clothes, and so forth). Women often gather in the kitchen or outside as they cook.

A visit may be long or short and may occur at any time, usually without prior notice. Urbanites with telephones may call ahead, but whether expected or not, company is always genuinely welcomed. In rural areas doors are kept open; people consider it strange to close them and not accept visitors. To Dominicans, privacy is unimportant; they perceive the desire for solitude as sadness and equate being alone with being

Dominican Republic

lonely. Sitting in *mesadoras* (rocking chairs) talking or just sharing time is common. Nearly all homes have *mesadoras*. Hosts offer visitors something to drink (coffee or juice) and invite them to eat if mealtime is near. Refusing such offers is not impolite.

If guests interrupt (or passersby happen upon) someone eating, the person will immediately and sincerely invite them to share what is left by saying *A buen tiempo* (You've come at a good time). Guests may decline by saying *Buen provecho* (Enjoy), or they may sit down and eat.

Eating. The main meal, *comida*, is served at midday and often lasts two hours. Families prefer eating at home. Urban workers unable to return home may eat at inexpensive cafés or buy from vendors. *Desayuno* (breakfast) usually is light: sweetened coffee and bread. People in urban areas often eat a bit more. *Cena* (the evening meal) is also light, often not more than a snack or leftovers from *comida*. Guests are served first, and sometimes separately and more elaborately. Table conversation is often lively. Dining out is popular among those who can afford it. A service charge is typically included in the bill.

LIFESTYLE

Family. Family ties are important; extended families commonly live together. Many households are led by women—widows, women who are divorced, women whose husbands work elsewhere, or older women with adult children and grandchildren. It is common for women, men, and boys to work outside the home. The boys shine shoes or sell snacks on the streets. Large families are the norm, and many rural villages are composed of interrelated families. Within the extended family, informal adoption is common: other family members take in and raise children whose parents need help. Siblings raised by one mother may have different fathers, but all children are cared for equally. Cousins are often as close as siblings. Some men have more than one wife and family. Smaller, nuclear families are more common among the educated urban population.

Most families live in small houses, either rented or self-built. They may be constructed of cement, wood, or palm bark. They are brightly painted, have cement or dirt floors, and are covered with zinc roofs. Electricity and running water are luxuries. Affluent urban houses are larger and often have walled and landscaped grounds. Urban apartments are becoming popular, as are newly constructed condominiums.

Dating and Marriage. Attending movies, discos, dances, baseball games, and sitting on park benches are social activities for couples. Dating is relatively open and increasingly free of parental control. Girls are more closely supervised than boys and often go out in groups. Some couples might have a sibling tagging along as chaperon. Marriages in the Dominican Republic are often common-law (*por la ventana*), but many couples also marry in a church or civil ceremony. Elaborate urban weddings are major social events.

Diet. If Dominicans do not eat rice and beans at midday, they feel they have not eaten. Most meals feature rice served in large quantities, along with such favorites as *habichuelas* (beans) and *yuca* (cassava). *Yuca* may be boiled, battered and deep-fried, or baked into rounds of crisp cracker bread called *casabe*. *Plátanos* (plantains) and bananas are plentiful. Mangoes, papaya, pineapples, guavas, avocados, and other tropical fruits (passion fruit, coconuts, and star fruit) are grown locally and eaten in season. People may eat small quantities of chicken, beef, pork, or goat with a meal. *Bacalao* (dried fish, usually cod) is eaten in some areas; fresh fish is eaten only along the coast. Food is generally not spicy.

The national dish is *sancocho*, a rich vegetable-and-meat stew served on special occasions. *Habichuelas con dulce* (a dessert similar to rice pudding but made with beans) is popular at Easter. Dominican coffee is usually served sweet and strong. National beers and rums are highly regarded and widely consumed. Bottled soft drinks and sweetened fruit juices are also popular.

Recreation. Playing the game of dominoes is a national pastime. Outdoor tables in front of homes, bars, and rural *colmados* (neighborhood markets) are surrounded by men who play for hours, especially on Sundays. Outdoor players are almost exclusively men, but everyone may play at home. Even young children become adept. Cockfighting is another national pastime, and cockfight gambling stakes can be high. The lottery also has high participation.

Baseball is the most popular sport. Competition is keen, and many Dominicans have become famous major league players in the United States and Canada. Boys also enjoy playing basketball, and boys and girls enjoy playing volleyball. Strolling in parks, visiting friends, and watching television are popular activities.

The Arts. Dominicans love music and dancing. Merengue is the national dance, and many people, including small children, know the steps. Its fast-paced, rhythmic music traditionally is performed using three instruments: a *tambora* (small drum), *melodeon* (similar to an accordion), and *guayano* (scraping percussion instrument). *Bachata* is a popular folk dance accompanied by accordions, drums, horns, and *guayanos*. Salsa and other Latino styles are popular, as are North American pop and jazz. Discos are found even in rural communities.

Literature from the Dominican Republic is well established. Much writing focuses on nationalistic themes, social protest, history, and everyday life. Common crafts include masks for *Carnaval*, colorful paintings, faceless dolls, and jewelry made from amber or *larimar* (a blue stone unique to the Dominican Republic).

Holidays. National holidays include New Year's Day, *Día de los Reyes* (Day of the Kings, 6 January), *Nuestra Señora de la Alta Gracia* (Our Lady of High Gratitude, 21 January), Duarte's Day (26 Jan.), Independence Day (27 Feb.), Easter, Labor Day (1 May), Corpus Christi, Restoration of Independence (16 Aug.), *Nuestra Señora de las Mercedes* (Our Lady of Mercies, 24 September), Columbus Day (12 Oct.), and Christmas.

Urban families go to the beach or mountains during *Semana Santa* (Holy Week before Easter). *Carnaval* is celebrated for several weeks in the early spring with costume parades, complete with masked participants hitting spectators with inflated, hardened pig bladders, and other festivities. Gifts are not exchanged at Christmas, but they may be given to children on 6 January. The government may call special holidays to celebrate an event or project completion.

Commerce. Business hours vary, but most establishments open first around 8 or 9 a.m., close between noon and 2 p.m., and open again until 5 or 6 p.m. Telephone offices remain open until 10 p.m. and do not close at midday. Banks close by 3 p.m. Most shops are closed on Sunday. Small *colmados* have their own hours. Street vendors are busiest at midday. Bargaining is common in open-air markets, in some owner-operated stores, and on the streets. Prices in supermarkets and elsewhere are fixed.

Dominican Republic

Family ties and social relationships are important in obtaining employment or doing business. Business arrangements are seldom made between strangers.

SOCIETY

Government. The Dominican Republic is divided into 29 provinces and one national district. The president, currently Leonel Fernandez, and vice president are elected by the people. A bicameral National Congress of 32 senators and 150 deputies is also directly elected, as are local officials. Major parties include the Dominican Revolutionary Party (PRD), the PLD, and the PRSC. National and local elections are held simultaneously every four years. The voting age is 18. A nine-member Supreme Court is appointed by the Senate.

Economy. The economy, once dependent on agriculture, is becoming more oriented toward service and tourism. Agriculture, however, still remains an important industry. Coffee, sugar, pineapple, cocoa, tobacco, and rice are key crops for both export and domestic use. Fluctuating world prices impact earnings and make the domestic market somewhat volatile. Dominicans living abroad often send earnings back to families in the Republic; the money constitutes an important source of revenue. Industrial activity includes sugar refining, cement, mining, and pharmaceuticals. Assembly plants for various products are located in duty-free zones. The environment has suffered from the exploitation of mineral and natural resources, but efforts at conservation are being made.

Among Latin American countries, the Dominican Republic's economic growth has remained strong despite hurricanes and the global economic downturn. However, even though real gross domestic product per capita has nearly tripled in the last generation, most people (particularly women) do not have access to economic prosperity. A wide gap exists between rich and poor. At least one-fourth of Dominicans live in poverty. Unemployment is high while underemployment is rampant. Inflation is relatively low. The currency is the Dominican *peso* (DOP).

Transportation and Communications. Main roads are paved and heavily traveled. Rural roads are often unpaved and may be impassable during rainy seasons. Public transportation includes motorcycle taxis, economical vans or buses called *guaguas* that are used for local or long-distance trips, or larger buses. Pickup trucks or small vans travel between rural villages, carrying passengers, animals, and cargo in a single load. Urban Dominicans travel by *conchos*, informal taxis that follow certain routes. Private cars are expensive but by no means rare. Motorcycles are more common.

Telephone service is available throughout the country, and middle- and upper-class families have phones. Daily newspapers are read widely. Postal service is slow and unreliable. Most businesses use private messenger services. Private radio and television stations broadcast regionally and nationally.

Education. Free public education is provided through the high school level. Attendance is mandatory through the sixth grade, but many children, particularly girls and those in the *campo*, cannot attend or do not complete school for various reasons (work, lack of transport, home and family responsibilities, or lack of money to buy required uniforms). While more than three-fourths of Dominicans begin school, only one-third finish. Parents and teachers must provide basic supplies such as pencils and paper. Textbooks and other materials are scarce. Many urban families send their children to private schools called *colegios*. University education is available, and trade schools provide technical training. The adult literacy rate is lower in rural areas.

Health. Public hospitals and clinics provide free care, but private doctors are preferred when affordable. Public institutions tend to be poorly equipped and understaffed. Village health care workers have enough training to administer basic services, but rural areas often have no doctors or medicine, and people must travel elsewhere for care. Many people still consult *curanderos* (native healers). Lack of early treatment and preventive care is a major concern. Vaccination campaigns are helping fight disease, but maladies such as intestinal parasites, dengue fever, and malaria pose serious challenges.

DEVELOPMENT DATA

Human Dev. Index* rank . . . . 98 of 177 countries
Adjusted for women . . . . 98 of 144 countries
Real GDP per capita $6,640
Adult literacy rate . . . . 84 percent (male); 84 (female)
Infant mortality rate . . . . 33 per 1,000 births
Life expectancy . . . . 64 (male); 69 (female)

AT A GLANCE

Events and Trends.

- In August 2004, newly elected president Leonel Fernandez took office. Fernandez was able to win 51 percent of the vote in May elections, in part because of his popularity during his first term as president, from 1996 to 2000. However, he angered many upon taking office this time when he appointed top government jobs to four men who were under investigation for fraud.
- In May 2004, weeks of torrential rains caused flooding throughout the island of Hispaniola. Although more deaths (1,660) occurred in Haiti, the Dominican Republic was also deeply affected. Hundreds of homes were swept away and almost 300 people were reported to have died there.
- In November 2003, eight people were killed in fights with soldiers during a one-day general strike protesting austerity measures that were being negotiated in an attempt to address the country's troubled economy.
- In April 2003, the country's second-largest bank collapsed amid charges or wrongdoing by those in leadership positions. The failure sent the economy into chaos.
- In July 2002, former president Joaquin Balaguer died at age 95. Thousands came out to honor the man who had dominated the nation's politics for so long.

Contact Information. Dominican Republic Tourist Office, 136 East 57th Street, Suite 803, New York, NY 10022; phone (888) 374-6361; web site www.dominicanrepublic.com. Embassy of the Dominican Republic, 1715 22nd Street NW, Washington, DC 20008; phone (202) 332-6280; web site www.domrep.org.

CultureGrams World Edition 2006

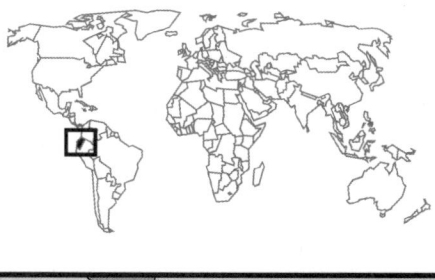

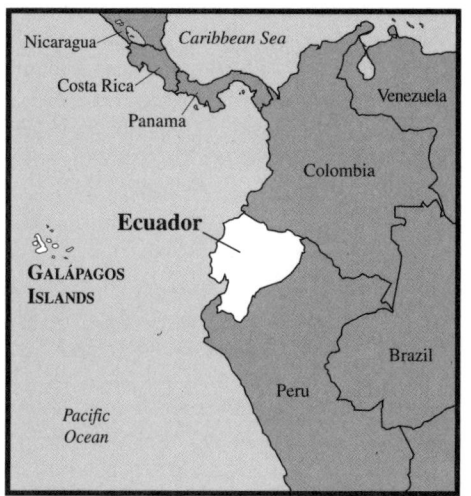

Republic of Ecuador

BACKGROUND

Land and Climate. Ecuador is just smaller than Nevada, covering 109,483 square miles (283,560 square kilometers). The country is located on, and named after, the equator. Ecuador has four major geographic regions: La Costa (coastal lowlands), which contains rich agricultural land; La Sierra (Andean highlands), with snowcapped mountains; El Oriente (eastern lowlands), beginning at the eastern Andean foothills and containing mostly tropical rain forest; and the Archipiélago de Colón (or Galápagos Islands), a group of islands in the Pacific about 600 miles (966 kilometers) off the coast. Charles Darwin developed his theories of evolution based on his observations of Galápagos wildlife. Ecuador is subject to earthquakes and volcanic eruptions. The country has 31 active volcanoes; many of them are near Quito, which is surrounded by the Avenue of the Volcanoes. The two highest peaks are Chimborazo at 20,561 feet (6,267 meters) and Cotopaxi at 19,347 feet (5,897 meters).

The climate varies with elevation more than with season, but the rainy season is generally from November to May. The driest months are June to September. The coastal lowlands are hot and humid, while the highlands include everything from subtropical valleys to frigid mountains. Quito's temperature averages 71°F (22°C) all year. The rain forest, which is part of the upper Amazon Basin, has a tropical climate. Temperatures in the Galápagos Islands average 76°F (24°C). Ecuador is located at the center of the El Niño weather pattern, which periodically causes destructive floods and mud slides and is often followed by the La Niña weather pattern, which causes drought.

History. Various groups of indigenous peoples, whose ancestors first inhabited Ecuador, were conquered in the latter 1400s by Incas from the south. The Incan Empire ruled the area until the Spanish conquered it in 1534. The Spanish claimed vast tracts of land and enslaved the local people. Nearly 300 years later, Antonio José de Sucre, a compatriot of Simón Bolívar, led a successful military campaign against the Spaniards. Ecuador (along with present-day Colombia, Panama, and Venezuela) gained its independence in 1822 and became part of *Gran Colombia*, a federation led by Bolívar that was dissolved a few years later. Ecuador declared itself a republic in 1830.

In 1941, Peru and Ecuador battled over ownership of an area in the southern Amazon region then controlled by Ecuador. A 1942 treaty granted Peru most of the territory, but because the treaty referenced obscure landmarks and denied Ecuador access to vital mineral wealth and the Amazon River system, the country later rejected it. The two neighbors continued exchanging hostilities from time to time. A January 1995 clash lasted for several days before international observers helped negotiate a settlement. A final agreement was signed in October 1998, granting Ecuador a small portion of land as well as navigation rights on some rivers in Peru.

Between 1830 and 1948, Ecuador had 62 presidents, dictators, and military leaders. In 1948, Galo Plaza Lasso became the first freely elected president to serve a full term. Civilian governments alternated with military rule until 1979, when a new constitution allowed for a freely elected president.

The 1996 elections marked Ecuador's fifth consecutive peaceful transition of power. Abdalá Bucaram, nicknamed *El Loco* (the Madman) for his flamboyant personality, won the presidency, promising to help Ecuador's poor. But in 1997, Congress voted to remove Bucaram for "mental incapacity" and charged him with corruption. An interim leader, Jamil Mahuad, was elected president in 1998, only to be ousted by

Ecuador

a military coup in 2000 and replaced by his vice president, Gustavo Noboa. In 2002, Lucio Gutierrez was elected and began the difficult task of stabilizing Ecuador's economy and maintaining order in the face of widespread discontent.

THE PEOPLE

Population. Ecuador's population of about 13.2 million is growing at roughly 1 percent annually. The majority (65 percent) is mestizo (of mixed indigenous and Spanish heritage). Indigenous peoples, whose culture differs from that of mainstream society, comprise about 25 percent of the population. Another 7 percent is of Spanish descent, and 3 percent is black. Quito, the capital, is one of the oldest continuously inhabited cities in the Western Hemisphere and is home to more than a million people. But the largest city is Guayaquil, which has almost 2 million residents. Approximately 60 percent of all Ecuadorians live in urban areas.

Language. Spanish is Ecuador's official language, although Quichua (also known as Quechua) is spoken by highland Indian groups, including the Quichua, Saraguro, Otavalan, Cañari, and Chimborazo. Quichua is recognized by the constitution as an important part of Ecuadorian culture, but it is not an official language. Many Quichua words have been adopted into colloquial language to supplement the Spanish vocabulary. Indigenous groups (Shuar, Auca, Cofan, Cecoya, Cayapa, and Colorado) in other regions speak their own languages. Many people from these groups are bilingual in a native tongue and Spanish. Spanish tends to be spoken faster on the coast than in the highlands. Some consonants are pronounced differently between the two regions.

Religion. While the constitution guarantees religious freedom, more than 80 percent of Ecuadorians belong to the Catholic Church. Many national and local holidays/festivals center on the Catholic faith. Rituals such as baptism, first communion, and confirmation are celebrated in the community, as well as among family. Many other Christian churches are growing in popularity, and people generally are tolerant of other beliefs.

General Attitudes. Ecuador encompasses a great diversity of cultures. In addition to ethnic differences, there are regional differences that tend to influence politics and internal relations. *Serranos* (people from highland areas, including Quito) are considered more formal, conservative, and reserved than *Costeños* (coastal inhabitants). Costeños are considered cosmopolitan, open, and liberal; they generally are the businesspeople of Ecuador. Serranos are associated with government and banks. The two groups, political rivals, distrust each other in many respects but are united in others.

A common trait of all Ecuadorians is the value they place on familial relationships and responsibilities. People are warm and hospitable. Relationships generally take precedence over schedules or timetables. A certain sentimentality is evident in popular songs and in the practice of exchanging or giving *recuerdos* (tokens of affection or remembrance). Oratory and leadership skills are admired, as are loyalty and honesty. Occupation, wealth, and family name indicate social status.

Long marginalized, indigenous groups have begun to organize themselves to regain lost rights, press for environmental protection of their lands, and achieve recognition for their language and culture. Today, there is greater contact and cooperation between indigenous peoples and other Ecuadorians than in the past. Still, most indigenous peoples who remain in their home regions (and many who move to urban areas) retain strong, traditional cultural identities.

Personal Appearance. In urban areas, many Ecuadorians wear standard Western-style clothing. Older women tend to prefer skirts, while younger women often wear pants. Every rural region has its own traditional styles, colors, and fabrics. These clothes are worn by rural and indigenous peoples. Women from these groups usually wear skirts and often wear hats—made of straw in coastal areas and wool or leather in the highlands. Generally, Costeños wear bright colors (white, yellow, and red), while Serranos prefer blues, browns, and blacks. Special celebrations call for new clothing, either purchased at a store or, more often, made by local tailors.

CUSTOMS AND COURTESIES

Greetings. People usually shake hands when first introduced. A handshake is then used in subsequent greetings, along with the exchange of good wishes. In rural areas particularly, one offers the wrist or arm rather than the hand when one's hands are soiled. Close friends greet with what seems like a kiss on the cheek—they actually touch cheeks while kissing the air. Men may embrace if well acquainted. It is customary to address a new acquaintance by title (*Señor, Señora, Doctor, Doctora*, etc.). Among friends, the title *Don* or *Doña*, followed by the first name, is a common greeting indicating respect and friendship.

Typical greetings include ¡*Buenos días!* (Good day) and ¿*Cómo está?* (How are you?). It is courteous to greet people in small stores or restaurants, or when passing on rural roads. Friends commonly greet each other with ¡*Hola!* (Hello). After a long absence, one might greet another with ¿*Cómo has pasado? A los tiempos que nos vemos* (How have you been? It has been a long time).

Gestures. Ecuadorians often use gestures to emphasize or replace verbal communication. During conversation, a person might touch another person of the same sex to show friendly concern. Drawing a circle or two in the air with the index finger means "I'll be back." To indicate "Sorry, the bus is full" or "Sorry, we're out of tomatoes" or anything along that line, a person sticks out the hand, as if to shake hands, and twists it almost as if waving. Yawning in public, whistling or yelling to get someone's attention, and pointing with the index finger are considered impolite. Ecuadorians might point by puckering or pursing the lips. One can also indicate "up the road" by lifting the chin, and "down the road" by lowering the chin.

Visiting. Relatives and friends usually visit for a meal and conversation. Unannounced visits are common and welcomed. If unexpected guests arrive during mealtime, they will be offered a full meal. Otherwise, they typically are offered something to drink. Refusing a meal, drink, or other refreshments generally is impolite. Hosts often offer departing guests a small gift of fruit, candy, or something else on hand. *Dios le pague* (God will repay you) is a common expression of thanks for a gift or an invitation. When inviting a guest to visit, the host will state the starting time, but specifying an ending time is considered bad taste. Instead, an ending time is generally understood depending on the nature of the visit. Guests are not expected to arrive on time and can be anywhere from 10 minutes to an hour late, depending on the event. This tendency to arrive late is jokingly referred to as *la hora Ecuatoriana* (Ecuadorian time). Dinner guests stay for conversation rather than leave right after the meal.

Evening socials and parties might extend past midnight. They usually involve eating, dancing, and drinking. Furniture is placed near the wall so everyone, including children, can dance in the middle of the main room. The hosts serve refreshments on trays; guests do not serve themselves from a central location. A late meal usually is served, after which some guests may stay for more socializing.

At small gatherings, arriving guests greet each person individually. The host introduces the guests to people with whom they are not acquainted. If guests fail to greet acquaintances, they show disrespect for the relationship. When leaving, one also says good-bye to each individual. Less formal customs are becoming the norm among the younger generation. For instance, young people often greet a whole group rather than each individual.

Eating. Food and eating habits play an important part in Ecuadorian culture. Each holiday is associated with a special kind of food and every town has a specialty dish. Mealtime is considered a good time for conversation—catching up, doing business, or socializing. At family meals, the mother generally serves food to the father first, followed by male children and then female children (who help prepare and serve the meal). The mother will eat only after everyone else has been attended to. Guests usually are served first and receive the largest amount and choicest cuts of food. Taking leftovers home is acceptable; leaving food on the plate is not. It is customary to say *Buen provecho* (roughly, *Bon appétit*) before beginning a meal. One should thank the person who prepared the meal before excusing oneself from the table. A host who invites a guest to a restaurant is expected to pay for the meal. Young people often split a bill.

LIFESTYLE

Family. Families generally are close-knit. The elderly are respected and treated well, and several generations may live under the same roof. While most families follow traditional roles, urban families are changing as more women work outside the home and more men share household duties. Still, mothers remain the emotional center of their families and are honored for their primary role of raising children. Many songs are devoted to mothers, and cities typically have a park or monument dedicated to motherhood. Children used to live with their parents until they married. Now they commonly leave to get an education or to work. Urban families average two children, while rural families average three children or more.

Dating and Marriage. Dating usually begins in groups, when young people get together for dances or other activities. As couples begin to pair off, a girl must ask for her parents' approval when invited out. In more conservative regions, the young man must personally visit with the girl's parents to gain approval. Girls often do not begin dating until after their *quinceañera* (coming-out party) at age 15. A Catholic ceremony officially presents the girl to society. If the family can afford it, a party with food and dancing follows.

Women usually marry by age 23 (younger in some rural areas), and men around age 25. Families often emphasize that young people should complete their education before marrying. Many urban couples do not live together before their church wedding, even if they have already been legally married. Common-law marriage, which is referred to as *estilo manabita*, is common and accepted as a legal marriage in rural, coastal areas (Manabi is a coastal region). For most of these unions, the ceremony is lacking only because of the expense of a wedding.

Diet. The main meal is eaten at midday. Serranos favor corn and potatoes, while Costeños favor rice, beans, and bananas, of which there are several varieties. Fresh fruits abound. Chicken, meat, and fish (on the coast) are dietary staples. Soup is almost always served at both the midday and evening meals. Hot bread is a popular afternoon snack. Some favorite dishes include *arroz con pollo* (fried chicken with rice), *locro* (soup with potatoes, cheese, meat, and avocados), *llapingachos* (cheese and potato cakes), *ceviche* (raw or cooked seafood marinated in lime and served with onions, tomatoes, and spices), *fritada* (fried pork), *empanadas* (pastries filled with meat or cheese), *arroz con menestra* (rice with spicy beans, barbecued beef, and refried plantains), *caldo de bola* (plantain-based soup with meat and vegetables), and *cuy* (roast guinea pig).

Recreation. Nationally, *fútbol* (soccer) is the favorite sport, followed by volleyball and basketball. Others include tennis, running, and boxing. Ecuadorian volleyball (*Ecuavolley*) is played with a heavy ball with three players on each side. Visiting and sightseeing are common leisure activities. People in coastal areas take advantage of nearby beaches. Many Ecuadorians participate in community groups (women's clubs, church groups, or sports clubs) and *mingas* (community improvement projects).

The Arts. Ecuador's music and dance reflect a mixing of cultures. String and wind instruments such as bamboo flutes and *rondadors* (panpipes) characterize indigenous music. "El Condor Pasa" is a traditional song from the highlands. Other folk music includes the *pasacalle*, *pasillo* (which has slow, waltz-like rhythms), and *yumbo*. The *bomba* is a rhythmic dance with African influences. Teens and young adults often gather at discos, where salsa music and dancing are particularly popular.

Folk arts are diverse and vary by region. Many people weave items such as carpets, bags, sashes, and Panama hats, which can take months to complete. Some make wood carvings of saints or Christ. Decorative crosses, musical instruments, jewelry, and leather work are other native arts.

Holidays. Ecuadorians mark the new year by burning images of the Old Year in the streets on New Year's Eve. These images, or effigies, represent problems they do not want to reencounter in the coming year. They celebrate the *Carnaval* season (in February or March) by dousing each other with water; *Carnaval* culminates in a weekend festival of parades, dances, and parties. Easter, Labor Day (1 May), and the Battle of Pichincha (24 May), which marks Ecuador's liberation, are all national holidays. *Inti Raymi* (Festival of the Sun) occurs in June at the Incan ruins near Cuenca. It features dancing and draws indigenous groups from Ecuador and other countries. Independence of Quito Day (10 Aug.) celebrates the nation's first efforts (in 1809) to gain independence. Independence of Guayaquil is celebrated 9 October. On All Souls' Day (2 Nov.) people visit cemeteries, eat bread-dough dolls, and drink *colada morada* (a thick drink made with berries, sweet spices, and purple flour). Communities celebrate Christmas and Easter with reenactments of religious events. Each city holds festivities marking the anniversary of its founding. The founding of Quito (6 Dec.) is celebrated with large festivals, bullfights, and sporting events.

Commerce. Stores generally are open weekdays between 8 a.m. and 6 p.m., with a lunch break from 12:30 to 2:30 p.m. Urban stores close at 12:30 p.m. on Saturday and do not open on Sunday. Some stores in rural areas may open on Sunday to accommodate farmers who cannot shop on other days. Banks close weekdays at 2 or 4 p.m.

Ecuador

Urban families often shop at supermarkets and department stores, but they also frequent open-air markets. Rural Ecuadorians usually shop at open-air markets and small local businesses. Open-air markets operate a few days a week and offer a variety of goods, including locally grown fruits and vegetables, food, clothing, household items, and crafts.

SOCIETY

Government. The executive branch of the Republic of Ecuador consists of a president (Lucio Gutierrez) and vice president (Alfredo Palacio). The unicameral legislature has 100 members elected by provinces. Elections are held every four years. All literate citizens 18 to 65 are required by law to vote. Voting is optional for other citizens. A number of political parties are active; the largest include the Democratic Left, Popular Democratic, Roldosista, and Social Christian parties and the Christian Democrats.

Economy. Ecuador's economy is slowly pulling itself out of its worst economic crisis in decades. The economy was devastated by natural disasters, low prices for oil and bananas, problems in the banking sector, and huge foreign deficits. However, rising oil prices, dollarization of the monetary system, and increased foreign investment have helped the economy. Nevertheless, unemployment is high and underemployment is extensive. Inflation has lowered but remains high. Foreign investment and trade are growing but are hampered by the uncertain political climate. Nearly half of the government's budget goes toward servicing debt. More than half of the population lives in poverty. These financial challenges make the country's substantial military spending a much-debated issue. The economic crisis has led to a general lack of faith in the government and increased the perception of foreign dependence. In March 2000, the U.S. dollar (USD) became Ecuador's new currency, replacing the *sucre* (ECS).

Roughly one-third of the population is employed in agriculture. Ecuador is the world's biggest banana exporter. Petroleum accounts for almost half of the nation's exports, followed by coffee, bananas, cocoa, shrimp, and fish. Fluctuations in global market prices for these products have a major impact on Ecuador's economy.

Transportation and Communications. In cities, transportation is provided by buses, taxis, and *colectivos* (minibuses that are more comfortable and faster than buses). In rural areas, *colectivos* are known as *busetas*. Roads connecting cities have been improved and about half are paved. Seaports provide shipping access to other nations. Air travel both to and within Ecuador is increasing. Most urban homes and many rural homes include a television and radio. Private telephones are much more common in upper-class and urban homes. Cities and towns generally have a pay-phone center where people can make local or long-distance calls. Newspapers are readily available in towns and cities.

Education. Beginning at age six, children attend six years of mandatory education. The school day lasts from 7 a.m. to 12:30 p.m. or from 1 to 6 p.m. Students usually wear uniforms. The government controls both public and private educational institutions. The school system is comprised of nursery schools, kindergartens, rural and urban primary schools, secondary and vocational schools, special-education schools and night schools. There are also 21 universities, the largest of which is in Quito and has around 45,000 students. Tuition is waved for various disciplines at state universities. Illiteracy is decreasing slowly as more children enroll in primary schools. Approximately 60 to 70 percent of school-aged children complete their primary education, but this percentage is lower in rural areas. Family economic need, inadequate facilities, and lack of personnel in rural areas contribute to the dropout rate.

Health. The government provides medical care to all citizens at low (and sometimes no) cost to the patient. However, healthcare professionals, facilities, and equipment are concentrated in urban areas. Those who can afford it might go to a private clinic or doctor. The country still battles diseases such as typhoid, cholera, polio, malaria, and yellow fever. Dengue fever is carried by mosquitoes in some coastal areas. Only about half of the rural population has access to safe drinking water. With improved medical care, the infant mortality rate has been cut nearly in half over the last decade.

DEVELOPMENT DATA

Human Dev. Index* rank . . . . 100 of 177 countries
　Adjusted for women . . . . 79 of 144 countries
Real GDP per capita $3,580
Adult literacy rate . . . . 92 percent (male); 90 (female)
Infant mortality rate . . . . 24 per 1,000 births
Life expectancy . . . . 68 (male); 73 (female)

AT A GLANCE

Events and Trends.

- In November 2004, opposition groups dropped their campaign to impeach President Gutierrez. Since coming to power in 2002, Gutierrez had lost much of his popularity. However, the opposition was unable to get 51 of the 100 members of Congress to support his impeachment. Some opposition leaders had accused Gutierrez of bribing members of Congress.

- In December 2004, Congress dismissed 27 of the Supreme Court's 31 judges. The dismissed judges were replaced with others who did not support the impeachment drive against Gutierrez. Gutierrez said the former court had been controlled by opposition leader and former president Leon Febres Cordero.

- In February 2004, inmates at a vastly overcrowded prison took more than 300 visitors hostage. The crisis ended when the government agreed to meet some of their demands, including building more prisons and releasing people who have been held without trial. But violence erupted again in April, when riots took place at two prisons and more hostages were taken. Although the crisis eventually calmed, tensions remain high.

Contact Information. Embassy of the Republic of Ecuador, 2535 15th Street NW, Washington, DC 20009; phone (202) 234-7200; web site www.ecuador.org.

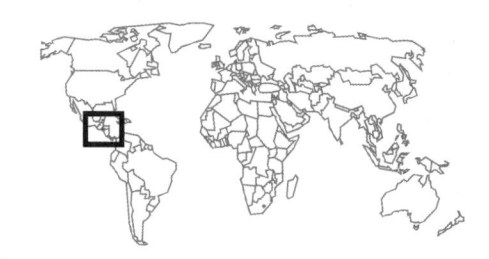

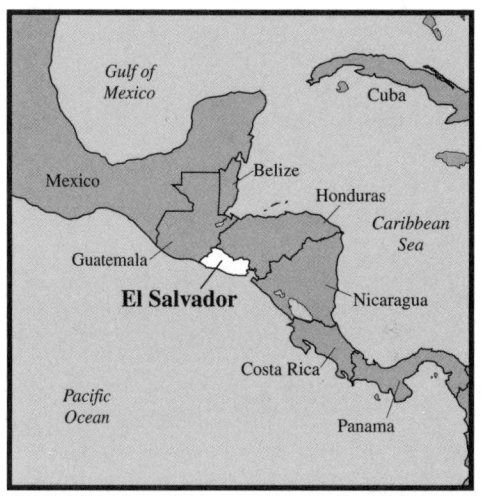

Republic of El Salvador

CultureGrams World Edition 2006

BACKGROUND

Land and Climate. With 8,124 square miles (21,041 square kilometers), El Salvador is just smaller than Massachusetts. A narrow band of coastal lowlands is divided from the mostly mountainous east and north by a central plateau. El Salvador is called Land of the Volcanoes for its more than two hundred extinct volcanoes that have enriched the country's soil. Some mountain peaks rise to between 6,000 and 8,000 feet (1,829–2,438 meters). Although deforestation has taken a heavy toll on the country's forests—the country has only about 2 percent of its virgin forests—the government and private citizens are working now to protect endangered species of animals and plants.

The climate is tropical in the lowlands, with an average annual temperature of around 85°F (29°C); semitropical on the plateau, with lower temperatures and less humidity; and temperate in the mountains. Temperatures rarely fluctuate more than 10 degrees year-round. El Salvador has only two seasons: a rainy season, from May to October, and a dry season. Most of the rain falls in short evening storms. San Salvador, the capital, lies on a plateau at the foot of the San Salvador Volcano. Small earthquakes are not uncommon; one region or another suffers a significant quake every 30 years or so.

History. Various native civilizations (including Maya, Lenca, and Nahuat) inhabited the area long before Spanish colonization. Ruins of their cultures remain at Tazumal, Joya de Cerén, and Quelepa. The Pipil, of Aztec origin, were those who encountered the Spaniards. The indigenous people called their land Cuscatlán. In 1524, Pedro de Alvarado conquered the area on behalf of Spain, which ruled for almost three hundred years. The indigenous population was nearly wiped out under harsh colonial rule. For most of its early history, El Salvador was a minor province of Guatemala. Attempts by Father José Matías Delgado to gain independence from Spain in 1811 and 1814 were unsuccessful but earned Delgado national recognition.

A wider regional attempt to gain independence was successful in 1821, but two years of instability followed as Mexico's emperor Agustín de Iturbide tried to annex Central America. When his empire collapsed, El Salvador and its neighbors formed the United Provinces of Central America, which disbanded in 1838. El Salvador claimed sovereignty in 1841 but was dominated intermittently by Guatemala until near the end of the century.

The 1871 constitution marked the true birth of the nation. During the relatively stable period that followed (1871–1931), most present-day educational, artistic, and government institutions and large businesses were formed. A new wave of upwardly mobile European and Palestinian immigrants also arrived during this time; their descendants comprise the bulk of today's affluent urban class. Much of their prosperity was built on the coffee industry. However, coffee became so successful that the government seized Pipil lands on which most of it was grown, marginalizing small farmers. In 1932, coffee prices collapsed, and already harsh treatment of natives was exacerbated, so the farmers rebelled. Many Pipil joined Augustín Farabundo Martí, a communist, in destroying property and killing scores of people. They were defeated quickly by government forces, who killed at least 10,000 indigenous people. Their culture nearly died with the massacre as the indigenous people feared to be thought of as anything other than Spanish.

For more than 50 years, El Salvador was plagued with internal strife and military dictatorships. Governments were hard

El Salvador

on those who voiced dissent. A rebel movement born in the 1960s began to mature in the late 1970s. In 1979, a rival faction of the military overthrew the government. The next year, rebel groups formed the Farabundo Martí National Liberation Front (FMLN), named for the executed leader of the 1932 rebellion. The FMLN launched a civil war to force a change in leadership. In the midst of war, a new constitution was adopted (1983) and the Christian Democratic Party's candidate, José Napoleón Duarte, was elected president in 1984. His government was accused of serious human-rights violations, corruption, and other abuses of power.

Alfredo Cristiani of the National Republican Alliance (ARENA) became president following 1989 elections. Violence marred the elections, peace talks broke down, and the war intensified. Cristiani reopened discussions with FMLN leaders in 1990, and both sides accepted the United Nations as a mediator. Eventually, key concessions from both sides led to a 1992 UN-sponsored peace agreement between the leftist FMLN and the right-wing government. As many as 75,000 people died during the years of violence.

Formal peace was declared in December 1992 amid huge celebrations. As part of the peace agreement, the FMLN became a legal political party, the size of the military was dramatically reduced, and a civilian national police force was established. The government has developed better trade relations with its neighbors, controlled inflation, and improved democratic institutions.

THE PEOPLE

Population. El Salvador's population of nearly 6.6 million is growing at about 1.8 percent annually. Roughly half of all people live in rural areas. Major cities include the greater San Salvador area, Santa Ana, and San Miguel. Nearly two million Salvadorans reside in the United States. The majority of Salvadorans (90 percent) are mestizos, or people of mixed European and indigenous ancestry, while about 1 percent are of pure indigenous blood. Most of the other people are white, though there is also a Palestinian presence.

Language. Spanish (also called *Castellano*) is the official language of El Salvador. Only a few thousand people continue to speak the indigenous language Nahua. School instruction is in Spanish, although English is strongly emphasized. Many Salvadorans with more formal education speak English in addition to Spanish.

Religion. El Salvador is a Christian nation; approximately 70 percent of the people belong to the Roman Catholic Church. Another 25 percent belong to a variety of other Christian faiths, including several Protestant movements whose memberships are growing. The state itself is secular; the only reference to religion in the constitution is a provision preventing clergy from holding public office. Still, priests usually pray or speak at school ceremonies and public meetings.

General Attitudes. Salvadorans are proud of their country and its accomplishments. Having endured 12 years of war, they now look forward to a future of peace and democracy. Past feelings of hatred and revenge gradually are being replaced with hope, optimism, and cooperation. Parents hope for a bright future for their children, even as they struggle with the devastation that war and natural disasters have brought to their country.

Salvadorans have a strong work ethic. Honest work is more important than income in determining social standing. All family members contribute to the family's well-being. Social status is also measured by occupation and landownership. Most people value personal relationships, friendships, and security. Devotion to the group is more important than individualism. Time is considered flexible: people are more important than schedules, and social events usually begin later than planned.

Some Salvadorans are offended when people from the United States introduce themselves as Americans because Salvadorans also consider themselves Americans. It is best to identify oneself as a U.S. citizen (*estadounidense*).

Personal Appearance. Because of the warm climate, summer clothing is suitable all year. For women, dresses are more common than slacks. During the dry season, light jackets are sometimes necessary at night. Although the poor do not have extensive wardrobes, they keep their appearance neat and clean. Daily showers are considered a must. People without running water will go to considerable lengths to keep themselves, or at least their children, bathed as frequently as possible.

CUSTOMS AND COURTESIES

Greetings. In urban areas, a brief, firm handshake is the customary formal greeting. People sometimes also slightly nod the head. Members of the opposite sex usually do not shake each other's hands. Weaker handshakes are common in rural areas. It is considered rude not to shake the hands of others around the area. Children appreciate adults shaking their hands. In cities, friends and relatives of the opposite sex kiss lightly on one cheek. Friends or relatives who have not seen each other for a while exchange hugs. Placing an arm around the shoulders of another person shows friendship. Friends often stand very close when conversing.

The most common daily greetings include *¡Buenos días!* (Good morning), *¡Buenas tardes!* (Good afternoon), and *¡Buenas noches!* (Good evening). *Adiós* or *Hasta luego* are formal parting terms, while less formal good-byes are *Chao* or *Nos vemos* (See you later).

When addressing people older than themselves, Salvadorans show friendly respect by using the title *Don* (for men) or *Doña* (for women) with the first name (e.g., *Doña Mélida*). *Niña*, a less formal title, is also used for women. Among peers, professional and courtesy titles are used with the family name (e.g., *Señor Moreno*) or with full names (e.g., *Doctora Isabel Pérez López*). Only close friends and relatives address each other by first name.

Gestures. In some circles, using excessive hand gestures is considered poor taste. But for many Salvadorans, hand gesturing is such an essential part of communicating that people jest they could not talk if their hands were tied. Although pointing directly at people with the index finger is impolite, pointing at objects or animals is acceptable. One points at an angle to the street to hail a taxi or bus. To indicate "no," one wags the vertical index finger from side to side. Touching the tip of the thumb and index finger together while facing the palm inward means "money," but facing the palm outward means "OK." A person can beckon to a friend with a hand wave, but strangers are summoned verbally.

Visiting. Friends and relatives visit one another frequently as a way to maintain strong relationships. Most people drop by without prior arrangement, although urban residents with phones try to call ahead when possible. Hosts usually serve guests refreshments or coffee. Visiting in the evening or on weekends is most popular. Visitors from out of town or who have not visited for a while commonly bring small gifts—fruit, pastries, and so on. Guests are expected to show dignity, courtesy, warmth, and friendship. It is appropriate to stand when a woman enters the room and when meeting other people. In rural areas, it is common for people to walk into each other's homes without knocking. Polite hosts entertain guests until the guests are ready to leave. At the end of a visit, hosts walk visitors to the door and wait there while they walk or drive away.

Eating. Families usually eat at least the main meal together, whether it is at midday or in the evening. In urban homes, food usually is served on dishes from which diners choose their portions. In rural homes, plates are more often served prepared.

Guests compliment their hosts on the meal as a way of assuring the hosts they feel welcome. Hosts usually offer second helpings and feel complimented when they are accepted. However, one is careful in a poorer home not to eat too much since the family may not have much food. Hosts will continue to offer food until the guest says *No, gracias; estoy satisfecho* (No, thank you; I am satisfied). It is less common to say *Estoy lleno* (I am full). In rural areas, the wife will eat alone after the guests have been properly fed and attended to. Men commonly stand when a woman leaves the table. People leaving the table say *Buen provecho* (roughly, "enjoy your meal").

LIFESTYLE

Family. The nuclear family is the basis of Salvadoran society. The father typically is head of the family, which has an average of five members. Single-parent families are also common, and many unwed women give birth at young ages. Some men consider it a sign of virility to father children by more than one woman. Families usually live close to each other. Most young adults remain at home until they marry. Excepting urban professionals, unmarried adults with children also usually live with their parents. Elderly parents often move in with their married children.

Women care for the children and household, but a large number are also employed in the labor force. They may till the ground, clean homes, sew, run a small store (*tienda*) inside their home, or work as skilled laborers. Men help with farm work or water transportation. The majority of families belong to the peasant class (*campesinos*, who work on the land but do not own it) and the blue-collar working class. The gap between rich and poor is wide and expanding. Domestic violence is a serious problem.

Dating and Marriage. Dating for both genders begins after the 15th birthday, when many girls celebrate a *quinceañera* (fifteen years) party—the traditional entrance for young women into the social world. Urban youth often begin dating earlier. Traditionally, it has been improper for couples to date openly unless engaged, but for the most part, only rural couples maintain this tradition today. Asking a young woman's parents for her hand in marriage is more or less a polite formality and often an occasion for a festive dinner. In most cases, wedding ceremonies follow Catholic traditions, even among the secularized population. In some rural areas, family and friends of the bride may celebrate at the bride's home while the groom's family and friends may celebrate separately at his home. *Campesinos* often enter into common-law relationships because they cannot afford the expense of formal weddings.

Diet. Salvadoran food is much less spicy than that of many other Latin American countries. Most people eat red beans (*frijoles*) cooked in many ways, thick corn tortillas, rice, eggs, and fruit. One of the most common dishes is *pupusas* (thick tortillas stuffed with meat, beans, or cheese). People who can afford it consume beef, chicken, or fish regularly for lunch and/or dinner. Poorer rural families eat tortillas, whatever they can grow, and an occasional pig or chicken, a number of which usually are kept around the house as domestic livestock.

Recreation. The national sport in El Salvador is soccer (*fútbol*). Basketball (*baloncesto*) is also popular. Most towns have a gym and athletic field. Young women play baseball or softball. In their leisure time, people like to visit, enjoy movies or music, or just relax. Many Salvadorans enjoy dancing at parties, discos (in larger cities), or dance halls (in smaller towns). Vacations are not common. Some people may take an excursion to the beach to get oysters or to enjoy the sunshine and fishing.

The Arts. With the end of the civil war has come a return to traditional handicrafts and arts. Ilobasco, a little town in the center of the country, is known for its beautiful pottery, especially *sorpresas* (surprises)—small egg-shaped cases that display miniature scenes and figures of everyday life.

National issues and daily life have been subjects for Salvadoran writers for centuries. Religious subjects are popular for sculpture and painting. A sculpture of Christ called *Salvator Mundi* in San Salvador's cathedral is one of the few major works left after natural disasters ruined older works. Colorfully painted scenes from Christ's life can be found as part of the works of Fernando Llort.

Holidays. The Salvadoran love for beauty and fun finds expression in the many colorful festivals during the year. National holidays include New Year's Day; Easter Week (*Semana Santa*); Labor Day (1 May); Mother's Day (10 May); Father's Day (17 June); August religious festivities (1–5 Aug.); Independence Day, which commemorates the day five Central American countries separated from Spain (15 Sept.); Columbus Day (12 Oct.); and Christmas. Each town has its holy day, which is celebrated over a long weekend or week. Holiday celebrations often include dances.

Commerce. Most businesses are open from 8 a.m. to noon and from 2 to 6 p.m., Monday through Friday. On Saturday they close at noon. Retail shops at large malls remain open through Sunday. Government offices open at 7:30 a.m. and close at 3:30 p.m. on weekdays. While fixed prices prevail in the stores, bargaining is common in open markets. People in small towns and in rural areas purchase produce and meat at open markets but other groceries (bread, milk, soap, rice, etc.) at small family-owned stores. In urban areas, this traditional retailing structure is quickly being replaced by *supermercado* (supermarket) shopping.

SOCIETY

Government. El Salvador is a democratic republic. The executive branch is led by a president and vice president. President Antonio Saca was elected in 2004 and will serve a five-year term. Both president and vice president are ineligible for immediate reelection. The unicameral, national Legislative Assembly has 84 members elected to three-year terms. Major political parties include ARENA, the FMLN, the Christian Democratic Party, and the National Conciliation Party. The voting age is 18. The country is divided into 14 departments and 262 municipalities. Although still weak, municipal power and autonomy, strengthened in the 1983 constitution, have been increasing steadily since 1990.

Economy. Because of the war and natural disasters, El Salvador has had one of the weakest economies in Latin America. But the economy recently has become more stable. Economic

El Salvador

growth is still low, but inflation remains under control.

Problems remain in areas such as income inequality, unemployment and underemployment (which affect more than half of the population), land reform, deforestation, and pollution. Opportunities for personal advancement are limited. Nearly 20 percent of the population is without access to the education, health care, and economic opportunities needed to rise above poverty. Training programs have been established to teach new skills, but a shortage of skilled labor remains a challenge. Salvadorans depend heavily on foreign aid and remittances from family members who have emigrated to the United States.

Coffee is the most important export, accounting for roughly one-third of all export earnings. It is grown on steep mountainsides: the higher the altitude, the higher the coffee-bean quality. Children often help their parents pick coffee during school vacations. El Salvador also exports sugar, cotton, shrimp, and clothing. Important domestic industries include food processing, cement, textiles, and petroleum processing. While agriculture employs about 30 percent of the workforce, the economy is becoming increasingly oriented toward manufacturing and services. In 2001, El Salvador adopted as its currency the U.S. dollar (USD), which will gradually replace the Salvadoran *colón* (SVC).

Transportation and Communications. Because few Salvadorans own cars, most travel by bus. Rural people also travel on foot or by pickup truck. Taxis are available in larger cities. Roads in and around cities are mostly pavement or gravel. However, rural roads are rarely paved and can be impassable during the rainy season. Many roads have not been rebuilt since they fell into disrepair during the war. Bridges and roads have been further damaged by the hurricane and earthquakes.

European firms have greatly improved the country's communications. Cell phones are common in urban areas, but some people in smaller towns don't have phones at all. Relatives who live apart and friends in rural areas often communicate through telegrams. The free press is growing, and there are several daily newspapers in addition to a few smaller ones. Of the eleven television stations in El Salvador, nine are privately owned. There are also many private radio stations.

Education. Only about 35 percent of all rural adults are literate. The government is engaged in a vigorous campaign to increase that rate, building rural schools and encouraging enrollment. Because many war-torn public schools are of poor quality, El Salvador has hundreds of private schools and dozens of private universities. In all, there are 45 colleges or universities (public and private) in the country.

Elementary school (for ages 7–12) is compulsory. It is followed by an optional three years of *educación básica* (basic education), after which students may choose between three years of technical school or three years of *bachillerato*, the college track. The school year begins in mid-January and runs through October. Most children wear uniforms. Although public schooling is free, including at the university level, most people stop attending school at various ages to begin working and contributing to the family income.

Health. Medical care in El Salvador is free at all state health facilities, but many were damaged either during the war or by natural disasters. Urban clinics and hospitals are in poor condition, and rural areas often lack clinics altogether. Patients often must provide their own sheets, syringes, and medicine. In cities, a large, higher-quality, private health care system is available to those who can afford it. The government is trying to improve health conditions through free immunizations, hygiene and sanitation education, water and sewage system development, and more modern hospital administration. Still, cholera, malaria, measles, intestinal disorders, dengue fever, and other diseases have increased recently, particularly in rural areas.

DEVELOPMENT DATA
Human Dev. Index* rank . . . . 103 of 177 countries
  Adjusted for women. . . . . 84 of 144 countries
Real GDP per capita $4,890
Adult literacy rate . . . . 82 percent (male); 77 (female)
Infant mortality rate . . . . 26 per 1,000 births
Life expectancy . . . . 68 (male); 74 (female)

AT A GLANCE
Events and Trends.
- Antonio Saca of the ruling ARENA party was elected in March 2004 to be El Salvador's new president. The party has been in power 14 years, and if the presidential results are any indication, ARENA will likely stay in power for some time. Saca, a former sports television announcer, promised to crack down on gangs, improve government transparency, and continue free-market reforms.
- In August and September 2004, violence erupted at three of El Salvador's prisons. In the August incident, riots broke out between Mara gang members and other prisoners. Thirty-one prisoners were killed by the time the riots were calmed. In September, inmates at two prisons held hostage visitors and prison workers in protest of overcrowding and poor living conditions.
- In December 2003, El Salvador, along with Guatemala, Nicaragua, and Honduras approved a free-trade deal with the United States. The Central American Free Trade Agreement (CAFTA) removed most trade barriers between the participating countries. The move was seen as a step toward a free-trade area that would include all of North and South America. However, some farmers and other businesses on all ends protested that the new plan would hurt them by allowing cheap competition.
- A series of gruesome murders of women took place in El Salvador and neighboring Guatemala during the early months of 2003. Police believe the killings are linked to the large numbers of gangs in the area, many of which require random killings for initiation.

Contact Information. Embassy of El Salvador, 2308 California Street NW, Washington, DC 20008; phone (202) 265-9671; web site www.elsalvador.org/home.nsf/home. Consulate General of El Salvador, 1724 20th Street NW, Washington, DC 20009; phone (202) 331-4032.

CultureGrams
People. The World. You.

ProQuest Information and Learning Company
300 North Zeeb Road, P.O. Box 1346
Ann Arbor, Michigan 48106 USA
Toll Free: 1.800.528.6279
Fax: 1.800.864.0019
www.culturegrams.com

© 2005 ProQuest Information and Learning Company and Brigham Young University. It is against the law to copy, reprint, store, or transmit any part of this publication in any form by any means without written permission from ProQuest. This document contains native commentary and original analysis, as well as estimated statistics. The content should not be considered strictly factual, and it may not apply to all groups in a nation. *UN Development Programme, Human Development Report 2004 (New York: Oxford University Press, 2004).

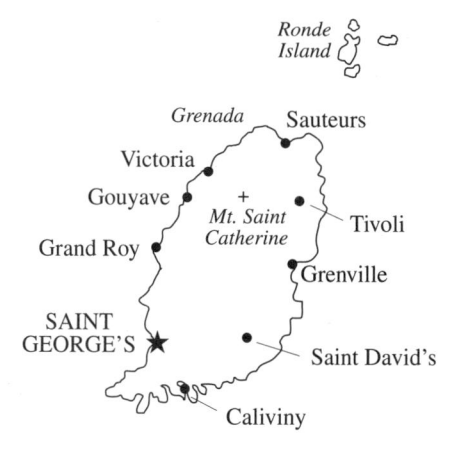

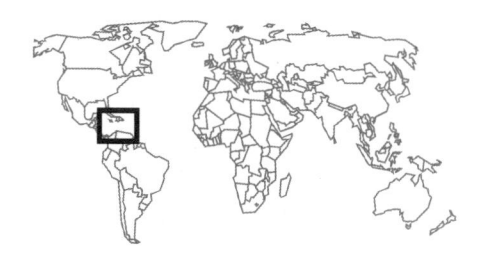

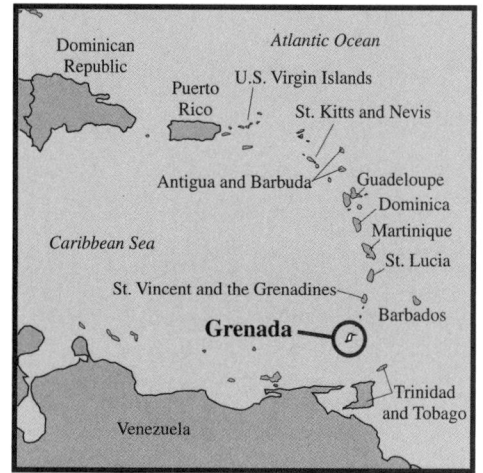

Grenada

BACKGROUND

Land and Climate. The nation of Grenada is made up of three islands: Grenada, Carriacou, and Petite Martinique. Together they occupy 131 square miles (339 square kilometers) of territory in the Caribbean. Grenada is some 100 miles (160 kilometers) north of Venezuela and about 20 miles (30 kilometers) from its sister islands. Marked by a central range of hills and mountains—the highest of which is Mount Saint Catherine (2,700 feet, or 823 meters)—the island is lush, tropical, and humid. Coastal areas are prized for fine beaches and warm surf. The rainy season runs from June to December, with November being the wettest month.

Carriacou and Petite Martinique are the drier and more barren of the islands and are marked by cactus. These small islands do not get much rainfall, presenting a water-supply problem for residents. Hurricane season is August to October. Average annual temperatures of 85°F (29°C) in the day and 74°F (23°C) in the evening vary only slightly, becoming hotter in July and August and cooler in January and February. The heat is moderated by a nearly constant breeze.

History. Grenada was originally inhabited by Arawak Indians, who were supplanted by the warlike Caribs. Christopher Columbus sighted the island (but did not land) in 1498 and named it Concepción. The origin of the name *Grenada* remains obscure. In 1650, the French government of Martinique purchased Grenada from a French company that had taken it from the Caribs. British forces captured the island in 1762. The Treaty of Paris (1763) formalized the acquisition and, except for a brief period of French occupation (1779–83), Grenada remained a British colony.

The French and then the British imported African slaves to work on plantations until slaves were emancipated in 1833. From 1855 to 1958, Grenada served as headquarters for the government of the British Windward Islands. From 1958 to 1962, Grenada was a member of the West Indian Federation.

In 1967, Grenada became a self-governing state in association with the United Kingdom. Eric Gairy, trade unionist turned politician, led Grenada to independence in 1974. As prime minister, he governed with a strong hand until March 1979, when the left-wing New Jewel Movement under Maurice Bishop staged a coup. Bishop formed the People's Revolutionary Government (PRG) and served as prime minister. He enjoyed popular support and is still regarded by many as a national hero. Many were drawn to Bishop's personality, if not his policies.

The PRG soon developed close ties with Cuba and the Soviet bloc, alienating neighboring states. Particularly alarming to these states was the size of Grenada's People's Revolutionary Army (PRA). In October 1983, General Hudson Austin of the PRA and Bernard Coard, PRG finance minister, led an internal coup that resulted in the violent execution of Bishop and several key government officials. On 25 October 1983, U.S. Marines and a coalition of Caribbean peacekeeping forces invaded to safeguard foreigners and restore law and order. Democratic elections were held in 1984 and the peacekeepers left in 1985.

Although subsequent elections in 1990 did not result in a clear mandate for any party, the New National Party received the most votes in June 1995 elections and has continued to be a major force in Grenadian politics. Faced with a high number of emigrating young people, the government is working to increase Grenada's employment opportunities.

Grenada

THE PEOPLE

Population. Grenada's population of about 89,500 is growing at 0.14 percent annually. Although the birthrate is high, emigration takes many from the island. Most people (94 percent) live on Grenada, 5 percent live on Carriacou, and several hundred reside on Petite Martinique. Saint George's, the capital and largest city, is home to about 7,500 people. Most people reside in small villages.

Most Grenadians (82 percent) are descendants of African slaves. Other groups include mulattoes (a mixture of European and African ancestry, 13 percent), East Indians (3 percent), and whites of European origin (1 percent). East Indians descend from laborers who came to work on plantations after the slaves were freed. Many East Indians also mixed with Africans to produce a group known locally as the *duglas*.

Language. English, the official language, is used in education, government, business, and the media. Grenadian English differs from U.S. English in idioms and some spellings. For instance, *Now for now* means "urgent," and *One time* means "at the same time." One says *Happy* (not *Merry*) *Christmas* or *Happy returns* (on holidays or special events). A car accident is a *bounce*.

Informally, Grenadians speak a French-English-African patois, sometimes referred to as *creole* or *broken English*. The dialect has no past or future tense. Inflection and body gestures are primary tense indicators. Rastafarians (see Religion) have influenced Grenadian patois to a small degree, introducing such terms as *Irie* (Everything is cool) and the affirmative *Yes I*. Children are urged to use Standard English in public, and Grenadians generally do not like outsiders to speak patois to them. But even spoken English contains patois elements, such as in the phrase "Don't *mamaguy* me" (Don't flatter me). Grenada's patois is noticeably different from that used on Carriacou and Petite Martinique.

Religion. Roughly 53 percent of the population is Roman Catholic, while most of the remainder belongs to various Protestant faiths (mostly Anglican). Small minorities practice Islam or Rastafarianism. Christians generally worship on Sunday morning, with prayer meetings throughout the week. Politicians freely invoke the powers of heaven, and schoolchildren pray at the beginning and end of the school day.

Rastafarianism is not practiced by many, but its influence (on fashion, vocabulary, etc.) is widespread. Practicing Rastas generally believe that Haile Selassie I (emperor of Ethiopia from 1930 to 1974) was "the living God," that marijuana is a sacred herb, that one's hair should be grown long in dreadlocks, and that all Afro–West Indians must eventually move to Ethiopia, the promised land.

General Attitudes. Grenadians are warm, friendly people who enjoy doing and returning favors. Their generous sense of humor helps them deal with difficult circumstances in a casual way. Disputes sometimes explode into angry shouting, but hard feelings seldom remain for long. Time schedules are not as important as people, and events usually start later than planned; it is customary to wait for everyone to arrive. Grenadians enjoy a strong sense of community. People often come together to finish a work project and share a meal or have a party. This cooperative effort is called a *maroon*.

An individual's feeling about the 1983 U.S. military occupation is summed up by how he or she describes the event: "American Rescue Mission" (positive), "American Intervention" (neutral), or "American Invasion" (negative).

Personal Appearance. Grenadians, especially women, take great pride in their public attire. They make it a point to appear neat and well dressed, particularly for church and certain social functions. Sloppy or very casual clothing is frowned upon, as are tourists who are scantily clad away from the beach. Men wear trousers and either a button-down shirt or *shirt-jac* (square-cut, untucked shirt). Women typically wear a skirt and blouse or a dress. In rural areas, or around one's home, dress is more casual. Men may be bare-chested and people often go barefoot.

Youth fashions include blue jeans, T-shirts, and basketball shoes. Schoolchildren wear uniforms. Boys often untuck their shirts or unfasten their belts in the fashion of rock/reggae musicians, which is known as *ragamuffin* style, much to the chagrin of older Grenadians. Rastafarian colors (red, yellow, and green) are ubiquitous in Grenada, seen on everything from belts to shoes to caps. These colors are also on the Grenadian flag, but their use in fashion is tied to Rastafarianism, not patriotism.

CUSTOMS AND COURTESIES

Greetings. Grenadians greet one another with a handshake. Friends sometimes nod upwards or tap clenched fists instead. In a formal setting or among strangers, *Good morning*, *Good afternoon*, and *Good night* are typical greetings, followed by *Mr.*, *Miss*, *Mistress* (for married women), or *Madam* (for married women of higher social status) and then the person's last name, if known. If the speakers know each other, they might combine the title with a first name. Grenadians exchange verbal greetings before conducting business, beginning a conversation, or asking a question. Failing to do so is considered rude.

Rural acquaintances and friends casually greet each other with such patois phrases as *W'happen dey?* (What's happening?) or *Hows tings?* (How are things?). Typical responses include *Ah dey* (I'm all right) or *Just cool* (Everything is fine). Throughout Grenada, friends address each other by a *call name* (nickname); a person's given name is generally unknown to any but the immediate family. It is considered rude to *pass a friend straight* in the street without at least nodding or saying hello. Grenadians often call out a friend's or relative's name as they pass his or her house and may stop briefly to chat if time permits. When parting, friends often say *Later!* or *We go see* (See you later). Formally, people might say *Until we meet again*.

Gestures. Waving the hand at waist level, palm down, means "no." The "thumbs up" sign means "good." To beckon, people wave the fingers with the palm facing down. Men and women hiss to get a friend's attention, but when a man hisses at a passing woman, she considers it suggestive and ignores it.

Visiting. Grenadians are considered to be among the friendliest people in the Caribbean; stopping to chat or socialize on the street or at a person's home is a favorite pastime. This time for impromptu visiting and relaxation, called *liming*, usually takes place in the afternoon or early evening. It may include sitting on the porch, chatting at the roadside, or going to sporting events with friends. Visitors verbally announce their presence and wait to be invited in. This practice is essential in rural areas, where a family watchdog might mistake a visitor for an intruder.

Grenadians nearly always offer guests refreshments, and it is impolite to refuse these entirely. If one cannot eat at a *fete* (party or gathering), it is polite to take something home for later. Funerals are social events. Men wear black suits and women wear hats with black or white dresses. People linger long at the graveside to talk. Men may go to a local *rum shop* to continue their conversations. Rural men often socialize at *rum shops*—small bars where they can drink and play dominoes, cards, or *draughts* (a game similar to checkers).

Women socialize less in the evening, except in family situations, and more through church and neighborhood organizations. They may also visit friends during the day.

Family visiting reaches a peak during Christmas. Relatives and close friends expect a visit during this season, and people typically visit from house to house for days. With each visit, they are offered food and something to drink (beer, rum, whiskey, black wine, or *sorrel*—a red, clove-spiced drink made from the flower of a sorrel bush).

Eating. Grenadians usually eat breakfast early in the morning, a main meal around noon, and supper at dusk. Families try to eat the main meal together. Supper is light, often consisting of bread and cheese. Most people eat from a bowl with a spoon. Wealthier families may also use a fork and a knife. People drink coffee with breakfast and tea in the afternoon, but with lunch or supper they prefer soft drinks, fruit juice, or water. When eating at restaurants, Grenadians normally do not tip the server.

LIFESTYLE

Family. The extended family is central to Grenadian society, and one household often consists of parents, children, grandparents, and cousins. Children might live at home well into adulthood. Family members look after one another and share resources and labor. Since most children are born out of wedlock, and men typically do not consider it their role to raise them, they are often nurtured by the mother, aunts, grandparents, and cousins. Women run the household, and men generally provide income. However, women are increasingly working outside the home as well. Wealthier and urban households more often include a nuclear family with both a father and mother.

Homes are constructed of wood and/or cinder block. They usually have one to three rooms, electricity, and water (except on Carriacou and Petite Martinique, which lack public water systems). Wealthy urban families often have other modern conveniences. Some rural homes have detached kitchens for cooking on coal pots. All Grenadians take pride in the appearance and cleanliness of their homes and yards. They often paint their houses bright colors and give them names (*Hideaway*, *De Fort*, *Fair Winds*, etc.). Domestic livestock (sheep, goats, chickens) share the rural yard with the dog. Each school day, children take sheep and goats to a grassy area for grazing and pick them up after school.

Dating and Marriage. Young people like to meet and date at dance halls or frequent street dances (*blockos*). Dancing (often called *wind and grind*) can be quite physical, and older Grenadians think it is lewd. Dating otherwise is inconspicuous, and public displays of affection generally are frowned upon. Couples often live together before or instead of marrying, but when weddings do occur, they are gala events. After a church ceremony, the entire village enjoys plenty of food, music, and dancing.

Diet. Staple foods include plantains, corn, rice, breadfruit, and peas. Common produce includes onions, green peppers, *callaloo* (a green, leafy plant similar to spinach), tomatoes, and carrots. Chicken, fish, mutton, goat, pork, and beef are the most popular meats. Grenadians also like *manicou* (a type of opossum) and iguana. The variety of available seafood includes reef fish (barracuda and parrot fish), shark, snapper, sea turtle, tuna, lobster, and *lambi* (conch), as well as canned sardines and salmon. Many staple items are imported, including powdered milk, canned vegetables and meats, salt pork and salt fish, rice, cheese, coffee, and tea.

Local favorite fruits include bananas, mangoes, grapefruit, coconuts, and *pawpaws* (papaya). Guavas are eaten fresh, stewed, jellied, or as *guava cheese* (a confection). A typical daily meal includes rice and *peas* (chickpeas or pigeon peas), a vegetable, and stewed meat. Soups, *souses* (boiled meat in a seasoned broth), fish broths, barbecues, and roasted foods are popular. Grenadians generously use hot pepper sauce, curries, and spices when cooking. The national dish is called the *oil down*, a stew of *callaloo*, breadfruit, meat or salt fish, and coconut oil. People also like *roti* (curried meat and vegetables wrapped in a flat bread) and *dahl* (curried chickpeas).

Recreation. Grenadians have a passion for cricket and closely follow the status of West Indian teams. Each town has cricket and *football* (soccer) teams, and boys begin playing at age 10. Basketball is becoming popular in urban areas. Girls play netball and watch other sports; both boys and girls participate in *athletics* (track-and-field). Men and boys like to fish, dive, or sail. Annual regattas draw fierce competition from around the region. Carriacou's Windward Village is widely known for its hand-built sailing vessels. Most people like to watch television, and urban residents go to movie theaters.

The Arts. Music is extremely popular, calypso being the favorite. People of all ages also love *soca* (a mixture of U.S. soul music and calypso), reggae, *ragamuffin* (a mixture of rock and reggae), *dub* (music in which disk jockeys rap street poems), and *pan* (or steel drum) music. Steel drums are used in many Grenadian music styles. U.S. and British pop music, particularly slower, romantic rock is also favored. Many Grenadians are competent on the guitar, violin, ukulele (often called *tenor banjo*), or drums. Jazz festivals are regular items on the yearly calendar, and a competition and parade of bands are held annually at Carnival celebrations. Potters, woodworkers, and silk screeners create and then market their crafts at the Grenada Craft Center, a government-sponsored institution.

Holidays. Grenadians celebrate Christmas, Good Friday, Easter (Saturday–Monday), Whitmonday, and Corpus Christi. Secular holidays include New Year's Day, Independence Day (7 Feb.), Labor Day (1 May), Thanksgiving (25 Oct.), Emancipation Day (first Monday in August), and Carnival. Thanksgiving, related to the 1983 U.S. intervention, typically is marked only by official ceremonies.

Grenada's national Carnival is held in August in St. George's. Celebrations (Sunday–Tuesday) involve street dancing, concerts, and colorful parades. Carriacou celebrates Carnival three days before Catholic Lent. Each region, or *parish* (Saint George's, John's, Mark's, Andrew's, Patrick's, and David's), has a festival to honor the saint for which it was named. Villages and towns also hold local festivals, including Fisherman's Birthday (St. Peter's Day) in Gouyave and Windward, Grenville's August Rainbow Festival, and Carriacou's August Regatta and December Parang Festival (a competitive folk-music event).

Commerce. Businesses typically are open weekdays from 8 a.m. to 4:30 p.m. and Saturday from 8 a.m. to noon. Longer hours are common in urban areas. Shops close on Sunday. Banks open from 8 a.m. to 2 p.m. on weekdays, except on Friday when they stay open until 5 p.m. Each large village or town has a Saturday open-air market for fresh fruits and vegetables.

Grenada

These markets are also a center for socializing. Supermarkets are found in larger urban areas. Rural people buy staples from small family-owned *cum-rum* shops, fresh produce from the open-air market, and meat and fish from roadside butchers and vendors. While in formal shops prices are usually fixed, street vendors are often willing to bargain. Street vendors are common and must be licensed to sell goods.

SOCIETY

Government. Grenada is a parliamentary democracy and a member of the Commonwealth of Nations. Hence, Britain's Queen Elizabeth II is the nominal head of state but is represented by a governor-general (Daniel Williams). The prime minister (currently Keith Mitchell) is head of government and is usually leader of the dominant party in the House of Representatives. Major parties include the New National Party, National Democratic Congress, and Grenada United Labour Party. Grenada's Parliament has two chambers: a House of Representatives with 15 elected members and a Senate with 13 appointees. There is an independent judiciary. The Privy Council in the United Kingdom is the final court of appeal. The voting age is 18.

Economy. Grenada's developing economy centers on agricultural exports and tourism. Known as the Isle of Spice, Grenada is the world's second largest nutmeg producer after Indonesia and is famous for cocoa, cinnamon, cloves, pepper, and ginger. Other exports include bananas, coconuts, and mangoes. Agriculture accounts for 40 percent of employment, most of it on small private plots. Tourism, important in and around St. George's, poses some ecological threats, as the construction of new resorts promotes rainforest and beach erosion.

Most Grenadians are able to meet their basic needs. However, the number of people in poverty doubled during the 1990s because of a lack of economic diversification. Despite growth in foreign investment and tourism, unemployment levels remain high. Almost one-third of the population lives in poverty. Remittances from Grenadians working abroad provide the country with needed income. The currency is the East Caribbean dollar (XCD).

Transportation and Communications. Air service and regular, inexpensive boat service link the islands. Paved roads connect major towns and villages. While there is a public bus system, most people rely on private minibuses for local transportation. Minibuses wait in market areas until full and then depart for their destination, dropping off and adding passengers along the way. Private taxis are available, and groups can charter a *board bus* (truck-turned-bus with a canvas top and wood sides) for special events. Especially in more remote areas, people commonly walk, rather than drive, short distances. Young people often ride bicycles.

Grenada has six radio stations, and television provides a mixture of local news and foreign programming (usually from the United States). Cable television is also available. Several weekly newspapers are published, but radio remains the primary source for news. Residential phone service is available, and most communities have public phones.

Education. Education is compulsory for ages five to sixteen. Churches own most schools, but the government sets the curriculum. Students may choose a school based on its religious affiliation, but the choice is most often based on a school's reputation, location, or other factors. About 90 percent of Grenadians finish primary school; students must then pass the Common Entrance exam to enter the secondary level. Of the roughly half who do advance, the vast majority graduate. Post-secondary education can be obtained at the University of the West Indies (which has a branch in St. George's), at various technical centers, or at a teacher-training college.

Health. Free health care is available to all Grenadians. Parishes and some towns have a clinic staffed with health assistants who perform preventive care and see minor cases. Government doctors make regular visits to the clinics. General Hospital in St. George's is somewhat crowded and underequipped. Two other hospitals (in St. Andrew's and Carriacou) provide basic services. High costs prohibit most Grenadians from visiting better private doctors. Water is safe to drink on the main island but is untreated elsewhere.

DEVELOPMENT DATA
Human Dev. Index* rank . . . . 93 of 177 countries
Adjusted for women . . . . NA
Real GDP per capita $7,280
Adult literacy rate . . . . 94 percent
Infant mortality rate . . . . 15 per 1,000 births
Life expectancy . . . . 63 (male); 66 (female)

AT A GLANCE

Events and Trends.

- Grenada suffered a direct hit from Hurricane Ivan in September 2004. With winds near 140 miles per hour, it was the most destructive hurricane in generations. The hurricane ruined buildings, downed power lines, and ripped up trees. Nearly 40 people were killed, and half of the island's 100,000 residents were left homeless. Prime Minister Mitchell declared that 90 percent of the island of Grenada had been damaged, although Carriacou and Petite Martinique were relatively protected. The island is rebuilding its infrastructure and tourism facilities.

- Prime Minister Keith Mitchell won a third term in office during November 2003 elections. Although his New National Party maintained control of 8 of the 15 parliamentary seats, the opposing National Democratic Congress—which had no seats before the election—picked up the remaining seven. The parties pledged to work together for the betterment of the nation.

- In late 2003, Grenada was forced to slash its economic growth forecasts as prices for nutmeg fell by one-third.

- In 2003, the Grenada United Labour Party was the first Grenadian political party to elect a woman (Gloria Payne-Banfield) as its leader.

Contact Information. Embassy of Grenada, 1701 New Hampshire Avenue NW, Washington, DC 20009; phone (202) 265-2561. Tourism Board, P.O. Box 1665, Lake Worth, FL 33460; phone (800) 927-9554; web site www.grenadagrenadines.com.

CultureGrams™
People. The World. You.

ProQuest Information and Learning Company
300 North Zeeb Road, P.O. Box 1346
Ann Arbor, Michigan 48106 USA
Toll Free: 1.800.528.6279
Fax: 1.800.864.0019
www.culturegrams.com

© 2005 ProQuest Information and Learning Company and Brigham Young University. It is against the law to copy, reprint, store, or transmit any part of this publication in any form by any means without written permission from ProQuest. This document contains native commentary and original analysis, as well as estimated statistics. The content should not be considered strictly factual, and it may not apply to all groups in a nation. *UN Development Programme, Human Development Report 2004 (New York: Oxford University Press, 2004).

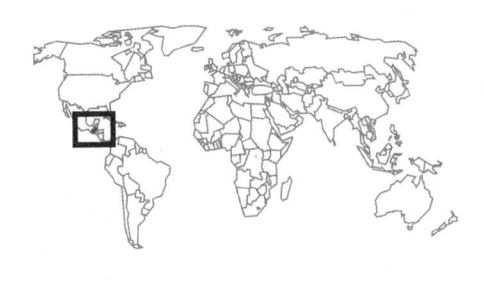

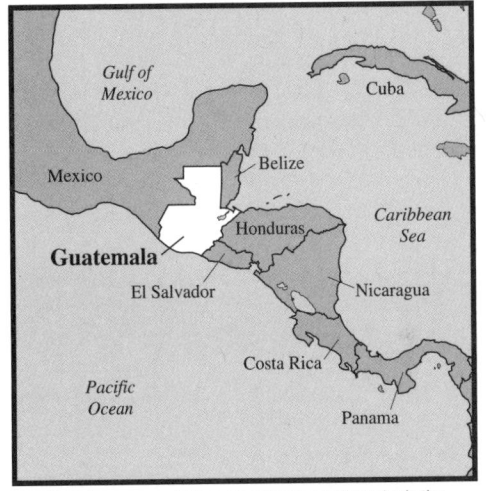

CultureGrams 2006 World Edition
Republic of Guatemala

BACKGROUND

Land and Climate. Covering 42,043 square miles (108,891 square kilometers), Guatemala is just smaller than Tennessee. About two-thirds of the country is mountainous. There are 32 volcanoes, some of which are active. Rich forests covering 40 percent of Guatemala, particularly in the northwest Petén region, are subject to rapid deforestation due in part to slash-and-burn agriculture and illegal logging. Use of wood for heating and cooking also has contributed to deforestation, which in turn has put archaeological sites and wildlife at risk. Most people live on the slopes of the highlands or in the fertile, well-watered lowlands along the Pacific coast.

The eastern-central portion of the country is hot and dry. In the coastal lowlands, hot, humid weather prevails. In the highlands, days are warm and nights are usually cool. The average annual temperature in the capital, which is located on a plateau 4,800 feet (1,400 meters) above sea level, is 75°F (24°C). Guatemalans often refer to their country as the Land of the Eternal Spring. November through April is the dry season. Rain is abundant from May through October. Guatemala's Caribbean coast is wet year-round.

History. The Mayan Empire flourished in what is now Guatemala for more than one thousand years until it began to decline in the 1100s. As one of the chief centers of the Mayan culture, Guatemala abounds in archaeological ruins, notably the majestic ceremonial city of Tikal in the Petén region. From 1524 to 1821, the Spanish ruled Central America. After winning its independence in 1821, Guatemala was briefly annexed by Mexico and then became a member of the Central American Federation until the federation dissolved in 1838.

Military dictatorships controlled Guatemala until a 1944 revolution. From 1945 to 1982, leaders tried to cure some of Guatemala's social ills, but full democracy proved elusive. Violence was common and an elected president (Jacobo Arbenz Guzmán) was overthrown by a U.S.-backed military coup in 1954. In 1960, rebels began a civil war that made political stability impossible until 1984, when an elected assembly wrote a new constitution.

In 1986, Guatemala returned to civilian rule under Marco Vinicio Cerezo Arévalo. Cerezo withstood two military coups, but the military had strong ties to the country's principal landowners and wielded more control over some regions than civilian authorities. Because the military was primarily responsible for human-rights abuses, such control presented enormous problems for political and economic progress.

Elections in 1990 brought the first transfer of power from one elected official to another. President Jorge Serrano Elías began peace talks with the rebels in 1991. However, in 1993, Serrano staged a "self-coup" backed by the army. He announced emergency rule, dissolving congress and the Supreme Court and suspending the constitution. As public protests mounted, the military withdrew its support, forcing Serrano to flee to Panama. Military leaders recalled congress, which chose its ombudsman for human rights, Ramiro de León Carpio, to finish Serrano's term.

New negotiations began when President Alvaro Arzú Irigoyen took office in 1996. In December 1996, the government and the rebels signed a series of agreements culminating in a UN-brokered peace accord. The accord ended Latin America's longest civil war—one that lasted 36 years, claimed more than 150,000 lives, and displaced about a million people. The agreements address military downsizing, the reintegration of soldiers and rebels into society, indigenous people's rights,

Guatemala

women's rights, resettlement of refugees, and socio-economic and agrarian reforms.

THE PEOPLE

Population. Guatemala's population of nearly 14.3 million is growing at a higher than average 2.6 percent annually. While 55 percent is *ladino* (people who descend from the Spanish and Maya but relate more to their Spanish heritage), 43 percent is composed of some 28 indigenous groups descended from the Maya. Some of the largest are the Quiché, Cakchiquel, Kekchí, Ixil, and Mam. They live throughout the country, but many reside in western highlands. Collectively, they refer to themselves as *indígenas* (indigenous) or Maya. A small black minority, the Garífuna, is concentrated on Guatemala's Caribbean coast. There is also a small white minority. Guatemalans as a group are known colloquially as *chapines*.

Language. Spanish is Guatemala's official language, but each indigenous group speaks its own language. While most indigenous male Guatemalans speak some Spanish, indigenous women have fewer opportunities to learn Spanish as they do not often attend school and have less contact with Spanish speakers. The Garífuna speak English, creole, and Spanish.

Religion. Roman Catholicism traditionally has dominated Guatemala, although many indigenous members combine it with Mayan beliefs. Some indigenous groups have not accepted Catholicism at all. Freedom of religion is guaranteed. While Catholicism influences most celebrations and habits, regardless of people's religious preference, devotion to the Catholic Church is declining. In the last 20 years, many have converted to Protestant and other Christian churches. About 45 percent of the people are now Protestants, known generally as *evangélicos* (evangelicals). Increased religious devotion is credited with decreasing alcoholism and other social problems. However, tension between Catholics and *evangélicos* is rising.

General Attitudes. Guatemalans are generous, warm, polite, and humble. They value honesty, family unity, personal honor, work, and education. Optimism is less common than the acceptance of misfortune. People often believe they are unable to change their condition, either for lack of empowerment or because some things are God's will. Personal criticism is taken seriously and should be avoided. Punctuality is admired but not strictly observed; people are considered more important than schedules. This type of keeping time is called *la hora chapina* (the Guatemalan hour). Guatemalans are gracious and strive to make any social interaction comfortable. The phrase *No tenga pena* (Don't worry) is commonly used to set others at ease.

Family status and wealth are important to *ladinos*. Many of them consider the Maya to be inferior and uncivilized, and they avoid contact with those who do not adopt *ladino* ways. The Maya, who have long been subjected to discrimination and human-rights abuses, desire to be treated as equals. Maya who wear Western clothing and assimilate into *ladino* culture are treated somewhat better.

While the peoples of Guatemala are diverse, they have in common a desire for a tranquil life. Guatemalans are cautiously optimistic that the 1996 accord has brought a true and lasting peace.

Personal Appearance. People usually wear Western-style clothing in cities. Most rural Maya, particularly women, have retained traditional dress. Each group's clothing has unique qualities, but basic features include a *faja* (woven belt worn by both sexes), a *corte* (wraparound skirt) for women, and knee- or calf-length trousers for men. Women may weave ribbons or fabric through their hair. Men generally wear hats made of straw or blocked felt. Clothing often is colorful. A woman treasures her *huipil* (blouse); its design identifies her social position and hometown. There are about 500 of these designs.

CUSTOMS AND COURTESIES

Greetings. When meeting for the first time, people greet with a handshake and ¡*Mucho gusto!* (Pleased to meet you). Among acquaintances, the most common greetings are ¡*Buenos días!* (Good day), ¡*Buenas tardes!* (Good afternoon), and ¡*Buenas noches!* (Good evening). After an initial greeting, one might ask ¿*Cómo está?* (How are you?). Friends often greet with a casual ¡*Buenas!* or ¿*Qué tal?* (How's it going?). Shaking hands heartily is common in most areas. Among friends, men usually shake hands and sometimes embrace, and *ladino* women kiss each other on the cheek. A younger woman will kiss a male friend, but older women kiss only male relatives. Some older women greet by grasping the person just below each elbow.

In small groups, it is important to greet each individual. In larger groups, it is acceptable to offer a group greeting or simply greet as many persons as possible. When addressing others, using a title (*Señor*, *Señora*, *Señorita*, *Doctor*, etc.) shows respect. People show special respect for older individuals by using *Don* and *Doña* with the first name. Common parting phrases include *Que le vaya bien* (May you go well), *Nos vemos* (See you later), and *Más tarde* (Later). Guatemalans generally begin all conversations by exchanging pleasantries; failure to do so implies lack of a personal relationship and makes the listener question the speaker's motives.

Gestures. Guatemalans beckon by waving the hand downward and in. A "tssst tssst" sound gets someone's attention. Pointing with the finger or hand can be misinterpreted because many finger and hand gestures are vulgar. To point, people often purse their lips in the direction of whatever they are indicating. To add emphasis, express surprise, or indicate "hurry," one shakes the hand quickly so that the index and middle fingers slap together and make a snapping sound. "No" can be indicated by wagging the index finger from side to side.

Urban couples tend to be more affectionate in public than rural couples. In rural areas, couples may hold hands but rarely show other affection. Personal space during conversation is relatively close, although touching is not common.

Visiting. Visiting friends and relatives is an important part of Guatemalan culture. Visiting frequently indicates a valuable relationship. People who live close, especially in rural areas, drop by unannounced (or send a child to announce the adults are coming later). A visit at nearly any time of day is acceptable. Socializing also takes place at the market, community meetings, church, or the water well. Still, it is proper to visit the home to show that a person's hospitality is valued. Any guest, expected or unexpected, generally is welcomed, ushered in, and served refreshments: coffee, tea, water, or another drink and sweet bread or other snack. Refusing is impolite.

Frequent visitors usually do not bring gifts to the hosts, but anyone staying more than one day will give flowers, chocolates, or something for the home. The longer the stay, the nicer the gift. Hosts often send dinner guests home with food or something from the garden. When leaving a home, guests graciously thank the hosts and often invite them to visit.

Eating. Most people eat three meals a day; poorer families might eat only one meal and then snack on tortillas the rest of the day. A rural breakfast may consist of tortillas and leftover beans. The main meal is eaten at midday; anyone in the family not working away from home eats this meal. A light dinner usually is eaten after 7 p.m. The entire family gathers for the main meal on weekends. In some cases, women serve the meal and eat later. Many people have coffee and sweet breads around 4 p.m., and men working in the fields might have a snack at midmorning. Schoolchildren are served hot cereal at 10 a.m.

Guatemalans generally use utensils but may eat some foods with the hands or use tortillas as a scoop. They keep hands above the table. Upon finishing the meal, each person (even the cook) thanks all others at the table with *Muchas gracias*, to which all reply *Buen provecho* (Good appetite).

Guests usually finish everything on their plates and wait for their host to offer more food. Asking for more might embarrass a host who is out of food, but eating more compliments the cook. When offered additional food, one first politely declines but then always accepts and eats it completely.

LIFESTYLE

Family. The extended family forms the basis of society and exerts significant influence on an individual's life and decisions. The father is the head of the family, but the wife controls the household; she is considered the heart of the family. Rural extended families often share a single home or live next to each other in a family compound. This community includes parents, married sons and their families, unmarried children, and often grandparents. Urban families generally live in nuclear family settings, although grandparents are often present. Unmarried adults live with their parents unless they must go elsewhere for work. Family members who work away from home usually send money back to help with expenses. Adult children are responsible for the care of their elderly parents.

Ladino women often work as secretaries, teachers, nurses, or in other professions. Mayan women also work, but less often in the formal workplace. They may sell produce at markets, embroider or weave products for sale, or work in community groups. Within the home, women are responsible for the food, household, children, education, and religion. Men may work in professional settings or in physically demanding jobs such as fieldwork. In poorer families, children must work as soon as they can help support the family.

Ladino families generally live in urban areas or towns in small single-family homes. Housing for indigenous groups follows their various traditions, such as a modest adobe or bamboo dwelling with a thatched or tin roof. Widespread poverty makes land ownership unavailable to most. Many rural families have no running water or electricity, although the cities are well equipped with these.

Dating and Marriage. Urban young people begin socializing in groups around age 15. They enjoy dining out, going to movies, or just being together. Young people in rural areas take walks, meet after school, visit at church or community events, or meet in town (at the market or water well). A girl's honor is important; a proper couple is "chaperoned" by younger siblings or cousins.

Among *ladinos*, social status is important in choosing a spouse. Traditionally, the man's parents asked for the woman's hand in marriage; now the man asks the woman's father. Women often marry by age 20 (earlier in rural areas) and men by 24. Common-law marriages are accepted and may be necessary if the groom cannot afford his responsibility to pay for the wedding, new clothes for the bride, and any celebrations. An indigenous couple's relationship is cemented through a series of formal meetings between the families. At the final meeting, the woman's parents ceremonially "give" her to her new parents-in-law.

Diet. Corn tortillas or, in many regions, *tamalitos* (cornmeal dough wrapped in corn husks and steamed) are eaten with every meal. Other foods include black beans, rice, greens, and fried *plátanos* (bananas) with honey, cream, or black beans. Meat (beef, pork, and chicken) usually is stewed, and sauces are important. Often a particular dish is unique to a certain village since key ingredients (such as spices) are found only in that village. Papaya, breadfruit, and other fruits are popular. Coffee often is served with a great deal of milk and sugar. The poorest rural families eat only tortillas (or *tamalitos*) and whatever food they can grow or gather in the forest.

Recreation. The most popular sports in Guatemala are fútbol (soccer), basketball, and volleyball. Family outings to a beach or lake are common holiday and festival activities. *Cofradías* (religious fraternities dedicated to a particular saint) offer a variety of recreational and leisure activities. Urban people enjoy watching television, but visiting is the most common leisure activity for all Guatemalans.

The Arts. Music permeates society. The *marimba*, which is similar to the xylophone, dominates indigenous Guatemalan music and can be played by up to six people at a time. Its keys are made of rosewood, found indigenously in Guatemala. The *marimba* is often accompanied by flutes, guitars, and various percussion instruments. North American and Mexican music also are popular among young Guatemalans.

Many ancient arts have survived in Guatemala, namely ceramics; silver-, gold-, and ironwork; and wood carving, especially of wooden masks. Rock sculptures and carvings are another ancient Mayan art form and stand in front of temples. Guatemala's textiles are famous for their vibrant colors and intricate patterns. The designs may reveal information about the wearer, such as marital status or place of birth. Black and green jade carvings and jewelry are popular and can be purchased at local markets.

Guatemala claims several internationally known writers, among them Nobel Prize winner Miguel Asturias. Like many Guatemalan authors, Asturias wrote about indigenous peoples, traditions, and individuality. The Mayan *Popol Vuh* is a literary work dating back to the mid-1500s; it recounts a creation story.

Holidays. A popular Guatemalan saying claims there are more celebrations than days in the year. Major celebrations are divided into two periods: Christmas and Easter. The Christmas season begins 7 December, when people clean house and burn their garbage to ceremonially cleanse their homes of evil in preparation to receive Christ. On Christmas Eve (*Noche Buena*), families set off firecrackers at midnight and then eat a large meal of *tamalitos* and hot chocolate. Firecrackers accompany most celebrations, especially New Year's. Easter is celebrated with Holy Week, during which numerous large processions fill the streets. In these, figures representing Christ are carried on special platforms by men wearing purple robes (black robes on Good Friday). On Saturday, effigies of Judas Iscariot are burned.

National holidays include Labor Day (1 May), Army Day (30 June), Independence Day (15 Sept.), *Día de la Raza* (Day of the [mestizo] Race, or Columbus Day, 12 October), Revolution Day (20 Oct.), and All Saints' Day (1 Nov.). The most

Guatemala

important holiday in rural towns is often the annual *feria* (fair) honoring the local patron saint.

Commerce. Business hours in rural areas vary but generally range from 8 a.m. to 6 p.m. in the cities, with a one- or two-hour break around noon. Urban residents purchase food and other basics from small shops and large supermarkets. Fresh produce is available at open-air markets. In rural areas, farmers grow some of their food and buy other products at open-air markets or small shops. Villages might have a market twice a week, offering only basic goods for one of the days. All neighborhood stores operated out of homes stock about the same items, so one buys from family and friends first.

SOCIETY

Government. Guatemala is a democratic republic. The president, currently Oscar Berger, is head of state and head of government. The Congress of the Republic has 158 seats; legislators are popularly elected to four-year terms. The Supreme Court and judicial branch of government exist but do not function well; the system has not yet recovered from years of war and dictatorship. The two largest political parties are the Guatemalan Republican Front (FRG) and the Party of National Advancement (PAN). A few minority parties also have representation in congress. The voting age is 18.

Economy. Guatemala is a relatively poor country, and three-fourths of the population lives in poverty. Wealth is concentrated among the upper class. Progress has been hindered by decades of civil war, the lack of a diverse manufacturing sector, and the existence of large commercial farms that produce for export but keep rural farmers landless and poor. More than half of the population is employed in agriculture. Coffee accounts for around one-fourth of all export earnings. Other leading products include cotton, cacao, corn, beans, sugarcane, bananas, broccoli, and livestock. Nickel, oil, fish, rubber, and chicle (used in chewing gum) are important natural resources. Tourism and manufacturing are also vital to the economy. The currency is the *quetzal* (GTQ).

Women earn roughly one-fifth of the nation's income, the lowest proportion among Latin American countries.

Transportation and Communications. Buses (many of them colorfully painted old school buses) provide the main form of long-distance travel. Paved roads connect the capital to major cities and neighboring countries, but most other roads are unimproved. Some villages are inaccessible by vehicle. For short distances, most people will walk, ride a bicycle or motorcycle, or take the bus. The wealthy have private cars. Commuter airlines fly domestically.

Telephones are widely used in cities but not in rural areas. Urban newspapers are available, but rural people rely on radio for news and entertainment. Television is popular where electricity is available.

Education. Although there are several thousand primary schools, more than half of primary-age children do not attend. The literacy rate is higher for males and for urban dwellers. However, girls now tend to stay in school longer than boys. Children often leave school because of family needs or inadequacies in the system. In rural areas, many children do not speak Spanish, the language of instruction. Facilities often are

DEVELOPMENT DATA
Human Dev. Index* rank . . . . 121 of 177 countries
    Adjusted for women. . . . . 98 of 144 countries
Real GDP per capita $4,080
Adult literacy rate . . . . 77 percent (male); 63 (female)
Infant mortality rate . . . . 37 per 1,000 births
Life expectancy . . . . 63 (male); 69 (female)

crowded, books in short supply, and teachers underpaid. After primary and middle school, students may attend three years of secondary schooling (vocational training). Those desiring to enter one of Guatemala's five universities must attend college preparation, which usually is available only to the wealthy.

Health. Guatemala faces serious health problems, including malnutrition, lack of potable water in many areas, and disease. Medical resources are concentrated in urban areas, although a national system is structured to provide health posts to outlying areas. However, most rural posts are not properly supplied. Care generally is free or costs a small fee, but medicines must be purchased. Many deaths are caused by preventable gastrointestinal and respiratory diseases.

AT A GLANCE
Events and Trends.

- In July 2004, the Guatemalan government took a major step toward healing the wounds left by the civil war by offering a first payment of US$3.5 million dollars to people who lost property or loved ones in the war. The payment was the first in a 13-year series of payments. While many people feel that the payments and other modest government programs don't go far enough, most are glad to see some fulfillment of promises.
- Guatemalan and U.S. authorities disagree over how to best fight the drug trade in Guatemala. Guatemalan police say they need more U.S. money to meet U.S. demands that they end trafficking. Meanwhile, the United States may impose sanctions against Guatemala if the Central American country is placed on a list of nations failing to fight drugs.
- In December 2003, Oscar Berger was elected as Guatemala's president. Former military ruler Efraín Ríos Montt—who briefly held power during the bloody civil war and is blamed for thousands of deaths—was one of the men Berger defeated. Berger immediately called for unity and asked Nobel Peace Prize winner Rigoberta Menchú Tum, an indigenous activist, to join his government.
- In May 2004, after losing the presidential race, military leader Efraín Ríos Montt was put under house arrest. Although he is believed to have been instrumental in many war crimes, his confinement is related to his possible involvement in the 2003 death of a journalist.

Contact Information. Embassy of Guatemala, 2220 R Street NW, Washington DC 20008; phone (202) 745-4952; web site www.guatemala-embassy.org.

CultureGrams™
People. The World. You.

ProQuest Information and Learning Company
300 North Zeeb Road, P.O. Box 1346
Ann Arbor, Michigan 48106 USA
Toll Free: 1.800.528.6279
Fax: 1.800.864.0019
www.culturegrams.com

© 2005 ProQuest Information and Learning Company and Brigham Young University. It is against the law to copy, reprint, store, or transmit any part of this publication in any form by any means without written permission from ProQuest. This document contains native commentary and original analysis, as well as estimated statistics. The content should not be considered strictly factual, and it may not apply to all groups in a nation. *UN Development Programme, Human Development Report 2004 (New York: Oxford University Press, 2004).

CultureGrams World Edition 2006

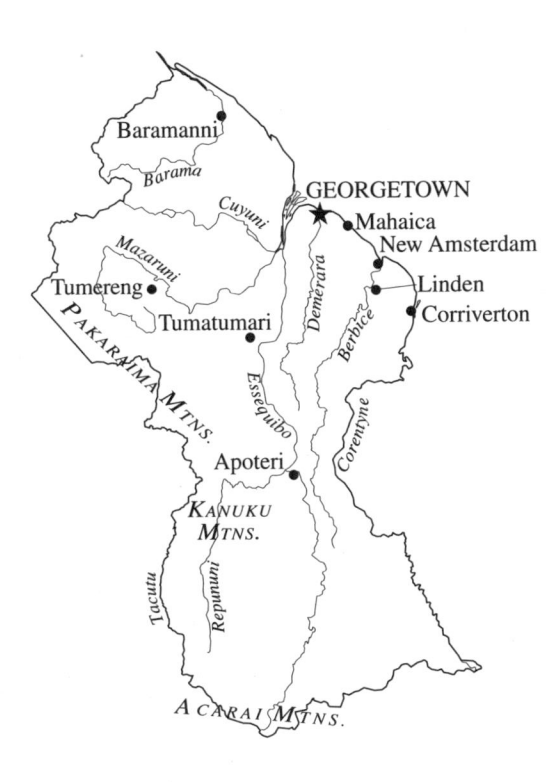

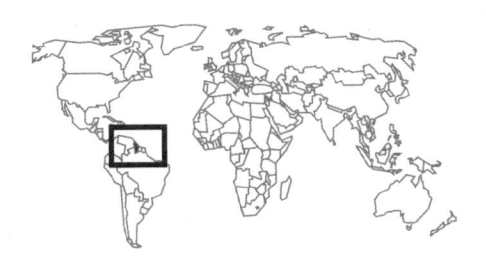

Cooperative Republic of Guyana

BACKGROUND

Land and Climate. Covering 83,000 square miles (214,970 square kilometers), Guyana lies just north of the equator and has a tropical climate. Trade winds moderate coastal humidity. Rain falls primarily between April and August and from November to January. Guyana is interlaced with rivers; the major ones flow north to the Atlantic. The coastal plain, which supports agriculture, lies slightly below sea level but is protected by drainage canals, dams, and walls. South of the coastal plain are white sand hills. Although unfit for agriculture, these hills support rain forests rich in hardwood trees and are home to a varied and abundant animal population. The interior is characterized by plateaus, flat-topped mountains, and savannas.

History. Little is known about the area's early inhabitants, but historians speculate they gradually migrated from central South America as early as A.D. 1000. These people were divided into at least nine tribes, including the Warrau, Wapisiana, Machushi, Patamona, Arawak, and Carib.

The Dutch established the first European trading post in Guyana in 1580 and were soon joined by the English, French, and Spanish. In 1621, the Netherlands established the Dutch West India Company and gave it control of their colony, known as Essequibo. Dutch colonies were later established on the Berbice River (1627) and Demerara River (1741), despite Spanish claims to the entire region. The colonies changed hands between the British, French, and Dutch with confusing frequency until the British purchased and united them and, in 1831, renamed the area British Guiana.

African slaves were brought to the area in the mid-1700s to meet labor needs, because the indigenous population had been nearly decimated through European colonization. By 1807, when the slave trade was abolished, about 100,000 Africans lived on plantations. After full emancipation in 1838, many freed slaves formed their own villages. Eventually, planters brought indentured workers from India. When the British government stopped officially supporting East Indian immigration in 1917, 341,000 Indians had settled permanently in British Guiana.

After World War II, the British prepared for the colony's independence. Political parties formed for elections; 1953 was the first year of universal suffrage. The most dynamic new party was the People's Progressive Party (PPP), established by Cheddi Jagan. The son of Indian immigrants, Jagan embraced Marxism while studying dentistry in the United States. The PPP splintered in the late 1950s after the British tried to halt its rise to power. Another party, the People's National Congress (PNC), was led by leftist Linden Burnham. His support came from the Afro-Guyanese, while Jagan's came from the East Indian or Indo-Guyanese community.

When Britain granted self-rule in 1961, an anticommunist party formed to challenge the PPP, which had gained a majority in 1961 elections. The party became the United Force (UF) and joined with the PNC and other groups to oppose the government. Violence and turbulence characterized the next few years.

In 1964, the PNC and UF formed a coalition government under Burnham's leadership. Independence was granted in 1966, and British Guiana became Guyana. The PNC consolidated power in 1968 elections, and Burnham used that power to commit Guyana to socialism. In 1970, he renamed the country the Cooperative Republic of Guyana, and by 1974, it was essentially a one-party state.

Guyana

After Burnham's sudden death in 1985, his successor, Vice President Desmond Hoyte, introduced political and economic reforms. Nevertheless, the standard of living remained low and Hoyte was urged to hold free and fair elections. The elections in 1992 were considered the country's first free elections and brought the PPP back to power. As president, Jagan continued to reform the systems that had been changed by Burnham, but Jagan died in March 1997 before he could complete his term.

Subsequent leaders have been unable to bring political cooperation to the nation. Because the two main parties tend to block each other's progress, political reform is a major challenge facing Guyana.

THE PEOPLE

Population. The population of Guyana is estimated to be about 700,000. Emigration has kept the annual population growth rate to less than 1 percent. About 30 percent of the population lives in urban areas, the largest of which are Georgetown, Linden, and New Amsterdam. The villages and fertile acres of the coastal lowlands are home to another 65 percent. The remaining 5 percent, mostly indigenous people, is scattered throughout the interior.

Guyana is ethnically diverse. The largest group is made up of descendants of the East Indian immigrants and comprises nearly 50 percent of the country's population. Next are the Afro-Guyanese (36 percent) and indigenous peoples (7 percent). The remainder includes people of mixed race as well as small groups of ethnic Chinese, English, and Portuguese.

Warrau and Arawak Catholics fled to British Guiana from Venezuela in the 19th century to escape religious persecution. Their settlements, such as Santa Rosa, are protected reservations. Today's indigenous peoples are seeking title to the lands they occupy, as they feel increasingly threatened by local and international companies looking for mineral and timber wealth. At the same time, many indigenous people are taking jobs with these companies in hopes of overcoming poverty on the reservations.

Language. English is the official language and is used in media, education, commerce, and government. However, the spoken English that many people use on a daily basis is a dialect known as Creolese. Unlike the French-based creoles of the Caribbean, this oral (unwritten) dialect is based on English. Creolese adds flavor to the country's cultural life and is especially popular for songs and colloquialisms like *Awe a go a Georgetown fore day morning* (We're going to Georgetown before sunrise). Older indigenous peoples speak their native languages in addition to English.

Religion. The Guyanese are a religious people. Even the country's socialist politicians usually have professed some religious beliefs. Christianity came to Guyana with the European colonists. Other religions followed with later immigrants. Under the British, the Anglican Church had official status, but today all major religious groups have equal recognition under the law.

More than half of the Guyanese are Christians. The major Christian congregations are Roman Catholic, Anglican, and various other Protestant denominations. Hinduism is practiced by 35 percent of the population; its adherents are almost exclusively Indo-Guyanese. East Indians also brought Islam to Guyana, and about 10 percent of Guyanese are Muslim. Unlike some other areas of the world, in Guyana there is no friction between Hindus and Muslims. Traces of African folk practices and the religious beliefs of indigenous peoples are still found.

General Attitudes. The Guyanese are warm, outgoing, friendly, and fun-loving. They are also resilient, as evidenced by how they survived terrible hardships associated with plantation life in colonial times. Many people's goals center on providing a better life and an education for their children. For example, rural men and women may work to purchase and develop a plot of land, acquire a milk cow and a good fishing net, and perhaps open a small shop—all while working several odd jobs if necessary. However, the sharp decline in the standard of living after independence has led thousands to seek a seemingly better life abroad. For most families today, the thing most desired is a visa to the United States or Canada.

Personal Appearance. The Guyanese generally follow North American and European fashion trends. At the same time, they value modesty, and skimpy clothing is frowned upon. Burnham had at one time decreed that all men would wear trousers and *shirt-jacs* (open-necked shirts with side pockets worn over the trousers). Although the *shirt-jac* is still popular, suits are now also common. Women generally wear dresses or suits (with a skirt, not pants) in the workplace. Informal dress includes slacks or shorts and T-shirts for both men and women. Special occasions call for women to wear dresses and considerable jewelry, often crafted from Guyanese gold. Schoolchildren wear uniforms, but after school they prefer T-shirts with slacks, jeans, or shorts.

CUSTOMS AND COURTESIES

Greetings. Relatives and friends may greet each other with a hug, and between women, a brief kiss on each cheek. A handshake is the norm between business and professional associates. Young people say *Hi* or *Hi, man, how you doin'?* They may add backslapping or a "high five." They might also ask *Wha' it saying?*, to which the response is either a "thumbs up" signal (for good) or an open palm turned down (for bad).

Tribal greetings vary according to the language. The Wapisiani use *Kaimen Pugar* (roughly, "Peace be with you"). The Machushi say *Morogeh koman honah* (I'm glad to see you) and respond with *Enah* ("Yes," meaning "Hello").

Young people may address adults who are not members of their families as *auntie* or *uncle*. If the adults are gray-haired, they are *grannie* or *grandpa*. Teachers and school personnel are addressed as *Miss* or *Sir*. Adults do not address each other by given name until they become close friends. Using the titles *Mr.*, *Mrs.*, *Miss*, *Professor*, *Doctor*, etc., with the family name is appropriate.

Gestures. The Guyanese talk with their hands, especially when angry or excited. They point their fingers in one another's faces to stress a point and shake the forefinger to show their displeasure. Most Guyanese do not wear shoes inside their homes. Guests entering someone's house for an informal gathering leave their shoes at the door as well.

Visiting. Unannounced visiting is an accepted practice. If the weather is nice, the host and caller may visit outside; otherwise, the visitor is invited in. Once the guest is seated, the host offers a cold drink and a snack. Such visits usually occur in the late afternoon or on weekends. Gifts are not expected at informal parties and family dinners, but guests may bring the hostess something from the garden or another small token.

An invitation to someone's home for a special event is an invitation to a feast. On arrival, one is offered a cold drink; dinner is served after most guests have arrived (which may be long after the appointed hour). If the event is a wedding or birthday, guests bring gifts, which are opened after the party.

Eating. Guyanese usually eat breakfast at home. Those working outside the home either carry their midday meal, eat it in a small restaurant, or buy it from a street vendor. Schoolchildren go home to eat, bring their lunch, or buy it from vendors who operate stands outside the schools. The family usually gathers for dinner, the main meal of the day. In addition to regular meals, Guyanese enjoy snacks. *Snackette* stands sell finger foods and drinks; vendors offer highly seasoned barbecued meat, and ice cream is popular anytime.

LIFESTYLE

Family. Urban couples customarily have three to five children; rural families may have five or more. Both urban spouses usually work outside the home; the husband is head of the household and primary breadwinner, and the wife is the homemaker. Men generally do not help with household chores. It is not uncommon for grandmothers to care for young children while mothers are at work. Indeed, extended family members may live together to share living costs and child-care responsibilities. People living in cities may help raise a rural sibling's children to afford them better opportunities. Although rural people generally marry within their respective ethnic groups, mixed marriages are common in cities.

The effect of historical practices can be seen on dating and marriage patterns today. For example, East Indian indentured laborers came and worked as families. Today, most Indo-Guyanese families are still close. Parents carefully monitor unmarried daughters, and should a young woman become pregnant before marriage, the entire family is disgraced. On the other hand, slavery did not encourage marriage, and it assigned child care to older women. The impact of this practice on the Afro-Guyanese, especially among lower-income families, is clear: when an unmarried girl bears a baby, she commonly brings it to her mother to raise. Grandmothers may rear the children of more than one daughter, and as a rule, both the mother and grandmother work to provide for the family. Such single-parent and multigenerational families are increasingly common among other ethnic groups as well.

Dating and Marriage. Young people socialize in groups until they finish their formal schooling. When couples date, they go to the cinema, public celebrations, church functions, and other activities they enjoy in groups. Weddings are important events and are celebrated according to traditional religious rites. A Christian marriage takes place in a church and is usually followed by a reception that includes food, drink, and dancing, as well as speeches honoring the couple and their parents. After a Hindu wedding, guests are served a traditional supper of seven vegetarian curries on a water-lily pad. They return the next day for a Western-style reception. Muslim festivities can last three days.

Diet. Guyanese cuisine is as diverse as the population, and each ethnic group contributes favorite foods. Rice, eaten at both lunch and dinner, is grown locally. Beef, pork, mutton, chicken, and both freshwater and saltwater fish are abundant. Many Guyanese, especially Hindus, are vegetarians.

Breakfast might include coffee and toast with perhaps a piece of fruit. Heartier eaters may add eggs, salt fish, or boiled *ground provisions* (plantains, cassava, yams). Meat pies, cheese rolls, *roti* (unleavened bread wrapped around chicken or beef and potatoes), and rice with bits of vegetables or meat are popular lunch items. Spicy curry is a favorite dinner. Another evening meal, *cook-up rice*, is made with coconut milk, rice, meat or fish, and—as the name implies—almost anything the cook has on hand. *Metemgee* is like *cook-up rice*, but with a *ground provision* instead of rice.

Adults drink soda, fruit juices, or beer with lunch and dinner. Coffee and milk are for breakfast; tea can be served at breakfast or between meals. Men drink substantial amounts of rum when they socialize.

Christmas calls for special treats: garlic pork, *pepper pot*, *black cake*, and ginger beer. No Christmas breakfast is complete without garlic pork. *Pepper pot*, served throughout the season, is a meat stew flavored with *casareep*, a cassava extract. Dried local fruits soaked in rum and caramelized sugar give *black cake* its unique color and distinct, sweet taste.

Recreation. Cricket is a national obsession, while *football* (soccer) comes in a distant second. Both men and women play field hockey, tennis, and golf. Large crowds attend regular car races near the Timehri International Airport. Boxing is popular among Afro-Guyanese men. Dominoes is a favorite table game at schools and in offices during the lunch hour.

The Guyanese like action movies made in India or the United States. Bars, discos, and karaoke clubs are places to relax with friends and enjoy the latest Caribbean music. Church and school fund-raising fairs draw crowds on weekends and provide an inexpensive and pleasant way for families to spend an afternoon.

The Arts. Guyana has produced several internationally respected painters and sculptors. Fine arts are represented in museums and galleries. Authors such as E. R. Braithwaite, who wrote *To Sir, with Love*, are also internationally known. The indigenous peoples are known for woven goods. Straw, grass, and thin strips of wood are woven into baskets, mats, and other household items. Other prominent crafts include wood carving and pottery.

Holidays. Nearly all Guyanese celebrate the Christmas season with gift-giving and feasting. Boxing Day (26 Dec.) is a day to relax after Christmas. New Year's Day is also quiet, as revelers recuperate from the parties of Old Year's Night. Republic Day (23 Feb.) marks the date Guyana became the Cooperative Republic of Guyana. The holiday is also known as *Mashramani*, a word used by indigenous people for the celebration at the end of a cooperative project. Fireworks and a presidential address are traditional on Independence Day (26 May). On CARICOM Day (first Monday in July), the Guyanese celebrate their ties with Caribbean nations. Freedom Day (first Monday in August) marks the end of slavery.

Easter (Friday–Monday) is popular and features kite flying along the seawall as a rite of spring. *Devali*, the fall Hindu Festival of Lights, features a light parade. *Phagwah* welcomes spring, and the Indo-Guyanese greet each other with a sprinkling of water, powder, and *abeer* (a red liquid). Official Muslim holidays are *Id ul Fitr*, the feast at the end of *Ramadan*, and *Id ul Azha*, the Feast of the Sacrifice. For the latter, people distribute food and clothing to the poor. Muslims also commemorate *Yaum an Nibi* (Muhammad's birthday), but it is not a public holiday.

Commerce. Major markets in Georgetown are open 24 hours a day. Other businesses and urban markets are open from 8 a.m. until 4:30 p.m.; markets close at noon on Wednesday and Saturday. Except for food vendors (open from 10 a.m. to 2 p.m.), urban markets are closed on Sunday. Village markets are open one or two days a week. Unlicensed street vendors flourish despite efforts to curb their activities. As part of the black market before 1992, they were essential to the local economy. Today, they mainly undermine established retailers.

Guyana

SOCIETY

Government. Guyana is a democratic republic within the British Commonwealth. The nation is divided into 10 regions. The president, currently Bharrat Jagdeo, serves as chief of state. The prime minister (Samuel Hinds) is appointed by the president and is head of government. All but 3 of the 68-seat National Assembly members are directly elected. The voting age is 18.

Economy. Guyana's economy has been growing slowly but consistently since the return to democratic governance in 1992. However, economic recessions have followed periods of political crises. Although government initiatives have privatized industries, increased foreign investment, improved infrastructure, lowered inflation and balance of debt payments, and increased industrial output, economic growth is hampered by poor roads, insufficient energy, a lack of skilled labor, and a large national debt.

Sugar and rice continue to be the chief exports. Gold and diamond mining have more potential than bauxite mining because the nation's substantial reserves are difficult to extract. Possible off-coast oil fields could present enormous revenue for the country. In addition to expanding fish processing, Guyana is experimenting with shrimp farming. Though the country has precious timber, an inadequate infrastructure and environmental concerns have spared Guyana's forests.

Much of the population lives in poverty, able to provide for their basic needs but little else. A disproportionate number of those affected by poverty are indigenous people. Due to the years of turmoil, most Guyanese still lack access to resources that would allow for personal advancement. Women earn about one-fourth of the nation's income. Expatriates often send money back to relatives in Guyana. The currency is the Guyanese dollar (GYD).

Transportation and Communications. Guyana's infrastructure is poorly developed. Bikes, scooters, cars, pedestrians, and horse- or donkey-drawn carts, compete with minibuses, *lorries* (small trucks), and *bush trucks* (four-wheel-drive trucks) for space on Guyana's roads. Minibuses have designated routes and fares but no schedules. Drivers wait at a *car park* until their bus is full (and crowded) before they set out. Outside the coastal plain, the only roads lead to the airport and to Linden. The rest of the country can only be accessed by water or air. Guyana Airways airline serves the interior, but seats are limited. Speedboats provide passenger and cargo service along the rivers. In many locations, the family boat is essential to get to the market, school, church, and nearest village.

Dependable phone service is available in most coastal areas. Efforts are underway to expand service. Communication with remote areas is possible via radiophone. A free press circulates several daily and weekly newspapers. Two radio stations, both owned by the government, broadcast nationwide, and Georgetown has a choice of television channels.

Education. Education is free and compulsory, but the cost of uniforms and books keeps some children from participating or advancing. Others cannot attend because their families need their labor. Children attend nursery school at age three, primary school by age six, and the first *form* (year) of secondary school by age ten. After the fourth *form*, a student may enter the job market, seek additional training, or prepare for a university. Education standards declined sharply after 1976, when the government took over private schools. Teachers are poorly paid and schools are not well supplied. More affluent parents send their children to after-school lessons for tutoring, and private schools are beginning to reopen. Higher education is offered through the University of Guyana, a teacher's college, technical institutions, and three schools of nursing.

Health. Guyanese receive free medical and dental care at public clinics and hospitals, but these facilities are not always well equipped. A national health insurance plan reimburses income lost to illness, maternity leave, or disability. Most clinics employ a *medex* (a person trained in primary health care), a nurse, or an untrained village matron. Community health workers provide basic care to interior villages. Several private (and expensive) hospitals operate in Georgetown.

DEVELOPMENT DATA

Human Dev. Index* rank .... 104 of 177 countries
　Adjusted for women .... 81 of 144 countries
Real GDP per capita $4,260
Adult literacy rate .... 99 percent (male); 98 (female)
Infant mortality rate .... 37 per 1,000 births
Life expectancy .... 60 (male); 66 (female)

AT A GLANCE

Events and Trends.

- A longstanding territorial dispute with neighboring Suriname over potential undersea oil fields has heightened tensions between the two nations. Attempts at resolution have included creating a joint border commission and appealing to the UN for help arbitrating the disagreement. The UN set up a tribunal to address the situation in June 2004.
- Guyana is facing political deadlock as the ruling People's Progressive Party (PPP) argues with the opposition People's National Congress (PNC) on a host of issues, including how to conduct local elections that have been put off for a decade. The parties also trade accusations that the other party is seeking to divide the country.
- In October 2003, Guyana's sugar industry was second on a list ranking the quality of international production. Although many Caribbean nations' sugar industries are failing, the executive director of the Sugar Association of the Caribbean said Guyana's industry was robust.
- In September 2003, Guyana's president, Bharrat Jagdeo, returned from a tour of India and announced that the Asian nation had forgiven Guyana's outstanding debt. Jagdeo, who is a descendant of East Indian immigrants, hopes to strengthen the strong ties between the two countries.

Contact Information. Embassy of the Cooperative Republic of Guyana, 2490 Tracy Place NW, Washington, DC 20008; phone (202) 265-6900; web site www.guyana.org.

CultureGrams World Edition 2006

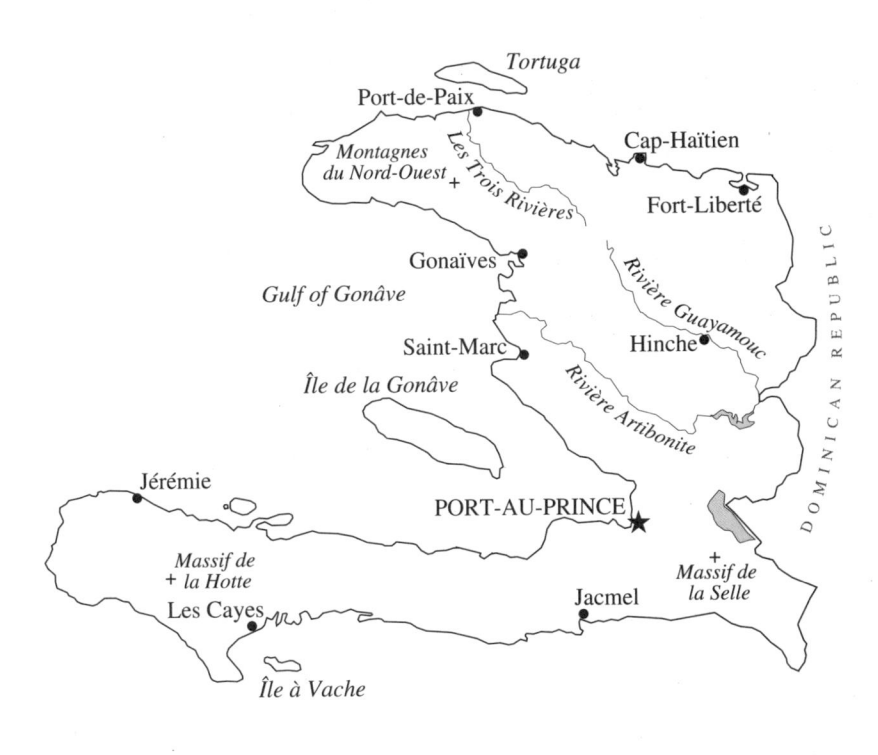

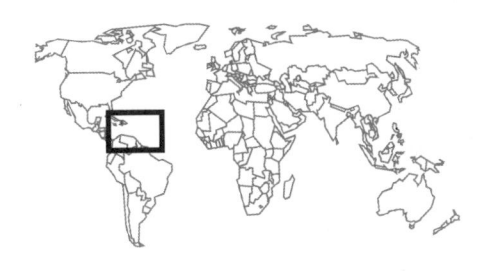

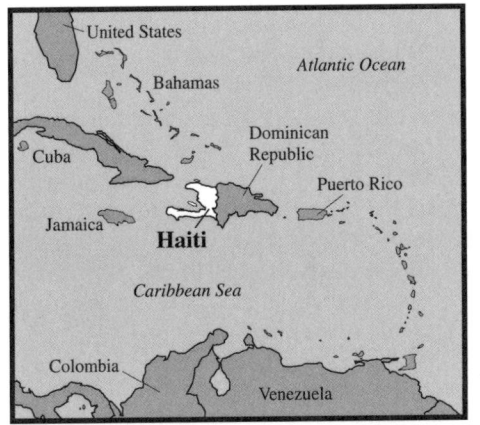

Republic of Haiti

BACKGROUND

Land and Climate. Haiti covers 10,714 square miles (27,750 square kilometers) of the island of Hispaniola, which it shares with the Dominican Republic. Just smaller than Maryland, Haiti is comprised of two peninsulas split by the Gulf of Gonâve. The mountainous, nearly barren island of Gonâve rests in the center of the gulf.

Haiti's portion of Hispaniola is significantly more mountainous, with successive mountain chains running east to west on both peninsulas. The northern Massif du Nord is part of the island's backbone, which Dominicans call the Cordillera Central. The southern peninsula boasts the Massif de la Hotte and Massif de la Selle. The highest peak, Pic la Selle, is located in the Massif de la Selle and rises to 8,793 feet (2,680 meters). Hills and valleys punctuate the mountains, and it is there where most people live and work. The four main plains include the Central, Northern, Artibonite, and Plaine du Cul-de-Sac (where the capital, Port-au-Prince, is located). Haiti is crossed by several large rivers, the longest of which is the Artibonite.

Haiti's climate is warm and only mildly humid. Frost, snow, and ice do not form anywhere—even at the highest elevations. The average temperature in the mountains is 66°F (19°C), while at Port-au-Prince it is 81°F (27°C). Spring and autumn are rainy, whereas December through February and June through August are dry. July is the driest summer month. The hurricane season lasts from June to October.

History. The island of Hispaniola was originally inhabited by Taíno and Arawak Indians. After Christopher Columbus arrived in 1492, opening Spanish colonization on Hispaniola, the indigenous peoples were enslaved. Within a few decades, a million of them died from starvation, hard labor in Spanish gold mines, and European diseases such as smallpox and measles. In a belated effort to save the remaining Indians and to help their sugar plantations prosper, the Spanish settlers began importing African slaves by 1517. By 1560, few Indians remained. The 2,000 Spanish settlers controlled the island and some 30,000 African slaves.

In 1697, Spain ceded the western third of Hispaniola to France, which soon enjoyed the coffee, sugar, and cotton riches of its new colony, Saint Domingue. France was given the entire island by 1795, although it didn't fully control the eastern half.

The slaves had begun revolting in 1791, but their efforts were futile until Toussaint L'Ouverture (a freed slave) led a revolt in 1798. He was eventually captured and subsequently died in a French prison. However, Jean-Jacques Dessalines became the next slave leader and gained victory over the French in 1803. Haiti declared its independence on 1 January 1804. French settlers who were not killed left the island. Dessalines became the emperor.

When Dessalines was killed in 1806, political chaos and rivalries led to General Henry Christophe gaining the throne in 1811. However, Christophe did not control the southern half of the nation. He ruled the north as King Henry I until he committed suicide in 1820. In 1822, north and south were reunited under President Jean-Pierre Boyer, who finally gained control over the Dominican Republic. Although Boyer was overthrown in 1844, the era still perpetuates tensions between the two neighbors. Power changed hands a few times until the 20th century, which found Haiti near anarchy. Under the United States's Monroe Doctrine, which essentially sought to maintain U.S. dominance in the Western Hemisphere, U.S. troops invaded and occupied Haiti from 1915 to 1934.

Haiti

The following years did not bring stability to Haiti, as people revolted against the government and elites who controlled it. In 1957, François Duvalier won presidential elections, despite charges of fraud. He killed his opponents and ruled with impunity, terrorizing the populace with his *Tontons macoutes*, the secret police. Before he died in 1971, "Papa Doc" Duvalier designated his son, Jean-Claude Duvalier, "Baby Doc," as his successor. Riots in 1985 forced Duvalier to flee Haiti in 1986.

A succession of military-led governments ruled Haiti until 1990, when Jean-Bertrand Aristide became the nation's first democratically elected president. Glee over his election was followed by impatience for reform and violence between Aristide's supporters and opponents. After just eight months in office, the military overthrew Aristide. General Raoul Cédras took power. Aristide made his way to the United States and set up a government in exile. His supporters in Haiti either went into hiding or were killed. The military dictatorship became increasingly brutal, and the international community decided to intervene with an embargo.

The embargo, ineffective at first, isolated Haiti in 1994 after the United States threatened further action. In September 1994, 20,000 U.S. soldiers landed in Haiti to overthrow the military. Two weeks later, Aristide returned from exile to rule for nearly a decade. However, he was overthrown again in 2004. Haiti continues to struggle with violent clashes between government and opposition groups, fraudulent elections, and economic devastation.

THE PEOPLE

Population. Haiti's population of 7.7 million is growing annually at about 1.7 percent. The country has a high birthrate, but emigration and poor health keep growth down. Most Haitians are descendants of African slaves who came to the island beginning in the 16th century. A small proportion (5 percent) are of mixed heritage or white. A large number of Haitians live in Florida and New York, although there are Haitian communities in other U.S. states as well.

Language. Haitian Creole is the language of daily conversation. French is used in government and business. Only educated adults or secondary school students speak French. Haitian Creole is a unique mixture of French and African languages. It is similar to Creole spoken on some other Caribbean islands, such as Guadeloupe and Martinique. Haitian Creole is traditionally an oral language, though it had a written form even in the 19th century. Use of written Creole began to spread after the 1940s with the introduction of adult literacy programs. People are increasingly interested in English, which is heard on television broadcasts from the United States. Also, because most Haitian families have a relative in the United States, English is used more often than in the past.

Religion. The majority (80 percent) of Haitians are Catholic. Protestants claim 16 percent or more of the population. The largest denominations are Baptist, Pentecostal, and Seventh-day Adventist. Perhaps as important as organized religion is voodoo, which is practiced to some degree by a majority of Haitians. It was given legal status equal to other religions in 2003. Though the practice is opposed by Catholic priests, voodoo has incorporated the worship of Catholic saints and the use of other Catholic rituals. Voodoo ceremonies and rituals, held in temples, usually are performed at night. Voodoo adherents believe that during the temple ceremonies, a voodoo god inhabits the body of a believer. Not all voodoo adherents practice the religion openly. Still, certain voodoo temples are the focus of annual pilgrimages.

General Attitudes. Haitians are warm, friendly, and generous. Their tradition for hospitality is clear in how they treat guests or go out of their way to help strangers find an address or something else they need. Haitians are proud of their culture and history. The stories of past Haitian heroes are not forgotten by today's youth. Some claim this is because the present offers no heroes, but others believe the past gives hope for the future.

Everyday life is hard for most Haitians, so parents strive to send their children to school, trusting that an education will give the next generation a better life. No matter society's conditions, Haitians celebrate life with joy, laughter, and dancing.

Rural and urban people have different perspectives on life, as their cultural practices and attitudes vary significantly. Urban people consider themselves to be more European or cosmopolitan than people from the countryside. The rural dwellers value their traditions and slower pace of life.

Personal Appearance. Whenever possible, people pay great attention to their public appearance. Urban Haitians prefer to wear Western-style clothing. Women may wear pants or colorful dresses. Some wear a headdress to match their outfit. Young people like to wear shorts; they follow the latest North American fashion trends. Sandals are the most popular footwear. Government officials and businessmen wear suits and ties. Rural men wear T-shirts and shorts or pants when working. Rural women wear dresses and head scarves, but they rarely wear pants. Almost all Haitian women enjoy jewelry and brightly colored clothing. Men also wear gold jewelry as a status symbol.

CUSTOMS AND COURTESIES

Greetings. Personal greetings are very important to Haitians. When entering a room or joining a group, a person is expected to physically greet each individual. Haitians usually shake hands when meeting a new acquaintance. Everyone else, from relatives to friends and casual acquaintances, receives a kiss on each cheek. The most common verbal greeting is *Bonjou, kouman ou ye?* (Good day, how are you?). The response usually is *Byen mèsi, e ou?* (Well, thank you, and you?).

Haitians address superiors or persons of status by title and last name (*Monsieur, Madame, Doctor*, etc.). Friends use first names or nicknames. An older person might be called "aunt" or "uncle" even if not related to the speaker.

Gestures. Haitians are an animated people who enjoy impromptu gatherings wherever they may be—at the market, in the street, at movie theaters. At such gatherings, people engage in loud conversation and laughing. Hand gestures usually accompany discussion or storytelling. If one is too busy to talk, one will greet a passerby by nodding the head up. To get someone's attention, Haitians often say "pssst."

Visiting. Visiting is a national pastime. Friends, neighbors, and relatives are welcome in the home at any time of day until about 8 p.m. It is not necessary to call ahead. Visitors arriving during a meal may be asked to wait in another room until the family finishes eating. Close friends might be invited to share the meal. They may accept or decline. It is also acceptable for guests to decline refreshments. Hosts typically offer fruit juice or soda. In addition to impromptu visits, Haitians enjoy inviting friends over for an evening of socializing or for dinner. When a visit ends, hosts accompany guests to the door. Rather than leaving, however, Haitians frequently extend their visit for a while by standing and talking with their hosts.

Special occasions also call for visits. Guests take gifts to hosts celebrating a communion, baptism, graduation, or wedding. The events may prompt people to organize an elaborate party. Friends and relatives also expect to visit the bereaved after a funeral.

Eating. Haitians eat three meals a day if they can afford it. Peasants may eat *cassave* (bread made from manioc) and coffee for breakfast, and they may not eat again until evening. The family gathers at the table for the main meal, which is usually at midday in cities. Diners take their portions from serving dishes on the table. If guests are present, they are given first opportunity to serve themselves. When no guests are present, family members often wait for the mother to begin eating before they eat. People eat at restaurants for special occasions. Sunday dinner traditionally is reserved as a family meal.

LIFESTYLE

Family. The basic unit of society is the extended family. Parents live with their married children and grandchildren. It is uncommon and generally unacceptable for the elderly to live alone or in a nursing facility. The father, if present in the home, is head of the household and responsible for earning an income. Single-mother households are very common, as men typically have children by more than one woman in their lifetime. Children stay with the mother in a divorce; the divorce rate is fairly high.

Urban families might have three or four children, while rural families have as many as ten or more. Most Haitians do not enjoy living in apartments, so houses are more common. Urban homes are built of cement block. The rural poor might use mud brick. Wherever possible, people have a garden next to their homes. Rural men work their fields, while women sell produce in the market. Rural and urban women care for the household and children. Urban families may have a servant to cook and do other chores.

Dating and Marriage. Although young Haitians socialize in groups, they do not usually begin dating until their late teens, when they finish school. Young people are free to choose their spouse; most parents do not greatly influence dating or marriage. When dating, the man will visit the woman at her home to become familiar with her parents and family members. Couples like movies, dancing, or other social events.

Urban couples typically have a church wedding followed by an evening reception. Receptions are usually held in private homes, where guests eat, dance, and socialize until late in the evening. In rural areas, a couple will not officially marry until they can afford a big wedding. They live together and have children as if married until they save enough money for the wedding.

Diet. Haitians usually eat rice and beans every day, although a main meal usually also includes meat, salad, and a vegetable. Rice and corn are staple grains. Spicy foods are most popular. *Piman zwazo* (small hot pimentos) and garlic are often added to dishes. Meat is marinated in sauces with ingredients such as sour orange juice, lemon juice, and hot peppers. For breakfast, one might eat the traditional urban fare of coffee, herring with plantains and avocados, corn with codfish, or liver with plantains. A lighter breakfast consists of bread, butter, and jam with coffee. A favorite daytime snack might be bread and butter or pastries.

Pork is the most popular meat, but Haitians also eat goat, chicken, guinea pig, and seafood (fish, shrimp, conch, crab, etc.). Meat-filled pastries are favorite snacks. Eggplant, yams, sweet potatoes, and a variety of fruits round out the diet. Haiti is especially known for its fresh-pressed juices made from passion fruit, oranges, *pamplemousse* (grapefruit), cherries, papaya, *zikak*, and other fruits.

Recreation. All Haitians have access to radios, and people generally listen to music and news throughout the day. A growing number of urban families are able to afford a television in their homes. Few people own VCRs, but they can watch videos at television stores. Haitian music videos are favored.

The most popular sport is soccer. Streets are empty if an important regional or world match is being televised. Children—both boys and girls—begin to play soccer at an early age. Leagues are organized throughout the country. Adult soccer stars are extremely popular among people of all ages. Men enjoy cockfights, usually held on Sunday afternoon. They also spend hours playing dominoes and cards.

The Arts. Music and dancing are integral to everyday life. Disco, reggae, and *konpa*, (related to big band music played in the United States during the 1940s) are popular in cities. *Meringue*, a mixture of African rhythms and European music, is the national dance. Urban residents enjoy a variety of North American music.

Haitian artists and sculptors are known for their unique images and striking colors. One popular art form is sculpture made from cut, pounded, and painted scrap metal. *Tap-taps*—brightly painted pickup trucks fitted with benches and covered tops—are both transportation and traveling art. Many artists choose Haitian history or daily life for their subject. Nature is also an important theme. Painted screens, papier-mâché art, wood carvings, basketwork, pottery, and painted wooden boxes are prominent crafts.

Oral literature is abundant and includes songs, proverbs, and riddles. Storytellers carefully craft their performance, acting out the story with their voice. Most written Haitian literature is in French, although Creole is now commonly used.

Holidays. Haiti's national holidays include New Year's, which is also Independence Day; National Heroes Day (2 Jan.); Constitution Day (29 Mar.); Easter; Flag Day (18 May); *Fête Dieu* (marks the institution of the sacrament or communion, first Thursday in June); and Christmas. Freedom from the Duvalier dictatorship is celebrated on 7 February. On New Year's Day, Haitians traditionally visit their parents and friends to wish them well in the new year.

Carnaval, held before the Catholic Lent, is a festive time for dancing and parades. People prepare for the holiday for weeks in advance; beginning just after New Year's, pre-*Carnaval* activities occur every Sunday. On the holiday itself, people awaiting the main parade dance to music they play on their own portable stereos. The partying continues all night and into the early morning hours for two or three days. Stores are open only in the morning on these days.

Various Catholic feasts are also marked but are not necessarily public holidays. *Fèt Gede* (2 Nov.) honors the dead, who are highly venerated in Haitian culture. Each village or town has a holiday for the local patron saint, celebrated with a morning mass, daytime festival, and evening ball. Some of these festivals are very large, such as the *Fête de Notre Dame*. From mid-January to Easter, local bands known as *Rara* dance and perform in the streets; they have their own rituals that carry some religious overtones. The holiday *Rara* is a more traditional version of *Carnaval*, which is not really celebrated in the countryside.

Commerce. Most businesses are open from 9 a.m. to 5 p.m., but shops may close at 3 p.m. during the summer. Open-air

Haiti

markets have varying hours, depending on their location. Most shops are closed on Sunday, except for urban supermarkets. The majority of people lack refrigeration and so shop daily for perishable foods. Rural people often grow their own food.

SOCIETY

Government. The Republic of Haiti is divided into nine departments (provinces), but the central government has most control over political affairs. The president, currently Boniface Alexandre, is head of state, and the prime minister, currently Gerard Latortue, is head of government. The constitution allows for a bicameral parliament, with a 27-seat Senate and an 83-seat Chamber of Deputies. The voting age is 18. The two most powerful political parties, *Fanmi Lavalas* (Lavalas Family Party) and the Struggling People's Organization, oppose each other in political conflicts.

Economy. Haiti's economy is based on agriculture, which employs more than two-thirds of the workforce. Large farms are rare, so production quantities are small. Around 80 percent of all Haitians live in poverty. Real wages have not risen in a generation. The most important cash crops include coffee, cacao, and sugar. However, little is actually exported, and international aid is necessary to develop future agricultural potential. Industrial activity is minimal, geared mostly for domestic needs (cement, sugar refining, etc.). A few industries make toys and clothing for export. The economy is experiencing little to no growth. Corruption, high unemployment, political instability, and inefficient state enterprises are major barriers to additional development. The government is working to privatize some state companies, but the process is slow and unpopular. Haiti's currency is the *gourde* (HTG).

Transportation and Communications. For short distances, most Haitians travel by foot. In cities, they may also ride buses, taxis, or a colorful *tap-tap,* which travels fixed routes but not on a fixed schedule. Intercity transportation is made by bus, boat, or plane. Few people own private cars.

Middle- and upper-income urban homes have phones. Otherwise, people go to a central telephone office. Phone booths are rare because of vandalism. The postal system is generally reliable but not protected against theft. A person can post a message on certain radio stations or send a written message via truck drivers. The drivers drop the messages at a store on their way and recipients can retrieve them. Haiti has two daily newspapers, about two hundred radio stations, and several television stations.

Education. Haiti's school system is patterned after the French model, with kindergarten, a primary school that lasts six years, and secondary school that lasts seven years. Many urban dwellers send their children to private schools, even though tuition can be a burden. In fact, two-thirds of all schools are private. Regardless of where children attend, their daily schooling is often interrupted by street demonstrations. Because these events can be very violent, parents tend to keep children home whenever a protest is announced or anticipated.

Students who complete secondary school may pursue higher education at a university or other private institutions. The country's main university is the State University of Haiti. Students who do not complete their education often work on family farms, especially in rural areas.

Health. Haiti's national health system is unable to meet the needs of most people due to the lack of funds, staff, and modern equipment. Malaria, hepatitis, HIV/AIDS, dengue fever, and other diseases combine with malnutrition to keep life expectancy rates low and infant mortality rates high. Most children do not receive proper vaccinations. Proper sanitation and clean water are also lacking.

DEVELOPMENT DATA

Human Dev. Index* rank . . . . 153 of 177 countries
 Adjusted for women. . . . . 123 of 144 countries
Real GDP per capita $1,610
Adult literacy rate . . . . 54 percent (male); 50 (female)
Infant mortality rate . . . . 74 per 1,000 births
Life expectancy . . . . 49 (male); 50 (female)

AT A GLANCE

Events and Trends.

- In February 2004, protests against the presidency of Jean Bertrand-Aristide culminated in rebels capturing several cities, both rebels and government troops suffering multiple deaths among their ranks, and Aristide leaving the country—possibly under threat of force. The UN Security Council voted to send troops to restore order in the area. Meanwhile, Supreme Court Chief Justice Boniface Alexandre was sworn in as interim president.
- In May 2004, Haiti was struck by severe floods that left hundreds dead and thousands homeless. On the heels of the floods came a moderate earthquake. Just when the nation seemed to be recovering, tropical storms again flooded the island in September, killing at least 1,500 people and displacing thousands more. With Haiti already in political turmoil, the natural disasters posed incredible problems.
- The international community rallied around Haiti in the wake of its political crisis and natural disasters. Brazil led an international peacekeeping force while countries like China contributed forces. Also, major donors promised an additional US$1 billion to help keep the island stable.
- In January 2004, Haiti marked 200 years of independence from France. The country's leaders praised Haiti for being the first black republic and for continuing to be an example to many countries. However, along with those enjoying the festivities, anti-government protestors took to the streets in several cities, and an air convoy carrying South African president Thabo Mbeki was fired upon. The president was not harmed, but several injuries among the protestors were reported.
- In October 2003, a global corruption index compiled by business leaders and academics rated Haiti's public officials and politicians the third most corrupt among 133 nations. Only Bangladesh and Nigeria were believed to be worse.

Contact Information. Embassy of the Republic of Haiti, 2311 Massachusetts Avenue NW, Washington, DC 20008; phone (202) 332-4090; web site www.haiti.org.

CultureGrams
People. The World. You.

ProQuest Information and Learning Company
300 North Zeeb Road, P.O. Box 1346
Ann Arbor, Michigan 48106 USA
Toll Free: 1.800.528.6279
Fax: 1.800.864.0019
www.culturegrams.com

© 2005 ProQuest Information and Learning Company and Brigham Young University. It is against the law to copy, reprint, store, or transmit any part of this publication in any form by any means without written permission from ProQuest. This document contains native commentary and original analysis, as well as estimated statistics. The content should not be considered strictly factual, and it may not apply to all groups in a nation. *UN Development Programme, Human Development Report 2004 (New York: Oxford University Press, 2004).

CultureGrams World Edition 2006

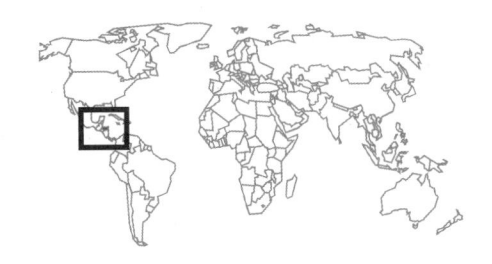

Republic of Honduras

BACKGROUND

Land and Climate. Covering 43,278 square miles (112,090 square kilometers), Honduras is just larger than Tennessee. Located in Central America, Honduras borders the Pacific and Atlantic Oceans. La Mosquitia, an area of wetlands, mountains, and tropical forests, covers the lower eastern coast. The largest pine forest in Latin America, the Olancho Forest Reserve, is about the size of Connecticut. The climate varies according to elevation: subtropical in the lowlands and temperate at higher levels. Tegucigalpa, the capital, enjoys a relatively mild climate year-round. The south is warmer than the rest of the country, excluding the north coast. The south is also drier. The rainy season extends from May to November, although rains sometimes may not begin to fall until as late as October. March through May is the hottest season. Summer highs reach 105°F (40°C).

While Honduras is mountainous, it is the only Central American country without volcanoes. The lack of volcanoes is a factor in its low food production because volcanic soils are usually good for agriculture. Due to the poor soil, many people have practiced migratory agriculture, moving every few years to clear new land and plant crops. This practice, along with timber operations, has caused Honduras to lose 30 percent of its forest over the past 25 years. Wildlife has also been affected. Many efforts are now underway to reverse this trend and preserve the forests for indigenous peoples, wildlife, and the environment. Precious woods, gold, silver, copper, lead, zinc, and other minerals are found in Honduras.

History. The great Mayan Empire flourished in present-day Honduras until about A.D. 800, when the Mayan population began to decline. Smaller empires controlled various regions until the arrival of Spanish *conquistadores*, explorers who battled and conquered the indigenous people. Columbus landed in 1502 and called the area Honduras ("depths") because of the deep waters off the north coast. Several groups of natives battled the Spanish until 1539, when the last of the Indian chiefs (Lempira) was killed. Lempira is still considered a national hero. That same year, the Spanish established a provincial capital at Comayagua. Honduras was incorporated into Spain's Captaincy General (colony) of Guatemala. Immigration increased when silver was discovered in the 1570s.

Preferring British rule to Spanish rule, the Misquito Indians of the Mosquitia region asked the British to invade the country. However, troops were only able to occupy the Mosquitia area, so they withdrew in 1859. Meanwhile, Honduras and four other provinces declared independence from Spain in 1821 and joined the Mexican Empire. Honduras became an independent republic in 1838. By the end of the 1800s, government instability led to the country to come under Nicaraguan influence. Instability continued until Tiburcio Carías Andino took power in 1932. His military rule ended in 1949, but military leaders continued to exercise control until 1981, when elections restored civilian rule.

Another civilian, Rafael Leonardo Callejas, took office in 1990, but the military still had a great deal of power and influence. Constitutional term limits prohibited Callejas from seeking a second consecutive term. Carlos Roberto Reina Idiaquez was voted president in 1993 elections. Reina worked to reduce the military's role in politics. He also pursued economic reform, attacked corruption, and promoted human rights. Presidential elections in 2001 brought Ricardo Maduro to office, marking the country's sixth democratic transfer of power since the end of military rule.

Honduras

Heavy rains and high winds from Hurricane Mitch pounded the country for a week in 1998. Nine thousand Central Americans died in the disaster, and billions of dollars in damage were sustained. Widespread devastation altered the nature, location, and course of many geographical features. Reconstruction loans, debt forgiveness, and foreign aid have helped Honduras recover from Hurricane Mitch, but much remains to be done. Honduras also must deal with ongoing social problems, such as government corruption, rampant crime, gang violence, vigilantes, and economic inequality.

THE PEOPLE

Population. About 6.8 million people live in Honduras, and the population is growing at around 2.2 percent annually. About half of Hondurans live in urban areas. The largest city is Tegucigalpa. La Ceiba and Puerto Cortés are important ports on the Caribbean Sea. Ninety percent of the population is mestizo—of mixed Spanish and indigenous heritage—while only 7 percent is of pure indigenous blood. Two percent is black and 1 percent is of European descent. The indigenous peoples live mostly in isolated regions, such as La Mosquitia and the mountains in the southwest. The principal indigenous ethnic groups include the Misquito, Payas, and Xicaques. Honduras's black population is primarily made up of the Garinagus, commonly known as Garífuna. There is also a group known as the Sambos—a mixture of black and indigenous inhabitants.

Language. Spanish is the official and dominant language. However, some Garinagu speak Garífuna, and the indigenous populations speak their own languages. About 10,000 people, mostly on the Bay Islands, speak Creole English. English is a required course in secondary schools, but few people are fluent. Major hotels have bilingual employees.

Religion. A majority of the population is Roman Catholic, but various other Christian groups are active, and freedom of religion is guaranteed by law. Protestantism is growing rapidly, with a variety of churches present in even the smallest towns. Most Protestants (or *evangélicos*) attend church regularly. Some follow specific rules affecting their lifestyle (no coffee, dancing, etc.). The Catholic Church maintains a strong influence on society through festivals, family celebrations, and politics. Many public holidays center on religious themes. Each town and city has a patron saint, for whom it holds an annual festival.

General Attitudes. In Honduras, as in much of Latin America, social philosophies such as fatalism, *machismo*, and *la hora latina* are evident. Fatalism exists partly due to the difficulties of life in poverty; people are aware of limited social mobility and try to accept their position in life as something they cannot control. This attitude often relieves frustration and allows people to focus on what is good in life rather than what is unpleasant. During conversation, people often add the phrase *Si Dios quiere* (God willing), particularly when making commitments. *Machismo* is indicative of a male-dominated society in which women are expected to remain submissive. Women comprise less than one-third of the formal labor force, and most rural women do not work outside the home. *La hora latina* refers to the concept of time and schedules. Since Hondurans consider individuals' needs to be more important than schedules, being late for appointments or social events is a way of life. For example, a person would not hesitate to stop and talk to a friend on the way to an appointment, even if it meant being late. This is true even in urban settings, where punctuality is a bit more important, because good relationships and personal contacts are often needed to conduct business and work with the government.

Hondurans value their Christian beliefs, as well as their ties to the land and to agriculture. Environmental issues are important to Hondurans, but financial concerns take precedence in many instances because many people live in poverty.

Personal Appearance. Hondurans normally wear Western-style clothing. Shorts rarely are worn in public except in the coastal areas, where it is hot and humid. Urban men often wear a *guayabera* (a decorative shirt of light fabric that hangs to just below the waist) instead of a more formal shirt and tie. Urban women are especially stylish with respect to clothing, hair, and makeup. In rural areas, where the majority is poor, many people wear secondhand clothing imported from the United States. Men wear rubber boots when working in the fields, while women wear flip-flops. Baseball caps or wide-brim hats are common. T-shirts with English slogans are popular throughout Honduras, even though the wearer often does not speak English. Dressing up for special occasions is important to Hondurans. People are careful to keep dress clothes separate from clothes worn at work and at home. The wealthy wear the latest Western fashions.

CUSTOMS AND COURTESIES

Greetings. A handshake is an appropriate greeting for men. Urban women are usually greeted with a kiss on the cheek, except in business settings where a handshake may suffice. Rural women greet one another by placing one hand on the upper arm of the other woman. An *abrazo* is a warm embrace shared by close friends and relatives. When meeting someone for the first time, a person addresses the other by official title or *Señor, Señora,* or *Señorita* (Mr., Mrs., or Miss). The titles *Don* (for men) and *Doña* (for women) are also used before first names to show respect. *Usted* (the formal version of "you" in Spanish) is appropriate among acquaintances or those meeting for the first time.

One customarily gives a general greeting when entering a room. In small groups, people greet and say good-bye to each person. People commonly say *Que le vaya bien* (May it go well with you) when parting. While passing someone on the street, one says *Adiós*. The word usually means "Good-bye," but in this case it is meant as a general greeting. One always says *Buen provecho* (Enjoy your meal) at the table before a meal. A person approaching or passing a table in a restaurant also says *Buen provecho* to the people at the table.

Gestures. Hand and body language is important to communication. Waving the index finger is often used to say "no." Clasping both hands indicates strong approval. Touching the finger below the eye warns caution. And a hand placed under an elbow usually means someone is thought to be stingy. People commonly point with their lips or chin because pointing with the index finger is rude. Beckoning with the index finger also is rude, so people beckon by waving the hand with the palm facing down. To express enthusiasm, they place their middle finger and thumb together and shake their hand, producing a snapping noise. Poorer people tend to avoid eye contact when conversing. Urban gang members have complicated hand signals that they use to communicate with each other from afar. These signs should not be imitated.

Visiting. Visiting is a common pastime on Saturday afternoons and Sundays, and people often visit unannounced. People in rural areas also visit on days when they are not in the fields. Hondurans are courteous and generous to guests in their homes. Hosts almost always offer their guests refreshments, such as juice, soda, coffee, or sweets; refusing is impolite. Unexpected visitors arriving at mealtime are often extended an invitation to eat with the family. Even people of humble circumstance will share whatever they have to make a guest feel welcome. If a guest does not feel like eating, the host may wrap up a little food to send home with him or her. When leaving a home, guests are especially respectful to the head of the household.

Social events may have an indicated starting time, but hosts and guests understand this is very flexible; being several minutes or even an hour late is not uncommon.

Eating. Hondurans eat breakfast between 6 and 8:30 a.m., the main meal around noon, and a lighter evening meal sometime between 6 and 8 p.m. Coffee breaks are customary in the late morning and midafternoon. Meals are eaten in a leisurely manner. Diners keep both hands (but not elbows) above the table. People customarily hold the fork in the right hand and knife in the left; rural people might use pieces of corn tortillas instead of utensils. Families do not necessarily eat together, either because they lack plates or table space or simply as a matter of convenience. At finer restaurants, a 10 to 15 percent tip is appropriate; tips are not necessarily expected at less formal restaurants.

LIFESTYLE

Family. Family ties are strong in Honduras. Members of the extended family, including grandparents and other relatives, often occupy the same household. Children rarely leave home until they marry. While the father is respected as the head of the household, the mother has the greatest responsibility and influence in everyday family life. Girls are expected to begin help with household chores and child care at a young age, but boys often do little until they are old enough to help in the fields. Hondurans carry both their paternal and maternal surnames. The father's surname is considered the family name; but it is the mother's surname that appears at the end of the entire name. Both surnames follow one or two given names. When a woman marries, her name does not change.

Unfortunately, a large number of families live in poverty. Most Honduran homes do not have modern conveniences. Small adobe houses with dirt floors are common in rural areas. Cities have both modern, luxurious housing and poor slums. People in remote areas usually lack electricity.

Dating and Marriage. Young women have their formal initiation into social life at age 15, when elaborate parties are held to recognize their coming of age. Teens begin dating in groups; a young woman is usually accompanied by one or more other young women. Later on, couples date without accompaniment. Activities are simple and usually just involve socializing. Couples often get together at dances.

In rural areas, most poor people will start their families without marrying, often as young as age 14. Common-law marriages generally are accepted, so many people never officially marry. Single mothers are common in all social classes, and many siblings in these families have only the mother in common. Young single mothers often return to live with their parents until they are older or find another spouse.

Diet. Red beans, corn, tortillas, and rice are the staple foods. Bananas, pineapples, mangoes, citrus fruits, coconuts, melons, avocados, potatoes, and yams are the most common fruits and vegetables. Special dishes include *tapado* (a stew of beef, vegetables, and coconut milk), *mondongo* (tripe and beef knuckles), *nacatamales* (pork tamales), and *torrejas* (similar to French toast and served at Christmas). *Topogios* or *charamuscas* (frozen fruit juice in plastic bags) are popular during the summer months. People also enjoy soft drinks. Coffee with or without milk is traditional and usually is served with the main meal of the day. North American fast food restaurants are prevalent in major cities and serve pizza, hamburgers, and other dishes.

Recreation. *Fútbol* (soccer) defines national recreation. Boys and men play regularly in leagues, and professional competition is available as well. Although in recent years more girls have become involved in *fútbol*, they are still more likely to play basketball. Many girls prefer dancing to sports. Boys and men in rural areas enjoy playing card and dice games. In villages on the north coast, men like to play dominoes after they return home from a day's work of fishing. Wealthy Hondurans enjoy cycle races, baseball, golf, tennis, and swimming. Movies are popular in urban areas.

The Arts. Honduras is known for brightly painted ceramics, carved wooden trunks, handmade musical instruments, and other woodwork. Metalwork, embroidery, and weaving are also common arts. Honduras is home to many Mayan ruins, including Copán, which is located near the Guatemalan border. Pottery and stone carvings have been discovered there.

Hondurans enjoy music and dance. A popular kind of music is known as *la punta*, which originated with traditional Garífuna music. It is often played with drums, a conch shell, and maracas and has a complex rhythm. The *marimba* (similar to a xylophone) is a common instrument; other traditional instruments include flutes and trumpets.

Holidays. Public holidays include New Year's; Day of the Americas (14 Apr.); Labor Day (1 May); Independence Day (15 Sept.); Birth of Morazán, the national hero (3 Oct.); Columbus Day (12 Oct.); Armed Forces Day (21 Oct.); and Christmas. Independence Day is the most popular national holiday. Schoolchildren practice for months in preparation for parades and programs. Constructing nativity scenes is a popular Christmas tradition. Since money is scarce, the scenes are made from scratch each year with clay figures and other natural resources.

During Easter's Holy Week (*Semana Santa*), businesses close from Wednesday through the end of the week. Many people go to the beach, while others may swim in the rivers. The Day of the Child (10 Sept.) is not an official holiday but is still popular. Children receive sweets and gifts at school, and adults congratulate the children when passing them on the street. Private home celebrations may also take place among the wealthy. In addition to national holidays, each community's most important holiday honors its patron saint. There are also regional *fiestas* such as *Carnaval* around La Ceiba.

Commerce. Government office hours are from 8 a.m. to 4 p.m. or 7:30 a.m. to 3:30 p.m., Monday through Friday. Private businesses operate from 8 a.m. to noon and 1 to 5 p.m., although some do not close at noon for the *siesta* (midday break). Banks usually close by 3 p.m., while post offices may remain open as late as 9 p.m., depending on the city. On Saturdays, most businesses close between noon and 2 p.m. In marketplaces and shops where prices are not posted, bartering is common; otherwise, prices are fixed. Small shops called *pulperias* operate out of people's homes in most communities. They sell food, medicine, and cleaning and school supplies and are open all day, every day.

Honduras

SOCIETY

Government. The Republic of Honduras is divided into 18 *departamentos* (provinces), each administered by a governor. The Honduran president (currently Ricardo Maduro) is chief of state and head of government. The president governs with a cabinet and serves one four-year term. The judicial branch of government is independent. The unicameral *Congreso Nacional* (National Congress) has 128 seats. All citizens are allowed to vote beginning at age 18. Two parties dominate in Congress, although smaller parties have representation. The two main parties are the Liberal Party (PLH) and the National Party (PNH). Party affiliation is taken seriously. Civilian rule in Honduras began in the 1980s, and great steps are taken to keep the government and military separate. However, the military continues to have considerable influence.

Economy. Honduras is one of the poorest countries in the Western Hemisphere. With more than half of the population living in poverty, many people do not earn an income sufficient for their needs. The economy is based largely on agriculture. The most profitable exports are bananas and coffee, followed by seafood, timber, cotton, sugar, and metals. Adverse weather conditions and fluctuating global prices for these raw materials can cripple the economy from one year to the next. Manufactured items are slowly becoming more important.

Economic reforms implemented in the early 1990s were beginning to improve some conditions prior to widespread devastation from Hurricane Mitch in late 1998. Damage to crops, farmland, and infrastructure from Mitch was substantial. The economy continues to struggle, although it is recovering. Obstacles to growth include an already weak infrastructure (services, roads, markets); large foreign debts; high interest rates; and a large, inefficient bureaucracy. Unemployment affects approximately a quarter of the population. The Honduran currency is the *lempira* (HNL).

Transportation and Communications. Roads and bridges throughout the country were destroyed by Hurricane Mitch; rebuilding in some areas may still be incomplete. Periodic floods also take their toll on roads. Highways connect Tegucigalpa with some other principal cities, but roads generally are in poor condition, particularly in more remote areas. People rely on buses and taxis for public transport because few own cars. Rural areas are isolated from cities because of poor transportation and communications. In areas without buses, truck owners may provide travel on specific routes. Several cities are accessible by airplane. Private telephones are found only in major cities. Most large towns have one public telephone and a telegraph service, usually used for urgent messages. Mail service is slow but fairly reliable.

Education. Schooling is required for six years beginning at age seven. However, while nearly all children begin their schooling, many drop out before the end—especially among the rural poor. Less than half of all children actually complete the full six years, and less than one-third advance to the secondary level. Children often are needed at home to help with farming or household chores, and having them gone all day at school can be too great a sacrifice for many families. Shortages of schools, teachers, educational texts, and supplies are also a problem. The National University of Honduras and some trade schools provide higher education, but only a small fraction of the population advances to those levels of study. Honduras has some of Central America's best agricultural and forestry schools.

Health. Various health challenges face Hondurans. Malaria is prevalent below about 3,000 feet (900 meters), and rabies, typhoid, hepatitis, parasites, dengue fever, dysentery, and intestinal disease present problems for the population. Vaccinations are provided free of charge, and nearly all people have access to them. But while most Honduran children are immunized, up to half suffer from malnutrition. Honduras has the highest number of AIDS cases in Central America.

Rural areas have health centers, but many villagers must walk hours to reach one. Facilities often are not equipped with medicine. Urban medical care is more adequate but still lacking by modern standards. Basic health care is subsidized throughout the country, but patients must pay small fees for each visit. Poorer citizens often cannot afford prescription medicine.

DEVELOPMENT DATA

Human Dev. Index* rank . . . . 115 of 177 countries
  Adjusted for women. . . . . 95 of 144 countries
Real GDP per capita $2,600
Adult literacy rate . . . . 80 percent (male); 80 (female)
Infant mortality rate . . . . 30 per 1,000 births
Life expectancy . . . . 67 (male); 71 (female)

AT A GLANCE

Events and Trends.

- In May 2004, a fire at a prison in northern Honduras destroyed a cellblock, killing more than 100 of the 186 gang members who were being kept there. The fire was blamed on faulty wiring. It was Honduras's second major prison fire in about a year. Prisons in Honduras face huge problems with overcrowding, especially after a law passed in August 2003 outlawed gangs and set up mandatory 12-year sentences for those convicted of gang activity.
- Honduras has seen an increase of Cuban refugees in 2004. Although many more Cubans attempt the 90-mile trip to Florida, about 100 each year are now attempting the 500-mile passage to Honduras because it may be easier to come ashore without being intercepted by the coast guard.
- In March 2003, the government said it would set up a commission to investigate the killings of more than 1,500 of an estimated 20,000 children living on the street. According to a UN report, the powerful security forces and gangs responsible for many of these killings had been acting without fear of punishment.

Contact Information. Embassy of the Republic of Honduras, 3007 Tilden Street NW, Suite 4M, Washington, DC 20008; phone (202) 966-7702; web site www.hondurasemb.org. Honduras Institute of Tourism, 299 Alhambra Circle, Suite 226, Coral Gables, Coral Gables, FL 33134; phone (800) 410-9608.

CultureGrams™
People. The World. You.

ProQuest Information and Learning Company
300 North Zeeb Road, P.O. Box 1346
Ann Arbor, Michigan 48106 USA
Toll Free: 1.800.528.6279
Fax: 1.800.864.0019
www.culturegrams.com

© 2005 ProQuest Information and Learning Company and Brigham Young University. It is against the law to copy, reprint, store, or transmit any part of this publication in any form by any means without written permission from ProQuest. This document contains native commentary and original analysis, as well as estimated statistics. The content should not be considered strictly factual, and it may not apply to all groups in a nation. *UN Development Programme, Human Development Report 2004 (New York: Oxford University Press, 2004).

CultureGrams World Edition 2006

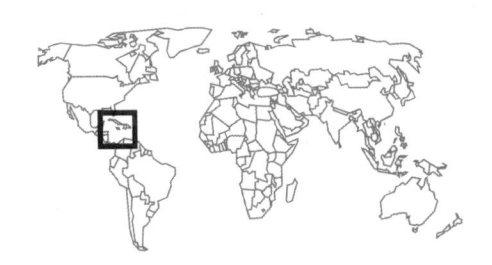

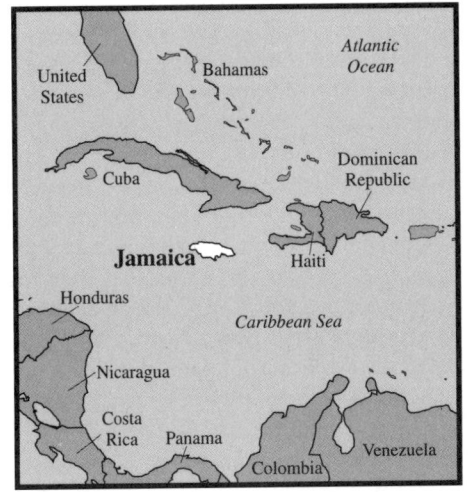

Jamaica

BACKGROUND

Land and Climate. Jamaica is part of the Greater Antilles, a chain of islands that forms the northern boundary of the Caribbean Sea. Its nearest neighbor is Cuba (about 90 miles, or 145 kilometers, to the north). Only 51 miles (83 kilometers) across at its widest point, Jamaica covers 4,244 square miles (10,991 square kilometers) and is just smaller than Connecticut. Eighty percent of the island is mountainous. Less than 20 percent is suitable for continuous cultivation. Jamaica has a tropical maritime climate, but rainfall varies depending on the region. The rainy seasons occur in May and October. Hurricanes are possible from June to November. The tropical island climate prevents extreme temperature variations; temperatures generally are 80 to 90°F (26 to 32°C). A natural port on the southern coast is home to Jamaica's capital, Kingston.

History. Jamaica's original inhabitants were the Arawak Indians, who called the island Xaymaca, meaning either "land of wood and water" or "land of springs." Columbus landed on the island in 1494. The Arawaks were virtually decimated within a few decades by European diseases and the harsh life settlers imposed on them. The Spanish occupied the island until 1655, when it was captured and colonized by the English. By the late 17th century, the English had established sugarcane plantations and were importing large numbers of slaves from Africa. Slavery was abolished in 1838. Some Spaniards stayed in Jamaica and eventually mixed with the African peoples. Today, these people are called the Maroons, a group that has some political autonomy.

In the 1860s, Jamaica's status was upgraded from colonial possession to British crown colony. During the 1930s, people began calling for self-determination. In 1938, serious social unrest was stirred up by long-standing injustices and labor problems. Alexander Bustamante, aided by Norman Manley, championed labor's cause and sparked important social change. The two also formed today's major political parties. A new constitution in 1944 ended rule by the British crown colony government and granted adult suffrage. However, Jamaica remained under nominal British rule until it gained full independence in 1962.

During the 1970s, Manley's son Michael headed a social-democrat government that concentrated on social issues and help for the poor. However, severe economic problems led to a 1980 victory for Edward Seaga and his conservative Jamaican Labour Party (JLP), which dominated government throughout the decade.

Most elections in the 1980s and 1990s were marked by fraud and violence, as political parties strove to maintain control over communities known as *garrison constituencies*, in which political parties joined forces with urban gangs to force citizens to vote for certain candidates. National elections in 1989 brought the social-democrat People's National Party (PNP) to power. A PNP leader, Percival James Patterson, has been prime minister since 1992. The government is faced with the challenges of addressing a struggling economy and stemming rising crime.

THE PEOPLE

Population. Jamaica's population of 2.7 million is growing at 0.66 percent annually. The majority of people are of African ancestry (76 percent). Afro-Europeans (15 percent) as well as Afro-East Indians and East Indians (3 percent) are significant minorities. The population also includes whites of European descent (3 percent), some Chinese, and other groups. More

Jamaica

than half of the population lives in urban areas. Kingston and Montego Bay are the largest cities. Because many people leave to seek greater opportunity, nearly as many Jamaicans live outside of Jamaica as on the island. Most expatriates live in England and the eastern United States.

Language. English is the official language of Jamaica. However, a Jamaican's ability to speak and understand standard English may vary depending on the person's level of education. *Patois*, an English-based creole with West African influences, is commonly used in everyday conversation. Jamaican speech, in English or *patois*, has a distinctive rhythmic and melodic quality.

Religion. Most Jamaicans (61 percent) are Protestants, and many major denominations are represented on the island. The Anglican Church is the official national church, although only about 5 percent of the population belongs to it. Other groups include the Church of God (21 percent), Baptists (9 percent), Seventh-day Adventists (9 percent), and Pentecostals (7.6 percent). Four percent of the people are Roman Catholic. Jamaicans commonly use the term *Christian* to mean practicing members of a Protestant (often evangelical) church. Non-Christians may practice ceremonies and rituals that have roots in India, China, or Africa but that have become uniquely Jamaican. There is also a long-standing Jewish community, whose first members arrived with Columbus as ship hands to escape the Spanish Inquisition.

Religious education commonly is included in school curricula. Religion plays an important role in society through the spiritual values and social opportunities it provides. Ecumenism (unity among all churches) is the norm among Jamaicans. The vast majority of Jamaican churchgoers are women and children; church gatherings are particularly popular among rural women.

The political and religious Rastafarian movement originated in Jamaica. Only about 5 percent of Jamaicans practice Rastafarianism, but it has had a profound impact on Jamaican and Caribbean culture. Adherents generally believe they should separate themselves from white people and regard Africa as the promised land. They consider Ethiopia's late ruler Haile Selassie I an incarnation of "the living God." Many also observe Old Testament laws, including dietary restrictions, and regard marijuana as a sacred herb.

General Attitudes. Jamaicans enjoy spending time together, having lively conversations, and generally being outgoing. People are warm and hospitable but may be reserved with strangers. It is considered important to be thoughtful, neighborly, and charitable. Selfish or standoffish behavior is looked down upon. Jamaicans have a fairly flexible approach to life. A common, good-natured answer to life's challenges is *No problem, man*, even if there is no solution at hand. Flexibility is also evident in attitudes toward time and schedules. A common phrase is *Soon come*, which can mean anything from five minutes to next week. Events and meetings often begin late, although people are more punctual in urban areas.

Jamaicans appreciate honesty and hard work. They are increasingly building a strong professional atmosphere in Urban areas. Financial security, prestige, homes, properties, and motor vehicles are valued possessions.

Personal Appearance. While Jamaicans may dress in a variety of ways, women generally try to keep themselves and their children well dressed, especially at church. Older women and women belonging to some religious sects usually wear dresses or skirts. Professional women wear business suits and skirts. Institutions such as banks and insurance companies may provide employees, particularly women, with uniforms. Children also wear uniforms for school.

Men wear casual clothing for most occasions. Youth fashions are often brightly colored and commonly follow trends from the United States and the music industry. On weekends, many young people wear *dance hall* (a popular form of music) outfits, which reflect current trends.

Rastafarians do not cut their hair, wearing it in long dreadlocks. Clothing and accessories worn throughout the island often feature Rastafarian colors (green, red, and gold).

CUSTOMS AND COURTESIES

Greetings. Jamaicans consider it important to recognize and greet others and to be recognized in return. Greetings range from a nod to a slap on the back to a kiss—depending on the people involved and the occasion. Strangers being introduced usually shake hands and say *Good morning*, *Good afternoon*, *Good evening*, or *Good night*. Professional or formal titles (*Mr.*, *Mrs.*, *Miss*) are used with the surname unless people are well acquainted. Children usually refer to adults who are not family members as *Sir*, *Mr.*, *Mrs.*, or *Miss*. Elderly people in rural areas may bow or curtsy when greeting. It is considered rude not to greet someone properly before beginning a conversation or asking a question. Friends and acquaintances passing on the road often call out greetings. A common phrase is *Whaapun?* (What's happening?) or *Alright, alright* (as if to bypass asking and responding to "How are you?"). Common parting phrases include *Later*, *Tomorrow then*, *Next time*, and *God bless*.

In casual situations, people often use nicknames. Jamaicans (particularly men) might have many nicknames given them by various friends or groups. The nickname usually refers to a physical trait or station in life. Examples include *Fatty* (a fat person; it is a compliment because it indicates life is treating that person well), *Whitey* (white person; also not an insult, but references to the "blackness" of a black Jamaican may be considered insulting), or *Juicy* (man who sells juice on the street). Family members more often call one another by a *pet name* or *yard name*, which often is a shortened or slightly altered version of a person's given name (*Nicky* for Nicholas).

Gestures. Jamaicans can be very animated when speaking and tend to use hand gestures to help make a point (especially men who are talking about cricket or politics). People sometimes show respect for or approval of shared ideas by touching fists. They emphasize greetings by holding on to an initial handshake or by touching the person's arm or shoulder. To hail a taxi, one keeps the hand down (rather than holding it above the head) and waves. To get someone's attention, one may clap hands or tap on a grill or gate of a home. Some people say "pssst" to attract another's attention, but this can be considered rude. Sucking air through the teeth may express exasperation or the idea of "Give me a break," but it also may be considered a rude way to say "You don't impress me."

Traditional social courtesies are common. Men offer seats on a bus to older women, women with young children, or pregnant women. Seated passengers commonly offer to hold packages or children for standing passengers. Men open doors for women in urban areas. Chewing gum, combing one's hair, or kissing extensively is not common in public.

Visiting. Informal visits take place at the house gate. Visitors simply knock, ring a buzzer, or otherwise call attention to themselves. Only close friends or relatives of the home's occupants will approach the door before being greeted and invited past the gate. Conversations held on the street are called *meet-and-greet* activities. Visitors inside homes usually are offered a drink and sometimes a meal. Guests sometimes bring their hosts a small gift (fresh produce, garden flowers, a bottle of wine). Families and friends get together often. Because telephones traditionally have been rare in Jamaica and many rural homes still lack them, visits commonly are unannounced. Surprise guests nearly always are welcome.

Eating. Rural families tend to eat dinner together each day after 4 p.m., while urban families may eat together only on weekends because of work and school schedules. Many Jamaicans say a prayer of thanks before or after meals.

Meals are usually sociable and not overly formal when guests are present. Buffet meals are popular, as is eating outdoors. Jamaicans eat in the continental style; the fork is in the left hand and the knife remains in the right. While family meals may be casual, good table manners in public are considered an important social refinement.

Restaurant bills usually include a service charge, but if not, one leaves a tip of 10 to 15 percent. Caterers, restaurants, and street vendors often sell *take-away* (take-out) meals served in boxes. Roadside stands or carts commonly feature pineapples, melons, and water coconuts sold as quick snacks or thirst quenchers. Because eating while walking is considered inappropriate, people often eat snacks on the spot.

LIFESTYLE

Family. The family structure varies in Jamaica according to several factors, including one's social standing. For example, families in lower socio-economic groups usually are larger than those in the middle or upper classes. In addition, some women in lower-income groups have several children by different men, known as *baby fathers*. The fathers refer to these women as *baby mothers* (as opposed to "wives" or "girlfriends"). Although baby mothers are common, many women prefer the social approval that comes with being married to their children's father. However, it is considered normal for both men and women to have more than one relationship, perhaps resulting in children, prior to marriage. While some associate motherhood with femininity or blessings and fatherhood with virility, caring for children generally is seen as a serious responsibility and financial commitment. Women assume the primary responsibility for child care, but children often live with grandparents, relatives, or godparents when the mother works outside the home. Therefore, in these circles the extended family plays a crucial role. Most families live in houses or town houses, built of concrete or (in rural areas) wood. Apartments are not common.

Dating and Marriage. Young people socialize at dances, movies, parties, church functions, the market, and on the street. Wealthier Jamaicans often date in pairs and marry in their twenties, before children are born. Lower-income youth tend to socialize in groups that often include neighbors, cousins, and close friends. Marriage ceremonies often are prohibitively expensive, with a church ceremony that includes decorations, formal clothing, a motorcade, and a party with much food, drink, and music. Therefore, lower-income couples may marry only after years together as a couple, usually after children are born. Family and neighbors may also help pay for the wedding. A formal marriage is sometimes associated with joining a church, giving up vices, and leading a responsible life.

Diet. Jamaican food generally is spicy. Breakfast often includes *saltfish* (salted, dried cod), which is the national dish. It may also include *ackee* (a rich red fruit) when it is in season. Fish may be eaten two or more times a week. Stews and curries (such as curried goat) are popular. *Jerk* (spicy barbecued pork or chicken, roasted in open pits or on makeshift grills) is often served with a bland, hard bread or with yams. *Bammy* (cassava bread), a staple food, is still prepared in the style of the Arawak Indians. *Bammy* or *festival* (fried dough) with fish is a frequent combination. Many Jamaicans enjoy Indian and Chinese dishes. *Box food* (food eaten out of a box when one is away from home) generally consists of fish, chicken, or goat served over rice and *peas* (any one of a variety of legumes). Boiled green bananas or fried dumplings are popular side dishes. Fruits (mangoes, bananas, papaya, pineapples, oranges, grapefruit, tomatoes) are plentiful, and one or more types of fruit usually are in season. Vegetables also play an important role in the diet. A typical salad includes lettuce and tomatoes or cabbage and carrots. Coffee, herbal teas, fruit juices, drinks made from boiled roots, and a variety of alcoholic beverages are common. All hot drinks (coffee, cocoa, green tea, etc.) are called *tea*. Beer and white rum are especially popular. Women usually drink less than men and do not generally drink alcohol from the bottle.

Recreation. Cricket and *football* (soccer) are the most popular sports in Jamaica. Many people also enjoy table tennis, field hockey, tennis, and *athletics* (track-and-field). Girls play netball (a game similar to basketball) in school. Dominoes is the favorite game among men and may be played indoors or outdoors. People attend discos, community centers, and clubs. A frequent pastime is listening to music from stereo systems outside of bars. Other leisure activities include going to movies and enjoying spectator sports such as boxing or team competitions. Various festivals, community events, and church activities provide entertainment and recreation. Jamaicans also take advantage of the outdoor activities their island offers, such as hiking and swimming.

The Arts. The most famous Jamaican musician, Bob Marley, used reggae music to advocate tolerance and justice. An annual festival commemorates his birthday (February 6). Reggae is still the most popular form of music, but Jamaicans are also fond of jazz, calypso, and gospel. Young Jamaicans enjoy *soca* (a mixture of soul music from the United States and calypso); *soca* is especially popular during Carnival. Another popular form of music is *dancehall*, which incorporates elements of reggae, disco, and rap.

Theatrical comedies performed in *patois* are popular. Galleries throughout the island display local fine art, and open-air markets sell folk art. These folk arts are produced primarily for tourists and include basketry, pottery, and textiles.

Holidays. Jamaican holidays include New Year's Day, Ash Wednesday, Easter (Friday–Monday), Labor Day (23 May, a day for community improvement projects), Independence Day (first Monday in August), National Heroes Day (third Monday in October), Christmas, and Boxing Day (26 Dec.). Boxing Day is a day to visit family and friends. Maroons celebrate 6 January as their independence day. Carnival is a springtime festival involving parades, costumes, and parties.

Commerce. Business hours generally extend from 9 a.m. to 5 p.m., Monday through Thursday, and until 4 p.m. on Friday. Banks close weekdays around 2 p.m.; on Fridays they stay open later. Grocery stores and other shops might open earlier and close later, depending on the town and type of shop. Street vendors sell goods and food from early in the morning until

Jamaica

late at night. Vendors at open-air markets often are willing to bargain on the price of merchandise. Produce prices, however, tend to be more fixed. Those from lower-income households shop often, as they have less access to refrigeration.

SOCIETY

Government. Jamaica's government is based on the British model of parliamentary democracy. The PNP and JLP are the only major political parties. Elections must be held at least every five years. The voting age is 18. Parliament consists of an elected House of Representatives with 60 members and an appointed Senate with 21 members. The prime minister (currently Percival James "P.J." Patterson) appoints 13 and the opposition appoints 8. The cabinet, led by the prime minister, holds executive power. Although Jamaica is independent, it is part of the Commonwealth of Nations and recognizes Queen Elizabeth II as head of state. She is represented in Jamaica by a governor-general (Howard Cooke).

Economy. Bauxite (an aluminum ore) and tourism are key elements of Jamaica's economy. Bauxite, aluminum, sugar, bananas, rum, and coffee are important exports. Agriculture employs more than 20 percent of the population.

Jamaica is part of the Caribbean Basin Initiative (CBI), a program designed to improve economic relations between Caribbean nations and the United States. It is also a member of the Caribbean Community and Common Market (CARICOM), a regional economic association. The currency is the Jamaican dollar (JMD).

A growing portion of the population earns a livable income, but unemployment is high. Slow economic growth inhibits greater prosperity, and both urban and rural poverty remain a challenge. About a fifth of the total population lives below the poverty line.

Transportation and Communications. Cars and buses are the most common form of transportation. Following the British tradition, traffic moves on the left side of the road. Most roads are paved but are often in poor repair. Buses serve all parts of the island and can be crowded; accurate schedules are not always available. *Route taxis* follow set local routes with set fares. Regular taxis, with negotiated fares, are plentiful. Jamaica's communications system is modern and adequate, although rural homes seldom have phones. Public phone booths, usually found near police stations and post offices, require phone cards, which are purchased at post offices and some stores. There are several radio and television stations as well as various daily newspapers.

Education. When and where children attend school may depend on their economic background. Lower-class children ages three through six attend basic schools, followed by primary schools until age twelve. Upper class children usually begin attending preparatory schools at age six and continue until age twelve. Secondary schools for youths ages twelve through seventeen include high schools, as well as technical, comprehensive, and vocational schools. Secondary enrollment is limited and admission is determined by competitive examinations. A lack of money for fees, uniforms, lunch, and transportation makes attendance difficult for some, although some government aid is available. More than 90 percent of children

DEVELOPMENT DATA
Human Dev. Index* rank . . . . 79 of 177 countries
   Adjusted for women . . . . 62 of 144 countries
Real GDP per capita $3,980
Adult literacy rate . . . . 84 percent (male); 91 (female)
Infant mortality rate . . . . 13 per 1,000 births
Life expectancy . . . . 74 (male); 78 (female)

who enter school finish the primary or prep level. About 60 percent of all eligible youth are enrolled in secondary schools.

Most Jamaican adults have completed at least five years of education. Young women increasingly recognize the economic benefits of an education. More young women than young men attend secondary school and graduate school. Higher education is provided at six teacher-training colleges; a college of art, science, and technology; a college of agriculture; schools of music, art, dance, and drama; and the University of the West Indies. The Caribbean Institute of Technology trains Jamaicans in programming and software development. University graduates who fail to find work in Jamaica often seek opportunities in North America or Europe.

Health. Most large towns or cities have a hospital. Medical clinics are community-based and available across Jamaica. The public healthcare system covers basic care for all citizens at low cost or for free. Payment might be required in some cases, especially for more complicated care. Private facilities are available. Piped water is safe to drink. Life expectancy has risen in recent years.

AT A GLANCE
Events and Trends.
- Hurricane Ivan hit Jamaica in September 2004, unleashing 155 mph winds in addition to flooding and huge tides. In the aftermath of the storm, it was discovered that at least 15 people had died, and homes and other buildings across the island were destroyed.
- In March 2004, Haiti's ousted president, Jean-Bertrand Aristide, sought temporary asylum in Jamaica before moving to South Africa. Aristide fled Haiti after a violent revolt but vowed to return and regain the presidency.
- Jamaica has one of the world's highest murder rates. More than 1,440 people were killed in 2004. The tally beat the previous record of 1,139 in 2001. Many of the deaths were related to gang violence. The government hopes to bring peace to Jamaica by boosting the size of the police force and is considering introducing the death penalty.
- In September 2003, Jamaican prime minister Patterson said he wants his country leave the British Commonwealth and become a republic by the time his term ends in 2007.

Contact Information. Embassy of Jamaica, 1520 New Hampshire Avenue NW, Washington, DC 20036; phone (202) 452-0660; web site www.emjamusa.org. Jamaica Tourist Board, 1320 South Dixie Highway, Suite 1101, Coral Gables, FL 33146; phone (800) 233-4582; web site visitjamaica.com.

CultureGrams™
People. The World. You.

ProQuest Information and Learning Company
300 North Zeeb Road, P.O. Box 1346
Ann Arbor, Michigan 48106 USA
Toll Free: 1.800.528.6279
Fax: 1.800.864.0019
www.culturegrams.com

Mexico (United Mexican States)

CultureGrams World Edition 2006

NORTH AMERICA

BACKGROUND

Land and Climate. Covering 761,602 square miles (1,972,550 square kilometers), Mexico is about three times the size of Texas, or one-fifth the size of the United States. It shares its northern border with the United States and its southern border with Guatemala and Belize. Mexico is rich in natural resources, including oil, natural gas, gold, silver, and coal. Temperatures and rainfall vary with elevation and region. The north is generally dry and hot, and there is a large desert region. Humidity is higher in the southeast, where tropical jungles are found, and along coastal areas. Rain falls mainly in the summer. The high and cooler central plateau, where Mexico City is located, is bounded by two mountain ranges: the Sierra Madre Oriental and Sierra Madre Occidental. Mountains, including some volcanoes, cover two-thirds of the country.

History. Mexico's history boasts a long line of advanced indigenous civilizations whose accomplishments rival those of the Egyptians and early Europeans. They built huge empires, were skilled artisans, and created accurate calendars. The Olmecs were among the first inhabitants of the area, around 2000 B.C. The Mayan Empire built incredible cities throughout North and Central America but fell in the 12th century. The Aztecs were the last great empire, conquered by the Spanish in 1521. While the Spanish assimilated some aspects of the Aztec and other native cultures, the destruction of these civilizations was widespread. Spaniards brought Christianity to the land and ruled until the 19th century.

Mexico was one of the first countries to revolt against Spain. Led by a priest named Miguel Hidalgo, the drive for independence began in September 1810 and ended in 1821. A constitution was adopted in 1824 and a republic was established. However, Antonio López de Santa Ana took power in 1833 and ruled as a dictator. During his regime, Mexico diminished in size as it lost territory comprising Texas and much of the current western United States. Santa Ana resigned in 1855 and Benito Juárez became president. In 1861, French troops invaded Mexico City and named the Austrian archduke Maximilian the emperor of Mexico. Forces under Juárez overthrew Maximilian in 1867. Dictator Porfirio Díaz came to power in 1877 and was overthrown in 1910, when Mexico entered a period of internal political unrest and violence. That period, which ended in the 1920s and produced a new constitution, became known as Mexico's social revolution.

Political unrest continued in the 1930s, but the situation stabilized in the 1940s. The Institutional Revolutionary Party (PRI) emerged as the national leader in 1929; it ruled the country as a single party and restricted political dissent for many years. Many changes did take place, but none challenged the PRI's domination. Elected in 1988, President Carlos Salinas de Gortari signed the North American Free Trade Agreement (NAFTA) with the United States and Canada. After his term he fled the country because of allegations of corruption.

Events in the mid-1990s helped weaken the PRI's power: The Zapatista National Liberation Army (EZLN) staged a 1994 rebellion in the state of Chiapas to protest government policy toward indigenous peoples. Charges of corruption against high-level government officials and the 1994 assassination of a PRI presidential candidate shocked the ruling party. The PRI replacement candidate took office in 1994 but immediately encountered an economic and currency crisis. In 1997 the PRI lost control of the lower house in Congress for the first time since its founding. In July 2000, Vicente Fox of the National Action Party (PAN) was elected president, ending

Mexico

more than 70 years of PRI control of the government. Government priorities include strengthening the economy, reducing violence and corruption, and improving living conditions for Mexico's citizens.

THE PEOPLE

Population. Mexico's population of around 105 million people is growing at about 1.2 percent annually. Roughly 60 percent of the population is of mixed Spanish and indigenous heritage. Roughly thirty percent belongs to various indigenous groups. Most of these are descendants of the Mayans and Aztecs. About 9 percent is of European ancestry. Most Mexicans tend to identify with their indigenous and Spanish heritage. Mexico City, the capital, is one of the largest cities in the world; its metropolitan area has a population of almost 22 million. Guadalajara and Monterrey are also major population centers.

Language. Spanish is the official language. The Spanish spoken in Mexico is somewhat unique in pronunciation and the use of idioms. One characteristic is the abundant use of diminutives to express small size, endearment or politeness: *chico* (small) becomes *chiquito*; *abuelo* (grandfather) becomes *abuelito*, etc. As many as one hundred indigenous languages are still spoken in parts of Mexico, including Tzotzil and Tzeltal (Mayan dialects), Nahuatl (Aztec), Otomi, Zapotec, and Mixtec. Most people who speak an indigenous language also speak some Spanish. English is taught at secondary schools, but competence in English is rare in most areas.

Religion. The majority of Mexicans (89 percent) are Roman Catholic, although many do not attend church services regularly. The Catholic Church has greatly influenced the culture, attitudes, and history of all Mexicans, and Catholic holidays are celebrated widely. The Virgin of Guadalupe is the patron saint of Mexico and a national symbol. According to legend, she appeared several times to an indigenous man named Juan Diego in December 1531. Other Christian churches are also active in Mexico; some are growing quite rapidly.

The Mexican constitution was drafted during the revolution in an attempt to transfer power from the Catholic Church to the people. It guaranteed freedom of worship but banned public displays of worship and forbid churches to own property or exist as legal entities. In 1992, the law was changed, endowing churches with more legal rights. Although many officials ignored the previous restrictions, the new law relieves tension between the state and various religions—without forcing the government to endorse a specific church.

General Attitudes. Mexicans value friendship, humor, honesty, hard work, and personal honor. They also respect individuals who use their ingenuity to solve daily problems. Social status is measured by wealth, family name, and education. *Machismo*, the ideal of a strong, forceful man, is still prevalent. The elderly are respected, particularly in indigenous communities. Mexicans are patriotic and generally proud of their country, despite its challenges. They may call people from the United States *americanos* or *norteamericanos* but may sometimes remind U.S. citizens that Mexico is also part of North America. The most common term used to refer to English speakers from the United States is *gringo*, a Spanish word meaning foreigner.

Mexicans traditionally have had a relaxed attitude toward time, although this is changing in urban areas. Generally, they believe individuals are more important than schedules.

Personal Appearance. Most Mexicans, especially in urban areas, wear clothing that is also common in the United States. Many indigenous groups wear traditional clothing—either daily or for festivals. In some areas, a man wears a wool poncho (*sarape*) over his shirt and pants when it is cold. He also may wear a wide-brimmed straw hat. Rural men and professional men in the north may wear cowboy hats, boots, and jeans. Rural women wear dresses or skirts, often covered by an apron. They may use a shawl (*rebozo*) to carry a child, cover the head or arms, or help support water buckets carried on the head. Fabric designs and colors can be characteristic of a specific region. People often dress up for special occasions.

CUSTOMS AND COURTESIES

Greetings. Mexicans usually greet with a handshake or nod of the head, although friends commonly embrace. People may also shake hands while saying good-bye. Women often greet with a kiss on the cheek, and men may greet close female friends in the same way. Common verbal greetings include *¡Buenos días!* (Good morning), *¡Buenas tardes!* (Good afternoon), *¡Buenas noches!* (Good evening/night), and *¿Cómo está?* (How are you?). A casual greeting is *¡Hola!* (Hello). Mexican males often make *piropos* (flirtatious personal comments) in passing to females, to which the females generally do not respond.

Mexicans commonly have more than one given name and two last names (e.g., *José Luis Martínez Salinas*). The next-to-last name comes from the father and functions as the official surname, while the final name is from the mother. Coworkers address one another by professional title followed by the first surname (e.g., *Doctor Martínez*). Acquaintances or coworkers without a title are addressed as *Señor* (Mr.), *Señora* (Mrs.), or *Señorita* (Miss), followed by the surname. Respected elders often are addressed as *Don* or *Doña*, followed by a given name.

Gestures. Mexicans typically stand close to each other while talking, sometimes touching their friend's clothing. They often use hand and arm gestures in conversation. Indigenous peoples generally are more reserved and often touch their mouth or cheek when they speak. A person can indicate "no" by shaking the hand from side to side with the index finger extended and palm outward. The "thumbs up" gesture expresses approval. Tossing items is offensive; one hands items directly to another person. If someone sneezes, a person may say *¡Salud!* (Health). If passing between conversing individuals is unavoidable, one says *Con permiso* (Excuse me). It is considered important to say *Gracias* (Thank you) for any favor or commercial service rendered.

Visiting. Mexicans are very hospitable. Unexpected visitors usually are welcomed and served refreshments, such as juice or a soft drink. Refusing refreshments may be considered impolite. Unannounced visits are fairly common, but as more people get telephones, it is becoming common to call ahead to ensure the hosts are home. Mexicans enjoy conversing and socializing with relatives or friends. At a dinner party, the meal might not be served until after 8 p.m. because people work late and enjoy socializing before eating. Guests are expected to relax and do not offer to help the host unless it is evident some help is needed. They stay for conversation rather than leave directly after the meal. It is considered rude to depart without taking leave of the hosts. On special occasions such as Mother's Day, gifts are important and in some areas serenading is still popular.

Eating. Although schedules for eating vary, many Mexicans eat four daily meals: a light breakfast, an early lunch, a main meal in the late afternoon, and a light snack called a *cena* or *merienda* at night. The main meal may consist of soup or salad, main dish, and dessert (*postre*). Eating as a family is common. Urban professionals often eat meals at restaurants or streetside stands. Food purchased on the street usually is eaten at the stand where the item is bought. It is inappropriate for adults to eat while walking on the street. Spicy food is called *picante*, while hot (temperature) food is called *caliente*. *Picante* dishes are often eaten with bland foods such as bread, tortillas, or rice to relieve the burning sensation. When eating, Mexicans keep both hands above the table. Some foods are eaten with utensils, while others are eaten by hand or by using pieces of tortillas to scoop food. Meals usually are not rushed. One should always ask to be excused when leaving a table or room.

LIFESTYLE

Family. Except in urban areas, where the trend is to have smaller families, Mexican families generally have more than three children. Family unity and responsibility are high priorities. The divorce rate is relatively low, partly because of the dominance of the Catholic faith, which does not approve of divorce. In many families, the father is the leader and provides economic support, while the mother is responsible for domestic duties. However, in some ethnic groups the mother is the leader, and more women from almost all groups are entering the formal workplace. Rural men and women often work together in the fields. A household, especially in rural areas, may include members of the extended family. Children generally live with their parents until they marry and sometimes after they marry.

Dating and Marriage. When dating, a young man often meets the young woman at a prearranged place rather than picking her up at her home. However, parental approval of the activity and of the boyfriend is important. In some rural areas, it is considered a mark of poor character for a young woman to go out alone after dark, so a young man may call on her at home. Many people marry first in a civil ceremony and then in a church, following Catholic traditions. Wedding celebrations include music, dancing, games, and food. Common-law marriage is also practiced and recognized. Teen pregnancy is common, and while abortion is not legal, it is available. However, unmarried women tend to keep the child and rear it with the help of their parents.

Diet. Staple foods include corn, beans, rice, and chilies. These typically are combined with spices, vegetables, and meats or fish. Some foods and dishes are regional, but others are common throughout the nation. Cornmeal or flour tortillas are eaten everywhere. Other common foods include *tortas* (hollow rolls stuffed with meat, cheese, or beans), *quesadillas* (tortillas baked or fried with cheese), *mole* (spicy or sweet sauce served with meat), and *tacos* (folded tortillas with meat or other filling). Popular soups include *pozole* (pork-and-corn soup), *birria* (goat soup), and *menudo* (spicy tripe soup). *Enchiladas* are tortillas filled with meat and covered in a chili sauce. *Tamales* are cornmeal dough stuffed with meat, cheese, fruit, or other filling; they are wrapped in a corn husk or banana leaf and steamed. People often make homemade fruit drinks, but commercially produced soda is everywhere. Popular "Mexican" foods and restaurants in the United States usually are very different from those found in Mexico.

Recreation. *Fútbol* (soccer) is Mexico's most popular sport; the national team has competed in several World Cups. Bullfighting draws the next highest number of spectators. Professional wrestling (*la lucha*) has a large following. Popular participation sports include baseball, basketball, tennis, and volleyball. Mexicans enjoy their own form of rodeo called *charreada*, which is often accompanied by a fair-like atmosphere. Many recreational activities include music and dancing. Daylong *fiestas* and weeklong festivals nearly always include fireworks, feasts, and bullfights. Watching television is a favorite leisure activity, especially in urban areas. *Telenovelas* (soap operas) are especially popular.

The Arts. Song and dance are integral to Mexican society. Originating in Mexico, *mariachi* music has found many international audiences. *Mariachi* bands vary in size but generally consist of a singer, violins, trumpets, and various guitars. *Corridos*, songs that tell stories, and *ranchera* are other forms of traditional music. Mexico has become a major recording and distribution center for the Americas. Dancing, such as the *jarabe tapatío* (Mexican Hat Dance), often accompanies traditional music and *fiestas*.

Revolutionary themes dominated all types of art the first half of the century and remain important today. For example, brightly colored murals commissioned by the government in the 1920s and 1930s decorate many public buildings. Diego Rivera and other Mexican artists inspired muralist movements worldwide. Museums feature the art of ancient civilizations as well as fine art. Textiles, pottery, and silverwork are popular and can be seen in many markets.

Holidays. National public holidays include New Year's Day; Constitution Day (5 Feb.), which also marks the beginning of *Carnaval*, the week of parties and parades before Lent; Birthday of Benito Juárez (21 Mar.); Labor Day (1 May); *Cinco de Mayo* (5 May), which celebrates an 1862 victory over the French; Independence Day (16 Sept.), which is marked by a presidential address and *El grito* (the cry of freedom) on the evening of 15 September; Columbus Day or *Día de la Raza*, which celebrates indigenous heritage (12 Oct.); Revolution Day (20 Nov.); and Christmas Day. Many offices close for a half day on Mother's Day (10 May), when schools sponsor special festivities.

Major religious holidays include St. Anthony's Day (17 Jan.), when children take their pets to church to be blessed; *Semana Santa* (Palm Sunday–Easter Sunday); Corpus Christi (May or June); and Assumption (15 Aug.). During the period known as *Día de los Muertos*, or Day of the Dead (1–2 Nov.), families gather to celebrate life while they honor the dead, sweep graves, build special altars to honor the newly dead, and place items on graves to accompany spirits on their journey to heaven. Day of the Virgin Guadalupe (12 Dec.) and *Noche Buena* (Christmas Eve) are so popular that most offices and businesses honor them as public holidays. Christmas celebrations begin on 16 December with nightly parties (*posadas*) and end on Day of the Kings (6 Jan.), when most children in central and southern Mexico get their presents.

Each town also has an annual festival that includes a religious ceremony, meal, and dance. Many people try to return home for these events.

Commerce. Businesses generally are open from 9 a.m. to 6 or 7 p.m., although many shops in smaller towns close between 2 and 4 p.m. for the midday meal, particularly in hotter areas. Legislation passed in March 1999 makes it impossible for government workers to take the traditional afternoon *siesta* break because it limits their lunches to one hour and does not allow them to work after 6 p.m. Private companies may offer midday breaks at their own discretion. Business contacts often are made during lunch breaks. These are largely social meetings,

Mexico

with business conducted in the last few minutes. Urban residents buy basic goods in supermarkets and smaller neighborhood stores. Street vendors and open-air markets are common and often open to bargaining. In small towns, weekly market days provide food and other goods. Government offices usually close by 4 p.m. Standard banking hours are 9 a.m. to 5 p.m.

SOCIETY

Government. Mexico's federal republic of 31 states and one federal district operates under a central government led by a president (currently Vicente Fox). While states technically are autonomous, the central government controls sectors such as education, security, and national industries. A president can serve only one six-year term, and a legislator cannot serve two consecutive terms. The legislature is composed of a 128-seat Senate and 500-seat Chamber of Deputies. Voting is considered a duty for adults 18 and older but is not enforced.

Economy. Service industries employ the highest proportion of Mexicans and create the largest part of the gross domestic product, although heavier industries such as mining, manufacturing, and petroleum also are important. Pemex, the giant government-owned petroleum company, is one of the world's largest oil companies. Tourism brings several billion dollars to the country. Agricultural pursuits employ one-fifth of the labor force. Another major source of income for the country is money sent home by those who have left the country. Money sent home by Mexicans in the United States totaled more than $10 billion in 2003.

The economy has seen some growth since 1993, when Mexico signed NAFTA with the United States and Canada. NAFTA lowered trade barriers and led to an increased number of *maquiladoras* (border industries), where U.S. investment employs Mexican labor. Economists are divided on how much NAFTA may have helped Mexico's economy. Although some sectors have grown, others, such as agriculture, have been harmed by competition from duty-free, heavily subsidized products from the United States. In addition, *maquiladoras* have drawn some criticism for not meeting typical U.S. guidelines for wages, safety, or environmental regulations. Mexico also has entered free-trade agreements with the European Union, much of Central America, and Israel.

Most Mexicans have access to basic resources; however, economic opportunities are fewer among the indigenous, rural, and southern populations. About 40 percent of Mexicans live in poverty. The currency is the Mexican *peso* (MXN).

Transportation and Communications. Personal cars are common in urban areas, but the majority of Mexicans rely on public transportation. Buses and minibuses are plentiful and inexpensive. Mexico City has a fine subway system. Taxis are numerous, but many operate illegally. The highway system has grown steadily over the last decade, and Mexico has an extensive system of roads, although many remain unpaved or semipaved. Most people use the private bus system for intercity travel. There are several domestic airlines. Communications are well developed and modern, although many rural families do not have telephones in their homes. Numerous radio and television stations and daily newspapers serve the public.

Education. Education is compulsory and free between ages six

DEVELOPMENT DATA

Human Dev. Index* rank .... 53 of 177 countries
   Adjusted for women........... 50 of 144 countries
Real GDP per capita $8,970
Adult literacy rate .... 93 percent (male); 89 (female)
Infant mortality rate .... 22 per 1,000 births
Life expectancy .... 70 (male); 76 (female)

and fifteen. However, attendance is not enforced and schools may require that students pay some fees. These obstacles have contributed to the literacy rate, which is about 91 percent nationally, being lower among indigenous and rural populations. After six years of primary education and three years of basic secondary education, students may enter one of two tracks: preuniversity education (three years) or a technical education program (two to three years). Obtaining a university degree takes from three to seven years. The essentially free National Autonomous University of Mexico (UNAM) is prestigious; only one-third of all applicants pass its entrance exams. Enrollment has increased rapidly in the last decade.

Health. By law, all citizens have access to medical services free of charge at government-operated facilities. Medical facilities are good in large cities but limited in remote areas. Traditional remedies and the use of herbs are common in rural areas. Sanitation and access to safe water are problems in some regions. Air pollution is a serious problem in big cities.

AT A GLANCE

Events and Trends.

- In January 2005, ten male gang members were convicted in the murders of 12 women around Ciudad Juarez in northern Mexico. Since 1993, more than 300 women have been raped and murdered in the area. Although the convictions were a small victory, other women in the area continue to be victimized. A federal-level investigation of the murders was finally opened in 2004.
- President Fox's PAN party suffered several defeats during regional elections held in July 2004. The candidates for the opposing PRI gained control from PAN incumbents in three northern states. PAN had already lost many parliamentary seats to the PRI in mid-term elections in 2003.
- In September 2003, World Trade Organization talks in Cancún collapsed after four days of heated debate and massive protests. One major issue was that wealthy countries often sell mass-produced goods to poor countries at prices lower than their own people can make them. However, the wealthy countries do not import a similar amount of goods in return, which forces many people in disadvantaged countries out of business.

Contact Information. Embassy of Mexico, 1911 Pennsylvania Avenue NW, Washington, DC 20006; phone (202) 728-1600; web site www.embassyofmexico.org (access English version). Mexico Tourism Board, (800) 446-3942; web site www.visitmexico.com.

CultureGrams
People. The World. You.

ProQuest Information and Learning Company
300 North Zeeb Road, P.O. Box 1346
Ann Arbor, Michigan 48106 USA
Toll Free: 1.800.528.6279
Fax: 1.800.864.0019
www.culturegrams.com

© 2005 ProQuest Information and Learning Company and Brigham Young University. It is against the law to copy, reprint, store, or transmit any part of this publication in any form by any means without written permission from ProQuest. This document contains native commentary and original analysis, as well as estimated statistics. The content should not be considered strictly factual, and it may not apply to all groups in a nation. *UN Development Programme, Human Development Report 2004 (New York: Oxford University Press, 2004).

CultureGrams World Edition 2006

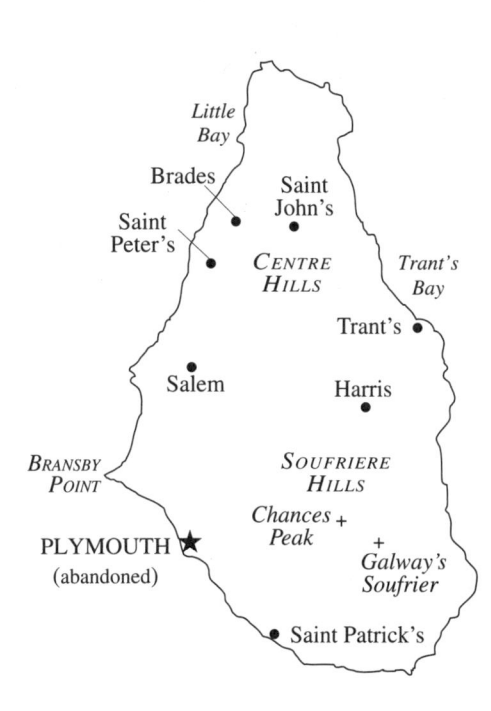

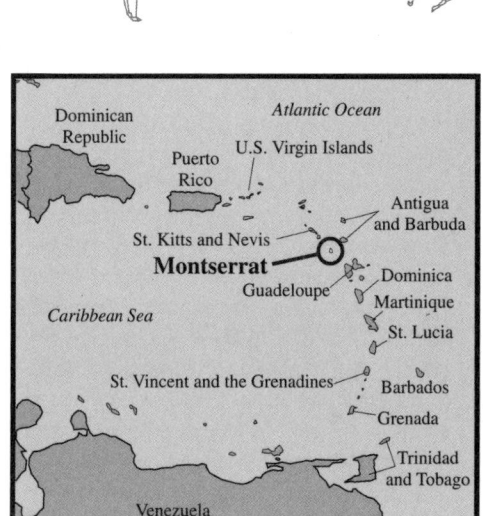

Montserrat

BACKGROUND

Land and Climate. Montserrat is located in the Caribbean Sea about 250 miles (400 kilometers) southeast of Puerto Rico. Part of the British West Indies, it is one of the Leeward Islands of the Lesser Antilles. Montserrat is known as the Emerald Isle, for both its early Irish settlers and its lush vegetation. The island is volcanic in origin and the ground in some volcanic areas still emits sulfur fumes, steam, and boiling water. Chances Peak, the highest mountain, has been the site of recent volcanic activity, which has resulted in the growth of its dome from 3,002 feet (915 meters) to more than 3,220 feet (977 meters). Montserrat's land area had been only 39 square miles (101 square kilometers), roughly half the area of Washington, D.C. Recent flows have increased the landmass slightly to 40 square miles (103 square kilometers). Natural vegetation is confined mostly to the summits of the Centre Hills. Sheltered bays are few and all beaches but one have black volcanic sand.

The climate is tropical; temperatures range from 76 to 86°F (24–30°C) year-round. Rainfall is abundant and there is a continual sea breeze. The wettest months are September through November, while the dry season lasts from March to June. The hurricane season usually occurs between June and November.

History. The pre-Columbian name of Montserrat was Alliouagana ("land of the prickly bush"); it was named by the Carib Indians who overtook the Arawak long before the coming of Europeans. Christopher Columbus sighted Montserrat in 1493, naming it after a monastery near Seville, Spain. However, the Spanish did not settle the island. In 1632, Thomas Warner began settling Montserrat with English and Irish Catholics who were uncomfortable in nearby Protestant Saint Kitts. Wealthy planters emerged as Montserrat developed into a sugar and slave colony in the 17th century. Repression eventually ignited a slave uprising, which failed on St. Patrick's Day in 1768.

In the 17th and 18th centuries, France and Britain fought for dominance over the sugar islands of the Caribbean, and Montserrat changed hands several times. The Treaty of Versailles in 1783 made Montserrat permanently British. It remains a dependent territory of the United Kingdom (UK).

In 1834, Britain's parliament abolished slavery in the Caribbean. Sharecroppers (or black laborers) began cultivating many of the properties that had become burdened by debt and sold. Limes and cotton eventually replaced the sugar industry. Montserrat lime juice was in demand by the British navy for combating scurvy and is believed to be the source of the term *Limey*, a derogatory nickname for people from the United Kingdom.

After the decline of cotton and limes in the 20th century, many Montserratians emigrated to Panama (to work on the Panama Canal), Cuba, the Dominican Republic, the United States, or the UK. When remittances from Montserratians abroad declined, the island turned to real estate and construction, building luxury winter homes for North American and British citizens.

A long-dormant volcano on Chances Peak began rumbling and spewing ash in July 1995. When the capital of Plymouth was ordered evacuated, many residents relocated in the north, while others left the island. The volcano claimed its first fatalities in June 1997 when part of the dome collapsed, sending a flow toward the eastern end of the island. Nineteen people who had returned to the "unsafe zone" were killed and seven villages were destroyed. The largest dome collapse occurred in December 1997, claiming no fatalities but damaging several

Montserrat

southern villages. The southern two-thirds of the island is now uninhabitable and 90 percent of the buildings are abandoned. A central buffer zone is open during daylight hours only, but the northern "safe zone" is not considered dangerous to live in.

In the north, aid from Britain has helped establish housing, government offices, utilities, and other services and institutions previously centered in Plymouth, the abandoned capital in the south. The British government also offered resettlement funds to those who wished to leave. In August 1997, Chief Minister Bertrand "Sonny" Osborne resigned amid public protests when Britain's aid package fell short of expectations. Upon taking office, new Chief Minister David Brandt openly criticized what he believed to be Britain's bias toward evacuation, rather than development, of the island. The governments of England and Montserrat have since begun cooperating on the creation and implementation of a sustainable development plan.

The overall level of volcanic activity decreased during 1998 and 1999, and scientists believed the eruptions had ended. The British government began financing the return of evacuees from the Caribbean and the UK in May and June of 1999. However, in November 1999, the volcano began spewing rock, and in March 2000, it erupted again, crushing many people's hopes to return to the island or to their homes.

In April 2001 elections, voters handed the New People's Liberation Movement (NPLM) a landslide victory. John Osborne became the new chief minister. The government hopes to rebuild the community, boost the economy, and build better relations with Britain.

THE PEOPLE

Population. Montserrat has a population of just over 9,000, concentrated in the safe zone. That number fluctuates, depending on economic opportunities or hardships experienced abroad. The population numbered about 12,000 in early 1995, but thousands have emigrated to Antigua, other Caribbean islands, Britain, or North America. Now that many who had left the island have returned, the population is growing at 1 percent. The majority of Montserratians are of African descent, but there has been a relatively recent infusion of North American, European, Caribbean, and East Indian residents. A number of tourists spend most of the year in Montserratian villas, which they rent or own.

Since the volcanic destruction of the southern part of the island, the once rural north has become more populated. For example, the village of Lookout was built to house displaced Montserratians, and many suburban areas are expanding.

Language. The official language is English, but most people speak a West Indian dialect. The dialect, referred to as *speaking Montserratian* or *speaking dialect*, is a form of English mixed with elements of Irish brogue and various African tongues. In Montserratian, *me* indicates both first person singular and past tense; therefore, *Me no me know* means "I did not know." *Fu true* is a common phrase that adds emphasis. For example, *Me vex fu true* means "I was really angry." Some people consider using the dialect improper, but most enjoy the way it makes speech more colorful and even poetic.

Religion. Montserratians are genuine about their religious devotion. This is manifest in the dignity and respect with which they treat each other and strangers. Anglican, Methodist, and Roman Catholic are the main Christian denominations. The Seventh-day Adventist Church, Pentecostal, and other Christian churches are assuming increasing importance. Religion affects many aspects of daily life. Public schools have daily prayer and gospel singing before classes begin. Most public functions are opened and sometimes closed with prayer.

General Attitudes. Montserrat's culture reflects African, European, and Caribbean influences. Television and other communication media are further modifying the culture. Montserratians take great pride in their country and, more recently, in their African roots. Friendliness, forthrightness, and honesty are viewed as desirable qualities. Interactions are easy and amiable, and most people display politeness, courtesy, and respect to all. The general attitude is one of tolerance and "live and let live." People generally take the time to talk with each other and consider relationships more important than schedules. Therefore, being late is not a problem, and an event will sometimes last much later than advertised. Montserratians are observant; very little goes unnoticed when they watch a passerby, a group, a scene, or an activity.

While the volcano has introduced a stressful element of uncertainty, most Montserratians face the future with optimism, perseverance, and humor. Many emigrants would like to return when housing is available and/or volcanic activity subsides. The destruction caused by the volcano has drawn remaining islanders together as they join in community improvement projects.

Personal Appearance. Montserratians wear their finest clothes to church or other important social functions. Women wear dresses or nice skirts and blouses to work, along with sandals or tennis shoes. Men wear sport shirts or a *shirt-jacket* (square-cut cotton shirt), slacks, and shoes. Tight-fitting clothing and ties are seldom worn because of the warm climate. Loose-fitting clothes made of lightweight fabric are most comfortable and therefore popular. Older rural women almost always wear skirts instead of pants, but younger urban women do wear pants.

CUSTOMS AND COURTESIES

Greetings. Montserratian greetings include the more formal *Good morning*, *Good day*, *Good evening*, and *Good night*, as well as the casual *You alright?*, which means "How are you?" The response is *Okay*. When parting, people might say *Goodbye* or *All the best*.

People often shake hands or touch when greeting. Friends may remain holding hands for some minutes while they converse. Young people sometimes touch clenched fists after a traditional handshake to show solidarity. When passing friends or acquaintances, people may raise the index finger of one or both hands, palms forward, as a silent acknowledgment. Drivers commonly honk horns or flash headlights (during the day) to greet friends who are walking or driving by.

When addressing friends and relatives, Montserratians use colorful nicknames that are usually acquired in childhood. Some nicknames also may be acquired in adulthood as a result of one's occupation, personality, body type, etc. Acquaintances might use one's nickname as well, but formal situations call for the use of given names and titles. An older person or superior at work might be called *Mas* (for men) or *Miss* (for women), but most people use *Mr.*, *Mrs.*, or *Miss*.

Gestures. Montserratians are affectionate and loving. They commonly touch each other's hands, arms, or shoulders while talking. Hand gestures might be used to emphasize verbal expressions, especially between friends. People often use a quick "pssst" or hissing sound to get one's attention while walking by or when in a crowd.

Visiting. Montserratians are friendly with their neighbors and often stop by to see how they are doing or to talk about the latest island news. Neighbors might bring homemade gifts such as banana bread or guava juice. People often have house parties for birthdays, anniversaries, graduations, or other special occasions. When they get together, the atmosphere is amiable, courteous, and relaxed. Invited guests usually are offered at least something to drink (soft drinks, juice, etc.). Visitors rarely leave empty-handed. Hosts send guests away with a gift (garden produce, tea leaves, canned goods) or make profuse apologies if nothing is available.

Men commonly socialize and discuss politics at the local *rum shop* (neighborhood tavern), where they watch television, play dominoes, listen to music, and eat chicken or bread. Women more commonly socialize in the home or at their children's activities.

Eating. Lunch and dinner are the main meals, as breakfast is usually light. Many Montserratians eat lunch at restaurants. They might have fried chicken and *chips* (french fries), a hamburger, or *pelau* (rice, beans, and chicken). Bread and cheese are eaten for a quick meal. Families usually eat dinner together at home. Barbecues are a popular activity for community or family gatherings.

LIFESTYLE

Family. The extended family is the primary social unit in Montserrat. Grandparents often live with their children's families and help raise the grandchildren. Siblings usually have the same mother but may have different fathers. Women generally hold the family together, caring for the household and commonly working outside the home. Men support their families and help raise children with a firm but loving hand. Discipline is stressed and children are well behaved.

Volcanic activity disrupted family life for many. Those from the south and east were forced to abandon their homes, land, and livestock. School and business closures, concerns for safety, and inadequate housing forced some families to splinter: women and children emigrated and men remained behind.

Most current residents are homeowners. Although many homes built since the volcano eruption reflect British and Caribbean influences, others are built after the Monserratian style. They include three to four bedrooms, a bathroom, laundry room, kitchen, and dining room. Concrete walls generally are painted in bright pastel colors, and floors are tiled. Poorer families build their houses of wood. Most homes have a porch and a plot of ground for flowers or vegetable gardens.

Dating and Marriage. Dating begins in secondary school and revolves around social or school functions. Young couples enjoy attending cricket matches, basketball games, or concerts. Nighttime drives are popular. At church *fetes* (parties for fund-raising), young people gather to enjoy the games, music, food, and fun.

Couples marry in their twenties or thirties and begin to raise a family. Churches stress formal marriage, but common-law unions are not unusual. There are many single mothers, but they generally receive support from the fathers of their children. Weddings traditionally are short ceremonies held in a church. After the ceremony, the newlyweds leave the church in a car adorned with ribbons, lace, and balloons. Drivers sound their horns as they parade through the streets behind the bridal car. A formal reception follows in which gowns and tuxedoes are standard attire. At the reception, the bride, groom, and their parents give testimonials in tribute to each other's families while toasting with champagne. Musical entertainment and dancing follow as guests enjoy drinks and food, including *goat water* (stewed mutton). Family and friends offer gifts and typically help defray the cost of the wedding. People may be offended if they are not invited to a wedding or involved in the preparations.

Diet. Because of the cost of imported goods, the island had attempted to become more self-sufficient in food production. However, volcanic activity destroyed much of the agricultural land. Still, Montserratians—even those living abroad or in temporary accommodations—take pride in their *kitchen gardens*. These small plots produce fruits (guavas, mangoes, papaya, etc.), *ground provisions* (root crops such as yams, sweet potatoes, and *tannia*), and herbs for tea. They might also include a small patch of sugarcane. Green bananas and breadfruit are common crops—often boiled and served with steamed fish. While fish and meats are popular, chicken is the most popular. Rice, white potatoes, and bread are also important; there are several small bakeries on the island.

Goat water and *mountain chicken* (actually frog) are popular dishes. Saturday lunch often consists of a highly seasoned stew made from vegetables (peas, pumpkin, sweet and white potatoes, etc.), meat, and flour dumplings. *Souse* (pork pickled in brine and served with cucumber slices) is typical Saturday evening fare. Sunday breakfasts usually consist of *saltfish* (reconstituted dried cod stewed with tomatoes, onions, green peppers, and garlic) served with boiled eggplant and *bakes* (fried flour dumplings). Most older Montserratians drink *bush* (herbal) teas first thing in the morning and last thing at night. Soft drinks, homemade fruit juices, beer, coffee, lemonade, and iced tea are other popular drinks.

Recreation. Cricket is the national sport. During a *test match* (an international cricket competition), schools and businesses often close for a half-day so people can watch Montserratian athletes compete. Basketball, women's netball (similar to basketball), *football* (soccer), tennis, swimming, biking, boating, jogging, and hiking have gained popularity. On weekends, friends enjoy music at *street blockoramas* (open-air parties). *Jumpups* (block parties that involve street dancing) are popular during the Christmas festival or on other special occasions.

The Arts. Cultural activities such as plays, school arts festivals, and folklore and gospel choir concerts enjoy community support. Churches and beaches serve as performance sites. Calypso, *soca* (a mixture of soul music from the United States and calypso music), reggae, gospel, folk, steel pan, and *dub* (disc jockeys rapping street poems) are favorite music genres.

Holidays. Christmas and Easter are the most important holidays. Traditional Christmas practices (giving gifts, singing carols, and attending church) combine with the Montserrat Festival, a carnival featuring cultural shows, calypso competitions, dancing, and parades. Many Montserratians who live overseas return for the festival, which culminates in a New Year's Day parade. Easter is a time for family gatherings and church services.

St. Patrick's Day (17 Mar.) is celebrated as a national holiday in memory of the 1768 slave uprising. Other important holidays include Emancipation Day (first Monday in August), Whitmonday (a church celebration about 50 days after Easter), Labor Day (first Monday in May), and Queen Elizabeth II's Birthday (second Saturday in June).

Commerce. Normal business hours are from 8 a.m. to 4 p.m., with an hour taken for lunch. Businesses close at noon on Wednesdays and Saturdays, and most are closed on Sundays.

Montserrat

Volcanic activity forced many businesses to close permanently, relocate abroad, or relocate several times in the north.

SOCIETY

Government. As a territory of the UK, Montserrat recognizes Queen Elizabeth II as head of state. She is represented on the island by a governor (currently Howard Fergus). The governor's Executive Council consists of a chief minister (currently John Osborne), the attorney general, financial secretary, and three members of the Legislative Council. Following legislative elections, the leader of the majority party generally becomes chief minister. Elections are held at least every five years. The Legislative Council has eleven members, nine of whom are elected. The legal system is based on English common law, and the highest judicial authority is the East Caribbean Supreme Court. The voting age is 18. As Plymouth remains abandoned, government offices are located in Brades.

Economy. Montserrat's economy is small and heavily dependent on imported goods. Despite the devastations of volcanic activity, the people continue to enjoy a decent standard of living. Low unemployment and gradual economic growth persist in the face of many changes. Before 1995, tourism accounted for about a third of the gross domestic product. It now accounts for much less, while government services and construction now provide more jobs. Although the majority of farming land has been rendered useless, agriculture, real estate, and some light industry (mostly assembly) are still important to the economy. Exports have declined sharply, but new hotels are opening, and businesses in the north continue to operate.

Some displaced families rent homes in the north while paying mortgages on their vacated homes in the south. A number of other families are purchasing land and building their own homes. The British government offers some housing and food subsidies, but rent and food costs have increased dramatically. The majority of insurers on the island canceled their property coverage in 1997.

The government is considering areas of potential economic development, including the small business sector, high-tech industries, and tourism. A number of offshore, government-regulated banks are in business. Montserrat is a member of the regional trade organization CARICOM (Caribbean Community and Common Market). The stable East Caribbean dollar (XCD) is the currency.

Transportation and Communications. Villages are linked to each other by paved roads on the western side of the island. Private cars and trucks account for a large portion of traffic. Buses run regularly between Saint John's and Salem; taxis are also available. Regular ferry and helicopter services connect Montserrat to Antigua. A port facility has been built at Little Bay.

Montserrat has reliable telecommunications services, and most homes have telephones and televisions. Privately owned radio stations use satellite technology to link nodes on Montserrat and various Caribbean islands. Satellites also facilitate service for local government-owned Radio Montserrat (ZJB). A weekly newspaper and newsletter are published and available electronically. A monthly newsletter also keeps residents up-to-date on volcanic activity. Many Montserratians, on the island and abroad, use the internet to keep in touch with each other and to stay updated about any new developments on the island.

DEVELOPMENT DATA
Human Dev. Index* rank . . . . NA
　Adjusted for women . . . . NA
Real GDP per capita $3,400
Adult literacy rate . . . . 97 percent (male); 97 (female)
Infant mortality rate . . . . 8 per 1,000 births
Life expectancy . . . . 76 (male); 81 (female)

Education. Given the reduction in students, staff, and facilities, only a handful of nursery schools, primary schools, and secondary schools operate on the island. The education system reflects a strong British influence. Primary and secondary schooling are free. Pupils traditionally attend school for 13 years, and most complete secondary school. After the final *form* (grade), students take *school-leaving* (graduation) exams, which are set by the Caribbean Examinations Council and the London and Cambridge syndicates.

Montserrat's Technical College remains closed. Some Montserratians seek higher education through home-study programs or colleges overseas. The University of the West Indies in Jamaica offers distance education programs.

Health. Montserrat traditionally has been a healthy island with an abundance of clean drinking water. Water storage and pumping facilities have been developed in the safe zone. Volcanic dust and ash measurements are taken regularly because of the concern that long-term exposure could cause lung problems. Hospital facilities are available in St. John's. Free care is provided to children, pregnant women, and the elderly. Working adults have health insurance to cover their medical costs. Private doctors are in practice, and specialists from other countries visit periodically to provide care. Patients requiring special care are flown to other Caribbean islands.

AT A GLANCE
Events and Trends.
- In August 2004, Montserratians who had been living in the United States since much of their island was destroyed were told they would have to return home. U.S. immigration services lifted the temporary protection status that had allowed about 300 islanders to live and work in the United States. Some of the Montserratians are fighting to be able to stay.
- In March 2003, more than 200 people signed a petition to get the island's governor fired, accusing him of harming the economy by keeping nearly two-thirds of the island off-limits because of safety concerns. However, the attempt to oust the governor failed. Eruptions in July 2003 and March 2004 spewed rock and ash over much of the nation's uninhabited areas.

Contact Information. Montserrat Tourist Board, P.O. Box 7, Olveston, Montserrat, West Indies; phone (664) 491-2230; web site www.visitmontserrat.com.

CultureGrams World Edition 2006

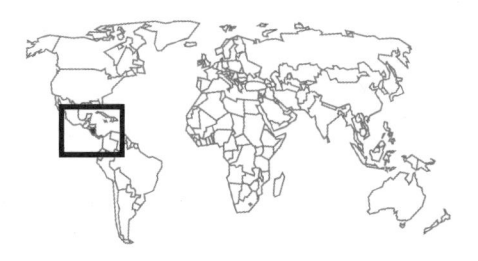

Republic of Nicaragua

BACKGROUND

Land and Climate. Covering 49,998 square miles (129,494 square kilometers), Nicaragua is about the size of Iowa. Although it is the largest country in Central America, only about 20 percent of the land is suitable for cultivation. Lago de Nicaragua is near the Pacific Ocean and is the only freshwater lake in the world known to have sharks, but many people believe the sharks are now extinct. Low central mountains and hills separate the populated west from the east. Forests cover about one-third of the country. Large pine forests are located in the northwest and mountain areas, while tropical rain forests and coastal wetlands spread across the east. Natural resources include gold, silver, copper, lead, zinc, and timber. Nicaragua's climate is tropical, although the highlands are cooler. Humidity is generally high and temperatures average 80°F (27°C). The dry season starts around November and ends around May. Several volcanoes along the Pacific coast are active; tremors and earthquakes are common. Nicaragua occasionally experiences destructive hurricanes and tidal waves.

History. In 1502, Columbus became the first European to visit Nicaragua. It was later settled by Spanish explorers—known as *conquistadores*—who battled and conquered the indigenous people. Spanish settlements date from the 1520s. Indigenous groups resisted the Spanish until finally being conquered in 1552. Britain established settlements along the Mosquito Coast (Costa de Mosquitos) in the 17th century and claimed sovereignty over the coast in 1740. However, Nicaragua essentially was ruled by Spain until it declared independence in 1821. With independence, it became a member of the United Provinces of Central America but chose to be an independent republic in 1838. Political power in the country alternated between liberals and conservatives over the next few decades. The competition sometimes led to violence.

When internal chaos threatened U.S. economic interests in 1909, the U.S. military intervened. During the 1920s and 1930s, guerrillas led by Augusto Cesar Sandino fought the U.S. occupation. A rival general, Anastasio Somoza García, gave orders for Sandino to be assassinated in 1934. In 1936, Somoza seized the presidency. He ruled as a dictator until his assassination in 1956. The Somoza family continued to rule the country, beginning with Somoza's son Luis Somoza Debayle, who died in 1967. He was succeeded by his brother, General Anastasio Somoza Debayle.

In 1962, the Sandinista National Liberation Front (FSLN) or *Sandinistas* revolutionary group was formed with the goal of overthrowing the Somozas. For the next 15 years, Sandinistas carried out various unsuccessful terrorist attacks on General Somoza's National Guard, which was armed by the United States. In 1972, a massive earthquake destroyed Nicaragua's capital city, Managua. During the disaster General Somoza stole relief supplies, which resulted in greater support for the Sandinistas.

Riots broke out in 1978 after a prominent anti-Somoza newspaper editor named Pedro Joaquín Chamorro was assassinated. Sandinistas stormed the national palace in Managua, and civil war followed. General Somoza was forced to flee the country in July 1979, when the Sandinistas took control. Fifty thousand people were killed in the civil war.

The new Marxist-oriented government seized the Somoza fortune, redistributed their lands to the peasants, suspended the constitution, and began tightening controls. Concerned that Sandinistas were aiding Marxist rebels in El Salvador, the U.S. government suspended economic aid to Nicaragua in 1981,

Nicaragua

beginning a decade of strained relations between the two nations. Throughout the 1980s, U.S. funds supported a guerrilla group known as the *Contras*, who were opposed to Sandinista rule. General elections officially brought Sandinista leader Daniel Ortega Saavedra to power in 1985. The United States responded by imposing a trade embargo that severely handicapped the country's economy.

Eventually, the Sandinista government agreed to ensure free elections if the Contras would disarm. In 1990, Ortega was defeated by Violeta Barrios de Chamorro, widow of the assassinated newspaper editor. The United States supported Chamorro's presidency, ended trade restrictions, and pledged aid to rebuild the economy. The Contras began to disband in 1990. Although sporadic violence erupted throughout the early 1990s, widespread fighting did not resume. Striving for national reconciliation and economic recovery, Chamorro's government made some progress: it lowered inflation, depoliticized the army and national police force, and initiated reparations for lands seized in the 1980s. However, Chamorro was unable to solve Nicaragua's severe economic problems.

The 1996 elections brought Arnoldo Aleman to power and marked the first time in a century that a democratically elected civilian president transferred power to another. In 1998 the country suffered widespread damage during Hurricane Mitch. The government's top priorities include rebuilding after a series of natural disasters, strengthening the economy, and addressing its large external debts.

THE PEOPLE

Population. Nicaragua's population of 5.4 million is growing at 2 percent annually. The majority (69 percent) is mestizo, or of mixed Spanish and Indian heritage. Approximately 17 percent is of European descent, about 9 percent is black, and 5 percent is purely indigenous. Most people live on the western plains. The population of Managua, the capital, is more than one million. The Caribbean side is sparsely populated—mostly by smaller ethnic groups. Nicaragua's population is young; nearly 40 percent is younger than age 14.

Language. Spanish is the official and predominant language. Along the Caribbean coast, small groups speak English or other ethnic languages. Creole and Garífuna are common languages among the black population, as are English and Spanish, while some indigenous groups speak Miskito, Sumo, or Rama. Some residents of Managua and other large cities speak English.

Religion. Approximately 85 percent of the population is Roman Catholic. Protestant, Evangelical, and other Christian organizations are also present. Although relations between the Catholic Church and the government were strained in the Sandinista period, the church has maintained a strong influence. Weekly attendance of mass is the norm. Catholic traditions, such as baptisms, communions, and weddings, remain a significant part of family life. Some older women attend mass daily. Religious icons, particularly pictures of the Virgin Mary, decorate many homes and vehicles. When making future plans, people often add *Si Dios quiere* (God willing) as a qualifier to their commitment. Freedom of religion is guaranteed.

General Attitudes. Nicaraguans enjoy being sociable. They value honesty, friendliness, respect, and good humor. They are kind, thoughtful, and willing to give to those in need, even if they themselves have little. Individuals are more important than schedules, so punctuality may be admired but not strictly observed. Nicaraguans defend honor vigorously, sometimes even physically. Those in power are esteemed for their opinions and generally are afforded wealth. Therefore, power is highly valued and often sought. Social status is measured by material possessions, land ownership, family name, and connections. Personal criticism is taken seriously and so is usually avoided. Getting a job, having a large family, and owning a home or plot of land are important long-term goals for Nicaraguans.

Politics is a favorite subject. The Sandinista influence still pervades civilian life. Collectivism and helping others are common values in all social classes. Years of strife have caused many to become wary and distrustful. Some now look at the government as a source of problems.

Machismo, the male attitude of proving one's manliness or superiority, continues to be a strong cultural influence. Excessive drinking and infidelity among men are widely tolerated.

Personal Appearance. Neatness and cleanliness in physical appearance are important to Nicaraguans. Even if they cannot afford expensive clothing, they will make special efforts to be neat and well groomed. All clothing is bleached and ironed.

People throughout the country wear lightweight clothing. In rural areas, men wear cotton shirts (button-down and T-shirts) and khaki pants. Jeans are also common. Rural women usually wear light cotton dresses or skirts and blouses. When working on daily agricultural tasks, both men and women wear *chinellas* (flip-flops), reserving regular shoes for trips to town or special occasions. Farmers might wear boots, sombreros, and old army fatigues.

Urban men wear cotton slacks and shirts (often long-sleeved). Urban women wear light cotton dresses, although many also wear pants. Men often wear a *guayabera* (an embroidered dress shirt) as semiformal wear instead of a tie and suit jacket. Suit coats are not worn during the hottest months of the year.

CUSTOMS AND COURTESIES

Greetings. When meeting another person for the first time, Nicaraguans smile, shake hands, and say either *Mucho gusto de conocerle* (Glad to meet you) or *¿Cómo está usted?* (How are you?). Inquiring about the health of family members demonstrates friendliness between acquaintances. Complete attention is given to the person being greeted. Common terms for greeting include *¡Buenos días!* (Good morning), *¡Buenas tardes!* (Good afternoon), and *¡Buenas noches!* (Good evening). A casual greeting, especially among the youth, is *¡Hola!* (Hi) or *¿Cómo le va?* (How's it going?). Men greet each other with a hearty handshake, and close friends hug and pat each other on the back. Men and women usually greet female friends with a kiss on the cheek and a gentle hug; rural women pat each other on the upper arm rather than hug. Those of higher social standing are greeted with titles such as *Señor*, *Señora*, or *Señorita* ("Mr.," "Mrs.," or "Miss") to show respect. One uses the titles *Don* and *Doña* with first names to indicate special respect, familiarity, or affection. Professional titles are also used before surnames.

Gestures. Nicaraguans use many gestures when speaking. To beckon, one waves all fingers with the palm facing down. One points by extending the chin or puckering the lips in the intended direction. If a person wants to pay for something, he or she may rub one index finger repeatedly down the other, similar to the U.S. gesture indicating shame. Many people snap the forefinger against the middle finger to emphasize that something is very rich, expensive, or difficult to accomplish.

Avoiding eye contact during conversation generally is not acceptable; however, some women may do so in deference to others. Offering a seat to pregnant women, the elderly, or women with children is common. Women may also offer to hold other people's children on their lap if the parents are standing. Upon entering a building, men remove their hats or caps. Raising one's voice or displaying affection in public generally is not acceptable.

Visiting. Nicaraguans are hospitable and enjoy visiting. In rural areas, people commonly (even daily) visit family and friends unannounced. Those in urban areas with access to telephones usually plan visits in advance. Relatives and friends who live in other areas often visit for weekends and holidays.

Because of the hot climate, hosts always offer their guests a cool drink. Water, juice, or natural beverages such as the corn-based *pinol* are most popular. Refusing a drink is considered a serious discourtesy. When one enters a home, it is important to greet everyone and wait for an invitation to sit. When visiting for a special purpose, guests first inquire about the health of the family before they discuss other matters. Good-byes may be drawn out and full of well-wishing. Visitors who arrive during mealtime are invited to join their hosts.

Guests tend to express admiration for their hosts rather than for material objects in the home. Dinner guests may take small gifts, such as flowers or candy, to the hosts. People also give presents on special occasions, such as anniversaries, birthdays, and Catholic ceremonies.

Eating. Breakfast usually is eaten at 6 or 7 a.m., although people in rural areas may eat earlier during busy agricultural seasons. Lunch, the main meal of the day, is eaten at midday and often is followed by a *siesta* (afternoon rest). In rural areas, the *siesta* is taken from noon to 2 p.m., the hottest time of day, when work is difficult. Most people in urban areas take only an hour break to eat lunch sometime between noon and 2 p.m. Dinner is usually between 7 and 9 p.m.

Rural families eat lunch together; but work and school schedules keep many urban families from doing the same. Most families make special efforts to eat together on weekends and holidays. In rural areas, people eat with a spoon or scoop their food with a tortilla. Sometimes the spoons are made from sections of a dried gourd shell. In urban areas, people may eat with a tortilla or spoon, but they also use knives and forks. Many fried foods are eaten with the hands. People keep both hands (not elbows) on or above the table. Hosts expect their guests to eat what is served. They may offer second helpings. Diners are expected to praise the quality of the meal.

LIFESTYLE

Family. The extended family is the basis of society and strongly influences an individual's life and decisions. Parents, children, aunts, uncles, and cousins commonly live together. The oldest male is the head of the family. Nearly all Nicaraguans aspire to have large families; both men and women gain social status by being a parent.

During the Sandinista period, women were given a greater role in society and the right to participate more actively in family matters. Military service was common for women under the Sandinista regime, and many became involved in civic affairs. About one-third of the labor force is female. Because a number of men died or were sent away during the civil war, many women became heads of families. While men are still seen as the authorities and women generally defer to them, women control most household affairs.

Rural homes are usually made of straw and wood. Many family members often share one bed or room. Urban homes and more expensive rural homes are made of concrete. Open areas and patios are common. The redistribution of land and homes seized by the Sandinista government remains a sensitive issue.

Nicaraguans have two family names. The name that comes last is the mother's family name, while the second-to-last name is the father's family name, which functions as the surname. Therefore, a person named José Muñoz Gómez would be called *Señor Muñoz*.

Dating and Marriage. A girl formally enters social life at age 15, and a large *fiesta* (party) is held in her honor. Thereafter, she is allowed to have a boyfriend and attend dances. Group dating is common among young people.

Civil marriages are the most common, although those who can afford it also have a large church wedding. Most marry between the ages of 16 and 23. In small towns, the bride and groom walk a full circle around the town directly after their ceremony.

Diet. For most Nicaraguans, a typical meal includes beans and rice; obtaining a well-balanced meal is difficult for many people who cannot afford more. Among wealthier families, the main meal of the day generally consists of rice, beans, some kind of meat, and a salad or vegetable. The meal is served with tortillas and fruit juice. Corn is an important ingredient in many foods. Oil is used frequently in cooking. *Gallo pinto* (a dish of rice and beans fried together) is eaten in many households for breakfast and dinner. Other typical dishes include tortillas, enchiladas, *nacatamales* (meat, vegetables, and corn meal cooked in a banana leaf), *mondongo* (tripe and beef knuckles), *vigorón* (vegetables with pork skins), and *baho* (meat, vegetables, and plantains). Tropical fruits generally are plentiful. Fried plantains (*plátanos*) are popular. Locally made cheeses also are very popular.

Recreation. Baseball is the national sport. Soccer, boxing, softball, basketball, and volleyball are also popular. Children and teens often socialize in the park until about 9 p.m. Dances are held on Friday and Saturday nights in local schools or on basketball courts. Nicaraguans of all ages love to dance, so most parties or large events include dancing. Going to the beach and participating in club activities are also common.

The Arts. Handicrafts such as ceramics, hammocks, wall hangings, hats woven of straw, embroidered blouses, and wood carvings are common. Rubén Darío made poetry a national pastime. A literary movement called *La Vanguardia* (the Vanguard) seeks to restore Nicaragua's cultural identity.

The national instrument is the *marimba* (which is similar to a xylophone) and is usually accompanied by guitars, maracas, and traditional flutes (*zuls*). Salsa is the most popular music. Folk music is prevalent at festivals. African culture influences music on the Caribbean coast.

Holidays. Public holidays include New Year's Day, Easter (Thursday–Sunday), Labor Day (1 May), Battle of San Jacinto (14 Sept.), Independence Day (15 Sept.), and Christmas. In addition to Christmas, *Gritería* Day (7 Dec.) and Feast of the Immaculate Conception (8 Dec.) both celebrate Christ's conception. Workers also receive a half-day vacation on Christmas Eve. Numerous holidays honoring local patron saints are the main annual events in towns and regions; celebrations may last from one day to two weeks. Because Catholics do not eat red meat during Lent, Nicaraguans traditionally eat iguanas as a paste or in *garrobo* soup before and during Easter.

Nicaragua

Commerce. Most merchants' shops are open from 8 a.m. to noon and 1 to 6 p.m., Monday through Friday, and from 8 a.m. to noon on Saturdays. Government offices generally are open from 7 a.m. to 5 p.m., Monday through Friday. While some businesses close for the *siesta*, many in urban areas do not. In rural areas, business hours vary depending on the crops cultivated. Most people purchase basic supplies at open-air markets, although supermarkets are available in large cities.

SOCIETY

Government. The Republic of Nicaragua consists of 15 *departamentos* (provinces) and 2 autonomous regions located on the Atlantic coast. The executive branch is composed of the president, currently Enrique Bolanos, the vice president, and the cabinet. Constitutional reforms in 1995 transferred many powers previously held by the executive branch to the legislative branch. The National Assembly has 93 members. Legislators are directly elected to serve six-year terms. While more than 20 political parties are active in Nicaragua, many are joined in coalitions. Some of the largest political parties include the Liberal Constitutionalist Party (PLC), the Sandinista National Liberation Front (FSLN), and the Conservative Party (PC). The voting age is 16.

Economy. Devastated by a decade of central planning under the Sandinistas, a civil war, the U.S. trade embargo, and natural disasters, the economy remains the country's greatest challenge. Economic stabilization plans have dropped inflation from more than 750 percent in 1991 to about 5 percent; however, expectations for change have greatly exceeded the government's ability to provide it. Unemployment and underemployment affect more than half of the population. Nicaragua's per capita foreign debt remains one of the highest in the world. The economy relies on agricultural exports, and about 40 percent of the labor force is employed in agriculture.

Nicaragua has the potential for a much stronger economy. However, damage to the country's infrastructure has set development back decades. Controversy surrounds property rights; settlement of land disputes is needed to increase foreign investment. More than half of the population lives in poverty. Despite the myriad of challenges, the economy is growing at a modest pace. The currency is the gold *córdoba* (NIO).

Transportation and Communications. Years of fighting, the poor economy, and natural disasters have damaged the transportation and communications systems. Outside of major cities, many roads are unpaved or are in disrepair. Many rural areas can be reached only by four-wheel drive trucks or by horseback. Buses provide service in cities and are generally affordable and efficient. Postal, telegraph, and telephone services are limited in rural areas. About 25 percent of the population has a phone, but cellular phone popularity is growing.

Education. Schooling is mandatory between the ages of six and thirteen. Most children begin primary school, but only about one-third complete it. Students have to pay for their own supplies, uniforms, tuition, and expenses, which often is too difficult for the poor. Those who complete primary training generally proceed to the secondary level. Nicaragua has five private and five state universities.

Health. Health care is limited, particularly outside of Managua. Community volunteers have become active in promoting prevention and early detection of diseases. However, many people, particularly those in rural areas, do not get adequate care. Patients who need to go to a hospital must provide their own dressings and medications; many cannot. Low wages have led to occasional strikes by medical professionals working in the public health system. Still, more than three-fourths of all infants are immunized and about the same number of women receive some prenatal care. Access to safe water and sanitation is a problem in rural areas.

DEVELOPMENT DATA
Human Dev. Index* rank . . . . 118 of 177 countries
    Adjusted for women . . . . 97 of 144 countries
Real GDP per capita $2,470
Adult literacy rate . . . . 77 percent (male); 77 (female)
Infant mortality rate . . . . 30 per 1,000 births
Life expectancy . . . . 67 (male); 72 (female)

AT A GLANCE
Events and Trends.
- Elections in November 2004 signaled that the opposition Sandinista candidates had gained popularity in the wake of a campaign-finance scandal surrounding center-right President Bolanos. Sandinista candidates won the races for mayor of Managua and 15 of 17 provincial capitals.
- Protests by university students in May 2004 left more than 40 students and police officers injured and one police officer dead. It is unclear whether students or police started the violence. The students were demanding that higher education receive the full 6 percent of the national budget, as stipulated in the constitution. But the government has said the country can't afford to spend that much.
- In January 2004, the World Bank agreed to forgive 80 percent (US$4 billion) of Nicaragua's debt and loan the country another US$75 million to fund poverty-reduction programs. The move was echoed by Russia in July 2004 when it wrote off billions of dollars of Nicaragua's debt from the Soviet era.
- In December 2003, the United States and five Central American nations, including Nicaragua, established a Central American Free-Trade Agreement (US-CAFTA), which will eliminate trade barriers with the United States and within the region.
- In September 2002, former Nicaraguan president Arnoldo Aleman was charged with money laundering, corruption, and embezzlement of US$100 million during his presidency. In December 2003, he was convicted and sentenced to 20 years imprisonment. Because of poor health, Aleman will likely serve his term under house arrest.

Contact Information. Embassy of the Republic of Nicaragua, 1627 New Hampshire Avenue NW, Washington, DC 20009; phone (202) 939-6570. Nicaraguan Institute of Tourism, Hotel Crowne Plaza, 1C Sur, 1C Oeste, Managua, Nicaragua; web site www.intur.gob.ni.

CultureGrams
People. The World. You.

ProQuest Information and Learning Company
300 North Zeeb Road, P.O. Box 1346
Ann Arbor, Michigan 48106 USA
Toll Free: 1.800.528.6279
Fax: 1.800.864.0019
www.culturegrams.com

© 2005 ProQuest Information and Learning Company and Brigham Young University. It is against the law to copy, reprint, store, or transmit any part of this publication in any form by any means without written permission from ProQuest. This document contains native commentary and original analysis, as well as estimated statistics. The content should not be considered strictly factual, and it may not apply to all groups in a nation. *UN Development Programme, Human Development Report 2004 (New York: Oxford University Press, 2004).

CultureGrams World Edition 2006

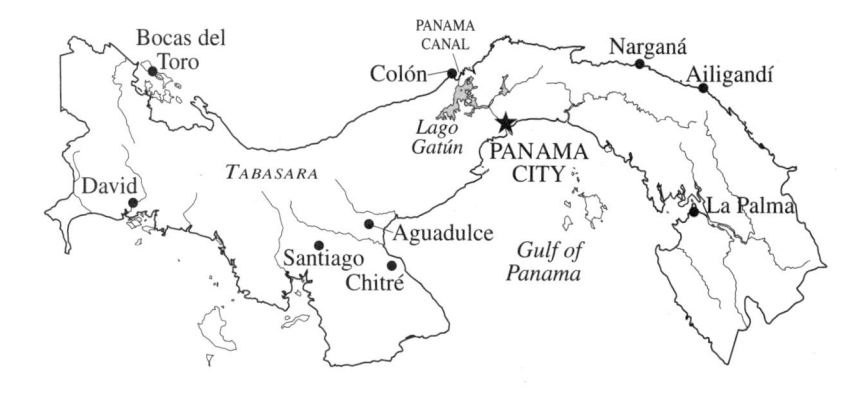

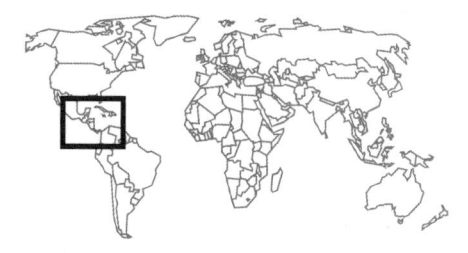

Republic of Panama

BACKGROUND

Land and Climate. Panama is a fairly rugged, mountainous country connecting Central and South America. Covering 30,193 square miles (78,200 square kilometers), Panama's total land area is just smaller than South Carolina. Volcanic activity has made the soil very fertile in some areas, and about half the country is forested. The Panama Canal, a man-made structure, runs from Panama City to Colón through Lago Gatún (Lake Gatún). The Canal Zone (*la zona*) stretches between and includes the two cities. Areas outside *la zona* are collectively called the interior (*el interior*). The Cordillera Central (Tabasara Mountains) forms a spine down the center of the western interior; there are also mountains in the eastern interior. The tropical climate is hot and humid except at higher elevations. The average annual temperature is 80°F (27°C). In the mountains, the average is about 55°F (13°C).

History. The history of Panama has been greatly affected by its strategic location between the Atlantic and Pacific Oceans. Columbus claimed the area for Spain in 1502. In the 16th and 17th centuries, Panama served as the route for shipping Incan treasures to Spain. In 1821, Spanish rule was overthrown, and Panama became a province of Colombia. During the 1880s, France attempted to build a canal across the narrow isthmus. Planning and financing were poor, and yellow fever claimed more than 20,000 lives.

In November 1903, Panama declared independence from Colombia, and the United States sent troops to support the new government. Canal rights were sold to the United States that same year. Construction of the Panama Canal began in 1907 and was completed in 1914. It quickly became an important passage for ships traveling between the Atlantic and the Pacific. In 1978, the U.S. Senate narrowly ratified a treaty signed by President Jimmy Carter that would allow Panama to assume control of canal operations in 1999; the United States would continue to guarantee the canal's neutrality.

Omar Torrijos Herrera, commander of Panama's national guard, seized control of the country in 1968. Although he ruled as a dictator, most Panamanians now revere him as a national hero. He turned daily government powers over to a civilian administration in 1978 and allowed free, multiparty legislative elections in 1980. After Torrijos died in a controversial 1981 plane crash, his defense minister, Manuel Antonio Noriega, became the leader of the Panama Defense Forces and de facto leader of the nation.

Arturo Delvalle Henríquez became president in 1985 but was ousted in 1988 for trying to fire Noriega, who had effectively suspended the constitution. Noriega ruled under a state of emergency and controlled the National Assembly. Following 1989 elections, he refused to allow the new president (who had opposed Noriega) to take office. Noriega's rule became increasingly repressive in Panama, and relations with the United States worsened.

When a 1989 coup attempt against Noriega failed, the United States sent troops to Panama in response to growing concerns about corruption, violence, and Noriega's threats against U.S. interests. Troops loyal to Noriega were defeated and he was taken prisoner. When the elected government was installed, Noriega was extradited to the United States to stand trial for various drug-trafficking charges. Convicted in 1992, he is serving a 40-year sentence in a U.S. prison.

After toppling Noriega, the United States installed President Guillermo Endara in 1989. Endara struggled to rebuild the nation as social unrest, poverty, and corruption hindered

Panama

progress. Free elections prevailed in 1994, and Ernesto Pérez Balladares was elected president. Pérez Balladares has been credited with stabilizing the economy, but he was not allowed to seek a second five-year term.

In December 1999, Panama assumed full control of the canal's operations. The government is considering how best to administer the canal, and further expansion of the canal is planned. Panama is also trying to find a productive use for the 70,000 acres of former U.S. military land and the more than five thousand buildings that reverted to Panama when the United States left the region.

THE PEOPLE

Population. Panama has just over 3 million people, and its population is growing by 1.3 percent annually. Next to Belize, Panama has the smallest population in Central America. About 70 percent of Panama's citizens are mestizos (people with mixed indigenous and European heritage). Fourteen percent of the people are black, descendants of laborers from the Caribbean (mostly the West Indies) who came to work on the Canal in the early 1900s. Ten percent of the people are white, having European ancestry. The rest are members of various indigenous groups who have their own rich cultural heritage and often have chosen not to integrate into Panamanian society. The largest groups are the Kuna, Ngöbe-Buglé, and Emberá (or Wounaan). Most of the country's urban population lives in Panama City, or in Colón. The life and culture of the *campesinos* (farmers) in the interior is drastically different from that of urban Panama.

Language. Spanish is the official language of Panama. However, about 14 percent of the people speak English as a native tongue, and many others speak English as a second language. English is rarely spoken outside of Panama City. Many black Panamanians speak creole English. Indigenous peoples speak various languages, according to their ethnic background. Most prevalent are Kuna, Ngäbere, and Ngöbe-Buglé. Ethnic minorities speak their native tongue and Spanish.

Religion. About 85 percent of the population is Roman Catholic. Most of the rest of the population belongs to various Protestant churches. There also are small numbers of Muslims, Jews, Hindus, and Baha'is in Panama. Although the Catholic Church has great influence on the lives of the people, Panamanian law maintains freedom of worship and separation of church and state. Many Catholics are critical of local ecclesiastical authorities but remain loyal to the pope.

General Attitudes. Although society is stratified in traditional social classes and there is some tension between different groups, most Panamanians consider all people to be of worth. They believe people should be treated with dignity and respect, regardless of their class. This value for the individual is also evident in Panamanians' respect for personal strength and charisma. Tradition, family loyalty, stability, and wealth are all important values in Panamanian society. Men are expected to be polite. However, *machismo*, the defining of a man as forceful, daring, and virile, is a large part of Panamanian culture. The ideal woman is well-bred, understanding, and feminine. People in large urban areas are more cosmopolitan in their approach to these traditions.

Nationalism is strong in Panama, a reflection of the country's strategic position in the world and the service it provides to all nations. Most citizens, even interior *campesinos*, are well informed on topics relating to national and international politics. Panamanians are also aware of their country's association with the United States. Many resent the relationship as unequal. Panamanians appreciate their Spanish heritage and, to a lesser extent, their indigenous roots.

Personal Appearance. Most people dress in styles similar to those worn in the United States. Bankers and other executives wear dark suits and ties. Many rural men wear collared, button-down shirts with four pockets called *guayaberas*. Panamanians, especially women, tend to pay careful attention to their public appearance. They admire a polished look and rarely wear sloppy clothing. However, dress habits may seem informal to U.S. observers, and sandals are common footwear. Traditional costumes are worn on special occasions. For women, this includes a *pollera* (a full-length dress with embroidery). For men, it is the *montuno* (baggy shorts and matching embroidered top), *cutarras* (leather sandals), and palm-fiber hats. Kuna women wear *mola* (appliquéd) shirts, Ngöbe-Buglé women wear *naguas* (colorful dresses), and Emberá women wear skirts but no top. Indigenous men usually wear Western-style dress.

CUSTOMS AND COURTESIES

Greetings. When greeting, many women (and sometimes members of the opposite sex) give an *abrazo* (hug). That is, they clasp hands as in a handshake, lean forward, and press cheeks. Men shake hands with one another, often while patting the other on the shoulder. *Campesinos* usually shake hands but usually do not hug when greeting. Verbally, they may also "howl" a *grita*, a personally styled cry used to express friendship, break the monotony of fieldwork, and show joy at *fiestas*.

The most common verbal greetings include ¡*Buenas!* (Good day), ¿*Cómo está?* (How are you?), ¿*Qué tal?* (What's up?), and ¿*Qué hay de bueno?* (What's good?). *Buenos días*, *Buenas tardes*, and *Buenas noches* (Good morning/afternoon/evening) are used more formally or with the elderly. Inquiring about the welfare of one's family members is polite after an initial greeting. For good-bye, one says ¡*Hasta luego!* (See you later), or ¡*Que le vaya bien!* (May things go well for you). In the cities, one says *Chao* (Good-bye). *Adiós* is rarely used because it is considered fairly permanent.

In formal situations among the educated, it is important to address people by educational title, such as *Maestro/a* (teacher), *Ingeniero/a* (person with a bachelor of science degree), or *Doctor/a* (Dr.). These titles usually are followed by the person's given name, not surname. Other titles include *Señor* (Mr.), *Señora* (Mrs.), and *Señorita* (Miss). *Don* and *Doña* are used for respected or elderly men and women. Informally, people often greet one another by given name or nickname. Using someone's nickname is not polite unless he or she is a close friend. People often address each other by terms of relationship: *hermano/a* (brother/sister), *amigo/a* (friend), *tío/a* (uncle/aunt), and so forth.

Gestures. People in the interior use nonverbal communication more often than those in urban areas. For example, they pucker their lips to point or to indicate "over there" or "time to go." One might ask "What's up?" by shrugging with the palms facing up. "No" can be expressed by wagging the index finger from side to side. Using a finger to draw a circle in the air means one is coming right back. Wrinkling a nose can mean "What's going on?" or "I don't understand."

Politeness is important and chivalry common. On public transportation, men offer their seats to women or the elderly. Deference to elders in any situation is important. Personal space generally is limited, and people sit or stand close to each other when they converse. Eye contact is important. It is polite to cover one's mouth when yawning.

Visiting. Panamanians enjoy hosting others in their homes. They are open, generous, and informal with their guests. Hosts customarily do not establish an ending time to a visit, as that might indicate to the guests that they are not as important as the hosts' schedule. It is polite for guests to allow their hosts to take care of them. That is, guests do not help with dishes, they take any offers of the best seat or food, and they graciously accept any good-bye gifts. When invited to dinner, guests usually do not take gifts to their hosts; this would imply the hosts are not expected to be thorough in providing hospitality. Rather than giving a gift, guests generally expect to return the favor of a dinner invitation.

A visit is a compliment in Panama, and friends and relatives visit one another often. Unannounced visitors are common and welcome. In the interior, relatives see each other almost daily, depending on their relationship and how far they live from one another. People in cities often enjoy Sunday visits. All visitors are offered refreshments, such as a fruit drink. A full meal is also often offered.

Eating. Urban residents generally eat three meals a day. People from the interior often have a big breakfast early, a main meal at midday, and a small dinner around 5 p.m. *Campesino* families usually follow the same schedule, but sometimes eat only breakfast and dinner. They may have snacks before or during work. Hands generally are kept above the table during a meal, and diners engage in light conversation.

Any guests present are served first, followed by the men, children, and the women and/or cooks. The cook or hostess usually prepares a plate for each person. Extra food might be put out for second helpings. Guests compliment the cook verbally and by finishing their food. City dwellers eat out often, but *campesinos* rarely do. Urban diners usually leave servers a tip of 5 to 10 percent.

LIFESTYLE

Family. The family is the basic unit of Panamanian society. In Panama, the mother generally takes responsibility for the home and child care. This traditional role is still quite admired and respected. Less than 30 percent of the labor force is composed of women. The father's main responsibilities are usually outside the home, but he is still considered the undisputed leader of the family. Because of the changing tempo of modern life, nuclear families are gaining prominence over the extended family. However, adult children still usually care for their aging parents, even if they do not live with them. In such cases, children send money or food, visit them, and arrange for their basic needs to be met. A large number of births take place out of wedlock, but many of these are within stable common-law marriages. Families in urban areas often live in rented apartments, while rural families may own small homes.

Dating and Marriage. Compared with girls of other Latin American countries or with girls from the interior, urban Panamanian girls enjoy a great degree of freedom; young women in the interior begin dating much later and are subject to parental restrictions. Most young women begin group dating around age 14. In both rural and urban areas, boys have nearly complete freedom. Although rural boys have farm responsibilities, they receive little supervision outside of school and have no domestic duties. When dating, couples enjoy dancing, going for walks, and watching movies.

Urban women usually marry in their early twenties; in the interior, women often marry by age 20. Common-law marriages are prevalent in the interior and are generally as well accepted and stable as legal marriages performed by the state. Couples desiring a church marriage must obtain a license; a registered religious official can then perform the marriage. Church weddings are common in urban areas.

Diet. In Panama, it is commonly said that one hasn't eaten if one hasn't had rice. Rice is served with nearly every meal, along with a source of protein (eggs, chicken, sardines, meat, fish, or beans). Corn and plantains are also staples. Fish is inexpensive and often made into a soup. People usually eat vegetables as part of the main dish or in a salad. Fruit is often eaten as a snack. *Chicha*, a popular drink, is made from fresh fruit, water, and sugar. Coffee is served often throughout the day. Common dishes in the interior include *sancocho* (chicken soup), *guacho* (rice soup), *bollo* (corn mush that has been boiled in the husk), corn tortillas, and *carne guisado* (stewed meat with tomatoes and spices). *Arroz con pollo* (rice and chicken) is eaten on special occasions. A wider variety of international foods are eaten in urban areas, along with traditional foods.

Recreation. In towns, many participate in team sports. *Futból* (soccer) is the national favorite. Baseball, boxing, and basketball are also popular. Panamanians enjoy attending horse races, cockfights, and movies. The twice-weekly national lottery is extremely popular. Socializing on the porch or visiting friends is an important leisure activity. Leisure time for rural women often revolves around domestic events; they may get together to make crafts or to socialize and make *bollos* when the new corn comes in. Dances are popular among people of European heritage and often last until dawn.

The Arts. Indigenous Panamanians create many handicrafts, including textiles, jewelry, baskets, ceramics, etc. Kuna women's *mola* shirts are known for their ornate designs. Poetry incorporates indigenous peoples' mythology, and dramatic poetry readings are popular. Most people in Panama love to dance, especially the *tamborito*, the country's national dance. The area's traditional music, called *típico*, is played by a band consisting of a singer and players with an accordion, a guitar, and some percussion. Lyrics usually pertain to love and life. *Típico* is more common in rural areas and is joined in cities by salsa, merengue, jazz, and reggae. On the Caribbean coast, drumming and singing to an African beat are popular.

Holidays. Official holidays include New Year's Day (1–2 Jan.), Day of the Martyrs (9 Jan.), Easter (Friday–Sunday), Labor Day (1 May), Independence from Colombia Day (3 Nov.), Uprising of Los Santos (11 Nov.), Independence from Spain Day (28 Nov.), Mother's Day (second Sunday in December), and Christmas. Each village or city holds celebrations to honor the local patron saint. *Carnaval* celebrations are always held the Saturday to Tuesday before Ash Wednesday (usually in February or March). Most businesses shut down during the holidays, as friends and family gather for parties, drinking, and socializing.

Commerce. The business day begins as early as 7 a.m. and ends by 4 p.m., but many stores stay open until 6 p.m. During holidays, they may be open until 9 or 10 p.m. Urban residents shop at large grocery stores and open-air markets for most basics. *Campesinos* may shop daily for small amounts of items they need; they also collect from their harvests and exchange produce with friends and relatives. When necessary, they travel to shops and markets in larger interior towns.

Panama

SOCIETY

Government. Panama is a multiparty democracy. Its president (currently Martin Torrijos) is chief of state and head of government. Presidents serve five-year terms and may not be reelected. The 71-seat national assembly has several active parties, including the Arnulfista Party (PA) and the Democratic Revolutionary Party (PRD), originally formed by Omar Torrijos. All citizens are required by law to vote beginning at age 18. The judicial branch is organized under a nine-member Supreme Court and includes all tribunals and municipal courts.

Panama is divided into nine provinces; the president appoints governors for each province. At the local level, communities elect a *junta local* (town council) to coordinate town events and functions. Each indigenous group also has its own form of government, and the Kuna have autonomy in their province.

Economy. Panama is working to revive its potentially strong economy after years of political instability, authoritarian rule, U.S. economic sanctions (1988–90), and the more recent removal of U.S. troops from the Canal Zone. Panama enjoys some successes in its banking industry, financial services, tourism, and trade. Economic growth was robust in the early 1990s after vital trade relations were restored with the United States. However, the country faces high unemployment and a shortage of skilled labor.

The economy reflects a widening gap between rich and poor; the richest 10 percent of the population controls about 35 percent of the nation's wealth, while the poorest 10 percent has only 1 percent of the wealth. More than a third of Panamanians live in poverty.

Key exports include bananas, shrimp, coffee, sugar, and clothing. The Panama Canal, a major international trade route, provides vital foreign-exchange earnings. Tourism is another important sector. About 21 percent of the labor force is employed in agriculture-related industries. The official currency is the *balboa* (PAB), which consists mostly of coins. Bills are U.S. dollars, which are legal tender.

Transportation and Communications. The highway system is the hub of transportation in Panama. Roads are generally in good condition, especially in and around urban areas. The Inter-American Highway runs from the Costa Rican border through Panama City, ending at the Darien Gap. The capital is linked to Colón by the Trans-Isthmian Highway. Some revenues from the national lottery help build and maintain roads. Domestic airlines and shallow waterways also provide transportation. In cities, buses, *chivas* (minibuses), and taxis are readily available. In the interior, people walk, use *chivas* or buses, or ride horses. The majority of the people do not own cars. Most telephones are owned by people living in urban areas. Centrally located public telephones are available in the interior. Communications facilities are well developed. A free press flourishes, and there are many newspapers.

Education. Primary education is compulsory and free between the ages of seven and fifteen. Most school-aged children (72 percent) complete primary schooling and go on to more specialized secondary education. Rural families may have difficulty sending children to secondary schools—usually located in larger towns—because they cannot afford to pay for daily transportation, uniforms and supplies, or room and board in the city. After completing the secondary level, a student may go on to one of several vocational schools or prepare to enter a university. Panama has a national university, established in 1935, as well as a Catholic university and other church-owned schools.

Health. Panama's public health program is part of the national security system. It provides such services as free examinations, care for the needy, and health education and sanitation programs. Most people have access to modern medical care of some kind, although the best facilities and personnel are in Panama City and Colón. Some rural health centers are understaffed or poorly equipped. Malaria and yellow fever are active in the eastern areas near Colombia.

DEVELOPMENT DATA

Human Dev. Index* rank . . . . 61 of 177 countries
   Adjusted for women . . . . 53 of 144 countries
Real GDP per capita $6,170
Adult literacy rate . . . . 93 percent (male); 92 (female)
Infant mortality rate . . . . 21 per 1,000 births
Life expectancy . . . . 72 (male); 77 (female)

AT A GLANCE

Events and Trends.

- The Panama Canal earned a record US$1 billion in 2004's financial year. The income was a huge boon to the Panamanian economy.
- Martin Torrijos was elected Panama's president in May 2004. Torrijos, a social democrat, announced plans to fight poverty, corruption, and despair. The new president is the son of former dictator Omar Torrijos, the man who is credited with getting the Panama Canal back from U.S. control.
- In November 2004, President Torrijos was able to restore diplomatic ties with Cuba, which had been broken after former president Mireya Moscoso pardoned four Cuban exiles who were accused of plotting to kill Cuban leader Fidel Castro.
- In November 2003, Panama marked 100 years of independence with ceremonies and parades that were watched by 14 foreign presidents and U.S. secretary of state Colin Powell. The country, which has always been greatly influenced by other nations, is looking to keep strong trade ties with countries like the United States while developing more independence.

Contact Information. Embassy of the Republic of Panama, 2862 McGill Terrace NW, Washington, DC 20008; phone (202) 483-1407. IPAT, Panamanian Institute of Tourism; phone (800) 231-0568; web site www.visitpanama.com.

© 2005 ProQuest Information and Learning Company and Brigham Young University. It is against the law to copy, reprint, store, or transmit any part of this publication in any form by any means without written permission from ProQuest. This document contains native commentary and original analysis, as well as estimated statistics. The content should not be considered strictly factual, and it may not apply to all groups in a nation. *UN Development Programme, Human Development Report 2004 (New York: Oxford University Press, 2004).

CultureGrams
People. The World. You.

ProQuest Information and Learning Company
300 North Zeeb Road, P.O. Box 1346
Ann Arbor, Michigan 48106 USA
Toll Free: 1.800.528.6279
Fax: 1.800.864.0019
www.culturegrams.com

CultureGrams World Edition 2006

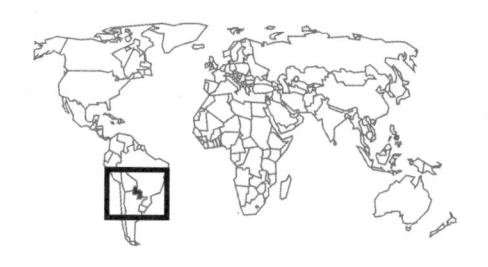

Republic of Paraguay

BACKGROUND

Land and Climate. Paraguay is a landlocked country in central South America. Covering 157,046 square miles (406,570 square kilometers), it is slightly smaller than California. About one-third of the country is forest or woodlands, although that amount is dwindling, as deforestation is a significant problem. About 6 percent of the land is suitable for cultivation. There are some hilly areas, but few high elevations.

The Río Paraguay (Paraguay River) divides the country into two regions. In the northwest lies the sparsely settled arid region known as the Gran Chaco, or simply Chaco. Near the river, the Chaco is mostly wetlands. Southeast of the river is the fertile Paraná Plateau, where the main population and agricultural centers are located. The plateau is subtropical and has a hot, humid, and rainy climate. Because Paraguay is south of the equator, the country's seasonal changes are opposite those in the Northern Hemisphere. The warm season is from September through May. The cooler rainy season is from June through August.

History. Spanish explorers came to Paraguay in 1524 and established Asunción in 1537. Colonial rule lasted until the 19th century. Paraguay peacefully gained independence in 1811, and José Gaspar Rodríguez Francia established the first in a long line of dictatorships. He closed the country to the outside world and ruled until his death in 1840.

The next ruler, Carlos Antonio López, began modernizing the country. But in 1865, his son Francisco Solano López took Paraguay into the War of the Triple Alliance against Brazil, Argentina, and Uruguay. Ultimately, Paraguay lost the war (1870), along with 55,000 square miles (142,450 square kilometers) of territory and as much as two-thirds of its adult male population. Foreign troops stayed until 1876, and Paraguay remained politically unstable for another generation.

In 1932, Paraguay waged the three-year Chaco War with Bolivia over a territorial dispute. Although Paraguay gained two-thirds of the disputed Chaco territory, even more of the country's male population died. Various dictators and one elected president ruled until 1954, when General Alfredo Stroessner, commander of the army, took control of the Paraguayan government and established a long-term dictatorship. Although his tenure brought some economic development (mainly in the form of three hydroelectric dams), his government was responsible for human-rights violations, corruption, and oppression.

A coup in 1989 ousted Stroessnerm, and the coup's leader, General Andrés Rodríguez Pedotti, was elected president. He restored civil rights, legalized political parties, and promised not to serve past 1993. Rodríguez was the first leader to successfully implement many democratic reforms. A new constitution was ratified in June 1992. Rodríguez's administration helped Paraguay emerge from its isolation under decades of dictatorship to join in regional and international organizations.

The nation's commitment to democracy was tested during an attempted coup in 1996. General Lino Oviedo, who led the coup, was sentenced to 10 years in prison. He ran for the presidency from his prison cell until a Supreme Court ruling forced him to withdraw his candidacy. His running mate, Raul Cubas, ran in his place and won in 1998. Oviedo received a presidential pardon, which was overturned by the Supreme Court, who ordered that Oviedo be returned to jail. In 1999, both Oviedo and Cubas fled the country after allegations that they were involved in the assassination of Paraguay's vice president, who was of an opposing party.

Paraguay

Since 1999 there have been two more presidents, the most recent being Nicanor Duarte Frutos of the Colorado Party. Although tainted by scandal, the Colorado Party has ruled Paraguay for more than 55 years. Despite this dominance, the president faces serious challenges because of societal unrest related to political corruption and economic hardships.

THE PEOPLE

Population. Paraguay's population of 6.2 million is growing annually at 2.5 percent. Paraguay is the most ethnically homogeneous country in South America, partially due to its many years of virtual isolation. As much as 95 percent of the population is mestizo, or of mixed Spanish and indigenous heritage. Pure indigenous Guaraní are few in number today; most live around Asunción or in northern Paraguay. Descendants of German and Italian immigrants have assimilated into mestizo society. Some Koreans (who generally are merchants), other Asians, and Arabs also reside in Paraguay, but they have not assimilated into Paraguayan culture. A small number of Mennonites, mostly around Filadelfia, maintain a distinct lifestyle based on their European agricultural heritage. About half of all Paraguayans live in urban areas. Roughly 38 percent of the population is younger than age 15.

Language. Paraguay has two official languages: Spanish and Guaraní. Spanish is the language of government, urban commerce, and most schooling, but Guaraní is the common language. In rural areas, some people speak only Guaraní, although many adults cannot read or write it. To remedy this, schools now teach students pure Guaraní as it is expressed in literature. Most people also speak or understand Spanish. Portuguese is spoken along the Brazilian border. Paraguay's Spanish is called *Castellano* (Castilian), not *Español*. Paraguayans mix many Guaraní words with Spanish, and many of their vocabulary words differ from those of other Spanish-speaking countries. They generally use the *vos* rather than the *tú* form for informal address.

Religion. About 90 percent of Paraguayans are Roman Catholic. Catholic rituals and holidays play an important role in society. However, various Protestant and other Christian churches also have members in Paraguay. Mennonites practice their own religion. Paraguayan women tend to be more religious than men. Many rural people mix Christian beliefs and traditional beliefs in their worship.

General Attitudes. Paraguayans are proud of being Paraguayan. They often define themselves by three aspects of their culture: speaking Guaraní, drinking *yerba* (herb) tea, and eating *mandioca* (cassava). Paraguayans say that Spanish is the language of the head, but Guaraní is the language of the heart. *Yerba* tea has been part of the culture for hundreds of years. *Mandioca* is served at nearly every meal. *Mate* (MAH-tay) leaves are made into a mildly stimulating *yerba* tea. Served cold, it is called *tereré*. Served hot, it is *mate*.

Paraguay is a traditional society. Large families, property, beauty, virility, money, and status are valued. A major goal for most people is to not have problems; they desire *tranquilidad* (tranquility). Deviations from traditional values and loud, disruptive behavior are not appreciated. Although most people are very welcoming, generations of isolation and wars with neighboring countries mean the population lacks experience with diverse groups. For example, the mestizo population tends to look down on people with darker skin tones, and negative attitudes toward unfamiliar religions or cultures may be encountered.

Paraguayans do not appreciate stereotypes about poverty and inferiority in developing countries; they are proud of their particular heritage. At the same time, they feel other countries take advantage of their nation. As South Americans, Paraguayans do not appreciate U.S. citizens referring to themselves as "Americans." They prefer to call residents of the United States *norteamericanos* (North Americans).

Personal Appearance. Western-style clothing is worn throughout Paraguay. Cleanliness is emphasized; even the poorest people have clean clothing and clean shoes. Adults do not wear shorts in public. Men generally do not wear sandals. Urban men wear slacks and a shirt for working, but suits and ties are less common because of the hot climate. Clothing is often lightweight; cotton is a popular fabric. Rural men wear work clothes and a hat when farming.

Women generally pay particular attention to their appearance, regardless of economic conditions. Styled hair, manicured nails, jewelry, and makeup are popular. Rural women nearly always wear dresses. Society generally considers beauty an important quality in women. Young people enjoy North American fashions.

CUSTOMS AND COURTESIES

Greetings. Spanish greetings, such as ¡*Mucho gusto!* (Pleased to meet you), are often used with strangers or for formal situations. Acquaintances might use less formal Spanish, such as ¡*Hola! ¿Cómo estás?* (Hi. How are you?), but friends and relatives more often use Guaraní greetings. The most common phrase is ¿*Mba'eichapa?* (pronounced "m-buy-ay-SHA-pah"), which means "How are you?" The reply is almost always ¡*Iporã!* (Just fine). In the countryside, it is friendly and polite to call out a greeting to a friend passing one's house. In this case, saying *adiós* (goodbye), but dropping the *s* and holding out the *o* is more common than saying *hola* (hello).

Except in the workplace, men and women always shake hands when greeting, even if for the second or third time in a day. Friends greeting for the first time in a day (if at least one is a woman) will kiss each other on each cheek as well as shake hands. Rural women are more likely to pat the other's arm than kiss. When departing, most people repeat whatever gesture they used in greeting.

Urban men are addressed respectfully by last name, often accompanied by *Don*. For women, *Doña* customarily accompanies the first name. Using a person's professional title also shows respect. Young people refer to each other by first name. In rural areas, *campesinos* (farmers) commonly address one another by first name, preceded by *Ña* (for women) or *Karai* (for men). Paraguayans often greet a respected elder by holding their hands in prayer position and waiting for the elder to bless them.

Gestures. Perhaps the most common hand gesture is a thumbs-up, which expresses anything positive or encouraging. A person uses the gesture when saying ¡*Iporã!* or when answering a question. Wagging a vertical index finger means "no" or "I don't think so." One beckons by waving all fingers of the hand with the palm facing out or down. Winking has romantic, even sexual, connotations; it is not used as a casual gesture.

Paraguayans are soft-spoken; they do not shout to get someone's attention. If making a "tssst tssst" sound does not work, a Paraguayan might whistle or run after the person. Paraguayan men usually give up their bus seats to older or pregnant women or women with babies. Seated bus passengers usually offer to hold packages or children for standing passengers. To make one's presence known at a home, one claps at the gate. It is impolite to enter the yard until invited.

Visiting. Paraguayans visit one another often. Unannounced visits are common and welcome. Paraguayans enjoy hosting friends and new acquaintances. Guests usually are offered refreshments. If the hosts are eating a meal or drinking *tereré*, they will usually invite visitors to join in. Otherwise, guests might be offered a soft drink (in the city), coffee, juice, or water. Hosts only give *tereré* to unannounced visitors if they want them to stay a while. People often drink the tea from a common *guampa* (container, usually made of wood, cattle horns, or gourds) through a *bombilla* (metal straw). The host passes the *guampa* to one person, who drinks and returns the container to the host, who makes another portion for the next person. Participants enjoy this important social custom while relaxing and conversing.

Urban residents like to invite friends to their homes for a meal; rural people generally extend invitations only for special occasions. Guests need not be punctual; being late is accepted and more comfortable for all involved. Invited dinner guests might bring a gift of wine, beer, or a dessert. Guests usually are expected to stay after a meal for conversation and tea.

Eating. Mealtimes and eating habits vary according to region and family. Rather than sit down to a daily family meal, rural people often eat when they can. Farmers might eat lunch in their fields, for example, rather than go home. Urban families usually eat their main meal together.

Children might eat before guests (who are not relatives) arrive or are served. Guests usually receive their plates of food fully served. They may take additional portions from serving dishes on the table. Not finishing one's food is considered an insult to the cook. Hosts usually insist their guests take second helpings. Proper etiquette is important in formal situations, including not placing hands in the lap (they rest on the table edge) and waiting for the hosts to begin eating.

Few people, especially in rural areas, drink during meals. At rural parties or celebrations, women eat after men do, or they eat at separate tables. The *asado* (barbecue) is a popular family gathering in many areas.

Street vendors sell a great deal of food on urban streets; eating or drinking in public is common. Sharing food or drink is a common custom. In restaurants, one rarely buys a drink for oneself; one orders a large pitcher for all at the table. Additional rounds are ordered by other diners. When eating a snack or small meal, Paraguayans offer the food to whomever is around. Declining the offer is not considered impolite. In restaurants, service is included in the bill and tips are not expected.

LIFESTYLE

Family. Paraguayan society centers on the extended family. Three or four generations might live in one home or on one farm. Most children are well behaved and polite. Adult children usually care for their aging parents. The father heads the family and the mother takes care of the household. Most rural women, like the men, are involved in agriculture. As much as 40 percent of the urban labor force is female.

Many rural families have electricity, televisions, and radios but do not have other modern conveniences such as plumbing. They live in wooden or brick homes with dirt floors and straw or tin roofs. Urban homes are made of concrete and have tile roofs. Nearly all homes in Asunción have running water and electricity.

Dating and Marriage. Most Paraguayan young women have an elaborate party at age 15 to celebrate becoming a *señorita*, or young woman. They are then allowed to go to dances. In traditional homes, they are not allowed to date for another year or two. Young people get to know each other at community *fiestas* (parties), large family gatherings, dances, and so forth. In rural areas, a young man must have permission from a young woman's parents to date her. Then he can only visit her on traditional visiting days (Tuesday, Thursday, Saturday, and Sunday). Later in a relationship, a relative of the young woman might chaperone the couple. Urban families are generally less strict on these rules, and young people in cities often hang out at dance clubs without chaperones.

Parents generally expect to approve of marriage partners. For a marriage to be legal, the wedding must be performed civilly. In addition, couples may have a church wedding. Many couples enter into common-law relationships. Others have children together but do not live together.

Diet. Breakfast usually consists of *cocido* (a hot drink of *mate*, cooked sugar, and milk) or coffee, bread and butter, and rolls or pastries. Lunch (the main meal) is eaten around midday and dinner often is served after dark when work is finished. The most important staple foods include *mandioca, sopa Paraguaya* (cornbread baked with cheese, onions, and sometimes meat), *chipa* (hard cheese bread), tortillas, and *empanadas* (deep-fried meat or vegetable pockets). Small rural gardens provide *campesino* families with tomatoes, onions, carrots, garlic, squash, watermelon, cabbage, and other produce. Surrounding trees and bushes provide fruit. Beef is a common part of the adult diet. Paraguayans also eat chicken and pork dishes.

Recreation. Soccer is the most popular spectator sport in Paraguay, but volleyball and soccer are both common participation sports. Urban men often play sports in the evenings. Many enjoy tennis and basketball. Women generally have not played sports in the past, but recently more have started participating. Urban people might go to the theater, the movies, or other cultural events. Most households have televisions, and families enjoy watching sports, the news, movies, and soap operas. Local radio broadcasts are also popular. Rural and urban people alike relax by drinking *tereré* and *mate* and visiting each other.

The Arts. Arts reflect the people's Spanish and Guaraní heritage. Paraguay's famous *ñandutí* lace, known for its intricate and delicate designs, was likely first introduced by the Spanish, although local legend says the indigenous people invented the art form. Other popular crafts include wood and stone carving, pottery, and embroidery. Several groups have been formed to preserve Guaraní culture.

Popular music tends to have Western influences and includes Latino polkas and ballads. Dancing is a popular form of recreation and shows heavy influence from Spain. Young people enjoy music with a distinct beat, (disco, rap, etc.). The Paraguayan harp is a famous instrument.

Holidays. Paraguayans celebrate New Year's Day, Epiphany (6 Jan.), *Carnaval* (a week of parades and parties in February), Heroes' Day (1 Mar.), *Semana Santa* (Holy Week before Easter), Labor Day (1 May), Independence Day (14–15 May), Mother's Day (15 May), the Chaco Armistice (12 June), *Día de la Amistad* (Friendship Day, 30 July), Founding of Asunción City (15 August, celebrated with large parades), Constitution Day (25 Aug.), Victory of Boqueron (29 Sept.), Columbus Day (12 Oct.), All Saints' Day (1 Nov.), Virgin of Cacupe (8 Dec.), and Christmas. *Semana Santa* is the most important

Paraguay

holiday period and is a week for family gatherings.

Commerce. Urban business hours extend from 7 a.m. to noon and from 3 to 6 p.m. Most people take a *siesta* during the three-hour break and eat their main meal of the day. Rural Paraguayans grow much of their own food; they purchase staples and other goods at small neighborhood stores, which are located in homes. People commonly shop on a daily basis because they lack refrigerators. Urban people purchase their food from supermarkets, grocery stores, or farmers markets.

SOCIETY

Government. Paraguay is a constitutional democracy divided into 17 *departamentos* (provinces) and the capital city. It is headed by an elected president who cannot serve two consecutive terms. The president, currently Nicanor Duarte Frutos, is chief of state and head of government. Legislators in the 45-seat Chamber of Senators and 80-seat Chamber of Deputies are elected to five-year terms. The voting age is 18; adults are required by law to vote until age 75. Paraguay's principal political parties are the Colorado Party and the Authentic Radical Liberal Party.

Economy. Paraguay's formal economy is based primarily on agriculture; most rural families grow cotton as their primary cash crop. Beef is an important export; cattle are raised on expansive ranches usually owned by foreigners. Many Paraguayans work in the country's large informal sector, involving the resale of consumer goods.

The government has sought ways to decrease dependence on cotton, but little progress has been realized. Rural families commonly send one or more members to other countries to work. Political instability, foreign debt, and lack of infrastructure inhibit economic progress. Other challenges include lack of a trained workforce and high unemployment. Deforestation has effectively ruined the potential for a sustainable timber industry. Land redistribution, foreign investment, and economic diversification are needed to improve conditions.

A small wealthy class has most of the nation's assets. While Paraguay's real gross domestic product has doubled in the last generation, more than a third of the population lives below the poverty line. Most economic opportunities are available only to urban residents.

In an effort to strengthen regional economic activity and boost foreign investment, Paraguay joined the Mercosur trade bloc, which includes Paraguay, Argentina, and Uruguay. However, the economy is still somewhat weak and unemployment remains high. Paraguay's currency is the *guaraní* (PYG) Currency inflation is another major problem: In 1999, one U.S. dollar was worth about 3,000 guaranís; in 2004 it was worth about 6,000.

Transportation and Communications. Paraguay has some paved highways, but most roads are not paved. Buses serve as the main form of public transportation throughout the country. Wealthier urban residents have cars, but rural people often walk. Taxis are available in Asunción. There are several television channels, and a private cable company services Asunción. Both AM and FM radio stations broadcast throughout the country. Most people do not have telephones, but public phones are available and cellular phones are becoming popular. The internet is widely used in the capital, and is becoming more common elsewhere.

DEVELOPMENT DATA
Human Dev. Index* rank . . . . 89 of 177 countries
   Adjusted for women . . . . 75 of 144 countries
Real GDP per capita $4,610
Adult literacy rate . . . . 93 percent (male); 90 (female)
Infant mortality rate . . . . 27 per 1,000 births
Life expectancy . . . . 69 (male); 73 (female)

Education. Public education is provided free of charge, but students must buy uniforms and are asked to help buy supplies. Schools tend to be crowded. Instruction is usually in Spanish, which can be a hardship on rural children whose primary language is Guaraní. Most children begin school, but less than half complete all six years of primary school. About one-third of eligible children attend secondary school. Opportunities for those who finish school are limited, and many either work in the fields or migrate to other countries to find work. There are some institutions of higher learning, but only 1 percent of the population attends college. The official literacy rate does not reflect reality in rural areas, where the literacy rate is substantially lower.

Health. The healthcare system includes hospitals and clinics. The smaller the town, the smaller the clinic. Rural health posts are staffed a few days a week by a nurse. Rural people use traditional herbs and cures to treat minor ailments. While Paraguayans value cleanliness, unsanitary conditions such as poor sewage systems contribute to poor health. Malnutrition affects children. Severe dental problems afflict a majority of the population. Other major issues include cardiovascular disease, parasites, and pneumonia.

AT A GLANCE

Events and Trends.
- In June 2004, former military general and coup leader Lino Oviedo returned to Paraguay after years of exile. He was hoping to regain the power he had once held. However, he was arrested in the airport and must first face several criminal charges before he can hope to have a political future.
- A shopping-center fire in the capital city claimed the lives of more than 420 people. The fire was believed to have started in a food preparation area inside the shopping center before spreading throughout the building. Three days of national mourning were declared for the victims.
- During much of 2004, many private lands were invaded and occupied for a short time by peasant farmers. The farmers were demanding land reform that would redistribute some properties from wealthy private owners to thousands of landless workers.

Contact Information. Embassy of Paraguay, 2400 Massachusetts Avenue NW, Washington, DC 20008; phone (202) 483-6960.

CultureGrams World Edition 2006

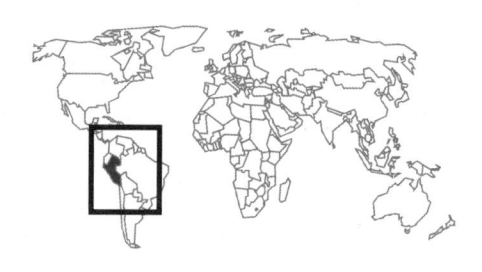

Republic of Peru

BACKGROUND

Land and Climate. Almost the same size as Alaska, Peru is the third largest country in South America. It covers 496,226 square miles (1,285,220 square kilometers). Peru is divided into three distinct geographic regions: the narrow, dry coastal plain (*costa*) in the west; the high Andes Mountains (*sierra*), roughly in the center; and the tropical lowlands of the Amazon Basin (*selva*) to the east. The Andes rise to elevations of 22,000 feet (6,706 meters). Forests, principally in the Andes and the Amazon Basin, cover more than half of the country. Only about 3 percent of the land is suitable for farming. The population is concentrated in the west. Peru's biodiversity allows for a wide variety of flora and fauna. Plant life ranges from desert vegetation to tropical forests. More than four hundred species of mammals—including jaguars, tapirs, alligators, llamas, alpacas, and monkeys—inhabit the interior of the country. Marine life and bird life are equally diverse; the government has set aside more than 50 areas as protected land.

Mild earthquakes are common, while more destructive quakes take place less frequently. Peru shares with Bolivia the highest navigable body of water in the world—Lake Titicaca. There is little rainfall along the coast, although the winter is foggy, humid, and cool. In the capital city of Lima, the temperature is moderate year-round, averaging 65°F (18°C). Temperatures vary significantly between the rugged Andes and the eastern jungles. The El Niño weather phenomenon periodically has a dramatic impact on Peru, often causing flooding and mudslides.

History. Several of South America's most advanced cultures lived in pre-Columbian Peru. The last of these groups was the great Incan Empire, which was unsurpassed in the art of stonecutting and also achieved a high degree of economic and political development. Chimu ruins at Chan Chan as well as Incan ruins at Cuzco and Machu Picchu make Peru a favorite destination for archaeologists and tourists. In 1532, the Spanish invaded Peru under the leadership of Francisco Pizarro. They conquered the Incas the next year. The area soon became the richest and most powerful Spanish colony in South America because of its location and many mineral treasures.

Under the leadership of South American liberator José de San Martín, Peru declared independence from Spain in July 1821. With the help of Simón Bolívar, the Venezuelan general who liberated several other countries, the fight for full independence was won in 1826. For a century, Peru worked to secure its territory and build its social institutions.

Peru's 1933 constitution mandated that the country be governed by a president and legislature elected to six-year terms; however, military leaders and dictators dominated Peru until the 1960s. A free multiparty election was held in 1963 and Fernando Belaúnde Terry was elected president. A military junta deposed him in 1968 and ruled for 12 years (a period called *la dictadura*). Belaúnde was reelected in 1980 when the military returned control of the government to civilians.

Economic troubles, which began during *la dictadura*, worsened under Belaúnde and were not resolved during Alán García's presidency (1985–90). In 1980, the Maoist group *Sendero Luminoso* (Shining Path) began a campaign of violent guerrilla warfare with the aim of overthrowing the government. The Shining Path and other terrorist organizations were responsible for some tens of thousands of deaths during the 1980s and 1990s. They held power in the Upper Huallaga Valley and were paid by drug traffickers for protection and the right to operate in the region.

Peru

Despite these problems, the country maintained democratic institutions and free elections. In 1990, Alberto Fujimori, a son of Japanese immigrants, was elected president. He promised government reform and vowed to overcome economic problems and terrorist violence. Saying he needed to make drastic changes to enable progress, Fujimori suspended the constitution, dissolved Congress, took emergency powers, and restricted civil liberties. A 1993 national referendum approved a new constitution that outlined a democratic, albeit more executive-centered, government and a free-market-oriented economy. Fujimori was reelected by a large margin in 1995, and his party gained a majority in Congress. Fujimori's popularity was heightened by his successful economic reform, the 1992 capture of Shining Path leader Abimael Guzmán Reynoso, and the resolution of Peru's long-standing border dispute with Ecuador.

Fujimori was elected for a third presidential term in May 2000, but accusations of misuse of power and public funds arose, and the leader fled to Japan and resigned in November 2000. In 2002, Peru issued arrest warrants for Fujimori. Despite pressure from Amnesty International, which cites Fujimori's alleged human-rights abuses, Japan has refused to extradite him.

After Fujimori fled, his opponent, Alejandro Toledo, was elected as the nation's first president of indigenous heritage. Toledo's main challenges include continuing to reduce the threat from Peru's rebel groups, rooting out government corruption, and making economic reforms effective in the lives of Peru's many poor.

THE PEOPLE

Population. The population of Peru is approximately 27.5 million and is growing at 1.4 percent annually. Population density is generally low. Peru's population is ethnically diverse. About 45 percent is of indigenous heritage, descendants of the Inca Empire. Many ethnic and linguistic divisions exist among indigenous peoples, some of whom are still fairly isolated in the Amazon jungle. Another 37 percent is of mixed indigenous and European heritage. Fifteen percent is of European descent (mostly Spanish), and the remaining 3 percent is composed of black descendants of West African slaves, as well as other groups, such as Japanese and Chinese immigrants. About one-third of the population is younger than age 15. Lima is the largest city, with approximately eight million residents. About three-fourths of the population lives in urban areas.

Language. Spanish and the indigenous languages Quechua and Aymara are officially recognized. Many Peruvians speak both Spanish and an indigenous language. Approximately 40 indigenous languages are spoken in the Peruvian Amazon alone and about 30 percent of the people speak no Spanish at all. Quechua was the language of the Inca Empire and is the root of English words such as *condor*, *guano*, *llama*, and *puma*. Aymara is spoken by about 300,000 Peruvians, mainly in southern Peru. Peruvians with more formal education often are taught English as a second or third language.

Religion. The Roman Catholic Church was the state church in Peru until 1979. Today there is freedom of religion and all churches enjoy equal political status, but about 90 percent of Peruvians are Roman Catholic and the church continues to play a significant role in their lives. Protestant and Evangelical churches also operate in the country. Many indigenous peoples who are Catholic mix traditional beliefs with Christian values, sometimes calling indigenous gods by Christian names.

General Attitudes. Peruvians are strong-willed and nationalistic. They have faced many challenges, both political and economic in nature, but maintain a strong desire to endure and succeed. The people have a good sense of humor and are accommodating and eager to please. Still, they may be sensitive about certain things. Jokes about their lifestyle, especially from foreigners, are offensive. Personal criticism, if necessary, is expected to be expressed in a positive manner.

The Peruvian concept of time is more relaxed than in industrialized nations. Appointments and other meetings may not begin on time, and Peruvians generally consider people to be more important than schedules. However, international visitors from countries where punctuality is more valued are expected to be on time for appointments.

Indigenous people are sometimes discriminated against by Peru's mestizo and European populations. Indigenous people usually live in rural areas, but even those who move to the city and adopt an urban lifestyle are not accepted. This has fueled great resentment and is one source of the country's social problems. Indigenous groups now place some hope in promises of increased investment from international organizations and the government.

Urban residents, particularly in Lima, are turning their attention to economic progress. People generally are optimistic about the country's future, especially with the return of democracy, the decrease in major insurgency movements, and economic reforms.

Personal Appearance. Western-style clothing is worn in Lima and other urban areas. People dress up when going to public places, such as the *plaza de armas* (town plaza). It is thought of as bad taste to leave the home wearing old or dirty clothes. Rural *campesinos* (farmers) often wear traditional outfits related to their ethnic background. Their clothes commonly are made of handwoven fabrics.

CUSTOMS AND COURTESIES

Greetings. When being introduced or meeting for the first time, members of the opposite sex usually shake hands. Women (and close friends of the opposite sex) commonly kiss each other on one cheek when meeting and parting. Men usually shake hands or pat each other on the shoulder. An arm around the shoulders or a pat on the back is a polite way to greet young people.

Typical greetings include ¡*Buenos días!* (Good morning), ¡*Buenas tardes!* (Good afternoon), and ¡*Buenas noches!* (Good evening/night). Friends address each other by first name. Professionals are addressed by their title (*Doctor/a*, *Profesor/a*, etc.). Older people are addressed as *Señor* (Mr.) or *Señora* (Mrs.), followed by their last name. Women and girls often are addressed by strangers as *Señorita* (Miss).

Gestures. Peruvians are often animated and use a lot of hand gestures while conversing. One beckons by holding the palm of the hand downward and waving all of the fingers. Personal space is limited. People stand very close to each other when they talk, often lightly touching the arm or shoulder of the person with whom they are speaking. Constant eye contact is important. On buses, men usually give their seat to women or elderly persons.

Visiting. Peruvians enjoy visiting one another. Most visits between friends and relatives are unannounced. However, when one visits other people, it is polite to make advance arrangements. Visitors are expected to feel at home and be comfortable. The traditional greeting *Está en su casa* (You are in your house) reflects Peruvian hospitality. Hosts always offer their guests drinks (water, juice, soda, etc.) and may offer other refreshments, but declining them is not impolite. In many areas, those visiting around 5:30 p.m. are invited to stay for *lonche*, a light breakfast-type meal served around 6 p.m. Hosts appreciate special acknowledgment of children in the home. It is polite to show concern for the health of the hosts' family and relatives. When visiting a home, one is not expected to bring gifts, but small gifts such as fruit or wine are welcome on any occasion. Dinner guests commonly bring such gifts.

Eating. Peruvians eat in the continental style, with the fork in the left hand and the knife in the right. They keep both hands (but not elbows) above the table at all times. Proper table manners are important. It is impolite to converse with only one person at the table without including the rest of the group. If this occurs, Peruvians will often repeat the saying *Secretos en reunión es mala educación* (It is bad manners to tell secrets in gatherings). Guests are expected to eat all of the food that is offered; excuses for not eating something are to be given tactfully. In a restaurant, one summons the server by waving. If service is not included in the bill, a tip is expected, and if service is included, a small tip is still given.

LIFESTYLE

Family. The family unit is important in Peru. Nuclear families have, on average, three children. The father is the head of the family. Because the mother usually spends most of her time at home, she is in charge of the children and their day-to-day activities. The father usually is consulted only for major matters. The mother directs and performs household duties. Women occasionally work outside the home, a trend that is more evident in urban areas. About one-third of the labor force is female. Most families live in humble circumstances without many of the modern conveniences common in more industrialized nations. Newly married couples often live in their parents' home until they can afford a place of their own.

Dating and Marriage. Young people in urban areas enjoy dancing at *fiestas* (parties) and social gatherings. Dating is exclusive: people do not date more than one person at the same time. Only after a couple breaks up are they allowed to date others. Men usually marry in their late twenties, while women generally marry in their early twenties. People in rural areas often marry at younger ages. Weddings usually include a civil ceremony, a church wedding, and a party for family and friends. The party frequently includes dancing and a one- or two-course meal. Common-law marriages are prevalent and widely accepted, except among the upper classes.

Diet. Main staples in the diet include rice, beans, fish, and a variety of tropical fruits. Soups are also common. Corn, native to Peru, is a staple among the indigenous people. Guinea pigs are eaten throughout the country and are raised in nearly all rural homes. *Ceviche* (raw fish seasoned with lemon and vinegar) is popular on the coast. *Papa a la Huancaina* is a baked potato topped with sliced eggs and a sauce (such as hot chili). Highland dishes often include potatoes, onions, and garlic. Fresh vegetables are eaten in season. People purchase most food on a daily basis, either in small corner stores (in cities) or large open-air markets. Bargaining is common in the markets but not in other types of stores.

Recreation. The most popular sport in Peru is *fútbol* (soccer). Peruvians enthusiastically follow World Cup competitions, especially when their national team is participating. Basketball, volleyball, and gymnastics are also favorites. Families enjoy picnics, and movies provide entertainment. Sunday is a favorite day for outings.

The Arts. Music is important to most Peruvians. International music is widespread, especially with the younger generation and along the coast, but traditional music is also very popular. Traditional songs often are about Peru, Peruvian culture, people's feelings, or animals. Three instruments used to play traditional music are the *charango*, a small guitar of sorts; the *antara*, an assortment of vertically placed flutes tied together; and the *quena*, which is similar to a recorder. Two types of music and dance from the mountains are *baile de las tijeras* (dance of the scissors) and *huayno*. Most cities have their own dances. The *cajón* is an athletic dance that is performed in Lima by those of African descent.

Folk arts, especially textiles, are integral to Peruvian culture. Many textiles are made from the wool of the *alpaca* (similar to a llama); clothing is made from this thick wool, along with wall hangings and other decorative art. Ruins like Machu Picchu, *alpacas*, condors, and people are frequently featured on these wall hangings. *Retablos*, another form of folk art, are wooden boxes that feature three-dimensional religious scenes or everyday moments. Pottery and metalworking are other prevalent crafts.

Like many other Latin Americans, Peruvians have written about the problems in society, specifically the problems concerning indigenous peoples. An indigenous literary genre known as *Indianista* focuses on indignities suffered by native peoples. Peruvian literature is often romantic, with mythological or fantastical themes.

Holidays. National holidays include New Year's Day, Easter (Thursday–Sunday), Countryman's Day (24 June), St. Peter and St. Paul's Day (29 June), Independence Day (28 July), National Day (29 July), St. Rose of Lima Day (30 Aug.), Navy Day (8 Oct.), All Saints' Day (1 Nov.), Immaculate Conception (8 Dec.), and Christmas. Independence Day is one of the most popular holidays. It is celebrated with fireworks and bands at the local *plaza de armas*. Schools usually take a one- or two-week break and businesses may close for such celebrations. Many local holidays honor patron saints or celebrate the harvest, as well as providing recreational opportunities.

Commerce. Peru's average workweek is slightly more than 48 hours, one of the longest in the world. Businesses are open at least six days a week. Some small businesses close between 1 and 3 p.m. each day for a *siesta* (break), but this is not as common today as it once was. Many shops remain open late into the evening. Business hours vary slightly according to the season but generally are between 8 a.m. and 5 p.m. Some government offices close as early as 1 p.m.

SOCIETY

Government. Peru is a republic. It is divided into 24 *departamentos* (similar to states) and the province of Callao. The president, currently Alejandro Toledo, holds executive power and serves a five-year term. Under the constitution, presidents may serve two consecutive terms. The executive branch is headed by the president and also includes two vice presidents and a Council of Ministers, the members of which are appointed by the president.

The unicameral Congress consists of 120 members, who serve five-year terms. The Supreme Court, composed of 16 judges, is the country's highest judicial authority. Major political parties include the Peru Possible Party, the National Unity Party, the Independent Moralizing Front, and the Popular

Peru

Action Party. Several other parties are also active. All citizens age 18 and older may vote.

Economy. The Peruvian economy faced severe strains in the early 1990s: inflation was high, output was low, and the standard of living was dropping. Government reforms have cut hyperinflation from 7,600 percent in 1990 to about 2.5 percent in 2004, attracted foreign investment, and produced stability and economic growth. However, the pace of economic growth has been slowed by global economic downturns and the recurring El Niño phenomenon. Unemployment remains high, and more than half of all Peruvians live in poverty.

Peru's natural resources include copper, silver, gold, iron ore, oil, timber, and fish. Peru has a relatively wide economic base with a variety of industries it can depend on for growth. Wheat, potatoes, sugarcane, rice, and coffee are important agricultural products. Agriculture accounts for about one-third of all employment. Peru's fishing industry is one of the largest in the world but recently has suffered setbacks because of El Niño. Peru is a member of the Andean Community trade bloc with Bolivia, Colombia, Ecuador, and Venezuela. The currency is the *nuevo sol* (PEN).

Economic dependence on the lucrative drug trade has been a major challenge for the country. Drug traffickers sell locally grown coca leaf (the basis of cocaine) to Colombian drug cartels for eventual export. Although many farmers would prefer to make a living raising crops like coffee or cacao, they cannot afford to stop growing the more profitable coca leaf. This is likely the main reason that Peru remains one of the world's largest producers of coca.

Transportation and Communications. Buses are the most popular form of transportation. Many middle- and upper-class families own a car but regularly use public transportation, because gasoline is expensive. In rural areas, people travel on foot or with the help of animals. Most roads are not paved. Two main roads, the Pan-American Highway and the Marginal Jungle Highway, run the length of the country from north to south. Train and air travel are available on a limited basis; some train routes are very scenic.

The privatization of the telecommunications system has increased and improved service. Telephone lines are available in most rural areas. Internet cafés, known in Peru as *cabinas internet*, now provide service, mostly in urban areas. Peru has several daily newspapers.

Education. Peruvians are generally well educated. Public education is free and compulsory between ages seven and sixteen. However, schools lack basic materials, and facilities are inadequate. Peru has increased efforts to extend primary schools into remote areas. However, the Shining Path controlled school facilities in some areas, so the government has attempted to reestablish control in these areas. Secondary education is also free in Peru. About half of eligible children are enrolled in secondary schools. Enrollment in both primary and secondary schools is increasing. The average adult has completed at least six years of school, and more young people are staying in school. The literacy rate is higher among teenagers than adults. Peru has more than 30 universities, including the University of San Marcos in Lima, one of the oldest in South America.

© 2005 ProQuest Information and Learning Company and Brigham Young University. It is against the law to copy, reprint, store, or transmit any part of this publication in any form by any means without written permission from ProQuest. This document contains native commentary and original analysis, as well as estimated statistics. The content should not be considered strictly factual, and it may not apply to all groups in a nation. *UN Development Programme, Human Development Report 2004 (New York: Oxford University Press, 2004).

DEVELOPMENT DATA
Human Dev. Index* rank . . . . 85 of 177 countries
  Adjusted for women. . . . . 74 of 144 countries
Real GDP per capita $5,010
Adult literacy rate . . . . 91 percent (male); 80 (female)
Infant mortality rate . . . . 33 per 1,000 births
Life expectancy . . . . 67 (male); 72 (female)

Health. Medical care is adequate in major cities but less developed in other areas. Quality care is available only through expensive private clinics. Hospitals are often short on medicine, food, and other supplies and equipment. Many Peruvians are superstitious about health care and are reluctant to use medical facilities. They prefer using home remedies made of herbs and roots before going to a doctor. Many people rely on the treatments of a *curandero/a* (native healer) as well. Care in small towns is often unreliable or altogether unavailable. Diseases such as typhoid, yellow fever, cholera, Chagas, and malaria are active in Peru. Water is not always safe to drink. Roughly 20 percent of the population suffers from malnutrition, and women and children are particularly affected.

AT A GLANCE
Events and Trends.
- In January 2005, about 150 military reservists took control of a remote police station, demanding President Toledo's resignation. Although the group agreed to withdraw a few days later, the uprising was a sign of President Toledo's deep unpopularity in Peru, where he usually gets about 10 percent approval ratings.
- Even though former president Fujimori has been living in exile in Japan for years, in October 2004 he announced his intentions to return to Peru and run for president in 2006. However, he is still wanted on charges for several crimes. In November 2004, Peruvian authorities again asked Japan to extradite Fujimori to Peru for trial.
- Meanwhile, Vladimiro Montesinos—the former head of intelligence and one of Fujimori's closest aides—was sentenced to another 15 years of jail for corruption, embezzlement, and conspiracy. It was the most recent in a long line of convictions for Montesinos.
- In November 2003, the United Nations Educational, Scientific, and Cultural Organization (UNESCO) said it would recommend that Peru change its tourism policy at Machu Picchu, reducing the number of tourists allowed. The organization believes that the more than 1500 tourists who visit the site each day are damaging the Incan ruins.

Contact Information. Embassy of the Republic of Peru, Consular Section, 1700 Massachusetts Avenue NW, Washington, DC 20036; phone (202) 833-9860. Commission for the Promotion of Peru; phone (866) 661-7378; web site www.peru.info/perueng.asp

CultureGrams
People. The World. You.

ProQuest Information and Learning Company
300 North Zeeb Road, P.O. Box 1346
Ann Arbor, Michigan 48106 USA
Toll Free: 1.800.528.6279
Fax: 1.800.864.0019
www.culturegrams.com

CultureGrams World Edition 2006

Commonwealth of Puerto Rico

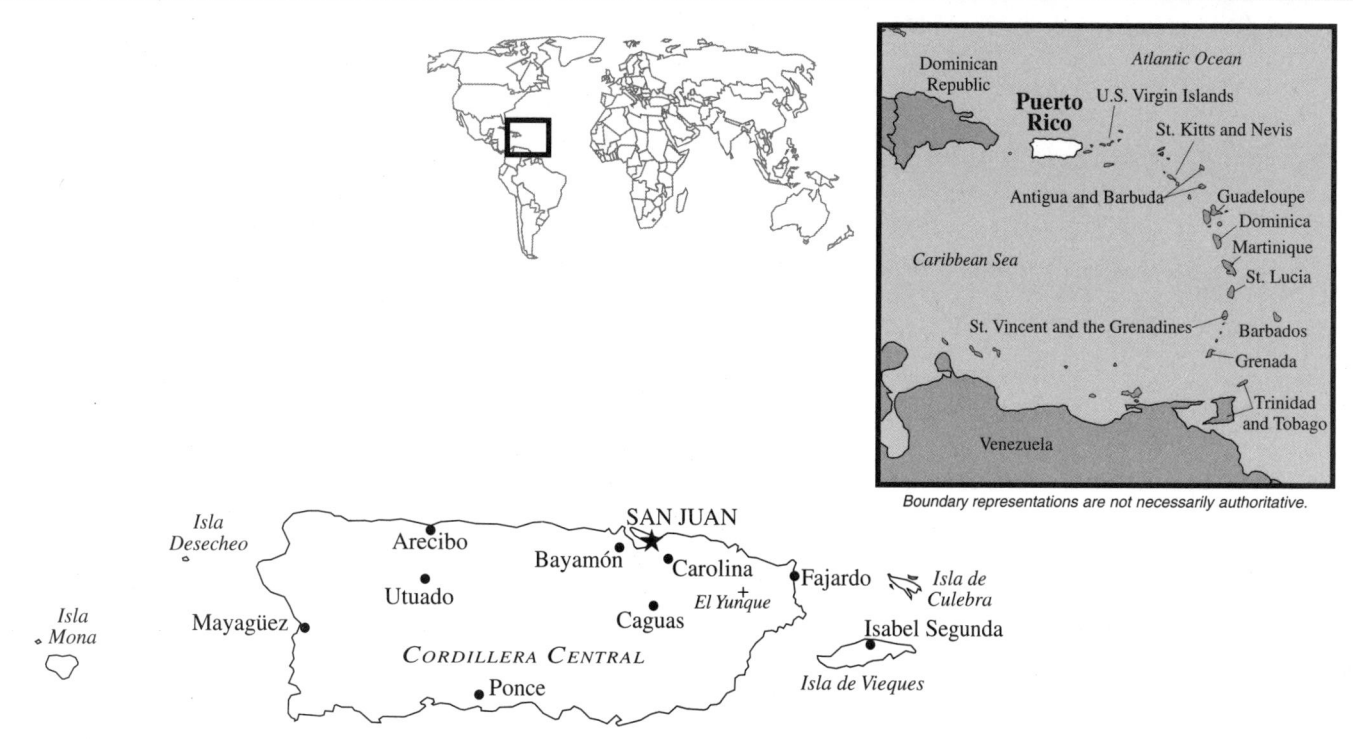

BACKGROUND

Land and Climate. Covering 3,515 square miles (9,104 square kilometers), Puerto Rico is about the same size as Delaware and Rhode Island combined. Its territory includes the islands of Culebra, Vieques, Desecheo, and Mona. The waters between Isla Mona (Mona Island) and the capital, San Juan, form a key shipping lane for vessels heading to the Panama Canal. San Juan has one of the best natural ports in the Caribbean. The island of Puerto Rico is characterized by the Cordillera Central (a high central mountain range), a dry southern coast, fertile northern coastal plains, low eastern mountains, and El Yunque rain forest. Relatively little land (4 percent) is available for cultivation. The coastal plains are densely populated. Widespread deforestation of the island in the early 1900s combined with the current level of industrialization and population density have left few animal species remaining in the wild. The government has set aside land to protect the nation's flora and fauna.

Puerto Rico's climate is mildly tropical, with warm and sunny weather. Rain falls mainly between May and December; it is moderate in coastal regions and heavier in the mountains. The island is often affected by excessive rains that accompany regional storms. Temperatures average 70 to 80°F (21–27°C) year-round. Several destructive hurricanes have hit the island.

History. The indigenous Taíno people were living in Puerto Rico when Columbus arrived in 1493. He named the island San Juan Bautista and claimed the island for Spain at that time, but colonization did not begin in earnest until 1508. The Spanish introduced slavery and diseases that decimated the indigenous population. In 1511, thousands of Taíno were killed and thousands more fled the island after a failed revolt. European settlers began to import African slaves in 1513. Slavery was not abolished until 1873.

The Spanish-appointed governor strictly controlled Puerto Rico. Despite protests, few promised reforms were ever implemented. An increasing sense of frustration led Puerto Ricans to rebel. The 1868 revolt, *El Grito de Lares*, ended swiftly and brutally, leaving hundreds of protestors dead. However, Spain began to slowly open the political process until in 1897 it granted Puerto Rico self-rule under the leadership of Luis Muñoz Rivera. Self-governance was short-lived, for in 1898, as part of the Spanish-American War, the United States invaded the island and conquered its Spanish defenders. Spain ceded the island to the United States that same year. In 1917, Puerto Rico officially became a U.S. territory and its people were granted citizenship. In 1946, President Harry S. Truman appointed Jesús Toribio Piñero as the first governor who had been born on the island. Two years later, Puerto Ricans directly elected a governor, Luis Muñoz Marín.

Puerto Rico became a commonwealth of the United States with its own constitution in July 1952. Opposition to commonwealth status has at times erupted into violence. In 1954, militants from Puerto Rico shot several congressional representatives in Washington, D.C., during a session of the House of Representatives. Since then, political groups have occasionally debated the island's status and its relationship with the United States. Puerto Ricans today remain divided by the issue of whether to request U.S. statehood or remain a commonwealth. A small group advocates full independence. Plebiscites in 1967 and 1993 approved the commonwealth status, but the margin of victory in 1993 was slim. A non-binding vote in 1998 also favored staying a commonwealth, although 47 percent of voters favored statehood.

Puerto Rico

THE PEOPLE

Population. Puerto Rico's population of about 3.9 million grows at an average annual rate of roughly 0.5 percent. Migration rates generally fluctuate relative to the strength of the U.S. economy. People tend to emigrate when there are better work opportunities on the mainland. About 80 percent of the population is of Hispanic origin, another 8 percent is black, others have a mixed Spanish, African, and Taíno heritage. The effects of the different cultures can be seen in the island's music, arts, food, and traditions. About one-third of the population lives in the greater area of San Juan, which includes Bayamón and Carolina. More than one million Puerto Ricans live in New York City, the destination of most emigrants. Another million reside elsewhere in the United States.

Language. Spanish and English share official status in Puerto Rico. For a short time in the early 1990s, Spanish was declared the only official language, but English has since regained equal status. Spanish is the language of school instruction and daily life. English is required as a second language in school and is used in business. Most people can speak English. The official status of either language often depends on the political climate surrounding Puerto Rico's relationship with the United States.

The close relationship Puerto Rico has with the United States and English has led people to mix many English words with spoken Spanish. Locally, people call this mixed speech *Spanglish*, and it is a comfortable, informal method of communication.

Religion. Roman Catholicism is the major Christian religion in Puerto Rico and claims about 85 percent of the population as members. Most of the remainder belong to various Protestant and other Christian churches, and their numbers are growing. Although there is a separation of church and state, Catholic traditions and customs prevail among the people. Puerto Ricans consider themselves religious and often attribute their good fortunes to Deity.

General Attitudes. Puerto Ricans are sensitive people, quick to express sympathy and equally quick to resent a slight. They are gregarious and fond of *fiestas* (celebrations). They admire people who are intelligent, hardworking, dedicated, and humble. Puerto Ricans consider open criticism, aggressiveness, and greed offensive. Many believe a person's destiny is God's will, although individuals must also watch for opportunities.

Puerto Ricans value a good education, and a large number of students not only finish high school but also attend college or another institution of higher learning. Gaining a good education is considered a key to a better future. Being able to buy land for a home or business is a universal goal. National and regional pride are strong. Political influence is desirable; individuals who have such power are admired.

The Puerto Rican concept of time is somewhat relaxed. People are considered more important than schedules. If a friend, relative, or business associate drops in unexpectedly, Puerto Ricans will stop everything they are doing to visit, even if they have other commitments.

Personal Appearance. Puerto Ricans take great pride in what they wear in public. Young people favor popular North American fashions and sporty styles. Sloppy, overly casual, or revealing dress is considered inappropriate. Because of the warm climate, people tend to prefer lightweight fabrics. Jeans are popular at all age levels for informal activities and outdoor work. Tennis shoes and sandals are the most commonly worn footwear. People living in interior towns may wear sweaters and jackets during winter months, as nighttime temperatures can be cool.

Shorts are acceptable casual wear. However, for most parties and social gatherings, formal clothing is expected, including suits with a shirt and tie for men, and dresses or skirts and blouses for women.

CUSTOMS AND COURTESIES

Greetings. People usually shake hands when greeting. Close friends often greet by grasping shoulders and kissing each other on the cheek. Women normally kiss women or men in this manner, but men do not greet other men this way. However, they may embrace a good friend or relative after a long absence. People stand very close when talking, and females often touch each other with their hands. Moving away, even slightly, may be considered an insult.

Although Spanish is most common, both Spanish and English greetings are used. One might hear *Good morning* or *¡Buenos días!*, *Good afternoon* or *¡Buenas tardes!*, *Good evening* or *¡Buenas noches!*, and *Hi* or *¡Hola!* When one meets a person for the first time, it is polite to say *How are you?* or *¿Cómo está?* Young friends often begin a conversation with *¿Qué tal?*, a casual way to ask "How are you?" The language speakers use depends on the situation (e.g., on the street, in a business meeting) and the relationship between the people talking.

When addressing others in formal situations, one may use titles of respect or profession alone or in combination with a person's surname. These might include *Señor* (Mr.), *Señora* ("Mrs." or "Ms."), *Señorita* (Miss), *Doctor/a* (Dr.), and so on. One respectfully addresses an older person by combining the title *Don* (for men) or *Doña* (for women) with the person's first name. Friends address each other by given name or nickname.

Most Puerto Ricans have two surnames in addition to one or two given names. The family name is the father's surname; this appears as the second-to-last name, while the mother's surname appears last. Therefore, a man named Victor Arocho Ramos would be called *Señor Arocho*. Women do not change their surnames when they marry.

Gestures. One beckons by waving all fingers with the palm down; beckoning people with the palm facing up is improper. Wiggling the nose is a way of asking "What's going on?" To point, people often purse or pucker their lips in the direction they are indicating. Rather than tossing or throwing small items, one hands them to the other person. During conversation, Puerto Ricans might interrupt each other; this generally is not considered rude. Although peers may tease each other in informal situations, such joking is not appropriate in formal settings.

A person can get another's attention by saying "pssst." This is common and not rude, but if a man does it to a woman, she will usually ignore him. Men often smile and stare at women, but it is considered improper for a woman to smile indiscriminately at strangers. It is appropriate for a man to offer his seat to a woman on public transportation. On longer trips, people often share food, and refusing such an offer is impolite.

Visiting. Visiting friends and relatives is considered a social obligation; people expect it as a basic courtesy. While inviting guests to the home is not uncommon, most casual visits occur in the early evening without prior arrangement. Visits are relaxed and the entire family participates. Guests are treated to refreshments such as juice, soda, crackers, and cookies. If visitors arrive at mealtime, the hosts generally invite them to join the meal. In most cases, guests politely decline the offer a few times before finally accepting.

Unannounced visits are usually short (one or two hours), but planned activities can last longer. Friends and relatives invited for dinner are expected to stay after the meal to relax and enjoy conversation with the hosts. Invited guests are not expected to bring gifts, except on special occasions. However, hosts may appreciate a gift of flowers, candy, or fruit. If offered, gifts are opened in the presence of the giver.

Eating. Puerto Ricans eat three meals each day, and dinner is the main family meal. The eating atmosphere is relaxed and cordial. Diners always keep both hands above the table. Spoons and forks are commonly used; knives are used when appropriate. Some foods are eaten with the hands. Food left on the plate may be interpreted as a sign that the guest did not enjoy the dish. Hosts might offer second helpings when guests finish their food, but guests may politely decline.

On the street, people normally eat food near the stand where they purchase it, but it is not uncommon for people to eat while walking in public. At a restaurant, leaving a 15 percent tip is customary when service is not included in the bill.

LIFESTYLE

Family. The Puerto Rican family is close-knit and supportive. Extended families usually do not share a household, but they often live in the same neighborhood or town. This proximity facilitates frequent visits among relatives and allows grandparents to provide child care when both parents work. Children often remain at home until they marry. Families have an average of three children. Parents consider themselves responsible for their children throughout life and expect to give adult children financial or emotional support if needed. Traditionally, children share the responsibility of caring for elderly parents; however, more elderly Puerto Ricans are being placed in nursing homes, often because of medical or economic concerns. If families emigrate to New York or elsewhere, one parent may move first and establish a home before the rest of the family joins him or her.

Dating and Marriage. Teens begin dating in groups but eventually pair off into boyfriend-girlfriend relationships. Dates may include going to the movies or on a picnic, dancing, or spending time at the beach. In rural areas, the relationship usually does not become serious until the young man has met the young woman's parents. Early dating leads some Puerto Ricans to marry, either formally or in a common-law partnership, at an early age (16–17). The majority of young women prefer marriage at a young age to single motherhood. However, an increasing emphasis on formal education has resulted in more Puerto Ricans marrying at a later age (19–21).

Whether a marriage is performed by a judge or in a church, a wedding is a time of great celebration and family gatherings. Families spend large amounts of money on decorations, food, and music, both traditional and modern.

Diet. Foods in Puerto Rico come from a variety of ethnic backgrounds, reflective of the people's mixed ancestry and colonial associations. The most commonly eaten main meal is beans and rice. Other popular dishes include *arroz con pollo* (rice and chicken), *bacalao con viandas* (boiled cod made with cassava and potatoes), *arroz con gandules y pernil* (rice with peas and roasted pork), and foods made with plantains. Plantains are a starchy banana-like fruit that must be cooked to be eaten. Chicken, pork, and beef are favorite meats. Seafood (shrimp, octopus, clams, fish) and fruits (pineapples, bananas, mangoes, papaya, grapefruit, and oranges) are also common in the diet. Pasta and fast foods tend to be popular among younger generations.

Packaged snack foods are as common as they are in the United States, but people also enjoy locally prepared snacks such as *frituras* (foods fried in oil). Popular varieties of *frituras* include *alcapurrias* (plantains with meat) and *sorullos* (corn flour). The local flat bread typically eaten with meals, *pan sobao*, is made with flour, water, and shortening.

Recreation. Puerto Ricans' favorite sport is baseball, but people also enjoy basketball and volleyball. Families enjoy going to the beach or parks for picnics. In their leisure time, people may visit one another or watch television or videos. Card and board games are also popular. A favorite strategy game is dominoes, in which two to four people play individually or on teams. The individual who places all of his/her tiles wins the game.

The Arts. The arts enjoy a wide following and reflect both African and Spanish influences. Long before the United States took possession of Puerto Rico, a strong tradition of literature and music, as well as scholarship, had been established. Indeed, art and music are fostered in the home; most Puerto Ricans can play a musical instrument, and a display of musical talent is usually expected at parties. Salsa, *bomba* (dance music influenced by West African rhythms and traditions), *plena* (folk music that deals with life's hardships), and *danza puertorriqueña* (Puerto Rican dance music) are the most popular forms of music for dancing and singing. The prestigious Pablo Casals Festival (late May–early June) features special concerts. Puerto Rican films and other cultural arts are known throughout the world. Among the most common folk arts are the carved religious figurines, called *santos*, which are found in almost every home. They represent the local patron saint or other Christian personages.

Holidays. Puerto Ricans celebrate New Year's Day as part of the Christmas season. The season ends with the Day of the Three Kings (6 Jan.), when each child receives a gift. Puerto Rico celebrates both local and U.S. national holidays. Holidays include the Birth of Eugenio María de Hostos (11 Jan.), Martin Luther King Jr.'s Birthday (second Monday in January), Presidents' Day (third Monday in February), the Abolition of Slavery (22 Mar.), Easter (including Good Friday), José de Diego's Birthday (third Monday in April), Memorial Day (last Monday in May), U.S. Independence Day (4 July), Luis Muñoz Rivera's Day (17 July), Constitution Day (25 July), José Celso Barbosa's Birthday (28 July), Labor Day (first Monday in September), All Souls' Day (2 Nov.), Discovery of Puerto Rico Day (19 Nov.), Thanksgiving, and Christmas. An important part of the Christmas season is the *parrandas*, when groups of friends sing Christmas songs door-to-door. They expect food and drinks in return for this entertainment.

Every town honors its patron saint annually with several days of activities, which include going to amusement parks, gambling, singing, dancing, and participating in religious ceremonies. A beauty queen is selected for almost every activity. *Carnaval* celebrations held before Lent (during February or March) are most visible in Ponce. Lively festivities there, as well as in Arecibo and other towns, feature "monsters" (*vejigantes*) who wear bells and elaborate papier-mâché masks with multiple horns. The *vejigantes* roam the streets, threatening to hit people on the head with a dried pig's bladder while children try to gather bells from their costumes.

Commerce. Business hours generally run weekdays between

Puerto Rico

9 a.m. to 5 p.m., although there are variations. Stores and shops may stay open 24 hours, and many retail outlets are open on Saturday. Some open on Sunday. The same national retail chains found throughout the United States also have stores in Puerto Rico. In the past, U.S. companies operating in Puerto Rico enjoyed a tax-exempt status because federal taxes did not apply in a commonwealth. This policy is changing and is scheduled to end completely by the end of 2005. Government offices are open from 8 a.m. to 4:30 p.m.

SOCIETY

Government. The Commonwealth of Puerto Rico has 78 municipalities. The chief of state is the U.S. president, currently George W. Bush, but the head of government is a locally elected governor. Anibal Acevedo Vila, a former non-voting representative in the U.S. Congress, is the current governor.

As commonwealth citizens, Puerto Ricans do not vote in U.S. national elections and do not pay federal income tax, but they do elect their own officials. They are subject to the draft and receive partial welfare benefits. They have no voting representation in the U.S. Congress and are restricted by federal controls in managing their territory. A locally elected resident high commissioner represents Puerto Rico in the U.S. House of Representatives. The high commissioner (Aníbal Acevedo-Vilá) cannot vote but can introduce legislation, express opinions, and engage in dialogue on issues that relate to Puerto Rico.

Puerto Rico's Legislative Assembly is composed of a 29-seat Senate and a 51-seat House of Representatives. All citizens age 18 and older may vote. Puerto Rico generally has a very high voter turnout rate. Elections are held on the same schedule as in the United States. Political parties include the pro-statehood New Progressive Party, the pro-commonwealth Popular Democratic Party, and the Independence Party.

Economy. Since World War II, industrialization and duty-free trade with the United States have transformed the once-poor agrarian island into a dynamic economy.

Only 3 percent of the population is now engaged in agriculture; 20 percent works in the industrial sector. The government, services, and tourism provide most of the nation's jobs. Unemployment is considerably higher than in the United States. Puerto Rico exports sugar, coffee, petroleum products, chemicals, pharmaceuticals, textiles, and electronic equipment. Drawbacks to industrialization include the fact that most foods must be imported, which makes them more expensive. But U.S. investment and labor laws have improved the standard of living for most people. The U.S. dollar (USD) is the official currency.

Transportation and Communications. Roads generally are in good condition, and most families have at least one car. Buses and taxis are available in large urban areas. *Públicos* serve most of the island. These large cars, fitting as many as six passengers, travel from each terminal to a fixed destination (with no stops in between). Air service operates domestically and internationally. Puerto Rico has numerous radio and television stations and newspapers. Most people have telephones and benefit from a modern communications network.

Education. Education is highly valued and the school system

DEVELOPMENT DATA
Human Dev. Index* rank . . . . NA
　Adjusted for women. . . . . NA
Real GDP per capita $16,800
Adult literacy rate . . . . 94 percent (male); 94 (female)
Infant mortality rate . . . . 8 per 1,000 births
Life expectancy . . . . 73 (male); 82 (female)

is continually improving. Primary and secondary schooling are the same as in the United States. Children begin kindergarten at age five or six. A high school diploma, earned upon completion of the 12th grade, is necessary to get a good job or go to college. The dropout rate is very low. Higher education is provided by several universities and colleges, including the University of Puerto Rico, with its nine campuses and 45,000 students. Other institutions include the Inter-American University, Catholic University, Turabo University, Sacred Heart University, and Puerto Rico Junior College. The literacy rate is higher among the youth than adults.

Health. A network of urban and rural health care centers and four medical schools (one public and three private) serve Puerto Rico's medical needs. The system of health care is similar to that in the United States, although people are not always eligible for the same federal funds.

AT A GLANCE
Events and Trends.

- In November 2004, Puerto Ricans went to the polls to vote for a new governor after Sila Calderón chose not to run for another term. However, the race between Anibal Acevedo Vila and Pedro Rosello was extremely close, with only 0.2 percent of votes separating them. Although the elections board eventually certified Acevedo Vila as the winner, debate about recounts raged on for some time.

- In 2004, several U.S.-based drug companies began moving some of their operations to Puerto Rico. The island offers advantages because it has several different types of tax breaks and has a superior infrastructure to other potential off-shore sites in Asia or Latin America.

- In May 2003, the U.S. Navy pulled out of the Island of Vieques, where it had been practicing bombing for more than 50 years. Eventually the land owned by the Navy will become a wildlife refuge. Although the base had been an economic boon to the island, residents opposed the Navy's presence. Protests intensified in 1999 after a stray bomb killed a civilian. Governor Sila Calderón, who had been elected in part because of her promises to end the Navy's presence on the island, helped to speed the process of the Navy's departure.

Contact Information. Puerto Rico Tourism Company, 666 Fifth Avenue, 15th Floor, New York, NY 10103; phone (800) 866-7827; web site www.gotopuertorico.com.

© 2005 ProQuest Information and Learning Company and Brigham Young University. It is against the law to copy, reprint, store, or transmit any part of this publication in any form by any means without written permission from ProQuest. This document contains native commentary and original analysis, as well as estimated statistics. The content should not be considered strictly factual, and it may not apply to all groups in a nation. *UN Development Programme, Human Development Report 2004 (New York: Oxford University Press, 2004).

CultureGrams
People. The World. You.

ProQuest Information and Learning Company
300 North Zeeb Road, P.O. Box 1346
Ann Arbor, Michigan 48106 USA
Toll Free: 1.800.528.6279
Fax: 1.800.864.0019
www.culturegrams.com

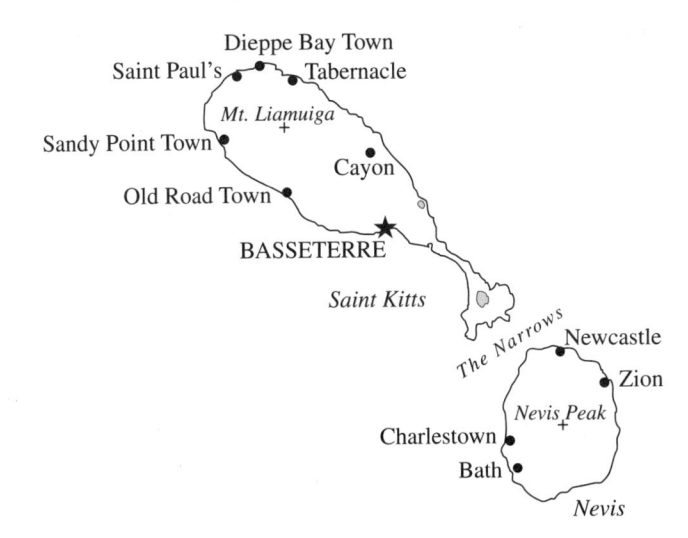

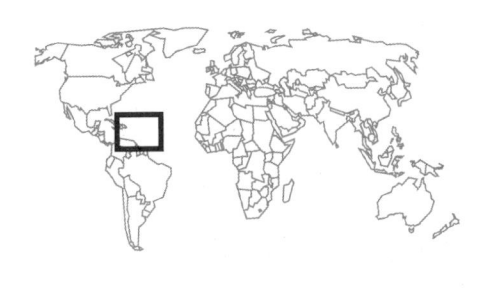

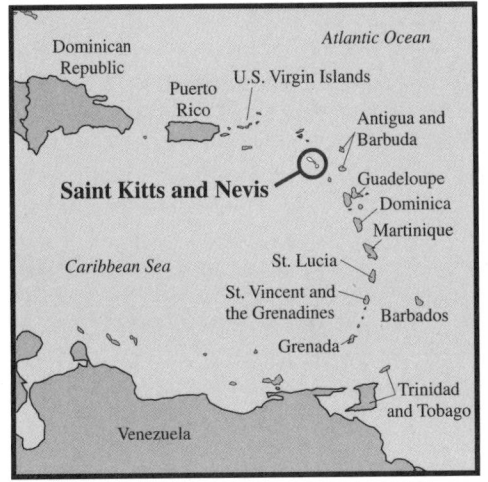

Federation of Saint Kitts and Nevis

CultureGrams World Edition 2006

BACKGROUND

Land and Climate. Saint Kitts, also called Saint Christopher, and Nevis are leeward islands in the Caribbean Archipelago about 200 miles (322 kilometers) southeast of Puerto Rico. They are separated by The Narrows, a channel only 2 miles (3.2 kilometers) wide at its narrowest point. St. Kitts is 65 square miles (168 square kilometers), while Nevis is 36 square miles (93 square kilometers). A mountainous central ridge extends across the length of St. Kitts. Its highest peak, Mount Liamuiga, rises to 3,792 feet (1,156 meters). On Nevis, Nevis Peak rises to 3,232 feet (985 meters). Both mountains are long-dormant volcanoes, but there is some evidence of volcanic activity in the form of hot sulfur springs and holes in the ground that emit smoke and gases.

Below 1,000 feet (305 meters), St. Kitts is a patchwork of cultivated fields, mostly sugarcane. Above these fields, slopes are covered with tropical rain forests. The peninsula has a number of salt ponds and is quite different from the rest of the island. Nevis is rockier, with clay soils and a higher concentration of natural vegetation. Cultivation is limited to small vegetable and fruit farms. Nevis's shoreline is ringed by coconut palms. The most valuable natural resources include the islands' beauty, tranquility, and unspoiled natural environment. The climate is dry and tropical. Temperatures range from 82°F (28°C) in December to 91°F (33°C) in July and August. The rainy season runs from July to December. Hurricanes are possible between July and November.

History. Prior to the arrival of Christopher Columbus, St. Kitts and Nevis were inhabited by Caribs who had migrated from South America. Liamuiga (Fertile Island) was the Caribs' name for St. Kitts, and Oualie (Beautiful Waters) was what they called Nevis. Columbus discovered St. Kitts and Nevis on his second Caribbean voyage in 1493. St. Kitts eventually was named San Cristóbal (St. Christopher), and Nevis was named Santa María de las Nieves (Our Lady of the Snows) because of the cloud cluster lying on Nevis Peak. *San Cristóbal* was later shortened to *St. Kitts* by its English colonists while *Nieves* became *Nevis*.

Sir Thomas Warner colonized St. Kitts (1624) and Nevis (1628). French settlers arrived in 1626 and St. Kitts was partitioned by formal treaty. Although the British and French were initially friendly with the Carib people and their king, Tegreman, the Europeans eventually massacred or expelled most Caribs; many of the indigenous people leapt from a sea cliff to their deaths.

The English and French coexisted peacefully until war broke out between Britain and France in 1666. The 1713 Treaty of Utrecht ceded the island entirely to the British. Little French presence remains besides historical sites and names (such as the capital, Basseterre).

Sugar production, begun in the 1650s, propelled the islands to 18th-century prosperity. Irish indentured servants, Dutch refugees, and Spanish and Portuguese Jews from Brazil all found their way to the islands. From 1675 to 1730, Nevis was also the headquarters of the African slave trade in the Leeward Islands. The African population eventually outnumbered Europeans ten to one.

The 19th century saw the decline of the sugar industry and the emancipation of the slaves (1833). A subsequent economic downturn was felt acutely by the African population, many of whom emigrated or protested conditions by rioting.

Riots in 1935 were followed by social and political change, including the establishment of trade unions, representative government, and universal adult suffrage (1952). The Crown Colony of St. Kitts-Nevis-Anguilla joined the short-lived West Indies Federation in 1958. In 1967, the three islands were given the status of Associated Statehood, making them responsible for their internal affairs. Anguilla left the union and later reverted to colonial status (1982). Labour Party leader Robert Bradshaw dominated the national political scene from the 1950s until 1980.

St. Kitts and Nevis have not always enjoyed harmonious relations. Independence in 1983 under the leadership of Prime Minister Kennedy Simmonds and his People's Action Movement (PAM) party made their association more permanent.

The possibility of Nevis's secession from St. Kitts remains at the forefront of relations between the two islands. In October 1997, the five-member Nevis Island Assembly voted unanimously to invoke a constitutional provision allowing Nevis to unilaterally withdraw from St. Kitts. In a 1998 referendum, Nevisians voted for the islands to remain together. Still, independence activists garnered 62 percent of the vote, just short of the two-thirds majority needed for Nevis to secede. The Nevis Reformation Party (NRP) wants to boost the economy before again considering secession. The government is evaluating ways to revise the constitution and grant Nevis greater autonomy.

THE PEOPLE

Population. The islands' total population numbers just under 39,000 and is growing at 0.25 percent annually. St. Kitts is home to nearly three-fourths of that total; one-fourth lives in the capital, Basseterre. Most inhabitants are of African descent, but a small percentage is European, Lebanese, or East Indian. A large number of St. Kitts and Nevis nationals live in North America, Britain, and other Caribbean nations, but their ties to the nation remain strong. Many European and North American expatriates own vacation homes on Nevis.

Language. English is the official language, although many residents use a local dialect for daily informal communication. The dialect (a combination of English and African words and syntax) is spoken most heavily in rural areas. It is known for its colorful expressions, folk wisdom, proverbs, and riddles.

Religion. Nearly everyone on the islands is Christian. The traditionally dominant churches—Anglican, Methodist, and Moravian—are being challenged in prominence by a growing number of Pentecostal, Seventh-day Adventist Church, and other Christian congregations. A small number of Rastafarians and Baha'is also live on the islands.

Religious beliefs and values have a noticeable influence on daily life. Not only do people regularly attend church services, but they (especially women) also participate in other church-sponsored activities. Most children are exposed to religious teachings while growing up. Major family events such as weddings, christenings, and funerals usually are observed in a church.

General Attitudes. People in St. Kitts and Nevis are sociable, outgoing, and friendly, both among themselves and toward strangers. They are flexible about time and are seldom in such a hurry that they cannot extend a greeting. Like members of most small communities, they take a keen interest in one another's affairs; rumors and gossip are common.

Social institutions and the law are generally respected. Therefore, major disputes are settled through litigation. People place considerable emphasis on politics and on personal relationships with lawyers, priests, doctors, and community leaders. They expect equality in social interaction.

Traditionally, inhabitants of Nevis are known for their thrift and for valuing land and livestock. In St. Kitts, greater importance is placed on material possessions. Residents of both islands value financial security and a good education, which is seen as the traditional route to social mobility.

Personal Appearance. Except when engaged in jobs that require old clothes or overalls, such as farming or fishing, people are meticulous about their appearance. Women are particularly fashion conscious, and they like jewelry. They also pay great attention to the grooming of their hair and that of their children.

Women usually wear dresses or skirts to work, reserving shorts and trousers for casual occasions. Swimsuits are worn only on the beach. Clothes are made of brightly colored, lightweight fabrics. People like colorful T-shirts, embroidered or tie-dyed Caribbean designs, or the latest North American fashions. The latter are popular with the youth. Children generally wear uniforms to school. Men may wear suits on formal occasions but prefer to work in light *shirt-jacs* (a pleated, square-cut shirt with pockets and light embroidery) and trousers. Jeans, shorts, and T-shirts are strictly casual wear.

CUSTOMS AND COURTESIES

Greetings. Common greetings on the islands include *Good morning*, *Good afternoon*, or *Good night*. Other more informal greetings are *Howdy*, *How you do?* or *Hey, wha' happ'nin'?* When leaving, one might say *Good-bye*, *See you*, or *Take care then till next time*. Older or rural people may still say *See you soon, D.V.* (*Deus Volunte*, or "God willing").

Remembering people's names is crucial. One addresses elders, those in important positions, or acquaintances as *Mr.*, *Mrs.*, or *Miss* with their surname or, less formally, their initial (e.g., *Mr. B.*). Older women may be addressed familiarly as *auntie*, *mother*, or *mama* (e.g., *Mother Saunders, Mama Liz*). Informally, one also may be addressed as *Darlin'*, *Me dear*, or *Sweetheart*. Many people have nicknames and seldom are called by their original names. Children are expected to address older people as *Mr.*, *Mrs.*, or *Miss* or as *auntie* or *uncle*.

Kittsians and Nevisians often touch hands or arms when meeting. A man may put his arm around a woman's shoulder or hold her hand in a friendly meeting. Hugging is more prevalent than kissing, particularly when people meet old friends and children. Formal introductions normally include a handshake.

Gestures. As in the rest of the Caribbean, individuals "talk with their hands," indeed many talk with the whole body. Speaking is accompanied by a variety of hand and arm movements, and the livelier the discussion, the more gestures there are. Women may put their hands on their hips when arguing or to signify defiance or aggression. Closely approaching someone during an altercation is also considered aggressive. Shrugging one's shoulders indicates uncertainty. People may pucker their mouths, toss their heads, and make a sideways motion with the thumb and hand when humorously mocking someone or indicating real derision. Individuals may purse their lips and make a sound by sucking air through their teeth (known as *sucking the teeth*) to indicate disgust or anger.

Men and younger people are expected to give up public transport seats or offer help to pregnant women, the elderly, and people with young children. Chewing gum during conversation or eating in the street is not well regarded.

Visiting. Residents of St. Kitts and Nevis tend to entertain for-

Saint Kitts and Nevis

mally for family celebrations such as weddings, christenings, or birthday parties or during festive seasons such as Christmas. Such occasions feature a great deal of food, drink, music, and perhaps dancing. Gifts are not expected, but for an evening party a guest might bring a bottle of something to drink.

Generally, people "drop in" unannounced for short visits. Hospitality is important; hosts always welcome visitors and usually offer them a cool drink and a snack, such as a slice of cake. On weekends, friends socialize on the veranda or in the garden. When expatriates return to the islands, they spend time visiting family members and old friends.

Eating. The average family eats three meals a day. Breakfasts are hurried and usually consist of a hot drink and eggs, cereal, or a sandwich. If family members have been working in the fields for several hours, breakfast may be later and heavier. The main family meal used to be at midday. However, because of work and school schedules, lunch often consists of a snack, and the family eats a substantial cooked meal together in the evening. This meal, preceded by a prayer, usually takes place around the table, but entertaining is often buffet-style. People eat out much more today than they did in the past. Many eat lunch at restaurants or snack bars.

LIFESTYLE

Family. The extended family structure is still a feature of life on the islands, but with socio-economic changes it is gradually being eroded. Families are close-knit. Many households are headed by women who are raising their children, their grandchildren, or the children of parents who work abroad. Elderly relatives may also live in the home.

Middle-class people are most likely to get married and have a traditional family. Common-law marriages are widespread among lower-income groups, and the children enjoy the same legal rights as do children of formally married couples. Men are encouraged to have contact with their children and are legally required to support them financially, even if they have not married the mother. It is not unusual for an individual, male or female, to have children by two or more partners. Women prize motherhood, while men try to show their superiority by their prowess with women and the fathering of children.

In general, women have the greatest responsibility for raising children. They may also be the sole or most consistent breadwinner for the household. Most women work outside the home, traditionally as farmers, domestic servants, nurses, teachers, or in commercial and administrative jobs. More recently, many have become self-employed in microenterprises or have found employment in the light-manufacturing sector.

Grown children are committed to improving their parents' lives by upgrading the family home and contributing to the family income, particularly if they migrate abroad. Unless they work some distance away, young unmarried people, particularly young women, continue to live with their parents.

Dating and Marriage. Young people go out together, although parents tend to control and supervise the activities of their teenage daughters. Boys and girls meet at school and church functions, at parties, on the beach, during festive occasions, at sporting events, or at spots where they simply "hang out."

Older couples may spend a lot of time together, especially on weekends. People generally marry between the ages of 20 and 35. Most weddings are performed in a church. They can be quite elaborate social events with many guests.

Diet. Popular traditional dishes include salt fish and dumplings (salted, dried codfish prepared as a stew with dumplings—a Good Friday staple), chicken and rice *pelau* with red beans or pigeon peas, and *goat water* (spicy stew made from goat, breadfruit, and dumplings). *Souse* is prepared from pickled pigs' trotters, cucumbers, and hot peppers. *Black pudding* is made from pigs' blood, rice, and herbal stuffing.

The islanders eat a lot of chicken and fish, both dried and fresh. Pork and mutton are also popular. Peas, beans, and lentils are important sources of protein. Bread is eaten for breakfast and snacks, while cooked staple carbohydrates include rice, breadfruit, yams, cooked cornmeal (usually eaten with steamed fish and okra), dumplings (or the fried version, *johnnycakes*), and macaroni.

Vegetables generally are cooked, although people do eat fresh lettuce, cucumbers, and coleslaw. Cabbage, carrots, eggplants, and sweet potatoes are also common. Local fruits include mangoes, sugar apples, soursops, pawpaws, plantains, golden apples, tomatoes, and guavas. The latter are turned into guava jelly or *guava cheese*, a chewy dessert made by boiling and puréeing guavas before mixing them with sugar.

At breakfast, people generally drink tea, coffee, *cocoa tea* (hot cocoa), or *bush tea* (herbal tea). Otherwise, they prefer cold drinks. Lunch and dinner are served with locally made lemonade, ginger beer, or drinks made from fruits such as tamarinds or passion fruit. The most popular Christmas drink is *sorrel*, a tart, acidic drink made from the petals of a sorrel plant.

Recreation. Popular team sports include cricket, *football* (soccer), and basketball for men; netball for women; and volleyball for both. Cricket and netball are national sports. Nevis prides itself on being the Caribbean territory that, for its population size, has produced the largest number of cricketers for the West Indies cricket team. Tennis is growing in popularity.

People also go to beaches or organize picnics or hikes. Men get together in bars or elsewhere to talk, drink, and play dominoes or cards. Women meet in their homes, at church-related social activities, or at various leisure spots. Community service clubs are also popular. Some, especially young people, seek out nightspots and enjoy themselves at dances. Watching cable television is a favorite leisure activity. Traveling throughout the Eastern Caribbean to visit family and to shop is common. The United States, Canada, and Britain are favorite holiday destinations.

The Arts. Many artists are engaged in the development of local music, drama, or folklore. Festivals such as the St. Kitts Music Festival in June bring artists together to compete in music contests featuring reggae, calypso, jazz, *soca* (a mixture of soul music from the United States and calypso music), gospel, samba, salsa, steel pan, and merengue, the rapid music that accompanies the ballroom dance also known as merengue. Nevis's Culturama Day provides opportunities for local artisans to display their crafts. A popular folk troupe named the Masquerades performs dances drawing on both traditional French and African sources.

The massive fortress of Brimstone Hill, constructed in the 17th and 18th centuries and since restored, is an important architectural piece. Slaves laboriously built the citadel and its 7-foot-thick walls over a period of nearly 90 years.

Holidays. National holidays include New Year's Day (1 Jan.), National Carnival Day (2 Jan.), Good Friday, Easter Monday, Labor Day (first Monday in May), Whitmonday (seven weeks after Easter Monday), Emancipation Day (first Monday in August), and Culturama Day (an annual August festival on

Saint Kitts and Nevis

Nevis). Independence Day is 19 September. The Christmas season includes Christmas Day and Boxing Day (26 Dec.). It is a time for family gatherings, gift giving, and related activities. The Carnival season runs for a week after the 26th and includes street dancing, costumed bands, calypso competitions, beauty contests, and beach parties.

Commerce. Stores are generally open from 8 or 8:30 a.m. to 4 or 5 p.m. Smaller stores may close for lunch at noon. Many are closed on Thursday afternoon but otherwise are open Monday through Saturday. Supermarkets and corner grocery stores may stay open later in the evening. Each island has public markets for vegetables, fruits, meat, and fish. The main market days are Thursday, Friday, and Saturday, but some vendors sell their goods every weekday. Most banks open from 9 a.m. to 3 p.m., Monday through Thursday, and later on Fridays. The National Bank is open Saturday morning.

SOCIETY

Government. The Federation of St. Kitts and Nevis is a parliamentary democracy with a federal constitution. The central government is based on St. Kitts. Nevis has a local government responsible for island administration. The National Assembly has eleven elected members—eight from St. Kitts and three from Nevis. In addition, two senators are appointed by the ruling party and one by the opposition. St. Kitts and Nevis is a member of the British Commonwealth. Queen Elizabeth II is head of state but is represented locally by a governor-general, currently Sir Cuthbert Montraville Sebastian. The prime minister (Denzil Douglas) is head of government. The voting age is 18; elections are held at least every five years.

Economy. Tourism, agriculture, and manufacturing are the most important sectors of the islands' economy. The principal export is sugar, but the recent diversification of agriculture has improved domestic self-sufficiency and provided links with the tourism industry. The sugar industry and 85 percent of arable land belong to a state-run corporation. Tourism is one of the most important industries in terms of foreign-exchange earnings. Manufacturing concentrates on textiles, data processing, electronic assembly, and computer software development. More than 20 percent of the labor force is employed in agriculture, another 20 percent in manufacturing, and about 15 percent in tourism. The government also employs one-fifth of the workforce. The currency is the East Caribbean dollar (XCD).

Transportation and Communications. Cars and buses are the primary forms of transport in St. Kitts and Nevis. Private buses operate routes between main towns and rural areas. There are 190 miles (306 kilometers) of road, including the Kennedy Simmonds Highway, which opened the southeast peninsula of St. Kitts to general development.

A government ferry operates five days a week between islands. Many private boats also ply the waters with freight and passengers or for fishing and sightseeing. St. Kitts has an international airport and Nevis is expanding its airport.

Most people have at least one radio; 70 percent have access to television. More than half of all households have a telephone. Two national newspapers, the *Democrat* and the *Labour Spokesman*, are owned by the major political parties.

DEVELOPMENT DATA
Human Dev. Index* rank . . . . 39 of 177 countries
Adjusted for women . . . . NA
Real GDP per capita $12,420
Adult literacy rate . . . . 98 percent
Infant mortality rate . . . . 15 per 1,000 births
Life expectancy . . . . 69 (male); 75 (female)

Regional newspapers from neighboring islands are also available. One government and one private television station broadcast to the nation. Cable television is also available.

Education. The education system consists of preschool, primary, secondary, and some postsecondary facilities. Education is free and accessible to all. Children are required to attend school between the ages of five and sixteen. A majority of children who enroll in school finish the primary level. About two-thirds of enrolled children pass to the secondary level. The dropout rate is higher among boys. Students who complete their secondary education but stay in the country can still obtain vocational and technical education, attend a teacher-training program, or study a handful of other subjects. For a university degree, students study at the University of West Indies branches in Jamaica, Barbados, or Trinidad, or go abroad elsewhere.

Health. Four hospitals and 17 clinics comprise the national healthcare system. There are fewer than 50 doctors. Health care is subsidized by the government, especially for lower-income groups. The government is also upgrading equipment and training to improve care. Hospitals in Jamaica, Barbados, and Guadeloupe take patients whose needs cannot be met on St. Kitts or Nevis. The nation has an excellent child immunization program.

AT A GLANCE
Events and Trends.

- After Prime Minister Denzil Douglas was reelected in October 2004 voting, he outlined broad plans for his third term in office. His goals included diversifying the economy; moving some resources from the sugar industry to producing an artificial sweetener called Stevia; and trying to ensure that wealth is evenly distributed throughout society.

- In a September 2004, Kittsian foreign minister Timothy Harris addressed the United Nations, calling for more cooperation among countries to combat the spread of HIV/AIDS. He encouraged governments to take "bold and sometimes controversial steps" to protect the public.

- In 2003, a large hotel complex was built on Frigate Bay on the east coast of St. Kitts. The complex will eventually boost the number of hotel rooms in the country by 60 percent and increase the number of tourism workers.

Contact Information. Embassy of St. Kitts and Nevis, 3216 New Mexico Avenue NW, Washington, DC 20016; phone (202) 686-2636; web site www.stkittsnevis.org or www.stkittsnevis.net.

© 2005 ProQuest Information and Learning Company and Brigham Young University. It is against the law to copy, reprint, store, or transmit any part of this publication in any form by any means without written permission from ProQuest. This document contains native commentary and original analysis, as well as estimated statistics. The content should not be considered strictly factual, and it may not apply to all groups in a nation. *UN Development Programme, Human Development Report 2004 (New York: Oxford University Press, 2004).

CultureGrams
People. The World. You.

ProQuest Information and Learning Company
300 North Zeeb Road, P.O. Box 1346
Ann Arbor, Michigan 48106 USA
Toll Free: 1.800.528.6279
Fax: 1.800.864.0019
www.culturegrams.com

CultureGrams 2006 World Edition — Saint Lucia

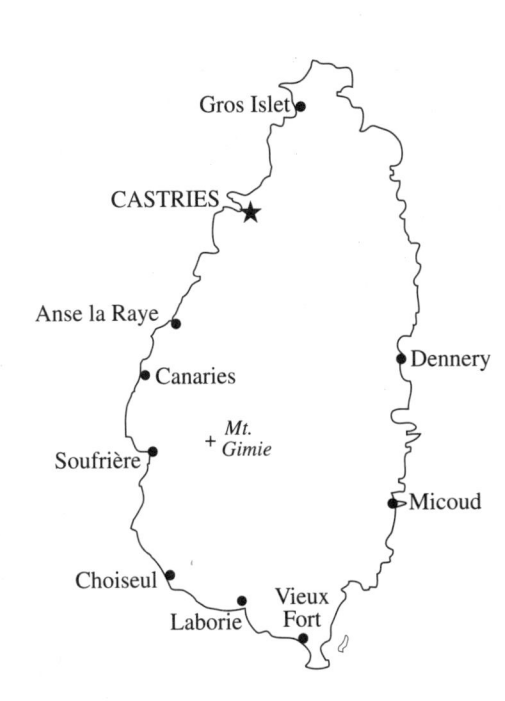

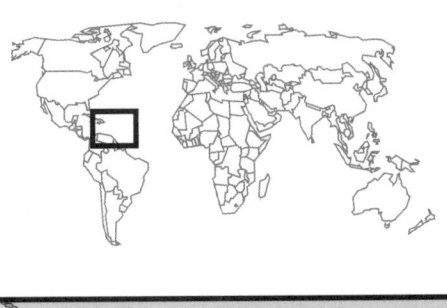

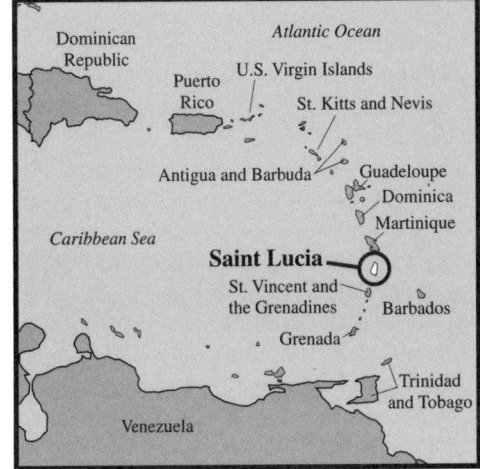

BACKGROUND

Land and Climate. Saint Lucia, often called the Helen of the West Indies for its beauty, lies about 1,300 miles (2,092 kilometers) southeast of Florida. It covers 239 square miles (620 square kilometers) and is about three times as large as Washington, D.C. The Caribbean Sea lies to the west of the island, while the Atlantic Ocean lies to the east. St. Lucia is a volcanic island with a subtropical climate. As such, it is mountainous and has a lush interior rain forest. The town of Soufrière is near the island's volcanic center. Both black and white sand beaches are found on the island. St. Lucia's two seasons (wet and dry) tend to be warm, with December to May the driest months and June to August the hottest. The rainy season (and hurricane season) extends from June to November; as much as 160 inches (406 centimeters) of rain can fall. Constant trade winds moderate the temperatures year-round. The average highs are 80 to 90°F (26–32°C).

History. St. Lucia originally was inhabited by Arawak Indians. By A.D. 800, they were replaced by Carib Indians. In the past, it was said that Christopher Columbus discovered St. Lucia in 1498, but that event is now discounted. There is no official record of the first European discovery of the island. The first English settlers came in 1605 and the French arrived in 1651. Eight years later, the two groups began fighting over land ownership. Hostilities endured for 150 years and St. Lucia changed hands between the powers 14 times. After the wars between the British and the French, the Caribs were expelled to the island of Dominica, and African slaves were imported to work on plantations. St. Lucia was finally ceded to the British in 1814, when France lost the Napoleonic Wars.

St. Lucia remained a British colony until 1967, when the West Indies Act extended self-rule over internal affairs. Full independence came in 1979, although St. Lucia remains a member of the Commonwealth.

John Compton's United Workers Party (UWP) prevailed in government from 1964 until independence, when the opposition St. Lucia Labour Party (SLP) managed to take office. By 1981, public discontent with the SLP led its leaders to resign, and John Compton became prime minister. The UWP dominated politics during the 1980s and early 1990s, but the SLP returned to power in 1997. The SLP government has been working to diversify the economy and reduce the island's widespread unemployment.

THE PEOPLE

Population. St. Lucia's population of about 164,000 is growing annually at 1.25 percent. About 90 percent of the population descends from African slaves; another 3 percent descends from East Indians who came as indentured laborers after slavery was abolished. Six percent is of mixed heritage, and there are significant minorities of Syrians and people with European heritage. Castries, the capital, is home to nearly 40 percent of the population.

Language. English is the official language. It is used in school instruction, government, and business. While most people speak English, some rural St. Lucians are not fluent. Creole, or *patois*, an oral language developed during French colonial rule, is the primary tongue for most rural and many urban residents. Except among the people of the upper class, who use English most frequently, *patois* is the language of daily communication. Urban residents often mix *patois* and English in conversation. There is a movement to preserve *patois* and develop a written form that could be taught in school.

Saint Lucia

Religion. Religion plays an important role in the lives of most St. Lucians. Business meetings, meals, the school day, and other events open with prayer. Most community activities are church-sponsored or church-related. Roman Catholicism is practiced by as much as 80 percent of the population. Most other St. Lucians are Christians of other denominations, including Anglicans (3 percent), Seventh-day Adventists, and Pentecostals.

General Attitudes. St. Lucians view themselves as friendly and accepting of others. They tend to be laid-back and make fun of others' perceived pretensions. St. Lucians can be confrontational at times, quickly engaging in an argument or (more rarely) a fight. But just as harsh words are easily spoken, tempers cool readily and conflicts are soon forgotten. Long-term confrontations are avoided because of local gossip.

While St. Lucians admire punctuality, they believe the pace of life should not be governed by the clock. Hence, on "Lucian time" everything starts late and no one expects otherwise. People do not like to schedule rigid appointments because they believe that events occur by the grace of God.

Class divisions cause tension among some St. Lucians. Prejudices are expressed verbally but rarely rise to a level of violence. The concept of coexistence prevails, and the country enjoys overall unity. St. Lucian men often express dominance over women through macho acts or sexually oriented language. Professional or otherwise economically independent St. Lucian women are becoming less tolerant of this attitude, so they are increasingly seeking partnerships based on equality and respect. St. Lucian women with fewer opportunities in life try to ignore the macho attitude or resign themselves to it as part of life.

Personal Appearance. St. Lucians try to dress neatly in unwrinkled, modest clothing. Bathing suits, short skirts, and other revealing clothing are not appropriate away from resort areas. Children must be dressed properly for church and social functions.

Attire indicates social status and occupation. Employees of many banks, hotels, and schools wear uniforms. Professional women might wear a skirt and blouse to work. Men often wear a *shirt-jac*: a pleated, square-cut shirt with pockets and light embroidery. Young people prefer fashions from the United States. Young urban men sometimes wear gold necklaces with medallions.

Some people wear the national costume for cultural events. Men have black trousers, a white shirt, and a cummerbund. Women wear a red-and-orange-checked skirt with a white frill underskirt, a white blouse with a triangle of checked fabric over one shoulder, and a fabric hat that is tied differently depending on one's marital status.

CUSTOMS AND COURTESIES

Greetings. Greeting strangers, acquaintances, and friends is important to St. Lucians. Formal greetings include *Good morning*, *Good afternoon*, and *Good night*. Such phrases are expected when one enters a place of business or boards public transportation. People passing on the street exchange a nod or short greeting (*Alright, Morning, Afternoon, Evening*). Greetings between friends are less formal. In *patois*, *Sa ka fet?* (What's happening?) is common. In English, an enthusiastic *Alright?* may be exchanged. Among friends, men might "high-five," *jam* (lightly touch closed fists), or shake hands vigorously; women may pat each other on the shoulder or brush a hand against one another's upper arm.

Nicknames are ubiquitous. In many cases, St. Lucians are referred to by nickname almost exclusively; one might not even know an acquaintance's given name. Daily radio obituaries list both the given name and nickname of an individual. Nicknames are derived from one's physical appearance, given name, characteristics, or an experience. For example, *Sparks* (meaning intelligent and knowledgeable) may be a nickname for a highly educated man.

Adults often address children in *patois* as *ish mwe* (my child), *ti ma mai* (my little one), *ti fi* (little girl), or *ti boy* (little boy). Out of respect, younger people call older people *auntie*, *uncle*, *mummy*, or *daddy*—even if not related. When titles (*Mr.*, *Miss*, *Teacher*, etc.) are used, they often are combined with a given name. Married, divorced, or widowed women may be called *Mrs.* or *Mistress*, followed by their husband's given name or nickname. As a Creole society, St. Lucians may also address women as *Ma* or *Madam*. Male peers often address one another as *garçon* (*patois* equivalent of "man" or "dude"), tacking the term onto the end of a statement or question.

Gestures. When conversing, St. Lucians express emotions with their face and hands. Clapping hands to show excitement or while laughing is common. Bending over while laughing is also common. People often nod to show agreement or shake their heads to show disapproval during conversation. Discussions may be punctuated with "eh-eh," which can mean disapproval, concern, or disbelief. People sometimes express extreme irritation by sucking air through closed teeth (known as *choopsing*). St. Lucians will point to indicate direction. To get another's attention, they say "pssst."

Visiting. St. Lucians visit friends and relatives often and unannounced. Visits rarely are the result of a formal invitation. People never seem too busy to stop at a friend's home. When one drops by, it is customary to first call out a greeting from outside the home. The residents may come out and engage in leisurely conversation. The visitors may or may not be invited inside for a drink or snack. The closer the people are, the more likely the invitation will be extended. Guests remove their shoes when they enter the home.

Arranged visits occur most often on weekends. One may be invited to a *fête* (party) or on an excursion to another part of the island. For a *fête*, it is acceptable but not required for guests to bring a beverage or food item to share. Evening parties start late and continue into the early morning hours. If a meal is served, it might be as late as 11 p.m.

Eating. St. Lucians usually rise early to begin work or chores before the hottest part of the day (11 a.m. to 3 p.m.). Therefore, they may eat breakfast early (before 7 a.m.). Breakfast usually is light, consisting of locally baked bread and butter. It may be accompanied by a hot drink, such as *tea* (green tea), coffee, or *cocoa tea* (Ovaltine drink).

Lunch (referred to as *dinner* or *the food*) is usually the main meal. Most St. Lucians begin preparing it in the morning before work. They return home at midday to enjoy the meal, which consists of rice, meat or fish, *peas* (any legume—including lentils, red beans, pigeon peas, etc.), *ground provisions* (foods grown in the ground, such as sweet potatoes or other root vegetables), and locally grown fruit (breadfruit, plantains, and bananas). Unripe bananas might be boiled and put in salads. For people unable to return home for *the food*, the main meal is supper. Otherwise, supper consists of bread and butter, fried fish or tinned meat, sometimes cheese, and *tea*. On Sundays, people eat a large meal in the early afternoon. It consists of meat or chicken, rice, *peas*, macaroni and cheese, and perhaps a *ground provision*. For special occasions, a goat or sheep may be roasted or stewed.

The spoon is the most common utensil used for lunch and supper. In traditional settings, St. Lucians may make a spoon from a calabash to eat with. Children might eat before the adults, especially when guests are present. To show appreciation for a meal, guests accept offers of second helpings.

LIFESTYLE

Family. Two or more generations often live together, but large traditional families are no longer the trend. Grandparents and other members of the extended family might help raise children and do household chores. St. Lucia has many families with single parents. Except among the elite and well educated, it is not uncommon to have a female head of household and several generations with no adult men. Men often date even when married; many consider it macho to father babies by different *baby mothers*. Even as a woman's partners change, her children remain with her and are raised together with half siblings. If the mother cannot care for a child, another relative or even a friend might raise it. St. Lucian society, as well as the law, is pressing fathers to take more financial responsibility for their offspring.

Adult children usually remain home until they marry. If they remain in their parents' home after marrying or having children, they are expected to help maintain the household. While some people live in apartments in Castries, most families have their own homes. Private ownership is high (more than 70 percent). The property on which the home sits may have been in the family for several generations. Urban houses are made of concrete and may be built on stilts. Rural houses may be built of concrete or brightly painted wood planks. Both styles have corrugated tin roofs. Around a home, families often plant a small garden with tropical flowers and *ground provisions*. Houses are small and simple, decorated with locally made wrought iron or wooden furnishings, as well as curtains and other accessories made from imported fabric.

Dating and Marriage. Most St. Lucians date individuals they know from their community. Relationships may also develop through school or church attendance and activities. Men prefer to date several women simultaneously, but more women are demanding monogamous relationships.

While marriage and monogamy are considered important, St. Lucians often do not get married or commit to one partner. Instead, they may live together in common-law arrangements. More dedicated couples marry after they have built a house, have begun to raise a family, or have lived together for a number of years. Common-law marriages are increasingly being recognized by the legal system for the purpose of child support and other family matters.

Diet. Rice, *ground provisions*, and *peas* are dietary staples. Beef and chicken are raised locally as well as imported. Certain fish (red snapper, dolphin, and tuna) are expensive and considered delicacies. Conch, goat, and sheep are eaten for special occasions. St. Lucians commonly utilize the entire animal in cooking; a favorite dish consists of a pig's feet, snout, and tail simmered in vegetable broth.

Cabbage, tomatoes, peppers, and onions are used in small quantities to garnish a dish. Seasonal fruits include tamarinds, oranges, limes, guavas, mangoes, passion fruits, papaya, and golden apples; they often are made into juice. Mangoes are peeled and eaten whole. Coconut water, drunk from green or immature coconut shells, is available year-round.

Urban residents (in Castries and Vieux Fort) eat more imported foods (such as canned fruit juice, frozen chicken, cheese, and canned or powdered milk). They also are more likely to eat in restaurants. Rural people rely on produce grown in their gardens, fruit they pick from local trees, or livestock they raise themselves. Locally caught fish is available near coastal villages. A common rural meal is the *one-pot* stew, which may vary in ingredients depending on availability and is usually cooked on an outdoor coal pot.

Recreation. *Football* (soccer) is St. Lucia's most popular sport, closely followed by cricket. Community leagues provide organized competition, but teams may also play against squads from other West Indian nations. Men listen to broadcasts of cricket matches that occur in other nations. St. Lucians love to play dominoes for pleasure or for money.

Carnival provides St. Lucians with a chance to dance, sing, and participate in calypso talent contests. Many people compete for the title of Calypso King and Queen; everyone follows the event closely. Winners are featured at Carnival events and hold the title for one year. Several weeks of preparation precede the calypso contests and *Jouvert*, a street parade that begins at sunrise with bands and costumed marchers. Spectators often join the parade.

Most people watch videos and enjoy television shows produced in the United States. St. Lucians go to the local beach for a barbecue or *fête*. Beach parties are usually impressive, with plenty of food served to casually dressed guests.

The Arts. As is the case in most Caribbean nations, music plays an important role in society. Local music is heavily influenced by Jamaican reggae. St. Lucians also enjoy calypso, *soca* (a mixture of soul music from the United States and calypso), *dub* (related to rap), country western music, and *cadance* (lively dancing music from the French Antilles). Quadrille dancing is also popular. St. Lucia hosts a world-renowned jazz festival each May at Pigeon Point.

The French, English, African, and Caribbean influences on St. Lucia have produced a unique blend of cultural arts. Architecture often follows European designs, although African styles and bright colors are also prevalent.

Holidays. Christmas is the primary religious holiday. The Christmas season begins on 13 December, which is also National Day (previously called Discovery Day for Christopher Columbus). The Christmas Eve Midnight Mass is widely attended. Special festivities begin after Mass and continue into Christmas Day. On Boxing Day (26 Dec.), St. Lucians like to relax and visit. Visitors may come throughout the holiday season, and people save for months to fix up their homes and have special foods to serve their many guests. Visits continue through New Year's. On New Year's Eve (*Old Year's Night*), friends and relatives toast the coming year at each home they visit.

Independence Day (22 Feb.) marks independence from Britain. At Easter, the emphasis is on family and religion. Labour Day is 1 May. Carnival takes place in July. Emancipation Day (first Monday in August) commemorates the end of slavery. Thanksgiving is held on the first Monday in October. Local festivals—such as *Jounet Creole* (Creole Day, celebrated 31 October)—are held in various communities throughout the year.

Commerce. Most government and business offices are open weekdays between 8 a.m. and 4 p.m.; banks close an hour earlier. Stores keep the same basic hours but are also open on Saturday until 12:30 p.m. Some small malls or local mini-markets

Saint Lucia

have extended evening hours. Castries has an open-air produce market that stays open until the food is sold or until dusk. Most stores close on Sunday.

SOCIETY

Government. St. Lucia is a parliamentary democracy that recognizes Britain's Queen Elizabeth II as head of state. She is officially represented by Dr. Pearlette Louisy, the island's first female governor-general. Prime Minister Kenny Anthony is head of government. In the bicameral parliament, the House of Assembly's 17 members are directly elected to five-year terms; the Senate's 11 members are appointed. Citizens are required to vote beginning at age 18.

Economy. Historically, St. Lucia's economy has been based on agricultural production. Bananas are the most important export, but the export of winter vegetables and organically grown produce is expanding. The island began to develop its tourism industry in the 1990s. Hotels and the supporting infrastructure were built along the beaches surrounding Castries, Soufrière, and Vieux Fort to attract tourists from the United States, Canada, and Europe. Tourism is now one of the nation's main sources of revenue.

St. Lucia does not have the resources to be self-sufficient and must import foods, fuel, and manufactured goods. Unemployment and underemployment are serious problems. Although most people have access to education and health care, economic opportunities are limited. Many people go overseas in search of work. Remittances from these workers provide vital income for St. Lucia. Light manufacturing is controlled mostly by foreign firms. The East Caribbean dollar (XCD) is St. Lucia's currency.

Transportation and Communications. The main paved road on St. Lucia runs the perimeter of the island. Several miles of it were constructed around Vieux Fort during World War II by U.S. military units wanting easy access to their airport, now Hewanorra International. All towns and villages are connected to the main road. Most urban streets are paved, but rural roads are not. Certain remote areas cannot be reached by road. On paved roads, the most popular form of travel is the *transport*. These private minivans run regular routes. They leave from a central location when full, picking up and dropping off passengers along the way. They often have a name or slogan painted on them; fares depend on where passengers board and exit. Many St. Lucians also own cars, and it is common for drivers to stop and offer pedestrians a ride.

St. Lucians without phones have access to public phones. Radio and television broadcasts reach most people. Radio is the main source of news; people are well-informed on local and regional matters.

Education. Education, based on the British system, is compulsory for children ages five to fifteen. Uniforms are required. About 80 percent of all eligible children attend school. Children are sometimes taken out of school to work on family banana farms.

At age 11, students take the Common Entrance Exam to determine where they will go to secondary school. Those who finish secondary school can take the Caribbean Examination Council (CXC) exam to enter Sir Arthur Lewis Community College. To graduate from there, students must take the British "A" level exam in one or more chosen disciplines (arts, science, general studies, teacher education, nursing, technical education, or management studies). To complete a full college degree, students must transfer to the University of West Indies in Jamaica, Barbados, or Trinidad. Some students gain an education abroad. St. Lucia is proud to have produced two Nobel laureates: Sir Arthur Lewis (Economics, 1979) and Derek Walcott (Literature, 1992).

Health. St. Lucia is striving to provide health care to all citizens. Free or low-cost care is available at public clinics and urban hospitals. Rural clinics are staffed by nurses, many of whom live on site; doctors visit weekly. Private doctors serve those who can afford their fees.

DEVELOPMENT DATA

Human Dev. Index* rank . . . . 71 of 177 countries
    Adjusted for women . . . . NA
Real GDP per capita $5,300
Adult literacy rate . . . . 95 percent
Infant mortality rate . . . . 14 per 1,000 births
Life expectancy . . . . 71 (male); 74 (female)

AT A GLANCE

Events and Trends.

- In November 2004, the St. Lucian government was in the process of trying to improve health care for all St. Lucians. The goal was to ensure all citizens access to hospital care and prescription drugs. However, there had been no decision on how to pay for the increased costs, though added taxes or salary deductions were discussed.

- St. Lucia's murder rate reached near-record levels in November 2004. Community leaders attributed the high rate in part to violence between feuding gangs. The gangs had been fighting for more than a year in communities around Castries and in Vieux Fort.

- In September 2004, St. Lucia volunteered to house 40 prisoners from Grenada after Grenada's prison was destroyed by Hurricane Ivan. It is not uncommon for the two island nations to exchange favors like this one: In 2002 when St. Lucia had a security crisis, Grenada hosted 16 of St. Lucia's prisoners.

- In 2003, several groups campaigned for social changes in St. Lucia, including the legalization of marijuana and the expansion of abortion rights. Rastafarians organized marches to persuade the government to allow cannabis, and women's groups demanded wider access to abortions—not just when the pregnancy endangers a woman's life or is the result of rape. However, the conservative Christian majority was not swayed by the groups' arguments.

Contact Information. Embassy of Saint Lucia, 3216 New Mexico Avenue NW, Washington, DC 20016; phone (202) 364-6792. Saint Lucia Tourist Board, 800 Second Avenue, Ninth Floor, New York, NY 10017; phone (800) 456-3984; web site www.stlucia.org.

© 2005 ProQuest Information and Learning Company and Brigham Young University. It is against the law to copy, reprint, store, or transmit any part of this publication in any form by any means without written permission from ProQuest. This document contains native commentary and original analysis, as well as estimated statistics. The content should not be considered strictly factual, and it may not apply to all groups in a nation. *UN Development Programme, Human Development Report 2004 (New York: Oxford University Press, 2004).

CultureGrams™
People. The World. You.

ProQuest Information and Learning Company
300 North Zeeb Road, P.O. Box 1346
Ann Arbor, Michigan 48106 USA
Toll Free: 1.800.528.6279
Fax: 1.800.864.0019
www.culturegrams.com

Saint Vincent and the Grenadines

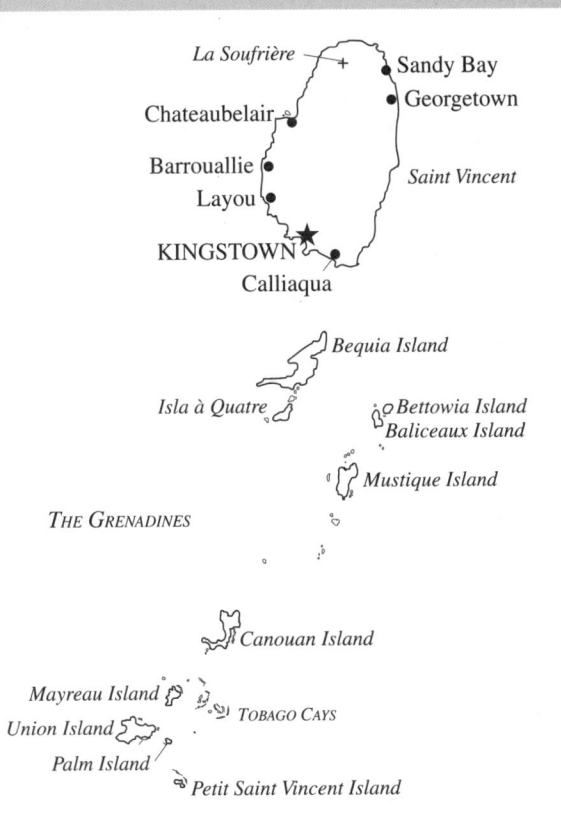

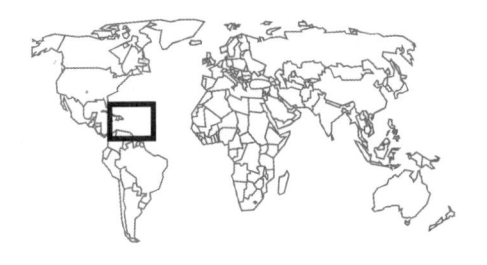

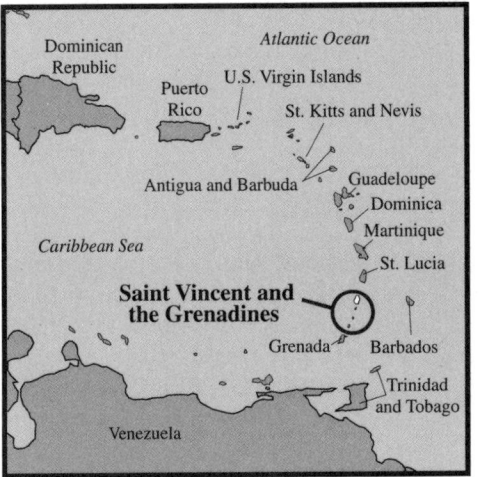

BACKGROUND

Land and Climate. Saint Vincent and the Grenadines consists of a chain of more than 30 volcanic and coral islands. St. Vincent (locally called *the mainland*) is a lush volcanic island with steep mountain ridges, valleys, and waterfalls. Its highest peak, the La Soufrière volcano, rises to 3,864 feet (1,178 meters) at the northern end of its mountain backbone. After an eruption in 1902 that took two thousand lives, La Soufrière lay dormant until the 1970s, when an active phase culminated in an eruption in 1979. No lives were lost, and since then the volcano has been relatively stable. From the island's central mountains, numerous streams flow east and west through the valleys to the sea.

The Grenadine Islands, which include many small coral cays, stretch between St. Vincent and Grenada (75 miles, or 121 kilometers, to the south). The Tobago Cays have been designated as a marine park. Palm Island and Petit St. Vincent are private resorts. Mustique, home to a number of wealthy foreigners, is owned by the Mustique Company. The combined land area of all the nation's islands is 150 square miles (389 square kilometers).

Temperatures vary according to elevation and time of year, ranging between 64 and 90°F (18–32°C). The coast is usually warm. The dry season extends from December to June, and the rainy season lasts the rest of the year. Hurricanes can threaten the area between June and October.

History. Prior to European domination that began in the 18th century, St. Vincent and the Grenadines was home to various tribes that had migrated from South and Central America. One early group was the peaceful Arawak, a tribe of skilled potters who also engaged in farming and fishing. By A.D. 1000, the more warlike Caribs overtook the Arawak on islands throughout the Caribbean. The Caribs' name for St. Vincent was Hairouna ("Home of the Blessed").

The traditional belief that Christopher Columbus landed on St. Vincent in 1498 has been refuted, but the island certainly was known to sailors and traders during his day. The Caribs fought the Europeans who landed there, so sailing vessels avoided St. Vincent for more than two hundred years. The Caribs did welcome other Caribs who had been defeated by Europeans on other islands, as well as escaped and freed African slaves. The Africans mixed with the Caribs and became known as Black Caribs, while the original Caribs were called Yellow Caribs because of their fair skin. Together, they proved nearly invincible to European conquerors. However, when the Black Caribs began to dominate the Yellow Caribs, the latter agreed to let the French build a settlement on St. Vincent in 1719.

The Black Caribs continued to resist the Europeans, and St. Vincent was declared a neutral island in 1748. For the next several years, the French, British, and Black Caribs all struggled to control the island. In 1795, the great Carib chief Chatoyer (the island's first national hero) was killed in battle by the British. His death allowed the British to eventually (in 1797) defeat the remaining five thousand Black Caribs and banish them to the Honduran peninsula. The remnant of the Yellow Caribs retreated to the island's northern tip, where their descendants live today.

For most of the colonial period, sugarcane production was the source of economic wealth. British landowners imported African slaves to work on their plantations. When slavery was phased out between 1834 and 1838, the African-origin population exceeded that of the Europeans, but most freed slaves could do little more than engage in subsistence agriculture,

Saint Vincent and the Grenadines

although some became skilled artisans. Gradually, plantation owners brought in Portuguese and East Indian indentured laborers, whose descendants live on the island today.

Until 1969, St. Vincent and the Grenadines was part of the Windward Islands colony. It then became an associated state with Britain, meaning it had internal autonomy but not full independence. The nation became an independent state within the Commonwealth in 1979 and has steadily developed socially and economically.

THE PEOPLE

Population. St. Vincent's population of about 117,000 includes the 10,000 people who live on various Grenadine Islands. The population is growing at about 0.3 percent annually. About 85 percent of the population is of African descent, either entirely or in part. Many people are also part English, Scottish, Portuguese, East Indian, or Carib. About 6 percent is East Indian and 2 percent is of Carib descent. Caribs live mainly at Sandy Bay. A growing number of Syrians live in the country. Ethnic patterns in the Grenadines are about the same as those on St. Vincent.

Language. English is the official language of St. Vincent and the Grenadines, but the French influence of the past has not been lost. Some villages, mountains, and islands still carry French names. A West African influence is also evident in the informal dialect people speak. Words like *boutou* (insult) and *nyam* (eat) stem from African languages, but phrases like *me na able* (I can't cope) illustrate how the dialect is English based.

Religion. Most residents in St. Vincent and the Grenadines are Christians. About 47 percent of the population is Anglican, 28 percent is Methodist, and 13 percent is Roman Catholic. Smaller groups include Hindus, Pentecostals, Baptists, Jehovah's Witnesses, Seventh-day Adventists, Latter-day Saints, and Baha'is. Nondenominational prayer groups are gaining popularity. Christianity is an important part of daily life. Schools begin and end the day with prayer. Most public and private functions also begin with prayer.

Rastafarians are few in number but have a significant impact on popular Caribbean culture. They are comprised mainly of African descendants who regard Africa as the promised land and Ethiopia's late ruler, Haile Selassie I, as "the living God."

General Attitudes. Vincentians are friendly and hospitable. They are known for their honesty, kindness, and willingness to share their resources and time with each other as necessary. They place great emphasis on family, church, and education. Social status is often measured by wealth and family name. People from all classes of society take great pride in the appearance of their homes. Vincentians are relaxed in their approach to time and schedules; therefore, meetings and events do not necessarily begin on time. U.S. culture and values introduced via television are changing people's lifestyles.

Personal Appearance. Vincentian dress is casual, conservative, and neat. A professional atmosphere prevails in offices and businesses, where women wear dresses or dress suits and men wear shirt jackets and dress pants or suits and ties. In many businesses and in all commercial banks, employees wear uniforms. All primary- and secondary-school students also wear uniforms. In less formal settings, women wear casual cotton tops with slacks or shorts. Men wear jeans or shorts with T-shirts or open-neck shirts. Vincentians do not wear swimwear on the street or in shops and restaurants. Young people's clothing varies from jeans and T-shirts to Jamaican *dancehall* styles and styles worn by rappers in the United States.

People buy imported clothing but also favor the creations of the many local tailors and seamstresses. Vincentians dress up for weddings, funerals, and festive occasions. Much emphasis is placed on hairstyling, and the many hair salons offer braiding, perming, cutting, and straightening. Rastafarians, both men and women, wear their hair in dreadlocks. Men also may shave their head or wear *pigtails* (a long, single braid at the back of the head).

CUSTOMS AND COURTESIES

Greetings. Greetings depend largely on the occasion and the relationship between the persons meeting. On the street, people use *Good morning*, *Good afternoon*, and *Good evening* to greet friends and strangers. Friends might also offer an informal *How you do?* or *How things?* to which *Good, good* and *Everything alright* are frequent responses. Friends and youth may use such local informal phrases as *Big up* (Hello), *Respect* (I respect you/It's nice to meet you), *Making a turn* (I am leaving), or *More times* (Until we meet again).

Fisting (hitting fists together) often replaces a handshake or embrace between friends when coming or going. *Fisting* is also typically used by West Indian cricketers (batsmen) to congratulate each other on playing well (for example, scoring a boundary). Men and boys frequently greet with backslapping and a variety of handshakes. Relatives often kiss and hug when greeting.

Elders or authority figures usually are addressed as *Sir*, *Mistress*, or *Miss*. Professional titles are used with surnames when appropriate. People are often known by their nicknames. For example, one might refer to West Indies cricketer Nehemiah Perry as *Nehemiah Perry a.k.a. Johnny*. Affectionately descriptive nicknames like *Tall boy*, *Shortie*, or *Yellowman* are common.

Gestures. Vincentians are usually very demonstrative while speaking. They often use their hands to reinforce an issue, point out a person or object, or show emotion. They may use facial expressions to communicate feelings, shrug their shoulders to express futility, or *stewps* (suck air through their teeth) to show exasperation. Friends in casual settings often *stewps*, but it can be considered rude when used as a response or when done in the presence of elders. Staring someone in the eye, called *bad eye*, is used to display anger. Throwing the hand in the air as if brushing the air with the back of the hand is considered a curse gesture. People sometimes hiss "pssst" to get someone's attention. "Excuse me" and "Pardon me" commonly are spoken.

Visiting. Vincentians enjoy visiting each other on an informal basis. Friends may drop in while passing by, announcing their arrival by calling from the gate or sounding the car horn. Calling in advance is also polite. Sunday afternoons and public holidays are popular times for visiting, and visitors commonly take small gifts of fruit, plants, vegetables, or local preserves. Sunday visiting often includes the whole family.

However spontaneous a visit, guests are always offered some refreshment, including fruit juice, tea, soda, or an alcoholic beverage with perhaps some home-baked cake or pie. In rural areas, people frequently remove their shoes at the front door, but this is rarely done in cities. The custom of frequent visiting is one reason many Vincentians take such pride in their homes.

Eating. Family members often eat at different times of day during the week, so lunch on Sunday is an important family meal.

Sunday breakfasts also tend to be larger than those served during the week. Sunday evening meals usually are light. Weekday breakfasts are light and often hurried. After work or school, people have a snack while waiting for the evening meal, which is served after 6 p.m. Most businesses and schools close for lunch between noon and 1 p.m. However, as life becomes increasingly hectic, more people bring their lunch to work or buy snacks instead of going home to eat. Families usually say a prayer to express thanks and bless the meal.

Entertaining at home continues to be a popular way of getting together with friends. Meals for these occasions range from an informal *cook-up* to very formal dinners with several courses. Unexpected visitors at mealtimes usually are invited to stay and eat.

LIFESTYLE

Family. The extended family is important to the social fabric in St. Vincent and the Grenadines. Since migration and emigration are primary avenues to financial progress, parents often leave their children in the care of grandparents, aunts, and uncles.

Family ties are usually strong, and families frequently come together on Sundays, holidays, and special occasions. Children often remain at home, regardless of age, until they marry or set up a permanent common-law relationship with someone. Common-law marriages are more prevalent than formal marriages. Many households are headed by single mothers or grandmothers.

Dating and Marriage. Young teens are not encouraged to date, so serious dating doesn't begin until around age 17. Young people often mix in family settings, at school and church functions, at social events (e.g., fairs and concerts), and through service clubs. Dating couples do not display affection in public. Once parents or guardians accept a relationship, the couple will meet often at each other's homes. Each person comes to be regarded as part of both families. Weddings usually are held on Saturday afternoons at a church, with a formal reception following at the bride's home or at a resort.

Diet. The main staples are rice, bananas, breadfruit, and ground provisions. Locally grown staple foods include sweet potatoes, yams, pumpkins, and plantains. Legumes and vegetables are also commonly eaten. Much of the country's food is imported, but the government is seeking to better use St. Vincent's fertile soil. Fish and shellfish caught by local fishermen complement the diet, as do local or imported meat and poultry. A variety of local fruits (sugar apples, golden apples, papayas, mangoes, bananas, and others) are sold at the central market and at occasional roadside stands. Some favorite Vincentian dishes are fried fish and roasted breadfruit, *pelau* (brown rice cooked with chicken), *boilin'* (fish boiled with green bananas and vegetables), and *boul-joul* (salted codfish sautéed in olive oil with vegetables). Seasonal fruits often are made into nutritious drinks.

Recreation. Cricket, *football* (soccer), and netball (for girls) are popular spectator sports. Cricket is especially loved, and Sunday village matches are a recreational focal point for men. Many successful Vincentian cricketers first developed their skills at these matches. The nation consistently has one of the leading netball teams in the Caribbean. Track-and-field meets are held throughout the school system just before Easter break. Table tennis and squash are two indoor sports gaining popularity. On weekends, men gather on porches or in bars to play cards, checkers, or dominoes for hours. Car racing also is becoming increasingly popular.

Friends and relatives of all ages enjoy getting together for beach picnics and river cookouts. In the Grenadines, people like to swim, windsurf, and water ski. The cinema is popular, but more people watch movies at home. On Friday nights, many Vincentians dance away the stress of the week. Adults also socialize in local bars, restaurants, and nightclubs.

The Arts. Drama and dance theater receive tremendous support, and music festivals attract individuals and choral groups from around the islands. Reggae and calypso music are popular, and many listen and dance to *soca* (a mix of soul music from the United States and calypso music). Festivals often include music and dancing. For example, carnival features street dances and a children's parade of bands. During Nine Mornings (see Holidays), people dance to the music of calypsos and carols at predawn street parties. Formal dances also take place on Old Year's Night.

Holidays. New Year's Day usually is celebrated with family reunions. It follows Old Year's Night (New Year's Eve), a time for *cook-ups* at home and church services. People often spend St. Vincent and the Grenadines Day (22 Jan.) visiting or at the beach. Easter weekend begins with Good Friday, the most important day of the year to attend religious services. It is customary to eat hot cross buns for breakfast and salmon or mackerel for lunch on this day. The weekend, including Easter Monday, offers such festivities as the Easterval water sports on Union Island and the sailing regatta at Bequia. Labor Day is 1 May.

Carnival is the biggest cultural event. Celebrations during the first two weeks in July coincide with CARICOM Day (second Monday in July, celebrating Caribbean unity). Carnival includes the Miss Carnival Show (a beauty pageant) and Mardi Gras shows. August Monday (first Monday in August) marks the abolition of slavery. Independence Day (27 Oct.) is observed with an official parade.

Nine Mornings, a uniquely Vincentian celebration, takes place during the nine days before Christmas (25 Dec.). It supposedly originated during slavery when the slaves who drove their masters to early morning *novenas* (nine days of prayer) would spend their time chatting and window-shopping. These days, Nine Morning revelers go walking, swimming, cycling, and window-shopping. Boxing Day (26 Dec.) is a day to relax and visit.

Commerce. Businesses generally open weekdays at 8 a.m. and close at 4 p.m., with an hour break for lunch at noon. Banks usually close at 1 p.m., except on Fridays when they reopen between 3 and 5 p.m. Businesses, but not banks, are open on Saturdays until noon. As commercial activity becomes increasingly centered in the capital, traffic jams are more common and more people are bustling about on Fridays and the days before public holidays.

Most retail and grocery businesses are located in or near Kingstown, which also boasts a central market that features fresh produce, boutiques, and specialty shops. Refrigerated fish and meat markets are near the central market. Local people control most of the food trade, but retailing and wholesale enterprises often have some foreign input or ties.

SOCIETY

Government. As a member of the British Commonwealth, St. Vincent and the Grenadines recognizes Queen Elizabeth II of Britain as its nominal head of state. She is represented by a governor-general (Frederick Ballantyne). The House of

Saint Vincent and the Grenadines

Assembly consists of fifteen elected representatives and six appointed senators (two of whom are nominated by the opposition). The prime minister (Ralph Gonsalves) is head of government. The prime minister and the cabinet of ministers constitute the country's highest decision-making body. The major political parties are the New Democratic Party (NDP) and the Unity Labour Party (ULP). Elections take place every five years. The voting age is 18.

Economy. Agriculture is an important part of St. Vincent's economy and employs a large portion of the labor force. Bananas account for much of the island's export earnings. However, destructive tropical storms and increasing competition for global markets have highlighted the need for the country to diversify its economy. Tourism and light industry are growing with the influx of foreign investment. This is especially true of the large hotels in the Grenadines and the flour and rice mills on St. Vincent. Financial institutions and the retail/wholesale trade are also growing and providing jobs. Despite these advances, the country suffers from high unemployment. The government remains the largest single employer. However, most people earn an income sufficient to meet their needs, and economic opportunities are improving. The currency is the East Caribbean dollar (XCD).

Transportation and Communications. Numerous minivans with colorful names such as *Wonder Not, Soon Come*, and *Rat Race* provide schoolchildren and workers with commuter service along fixed routes. Taxis are common but unmetered. Fares are published and usually agreed on before departure. Vincentians use bicycles mainly for recreation. Half of all vehicles (including motorcycles) are privately owned. Traffic moves on the left side of the road.

An efficient ferry service links the Grenadine Islands to each other and to the mainland. Light aircraft provide domestic service and also link the islands to international airports in Barbados, Saint Lucia, Grenada, and Trinidad.

St. Vincent has an efficient postal system and a modern digital telephone service. Broadcast and cable television are available, as are privately owned newspapers and radio stations.

Education. By the time they enter primary school at age five, many children have had some basic education at a private kindergarten. After six years of primary school, students take a Common Entrance Exam, which determines whether and where they will attend secondary school. Children may end their education at age 15 by taking a School Leaving Exam. Some students drop out before this. Education is provided free of charge, but parents must pay for uniforms, books, transportation, and lunch.

The Caribbean Examination Council exams (given throughout the Caribbean) are offered in the final (fifth) year of high school. At this level, girls tend to perform better than boys and account for more than double the enrollment of boys. Higher secondary education is available at a grammar school, a technical college, a teacher-training college, and other institutions. There are no four-year universities, but students may pursue further education at a campus of the University of the West Indies or in North America. Local adult-education classes have helped Vincentians achieve a higher literacy rate than in the past.

DEVELOPMENT DATA
Human Dev. Index* rank . . . . 87 of 177 countries
Adjusted for women . . . . NA
Real GDP per capita $5,460
Adult literacy rate . . . . 83 percent
Infant mortality rate . . . . 14 per 1,000 births
Life expectancy . . . . 73 (male); 76 (female)

Health. Government health clinics offer outpatient services and general dental care in all districts. Kingstown's General Hospital provides basic surgical, obstetric, and medical care. Three smaller hospitals offer more auxiliary treatment. Private medical care is available to those who can afford it.

AT A GLANCE
Events and Trends.
- In November 2004, thousands of supporters of the New Democratic Party (NDP) staged the latest in a yearlong series of protests against the government. The protesters said that the government was corrupt and that it was misusing money that had been designated to build a cross-country road. The protesters were also angry about the nation's rising crime rate.
- In September 2004, a high-ranking government medical official sounded a warning bell about the steady increase in HIV/AIDS patients over the past 20 years. Helped by millions of dollars of international funding, the country has made important steps—such as providing sex education and free antiretroviral drugs—but still must do more to stem the flow of new cases.
- Along with many other areas of the Caribbean, Hurricane Ivan in September 2004 damaged St. Vincent and the Grenadines. Homes, public buildings, and roads were harmed by the 120-mph winds and huge waves. It was estimated that it would take millions of dollars to recover from the storm. A 2002 hurricane caused nearly US$15 million of damage and harmed about 300 homes.
- St. Vincent owes a recent surge in tourism to a unique source: the blockbuster movie Pirates of the Caribbean. The successful movie was filmed on the island nation, and now 13 percent more tourists and 30 percent more cruise ships are stopping to see the scenery. A sequel to the movie may also be shot on the islands.
- St. Vincent's economy is becoming increasingly diversified from bananas as it develops services—tourism, telephone- and internet-based marketing, and offshore financial services. The government has taken ambitious steps to increase the rate of growth while decreasing unemployment and poverty rates.

Contact Information. Embassy of St. Vincent and the Grenadines, 3216 New Mexico Avenue NW, Washington, DC 20016; phone (202) 364-6730; web site www.embsvg.com. St. Vincent and the Grenadines National Tourist Office, 801 Second Avenue, 21st Floor, New York, NY 10017; phone (800) 729-1726; web site www.svgtourism.com.

CultureGrams World Edition 2006

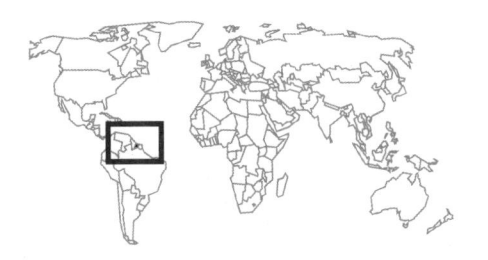

Republic of Suriname

BACKGROUND

Land and Climate. Suriname is located on the northeastern shoulder of South America. With an area of 63,039 square miles (163,270 square kilometers), it is nearly as large as Florida. The population is concentrated along the Atlantic coast, leaving about 80 percent of the country covered with pristine tropical rainforest. The absence of roads and the difficult navigability of Suriname's rivers have long protected rainforest biodiversity in the interior, but the growth of the logging and mining (bauxite and gold) industries now threatens some regions. Rainforest wildlife includes eight primate species, the cock-of-the-rock bird, and the spectacled caiman alligator. Coastal species include the giant leatherback sea turtle.

Positioned just north of the equator, Suriname has a warm tropical climate with little seasonal variation in temperature. Daytime coastal temperatures usually stay between 73 and 88°F (23–31°C) year-round. Suriname experiences two rainy seasons (December to January, May to mid-August) and two dry seasons (February to April, mid-August to November). Rainfall averages 87 inches (2,200 millimeters) per year.

History. Amerindians were the original inhabitants of what is now Suriname. As many as 70,000 Amerindians lived in the region when European explorers arrived in the 16th century. Warfare, slavery, and disease soon decimated their population.

The English colonized Suriname in the early 17th century but ceded control to the Netherlands in 1667. Sugarcane and coffee plantations, the backbone of the colonial economy, depended on African labor. Roughly 200,000 Africans arrived on slave ships in just over two centuries. Despite harsh punishments, many slaves escaped. Called Maroons, the escaped slaves formed groups in the forested interior. Expensive but failed attempts to exterminate the groups forced the Dutch to conclude peace treaties with them in the 1760s.

Despite resistance from plantation owners, slavery was officially abolished in 1863 (though the colony's 33,000 slaves were required to work on the plantations another 10 years). To compensate for the resulting labor shortage, the Dutch colonial government recruited contract laborers from China, India, and the Indonesian island of Java. Poor working conditions led many disillusioned laborers to return to their homelands after their contracts had ended, but the majority settled in Suriname and became small-scale farmers, wage laborers, and traders.

After two decades of internal autonomy, Suriname was granted full independence on 25 November 1975. Economic development lagged far behind expectations, so many Surinamers did not protest when a February 1980 coup installed a leftist military government. Led by Desi Bouterse, the regime dissolved parliament, suspended the constitution, and executed 15 supporters of the democratic opposition movement in 1982. To protest the regime's tactics, the Netherlands cut off aid to Suriname. The Surinamese Liberation Army (SLA), a group of mostly Maroon anti-government insurgents, began strikes on strategic economic targets in 1986. The army responded with attacks on Maroon villages suspected of supporting the rebels. Many Maroons were killed or forced to seek refuge abroad.

Under international pressure, Bouterse allowed elections and a return to civilian rule in 1988. Bouterse seized power again in 1990 but allowed elections the following year. Ronald Venetiaan, the elected president, signed a peace accord with the SLA in 1992 but failed to materialize economic recovery, leading to the election of Jules Wijdenbosch in 1996. Public expenditures under Wijdenbosch were offset by massive price

Suriname

increases. Street protests forced Wijdenbosch to step down, and Venetiaan was voted back into power in 2000. The currency has since stabilized, and inflation has been brought under control.

THE PEOPLE

Population. Suriname has a population of more than 480,000. About 90 percent of Surinamers inhabit the coastal plain. Roughly 75 percent live in urban areas, concentrated in the capital city of Paramaribo. Suriname's interior is inhabited primarily by Amerindians and Maroons in small villages. Population growth is low due to a high rate of migration, largely to the Netherlands.

An estimated 37 percent of Surinamers are Hindustanis (descendents of indentured laborers from India). About 31 percent are Creoles (descendents of African slaves and people of mixed African-European heritage). The remainder consists of Javanese (15 percent), Maroons (at least 10 percent), Amerindians (3 percent), Chinese (2 percent), Lebanese, Europeans, Haitians, and Brazilians. Maroons are divided into six distinct groups: Ndyuka, Paramaka, Aluku, Saramaka, Matawai, and Kwinti. Amerindians include the Arawak and Carib peoples on the coast and the Trio and Wayana in the interior.

Language. Most Surinamers speak Dutch, the nation's official language, but Sranan Tongo is the most common language for informal conversation. English is also widely spoken. Sranan Tongo (literally, "Suriname language") is a creole language formed by the slaves brought to Suriname. It is often called Taki-taki (literally, "Talking"). Most words can be traced to English, Dutch, or Portuguese, while the grammar contains African elements. In everyday speech, people often switch back and forth between Sranan Tongo and Dutch. Also spoken are Sarnami (among Hindustanis) and Javanese (among Javanese), though the elderly are more likely to use them than younger people. The Hakka Chinese dialect is spoken among Chinese. Each of the six Maroon groups speaks its own language. In one language group are Ndyuka, Paramacca, Aluku, and Kwinti, while Saramaccan and Matawai belong to another. The Amerindian groups speak their respective languages: Arawak, Carib, Trio, and Wayana.

Religion. Christians comprise 45 percent of the population, with about half of them Roman Catholic, one-third Moravian Protestant, and the remainder largely of other Protestant denominations. Most Hindustani people are Hindus (27 percent of the population), while most Javanese and some Hindustanis are Muslims (20 percent). About 6 percent follow indigenous religions. The remaining 2 percent belong to other faiths or claim no religious affiliation.

One of Suriname's most widely practiced indigenous religions is the Winti faith. Originally practiced by Creoles and Maroons, Winti is now also popular among people of other ethnicities. Through music, singing, trances, and rituals, practitioners consult the spiritual world to solve a problem or illness believed to have been caused by supernatural forces. For many Javanese, *agama Djawa* (Javanese religion) is at least as important as Islam. Incorporating elements of Hinduism, Buddhism, and animism, this belief centers on the world of spirits, which need to be appeased with food sacrifices (*sadjèn*). Harmony between the spirits and the living can be strengthened or repaired by holding a ritual feast (*slametan*), typically held for births, circumcisions, marriages, and funerals.

General Attitudes. Surinamers take great pride in their nation's cultural diversity and tolerance. Ethnic conflict is rare, and people of different groups routinely socialize and work together. Generosity is also highly valued. When a child does not share, or when someone finishes a plate of food without offering some to others, people call out *Saaang, I gridi!* (You are greedy!). Sharing is also at the root of Maroon and Amerindian subsistence economies. A successful hunter gives everyone in the village a portion; the next time he is less fortunate, he knows someone else will share food with him. Villagers who are considered greedy risk social isolation.

Education and owning a business are seen as high achievements due to the basis they provide for financial independence. Many Surinamers maintain a formal job for its pension and health benefits, while relying on the informal selling of goods and services (a practice known as *hosselen*) to earn extra money without the interference of a boss or the government. *Hosselen* may consist of baking for birthday celebrations, selling imported secondhand clothing, repairing bicycles, driving one's private car as a taxi, or other activities. Financial independence has a particular importance for women, as it enhances their power in relationships with men.

Personal Appearance. Most Surinamers wear casual Western clothing. For men, typical attire consists of jeans or cotton trousers with a T-shirt or buttoned shirt. Young women wear the same, as well as more open tops and skirts. Older women usually prefer more formal dresses. Suits and other business attire are common in offices.

Traditional ethnic clothing may be worn on special occasions. The *koto* is a Creole dress consisting of many layers of colorful fabric; it is accompanied by a head scarf (*angisa*). For Hindustani women, traditional attire consists of a *salwar* (a long blouse worn over long pants with a matching shawl), *gharara* (a long blouse worn over a long skirt with a matching shawl), or *sari* (a brightly-colored wraparound dress). On formal occasions, Javanese women may wear a *sarong* (a long wraparound skirt) with a *klambi koeroeng* (a tight-fitting jacket) and *slendang* (a shoulder drape).

Western clothing is increasingly common among rural Maroons and Amerindians. However, many Maroon women continue to wear a traditional wraparound dress called a *pangi* (in Ndyuka) or *kosu* (in Saramaccan), and some Amerindian men wear the *kamisa* (a cotton loincloth). Trio and Wayana Amerindians may still decorate their faces (and sometimes the entire body) with red and black paint as well as wear head dresses (*pumari*) made of toucan and parrot feathers.

CUSTOMS AND COURTESIES

Greetings. A woman may greet a friend she has not seen for a while with a hug (*brasa*) and three kisses on alternating cheeks. In everyday encounters, however, greetings tend to be informal; people merely exchange oral greetings. In Sranan Tongo one might say "How are you?" with the greetings *Fa waka?* (How are you walking?), *Fa'y tan?* (How are you staying?), or *Fa'y go?* (How are you going?). The reply is *Mi de* (I'm fine) or *A'y go* (It goes). In Dutch, one could start the day with *Goedemorgen* (Good morning) or greet with *Hoe gaat het?* (How's it going?). Young men may greet one another by bumping their right fists against the other's and then on their own chests. In Maroon forest communities, one is expected to start the day by greeting neighbors in a lengthy exchange. Such an exchange in Ndyuka would begin with *U-weekii* ("Good morning," literally "You have awakened") and include questions such as *I siibi mooi?* (Did you sleep well?) and *Fa fu den sama?* (How is your family?).

Gestures. Surinamers express dissatisfaction or annoyance by using the *tjuri*: one points the lips and sucks in air between the teeth and lips, while looking away. Disapproval can also be expressed with the *skir ai* (rolling and blinking the eyes) and by drawing the corners of the mouth down and the lower lip out. Men use a wide variety of whistles, kissing sounds, and "psss-psss" sounds to draw the attention of women. Surinamers also use many gestures common to North Americans, such as tapping the index finger on the forehead to question someone's intelligence.

Visiting. It is common for family and friends to visit one another at home without prior notice. The host always provides something to drink or eat. Visits are not segregated by gender and can last anywhere from five minutes to several hours. If parents bring their children, the children are expected to play quietly and not interfere with the adults' conversation. Visits are usually informal, so the host is not expected to be nicely dressed or keep the visitor entertained. For example, a woman receiving a female friend may continue cooking, washing clothes, or completing other household tasks while they talk. The friend, in turn, will not wait to be offered a chair and may look in the fridge for something to drink.

Eating. Families do not necessarily sit down together for meals. Children and adults who leave and arrive home at different times will eat whenever they are hungry. Generally, they have a simple breakfast before children go to school and parents leave for work. Lunch is the main meal of the day. It may be eaten at around 1 p.m., though it is more commonly eaten in late afternoon, when children are home from school and many adults end their workday. Around 7 or 8 p.m., people may have a sandwich or another light dinner. Options for dining out include restaurants, cantinas, and inexpensive street stands. Tipping is uncommon, but people may leave the change if they are pleased with the food.

LIFESTYLE

Family. Surinamers tend to live in nuclear units, though expensive housing often forces three or more generations to live in the same household. Elderly parents frequently live with their adult children.

Living together in a common-law relationship is customary among Creole, Maroon, and (to a lesser extent) Javanese couples. A large share of women are single mothers. In Hindustani society, living together and single motherhood are generally frowned upon, though families in Paramaribo tend to be more liberal than families elsewhere. It is not unusual for Surinamese men in common-law relationships to have a *buitenvrouw* (outside woman). This may be a short-term mistress or a more formal partner (with children) over several years. In traditional Maroon culture, a man is permitted to marry as many women as he can support (with their children). However, many modern urban Maroon men have multiple relationships without providing the required support.

Women represent one-third of the formal work force, and at least half of the informal work force. Even if she is working full-time, the woman usually takes care of the children and the household. Some men discourage their wives from working outside the home, but economic necessity often overrules such objections.

Dating and Marriage. Youths may go out in couples or with groups of friends. Popular weekend spots in Paramaribo are shopping streets, malls, and river and creek beaches. On weekend nights, young people gather at dance clubs and pool cafés.

Among Creoles and Maroons, sexual relationships among unmarried couples are common and accepted (though more so for boys than for girls). Young Hindustani women are usually more strictly guarded by their families. Hindustani parents may arrange their daughter's marriage to a selected partner, though women from more liberal families select their own partners. Among Javanese families, arranged marriages have fallen out of custom, but the parents of the prospective groom still go to the young woman's parents to ask for her hand in a formal ritual called the *panglamaran*. Although Suriname prides itself on its cultural tolerance, interracial dating can cause friction. For example, even though a Hindustani family may be good friends with their Creole neighbors, they are likely to oppose their daughter dating a Creole man.

Wedding customs differ by religion and ethnicity. Javanese families may celebrate a marriage by holding a dance party called a *tajub*. A traditional Hindu wedding ceremony can last many hours, with prayers, readings, and rituals that include the bride and groom walking seven times around a sacrificial fire with the bridal *sari* and the groom's scarf tied together.

Diet. Surinamers of all ethnic groups enjoy cuisine with Asian, African, and European influences. Breakfast often includes milk or tea and a white bread bun with peanut butter, cheese, or jam. Lunch, the main meal, typically consists of rice, vegetables, and meat or fish. Popular vegetables include legumes and tropical vegetables such as *sopropo* (bitter melon). Favorite dishes include *pom* (a Creole dish named for the ingredient *pomtayer*, a local root), *bami* (a Javanese noodle dish), and *roti* (a Hindustani dish of curried chicken, vegetables, and potato, wrapped in a flour pancake). Meals may be accompanied by water, soft drinks, juice, ginger beer, milk (for children), or *stroop* (a sweet drink available in many flavors). The day is concluded with a light meal and tea. Surinamers enjoy tropical fruits such as plantains, mangos, watermelons, and mandarins. Baked goods include *boyo* (a coconut flavored pastry) and *viadu* (a sweet raisin-almond bread).

Recreation. Suriname's most popular sports are soccer, basketball, and swimming. Residents of Paramaribo often spend free time on the beaches of the city's rivers and creeks, where they picnic, swim, and socialize. Surinamers of all groups and ages enjoy listening and dancing to live music, which is performed in many locations on weekends. Music festivals are common in August and September and during the December holiday season. The majority of Surinamers cannot afford to travel internationally, but the wealthy travel to the Netherlands (usually to visit family) and nearby Caribbean countries.

The Arts. Suriname's vibrant musical styles include *kaseko*, which combines traditional Creole music and Caribbean rhythms (calypso, salsa, and *zouk*) and uses call-and-response singing and percussion instruments such as the *skratsji* (a low wooden bench played with sticks). *Sranan bubbling*, a local variant of reggae music, is most popular among Creoles and Maroons. Traditional Javanese music centers on the *gamelan*, an orchestra with gongs, xylophones, drums, and other percussion instruments. Music favored by the Hindustani population combines classical East Indian music with modern house, techno, and rock music. These styles may mix sounds of traditional instruments (such as the *sitar*, a lute with a long neck) with synthesizers, electric guitars, and other modern electronic instruments. *Hindi-pop*, for example, is a blend of East Indian music, traditional Creole music, European pop, and Caribbean rhythms. Amerindian music incorporates flutes and percussion instruments such as the *seke-seke* (a closed piece of metal

Suriname

pipe with seeds or gravel, shaken to the rhythm). Other popular art forms include folk theater, painting, and sculpture.

Holidays. National holidays are New Year's Day, Easter (Good Friday–Easter Monday), *Holi Phagwah* (the Hindustani spring festival, March or April), *Id ul Fitre* (the festival to end *Ramadan*, the Muslim month of fasting), Labor Day (1 May), Freedom Day (1 July), Independence Day (25 Nov.), Christmas (24–25 Dec.), and Boxing Day (26 Dec.).

Commerce. Most businesses and shops are open 7:30 a.m. to 4:30 p.m., Monday to Friday. Some may also open on Saturday from 7:30 a.m. to 1 p.m. Hours for government offices are 7 a.m. to 3 p.m., Monday to Thursday, and 7 a.m. to 2:30 p.m. on Friday. Surinamers often buy fresh fruits and vegetables at open-air markets and street stalls; prices are usually open to negotiation. Supermarkets sell groceries at fixed prices.

SOCIETY

Government. The president (currently Ronald Venetiaan) is chief of state and head of government. Elected by the 51-seat National Assembly, the president is generally the leader of its majority party or coalition. Elections are held every five years. The voting age is 18. Many political parties are predominantly comprised of one ethnic group, though membership is not exclusively limited. In the interior, Maroon and Amerindian leaders known as *kapiteins* (chiefs) receive public salaries and have authority over some local matters.

Economy. Mining dominates the economy. Bauxite mining accounts for 70 percent of export earnings. Large-scale corporate gold mining is expanding, though most profits flow out of the country. Other formal industries include logging, oil drilling, and food processing. Small-scale gold mining (typically informal and illegal) provides subsistence to thousands of people in the interior. In the agricultural sector, rice is the major crop, followed by bananas, palm kernels (for oil), coconuts, plantains, peanuts, and citrus fruits. Tourism offers potential for growth.

Suriname enjoys a high standard of living compared to other countries in the region, but large sections of the population remain impoverished due to the nation's history of economic instability. Development aid remains a vital component of the economy, and the government is a major employer. Most people earn at least part of their income in the informal economy. The currency is the Suriname dollar (SRD). Large purchases (such as cars) are usually made in U.S. dollars or euros.

Transportation and Communications. In urban areas, Surinamers travel by car, minibus, motorcycle, and bicycle. Increases in car ownership have made Paramaribo heavily congested. Privately owned minibuses have no fixed schedules and leave from the stations when they are full. Most interior villages can only be accessed by motorized river canoes (*korjaals*). In the dry seasons, drops in river water levels make some villages inaccessible. Small private planes fly to the interior, but the unpaved airstrips become muddy and unusable during the rainy seasons.

Most urban households have a telephone connection, and most people own a mobile phone. Paramaribo internet cafés have reliable service. Telephones are almost non-existent in the interior, where people communicate via a radio network that broadcasts news and local information. Several privately-owned daily newspapers are published in Paramaribo. Most urban families have a television; broadcasts include local, Dutch, U.S., and Indian programs. In forest villages (where electricity is rare), a wealthy person with a personal generator may show videos or DVDs for other villagers.

DEVELOPMENT DATA
Human Dev. Index* rank . . . . 67 of 177 countries
Adjusted for women . . . . NA
Real GDP per capita $6,590
Adult literacy rate . . . . 95 percent (male); 91 (female)
Infant mortality rate . . . . 24 per 1,000 births
Life expectancy . . . . 68 (male); 74 (female)

Education. The education system consists of preschool (two years), primary school (six), junior secondary school (four), and senior secondary school (two to four), followed by vocational training or university studies. Primary education is compulsory between the ages of 6 to 12. Families who cannot afford uniforms, shoes, books, and the small school fee can apply for public support. At the secondary level, enrollment drops to less than 65 percent. Many students drop out to find work. In remote areas, progression above primary school is hindered by limited transportation and the scarcity of qualified teachers. Also, students in remote areas usually speak a local language at home, so they have difficulty understanding classes in Dutch.

Health. Government employees receive public health insurance. Most other people are covered by their employer's health insurance or have private insurance. Registered low-income families receive free medical care. Public hospitals offer a good standard of health care, though the technology and specialist knowledge are better at more expensive, private hospitals. Virtually all specialists have been educated in the Netherlands. Nurses are locally trained. Both rural and urban residents continue to rely on a variety of forest medicines (*busi dresi*) and home medicines (*oso dresi*) typically linked to traditional religious rituals. Major health concerns are malaria and the spread of HIV/AIDS.

AT A GLANCE

Events and Trends.
- Suriname's Rosebel gold mine produced nearly 700,000 ounces of gold in 2004, a record for the Canadian company that operates the mine. The mine's financial success has resulted in criticism of the government for negotiating a poor deal with the mine operator and securing only a fraction of the profits.
- Since 2004, a UN tribunal has evaluated a maritime border dispute between Suriname and Guyana. Potential offshore oil reserves are at stake. Suriname also has longstanding disputes over its southwestern border with Guyana and its southeastern border with French Guiana.

Contact Information. Embassy of Suriname, 4301 Connecticut Avenue NW, Suite 460, Washington, DC 20008; phone (202) 244-7488; web site www.surinameembassy.org.

CultureGrams™
People. The World. You.

ProQuest Information and Learning Company
300 North Zeeb Road, P.O. Box 1346
Ann Arbor, Michigan 48106 USA
Toll Free: 1.800.528.6279
Fax: 1.800.864.0019
www.culturegrams.com

© 2005 ProQuest Information and Learning Company and Brigham Young University. It is against the law to copy, reprint, store, or transmit any part of this publication in any form by any means without written permission from ProQuest. This document contains native commentary and original analysis, as well as estimated statistics. The content should not be considered strictly factual, and it may not apply to all groups in a nation. *UN Development Programme, Human Development Report 2004 (New York: Oxford University Press, 2004).

CultureGrams World Edition 2006

Republic of Trinidad and Tobago

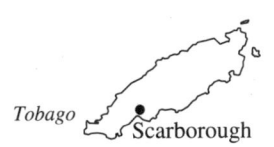

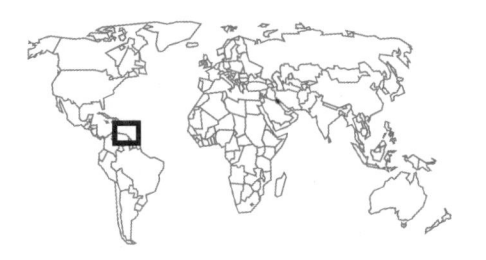

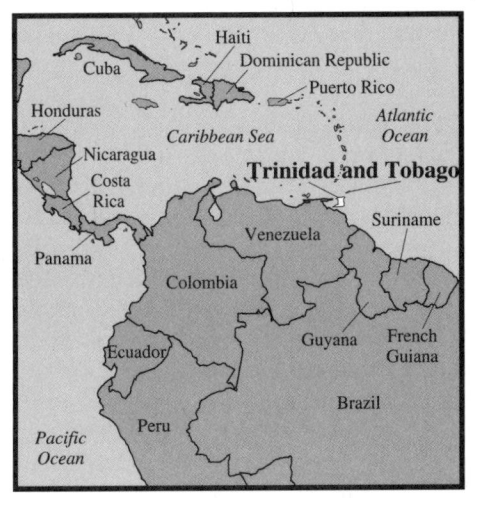

BACKGROUND

Land and Climate. Trinidad and Tobago is a two-island republic in the Caribbean Sea, just 7 miles (11 kilometers) off the coast of Venezuela. Trinidad is the larger island at 1,864 square miles (4,828 square kilometers), while Tobago is just 116 square miles (300 square kilometers). Together, the islands are slightly smaller than Delaware. Port of Spain is both the national capital and the capital of Trinidad. Tobago's capital is Scarborough.

Once a part of the South American continent, the islands were divided from Venezuela through tectonic movement. The islands are still home to many plants and animals that are native to South America. For example, a bird known as the scarlet ibis breeds in Suriname and Venezuela but spends much of its life feeding on the islands. Both islands are mostly covered by plains but also have some hills and low mountains. The highest mountain is Trinidad's Cerro del Aripo, which rises to more than 3,000 feet (940 meters).

The nation has a tropical climate, with an average annual temperature of 78°F (25.5°C). Temperatures remain relatively stable all year, but the islands experience a dry season from January to early June and a wet season from late June through December. During the wet season, rainstorms are frequent but usually short, and although about 75 percent of the annual rainfall comes during this season, sunshine is also common. Tobago is slightly cooler and drier than Trinidad.

History. The first inhabitants of Trinidad and Tobago were the Carib and the Arawak tribes, who are thought to have inhabited the Caribbean as long as 6,000 years before Europeans arrived. The warlike Caribs greatly reduced the Arawak population, but the dominance of the Caribs ended when European settlers moved in. Despite the Caribs' fierce resistance, Europeans eventually enslaved many of the indigenous inhabitants. Colonizers largely wiped out both tribes, and most of the survivors were gradually assimilated. Few, if any, identifiable descendants of Caribs are left on the islands.

Christopher Columbus sighted Trinidad in 1498 and claimed the island for Spain, calling it La Isla de la Trinidad ("Island of the Holy Trinity"). However, because Trinidad had no gold, the Spaniards paid little attention to the area, and it was nearly a hundred years before the first permanent Spanish settlement was established. Few attempts were made to colonize Tobago until much later, but it did change hands between colonial powers more than 20 times.

In the late 18th century, Spain offered land grants in Trinidad to Catholics, so an influx of French Catholics established sugar and cocoa plantations there. However, Spain reaped few rewards from the deal, as Britain captured Trinidad in 1797 and gained final control of Tobago in 1814.

Both French and English plantations made heavy use of slave labor, and after slavery was abolished in the 1830s, the English brought thousands of indentured laborers from India to serve on the islands. Today, most residents of Trinidad and Tobago are descendants of either African slaves or East Indian laborers.

In the 1880s, Tobago's economy began to falter, and the British combined the two islands into one colony. The Depression of the 1930s spawned a labor movement, which soon led to demands for greater self-determination on a national scale. The British granted universal suffrage in 1946, and in 1962 the nation gained independence and became a parliamentary democracy. Trinidad and Tobago became a republic within the British Commonwealth in 1976.

Trinidad and Tobago

Throughout the 1900s, the country's vast oil industry helped make the nation one of the richest in the Caribbean, but fluctuating oil prices have occasionally hurt the economy. Although political stability has been the norm, a group of militant Muslims attempted a coup in 1990. They took the prime minister and 45 other people hostage. After six days and 24 deaths, the hostages were released. The captors were imprisoned, but eventually released on a technicality.

Today politicians sometimes use racial issues in their campaigns, and voting often follows racial lines, with much of the black population supporting People's National Movement and many East Indians backing the United National Congress. This trend has contributed to a recent deadlock in parliament. Other current challenges include diversifying the economy to withstand fluctuating oil prices, battling drugs and violence, and promoting the nation's small but growing tourist industry.

THE PEOPLE

Population. Trinidad and Tobago's population of 1.1 million is shrinking at an annual rate of 0.68 percent as some people choose to have fewer children and others migrate to North America or Europe. About 95 percent of the population lives on Trinidad, while Tobago has just 50,000 residents.

The nation prides itself in its ethnic diversity, with inhabitants having roots in Africa, India, Europe, Asia, and the Middle East. Most people are either East Indian (40 percent) or black (40 percent). The rest of the population includes people of mixed race (18 percent), Chinese and other Asians (1.2 percent), whites (0.6 percent), and small numbers of Portuguese, Syrians, and Lebanese. In Trinidad, many races live near each other, while Tobago's population is mostly black.

Language. Almost everyone speaks English, the country's official language. English is used in formal situations and follows British rules of grammar and spelling; however, other languages are used informally. The older generation speaks a French-based Creole language called *patois*, while the younger generation speaks a slang-filled language called *Trini*. *Trini* is English with French, Spanish, Hindi, and African influences and is often difficult for visitors to understand. Words and phrases include *Yuh stickin'* (you are moving too slowly), *bowgee* (sister-in-law), *mamaguy* (trying to fool someone), and *jumbie* (unpleasant spirit or ghost). Many East Indians speak Hindi, and other minorities speak French or Spanish, which are also taught in schools.

Religion. Most Trinidadians are Christian, with the largest denominations being Roman Catholic (29 percent), Anglican (11 percent), and Presbyterian (3.4 percent). East Indians and Asians on the islands practice Hinduism (24 percent), Islam (6 percent), Buddhism, and Taoism. Followers of the Shango and Spiritual Baptist faiths mix Christian beliefs with traditional African rituals and the worship of nature.

Although followers of non-Christian religions suffered systematic discrimination during the colonial era, both Christian and non-Christian religions flourish on the islands today. Most residents are quite religious and attend church weekly. The government acknowledges the importance Trinidadians place on religion by discussing matters of national interest with religious leaders. Various churches also do humanitarian work, including feeding and housing the islands' poor.

General Attitudes. Trinidad sees itself as a vibrant cosmopolitan island, while Tobago considers itself more relaxed. People on both islands are known for their friendliness, and they respect people who are strong-willed, educated, and loyal. The elderly and members of the clergy are held in high esteem. Trinidadians are proud of their rich heritage and will defend their country in the face of criticism. They also tend to have a relaxed attitude toward punctuality. The phrase *Any time is Trini time* refers to the fact that Trinidadians often arrive well after an event starts, and being late not considered rude.

The islands' peoples have long been known for their ability to get along with each other, and all groups refer to themselves as Trinidadians. However, races tend to associate within their own groups. Racial characteristics such as skin color are also discussed openly.

Poor Trinidadians see North America and Europe as a way out of poverty, and many migrate to these areas seeking better opportunities. Another reason North American culture influences the islands is because most television and radio programs are from the United States. Trinidadians believe the North American influence has brought technology and education but also the glamorization of sex and violence.

Personal Appearance. Appearance matters a great deal to Trinidadians. Urban professionals wear suits or uniforms and dress shoes. Schoolchildren also wear uniforms. In casual situations, people wear brightly colored, lightweight clothes. T-shirts, pants, and skirts are common. East Indian women wear a traditional gown called a *sari* during festivals.

U.S. fashions are popular among Trinidadians. Men wear shorts fairly often, but women are more likely to wear skirts. Sleeveless shirts, crop tops, and short skirts are fairly common. Young people wear t-shirts, jeans, and sneakers. Sweaters and long-sleeved shirts are rare.

CUSTOMS AND COURTESIES

Greetings. It is impolite not to greet someone when one first sees him or her for the day. Greetings include *Good morning*, *Good night*, *Hello*, *How are you going?*, *Wuh yuh sayin'?* (How are you?), or simply *Aaaaall-right*. A proper response might be *Just cool* (I'm doing well). Close friends may shake hands or hug. Women or mixed couples may kiss once on the cheek. Men may greet with a *bounce*, in which each man touches the closed fist of the other. It is customary to ask a friend about his or her health during the greeting.

First names and nicknames are used only among friends and family members. *Doo doo* (someone who looks good) is a common term of endearment used among friends of the opposite sex. It is proper to address coworkers or strangers with the title *Mr.*, *Ms.*, or *Mrs.*, followed by their family name.

Gestures. Trinidadians are expressive and often use their hands to emphasize speech. Conversations usually include laughter and touching, especially between close friends. Females and young people accompanying the elderly often walk hand in hand. On buses, younger people offer seats to the elderly. A common way to display disgust, frustration, or disapproval is to make a tooth-sucking noise known as *steupsing*. It is rude for a younger person to do this to an elder.

Visiting. Trinidadians generally enjoy socializing, and friends often see one another informally. This kind of socializing is called a *lime* and can take place nearly anywhere or at any time. *Liming* activities include listening to music, chatting, and relaxing. Dropping by a home unannounced is acceptable, but staying past 10 p.m. during such a visit is rude. However, when one is invited, visits often start after 7 p.m. and go late into the night.

The greatest number of visits occurs around Christmastime. Often, homes will be packed with family and friends during this season, and unlike at other times of the year, guests generally bring the host a gift. Groups of friends may also go *paranging* (going from house to house singing Spanish Christmas carols called *parang*), as well as dancing, eating, and playing homemade instruments.

Eating. Trinidadians love to cook and eat. In addition to eating three meals a day, many Trinidadians snack between meals. Breakfast is usually light and may consist of tea or juice with cereal or bread and cheese, meat, or eggs.

The biggest meal is eaten at lunchtime. While many people bring home-cooked meals to work, others eat at food courts or restaurants. Some prefer to eat a light lunch in favor of having a larger meal with the family at dinner. Fast food is popular among the younger generation, and American-style chain restaurants and street vendors selling local specialties have become very common.

In private, most Trinidadians like informal eating and will use their hands or a fork or spoon as their only utensil. In public, they eat with a fork in the left hand and a knife in the right. Asking for second servings and speaking while eating are common at home or with friends but rare during formal meals. For formal occasions, only one serving is taken and conversation is saved for after the meal.

LIFESTYLE

Family. Young people usually live with their parents until they marry. Even married couples may live with family until the couple is financially able to move out. Single-parent families also stay with their extended families. Urban families tend to live in apartments, which are plentiful and generally affordable. Most rural families own their homes, and many do agricultural work on their land to supplement their incomes. The average urban family usually has no more than two children, but rural families may have as many as five.

Young and elderly Trinidadians receive special care. Women do most household chores and cooking, but men also may help around the house. Grandmothers, aunts, and other relatives pitch in to help care for children. Adult children are expected to care for the elderly.

Dating and Marriage. Young people meet at movies, parties, malls, or dance clubs, and they begin dating around age 16. Women usually get married between ages 17 and 23, while most men marry between ages 20 and 30. Most Trinidadians expect to marry and have children at some point, but out-of-wedlock births and common-law marriages are prevalent. Because many people never officially marry, the divorce rate is relatively low. Arranged marriages are occasionally still practiced in rural areas and among members of the East Indian community. However, it is now more common for the bride and groom to simply seek parental approval before marrying. Muslims are usually expected to marry other Muslims.

Weddings generally feature a ceremony at a church, where all civil matters are also dealt with. The ceremony is followed by a reception at a large hall. Guests bring gifts for the newlyweds and enjoy eating, drinking, and dancing. After this celebration, many couples go on a honeymoon.

Diet. Trinidadians prefer chicken or fish with most main dishes. Pork, beef, goat, and lamb are less common, but are also popular. Main meals include *macaroni pie* (macaroni baked with cheese, butter, and milk), *callaloo* (a local plant that is cooked with coconut milk, pepper, and pumpkin), *stewed chicken* (chicken simmered in caramelized sugar and oil), *bake* (a small, flat bread that is fried instead of baked), and *saltfish* (fish cured in salt), which is cooked with vegetables. Many dishes are served with rice, which is called *pelau* when it is prepared with chickpeas or *spanish rice* when it is cooked with vegetables. Among the East Indian population, the most common foods are curried meat and vegetables served with rice or *roti*. *Roti* is similar to pita bread and has gained widespread popularity as a local fast food. Another popular fast-food Indian dish is called *doubles* and consists of fried dough stuffed with chickpeas and hot sauce. Dessert is not a traditional part of a Trinidadian meal, but those who eat it may have ice cream, fruit cocktail, or gelatin. A wide variety of foreign foods are also available, including Asian, European, and U.S. cuisines.

Recreation. Trinidadians enjoy outdoor activities such as cycling, walking, jogging, hiking, and swimming at the beach. Water sports are more common on Tobago, where there is a greater emphasis on tourism. Shopping at malls and watching movies are other popular activities. Hollywood movies come to the islands soon after they are released in the United States. When school is out during July and August, many children attend summer camps.

Cricket is the favorite sport on the islands, and the nation sends players to the popular West Indies cricket team. The islands also have their own professional soccer team, but it is relatively new and does not yet have a large following. Both teams play internationally. Many people play basketball and tennis, but in general, Trinidadians do not follow sports with the same vigor as people in the United States.

The Arts. *Calypso* music is a favorite among Trinidadians. *Calypso* is a form of social commentary invented in Trinidad and sung by performers called *calypsonians*. *Steel drums* also feature prominently in local music; they are made from the lids of oil drums that have been hammered into the shape of an inverted turtle shell. Local music is at its best during Trinidad and Tobago's extensive Carnival celebration. Preparations for Carnival—also known as *Mas* (short for masquerade)—begin in late December and the festivities culminate a few days before Lent. Trinidadians flock to *calypso* tents to hear the latest music. *Calypsonians* and *steel drum* bands compete to be named best in the nation. During the final days of Carnival, Trinidadians don elaborate costumes and dance through the streets, accompanied by music.

There are also strong traditions of art, dance, literature and theater. Pottery, sculpture, basketry, and leatherwork are popular crafts. African-inspired arts include stick fighting and limbo dancing, while common East Indian arts include traditional singing and playing *tassa drums* (cone-shaped drums made of clay and goat skins).

Holidays. Trinidadians celebrate a variety of religious public holidays. Christian holidays include Carnival, Good Friday, Easter, Corpus Christi, and Christmas. *Divali* (October or November) is the Hindu festival of lights and emphasizes truth and light triumphing over darkness. The Muslim holiday *Eid-ul-Fitr* is a feast at the end of the Muslim holy month of fasting, which is known as *Ramadan*. Spiritual Baptist Liberation Day (30 Mar.) commemorates the abolition of a British law forbidding participation in the African-influenced Spiritual Baptist religion.

Other national holidays include New Year's day; Indian Arrival Day (30 May), which celebrates the arrival of East Indians to the country; Labor Day (19 June), which honors the period in the 1970s when the labor movement was born; Emancipation Day (1 Aug.), which marks the abolition of sla-

Trinidad and Tobago

very in 1845; Independence Day (31 Aug.), which celebrates the nation's 1962 independence from Britain; Republic Day (24 Sept.), which commemorates the day the country became a republic; and Boxing Day (26 Dec.), which originates from the British tradition of giving small boxed gifts to employees or the poor, and is now a day to visit friends and relatives.

Commerce. The average workweek for office employees is 40 hours. Most offices are open from 8 a.m. to 4 p.m., Monday through Friday, and 8 a.m. to noon on Saturdays. Banks usually close earlier. Many people in the industrial and services sectors work longer hours and extra days to supplement their incomes; the minimum wage is about US$1.35 per hour.

Malls are open from 10 a.m. to 8 p.m., Monday through Saturday, with shorter hours on Sunday. Trinidadians tend to shop for most food and household items once every two or three weeks, while buying produce on a weekly basis. Supermarkets are common; open-air markets are prevalent in rural areas.

SOCIETY

Government. Trinidad and Tobago is a parliamentary democracy. George Maxwell Richards is the president, but his position is largely ceremonial. Patrick Manning is the prime minister and leads the People's National Movement (PNM), the political party with the most seats in the House of Representatives. The PNM has dominated politics since independence; the other main parties are the United National Congress (UNC) and the National Alliance for Reconstruction (NAR). While the NAR and UNC have won elections, each managed only one term with their prime minister in office. Parliament consists of the 36-member House of Representatives and the 31-member Senate. The voting age is 18.

Economy. The economy of Trinidad and Tobago is one of the Caribbean's strongest. Although sugar had long been a source of wealth for the islands, the industry has been sagging for decades. The economy is now anchored by oil drilling, manufacturing, and services. With the continuing discovery of more oil, the country is entering an economic boom period. There was a similar period in the early 1970s, but the boom ended in the late '80s, which led to hardship for many locals. The economy began to pick up again in the mid-'90s and foreign companies have started reinvesting in the country. However, unemployment is still a major problem.

The country has a large energy and industrial sector and is a major refiner and exporter of oil, natural gas, and petrochemicals, which account for 70 percent of the country's exports. Asphalt, which is naturally produced at the La Brea Pitch Lake, is another major export. Agriculture and tourism also contribute to the economy.

Transportation and Communications. In urban areas, the majority of people use *maxi-taxis* (mini-buses) and taxis. Taxis are shared and used mostly by tourists. The national train system was abolished more than two decades ago because of maintenance difficulties, but the public bus system is popular. Many families also own cars, which are becoming so plentiful that the government is building and improving roads to accommodate them. Each island has an international airport.

The communication system is well developed. A monopoly phone company provides local and international service.

DEVELOPMENT DATA
Human Dev. Index* rank . . . . 54 of 177 countries
   Adjusted for women . . . . 47 of 144 countries
Real GDP per capita $9,430
Adult literacy rate . . . . 99 percent (male); 98 (female)
Infant mortality rate . . . . 25 per 1,000 births
Life expectancy . . . . 69 (male); 75 (female)

Three television stations show local and international programs. Cable has made U.S. and European culture much more common on the islands. Eighteen radio stations provide music and talk radio. There are three daily newspapers and four weekly papers. Ten percent of the population uses the internet.

Education. Education is compulsory between ages 6 and 12 and free between ages 6 and 18. Trinidadians must pay for university education. The government guarantees all qualified children education in secondary schools, but students who place high on a competitive exam go to college-preparatory schools; others may be sent to vocational schools. Wealthy families often send their children to private secondary schools. The University of Trinidad and Tobago and the University of the West Indies as well as technical colleges and teachers colleges offer higher education.

Health. Health care at government-owned clinics is free to all citizens. However, it is fairly common for patients to be put on long waiting lists for elective procedures and for medical equipment to be in poor condition. Those who can afford it often seek care in private hospitals, which are much more modern and which have recently become more common. Medication costs are high, but the government attempts to assist the elderly by providing some medicines for free. Major health concerns include heart disease, cancer, diabetes, and AIDS.

AT A GLANCE
Events and Trends.
- In August 2004, the first president of the Caribbean Court of Justice (CCJ) was sworn in. Although the CCJ had not begun deciding cases by late 2004, it was expected to become the highest court in the Caribbean. For years, London judges had decided the most important cases.
- The disparity between Caribbean and British values could be seen in November 2003, when Trinidad and Tobago's mandatory death sentence for murderers was overturned in London. Trinidad and Tobago had reinstated the death penalty in 1999 to combat a rising murder rate.
- The University of Trinidad and Tobago (UTT) was launched in November 2004, becoming the second university on the islands. The creation of UTT was intended to increase number of skilled workers in the country, in turn helping the economy.

Contact Information. Embassy of Trinidad and Tobago, 1708 Massachusetts Avenue NW, Washington, DC 20036; phone (202) 467-6490; web site http://ttembassy.cjb.net. For tourist information, write P.O. Box 222, Maritime Centre, 29 Tenth Avenue, Barataria, Trinidad, West Indies; call (868) 675-7034; or visit www.visittnt.com.

© 2005 ProQuest Information and Learning Company and Brigham Young University. It is against the law to copy, reprint, store, or transmit any part of this publication in any form by any means without written permission from ProQuest. This document contains native commentary and original analysis, as well as estimated statistics. The content should not be considered strictly factual, and it may not apply to all groups in a nation. *UN Development Programme, Human Development Report 2004 (New York: Oxford University Press, 2004).

CultureGrams™
People. The World. You.

ProQuest Information and Learning Company
300 North Zeeb Road, P.O. Box 1346
Ann Arbor, Michigan 48106 USA
Toll Free: 1.800.528.6279
Fax: 1.800.864.0019
www.culturegrams.com

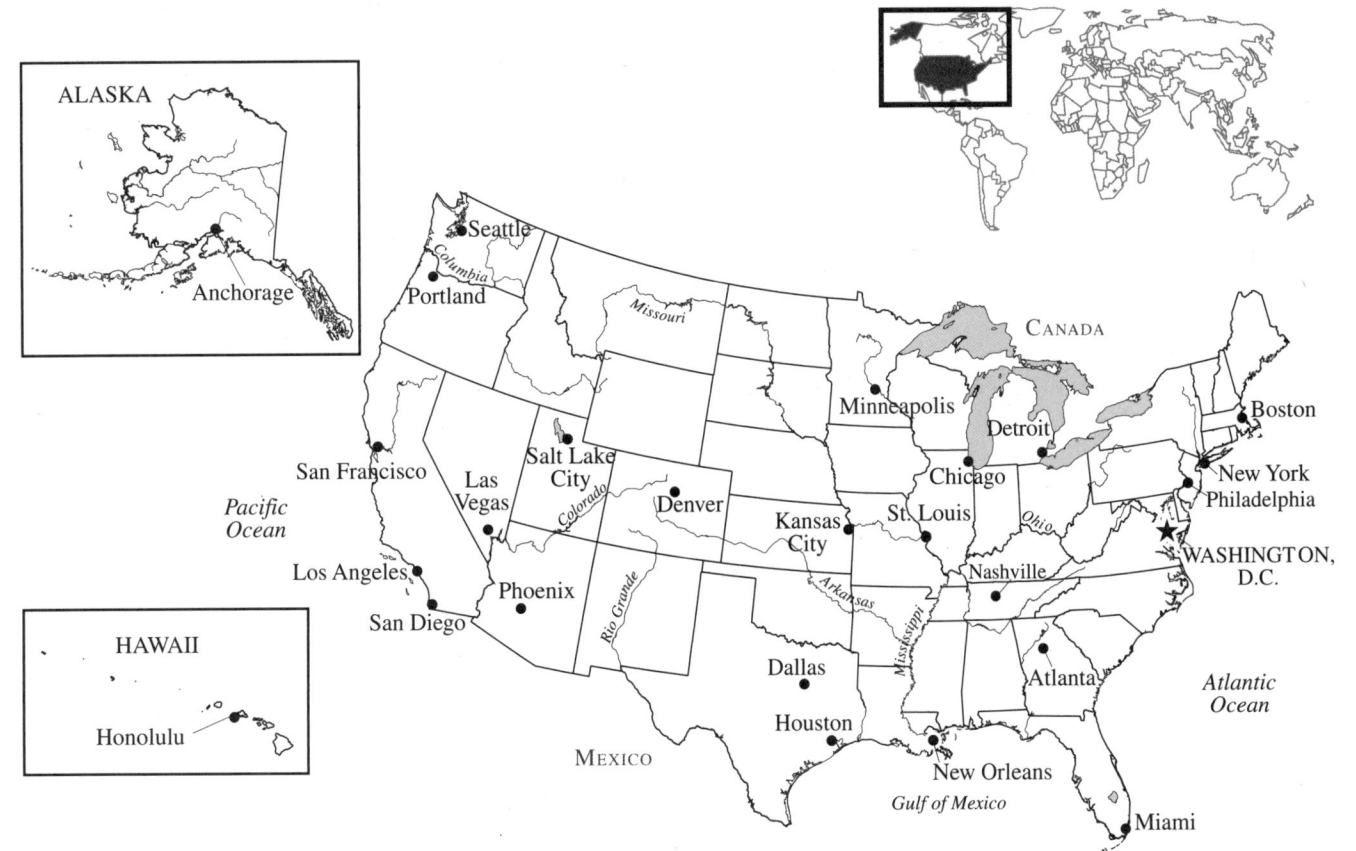

CultureGrams World Edition 2006
United States of America

BACKGROUND

Land and Climate. The United States covers the central portion of North America and includes Alaska in the far northwest and the Hawaiian Islands in the Pacific Ocean. Covering 3,618,765 square miles (9,372,558 square kilometers), it is the fourth largest country in the world. Because of its size and location, the United States has a variety of geographical features and climates. Imposing mountains, vast deserts, wide canyons, extensive coasts, subtropical forests, wetlands, rolling hills, prairies, and tundra are all part of the country's natural diversity. Beyond the beaches and mountains of California, the Rocky Mountains in the west give way to a vast central plain, which merges with the rolling hills and low mountains of the east. Hawaii's rugged volcanic topography is lush and green year-round. Alaska has a varied landscape, with towering mountains, broad valleys, and glaciers.

Climates throughout the country are as varied as the terrain. Natural resources include coal, copper, lead, uranium, bauxite, gold, silver, iron, petroleum, natural gas, timber, and much more. Natural disasters such as droughts, floods, hurricanes, tornadoes, earthquakes, and severe winter storms affect various regions.

History. North America's history before Europeans arrived is not completely known, but many of the original inhabitants had advanced civilizations. From the 17th century on, Native Americans were displaced by European settlers, who came for riches, territory, and religious freedom. Between 1607 and 1730, 13 British colonies were established on the East Coast. The American Revolution (1775–83) led to independence from Britain and a loose confederation of states. A constitution was created, which prescribed a system of government, balanced the rights of the states and federal government, and protected free speech and other civil liberties. Explorers and pioneers headed west and settled large areas of land. The United States acquired territory from France, Mexico, Russia, and Spain throughout the 19th century, expanding its borders from the Atlantic to the Pacific Ocean.

In 1861, civil war broke out between Union states in the north and Confederate states in the south over issues of states' rights, economics, and slavery. Under President Abraham Lincoln, Union forces were victorious in 1865. Slavery was abolished and the Union was restored, although it took many years for the nation to heal from the conflict. Legal discrimination based on race continued until the civil rights movement of the 1950s and 1960s prompted counterlegislation.

In the late 19th and early 20th centuries, immigration boomed, the economy grew substantially, and government policy focused on finding world markets. Initially wary of involvement in European affairs, the United States provided troops toward the end of World War I, which ended in 1918. By 1942, it was a major combatant in World War II and emerged after the war as the strongest economic and military power in the world.

In the latter half of the twentieth century, the United States became an important donor of financial, technological, and

United States of America

military aid to developing countries in an effort to engender allegiance and stop the spread of Soviet-sponsored communism. With the U.S. defeat in Vietnam in 1973, American influence abroad declined, although this trend seemed to reverse in the 1980s and 1990s. U.S. leadership was pivotal in the 1991 Gulf War as well as conflicts in Bosnia, Somalia, and Kosovo.

In the 2000 presidential elections, George W. Bush was declared the winner over former vice president Al Gore after numerous vote recounts and court decisions. Initially working to reduce the country's part in international disputes, Bush changed his approach after the terrorist attacks of September 11, 2001. He declared a war on terror, which eventually led to military action against Afghanistan (2001) and a controversial war in Iraq (2003). A leader in the global economy and foremost among the world's military powers, the United States continues to have a far-reaching worldwide influence.

THE PEOPLE

Population. The population of the United States (about 293 million) is the third largest in the world, after China and India, and is growing at roughly 0.9 percent per year. A large portion of the population (69 percent) is white. Hispanics, also known as Latinos, (13.5 percent) are the fastest-growing minority group. They recently became the country's largest ethnic minority, surpassing the black population (13 percent). Other groups include Asians and Pacific Islanders (4 percent) and Native Americans (1 percent). About 2.4 percent of the population claims more than one race.

Although members of any ethnic group can be found anywhere in the country, populations vary by region. For example, the black population lives mostly in the east and southeast, while Hispanics reside mostly in the west and southwest. In Hawaii, more than half of the people are Asians or Pacific Islanders. Minority populations also tend to be concentrated in urban areas. About one-fourth of the population is younger than 18 years of age, and nearly 80 percent of all Americans live in metropolitan areas.

Language. English, the predominant language, is spoken by most citizens. The English spoken in the United States is referred to in other English-speaking nations as American English. It is characterized by unique idioms as well as spelling and pronunciation variations from British English. Spoken English is very flexible, while written English is more formal and standardized. Many immigrants of the first, second, or even third generation also speak their native tongue. In fact, one in seven Americans speaks a language other than English in the home. Spanish is spoken in many communities. Native Americans speak a variety of languages.

Religion. Although the United States has never had an official state church, about 90 percent of the population professes some religious belief. Most Americans (roughly 80 percent) are Christians. Early European settlers were primarily Christians, and the Constitution and Bill of Rights are based, in part, on Christian values and principles. However, the Constitution dictates that church and state remain separate. Many different Christian churches are found throughout the country. As much as 55 percent of the population belongs to Protestant organizations, with Baptists, Methodists, and Lutherans being the largest Protestant groups. About 25 percent of the population is Roman Catholic. Other Christian denominations account for another 3 to 5 percent of the total. There are also substantial numbers of Jews (1–2 percent), Muslims (1 percent), Buddhists, and other religions. Between 40 and 45 percent of Americans attend religious services weekly. About 10 percent has no religious affiliation but may still have spiritual convictions. Religion is generally a personal matter for Americans, but some openly discuss their beliefs with others.

General Attitudes. Americans tend to be frank and outspoken. In general, they appreciate people who are candid. They voice their opinions and share their views on a variety of subjects; there are few subjects they will not discuss. Of course, there are exceptions, and religious values may keep some from discussing certain issues. Those who are not close friends avoid extremely personal questions. Americans value innovation, industry, and integrity. They enjoy a good sense of humor, including sarcasm. Most people have the ability to laugh at themselves as well as at others. Even though Americans may criticize the government, most are patriotic and believe the United States is one of the greatest countries in the world. People in the United States consider their country to be a guardian of democracy and freedom. They strongly value their freedom and independence, as a nation and as individuals. Individualism, as opposed to conformity, is often cited as an American characteristic. Even when working as a team, Americans usually think in terms of several distinct individuals blending their efforts rather than a group working as one unit.

Personal Appearance. Although fashion trends affect how people dress, Americans generally feel free to wear whatever they please. Some use clothing to make a social or personal statement. Americans emphasize cleanliness but may purposely wear tattered clothing or casual attire in public. Dressing "down" (casually) is a trend in the workplace; still, suits for men, and pantsuits, dresses, or skirts for women are standard attire in many offices. Formal clothing is worn for certain social occasions. Appearance, in general, is important to the individual American.

CUSTOMS AND COURTESIES

Greetings. Both men and women usually smile and shake hands when greeting. The American handshake is usually firm. Good friends and relatives may embrace when they meet, especially after a long absence. In casual situations, people may wave rather than shake hands. Friends also wave to each other at a distance. Americans may greet strangers on the street by saying *Hello* or *Good morning* (in Spanish, *Hola* or *Buenos días*), although they may pass without any greeting. Among young people, casual verbal greetings or hand-slapping gestures are common. Except in formal situations, people who are acquainted generally address one another by given name. Combining a title (*Mr.*, *Ms.*, *Dr.*, for example) with a family name shows respect. When greeting someone for the first time, Americans commonly say *Nice to meet you*. A simple *Hello* or *Hi* is also common. Regional variations exist, such as *Aloha* (Hello) in Hawaii. Friends often greet each other with *How are you?* and respond *Fine, thanks*. Americans do not usually expect any further answer to the question.

Gestures. When conversing, Americans generally stand about 2 feet (.6 meters) away from each other. However, they may spontaneously touch one another on the arm or shoulder during conversation. Members of the opposite sex often hold hands or show affection in public. To point, a person extends the index finger. One beckons by waving all fingers (or the index finger) with the palm facing up. Direct eye contact is not necessary for the duration of a conversation, but moments of eye contact are essential to ensure one's sincerity. In informal settings, it is not impolite for people to prop their feet on chairs, sit with poor posture, place the ankle of one leg on the knee of the other, cross legs at the knee (more common for women), or if one is wearing pants, to sit with legs spread apart. It is not uncommon for people to toss items to friends. Winking to children is a gesture of friendliness; when adults wink it usually means that they or someone else is joking.

Visiting. Although Americans are informal, they generally are conscious of time. Appointments are expected to begin promptly. Guests invited to a home for dinner should arrive on time because the meal is often served first. Hospitality takes many forms: a formal dinner served on fine dishes, an outdoor barbecue with paper plates, or a leisurely visit with no refreshments. Hosts generally want guests to feel at ease, sit where they like, and enjoy themselves. It is not unusual for either guests or hosts to agree on a reasonable limit of time for the visit if schedules are pressing. Guests are not expected to bring gifts, but a small token such as wine or flowers might be appreciated. Hosts inviting close friends to dinner may ask them to bring a food item to be served with the meal. Americans enjoy socializing; they gather in small and large groups for nearly any occasion, and they enjoy talking, watching television or a movie, eating, and relaxing together.

Eating. Eating styles and habits vary among people of different backgrounds, but Americans generally eat with a fork in the hand with which they write. They use a knife for cutting and spreading, setting it down as they begin to eat. When a knife is used for cutting, the fork is switched to the other hand. People eat foods such as french fries, fried chicken, hamburgers, pizza, and tacos with the hands. They generally place napkins in the lap. Resting elbows on the table is often considered impolite. After-dinner refreshments such as dessert or coffee are frequently served away from the dining table. Guests are expected to stay a while after the meal to visit with the hosts. In restaurants, the bill usually does not include a service charge; leaving a tip of 15 percent is customary.

LIFESTYLE

Family. The immediate family is the basic unit of society, but the composition of the average family has been changing. Traditionally, the average household consisted of a mother, father, and two or more children. This nuclear family often maintained important ties to members of the extended family. Today, only about one-fourth of all households consist of a mother, father, and one or two children. While another 29 percent of households are married couples with no children in the home, other family structures are becoming more common, including families with a single parent and unmarried couples with or without children. One-third of all children are born out of wedlock. Children may live with or be cared for by grandparents, especially if the parents are young and unmarried.

A generation ago, men were the traditional breadwinners. Today, nearly half of all working Americans are women. In homes where both the husband and wife work, men are now expected to share household chores, although women still perform most domestic duties. Men often play an important role in raising children as well. With both parents working, the use of day-care facilities is increasing. Single-parent families also rely heavily on day care. Elderly individuals who cannot care for themselves may live in retirement communities or other institutions, or they may live with their adult children. Otherwise, the elderly live in their own homes and comprise a rapidly expanding segment of the population. More than half of all young, unmarried adults (ages 18–24) live with their parents. The American family is mobile. People frequently move from one region of the country to another for education, employment, or a change in living conditions.

Dating and Marriage. Dating is a social pastime. Some adolescents begin dating in couples as early as age 13, although group activities are more common at that age. More serious dating begins around age 15. Going to movies, dancing, having picnics, playing sports or watching sporting events, and dining out are popular activities. Casual sexual relationships are common. Many couples choose to live together before or instead of marrying. Still, many consider marriage to be the preferred living arrangement. Weddings can be either lavish or simple, depending on factors including region, religious affiliation, and the family's economic status. On average, men get married at age 27 and women at age 25.

Diet. It is difficult to name a national dish. The abundance of fast-food restaurants in the United States would seem to indicate that the national foods are hamburgers, french fries, pizza, and chicken. While these foods are popular among most segments of the population, they reflect a busy lifestyle as much as preference. Many popular "American" foods are adopted from the national cuisines of immigrants; these include Mexican, Chinese, and Italian foods, as well as many others. People in the United States eat beef, pork, chicken, and turkey in relatively large quantities. Fresh vegetables and fruits are available year-round. Many people also consume large amounts of "junk food," including potato chips, soda, candy, and ice cream. Most Americans are open to trying new foods, and the culture easily adapts to new tastes.

Recreation. Basketball, American football, and baseball are the most popular U.S. sports. Public schools and local organizations sponsor team sports for young people. Professional sports are an important part of the culture. Americans also enjoy soccer, cycling, racquetball, hockey, tennis, swimming, golf, bowling, jogging, and aerobic exercise. Leisure activities include watching television, going to movies, reading, surfing the internet, spending time with friends, attending music concerts, and traveling.

The Arts. Galleries and museums nationwide exhibit many art styles and mediums. Government and private organizations provide financial support to artists and art education programs. Larger cities usually have a professional orchestra and at least one theater. Broadway musicals are quite popular, and the best tour the nation. The U.S. entertainment industry, including movies and music, is known worldwide. Pop music is the most common form of music. However, several rock and roll styles, jazz, blues, country, and bluegrass all originated in the United States and have large followings. Realistic fiction is the most popular literary form in the country.

Holidays. Each state has its own public holidays, and each city may have local celebrations. National public holidays include New Year's Day, Martin Luther King Jr.'s Birthday (third Monday in January), Presidents' Day (third Monday in February), Memorial Day (last Monday in May), Independence Day (4 July), Labor Day (first Monday in September), Columbus Day (second Monday in October), Veterans' Day (11 Nov.), Thanksgiving (fourth Thursday in November), and Christmas. Although they are not official holidays, other observances include Groundhog Day (2 Feb.), Valentine's Day (14 Feb.), St. Patrick's Day (17 Mar.), Easter, Mother's Day (second Sunday in May), Father's Day (third Sunday in June), Flag Day (14 June), and Halloween (31 Oct.).

United States of America

Commerce. Business office hours usually extend from 8 or 9 a.m. to 5 or 6 p.m. However, retail and grocery stores often remain open until 9 or 10 p.m., and many are open 24 hours a day, seven days a week. Suburban Americans shop for groceries in supermarkets and other goods in large enclosed malls, smaller open-air strip malls that feature specialty shops, and chain discount stores. Urban residents shop in many of the same stores but might also buy goods at small neighborhood shops that are part of large office or apartment buildings.

SOCIETY

Government. The United States is a democratic federal republic guided by a constitution. Individual states hold sovereignty over their territory and have all rights that are not reserved by the federal government. Each state has its own legislature for enacting laws. Free elections have always determined the country's leadership, and citizens may vote at age 18. The U.S. president (currently George W. Bush) is elected by an electoral college, which represents the vote of the people in each state. Presidential elections are held every four years. The bicameral legislature (Congress) has two houses: the 435-seat House of Representatives, whose members serve two-year terms, and the 100-seat Senate, whose members serve six-year terms. Congress is dominated by the Republican and Democratic Parties. Smaller parties are active throughout the country. The government also has a separate judicial branch. The U.S. Supreme Court is the highest judicial authority. Its justices are appointed by the president and approved by the Senate.

Economy. The United States has the world's largest, most diverse, and most technically advanced economy. While American society as a whole is prosperous, there is a widening gap between the wealthy and the poor, and even between those who earn a comfortable income and those who struggle to meet basic needs.

The country's economic strength is based on diversified industrial and service sectors, investments abroad, the dollar as a major world currency, a demand-driven consumer society, and exports. The service sector employs more people than manufacturing, but the United States remains a world leader in industry and high technology. It exports capital goods, cars, consumer goods, food, and machinery. It also exports pop culture (e.g., movies, music, television, fashion, sports), which fuels demand for American goods. The United States is a key world financial center, and its economic fortunes affect global markets and international economic growth. The currency is the U.S. dollar (USD).

Transportation and Communications. The United States has an extensive network of paved highways, and people use private cars to get around. In large cities, urban mass-transit systems are common. In many areas, however, public transportation systems are not well developed. Many people travel by air, and the United States has the largest number of private airline companies in the world. Passenger train travel is limited to short commuter distances and relatively few cross-country routes; trains more frequently transport goods.

The communications network is extensive and modern. Almost all households have a telephone (and often a cellular phone) and one or more television sets. Most homes have cable or satellite television. There are thousands of radio and television stations in operation throughout the country; most are privately owned. Freedom of the press is guaranteed. Although newspapers are available everywhere, only about half of all Americans read one every day. Others watch television or use the internet for news. More than 70 million households have internet access.

Education. Each state is responsible for its educational system. Education is compulsory for ages five through sixteen and free through the secondary level. Most children attend public schools, but a growing number attend private schools or are taught at home. Most students complete their high school education at grade 12 (at age 17 or 18). About 75 percent of high school graduates seek some higher learning in technical school or at a university, but many enter the labor force at that time. Although nearly all Americans can read, low-level literacy is a problem for some people.

Health. The health problems facing Americans are different from those in some other countries, in that the two greatest causes of adult health problems are a sedentary lifestyle and risky physical behavior. The United States is the only industrialized country in the world without a national (public) healthcare system. Most people must have private insurance to receive medical care without paying very high prices. The health network is extensive and modern, except in some rural areas. Each state has its own regulations regarding health care, and there are some national standards as well. Public and private reform movements are changing how health care is provided and paid for. The United States is a world leader in medical research and training.

DEVELOPMENT DATA
- Human Dev. Index* rank .... 8 of 177 countries
- Adjusted for women .... 8 of 144 countries
- Real GDP per capita $35,750
- Adult literacy rate .... 99 percent (male); 99 (female)
- Infant mortality rate .... 7 per 1,000 births
- Life expectancy .... 74 (male); 80 (female)

AT A GLANCE

Events and Trends.
- In January 2005, Republican president George W. Bush was inaugurated for a second term. He had won the presidential election in November of the previous year, beating out Democratic candidate John Kerry.
- The United States invaded Iraq in 2003. The move was controversial in the United Nations and among people around the world. The occupation has proven difficult; by 2005, U.S. forces were still attempting to quell ongoing insurgency.

Contact Information. U.S. Department of State, 2201 C Street NW, Washington, DC 20520; phone (202) 647-6575; web site www.state.gov.

© 2005 ProQuest Information and Learning Company and Brigham Young University. It is against the law to copy, reprint, store, or transmit any part of this publication in any form by any means without written permission from ProQuest. This document contains native commentary and original analysis, as well as estimated statistics. The content should not be considered strictly factual, and it may not apply to all groups in a nation. *UN Development Programme, Human Development Report 2004 (New York: Oxford University Press, 2004).

CultureGrams
People. The World. You.

ProQuest Information and Learning Company
300 North Zeeb Road, P.O. Box 1346
Ann Arbor, Michigan 48106 USA
Toll Free: 1.800.528.6279
Fax: 1.800.864.0019
www.culturegrams.com

CultureGrams™ World Edition 2006

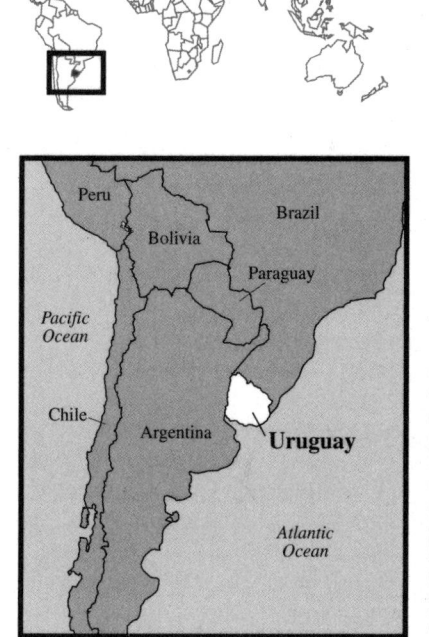

Oriental Republic of Uruguay

Boundary representations are not necessarily authoritative.

BACKGROUND

Land and Climate. Uruguay covers 68,039 square miles (176,220 square kilometers) and is about the same size as Washington State. Bordered by the Atlantic Ocean, the estuary of the Río de la Plata, and two other rivers (Uruguay and Cuareim), Uruguay is nearly enclosed by water. Rolling lowland plains covered with prairie grass extend across most (about 78 percent) of the country. These plains provide excellent pastures for ranching and farming. Forests and hills dominate the northeast region. Uruguay's coastline has several fine beaches. Because the land is free of many natural disasters, it has remained relatively unchanged over time. The climate is temperate and the seasons are opposite those in North America. Temperatures in July average 52°F (11°C); January is the warmest month, with temperatures averaging 73°F (23°C).

History. Originally, Uruguay was home to small groups of indigenous tribes, including the Guaraní and Charrúas. Although the tribes traded with the colonists early on, nearly all the indigenous population was conquered, killed, or driven out during European colonization. Spanish explorers first landed in the area in 1516. The Portuguese founded Colonia del Sacramento in 1680 and maintained a presence in the region until 1726, when the Spanish drove them out and began to colonize, founding Montevideo.

In conjunction with a general uprising throughout South America, a Uruguayan war of independence from Spain began in 1811. Under the leadership of José Gervasio Artigas, Uruguayans joined forces with Argentina to make significant gains against the Spanish, even achieving unofficial independence for a time. However, in 1816 Portuguese forces from Brazil saw an opportunity to seize unprotected territory, and when Artigas was unable to stop them, he fled to Paraguay. Even so, Artigas is considered the "father of Uruguay." His efforts inspired another uprising in 1825, when patriots known as the Thirty-Three Immortals rebelled against Portuguese domination and declared independence. Three years later, Brazil granted Uruguay full independence.

Civil war raged between conservative, landowner *Blancos* (Whites) and liberal, urban *Colorados* (Reds) from 1839 to 1851; these two groups dominated Uruguayan politics for much of the 19th and 20th centuries. War with Paraguay (1865–70) was followed by a period of dictatorship. A president, José Batlle y Ordóñez, was finally elected in 1903. Ordóñez was a major force in national politics for two decades and laid the groundwork for a modern democracy. Throughout the first part of the 20th century, successive liberal governments instituted a variety of social programs. Uruguay became one of the first South American countries to legalize divorce (1907), give women the right to vote (1932), and recognize the rights of trade unions (1934).

Severe economic problems in the 1950s and 1960s led to unrest and urban terrorist violence. In the early 1970s, under pressure from the military, President Juan María Bordaberry attempted to restore order by suspending the constitution, dissolving the legislature, and banning all political activity. By 1976, the military had ousted him from power. A decade of brutal military rule followed, during which thousands were detained and tortured. A vote in 1980 determined that the armed forces should relinquish control of the government, but the military refused to recognize the results and appointed General Gregorio Alvarez president in 1981.

Public pressure paved the way for general elections in 1984. The military stepped down when the elected president, Julio

Uruguay

María Sanguinetti of the Colorado Party, took office in 1985. The new government restored basic human rights, and to avoid clashes with the military, granted amnesty to personnel suspected of human-rights violations. The 1989 elections marked the first democratic transfer of power from one elected government to another since 1971.

In 1999, Jorge Batlle Ibañez of the Colorado Party became president at the age of 72. He moved cautiously toward implementing free-market reforms and attracting foreign investment while retaining the country's social programs. However, some of his reforms were unpopular. In 2004, a candidate from Batlle's Colorado Party lost presidential elections to liberal politician Tabare Vazquez. As a member of the Broad Front Coalition, Vazquez ended 170 years of rule by the Colorado and Blanco parties.

THE PEOPLE

Population. Uruguay has a population of 3.4 million. Unlike most other nations in South America, it has a low annual growth rate of 0.5 percent. People of European descent, mostly of Spanish, Italian, and Portuguese heritage, account for 88 percent of the total population. This heritage is also dissimilar to most South American countries, where mestizos—people of mixed European and indigenous blood—are usually the majority ethnic group. In Uruguay, mestizos comprise only 8 percent of the population. Four percent of the people are black (descendants of slaves who were imported by the Spanish). More than 90 percent of the people live in urban areas. Montevideo (MOAN-tay-vee-DAY-oh) is the capital and largest city, with about 1.5 million people. It is the country's financial, political, and cultural center.

Language. Spanish is the official language of Uruguay and is spoken by nearly the entire population. People in northern towns that border Brazil often speak a mixture of Spanish and Portuguese known as *Portuñol* or *Brazilero*. The Uruguayan accent is quite different from those in other Spanish-speaking countries. Most notable is the Uruguayan "sh" pronunciation of *y* and *ll*. For instance, *yo* (I) is pronounced more like "show" than "yoh." Portuguese and English are common second languages. Small minority groups speak Italian and other languages.

Religion. Uruguay is one of the most secular countries in Latin American. There is no official religion, church and state are strictly separated, and religious freedom is guaranteed. Because of this secularism, few statistics exist on religion. It is believed that 50 to 65 percent of the population belongs to the Roman Catholic Church, although less than half regularly attend services. Non-Catholic Christians make up between 2 and 16 percent of the population. A little more than 1 percent is believed to be Jewish. The rest of the population belongs to various other organizations or professes no religion at all.

General Attitudes. Uruguayans often view their country as one of the more culturally advanced nations in South America. They are also proud of their country's traditions and symbols, such as the *gaucho* (a cowboy-like figure), which is regarded as an example of the country's rugged independence. People are conservative and often distrustful of change. Uruguayans can be pessimistic, opinionated, and individualistic, but they do not appreciate aggressiveness or arrogance. Occupation, power, and money may grant social status, but flashy displays of wealth or power are frowned upon. Education is held in high esteem. The democratic view that *Nadie es más que nadie* (No one is better than anyone else) is shared by most. Although the government is considered bureaucratic and inefficient, many people think it should run the economy rather than foreign companies, which are generally viewed with suspicion.

Punctuality is admired but not always practiced. Arriving later than a scheduled time is not improper. However, the more formal an appointment, the more important it is to be on time. Uruguayans are extremely proud of their country, but they are also aware of its problems. They do not appreciate individuals who praise other countries more than Uruguay—not because they dislike other countries but because they do not want to be treated as inferior.

Uruguayans value education, and parents go to great lengths to ensure their children have good schooling. The elderly are respected, and adult children often care for aging parents.

Personal Appearance. Conservative, well-tailored clothing is the general rule in Uruguay. Subdued colors (blue, brown, and gray) are pervasive. Fashion generally indicates a person's social status. European fashions are common. Women do not usually wear much makeup or jewelry, but they wear dresses more often than do women in the United States. Popular casual clothing includes jeans and T-shirts. In interior (rural) areas, some men wear *bombachas* (loose-legged trousers) with wide belts, boots, and hats or berets.

CUSTOMS AND COURTESIES

Greetings. Men usually greet others with a warm, firm handshake. With family or close friends they may offer an *abrazo* (hearty hug) and occasionally a kiss. Women (and sometimes men) appear to kiss one cheek when they greet each other. Actually, they only brush cheeks and "kiss the air." If a woman greets a person with an *abrazo*, it is always accompanied with a "kiss." Verbal greetings depend on the time of day or situation. *¡Hola!* (Hi) and *¿Cómo estás?* (How's it going?) are common casual greetings. The *usted* form of greeting (*¿Cómo está?*) is used toward older people and to show respect. A greeting that is especially popular in the morning is *¡Buen día!* (Good day).

People generally do not greet strangers when passing on the street, particularly in cities. The other person might misunderstand if one were to extend a greeting or even a smile. Rural people are more open and more likely to greet passing strangers with *¡Chau!* (Good-bye). They use *¡Chau!* because they are passing (not stopping) and therefore saying "good-bye" more than "hello."

One greets all individuals in a small group when one arrives at a social function. Group greetings and farewells are considered impolite. In general, people address each other by an appropriate title and surname. For example, *Señor* (Mr.), *Señora* (Mrs.), or *Señorita* (Miss) is used with the family name. Only close friends and family members address each other by given name.

Gestures. To beckon, one snaps the fingers or makes a "ch-ch" sound. The "ch-ch" sound is used for many purposes, such as getting someone's attention or stopping a bus. People often use hand gestures in conversation. One avoids hiding the hands or fidgeting with them when conversing because such actions can convey unintended messages. Forming a zero with the index finger and thumb is extremely rude. Brushing the back of the hand under the chin means "I don't know." Raising one's shoulders quickly can mean "What's up?" Placing the thumb and index finger on the upper lip in an upward "V" is called a *bigote para arriba* (upward mustache) and means "Everything is all right." People do not sit on tables or ledges or rest their feet on objects in a room. On public transportation, it is polite for a man to offer his seat to a woman.

Visiting. Uruguayans commonly visit for hours at a time in cafés and bars. Visiting friends and relatives at home is important, but busy schedules make this increasingly difficult. People in rural areas often visit in the late afternoon or early evening. It is impolite to visit unannounced during regular mealtimes. Invited guests are not expected to bring gifts to their hosts, but flowers or chocolates are considered a nice gesture. Guests invited to a meal may bring wine or a dessert. Hosts always offer their guests refreshments (soft drinks, tea, coffee, etc.). The length of a visit often depends on the familiarity between host and guest, but a guest may leave comfortably after eating and staying for coffee or tea. It would be rude for a host to suggest that a guest leave.

On weekends or during the summer, hosts may invite lunch guests to stay for the afternoon *siesta* (rest) and a round of *mate* (pronounced "MAH-tay"). *Mate* is a strong, bitter herb tea that is drunk from a gourd through a silver straw (*bombilla*). The gourd is filled almost to the brim with *mate* and is repeatedly filled with hot water for each person to finish and pass on to the next. Holding on too long to a passed *mate* is impolite. Many Uruguayans, particularly men, appreciate having friends come by to discuss sports, politics, or family matters and share a round of *mate*. Women commonly share *mate dulce* (*mate* with sugar). Sharing *mate* with someone is a sign of acceptance, and strangers are seldom invited to participate in a round. The activity has become a cultural ritual for many. Uruguayans drink *mate* at any time and any place (in a park, walking on the street, etc.).

Eating. Uruguayans eat in the continental style, with the fork in the left hand and the knife in the right. During the meal, they keep the hands (not elbows) above the table rather than in the lap. People often wipe their plates clean with bread as they finish eating. Taking second helpings indicates one likes the food. When finished, one places the utensils side by side on the plate. Dinner guests remain at the table until all have finished eating. Using a toothpick in public or reading a newspaper at the family table is impolite.

Although habits in urban areas are changing to accommodate schedules, Uruguayans traditionally eat a light breakfast of coffee and bread. They have their main meal at 1 or 2 p.m. When possible, the whole family will go home for this meal. Supper is lighter and later in the evening (8 or 9 p.m.). Children usually have a snack when they get home from school, and adults may snack around 5 p.m.

LIFESTYLE

Family. Strong ties traditionally unite the family. The average family has two children, and nuclear families are the norm. Although extended families do not live together, they play a significant role in the social lives of Uruguayans. The father presides in the home. This patriarchal order is still predominant, but the role of women is increasing in significance. A large percentage of women work or study outside the home. Uruguay has more professional women than men; however, men are still expected to earn the better salary. Many couples today share family responsibilities more evenly. Nannies or family members often care for children while the mother is at work. Because of housing shortages, children remain at home until they marry, regardless of their age. Young university students from the interior may stay with relatives in Montevideo while attending college.

A small number of wealthy families generally control politics and the economy. The majority of families live in more humble circumstances, although few are without basic modern conveniences. Most rent their home or apartment because of the difficulty and cost involved in purchasing a home.

Dating and Marriage. Dating customs are similar to those in the United States, although young people usually date only one person at a time. Some rural families have retained traditional European customs in which the young man asks the parents' permission to date the young woman for the first time. He must also ask her parents' permission before getting engaged. Young people enjoy dancing, dining out, going to the beach, and watching movies. Men and women usually marry in their mid- to late twenties. Both families play a large role in preparing for the wedding and often associate closely after their children are married. The marriage reception usually includes a formal, catered party, from which the couple generally leaves early.

Diet. Uruguay produces most of its own food. Wide varieties of meat, fish, vegetables, and fruits are available. Wheat and rice are the principal grains. Beef is consumed in some form almost daily. Pasta usually is served with the main meal. Families often eat roasts and stews served with potatoes and carrots. Meat pies are popular menu items. Traditional dishes include *asado* (grilled beef), *chivito* (steak and egg with cheese and mayonnaise), *milanesa* (fried, breaded steak), and *guiso* (ground beef with rice, onion, and egg). Homemade pasta is also common: *tallarines* is like spaghetti, and *ñoquis* is similar to the Italian dumpling dish called gnocchi.

Recreation. *Fútbol* (soccer) is the national sport. Uruguayans closely follow the country's national team, especially in World Cup competitions. Basketball, volleyball, cycling, swimming, and other water sports are also popular. Rowing is popular among city dwellers who live near rivers and the coast. *Asados* (barbecues) are common social events. Beaches in the southeast are popular destinations during summer vacations in January. Uruguayans enjoy watching movies or television and attending cultural events.

The Arts. Uruguay has a rich national tradition in the arts and literature. Painting is influenced by international trends but often focuses on local themes such as rural life, history, and the *gaucho*. Indigenous groups carve *mate* gourds, crochet items, and make textiles.

The dance and the music of the tango are very popular. Other traditional dances include the *milonga* and the *vidalita*. The *candombe*, an African-influenced rhythm, is played with three *tambores* (drums) and is often performed at Carnival. Carnival theater productions are performed on *tablados* (stages) throughout Montevideo. Especially popular are *las murgas*, small groups of singers and actors who present parodies of the year's main events.

Holidays. The most important holidays are New Year's Day, Children's Day (6 Jan.), Carnival, Easter (including Holy Thursday and Good Friday), Landing of the Thirty-Three Patriots (19 Apr.), Labor Day (1 May), Constitution Day (18 July), Independence Day (25 Aug.), Christmas Eve, and Christmas. Most Catholics have celebrations to honor local patron saints, and some celebrate name days (a day honoring the saint for whom one is named). Christmas Eve and New Year's Eve are celebrated with large family parties and midnight fireworks. The week preceding Easter is also known as *Semana de Turismo* (Tourism Week), when people travel throughout the country and participate in local festivals.

Uruguay

Commerce. Business hours are from 9 a.m. to 7 p.m., Monday through Friday. Businesses in interior towns often close for a *siesta* at midday; a *siesta* may last from two to four hours, depending on the season (they are longer in summer). Government hours vary between the seasons, running primarily in the morning during the summer and in the afternoon and evening during the winter.

SOCIETY

Government. Uruguay is a democratic republic divided into 19 *departamentos* (provinces). The executive branch is headed by the president, currently Tabare Vazquez, and the vice president. The constitution prohibits consecutive presidential terms. The legislature, or *Asamblea General* (General Assembly), has two houses: a 30-seat Chamber of Senators and a 99-seat Chamber of Representatives. Uruguay's major political parties include the Colorado Party, National (Blanco) Party, and Broad Front Coalition. A few smaller parties also have legislative representation. Uruguayan parties had presidential primary elections for the first time in April 1999. Beginning at age 18, all citizens are required to return to their place of birth to vote.

Economy. Uruguay's greatest natural resource is its fertile land, with much of it being used for agriculture and livestock production. Uruguay is a world leader in the production of cattle and wool. Other products include wheat, rice, corn, and sorghum. The industrial sector is tied to agriculture as well. The chief industries are meat processing, wool and hides, footwear, leather apparel, and fish processing. The services sector is growing in importance. Uruguay has been a member of Mercosur (Southern Common Market) since 1995.

The return to democracy and subsequent economic reforms initially spurred economic growth. For example, inflation lowered by more than 100 percent in less than 10 years. However, the economy has struggled since 1999, largely because of economic problems in Argentina and Brazil. During the past several years, inflation, low wages, and high unemployment have been consistent issues. Still, incomes are generally sufficient to meet basic needs. Uruguayan women earn roughly one-third of their nation's income, the largest share among Latin American countries. People generally have access to education and health care. The country's currency is the Uruguayan *peso* (UYU).

Transportation and Communications. Buses are the primary form of public transportation. Many Uruguayans also travel in private automobiles. Taxis are readily available in the cities. Roads are generally developed around major urban areas but are less so in rural areas. Key highways are paved and well maintained. Uruguay has international airway links. The communications system is developing rapidly; the best facilities are in Montevideo. Private telephone lines are becoming increasingly accessible. The country has a national radio relay system and a number of radio and television stations. Most people own a radio and television. Several newspapers are widely circulated.

Education. Uruguay has one of the highest literacy rates in South America, at about 98 percent. Primary schooling is compulsory for nine years. Afterward, students may choose to enter a government-subsidized *liceo* (secondary school) or receive technical training at a vocational school. While the government provides education free of charge through postgraduate studies, general economic conditions do not allow everyone to continue their studies. Still, Uruguay boasts a large percentage of professionals (lawyers and doctors, for example). The University of Montevideo, founded in 1849, and the Catholic University in Montevideo have fine reputations throughout South America.

Health. Health care is free and available to all citizens. Uruguay has good health standards, with modern facilities available in Montevideo. Health and other social programs are highly valued, but the government spending on health care has become a drain on the national budget. Private health organizations with better facilities also provide care for those who can afford it. Sanitation is generally good.

DEVELOPMENT DATA
- Human Dev. Index* rank .... 46 of 177 countries
- Adjusted for women .... 41 of 144 countries
- Real GDP per capita $7,830
- Adult literacy rate .... 97 percent (male); 98 (female)
- Infant mortality rate .... 12 per 1,000 births
- Life expectancy .... 72 (male); 79 (female)

AT A GLANCE

Events and Trends.
- The November 2004 election of Broad Front Coalition candidate Tabare Vazquez to become president marked the end of 170 years of two-party rule in Uruguay. It was also part of the trend of Latin American nations to elect left-leaning leaders who promise social programs for the underprivileged. Other prominent leftists include Venezuela's Hugo Chavez, Brazil's Luiz Inacio Lula da Silva, Chile's Ricardo Lagos, and Argentina's Nestor Kirchner.
- In May 2004, Uruguayan senators voted 17–13 against legalizing abortion in the country. Uruguay would have been the only other Latin American nation, after Cuba, to allow the procedure. The bill, which also included provisions on sex education, contraceptive distribution, and maternal health care, had already passed the Chamber of Representatives.
- In December 2003, 60 percent of Uruguayans voted to renationalize the country's oil industry, which had recently been opened to private ownership. The vote signaled a turn away from free-market reforms and away from the ruling Colorado and Blanco parties. The results favored the Broad Front Coalition, a party that supports keeping Uruguay's European-style welfare state.

Contact Information. Embassy of Uruguay, 1913 I Street NW, Washington, DC 20006; phone (202) 331-1313; web site www.uruwashi.org.

CultureGrams World Edition 2006

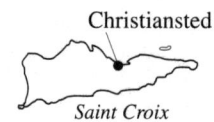

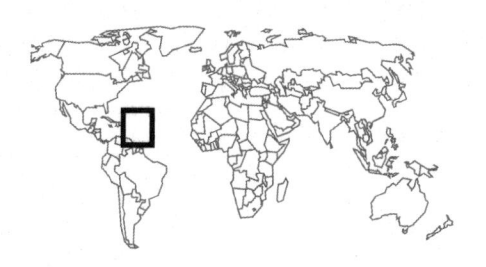

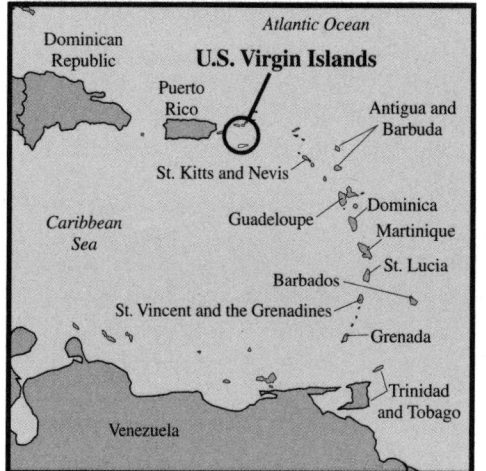

U.S. Virgin Islands

BACKGROUND

Land and Climate. The U.S. Virgin Islands (USVI) is made up of 68 islands in the Greater Antilles, covering a total of 135 square miles (349 square kilometers). The three largest islands are Saint Croix (83 square miles), Saint Thomas (31 square miles), and Saint John (20 square miles). St. Thomas is about 40 miles from Puerto Rico. The remaining islands are small and mostly uninhabited.

USVI's highest point is Crown Mountain (1,550 feet, or 368 meters), located on rugged St. Thomas. This island is also home to Charlotte Amalie, a natural port and the territorial capital. St. John is characterized by moderately sloping mountains that meet the shorelines. St. Croix is dry and windswept in the east and lushly tropical in the west. Central high pastures are favorable to agriculture.

Constant trade winds moderate the subtropical climate; the temperature averages 79°F (16°C). The country receives about 43 inches (109 centimeters) of rainfall each year, although droughts are possible. Hurricanes occur periodically and can inflict serious damage.

History. Before they ever became a nation, the Virgin Islands had a long and active history. Artifacts show that the area's first inhabitants were the *Igneri*, or "Ancient Ones" (A.D. 50–650). They preceded the peace-loving Arawak tribes, who were eventually dominated by the fierce Caribs. It was the Caribs who greeted Christopher Columbus with arrows at the Salt River on St. Croix. Columbus named this island *Santa Cruz* (Holy Cross). Sailing north, he compared the multitude of other islands to St. Ursula's 11,000 virgins (hence, the name Virgin Islands).

Spain made little effort to colonize the Virgin Islands, and for the next two hundred years, the French, Dutch, and English traded them back and forth. By the 1700s, Denmark had planted its flag on St. Thomas, adopted St. John, and purchased St. Croix (the French name for Santa Cruz) from the French. Britain secured the islands that are now the British Virgin Islands from the Dutch.

Denmark went on to promote the islands as thriving sugarcane and trading centers. By the late 18th century, St. Croix had 264 sugar mills (many of which remain as ruins) and more than 24,000 African slaves. The sugar-based economic system began to decline when the European sugar beet was introduced and when the Danes proclaimed slave trading (but not slave labor) illegal in 1803. After an organized slave protest in 1848, Governor Peter von Scholten promised emancipation for all "unfree" persons. When the Danish government subsequently enacted harsh labor laws, further conflict ensued. In the Great Fire Burn of 1878, laborers destroyed or burned more than 40 estates and miles of plantations, ultimately putting an end to the sugarcane industry.

The United States decided to buy the Danish Virgin Islands in 1917 to block any enemy approach to the Panama Canal during World War I. In 1927, the territory's residents were granted U.S. citizenship. The U.S. Navy administered the islands until 1931, when the Department of the Interior assumed jurisdiction. The first locally elected legislature of 11 members was elected in 1954; it was not until 1970 that a governor was popularly elected. In 1972, the U.S. Virgin Islands received a nonvoting seat in the U.S. Congress.

Today, the primary challenges facing the territory's government include reducing the public debt, securing more rights for the territory, balancing the rights of individual islands, and stimulating growth in the private sector.

U.S. Virgin Islands

THE PEOPLE

Population. The population of the U.S. Virgin Islands is about 108,000 and is shrinking at an annual rate of 0.5 percent. St. Croix is the largest and most populous island, with more than 53,000 spread throughout its area. About 51,000 people live on St. Thomas; many of them live in Charlotte Amalie, which is the island's largest city and national capital. More than 4,000 people live on St. John, most of them in Cruz Bay. Approximately 78 percent of the population is of African descent, 10 percent is white, and 12 percent is of mixed heritage or another background.

Interestingly, much of the population was not born in the Virgin Islands. This is because the creation of new industries in the 1960s caused a severe labor shortage. Thousands of workers from surrounding nations and other areas came to the islands, nearly tripling the population. In 1985, Congress passed legislation that offered legal status to these individuals. As a result, the Virgin Islands' strong culture is influenced by a number of other cultures. Today about 49 percent of the population is native to the country. Another 32 percent is from elsewhere in the West Indies, 13 percent is from the U.S. mainland, and 4 percent is from Puerto Rico.

Language. English is the official language, but Virgin Islanders converse with one another in a local dialect (English Creole) that incorporates many languages. For example, *Man, yoh overtake meh* (Friend, you surprised me) has its roots in English, but *What a pistarkel* (What a spectacle) stems from the Dutch Creole *Spektakel* or the Danish *Spetakel*, meaning "noise" or "din." St. Thomians, St. Johnians, and Cruzians speak the same dialect but have slightly different accents. A St. Thomian would say *Com hare* (Come here) and a Cruzian would say *Com yah* or *Com heh*.

On St. Croix, 45 percent of the population speaks Spanish. French Creole (*Patois*), Dutch Creole (*Papiamento*), East Indian, and Arabic also are spoken in smaller communities.

Religion. Religion is important to Virgin Islanders. Most people are Christians. Of the 35 Christian denominations active in the Virgin Islands, the Baptist (42 percent), Catholic (34 percent), and Episcopalian (17 percent) faiths are the largest. Most people attend church services. To be honest and considered a good Christian is highly regarded. Many native islanders often carry scriptures with them and read them in spare moments or while waiting for buses and taxis. Non-Christian communities (including Rastafarians, Muslims, and Hindus) also have a presence on the islands. One Jewish synagogue serves the small Jewish population.

General Attitudes. Virgin Islanders have a tradition of being gracious and somewhat conservative. They enjoy their privacy and strive to be morally respectable. Many social values were adopted from other West Indian islands, but current social values are coming more from the United States. For example, women are now less tolerant of the classic West Indian male-dominant relationship. Also, events that begin on time rather than on "island time" or "Cruzian time" (i.e., later than planned) are viewed as more professional than other events.

Islanders vote regularly in local elections and show great interest in current affairs reported by the media. Whether heated or lighthearted, daily discussions about politics and the economy are prevalent. It is acknowledged that an educated person will often have more opportunities. Therefore, children are encouraged to go to school, and parents do their best to provide the means.

Each island prides itself on different aspects of its culture and landscape. St. Thomas accommodates tourism, St. Croix highlights private industry, and St. John values its natural beauty. The three sister islands share an attitude of good-natured competition.

Personal Appearance. Islanders wear conservative clothing that is pressed and clean. Children wear cotton school uniforms with shoes or sneakers. Men wear shirts and long pants with shoes or sandals. Traditional men often wear *guayabera* shirts; these cotton shirts have short sleeves, a square cut, pleats, light embroidery, and four pockets on the front. Women dress in stylish skirts, dresses, or pantsuits with sandals or high heels. Hats or umbrellas are donned by those walking or sitting in the sun. The younger generation prefers styles from the U.S. mainland, such as T-shirts, jeans, or shorts. Gold jewelry is popular, especially with young people. Islanders wear formal, even elegant, clothing to church services, graduations, funerals, and weddings.

CUSTOMS AND COURTESIES

Greetings. Courtesy is essential to greetings in the Virgin Islands. People say *Good morning*, *Good afternoon*, and *Good night* when greeting a stranger or a group. These formal greetings also precede daily conversations. It is considered rude, for example, to not say *Good morning* before asking a store clerk a question or upon entering a waiting room containing several people. Islanders shake hands, particularly when being formally introduced. Formal titles are used more often in professional situations rather than for social introductions.

Greetings between friends are more casual, with *Hi*, *Hello*, *Ya alright?* or *Hey, how's it going?* being typical. Male friends shake hands or may say the other's nickname while tapping fists. Women commonly refer to each other as *dear* or *sweetheart*. A casual "pssst" will get another person's attention. The older generation usually addresses strangers or acquaintances as *Miss* or *Mister*. Traditionally, but now less often, children have been taught to use *Miss* and *Mister* plus the person's first name.

Gestures. Gestures of courtesy—such as holding a door open for someone or covering one's mouth when yawning or coughing—are important to Virgin Islanders. It is considered improper for a woman to drink directly from a bottle or can; she usually asks for a cup or straw.

Hand gestures and facial expressions are used often during conversation. Men, especially those of Spanish descent, tend to be the most animated in their discussions. To widen the eyes and raise the eyebrows with a slight nod of the head indicates surprise or disbelief. This is often accompanied by *Whaaa?* The act of sucking one's teeth to make a mild noise, called *chuups*, is used to express annoyance (e.g., as when waiting in a long line). Patting the air several times with a flat hand is the signal for "stop." Islanders use this gesture to hail taxis or to tell traffic behind them to slow down or stop, usually to avoid a collision.

Visiting. People usually visit one another at home on weekends and holidays. The visits typically are prearranged, and guests will *carry* something such as fruit or pastries to give to the host. When arriving, guests knock on the front door and wait to be invited in. Guests rarely wander through a home unless invited to do so by the hosts. Children formally greet the adults and then go off to play. Guests are offered something cool to drink. If a meal is to be served, the hostess usually serves each seated guest after offering to fix a plate for him or her. Departure courtesies are drawn out and can take up to an hour: guests get up to leave, talk with the hosts, walk together over to the door and talk some more, and then walk out to the car and chat some more before finally leaving.

Unannounced visits normally involve close neighbors or family and usually have a purpose, such as to borrow something or to discuss a bit of news. Friends commonly drop in just to *check on* each other and see how each is doing. In the summer, friends and families often spend the day picnicking at the beach. Many of the young people socialize in the evenings at clubs or music events. *Hey de mon, leh we go limin* is a typical invitation between male friends to go out on the town.

Eating. Workdays usually begin with an early breakfast consisting of foods such as eggs, cereal, and toast. Many people drink a cup of hot *bush tea* in the morning. This is a drink made of steeped basil leaves, mint, lemon grass, or a combination of ingredients. *Bush tea* is also said to have medicinal value when blended in certain ways. Lunch is traditionally the main meal, and people try to go home to eat lunch if their work schedules allow. Otherwise, people meet friends for lunch at local restaurants and eat their main meal in the evening. For the rural worker, privately owned food vans or women carrying baskets come around at lunchtime selling meat, fish *pates* (similar to turnovers), or other hot entrées.

Evening meals usually are eaten at home, since this is the time the family can sit at the table and eat together. The atmosphere is casual. It is generally acceptable to eat certain foods with the fingers, although utensils are used for most dishes. Special occasions, holidays, and Sunday afternoons call for roasted goat or pig with all the trimmings. Such meals are served buffet style, although the hostess may *fix a plate* for special guests.

LIFESTYLE

Family. Families are large and play an important role in the lives of Virgin Islanders. In a two-parent family, the woman is expected to raise the children and handle household responsibilities. The father is expected to support the family financially, although more women are now earning an income. Grandmothers often take care of their grandchildren while parents are working or living off-island (usually in the United States) for economic reasons. Elderly people often live with a daughter's family rather than in a retirement home.

It is not unusual for a woman to be the head of household. Young single mothers are also not uncommon and they rely on their families for support. Half siblings live together with their mother. Children tend to maintain friendships and socialize with their cousins and other family members close to their age. It is common for close friends to participate within a family as godparents.

Dating and Marriage. Young people meet and socialize at school, church, beach outings, music events, movies, and holiday affairs. Dating habits are similar to those in the United States. Weddings are formal and elegant. One tradition unique to the Virgin Islands is the *black cake*. This is prepared by soaking a heavy cake, consisting mostly of raisins and currants, in brandy for several days until it turns dark. The cake is then cut into small pieces, each of which is nicely wrapped and placed in a small box as a gift for each wedding guest.

Diet. The Virgin Islands imports a wide variety of food from the mainland United States. However, many locally produced foods and drinks are also available. Traditional dishes include chicken, conch, goat, fish, and pork. These are served with seasoned rice, pigeon peas, sweet potatoes, or plantains. Okra, eggplant, pumpkin, or dumplings are often added to a stew or sauce. Nutmeg, thyme, and cloves are standard seasonings. *Johnnycakes* (deep-fried, dumpling-like bread) are popular; they are sold regularly on the street or at festivals and are prepared for any gathering or special occasion.

Kallaloo, a special dish of African origin, traditionally is made with pig tail, conch, blue fish, land crab, salt beef, or oxtail. It gets its name from the *kallaloo* bush, which seasons this elaborate stew. Today, some of the ingredients are hard to find, so canned crab may be substituted for land crab and spinach often is used instead of the *kallaloo* greens. It is not uncommon to find a modern version of *kallaloo* on the menu in local restaurants. *Fungi*, cooked cornmeal with okra, usually is served with *kallaloo*. Other favorite foods include red kidney bean soup, curried goat or chicken, and salt fish. Local fruits such as mangoes, guavas, papaya, bananas, and smooth-skinned avocados (called *pears*) are seasonally abundant.

Recreation. Fishing is a passion among Virgin Islanders. The Virgin Islands is host to annual fishing tournaments because USVI waters are considered some of the best for sportfishing tuna, sailfish, marlin, or wahoo. Most fishermen stay offshore, trolling in small motorboats.

Friends and relatives like to gather on the many public beaches to relax and socialize. Large sound systems are set up right on the beach, and music is played quite loudly. Islanders picnic in this festive atmosphere, but they do not usually go swimming. West Indians, including Virgin Islanders, generally do not know how to swim. If they go in the water at all, it is to stand shoulder deep and chat in a group; this is referred to as *coolin' out*. Hanging out with friends is called *limin* or being *out on a lime*.

The Arts. Virgin Islanders love music. *Soca*, which has a Latin reggae beat, is a favorite at parties and on festive occasions. Reggae, calypso, and other forms of contemporary music are also popular. Musicians often use unconventional instruments, such as washboards, to make their music livelier. Older people still enjoy *quadrille* dancing, which is similar to square dancing, but with an island beat. Artists and musicians draw inspiration from plants, animals, and the ocean. The North Shore Shell Museum has a large collection of shells and handicrafts.

Holidays. The Virgin Islands celebrates all U.S. federal holidays and a few of its own. These include Transfer Day (31 Mar.), which celebrates the transfer from Danish rule to U.S. rule; Organic Act Day (21 June), the day when the Virgin Islands was granted local rule; Emancipation Day (3 July), honoring freedom from slavery; Hurricane Supplication Day (29 July) at the beginning of the hurricane season; Hurricane Thanksgiving Day (21 Oct.) at the end of the hurricane season; and Boxing Day (26 Dec.), or *Christmas Second Day* as it is sometimes called. In July, St. Thomians celebrate French heritage week in conjunction with Bastille Day (14 July). Columbus Day (second Monday in October) is also called Virgin Island/Puerto Rico Friendship Day.

Carnival holidays are some of the happiest of times in the Virgin Islands. The days are filled with crowded food fairs and parades that feature costumed dancers, music, and elaborate floats. At night, people enjoy calypso contests and more food and music at the Carnival Village. St. Thomas holds its Carnival at the end of April; St. John's is on 4 July. Three Kings Day—which is also known as the Cruzian Christmas Festival (6 Jan.)—marks the climax of St. Croix's Carnival.

Commerce. Downtown shops have normal business hours, but these stores attract mostly tourists. Virgin Islanders do most of

U.S. Virgin Islands

their shopping at *plazas* (large parking areas that have supermarkets, banks, department stores, post offices, fast-food restaurants, and so on). At Saturday-morning markets, local farmers sell fresh vegetables and fruits. Many well-trafficked corners have roadside stands where vendors sell fresh local fish, fruits, and vegetables, as well as charcoal, sweets, and cold drinks.

SOCIETY

Government. The U.S. Virgin Islands is governed by the Revised Organic Act of 1954. This document allows for executive, legislative, and judiciary branches of government that function similarly to state governments on the U.S. mainland. The local government is free to make laws that do not conflict with the U.S. Constitution. Ultimate jurisdiction resides with the U.S. Congress. The governor (Charles Turnbull) and lieutenant governor (Vargrave Richards) are elected to serve four-year terms and are limited to two terms.

The territory is grouped into two legislative districts: St. Thomas/St. John and St. Croix. Each district elects seven senators, and all three islands together elect the 15th senator from St. John. Senators serve two-year terms with no term limit. Islanders also elect a delegate to the U.S. House of Representatives. Although they are U.S. citizens, Virgin Islanders have no vote in national elections, and the delegate to Congress votes in committees only (not on the floor). In the judiciary branch, the Territorial Court tries most local cases and a federal judge handles all matters involving violations of federal law.

Economy. Tourism is the largest sector of the economy and employs more than half of the labor force. The government also employs a large percentage of the population. Unemployment is a persistent problem, causing many to leave the islands.

Industry is dominated by the Hess Oil Refinery, one of the largest oil refineries in the Western Hemisphere; it employs as much as 10 percent of St. Croix's workers. The islands are also an important tax haven for corporations from the United States and elsewhere. The currency is the U.S. dollar (USD).

Transportation and Communications. The Virgin Islands have more than 530 miles (850 kilometers) of roads, many of which are paved and in good condition. All vehicles (except public buses) are designed for right-hand driving; however, traffic moves on the left. Under these circumstances, it becomes faster and safer for drivers on the straightaway to yield to side-street traffic.

The public bus system services St. Thomas. Private taxi vans stop and pick up passengers on the side of the road and run unscheduled service between main towns. The seaplane and a handful of commuter airlines offer regular flights between St. Thomas and St. Croix. St. John can be reached only by sea; it is linked to St. Thomas by a comprehensive ferry system.

There are two local newspapers, one of which (the *Virgin Islands Daily News*) won a Pulitzer Prize in 1995 for public service journalism. There are about a dozen radio stations, two television stations, and two cable companies. The phone company offers good service; a call between islands is considered a local call. USVI is part of the U.S. domestic postal system.

© 2005 ProQuest Information and Learning Company and Brigham Young University. It is against the law to copy, reprint, store, or transmit any part of this publication in any form by any means without written permission from ProQuest. This document contains native commentary and original analysis, as well as estimated statistics. The content should not be considered strictly factual, and it may not apply to all groups in a nation. *UN Development Programme, Human Development Report 2004 (New York: Oxford University Press, 2004).

DEVELOPMENT DATA
Human Dev. Index* rank . . . . NA
   Adjusted for women. . . . . NA
Real GDP per capita $17,200
Adult literacy rate . . . . 90 percent
Infant mortality rate . . . . 8 per 1,000 births
Life expectancy . . . . 75 (male); 83 (female)

Education. Education is mandatory and free for all children between the ages of 5 and 16. There are 35 public schools (elementary to high school) and many private schools. Public schools require uniforms; private school students wear street clothes. Many St. John students take a daily ferry to attend high school on St. Thomas. The University of the Virgin Islands has campuses on St. Thomas and St. Croix. Many of its 3,200 students come from other Caribbean islands.

Health. Local hospital boards, together with the U.S. Department of Health and Human Services, operate the territory's hospitals. St. Johnians needing hospitalization are ferried to the hospital on St. Thomas. All three islands have ample outpatient facilities. The Department of Health administers home health care, diagnostic clinics, specialized programs, and free immunizations.

AT A GLANCE

Events and Trends.

- By November 2004, about 5,500 residents of St. Croix had signed a petition asking the U.S. Congress to make the island its own territory. The change seemed unlikely because the number of people on the petition amounted to only about 20 percent of island's registered voters, and because such a change would require huge administrative changes. Still, many on the island believed it would help the island have more autonomy as well as better access to U.S. funding.

- In September 2004, IRS agents began cracking down on wealthy taxpayers from the U.S. mainland who had claimed residency in the Virgin Islands. The agents wanted to make sure the taxpayers were actually living in the Virgin Islands, not just keeping an empty house there to enjoy the low 3.5 percent income tax. While Virgin Islands leaders were eager to have all residents comply with U.S. tax laws, they also wanted to maintain the higher tax revenues that had come with the mainland residents.

- In September 2003, the St. Croix Federation of Teachers launched an effort to recall Gov. Charles Turnbull because the union accused him of incompetence that had led to public high schools in the U.S. Virgin Islands losing federal accreditation.

Contact Information. U.S. Virgin Islands Department of Tourism, PO Box 6400, Charlotte Amalie, St. Thomas, USVI 00804; PO Box 200, Cruz Bay, St. John, USVI 00831; or PO Box 4538, Christiansted, St. Croix, USVI 00822; phone (800) 372-8784; web site www.usvitourism.vi.

CultureGrams
People. The World. You.

ProQuest Information and Learning Company
300 North Zeeb Road, P.O. Box 1346
Ann Arbor, Michigan 48106 USA
Toll Free: 1.800.528.6279
Fax: 1.800.864.0019
www.culturegrams.com

Bolivarian Republic of Venezuela

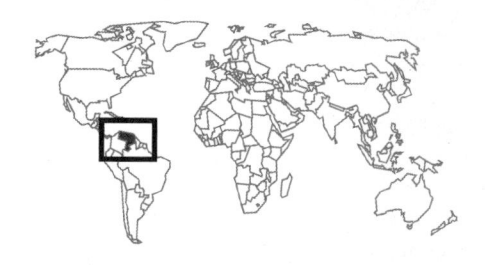

BACKGROUND

Land and Climate. Venezuela is a tropical land located at the top of South America. Covering 352,143 square miles (912,050 square kilometers), it is slightly larger than Texas and Oklahoma combined. The country is divided roughly into four geographic zones: west, central, east, and south. The Andes Mountains dominate the west, where the highest peak, Pico Bolívar, rises 16,427 feet (5,007 meters) above sea level. The central zone includes the northern coast and Venezuela's largest cities. To the east of the Orinoco River is Los Llanos ("the plains"), a region occupying one-third of the country. High plateaus and jungle are common in the west. Angel Falls, the highest waterfall in the world, at 3,212 feet (979 meters), is in southeastern Venezuela. In the far south is a reserve for the country's 14,000 Yanomami tribes. Covering 32,000 square miles (almost 83,000 square kilometers), the area is off-limits to farmers, miners, and all non-Yanomami settlers.

There are two seasons in most of Venezuela: wet and dry. The rainy season is from May to November. Temperatures average 70–85°F (21–29°C), but the mountains can experience cool temperatures, and some Andean peaks are snow-capped year-round. Earthquakes are not infrequent.

History. Before the arrival of Columbus, Venezuela was inhabited by a number of indigenous groups, including the Caracas, Arawak, and Cumanagotos. In 1498, Columbus became the first European to explore the area. The Spanish soon began conquering offshore islands and coastal regions. They named the area Venezuela ("little Venice") because the coastal homes were built on stilts, reminding them of Venice, Italy. Caracas, the capital, was founded in 1527. The Spanish Crown, which claimed the territory, controlled Venezuela through the 18th century. After various failed revolts by American-born Spanish elite, a congress formed and declared independence in 1811. This began a 10-year struggle to create a truly free and united country. Finally, in 1821, the forces of Simón Bolívar were victorious at the Battle of Carabobo, and a republic was established. The republic (*Gran Colombia*) contained Venezuela, Ecuador, and Colombia. The republic dissolved in 1830 and Venezuela became an independent country.

Venezuela experienced instability and dictatorships for many years. The 20th century began under the dictator Cipriano Castro. He was deposed by his vice president, Juan Vicente Gómez, who ruled as a brutal dictator until his death in 1935. More political instability and military coups followed.

A freely elected president came to power in 1958, and democratic elections have taken place since. For a time, Venezuela was the most stable South American country and was also one of the wealthiest in the region. It has some of the world's largest oil reserves outside of the Persian Gulf area, and it benefited from high oil prices in the 1970s and 1980s. Carlos Andrés Pérez, who became president in 1989, introduced a controversial economic austerity plan to address the plummeting price of oil and rising foreign debt. The reforms boosted gross domestic product, but the wealth was concentrated in the hands of a few. Poverty, inflation, and unemployment increased, and violent opposition soon rose to challenge Pérez. He was nearly overthrown by two coups in 1992. Pérez was impeached in 1993 and later imprisoned for misusing government security funds.

December 1993 elections brought a former president, Rafael Caldera, to office. He promised to end corruption, stabilize the economy, and slow privatization begun under Pérez, but austerity measures and high inflation sparked public protests, and

Venezuela

the standard of living for most Venezuelans declined dramatically under Caldera's leadership.

Record-low oil prices in the late 1990s deepened Venezuela's economic crisis. Claiming to represent the needs of the poor, Hugo Chávez Frias was elected president by a large majority in the December 1998 elections. Chávez, who had led a coup attempt in 1992, began to transform Venezuela's political system after coming to office, promising complete social reform. Under a new constitution in 1999, Chávez dissolved the bicameral parliament, established a single National Assembly, and gave greater powers to the president. Chávez's reforms increasingly polarized the country and led to violent antigovernment protests. In April 2002, a military coup temporarily replaced Chávez with businessman Pedro Carmona as president. However, two days later, Chávez was returned to power. Political struggles continued with a 9-week general strike that paralyzed the nation and a referendum on Chávez's rule. Although Chávez survived the strike and referendum, some turmoil continues as the government and opposition fight for power.

THE PEOPLE

Population. Venezuela has a population of about 25 million, which is growing at 1.4 percent annually. The country is the most urbanized in South America; approximately 90 percent of the people live in urban areas. Caracas has 4.5 million inhabitants. Venezuela's other major cities include Maracaibo, Valencia, and Maracay. In general the population is a racial mixture, and the majority of the population (about 67 percent) is of mixed European and indigenous or black heritage. About twenty-one percent is white, of European (mostly Italian or Spanish) descent. About 10 percent of the population is black. Two percent of the population is made up of indigenous peoples, including the Goajiros, who live in the west, and the Yanomamis, who live in the south.

Language. Spanish is the official language and is spoken by almost everyone, with the exception of some indigenous people living in remote areas. These indigenous groups speak a variety of languages. The Spanish spoken in Venezuela is known for its many unique words and phrases. *Chévere* means "very well" or "cool." *Estar pelado* (to be bald) and *estar limpio* (to be clean) can also mean "to be broke," or out of money. *Ponerse las pilas* (to insert batteries) means "to be aware" or "watch out." *Echar una zorrita* (to throw a little fox) means "to take a nap." Students are required to take English courses in high school.

Religion. Religious freedom is guaranteed by the constitution. Still, the Roman Catholic Church has historically had a large voice in government, Catholicism is deeply ingrained in the culture, and as much as 90 percent of the population is Roman Catholic. While many Catholics do not attend church services regularly, most profess some faith in God, the Catholic saints, and the Virgin Mary. Protestant and other Christian faiths are becoming more prevalent. In general, Venezuelans are somewhat less religious than other Latin Americans. Rural people tend to be more devoted to their faith than are urban residents.

General Attitudes. Venezuelans take great pride in their country and the heroes of the independence movement. The South American liberator Simón Bolívar was Venezuelan, and while he is honored in many other nations, he is a national treasure to Venezuela. Most cities have a *Plaza Bolívar* that occupies a block near the city center. It is rude to behave disrespectfully in that plaza or to refer negatively to Bolívar.

Venezuelans admire honesty, generosity, and a good sense of humor. Their fondness of talking, joking, laughing, and spontaneity often creates a party-like atmosphere wherever they happen to be. Venezuelans feel that the needs of an individual or the joy of an event are more important than the demands of a time schedule. Therefore, they may be late for appointments, and scheduled events may last longer than expected. Venezuelans are proud of the beauty of their country and of Venezuelan women; they proudly point out that winners of international beauty contests are frequently from Venezuela. Loss of prosperity over the last decade has affected the outlook of many, as Venezuela's once relatively large middle class now focuses on making ends meet. Still, many are optimistic that they can work out their current problems.

Personal Appearance. Most people feel it is important to look their best and be properly groomed. Venezuelans tend to be quite fashion-conscious; urban people dress in current European styles. Professional men and women wear suits or more casual clothing, which is always neat and clean. In Caracas, business dress tends to be more formal. In the summer, cotton clothing is the most common and comfortable. Shorts and swimwear are worn only in urban recreation areas and at the beach. Native peoples may wear European or traditional dress or a combination of both.

CUSTOMS AND COURTESIES

Greetings. Men greet close friends with an *abrazo* (a full embrace, while patting each other on the back); women greet and part with an *abrazo* and a kiss on the cheek. Usually a man and a woman exchange an *abrazo* only if they are close friends or relatives. A firm handshake is a common greeting and parting gesture among acquaintances and strangers. It may be accompanied by a pat on the back, or among closer acquaintances, an *abrazo*.

During conversation, most people in Venezuela stand closer than do people in the United States, and backing away is usually improper. However, people in the Andes region often stand farther apart than other Venezuelans. Common greetings include ¡*Buenos días!* (Good morning), ¡*Buenas tardes!* (Good afternoon), and ¡*Buenas noches!* (Good evening). Young people generally use the casual ¡*Hola!* (Hi). Greetings often include polite inquiries about a person's health. Common parting phrases include *Hasta luego* (Until later), *Nos vemos* (We'll see you), and *Chao* (Good-bye). *Adiós* (Good-bye) is rarely used as it implies a permanent farewell.

Friends often address one another by nickname. Acquaintances and professionals are addressed by title (*Doctor*, *Señor*, *Señora*, etc.), usually followed by the surname. The elderly and other respected people may be addressed as *Don* (for men) or *Doña* (for women), followed by the first name.

Gestures. Venezuelans generally use their hands during conversation to communicate or emphasize a point. They may also use a gesture to communicate without speaking. For example, one can ask the price of an item or request payment by rubbing the thumb and index finger together while rotating the palm up. It is courteous to maintain eye contact while conversing. When sitting, a person does not slouch or prop the feet up on any object. Pointing with the index finger is considered rude; motioning with the entire hand is more polite. Passing between conversing individuals or interrupting a conversation is also rude; in such circumstances, one is expected to say *Con permiso* (With permission). People often offer their seats to the elderly on public transportation.

Visiting. Venezuelans enjoy visiting friends and relatives. Friends may visit unannounced, but such visits generally are short and not at mealtimes. People typically only invite close friends to their homes; business contacts and other visitors usually are invited to dine at a restaurant. Venezuelans are careful to provide for their guests. When visitors arrive at a home, business, or office, they often are served *un cafecito* (thick black coffee) in a very small cup. This is a gesture of hospitality and friendship. Polite discussion usually precedes any business matters. In the home, hosts may offer guests refreshments in addition to coffee. It is polite for guests to inquire about the health of the host's family members. As a guest, one should greet each person upon one's arrival and departure. Hosts generally do not expect gifts from visitors.

Eating. Lunch is the main meal of the day. Families traditionally eat together for midday and evening meals; however, this custom varies by region. Families in big cities no longer eat midday meals together. Parents usually sit at the head and foot of the dinner table. Some Venezuelans eat in the continental style, with the fork in the left hand and the knife in the right. Others use the style more common in the United States, with the fork in the right hand, unless the knife is picked up to cut something. When a person is finished, he or she places the utensils together or in an "X" at the center of the plate. It is inappropriate for adults to eat on the street. Dining out, especially on business, is common. In restaurants, the bill usually includes a service charge (10 percent), but patrons are expected to leave a small additional tip.

LIFESTYLE

Family. Family ties are strong and most families are close-knit. However, about half of all births in Venezuela are out of wedlock or in common-law marriages. Households commonly include members of the extended family, usually grandparents. The father dominates in the home, but the responsibility for raising the children and managing the household traditionally rests with the mother. More couples are sharing responsibilities as an increasing number of women work outside the home, especially in Caracas. While women comprise almost half of the labor force, less than 10 percent of employers and managers are women. If members of a family are affluent, they customarily share their wealth with less-fortunate relatives.

Dating and Marriage. Dating and courtship traditions in Venezuela are similar to those in other Western countries. Young people enjoy socializing and choosing their companions. Weddings are social events for many Venezuelan families. Most weddings include two marriage ceremonies: a civil ceremony for legal recognition and an optional religious ceremony. Religious ceremonies are an important part of the Venezuelan culture because of the Roman Catholic tradition. Parties are usually held after the religious ceremony.

Diet. Common foods in Venezuela include pasta, rice, beans, plantains, white cheese, chicken, potatoes, and fish. Corn is the basis of many dishes, and fried foods are popular. One favorite is the *arepa*, a deep-fried thick pancake made from white corn flour and sometimes filled with butter, meat, and cheese. *Hallacas* are similar to *arepas* but are stuffed with stewed meat, potatoes, olives, raisins, and other spices; they are especially popular at Christmastime. Casseroles, meat pies, meatloaf, and stews are well liked, although rising prices have diminished meat's popularity somewhat. *Puntatrasera* is a favorite tender steak. *Pabellón criollo* consists of black beans, rice, shredded meat, plantains, and *arepas*.

In most cities, open-air markets provide a large variety of tropical fruits and fresh vegetables. Popular fruits include mangoes, *lechoza* (papaya), bananas, and watermelon. These may be eaten or made into *batidos de fruta* (fruit shakes), which are sold on the street at *refresquerias* (fruit-and-drink stands). *Raspaitos* (shaved ice) are another common treat. Although soda and coffee are favored drinks, hot chocolate is also common, particularly in the cooler Andean states.

Recreation. The most popular sport in Venezuela is baseball, followed by basketball. Soccer is much less popular than in other Latin American countries. Venezuelans enjoy watching horse racing and bullfighting. Fishing, swimming, cycling, and tennis are common participation sports. *Bolas criollas* is a well-liked game similar to lawn bowling. Many women enjoy walking, cycling, and playing softball. For entertainment, Venezuelans like to go dancing, to movies, or to cultural events. Playing dominoes and visiting are favorite leisure activities. *Telenovelas* (nighttime soap operas) have a large following, particularly among women. Going to the beaches or the mountains is a common vacation activity.

The Arts. *Llaneros* (similar to cowboys) are often depicted in Venezuela's arts. The *Joropo* (traditional music of Los Llanos) is the national dance. *Maracas* (rattles made of gourds) and the *cuatro* (a small guitar) often accompany it. Annual music festivals feature such popular music as salsa, merengue, *gaitas* (traditional Christmas music), and *aguinaldos* (traditional Christmas songs). Classical music is appreciated, and there are orchestras in many cities.

Literature developed substantially in the 20th century and is often characterized by nationalism. Many people produce crafts such as canoes, saddles, and musical instruments.

Holidays. Official public holidays include New Year's Day, *Carnaval* (two days before Ash Wednesday), Ash Wednesday, Easter (Thursday–Sunday), Declaration of Independence Day (19 Apr.), Day of Workers (1 May), Battle of Carabobo (24 June), Independence Day (5 July), Simón Bolívar's Birthday (24 July), Columbus Day (12 Oct.), Christmas Eve, Christmas, and New Year's Eve.

Many families vacation at the beach or in the mountains during the week preceding Easter, which is called *Semana Santa* (Holy Week) and during August. *Carnaval* is celebrated most in eastern Venezuela, where water fights, parades, dancing in the streets, and other activities are common.

Towns and cities hold annual *ferias* (festivals), honoring their local patron saint. The three most important *ferias* include the *Feria de San Sebastian*, in San Cristóbal; the *Feria del Sol*, in Mérida; and the *Feria de la Chinita*, in Maracaibo. Festivities include bullfighting, street dances, craft exhibits, and beauty contests. Flowers are important in Venezuelan celebrations. During each holiday, statues of Simón Bolívar, the "father of Venezuela," are decorated with colorful wreaths.

Commerce. Business hours generally extend from 8 a.m. to 6 p.m. (with a one- or two-hour break), Monday through Friday. Government offices maintain similar hours, with regional variations. Standard banking hours are from 9 a.m. to 3:30 p.m. City dwellers purchase basic goods from larger stores and shopping centers, while rural residents rely on local markets, small specialized shops, and their own labor for basic items.

It is customary for service personnel, such as garbage collectors and postal carriers, to present a calling card requesting a *regalo* (gift) in the form of money at Christmastime. The expediting of needed services or supplies sometimes requires a tip in advance.

Venezuela

SOCIETY

Government. Venezuela is a republic headed by a president who serves a six-year term. As chief of state and head of government, President Hugo Chávez governs with a Council of Ministers. The new constitution abolished the 52-seat Senate and 207-seat Chamber of Deputies and replaced it with a single 165-seat National Assembly. Venezuela's traditional political parties, most notably the Democratic Action Party (AD) and the Social Christian Party (COPEI), have been challenged by new political parties such as the Movement for a Fifth Republic (MVR) and Proyecto Venezuela. The voting age is 18.

Economy. Venezuela is a member of OPEC (Organization of Petroleum Exporting Countries), and petroleum is the cornerstone of the economy. It accounts for more than 80 percent of all export earnings and a substantial portion of all government revenues. Those revenues have allowed the country to develop a modern infrastructure. However, oil has also made Venezuela subject to market fluctuations. When the price of oil drops, the entire economy suffers. Therefore, the government stresses economic diversification. Tourism, petrochemical, and gas sectors are potential sources of revenue. The country also exports some minerals and other raw materials. Agriculture employs about 10 percent of the population and produces grains, sugar, fruits, coffee, and rice.

Economic growth has been somewhat erratic in the 1990s. Several major banks went bankrupt in 1994, which led to a severe currency devaluation of the *bolívar* (VEB) and added to concerns about economic stability. Unemployment and inflation are relatively high. Fluctuating oil prices, a large external debt, and strikes in 2002 and 2003 have severely damaged the economy.

The standard of living of most Venezuelans is falling. A large portion of the population lives in poverty. The gap between rich and poor is widening as Venezuela's middle class continues to shrink. Benefits from Venezuela's oil wealth have eluded a significant proportion of the population. Access to health care, education, and a decent standard of living is somewhat limited for the general population.

Transportation and Communications. Most people use public transportation; few Venezuelans can afford to own a private car. Buses and taxis are common, but the *por puesto* is the most popular and cheapest form of transportation. It features a system of taxi-like automobiles that travel a regular route throughout the city, picking up and letting off passengers at any point. The cost is less than a taxi but more than a bus. Highways are excellent in Venezuela, but driving is often hazardous. Railroads generally are not used for passenger travel. Caracas has a modern underground subway system.

The communications system is modern and expanding. Private phones are expensive, but public phones are readily available. The popularity of cellular phones is growing. Several radio and television stations broadcast in Venezuela. A number of daily national and regional newspapers also service the country.

Education. Education is compulsory (though not enforced) from ages seven to fourteen. All education, including university level, is free in public institutions. The government has taken great strides in improving the literacy rate. About three-fourths of all students complete primary school (nine years), and many of those children go on to secondary school (two years). However, about two-thirds of the overall school-age population does not attend a secondary school. Secondary school tracks are available in the sciences, humanities, and technical fields. Many families are unable to afford the necessary books and transportation. The school year begins in October and ends in July of the following year. After secondary school, students may choose from a variety of three-year vocational schools or take an aptitude test to enter a university.

Health. Good medical facilities can be found in urban areas, but the best are private and very expensive for the average citizen. Many facilities, particularly in rural areas, lack staff, equipment, and supplies. Strikes involving medical-care personnel are relatively frequent. Only about two-thirds of all infants are immunized against childhood diseases, but the government is trying to improve that percentage. Malnutrition is a challenge faced by many. Malaria, cholera, and dengue fever are active, especially in certain rural areas.

DEVELOPMENT DATA
- Human Dev. Index* rank . . . . 68 of 177 countries
- Adjusted for women . . . . 58 of 144 countries
- Real GDP per capita $5,380
- Adult literacy rate . . . . 94 percent (male); 93 (female)
- Infant mortality rate . . . . 23 per 1,000 births
- Life expectancy . . . . 71 (male); 77 (female)

AT A GLANCE

Events and Trends.
- In January 2005, President Chávez began implementing a land reform deal that aimed to equalize some of the country's wealth. He wanted to change the fact that less than 5 percent of the Venezuelan population has controlled more than 80 percent of the land. Chávez said the government would negotiate with individual landowners before redistributing portions to the landless. While the move was greeted with joy among many of the underprivileged, some landowners vowed to fight the changes.
- The Venezuelan legislature appointed 17 new justices to the nation's highest court in December 2004. The move filled 5 vacancies and added 12 new justices, expanding the court from 20 to 32 justices. The government said it hoped the move would help the court become less corrupt and more efficient. However, some groups said government leaders were trying to pack the court with judges who shared their political beliefs.
- In August 2004, President Chávez survived a referendum on his rule with 59 percent of the electorate's support. The results meant Chávez could continue to serve for two-and-a-half more years. The referendum was the latest event in a series of political upheavals, which involved a coup attempt, followed by nationwide strikes and street riots.

Contact Information. Embassy of the Republic of Venezuela, 1099 30th Street NW, Washington, DC 20007; phone (202) 342-2214; web site www.embavenez-us.org.

Country Data Tables

▼ CAPITALS
　POPULATION AND AREA
　DEVELOPMENT DATA

Nation or Territory	Capital
Afghanistan	Kabul
Albania	Tirana
Algeria	Algiers
American Samoa	Pago Pago
Angola	Luanda
Antigua and Barbuda	Saint John's
Argentina	Buenos Aires
Armenia	Yerevan
Australia	Canberra
Austria	Vienna
Azerbaijan	Baku
Bahamas	Nassau
Bahrain	Manama
Bangladesh	Dhaka
Barbados	Bridgetown
Belarus	Minsk
Belgium	Brussels
Belize	Belmopan
Benin	Porto-Novo
Bhutan	Thimphu
Bolivia	La Paz
Bosnia and Herzegovina	Sarajevo
Botswana	Gaborone
Brazil	Braslia
Bulgaria	Sofia
Burkina Faso	Ouagadougou
Cambodia	Phnom Penh
Cameroon	Yaoundé
Canada	Ottawa
Cape Verde	Praia
Central African Rep.	Bangui
Chad	N'Djamena
Chile	Santiago
China	Beijing
Colombia	Bogot
Comoros	Moroni
Congo, Dem. Rep. of	Kinshasa
Costa Rica	San Jos
Croatia	Zagreb
Cuba	Havana
Czech Republic	Prague
Denmark	Copenhagen
Dominican Republic	Santo Domingo
Ecuador	Quito
Egypt	Cairo
El Salvador	San Salvador
England	London
Equatorial Guinea	Malabo
Eritrea	Asmara
Estonia	Tallinn
Ethiopia	Addis Ababa
Fiji	Suva

Nation or Territory	Capital
Finland	Helsinki
France	Paris
French Polynesia	Papeete
Gabon	Libreville
Gambia	Banjul
Georgia	Tbilisi
Germany	Berlin
Ghana	Accra
Greece	Athens
Grenada	Saint George's
Guam	Hagta
Guatemala	Guatemala City
Guinea	Conakry
Guinea-Bissau	Bissau
Guyana	Georgetown
Haiti	Port-au-Prince
Honduras	Tegucigalpa
Hong Kong	Hong Kong
Hungary	Budapest
Iceland	Reykjavk
India	New Delhi
Indonesia	Jakarta
Iran	Tehran
Iraq	Baghdad
Ireland	Dublin
Israel	Jerusalem
Italy	Rome
Ivory Coast	Yamoussoukro
Jamaica	Kingston
Japan	Tokyo
Jordan	Amman
Kazakstan	Astana
Kenya	Nairobi
Kiribati	Bairiki
Kuwait	Kuwait City
Kyrgyzstan	Bishkek
Laos	Vientiane
Latvia	Rīga
Lebanon	Beirut
Lesotho	Maseru
Libya	Tripoli
Liechtenstein	Vaduz
Lithuania	Vilnius
Luxembourg	Luxembourg
Macedonia	Skopje
Madagascar	Antananarivo
Malawi	Lilongwe
Malaysia	Kuala Lumpur
Mali	Bamako
Malta	Valletta
Marshall Islands	Majuro
Mauritania	Nouakchott

Capitals

Nation or Territory	Capital
Mauritius	Port Louis
Mexico	Mexico City
Micronesia	Palikir
Moldova	Chisinau
Mongolia	Ulaanbaatar
Montserrat	Plymouth
Morocco	Rabat
Mozambique	Maputo
Myanmar	Yangon
Namibia	Windhoek
Nepal	Kathmandu
Netherlands	Amsterdam
New Zealand	Wellington
Nicaragua	Managua
Niger	Niamey
Nigeria	Abuja
Niue	Alofi
North Korea	Pyongyang
Northern Ireland	Belfast
Norway	Oslo
Oman	Muscat
Pakistan	Islamabad
Panama	Panama City
Papua New Guinea	Port Moresby
Paraguay	Asuncin
Peru	Lima
Philippines	Manila
Poland	Warsaw
Portugal	Lisbon
Puerto Rico	San Juan
Qatar	Doha
Romania	Bucharest
Russia	Moscow
Rwanda	Kigali
Saint Kitts and Nevis	Basseterre
Saint Lucia	Castries
Saint Vincent and the Grenadines	Kingstown
Samoa	Apia
Saudi Arabia	Riyadh
Scotland	Edinburgh
Senegal	Dakar
Serbia and Montenegro	Belgrade
Sierra Leone	Freetown
Singapore	Singapore
Slovakia	Bratislava
Slovenia	Ljubljana
Solomon Islands	Honiara
Somalia	Mogadishu
South Africa	Pretoria
South Korea	Seoul
Spain	Madrid
Sri Lanka	Colombo

Nation or Territory	Capital
Sudan	Khartoum
Suriname	Paramaribo
Swaziland	Mbabane
Sweden	Stockholm
Switzerland	Bern
Syria	Damascus
Taiwan	Taipei
Tajikistan	Dushanbe
Tanzania	Dodoma
Thailand	Bangkok
Togo	Lom
Tonga	Nuku'alofa
Trinidad and Tobago	Port of Spain
Tunisia	Tunis
Turkey	Ankara
Turkmenistan	Ashgabat
Tuvalu	Funafuti
Uganda	Kampala
Ukraine	Kyiv
United Arab Emirates	Abu Dhabi
United States of America	Washington, D.C.
Uruguay	Montevideo
U.S. Virgin Islands	Charlotte Amalie
Uzbekistan	Tashkent
Venezuela	Caracas
Vietnam	Hanoi
Wales	Cardiff
West Bank and Gaza	None
Yemen	Sana'a
Zambia	Lusaka
Zimbabwe	Harare

Nation or Territory	Population	Area (sq. mi.)	Area (sq. km.)
Afghanistan	28,513,677	251,773	652,090
Albania	3,544,808	11,100	28,750
Algeria	32,129,324	919,590	2,381,740
American Samoa	57,902	77	199
Angola	10,978,552	481,354	1,246,700
Antigua and Barbuda	68,320	170	440
Argentina	39,144,753	1,068,296	2,766,874
Armenia	2,991,360	11,506	29,800
Australia	19,913,144	2,967,892	7,686,850
Austria	8,174,762	32,375	83,850
Azerbaijan	7,868,385	33,436	86,600
Bahamas	299,697	5,353	13,860
Bahrain	677,886	240	620
Bangladesh	141,340,476	55,599	144,000
Barbados	277,264	166	430
Belarus	10,300,483	80,154	207,600
Belgium	10,348,276	11,780	30,510
Belize	272,945	8,866	22,963
Benin	7,250,033	43,482	112,620
Bhutan	2,185,569	18,147	47,001
Bolivia	8,586,443	424,165	1,089,581
Bosnia & Herzegovina	4,007,608	19,775	51,233
Botswana	1,561,973	231,800	600,370
Brazil	186,112,794	3,286,488	8,511,965
Bulgaria	7,517,973	42,823	110,910
Burkina Faso	13,574,820	105,869	274,200
Cambodia	13,363,421	69,900	181,040
Cameroon	16,063,678	183,567	475,440
Canada	32,507,874	3,851,788	9,976,085
Cape Verde	415,294	1,557	4,033
Central African Rep.	3,742,482	240,533	622,980
Chad	9,538,544	495,755	1,284,000
Chile	15,823,957	292,260	756,950
China	1,298,847,624	3,705,820	9,598,032
Colombia	42,310,775	439,773	1,138,910
Comoros	651,901	838	2,171
Congo, Dem. Rep. of	58,317,930	905,563	2,345,410
Costa Rica	3,956,507	19,730	51,100
Croatia	4,496,869	21,829	56,538
Cuba	11,308,764	42,803	110,860
Czech Republic	10,246,178	30,387	78,703
Denmark	5,413,392	16,629	43,070
Dominican Republic	8,833,634	18,815	48,731
Ecuador	13,212,742	109,483	283,560
Egypt	76,117,421	386,662	1,001,149
El Salvador	6,587,541	8,124	21,041
England	49,855,700	50,363	130,357
Equatorial Guinea	523,051	10,830	28,050

Nation or Territory	Population	Area (sq. mi.)	Area (sq. km.)
Eritrea	4,447,307	46,842	121,320
Estonia	1,341,664	17,462	45,226
Ethiopia	67,851,281	435,184	1,127,127
Fiji	880,874	7,054	18,270
Finland	5,214,512	130,127	337,030
France	60,424,213	211,208	547,030
French Polynesia	266,339	1,413	3,660
Gabon	1,355,246	103,347	267,670
Gambia	1,546,848	4,363	11,300
Georgia	4,693,892	26,912	69,700
Germany	82,424,609	137,803	356,910
Ghana	20,757,032	92,100	238,540
Greece	10,665,989	50,942	131,940
Grenada	89,357	131	339
Guam	166,090	212	538
Guatemala	14,280,596	42,043	108,890
Guinea	9,246,462	94,000	243,460
Guinea-Bissau	1,388,363	13,946	36,120
Guyana	705,803	83,000	214,970
Haiti	7,656,166	10,714	27,750
Honduras	6,823,568	43,278	112,090
Hong Kong	6,855,125	421	1,092
Hungary	10,032,375	35,919	93,030
Iceland	293,996	39,768	103,000
India	1,065,070,607	1,269,338	3,287,590
Indonesia	238,452,952	741,096	1,919,400
Iran	69,018,924	636,293	1,648,000
Iraq	25,374,691	168,754	437,072
Ireland	3,969,558	27,135	70,280
Israel	6,199,008	8,020	20,770
Italy	58,057,477	116,305	301,230
Ivory Coast	17,327,724	124,500	322,460
Jamaica	27,131,130	4,243	10,989
Japan	127,333,002	145,882	377,835
Jordan	5,611,202	35,475	91,880
Kazakstan	15,143,704	1,049,155	2,717,300
Kenya	32,021,856	224,961	582,650
Kiribati	100,798	313	811
Kuwait	2,257,549	6,880	17,820
Kyrgyzstan	5,081,429	76,640	198,500
Laos	6,068,117	91,430	236,800
Latvia	2,306,306	24,750	64,100
Lebanon	3,777,218	4,015	10,400
Lesotho	1,865,040	11,718	30,350
Libya	5,631,585	679,362	1,759,540
Liechtenstein	33,436	62	163
Lithuania	3,607,899	25,174	65,200
Luxembourg	462,690	998	2,586

Population and Area

Nation or Territory	Population	Area (sq. mi.)	Area (sq. km.)
Macedonia	2,071,210	9,928	25,713
Madagascar	17,501,871	226,656	587,040
Malawi	11,906,855	45,747	118,484
Malaysia	23,522,482	127,317	329,750
Mali	11,956,788	478,764	1,240,000
Malta	396,851	122	316
Marshall Islands	57,738	70	181
Mauritania	2,998,563	397,953	1,030,700
Mauritius	1,230,602	718	1,860
Mexico	104,959,594	761,602	1,972,550
Micronesia	108,155	270	700
Moldova	4,455,421	13,010	33,700
Mongolia	2,751,314	604,250	1,565,000
Montserrat	9,245	40	103
Morocco	32,209,101	172,413	446,550
Mozambique	18,811,731	309,574	801,590
Myanmar	50,100,500	262,000	678,500
Namibia	1,954,033	317,816	823,144
Nepal	27,070,666	54,362	140,800
Netherlands	16,318,199	16,036	41,532
New Zealand	3,993,817	103,737	268,680
Nicaragua	5,359,759	49,998	129,494
Niger	11,360,538	489,206	1,267,000
Nigeria	137,253,133	356,668	923,770
Niue	2,156	100	260
North Korea	22,697,553	47,250	120,540
Northern Ireland	1,702,600	5,482	14,199
Norway	4,574,560	125,182	324,220
Oman	2,903,165	119,498	309,500
Pakistan	159,196,336	310,410	803,940
Panama	3,000,463	30,193	78,200
Papua New Guinea	5,420,280	178,259	461,690
Paraguay	6,191,368	157,046	406,570
Peru	27,544,305	496,226	1,285,220
Philippines	86,241,697	115,830	300,000
Poland	38,626,349	120,728	312,685
Portugal	10,524,145	35,672	92,391
Puerto Rico	3,897,960	3,515	9,104
Qatar	840,290	4,416	11,437
Romania	22,355,551	91,700	237,500
Russia	143,782,338	6,592,734	17,075,200
Rwanda	7,954,013	10,170	26,340
Saint Kitts and Nevis	38,836	101	261
Saint Lucia	164,213	239	620
Saint Vincent & the Gr.	117,193	150	389
Samoa	177,714	1,133	2,934
Saudi Arabia	25,795,938	750,965	1,945,000
Scotland	5,057,400	30,421	78,789
Senegal	10,852,147	75,749	196,180
Serbia and Montenegro	10,825,900	39,518	102,350
Sierra Leone	5,883,889	27,699	71,740
Singapore	4,425,720	244	633
Slovakia	5,423,567	18,859	48,845
Slovenia	2,011,473	7,820	20,253
Solomon Islands	523,617	10,634	27,540
Somalia	8,304,601	246,300	638,000
South Africa	42,718,530	471,445	1,221,043
South Korea	48,598,175	38,023	98,480
Spain	40,280,780	194,897	504,782
Sri Lanka	19,905,165	25,332	65,610
Sudan	39,148,162	967,494	2,505,810
Suriname	481,146	63,039	163,270
Swaziland	1,169,241	6,704	17,363
Sweden	9,013,109	173,732	449,964
Switzerland	7,450,867	15,942	41,290
Syria	18,016,874	71,498	185,180
Taiwan	22,749,838	13,892	35,980
Tajikistan	7,011,556	55,251	143,100
Tanzania	36,588,225	364,899	945,090
Thailand	64,865,523	198,455	514,000
Togo	5,556,812	21,930	56,790
Tonga	110,237	277	718
Trinidad and Tobago	1,096,585	1,980	5,128
Tunisia	9,974,722	63,170	163,610
Turkey	68,893,918	301,382	780,580
Turkmenistan	4,863,169	188,500	488,100
Tuvalu	11,468	10	26
Uganda	26,404,543	91,135	236,040
Ukraine	47,732,079	233,090	603,700
United Arab Emirates	2,523,915	32,400	83,900
United States	293,027,571	3,618,765	9,372,558
Uruguay	3,399,237	68,039	176,220
U.S. Virgin Islands	108,775	135	349
Uzbekistan	26,410,416	172,740	447,400
Venezuela	25,017,387	352,143	912,050
Vietnam	82,689,518	127,243	329,560
Wales	2,938,000	9,018	20,769
West Bank and Gaza	3,636,195	2,367	6,130
Yemen	20,024,867	203,849	527,970
Zambia	10,462,436	290,583	752,610
Zimbabwe	12,671,860	150,803	390,580

Nation or Territory	Human Dev. Index Rank*	HDI Adjusted for Women*	Real GDP per Capita**	Adult Literacy	Literacy (Male)	Literacy (Female)	Infant Mortality (per 1,000 births)	Life Expectancy (Male)	Life Expectancy (Female)
Afghanistan	NA	NA	$700	36%	51%	21%	166	43	43
Albania	65 of 177	54 of 144	$4,830	99%	99%	98%	22	71	77
Algeria	108 of 177	89 of 144	$5,760	69%	78%	60%	32	68	71
American Samoa	NA	NA	$8,000	98%	98%	97%	9	72	79
Angola	166 of 177	NA	$2,130	42%	56%	28%	193	39	42
Antigua and Barbuda	55 of 177	NA	$10,920	86%	NA	NA	20	69	74
Argentina	34 of 177	36 of 144	$10,880	97%	97%	97%	16	71	78
Armenia	82 of 177	65 of 144	$3,120	99%	99%	99%	24	69	76
Australia	3 of 177	3 of 144	$28,260	99%	99%	99%	5	76	82
Austria	14 of 177	17 of 144	$29,220	99%	99%	99%	5	75	81
Azerbaijan	91 of 177	NA	$3,210	98%	99%	96%	82	69	75
Bahamas	51 of 177	46 of 144	$17,280	96%	95%	96%	17	64	70
Bahrain	40 of 177	39 of 144	$17,170	88%	92%	84%	18	72	76
Bangladesh	138 of 177	110 of 144	$1,700	41%	50%	31%	64	61	62
Barbados	29 of 177	27 of 144	$15,290	99%	99%	99%	13	74	79
Belarus	62 of 177	51 of 144	$5,520	99%	99%	99%	13	65	75
Belgium	6 of 177	7 of 144	$27,570	99%	99%	99%	5	76	82
Belize	99 of 177	80 of 144	$6,080	77%	77%	77%	26	70	73
Benin	161 of 177	130 of 144	$1,070	41%	55%	26%	86	49	53
Bhutan	134 of 177	NA	$1,969	42%	56%	28%	103	62	64
Bolivia	114 of 177	92 of 144	$2,460	87%	93%	81%	55	62	66
Bosnia & Herzegovina	66 of 177	NA	$5,970	95%	98%	91%	22	71	77
Botswana	128 of 177	102 of 144	$8,170	79%	76%	82%	70	40	42
Brazil	72 of 177	60 of 144	$7,770	87%	86%	87%	30	64	73
Bulgaria	56 of 177	48 of 144	$7,130	99%	99%	98%	21	67	75
Burkina Faso	175 of 177	143 of 144	$1,100	14%	19%	8%	99	45	46
Cambodia	130 of 177	105 of 144	$2,060	70%	81%	59%	74	55	60
Cameroon	141 of 177	111 of 144	$2,000	69%	77%	60%	69	46	48
Canada	4 of 177	4 of 144	$29,480	99%	99%	99%	5	77	82
Cape Verde	105 of 177	83 of 144	$5,000	77%	85%	68%	49	67	73
Central African Rep.	169 of 177	138 of 144	$1,170	50%	65%	34%	92	39	41
Chad	167 of 177	135 of 144	$1,020	47%	55%	38%	95	44	46
Chile	43 of 177	40 of 144	$9,820	96%	96%	96%	9	73	79
China	94 of 177	71 of 144	$4,580	91%	95%	87%	25	69	73
Colombia	73 of 177	59 of 144	$6,370	92%	92%	92%	22	69	75
Comoros	136 of 177	108 of 144	$1,690	57%	64%	49%	77	59	62
Congo, Dem. Rep. of	168 of 177	136 of 144	$650	63%	74%	52%	95	40	42
Costa Rica	45 of 177	44 of 144	$8,840	96%	96%	96%	10	76	81
Croatia	48 of 177	43 of 144	$10,040	98%	99%	97%	7	70	78
Cuba	52 of 177	NA	$5,259	97%	97%	97%	6	75	79
Czech Republic	32 of 177	32 of 144	$15,780	99%	99%	99%	4	72	79
Denmark	17 of 177	13 of 144	$30,940	99%	99%	99%	5	74	79
Dominican Republic	98 of 177	98 of 144	$6,640	84%	84%	84%	33	64	69
Ecuador	100 of 177	79 of 144	$3,580	91%	92%	90%	24	68	73
Egypt	120 of 177	99 of 144	$3,810	56%	67%	44%	34	67	71

*UN Development Programme, Human Development Report
**U.S. Dollars

Development Data

Nation or Territory	Human Dev. Index Rank*	HDI Adjusted for Women*	Real GDP per Capita**	Adult Literacy	Literacy (Male)	Literacy (Female)	Infant Mortality (per 1,000 births)	Life Expectancy (Male)	Life Expectancy (Female)
El Salvador	103 of 177	84 of 144	$4,890	80%	82%	77%	26	68	74
England	12 of 177	9 of 144	$26,150	99%	99%	99%	5	76	81
Equatorial Guinea	109 of 177	86 of 144	$29,780	85%	93%	76%	87	48	51
Eritrea	156 of 177	127 of 144	$890	57%	68%	46%	76	51	54
Estonia	36 of 177	33 of 144	$12,260	99%	99%	99%	12	66	77
Ethiopia	170 of 177	137 of 144	$780	42%	49%	34%	102	45	46
Fiji	81 of 177	69 of 144	$5,440	93%	95%	91%	13	68	71
Finland	13 of 177	10 of 144	$26,150	99%	99%	99%	4	74	81
France	16 of 177	15 of 144	$26,920	99%	99%	99%	4	75	83
French Polynesia	NA	NA	$17,500	98%	98%	98%	9	73	78
Gabon	122 of 177	NA	$6,590	64%	74%	53%	54	56	58
Gambia	155 of 177	125 of 144	$1,690	38%	45%	31%	73	53	55
Georgia	97 of 177	NA	$2,260	99%	99%	98%	19	69	78
Germany	19 of 177	19 of 144	$27,100	99%	99%	99%	4	75	81
Ghana	131 of 177	104 of 144	$2,130	74%	82%	66%	52	56	59
Greece	24 of 177	24 of 144	$17,740	98%	99%	96%	6	76	81
Grenada	93 of 177	NA	$7,280	94%	NA	NA	15	63	66
Guam	NA	NA	$21,000	99%	99%	99%	7	75	81
Guatemala	121 of 177	98 of 144	$4,080	70%	77%	63%	37	63	69
Guinea	160 of 177	NA	$2,100	36%	50%	22%	92	49	49
Guinea-Bissau	172 of 177	141 of 144	$710	40%	55%	25%	109	44	47
Guyana	104 of 177	81 of 144	$4,260	99%	99%	98%	37	60	66
Haiti	153 of 177	123 of 144	$1,610	52%	54%	50%	74	49	50
Honduras	115 of 177	95 of 144	$2,600	80%	80%	80%	30	67	71
Hong Kong	23 of 177	23 of 144	$26,910	94%	97%	90%	3	77	82
Hungary	38 of 177	35 of 144	$13,400	99%	99%	99%	9	67	76
Iceland	7 of 177	6 of 144	$29,750	99%	99%	99%	3	78	82
India	127 of 177	103 of 144	$2,670	58%	69%	46%	58	63	64
Indonesia	111 of 177	90 of 144	$3,230	88%	93%	83%	37	65	69
Iran	101 of 177	82 of 144	$6,690	77%	84%	70%	43	69	72
Iraq	NA	NA	$1,500	40%	55%	24%	53	59	62
Ireland	10 of 177	14 of 144	$36,360	99%	99%	99%	6	74	80
Israel	22 of 177	22 of 144	$19,530	95%	97%	93%	7	77	81
Italy	21 of 177	21 of 144	$26,430	99%	99%	98%	6	76	82
Ivory Coast	163 of 177	132 of 144	$1,520	49%	60%	38%	97	42	41
Jamaica	79 of 177	62 of 144	$3,980	88%	84%	91%	13	74	78
Japan	9 of 177	12 of 144	$26,940	99%	99%	99%	3	78	85
Jordan	90 of 177	76 of 144	$4,220	91%	96%	86%	18	70	72
Kazakstan	78 of 177	63 of 144	$5,870	99%	99%	99%	31	61	72
Kenya	148 of 177	114 of 144	$1,020	85%	90%	79%	63	44	46
Kiribati	NA	NA	$800	80%	80%	80%	50	58	64
Kuwait	44 of 177	42 of 144	$16,240	83%	85%	81%	10	75	79
Kyrgyzstan	110 of 177	NA	$1,620	98%	99%	96%	37	65	72
Laos	135 of 177	107 of 144	$1,720	67%	77%	56%	87	53	56
Latvia	50 of 177	45 of 144	$9,210	99%	99%	99%	10	65	76

*UN Development Programme, Human Development Report
**U.S. Dollars

Development Data

Nation or Territory	Human Dev. Index Rank*	HDI Adjusted for Women*	Real GDP per Capita**	Adult Literacy	Literacy (Male)	Literacy (Female)	Infant Mortality (per 1,000 births)	Life Expectancy (Male)	Life Expectancy (Female)
Lebanon	80 of 177	64 of 144	$4,360	87%	92%	81%	25	72	75
Lesotho	145 of 177	117 of 144	$2,420	82%	74%	90%	85	33	39
Libya	58 of 177	NA	$7,570	82%	92%	71%	26	71	75
Liechtenstein	NA	NA	$25,000	99%	99%	99%	5	76	83
Lithuania	41 of 177	37 of 144	$10,320	99%	99%	99%	7	67	78
Luxembourg	15 of 177	16 of 144	$61,190	99%	99%	99%	5	75	81
Macedonia	60 of 177	NA	$6,470	96%	97%	94%	12	71	76
Madagascar	150 of 177	121 of 144	$740	68%	74%	61%	79	52	55
Malawi	165 of 177	134 of 144	$580	63%	76%	49%	104	38	38
Malaysia	59 of 177	52 of 144	$9,120	89%	92%	85%	18	71	76
Mali	174 of 177	142 of 144	$930	20%	27%	12%	118	48	49
Malta	31 of 177	31 of 144	$17,640	93%	92%	93%	4	76	81
Marshall Islands	NA	NA	$1,600	94%	94%	94%	31	68	72
Mauritania	152 of 177	124 of 144	$2,220	42%	52%	31%	72	51	54
Mauritius	64 of 177	55 of 144	$10,810	85%	88%	81%	16	68	76
Mexico	53 of 177	50 of 144	$8,970	91%	93%	89%	22	70	76
Micronesia	NA	NA	$2,000	90%	91%	88%	31	68	71
Moldova	113 of 177	91 of 144	$1,470	99%	99%	99%	40	65	72
Mongolia	117 of 177	94 of 144	$1,710	98%	98%	98%	56	62	66
Montserrat	NA	NA	$3,400	97%	97%	97%	8	76	81
Morocco	125 of 177	100 of 144	$3,810	51%	63%	38%	43	67	70
Mozambique	171 of 177	139 of 144	$1,050	47%	62%	31%	137	37	40
Myanmar	132 of 177	NA	$1,027	85%	89%	81%	69	55	60
Namibia	126 of 177	101 of 144	$6,210	84%	84%	83%	70	44	47
Nepal	140 of 177	116 of 144	$1,370	44%	62%	26%	69	60	59
Netherlands	5 of 177	5 of 144	$29,100	99%	99%	99%	5	76	81
New Zealand	18 of 177	18 of 144	$21,740	99%	99%	99%	6	76	81
Nicaragua	118 of 177	97 of 144	$2,470	77%	77%	77%	30	67	72
Niger	176 of 177	144 of 144	$800	17%	25%	9%	123	46	46
Nigeria	151 of 177	122 of 144	$860	67%	74%	59%	70	51	52
Niue	NA	NA	$3,600	95%	95%	95%	29	69	71
North Korea	NA	NA	$1,300	99%	99%	99%	25	61	66
Northern Ireland	12 of 177	9 of 144	$26,150	99%	99%	99%	5	76	81
Norway	1 of 177	1 of 144	$36,600	99%	99%	99%	4	76	82
Oman	74 of 177	68 of 144	$13,340	74%	82%	65%	20	71	74
Pakistan	142 of 177	120 of 144	$1,940	41%	53%	29%	74	61	61
Panama	61 of 177	53 of 144	$6,170	93%	93%	92%	21	72	77
Papua New Guinea	133 of 177	106 of 144	$2,270	65%	71%	58%	53	57	59
Paraguay	89 of 177	75 of 144	$4,610	92%	93%	90%	27	69	73
Peru	85 of 177	74 of 144	$5,010	86%	91%	80%	33	67	72
Philippines	83 of 177	66 of 144	$4,170	93%	93%	93%	24	68	72
Poland	37 of 177	34 of 144	$10,560	99%	99%	99%	9	70	78
Portugal	26 of 177	24 of 144	$18,280	93%	95%	90%	5	73	80
Puerto Rico	NA	NA	$16,800	94%	94%	94%	8	73	82
Qatar	47 of 177	NA	$19,844	84%	85%	82%	19	70	75

*UN Development Programme, Human Development Report
**U.S. Dollars

Development Data

Nation or Territory	Human Dev. Index Rank*	HDI Adjusted for Women*	Real GDP per Capita**	Adult Literacy	Literacy (Male)	Literacy (Female)	Infant Mortality (per 1,000 births)	Life Expectancy (Male)	Life Expectancy (Female)
Romania	69 of 177	56 of 144	$6,560	97%	98%	96%	27	67	74
Russia	57 of 177	49 of 144	$8,230	99%	99%	99%	17	61	73
Rwanda	159 of 177	129 of 144	$1,270	69%	75%	63%	102	38	39
Saint Kitts and Nevis	39 of 177	NA	$12,420	98%	NA	NA	15	69	75
Saint Lucia	71 of 177	NA	$5,300	95%	NA	NA	14	71	74
Saint Vincent & the Gr.	87 of 177	NA	$5,460	83%	NA	NA	14	73	76
Samoa	75 of 177	NA	$5,600	99%	99%	98%	29	67	73
Saudi Arabia	77 of 177	72 of 144	$12,650	77%	84%	70%	14	71	74
Scotland	12 of 177	9 of 144	$26,150	99%	99%	99%	5	76	81
Senegal	157 of 177	128 of 144	$1,580	40%	49%	30%	57	51	55
Serbia and Montenegro	NA	NA	$2,200	93%	97%	89%	13	72	77
Sierra Leone	177 of 177	NA	$500	32%	45%	18%	145	33	36
Singapore	25 of 177	28 of 144	$24,040	93%	97%	89%	4	76	80
Slovakia	42 of 177	37 of 144	$12,840	99%	99%	99%	8	70	78
Slovenia	27 of 177	27 of 144	$18,540	99%	99%	99%	5	73	80
Solomon Islands	124 of 177	NA	$1,590	62%	68%	56%	22	68	71
Somalia	NA	NA	$500	38%	50%	26%	119	46	49
South Africa	119 of 177	96 of 144	$10,070	86%	87%	85%	62	46	52
South Korea	28 of 177	29 of 144	$16,950	98%	99%	97%	7	72	79
Spain	20 of 177	20 of 144	$21,460	98%	99%	97%	4	76	83
Sri Lanka	96 of 177	73 of 144	$3,570	93%	95%	90%	15	70	76
Sudan	139 of 177	115 of 144	$1,820	60%	71%	49%	64	54	57
Suriname	67 of 177	NA	$6,590	93%	95%	91%	24	68	74
Swaziland	137 of 177	109 of 144	$4,550	81%	82%	80%	68	34	37
Sweden	2 of 177	2 of 144	$26,050	99%	99%	99%	3	78	83
Switzerland	11 of 177	11 of 144	$30,010	99%	99%	99%	4	76	82
Syria	106 of 177	88 of 144	$3,620	83%	91%	74%	31	71	73
Taiwan	NA	NA	$23,400	95%	98%	92%	7	74	80
Tajikistan	116 of 177	93 of 144	$980	99%	99%	99%	112	66	71
Tanzania	162 of 177	131 of 144	$580	77%	85%	69%	102	43	44
Thailand	76 of 177	61 of 144	$7,010	93%	95%	91%	21	65	73
Togo	143 of 177	119 of 144	$1,480	60%	74%	45%	68	48	51
Tonga	63 of 177	NA	$6,850	99%	99%	99%	13	68	69
Trinidad and Tobago	54 of 177	47 of 144	$9,430	99%	99%	98%	25	69	75
Tunisia	92 of 177	77 of 144	$6,760	73%	83%	63%	26	71	75
Turkey	88 of 177	70 of 144	$6,390	87%	94%	79%	43	68	73
Turkmenistan	86 of 177	67 of 144	$4,300	99%	99%	98%	73	64	70
Tuvalu	NA	NA	$1,100	96%	96%	96%	21	65	70
Uganda	146 of 177	113 of 144	$1,390	69%	79%	59%	86	45	46
Ukraine	70 of 177	57 of 144	$4,870	99%	99%	99%	21	65	75
United Arab Emirates	49 of 177	NA	$22,420	79%	76%	81%	15	73	77
United States	8 of 177	8 of 144	$35,750	99%	99%	99%	7	74	80
Uruguay	46 of 177	41 of 144	$7,830	98%	97%	98%	12	72	79
U.S. Virgin Islands	NA	NA	$17,200	90%	NA	NA	8	75	83
Uzbekistan	107 of 177	85 of 144	$1,670	99%	99%	99%	71	67	72

*UN Development Programme, Human Development Report
**U.S. Dollars

Development Data

Nation or Territory	Human Dev. Index Rank*	HDI Adjusted for Women*	Real GDP per Capita**	Adult Literacy	Literacy (Male)	Literacy (Female)	Infant Mortality (per 1,000 births)	Life Expectancy (Male)	Life Expectancy (Female)
Venezuela	68 of 177	58 of 144	$5,380	94%	94%	93%	23	71	77
Vietnam	112 of 177	87 of 144	$2,300	91%	94%	87%	30	67	71
Wales	12 of 177	9 of 144	$26,150	99%	99%	99%	5	76	81
West Bank and Gaza	102 of 177	NA	$750	81%	89%	72%	22	71	74
Yemen	149 of 177	126 of 144	$870	50%	70%	29%	63	59	61
Zambia	164 of 177	133 of 144	$840	80%	86%	74%	98	33	33
Zimbabwe	147 of 177	118 of 144	$2,400	90%	94%	86%	67	34	34

*UN Development Programme, Human Development Report
**U.S. Dollars

Concepts and Terminology

The following is a list of some common concepts found in CultureGrams™. These are not necessarily definitions; they are explanations of how the terms are used in the series, what significance they hold in regard to understanding cultures, and often how they are calculated. For explanations of international organizations (United Nations, European Union, and others), please refer to reference sources in a library.

Cash Crops. A cash crop is an agricultural product that is grown for sale, not for the farmer's consumption. It is often a crop (coffee, cotton, sugarcane, rice and other grains) that requires manufacturing or processing. It may also be a crop (oranges, potatoes, bananas) that can be consumed upon harvest but is cultivated primarily to be sold. Cash crops are produced most effectively on a large scale, but they can be grown on small plots of land. When grown on a large scale, the crops are more likely to be exported than consumed locally, although small growers in developing countries may sell to a local buyer who then sells larger quantities domestically and abroad. The economies of many countries depend heavily on the sale of cash crops.

Diversified Economy. An economy is considered diversified if its stability relies on a variety of industries rather than one or two commodities. For example, oil-rich countries that rely almost solely on the petroleum industry for their income are vulnerable to changes in the price of oil on the world market. When the price drops significantly, the countries are suddenly unable to pay debts or finance social development projects. The same is true for countries that rely on agricultural products such as coffee or on minerals such as copper for their income. Countries whose economies are based not only on agricultural products but also manufacturing, services, technology, and so forth are better able to withstand global price changes. Thus, the more diversified a country's economic base, the better.

Foreign Language Phrases. Most CultureGrams contain phrases and words in the target culture's official or common language. In general, CultureGrams do not provide a pronunciation guide for these phrases, due to limited space. Also, including pronunciation and a translation tends to interrupt the flow of the text. CultureGrams are not designed to teach foreign languages. Rather, the phrases contained in CultureGrams are there to facilitate the description of how people interact with one another. Their translation often provides insights about the culture, but pronunciation is not necessary to gain that insight. In the few cases where pronunciation hints are provided, they are necessary for English speakers to properly pronounce a word. For instance, the country Lesotho is not pronounced as it would seem. Instead of saying "le-SO-tho," one should say "le-SUE-too."

Free and Compulsory Education. Most countries provide free education to their citizens, meaning the government operates a public school system open to all children who are in a certain age group. It does not necessarily mean there are no costs involved in attending school. Students may be required to wear uniforms (which must be purchased), might live far from the nearest school (and transportation must be paid for), or may need to supply their own books, pencils, and other basic items. In addition, having a child in school can cost a rural family one laborer on the family farm. This can become such a burden to poorer families that free education is still not accessible to them.

Compulsory education refers to the fact that the law requires children to attend school for a certain number of years. In many countries this rule is seldom enforced. Therefore, it may reflect the government's target for how long children should remain in school to obtain a basic education rather than how long they actually are required to attend. Compulsory education usually encompasses six to nine years, and optional schooling usually continues for three or more years.

Gross Domestic Product (GDP) Per Capita. This economic statistic refers to the value of all goods and services produced annually in an economy per person. Naturally, not every person produces goods and services, but the total is averaged for the entire population. If the term is expressed as "gross national product" (GNP), it is essentially the same statistic except for the addition of income earned abroad minus the income earned in the country by noncitizens. This is significant when part of the population works in other countries and sends back money to their families. It is also significant for countries that have substantial investments abroad. For most countries, the two statistics, GDP and GNP, are almost interchangeable.

In the past, GDP was calculated in terms of the U.S. dollar after conversion from the local currency at official exchange rates. This caused accuracy problems because of artificially set exchange rates and because a dollar may not buy the same amount of goods in the United States as it does in another country. Social scientists recently have developed the concept of Purchasing Power Parity (PPP), a measurement that tries to account for the inconsistencies of the past. When GDP is figured in terms of PPP, an international dollar not affected by exchange rates is used. Likewise, PPP attempts to express the relative ability of a person to purchase goods with the local currency. Therefore, measured with PPP, five hundred dollars will buy essentially the same things in the United States as it will in Brazil or Japan. For many countries, PPP data does not yet exist, and only estimates are available for others.

Most CultureGrams use PPP with GDP, as expressed by the phrase "real gross domestic product." When the word "real" is absent, only the GDP has been calculated. The real GDPs in CultureGrams usually are taken from the *Human Development Report* (New York: Oxford University Press). In cases where the real GDP is low (less than one thousand dollars, for example), one can assume that people have very little disposable income. But one should also remember that rural families may grow their own food and therefore need less disposable income

Concepts and Terminology

to meet basic needs. In other cases, such a low figure indicates people indeed may be without food, shelter, clothing, or other necessities.

Hard Currency. Many countries have currencies that are not acceptable as currency for international purchases or exchanges. These currencies are considered inconvertible (not a medium of exchange) outside of their sponsoring nation. Such countries must pay for imports with a convertible currency that is accepted as a medium of exchange among countries. A convertible currency often is called hard currency because it is worth something outside its own borders. The U.S. dollar, Japanese yen, British pound, European Union euro, and a few others are global hard currencies. The currencies of most advanced economies are also convertible. Regional hard currencies also exist, such as the *CFA franc*, a currency used in many West African nations (former French colonies) as both a domestic and regional exchange currency. However, the *CFA franc* would not be accepted as a global hard currency. Developing countries without convertible currencies use hard currencies to import goods and services. They obtain hard currency through their goods and services exports, their expatriate workers, tourism, and international lending or aid.

Human Development and Gender-Related Development Indexes. Originating with the United Nations Development Programme (UNDP), the human development index (HDI) and gender-related development index (GDI) attempt to compensate for the inability of traditional economic indicators to portray accurately the environment in which people live—whether that environment nurtures personal development or hinders it. The project functions under the assumption that human development is a process of "expanding [people's] choices to live full, creative lives with freedom and dignity." (UNDP 2003, 28). The three essential capabilities that people must have in order to expand their choices are "living a long and healthy life, being educated and having a decent standard of living." (UNDP 2003, 2). Accordingly, the basis of the HDI is statistics related to infant mortality, life expectancy, literacy, and real GDP. If people have access to adequate education, health care, and wages, they are more likely to be involved in community affairs, join the middle class, and contribute skills and time to society. Such societies are more often democratic and respectful of human rights.

Each country is ranked in relation to the others according to an index value that falls between 0 and 1. The HDI "shows how far a country has to travel to provide . . . essential choices to all its people. It is not a measure of well-being. Nor is it a measure of happiness. Instead, it is a measure of empowerment" (UNDP 1995, 12). The GDI measures progress in the same way as the HDI, but it is adjusted to account for inequality between men and women. It is common for men to have access more quickly than women to the same basic resources and choices. Only 144 nations have been ranked for the GDI, whereas 175 have been listed for the HDI. Each CultureGram for which HDI and GDI data are available lists the country's rank. For more detailed analysis and additional data, refer to the entire *Human Development Report*, which is updated annually.

Income Distribution. This phrase generally is used in connection with the gap between what the poorest people in a country earn and what the richest earn. If income distribution is highly unequal, a small wealthy class generally controls the economy (and often the government) and owns most property. The much larger poor class is often landless, which is significant since the people are probably farmers who must rent property and receive only a small share of the benefits from their labor. An unequal, but not highly unequal, income distribution often indicates that a middle class is beginning to grow. When the distribution is fairly equal, as is the case in a minority of countries, it is due mostly to a large and prosperous middle class. However, it also can indicate the presence of a broad poor class and absence of a wealthy elite. Generally, having a highly unequal income distribution means the economy is unhealthy, whereas the existence of a strong middle (consumer) class is good for an economy.

Infant Mortality Rate. This statistic is expressed as the number of children per 1,000 live births who die before their first birthday. It is an important indicator of the overall health of a population, since infants who die at this age usually are subject to preventable diseases or birth defects related to the mother's health. Those who die at birth often do so because of a lack of prenatal care and medical attention at birth. People who have access to health care, clean water, nutritious food, and education are more likely to have a low infant mortality rate than people without such access. Industrialized countries generally have a low rate (fewer than 10 per 1,000), while developing countries usually have a higher rate (averaging more than 30). The poorest countries may have rates exceeding 100.

Life Expectancy. This measurement refers to how long a person can expect to live from birth if mortality patterns remain unchanged. Someone born today may be expected to live 80 years if living in some European countries but only 58 years if living in parts of Africa. However, since mortality patterns do change throughout a person's lifetime, the statistic is really a better reflection of how long an adult who is currently living can expect to live. So a person who is 50 today can expect to live until 80 in some countries or only a few more years in others. Women live longer than men in most countries, and people in industrialized countries live longer than those in developing countries. People in countries with high pollution have lower rates of life expectancy.

When a CultureGram lists only one average age, it is the average of the male and female averages. This statistic, like infant mortality, helps the reader understand the overall health of a population and whether the people have access to nutritious food, clean water, health care, and proper sanitation.

Literacy Rate. CultureGrams list a literacy rate for the general adult population. These data usually are taken from the *Human Development Report*, which defines adult literacy as "The percentage of people aged 15 and above who can, with understanding, both read and write a short, simple statement related to their everyday life" (UNDP 2003, 354). This is the global standard for reporting literacy, although a few countries will certify persons literate if they can write their name or if they have ever been enrolled in school. Most educational experts agree that such definitions are misleading, since being able to write a name or a short sentence does not imply a person can understand such things as a ballot, a newspaper, or work instructions. Were it possible to report functional literacy, many countries would have far lower literacy rates than are presented. But no uniform standard exists for reporting functional literacy. Therefore, readers should keep in mind that an official literacy rate is only one indicator of a nation's overall educational level.

On the other hand, many developing countries report their literacy rates based on an official language that a majority or significant group of people does not even speak, let alone read. In these cases, people may be functional in a local language or an oral language but not functional in the "official" language. Although one cannot read and write an oral language, one can use it to recount history, calculate numbers, share information, relate instructions, and so on. In some areas, the ability to read may not be considered a necessary life skill. In other words, one cannot equate intelligence or skill with literacy.

Population and Population Growth Rate. The figure for population listed in each CultureGram is an estimate for the year previous to publication (i.e., 2003 population for text published in 2004). The estimate is based on the actual population at the last census, multiplied by an annual growth rate. The estimate may seem to conflict with other sources, since other sources often only print the population as of the latest census (whenever it may have been taken) or an estimate made in a base year (e.g., 2000).

CultureGrams estimates are in keeping with figures in U.S. government and UN publications, but they sometimes are modified by information from the target culture's government. Each population estimate is revised annually.

The population growth rate is an estimate based on the previous year's difference between births and deaths and the net number of migrants leaving or entering the country. The growth rate may change substantially in a single year if there is a large influx of immigrants, a massive emigration, a natural disaster, or an epidemic. Growth rates tend to be low in industrialized countries because families are small, averaging one or two children. Growth rates are generally high in developing countries, especially in areas where subsistence farming is the primary economic activity. These cultures require large families to help farm the land, but they often have a high infant mortality rate; many children are conceived to ensure that enough will survive into adulthood. In small nations, the growth rate may be low due to emigration, as people must go elsewhere to find work.

Poverty. Poverty is noted in CultureGrams in two ways. Sometimes poverty is described in general terms to indicate a low standard of living according to various governmental or societal criteria. Other references to poverty (those marked by an asterisk) are based on the Human Poverty Index (HPI) from the *Human Development Report 2003*. The HPI measures deprivation in three main areas—"a long and healthy life, knowledge and a decent standard of living" (UNDP 2003, 353). These figures, expressed sometimes as percentages and sometimes as fractions, indicate what portion of a population not only lives in poverty but also lacks access to adequate education, health care, safe water, and economic opportunity to escape the poverty they face.

Staple Food. Staple foods are those foods that supply the majority of the average person's calories and nutrition. A people's primary staple food is usually starchy, such as cassava (manioc), corn, rice, millet, or wheat. Staple foods also include any meats, fruits, and vegetables eaten frequently or in large quantities.

Subsistence Farming. Subsistence farming refers to farming as the main source of a family's livelihood. That is, a family will grow its own food, raise its own livestock, build its own home, and often make its own clothing. Members of such a family generally do not earn a wage by working at a job, but they usually are not entirely without a cash income. Family members might sell surplus produce or livestock, or make crafts or other items (blankets, baskets, etc.), in order to buy things they cannot provide for themselves. These usually include items such as sugar, cooking oil, clothing, rice or another staple food, and so forth. Subsistence farmers also may set aside part of their land to grow cash crops in order to earn money. Subsistence farmers generally do not grow an abundance of anything. They often live on small owned or rented plots of land, and they seldom enjoy the luxuries of running water or electricity.

Underemployment. Underemployment refers to when workers are not officially unemployed but either are unable to find enough work in their profession or are working in jobs below their skill level. For example, if a country's universities graduate many people in engineering or other professional fields but the economy is not diversified or well developed, those people may find themselves underemployed, working in jobs that do not take advantage of their skills, or only working part-time in their field of study. In the latter case, they may return to farming or local retailing. In too many cases, the most educated people simply emigrate to another country to find work, resulting in what is called a "brain drain."

Government unemployment figures generally do not include underemployment; it must be estimated. However, when unemployment is high (more than 10 percent), one usually can assume that underemployment affects at least as many or more workers. This condition reflects an economy that is not growing, and it can lead to social unrest. High underemployment (more than 40 percent) often leads to political turmoil and violence. Employing and paying people according to their skill level helps secure social stability and encourage economic growth.

Western/Western-style. This term usually refers to the dress, eating customs, culture, and traditions of Western Europe, the United States, and Canada. This culture often is referred to as Western because of its common ancient (primarily Greek and Roman) philosophical, legal, political, and social heritage. The term Western can also refer to cultures that have a Judeo-Christian value system and religious orientation.

Glossary of Cultural Terms

This glossary lists key cultural terms used in CultureGrams™ texts. The text a term appears in (usually a specific country) follows in parentheses after the entry. However, since neither CultureGrams texts nor our glossary is intended to provide exhaustive information, note that the term might apply to other countries not listed. The spellings used are those given by our native writers and reviewers.

Aaaaall-right. "How are you?" (Trinidad and Tobago).
Aam. "Uncle." An Arabic term of address for an older man. (Syria).
Aamaa. The Nepali word for "grandmother." (Bhutan).
Aba. "The land" or "people of the land." (Kiribati). *See also* **Mane, Maneaba(s).**
Ab'a. (United Arab Emirates). *See* **Abaya.**
'Aba. A light wool cloak worn by laborers and village men. (Iraq).
Abaa. A hut made of bamboo and palm leaves where elderly men socialize and work on crafts. (Equatorial Guinea).
Abaaya. (Saudi Arabia). *See* **Abaya.**
Abambo. (Malawi). *See* **Bambo.**
Abaya. [NOTE: Spelling varies because it is a transliteration of Arabic.] A full-length black robe worn by women over their clothing. (Bahrain, Kuwait, Oman, Qatar).
'Abayah. (Iraq). *See* **Abaya.**
Abeer. A red liquid. Used along with water and powder by the Indo-Guyanese during **Phagwah**. (Guyana).
Abendbrot. A light evening meal commonly consisting of open-faced sandwiches. (Germany).
Abendessen. An evening meal. (Austria).
Abi. A Turkish term for "brother." Used to address an older man. (Turkey).
A bientôt. "See you soon!" A common French parting phrase, less formal then **Au revoir**. (France).
Abitur. An exam taken at the end of **Gymnasium**. Passing the exam is required for admittance to university. (Germany).
Abla. "Sister." A term added to the end of an older woman's name. (Turkey).
Abrazo. A hug often given when greeting close friends and family members. Characteristics vary depending on the country. (Bolivia, Chile, Colombia, Honduras, Panama, Spain, Uruguay, Venezuela).
Abu. "Father of." An Arabic title combined with a child's name to show respect. (Afghanistan, Bahrain, Iraq, Jordan, United Arab Emirates, West Bank and Gaza).
A buen tiempo. "You've come at a good time." A Spanish phrase used to invite guests or passersby to join the ongoing meal. (Dominican Republic). *See also* **Buen provecho.**
Abu ghayib. "Awaiting father." A respectful term used to address a man without children. (Iraq). *See also* **Um ghayib.**
Académie française France's official authority on the French language. It tries to keep the language pure. (France).
Accara. Fried bean flour. Can be eaten for breakfast. (Gambia).

Achachila. God of the mountains, part of traditional beliefs. (Bolivia). *See also* **Ch'alla, Pachamama.**
Achar. Chutney. (Nepal).
Achoura. [NOTE: Muslim holidays are set according to the lunar calendar.] A Muslim religious holiday celebrated one month after **Aid al Adha**. (Algeria).
Ackee. A rich red fruit often eaten at breakfast. (Jamaica).
Adab. "Hello." A common Hindu greeting. (Bangladesh).
Äddi. "Good-bye." A casual Luxembourgish parting phrase. (Luxembourg). *See also* **Au revoir.**
Äddi, bis mar. "Until tomorrow." A common Luxembourgish parting phrase used among friends and acquaintances. (Luxembourg). *See also* **Bis eng aner Kéier, Bis härno.**
A de go. "I'm going." A common Krio parting phrase. (Sierra Leone).
Adeus. "Good-bye." A common parting phrase. (Portugal).
Adharma. A Hindi term for "darkness." (Mauritius). *See also* **Divali.**
Adijo. "Adieu." A common phrase used when parting or exiting a room or an elevator, even if one does not know the others present. (Slovenia).
Adió. (Paraguay). *See* **Adiós.**
Adiós. (1) "Good-bye." A common term used in partings. In a few countries, such as Venezuela, the term is rarely used because it implies a more permanent farewell. Used in Spanish-speaking countries.. (2) A quick greeting on the street or in the countryside. Used in Latin American Spanish-speaking countries..
Adji. A mathematical and probability game. (Benin).
Adjö. The more formal Swedish word for "Good-bye." (Sweden). *See also* **Hej då.**
Adlea. Civil code. (Qatar).
Adobo. A stew made of chicken and pork in garlic, soy sauce, and vinegar. (Philippines).
Aezor. Long pants worn by women under a traditional dress (**Curta**). (Tajikistan). *Also called* **Pajomah.**
A fair go. "A fair chance." A phrase expressing the value that Australians place on fairness. (Australia).
Afé al hamdulilah. "Fine, praise be to **Allah**." The appropriate response to **Kaif al hal?** (Chad).
Afghani. Afghanistan's national currency. (Afghanistan).
Afindrafindrao. Malagasy line dancing. One couple leads off dancing and the other couples follow like a train. (Madagascar).
Afio mai. "Welcome" or "Come in." A respectful greeting. (American Samoa, Samoa).
Afiyet Olsun. "May what you eat bring you well-being." A Turkish phrase used to begin or to end a meal. (Turkey).
A fon dagbe a? "Did you wake up well?" A common Fon greeting. (Benin).
Aga. This term is added to a male senior acquaintance's name to show respect. (Turkmenistan). *See also* **Kaka.**

Glossary of Cultural Terms

Agai. "Older brother." A Kyrgyz title used to address a man older than the speaker. (Kyrgyzstan).

Agal. (United Arab Emirates). See **Ogal**.

Agama Djawa. Literally, "Javanese religion." This belief centers on the world of spirits, which need to be appeased with food sacrifices (**Sadjèn**). (Suriname). See also **Slametan**.

Agay. The Dzongkha word for "grandfather." (Bhutan).

Agbada. A top worn by men at formal occasions. (Benin, Togo).

Agbogbo. The local god in Notsé. (Togo).

Agbogbozan. A rite in the Notsé region that celebrates people's escape from the reign of King Agokoli and honors the local god, **Agbogbo**. (Togo).

Agha. "Older brother." A Kazak term added to the end of a name to show respect to an older man. (Kazakstan).

Aglipayan. The Philippine Independent Church. (Philippines).

A-go. An expression a vistor calls out to announce one's presence before entering a door. (Ghana).

Agouti. Sugarcane rat, a special delicacy. (Benin).

Aguayo. A woven square cloth worn by Bolivian women for a variety of purposes, such as carrying babies on their backs. (Bolivia).

Aguinaldos. Traditional Christmas songs. (Venezuela). See also **Gaitas**.

Agyz Acar. A three-day holiday celebrating the end of **Ramadan**. (Turkmenistan). See also **Aid al Fitr**.

Ah dey. "I'm alright." A typical Grenadian creole response to the questions **W'happen dey?** or **Hows tings?** (Grenada). See also **Just cool**.

Ahiga. Community hall. (Tuvalu). Also called **Maneapa(s)**. See also **Fakaala**.

Ahimaa. A Tahitian word for "ground oven." (French Polynesia). Also called **Umu**.

Ahimsa. The Jain practice of reverence for life. Literally means "nonviolence." (India).

Ahlan Wasahlan. (Morocco). See **Ahlan wa sahlan**.

Ahlan wa sahlan. An expression of welcome. Used in Arabic-speaking countries..

Ahn-ahn-ahn. Said while a person shakes his or her head from left to right to indicate "no." (Madagascar). See also **Uhn-uhn**.

Ah-nar-deh. The reluctance to bring about a loss of face or to cause trouble or inconvenience. Roughly translated as "having consideration for others." Often described as a Myanmar national characteristic. (Myanmar).

Ahoj. "Hi" or "Good-bye." Used casually in greeting or parting. (Czech Republic, Slovakia).

Ah sey! "I say." A Krio phrase used to get someone's attention. (Sierra Leone).

Aht Chabysh. Long-distance races on horseback. (Kyrgyzstan).

Ahu. Coconut candy, a dessert. (Guam).

Aib. "Shame." If guests visit without prior arrangement, it is considered an offense or *aib* not to invite them in for refreshments. (United Arab Emirates).

'Aid al Adha. (Egypt, West Bank and Gaza). See **Eid al-Adha**.

Aid al Adha. (Algeria). See **Eid al-Adha**.

Aid al Fitr. [NOTE: Spelling varies because it is a transliteration of Arabic. Also, Muslim holidays are set according to the lunar calendar.] A two- or three-day feast at the end of **Ramadan**. Celebrated in Muslim-populated countries. (Algeria, Chad, Egypt, West Bank and Gaza). See also **Aid al Saghir**.

Aid al Kebir. [NOTE: Spelling varies because it is a transliteration of Arabic. Also, Muslim holidays are set according to the lunar calendar.] Feast of the Sacrifice. A Muslim holiday that commemorates Abraham's willingness to sacrifice his son. (Morocco). Also called **Eid al Adha**.

Aid al Saghir. [NOTE: Spelling varies because it is a transliteration of Arabic.] A two- or three-day feast at the end of **Ramadan**. (Morocco). Also called **Aid al Fitr**.

Aid-e-adha. (Iran). See **Eid al-Adha**.

Aid-e-fitr. (Iran). See **Aid al Fitr**.

Aid-e-khadir. [NOTE: Spelling varies because it is a transliteration of Arabic. Also, Muslim holidays are set according to the lunar calendar.] Celebrates Muhammad's choosing of Ali (his son-in-law) as his successor. This holiday is celebrated by Shi'ite Muslims. (Iran). See also **Shi'i**.

Aid el Adha. (Togo). See **Eid al-Adha**.

Aid el Fitr. (Togo). See **Aid al Fitr**.

Aid El Kebir. (Tunisia). See **Aid al Kebir**.

Aid El Seghir. (Tunisia). See **Aid al Saghir**.

Aiga. Extended family or kinship group. (American Samoa, Samoa).

Aii. "Elder brother." A Lao term used to address a male with no specific title. (Laos).

Airag. Fermented mare's milk. (Mongolia).

Aish. Bread. Literally, the Arabic word for "life." (Egypt).

Aisse. "Friend." Used to get the attention of a nearby person. (Malawi).

Aitys. Singing debate. Two people sing their arguments and rebuttals, accompanied by music from a **Dombra**. (Kazakstan).

Aiya. "Older brother." A Sinhala term of address for a close male friend or relative. (Sri Lanka).

Ajsino oro. A folk dance. (Albania).

Ajua. A traditional strategy game played with pebbles or seeds. (Kenya). Also called **Bao**.

Ajvar. A pepper and tomato spread that Macedonians make in early October and eat with bread. (Macedonia).

Aka. "Big brother." An Uzbek term used to address male strangers. (Uzbekistan).

Akam jirta? "How are you?" An Oromifaa greeting. (Ethiopia).

Akaryna. A traditional ceramic flute. (Belarus).

Akimbo. Placing one's hands on one's hips. Can show defiance, anger, or frustration. (Barbados).

Akory. "How are you?" A Malagasy greeting, popular in coastal areas. (Madagascar).

Akoumé. The Ewe word for a stiff porridge made of cornmeal and water and served with a spicy sauce of okra, spinach, and fish or meat. (Togo). Also called **Pâte**.

Aksakal. A "white-bearded" elder. (Turkmenistan).

Aksanti. "Thank you" in Swahili. (Congo).

Alaja. A woven camel-hair talisman. It is often tied to the steering wheel for good luck. (Turkmenistan).

Alambamento. A ceremony in which the prospective groom offers a bride-price to the bride's family and conditions of the marriage are discussed. (Angola).

Alaps. Lords. A position in the traditional social system that is now incorporated into the formal government. (Marshall Islands). See also **Irooj, Rijerbal**.

Al-ardah. A sword dance for men. This national dance is accompanied by drums and a poet who chants verses. (Saudi Arabia).

Glossary of Cultural Terms

Ala yeke senge? "Are you OK?" Part of a common Sango greeting, it usually follows the phrase **Bara ala** or **Bala mo** (Greetings to you!). (Central African Republic).

Alba-ca-Zapada. Snow White, the granddaughter of Santa Claus. (Moldova). *See also* **Mos Craciun.**

Al-Badiyah. The common name for the Syrian Desert. (Syria).

Albarka. An Arabic term that credits **Allah** for food. A host's reply to an appreciative guest. (Guinea).

Alcapurrias. Fried plantain dough with a meat filling. A locally prepared variety of **Frituras**. (Puerto Rico).

Alchiki. A game similar to marbles, but played with dried sheep bones. (Kazakstan).

Alendo ndi mame. "Visitors are like dew." A Chichewa proverb that means a visitor's presence is short-lived and hence precious. (Malawi).

Al-haj. (Jordan). *See* **Hadj.**

Al-hajjah. (Jordan). *See* **Hadjia.**

Al hamdo lellah. (Jordan). *See* **Al hamdu lillah.**

Al-hamdu lilah, bahi. Arabic phrase meaning "Praise to God, very well"; it is a common response to **Kayf halak?** (Libya).

Alhamdul'illah. (Comoros). *See* **Al hamdu lillah.**

Al hamdu lillah. [NOTE: Spelling varies because it is a transliteration of Arabic.] An Arabic phrase meaning "Praise be to God" or "Thanks be to God." Used by Arabic speakers. (United Arab Emirates).

Al-hamdu lillah, zein. "Praise to **Allah**, well." An Arabic response to the greeting **Kayf halak?** (Oman).

Alikalo. Village chief. Has local power and settles village disputes. (Gambia).

Aliki. Traditional chiefs. *Aliki* still play a significant role in influencing island events. (Tuvalu).

Alikum essalam. The usual response to the greeting **Assalam alikum**. (Bahrain).

Aling. (1) A Pilipino title for an unmarried woman. Added before her given name. (Philippines). (2) A Pilipino title added before an elderly woman's name. (Guam).

Al-Isra walmi'raj. [NOTE: Muslim holidays are set according to the lunar calendar.] A Muslim holiday celebrating the occasion of Muhammad's ascension to the sky. (United Arab Emirates).

Al-jil. Contemporary Egyptian pop music with a more-educated audience appeal. (Egypt). *See also* **Shaabi.**

Aljotta. Fish chowder. (Malta).

Allah. The Arabic word for "God." Used in countries with Muslims or Arabic speakers..

Allahaısmarladık. A parting phrase used to ask for blessings from **Allah**. (Turkey). *See also* **Güle güle.**

Allah akbar. "God is great." Used to call faithful Muslims to prayer five times a day. (Mauritania).

Allah ghalib. "God is stronger." An Arabic phrase used to express hopes or intentions. (Tunisia). *See also* **Inshallah.**

Al-lahjah Al-Ordoniah. The Jordanian dialect of Arabic. It is considered to be the closest to classical Arabic. (Jordan).

Alles goed? "Is everything all right?" A common Dutch greeting. (Netherlands).

Alloco. Fried plantains eaten as a snack food. (Ivory Coast).

Almacenes. A Spanish term for neighborhood shops. (Argentina). *See also* **Kioskos.**

Al-Mahdi. An Arabic word for "guide." (Sudan).

Al Mawlid. (Algeria). *See* **Mouloud.**

Al-Mawlid. (Egypt). *See* **Mouloud.**

Al-mizmar. A traditional dance that features the oboe-like *al-mizmar* instrument. (Saudi Arabia).

Almuerzo. The Spanish word for "lunch." (Cuba).

Al-nay. A simple bamboo pipe. (Libya).

Alo. "Hi." A colloquial greeting used among urban youth. Others include **Olá** and **Oi**. (Mozambique).

Aloalo. Tall wooden poles that decorate tombs with carved figurative images and depictions of past events. (Madagascar).

Aloha. A Hawaiian greeting. It has many meanings depending on usage. (United States of America).

Alpaca(s). An animal similiar to a llama. Its wool is used for textiles. (Peru).

Alright. A common informal greeting. (Antigua and Barbuda, Saint Lucia).

Alright alright. A common greeting, as if to bypass asking and responding to "How are you?" (Jamaica). *See also* **Whaapun?**

Al-Salaam 'Alaykum. (West Bank and Gaza). *See* **Assalaam alaikum.**

Al-salamu 'alaykum. (Iraq). *See* **Assalaam alaikum.**

Al Tarawiah. Special prayers offered during the Muslim holiday of **Ramadan**. (United Arab Emirates).

Alta velocidad. A high-speed train. (Spain).

Althingi. Iceland's national assembly, one of the world's oldest. (Iceland).

'Alu a. Literally "You go." A response to the parting phrase **Nofo a**. (Tonga).

'Am. (Iraq). *See* **Aam.**

Amakuru? "How's the news?" A phrase that usually follows the initial greeting **Muraho**, **Mwaramutse**, or **Mwiriwe**. (Rwanda).

Amala. Yam flour. Can be used to make a stiff porridge. (Benin). *Also called* **Loubo.**

Amarillo. "Traffic official" in Cuban Spanish. The literal Spanish meaning is "yellow." (Cuba).

Amca. "Uncle." A Turkish term of address for an older man. (Turkey).

Ami. "Uncle." A title used after a man's given name. (Azerbaijan).

Amiga. "Friend." A feminine term of address. (Guinea-Bissau, Panama). *See also* **Amigo.**

Amigo. "Friend." A masculine term of address. (Guinea-Bissau, Panama). *See also* **Amiga.**

Amin Aleikum Salaam. "Come in peace." A response to the phrase **Salaam Aleikum**. (Niger).

Amiwo. Corn flour. Used to make a stiff porridge. (Benin). *Also called* **Wo.**

Ammo. The Arabic word for a paternal uncle. (West Bank and Gaza).

Ampesi. Boiled yams, plantains, or other root crops with sauce. (Ghana).

Amshee afé. "Go in peace." An Arabic parting phrase. (Chad).

Amto. The Arabic word for a paternal aunt. (West Bank and Gaza).

Amzhad. A single-stringed instrument often used to accompany poetry. (Morocco). *Also called* **Ribab.**

Andriamanitra. A supreme being of Malagasy indigenous beliefs. (Madagascar). *Also called* **Zanahary.**

Anesaty. (Syria). *See* **Aneseh.**

Glossary of Cultural Terms

Aneseh. [NOTE: Spelling varies because it is a transliteration of Arabic.] "Miss." An Arabic title used with the last name. (West Bank and Gaza).

Angisa. A head scarf that accompanies the **Koto** dress. (Suriname).

Angkor Wat. A Khmer temple built in the 12th century. It is the world's largest religious building and a cherished national symbol. (Cambodia).

Angling. Fishing. (England).

Ang pow. A red envelope with money given on special occasions such as New Year's, weddings, etc. (Singapore).

Anh. "Brother." A Vietnamese term used to address a man the same age as one's brother. (Vietnam).

A ni sogoma. "Good morning." A common Dioula greeting. (Burkina Faso).

An moho. "On you no evil." A Soninke greeting. (Mauritania). *See also* **Jam.**

Annyong? [NOTE: Spelling varies because it is a transliteration of Korean.] "Are you at peace?" A common greeting among children. (South Korea). *See also* **Annyong haseyo?, Annyong hashimnikka?**

Annyong haseyo? [NOTE: Spelling varies because it is a transliteration of Korean.] "Are you at peace?" A common greeting between peers or to subordinates. (South Korea). *See also* **Annyong?, Annyong hashimnikka?**

Annyong hashimnikka? [NOTE: Spelling varies because it is a transliteration of Korean.] "Are you at peace?" A common greeting used to show respect to a social superior. (South Korea). *See also* **Annyong?, Annyong haseyo?**

Anong balita? "What's new?" A common Pilipino greeting used among friends. (Philippines). *See also* **Ayos ba tayo 'dyan?**

Antara. An assortment of vertically placed flutes tied together. Used to play traditional music. (Peru). *See also* **Charango, Quena.**

Anyong? (North Korea). *See* **Annyong?**

Anyonghaseyo? (North Korea). *See* **Annyong haseyo?**

Anyonghashimnikka? (North Korea). *See* **Annyong hashimnikka?**

Any time is Trini time. Refers to the fact that Trinidadians often arrive well after an event starts, and being late is not considered rude. (Trinidad and Tobago).

Ao dai. A long traditional dress with front and back panels worn by women over satin trousers on special occasions. (Vietnam).

Apa. "Older sister." A Bangla term used to address an older woman. Can be added as a suffix or used by itself. (Bangladesh).

Apa khabar? "How are you?" A common Malay greeting. (Malaysia).

Aparima. A slow hula performed by the bride for the groom at their wedding feast. (French Polynesia). *See also* **Tamaaraa.**

Api. A hot drink made of corn, spiced with sugar and cinnamon. (Bolivia).

Apinun. "Good afternoon." A common Melanesian Pidgin greeting for acquaintances. (Papua New Guinea).

Apinun kaikai. "Afternoon food." The Melanesian Pidgin word for dinner. (Papua New Guinea).

Aqal. A cord that holds a headscarf in place. (Iraq).

Arachide. Peanut sauce. (Togo).

Arahaba. "Hello." A common Malagasy greeting. (Madagascar).

Araijem. "See you later." A common Armenian parting phrase between friends. (Armenia).

Arak. A traditional strong liquor that is served with Middle Eastern foods, except among devout Muslims. (Lebanon).

Arback. Living ancestral spirits. Part of traditional Kyrgyz beliefs. (Kyrgyzstan).

Ardha. A traditional dance involving the use of the sword. Accompanied by drums and poetry reading. (Kuwait).

Ardin. A harp used to accompany vocalists in traditional musical performances. (Mauritania).

Arefa. [NOTE: Muslim holidays are set according to the lunar calendar.] Feast of the Sacrifice. A Muslim holiday that commemorates Abraham's willingness to sacrifice his son. (Ethiopia). *Also called* **Eid al-Adha.**

Arepa(s). A cornmeal pancake. (Colombia, Venezuela).

Arequipe. Caramel sauce. (Colombia).

Ariary. The national currency. (Madagascar). *See also* **Franc.**

Aright. A common Scottish greeting. (Scotland).

Armudi stakan. Small pear-shaped glasses used to serve tea. (Azerbaijan).

Arrivée de l'Evangile. Missionary Day. Celebrated on 5 March. (French Polynesia).

Arros negre. Rice with calamari ink. (Spain).

Arroz con gandules y pernil. Rice with pigeon peas and roasted pig. (Puerto Rico).

Arroz con menestra. Rice with spicy beans, barbecued beef, and refried plantains. (Ecuador).

Arroz con pollo. Rice with chicken. (Colombia, Costa Rica, Ecuador, Panama, Puerto Rico).

Arroz de coco. Rice pudding with coconut and rum. (Colombia).

Arroz y frijoles. Rice and beans. A traditional staple food. (Cuba).

Asado. (1) A Spanish term for barbecue, a popular social event. (Argentina, Paraguay, Uruguay). (2) A Spanish term for grilled beef. (Uruguay).

Asalaam alaikum. (Comoros). *See* **Assalaam alaikum.**

Asalaam alaykum. (Syria). *See* **Assalaam alaikum.**

Asalaamu aleikum. (Somalia). *See* **Assalaam alaikum.**

Asalaha Bucha. An important Buddhist holiday. Set according to the lunar calendar. (Thailand).

Asamblea General. Uruguay's General Assembly. It consists of two houses: a 30-seat Chamber of Senators and a 99-seat Chamber of Representatives. (Uruguay).

Asante. Swahili for "Thank you." An adopted form. (Tanzania).

Aseeda. A thick porridge. (Sudan).

Ashak. A pasta dish. (Afghanistan).

Ashi. (1) "So long." A common parting phrase. (Bangladesh). (2) Female royalty. (Bhutan).

Ashugh. (Armenia). *See* **Ashugs.**

Ashugs. Poet-singers. (Azerbaijan).

Ashura. [NOTE: Spelling varies because it is a transliteration of Arabic. Also, Muslim holidays are set according to the lunar calendar.] A holiday during which Shi'ite Muslims reenact the suffering of the martyr Hussain, the grandson of Muhammad. (Afghanistan, Iraq, Syria). *See also* **Shi'i.**

Assalaam alaikum. [NOTE: Spelling varies because it is a transliteration of Arabic.] "May peace be upon you." A common greeting. It is usually answered with **Waalaikum assalaam**. Used in countries with large or predominantly Muslim populations..

Glossary of Cultural Terms

As-salaam aleikum. (Oman). *See* **Assalaam alaikum.**
Assalaam alikum. (United Arab Emirates). *See* **Assalaam alaikum.**
Assalaamu alaikum. (Bangladesh). *See* **Assalaam alaikum.**
As-Salaamu 'Alaykum. (Saudi Arabia). *See* **Assalaam alaikum.**
As-Salaamu Alaykum. (Kuwait, Qatar). *See* **Assalaam alaikum.**
Assalaamu alaykum. (Yemen). *See* **Assalaam alaikum.**
Assalama Allekuhm. (Tunisia). *See* **Assalaam alaikum.**
Assalam Alaikum. (Jordan, Singapore). *See* **Assalaam alaikum.**
Assalam alikum. (Bahrain). *See* **Assalaam alaikum.**
Assalam Oualaikoum. (Morocco). *See* **Assalaam alaikum.**
Assalamu alaikum. (Indonesia). *See* **Assalaam alaikum.**
Assalamu alikum. Arabic greeting meaning "I offer you peace." (Libya).
Assemblée Nationale. The French term for National Assembly. (Gabon, Senegal).
Assembleia Nacional. The National Assembly. (Angola).
Ass'lama. An Arabic term for "Hello." (Tunisia).
Assura. (Bahrain, Kuwait). *See* **Ashura.**
Atangas. A violet, bitter fruit about the size of a golf ball. (Gabon).
A tel God tanki. "I give thanks to God." A Krio response to the greeting **Ow di bodi?** (Sierra Leone).
Até logo. "See you soon." A common parting phrase. (Brazil).
Atenteban. A wooden flute. (Ghana).
Athletics. Track-and-field. (Grenada, Jamaica, New Zealand).
Atlas. Colorful patterned silk. (Uzbekistan).
Attan. Originally a Pashtun dance, now common throughout Afghanistan. Performed at feasts and other celebrations. (Afghanistan).
Attaya. Green tea with sugar. (Gambia).
Auf Wiedersehen. "Until we meet again." A common German phrase. (Switzerland).
Aunt(ie). A term a younger person uses to address an older woman, even if they are not related. (Barbados, Gambia, Ghana, Guam, Guyana, Saint Kitts and Nevis, Saint Lucia, Sierra Leone, Uganda). *See also* **Uncle.**
Au revoir. "Good-bye." A common French parting term. (Canada, France, Luxembourg).
Aurora borealis. The northern lights. (Norway).
Ausgleich. A compromise that led to the establishment of a dual monarchy with Hungary. (Austria).
Aussies. Australians. (Australia).
Autobahn. Expressway or freeway. (Germany, Liechtenstein).
Autogare. A central gathering point in each city for "bush-taxis." (Niger). *See also* **Taxis de brousse.**
Autonomie Interne. A holiday that celebrates Tahitian self-rule. Celebrated on 29 June. (French Polynesia).
Avo tata. A wraparound cloth worn by women. The term is used in the south. In the north the terms used are **Bsawao** or **Sata**. (Togo).
Awa in Majel. Marshallese time. A concept that interpersonal relations are more important than time. Meetings and appointments begin when they start and not always at a specific hour. (Marshall Islands).
Aw lafia. "Go in peace." A Sara parting phase. (Chad).
Ayatollah. (Iran). *See also* **Shi'i.**

Ayaz Ata. The Kazak name for Grandfather Frost. At the beginning of a new year, he delivers gifts to children. (Kazakstan). *See also* **Dyed Morosz, Zhanga Zhyl.**
Aye. (1) "Yes." (Scotland). (2) An expression of surprise or shock. One can also say **Mama**. (Central African Republic).
Ayendi, ki kati? "I'm fine, what's up?" A Luganda response to the greeting **Ki kati?** (Uganda).
A'y go. "It goes." A Sranan Tongo response to a greeting such as **Fa waka?**, **Fa'y tan?**, or **Fa'y go?** (Suriname).
Aynalayin. "Darling." Often used by elderly Kazaks to call to children. (Kazakstan).
Ayos ba tayo 'dyan? "Is everything all right?" A common Pilipino greeting used among friends. (Philippines). *See also* **Anong balita?**
Ayubowan. "May you be blessed with the gift of a long life." A Sinhalese phrase that accompanies the traditional greeting of placing one's palms together in front of the chest and bowing the head slightly. (Sri Lanka).
Ayurvedic. Traditional medicine that stresses the use of herbs and natural cures. (Sri Lanka).
Ayyalah. A popular traditional dance in which the dancers reenact a battle scene. (United Arab Emirates).
Azmaris. Traveling singers. (Ethiopia).
Azulejo(s). Glazed tile widely used to decorate the floors, walls, and facades of buildings. (Portugal).
Azumi. The Hausa word for **Ramadan**. (Niger).
Ba-. A prefix used when referring to more than one person. (Botswana). *See also* **Batswana, Mo-, Motswana.**
Baba. (1) "Father." An Arabic term of address used by children. (Qatar). (2) "Father." A Sango and Zulu term of address for older males. (Central African Republic, South Africa).
Babai. A taro-like, starchy root crop. (Kiribati).
Babban sallah. [NOTE: Muslim holidays are set according to the lunar calendar.] "Big feast." A Muslim holiday that commemorates Abraham's willingness to sacrifice his son. Celebrated 40 days after the **Ramadan** feast. (Niger). *Also called* **Tabaski.** *See also* **Eid al-Adha.**
Babe. A social title added to an adult male's name to show respect. Pronounced "BAH-bay." (Swaziland).
Babi-taxis. Three-wheeled motor scooters. (Bangladesh).
Babu. Lying down to converse and propping one's head with a large stone, coconut, or windowsill. (Marshall Islands).
Baby fathers. Men who have several children by different women. (Jamaica).
Baby mothers. Women who have children by different men. (Jamaica, Saint Lucia).
Bac. (1) The baccalaureate exam that is taken at the end of 13 years of education. (Gabon). (2) "Uncle." A term used to address a man the age of one's father. (Vietnam).
Bacalao. Dried fish, usually cod. (Dominican Republic).
Bacalao con viandas. Boiled cod with cassava and potatoes. (Puerto Rico).
Bacalhau. Codfish, usually dried and salted. (Portugal).
Baccalaureat. A certificate of completion that Ivorian students receive after successfully completing seven years of secondary school. After receiving the certificate, students may then attend university, train to be a teacher, or learn a trade. (Ivory Coast).
Bachata. A popular folk dance accompanied by accordions, drums, horns, and **Guayano(s)**. (Dominican Republic).

Glossary of Cultural Terms

Bachillerato. Three years of education that prepare students for college. (El Salvador).

Backhendl. Fried, breaded chicken. (Austria).

Bac si. "Doctor." A Vietnamese title. (Vietnam).

Bad eye. Staring someone in the eye. The gesture is used to display anger. (Saint Vincent and the Grenadines).

Badjan. Minibus used in Ivory Coast. (Ivory Coast). *See also* **Dyna, Gbaka.**

Bagaimana kabarnya? "How is your news?" A common verbal greeting. (Indonesia).

Baganda. Historically, the people of the Buganda Kingdom. Today, a person belonging to the Buganda ethnic group. (Uganda).

Baguettes. French bread. (Madagascar).

Bahala na. "Accept what comes and bear it with hope and patience." A common Pilipino expression. (Philippines).

Bahasa Indonesia. Indonesian, the official language. (Indonesia).

Bahasa Melayu. Malay, the official language. (Malaysia).

Bahini. "Younger sister." A Nepali term of address. (Bhutan, Nepal).

Bah kut teh. Chinese pork soup. (Malaysia).

Baho. Meat, vegetables, and plantains. (Nicaragua).

Baht. Thailand's national currency. (Thailand).

Bai. "Younger brother." A Nepali term of address. (Nepal).

Baiga. Traditional horseback competitions. (Kazakstan). *See also* **Kokpar.**

Baikay. "Older brother." A Kyrgyz title used to address a man older than the speaker. (Kyrgyzstan).

Baile de las tijeras. The term means "dance of the scissors," and includes both the dance and the music that accompanies it. The dance originated among the mountain people of Peru. (Peru).

Bairn. A Gaelic word meaning "baby." (Scotland).

Baisakh. The first month in the Nepali calendar **Bikram Samvat.** (Nepal).

Baisakhi. The New Year celebration in northern India. Also, the start of Punjab's harvest season. (India).

Baiza. A form of Omani currency. One thousand *baiza* equal one **Rial Omani**). (Oman).

Baja mar. Spanish for "shallow sea." The name of the Bahamas originates from this phrase. (Bahamas).

Bajans. Barbadians, the people of Barbados. (Barbados).

Bajella. Boiled beans. (Bahrain).

Bake. A small, flat bread that is fried instead of baked. (Trinidad and Tobago).

Bakes. Fried flour dumplings. (Montserrat).

Bakhour. The Arabic word for "incense." (Bahrain, Qatar).

Bakkala. Small shops that contain basic goods. (Kuwait).

Baklava. A layered pastry with syrup and a nut filling. (Albania, Bosnia and Herzegovina, Bulgaria, Turkey).

Baklawa. (Libya). *See* **Baklava.**

Bala. A type of xylophone. (Guinea-Bissau).

Balafon. A type of xylophone. (Burkina Faso, Ghana, Guinea, Ivory Coast).

Balalaica. A traditional two-piece safari suit. (Mozambique).

Bala mo. "Greetings to you." A common Sango greeting. One can also say **Bara ala.** (Central African Republic).

Balboa. Panama's national currency. (Panama).

Balendėlai. Stuffed cabbage leaves. (Lithuania).

Bali shani. "How are you?" A Bemba greeting to a superior. Shows more respect than **Muli Shani?** (Zambia).

Baloncesto. The Spanish word for "basketball." (El Salvador).

Balot. A fertilized duck egg with an embryo, sold by street vendors. (Philippines).

Bals. The Malagasy word for "dances." (Madagascar).

Baltmaize. Latvian word for "white bread." (Latvia).

Balutan. A plate of food to take home. Offered to guests as they prepare to leave. (Guam).

Balzāms. A thick herb and alcohol mixture. (Latvia).

Bambo. "Man." Placing the prefix "a-" before the name, *abambo*, would show respect. (Malawi).

Bambuco. The national song and dance. Originated in the Andes Mountains. (Colombia).

Bami. A Javanese noodle dish. (Suriname).

Bammy. Cassava bread. (Jamaica).

Banca. A local outrigger boat. (Philippines).

Bandoneón. A musical instrument similar to an accordion. (Argentina).

Bands. Groups of people in brightly colored costumes. They participate in holiday celebrations. (Barbados).

Bandura. A stringed musical instrument. The Ukrainian national instrument. (Ukraine).

Bandy. A sport similar to hockey. (Sweden).

Banian. A sleeveless shirt, worn by men. (Sri Lanka).

Banitsa. A layered pastry. (Bulgaria).

Banners. Local fiefs. (Mongolia).

Bansh. A boiled dumpling stuffed with diced meat, onion, cabbage, garlic, salt, and pepper. (Mongolia).

Banya. The Russian word for "sauna." (Kazakstan).

Bao. A strategy game played with pebbles or seeds on a carved-out board. (Kenya, Malawi, Tanzania).

Bapak. "Father." A respectful Indonesian term of address for older men. (Indonesia).

Bara ala. "Greetings to you." A common Sango greeting. One can also say **Bala mo.** (Central African Republic).

Bara ala kwé. "Greetings, everyone." A common Sango greeting for a large group. (Central African Republic).

Bara brith. Currant cake. (Wales).

Baraholka. An open-air market where clothes, shoes, and household goods are sold. (Kazakstan).

Bara lawr. A mixture of seaweed and oatmeal that is fried and then served with bacon. (Wales). *Also called* **Laver bread.**

Barambo. The Sango word for "stool." (Central African Republic).

Barangays. A region similar to a county. (Philippines). *See also* **Barrios.**

Barbie. Barbecue. (Australia).

Barev. "Let good be with you." An Armenian greeting used as a casual "Hello." The plural form, **Barevdzez**, signifies more respect and formality. (Armenia).

Barevdzez. (Armenia). *See* **Barev.**

Barika. A Dyula, term meaning "strength," as in "May the Lord put strength in this meat." Ivorians might say it after a meal. (Ivory Coast).

Baris gede. A male military dance. (Indonesia).

Bariza. A Shingazidja word that can be used before anything to form a greeting. (Comoros). *See also* **Bariza hazi?, Bariza husha, Bariza masihu.**

Bariza hazi? "How is work?" A common Shingazidja greeting. (Comoros). *See also* **Bariza.**

Bariza husha. "Good morning." A common Shingazidja greeting. (Comoros). *See also* **Bariza.**

Glossary of Cultural Terms

Bariza masihu. "Good evening." A common Shingazidja greeting. (Comoros). *See also* **Bariza.**

Barong. An embroidered shirt worn by men that hangs over the pants. (Guam, Philippines).

Barov gnas. "Go with peace." A formal Armenian parting phrase used for long separations. (Armenia). *See also* **Barov mnas.**

Barov mnas. "Stay with peace." A formal Armenian parting phrase used for long separations. (Armenia). *See also* **Barov gnas.**

Barrios. (1) The Spanish word for "neighborhoods." (Dominican Republic). (2) Small villages or suburbs. (Philippines). *See also* **Barangays.**

Barščai. Beet soup. (Lithuania).

Basi. A ceremony involving offerings, food, rice wine, and religious chanting by a holy person. (Laos).

Basmachi. A resistance movement against the government of the Soviet Union in the early 20th century. (Uzbekistan).

Basmachi(s). Small bands of fighters that resisted the Soviets. (Turkmenistan).

Basturma. Salted beef with a spicy coating. (Armenia).

Bateys. Sugarcane villages where many Haitian workers live. (Dominican Republic).

Batidos de fruta. Fruit shakes. (Venezuela).

Batik. A traditional type of fabric with hand-colored patterns made using a hot-wax process on dyed cloth. (Indonesia, Malaysia, Niger).

Bâton de manioc. A dough-like paste made from cassava. (Gabon).

Batono. "Sir." A Georgian term of address used with the first name. (Georgia).

Batrana. Older rural women. (Moldova).

Batsakatsi. Witches. They can be paid to place or remove a curse on someone. A traditional practice. (Swaziland). *See also* **Muti, Sangoma, Tinyanga.**

Batswana. "Tswana people." Also, citizens of Botswana, regardless of ethnicity. (Botswana). *See also* **Ba-, Mo-, Motswana.**

Baurua. A traditional canoe made from driftwood lashed together with coconut fibers. (Kiribati).

Bayan. A traditional instrument similar to the accordion. (Belarus).

Bea bilong Solomons. "Beer of the Solomons." Betel nut chewed with pepper leaf and lime. It is mildly intoxicating. (Solomon Islands).

Beaucoup. A French term meaning "many" or "much." (Gabon).

Becak. A pedicab. (Indonesia).

Bedu. The Bedouin people. (Kuwait, United Arab Emirates).

Begena. A lyre, a musical instrument. (Ethiopia).

Beh-thwa-ma-lo-leh? "Where are you going?" A common Burmese greeting. (Myanmar).

Beignets. Deep-fried, doughnutlike food. (Gabon, Niger).

Beijinhos. "Little kisses." A small kiss on each cheek given at greeting and parting among relatives and friends. (Portugal).

Belarusian ruble. Belarus's national currency. (Belarus).

Belembaotuyan. A gourd with a long neck and one string; the musician strikes the string with a stick. A traditional musical instrument played by older men. (Guam).

Belo. The Melanesian Pidgin word for "lunch." (Papua New Guinea).

Belum. The Indonesian word for "not yet." (Indonesia).

Benachin. Jollof rice. (Gambia).

Bendición. A word used by children in asking blessings of their parents and other relatives. (Dominican Republic). *See also* **Dios te bendiga.**

Benga. A type of contemporary dance music. It fuses traditional rhythms of the Luo ethnic group with modern instruments such as the electric guitar. (Kenya).

Berbere. A red hot pepper that is often used to spice **Wat(s)** or served separately with raw meat. (Ethiopia).

Beretitenti. The Kiribati word for "president." (Kiribati).

Ber ibuto aber? "Fine, and you?" A Luo response to the greeting **Ibuto aber?** (How did you sleep?). (Uganda).

Beritta. A traditional Maltese cap. (Malta).

Beryani. Rice with meat, a common lunch item. (Bahrain).

Bes. The Arabic word for "enough." (Saudi Arabia).

Besa. "Sworn truce." Adherents believe family honor, hospitality, and a patriarchal order are the basis of successful relationships. (Albania).

Besbarmak. (Kazakstan). *See* **Beshbarmak.**

Beshbarmak. A dish of noodles and meat eaten with the fingers. (Kyrgyzstan).

Besht. (Bahrain). *See* **Bisht.**

Beso-beso. A kiss on each cheek, given in greeting. (Philippines).

Bey. A title used after a man's given name. (Azerbaijan, Turkey).

-bhabi. "Wife of older brother." A Bangla suffix used as a term of address. A man adds the suffix to the name of his friend's wife. (Bangladesh).

Bhaku. A wraparound jumper worn by married Tibetan women. (Nepal).

Bharata Natyam. A classical Indian dance. (Singapore).

Bhinneka Tunggal Ika. "Diverse yet unified." Indonesia's motto. (Indonesia).

Bhoot. The Nepali word for "ghost." The Nepalese believe *bhoot* can cause disease, crop failures, or accidents. (Nepal). *See also* **Bokshi, Graha dasha, Pret.**

Bhoto Jatra. A great festival that takes place around April or May. (Nepal).

Bhuti. A social title added to a boy's name to show respect. (Swaziland).

Bica. A strong espresso-type coffee. (Portugal). *Also called* **Cimbalino.**

Bidayuhs. Land Dayaks. An indigenous people in Malaysia. (Malaysia).

Bife à cavalo com fritas. Meat with egg and french fries. (Brazil).

Bigos. A common dish consisting of sausage, mushrooms, and pickled cabbage. (Poland).

Bigote para arriba. The gesture of placing the thumb and index finger on the upper lip in an upward "V." Literally, "upward mustache." The gesture means "Everything is all right." (Uruguay).

Big up. "Hello." An informal phrase used among friends. (Saint Vincent and the Grenadines).

Biharis. Muslims who immigrated to Bangladesh from Bihar, India. (Bangladesh).

Bikhair al-hamdu lillah. "Good, praise be to God." A common response to the greeting **Kaif halak?** (United Arab Emirates).

Bikkhu. A Buddhist priest. (Laos).

Glossary of Cultural Terms

Bikman. "Big man," or leader. There is one in each village. (Papua New Guinea). *Also called* **Kukurai**.

Bikram Samvat. Nepal's calendar. The New Year takes place in mid-April. (Nepal).

Bikutsi. An indigenous musical style. (Cameroon).

Bili-bili. Millet beer. (Chad).

Bilo. A coconut shell used to drink **Yaqona**. (Fiji). *See also* **Tanoa**.

Biltong. A jerky-like meat snack. (Namibia, South Africa).

Bilum(s). A woven string bag used by men and women. (Papua New Guinea).

Bin. "Son of." An Arabic title combined with the father's name. (Bahrain, Oman, Singapore). *See also* **Ibn**.

Bindi. A red dot worn on the forehead by Hindu women. (India).

Bint. (Oman). *See* **Binti**.

Bint-al-sahn. A popular festive bread cooked in layers and served hot with clarified butter and warm honey. (Yemen).

Binti. "Daughter of." An Arabic title combined with the father's name. (Malaysia, Singapore).

Birr. Ethiopia's national currency. (Ethiopia).

Birria. Goat soup. (Mexico).

Biryani. Rice with meat and spices. (Pakistan, United Arab Emirates).

Biscuits. Cookies. (Australia, England, Mauritius, New Zealand, Scotland, Wales).

Bis eng aner Kéier. "See you later." A parting phrase used between friends and acquaintances. (Luxembourg). *See also* **Äddi, bis mar, Bis härno**.

Bis härno. "See you later." A parting phrase used between friends and acquaintances. (Luxembourg). *See also* **Äddi, bis mar, Bis eng aner Kéier**.

Bisht. A robe worn on formal occasions over the **Dishdasha**. (Kuwait, Oman).

Bism Allah. [NOTE: Spelling varies because it is a transliteration of Arabic.] A Muslim blessing meaning "In the name of God." (United Arab Emirates).

Bismi Allah. (Algeria). *See* **Bism Allah**.

Bismilla. (Turkmenistan). *See* **Bism Allah**.

Bissimilai. A blessing often used over food. It can be used in a variety of situations. (Gambia).

Bisslama. "Good-bye." A standard parting phrase. (Tunisia).

Bissm Allah. (Jordan). *See* **Bism Allah**.

Bissm Allah arrahman arrahim. "By the name of God, most gracious and most merciful." A blessing said before a meal. (Jordan).

Bite se? "How are things going?" A phrase that follows the initial greeting **Muraho**. (Rwanda). *See also* **Amakuru?, Ni meza**.

Bit of a dag. A phrase meaning "a humorous character." (New Zealand).

Black buns. A fruit cake on a pastry base. (Scotland).

Black cake. A cake for special occasions made with fruit that is soaked in brandy. (Guyana, U.S. Virgin Islands).

Black pudding. Blood sausage. (Antigua and Barbuda, Saint Kitts and Nevis).

Blancos. "Whites." The name of the conservative landowners during the civil war, which lasted from 1839 to 1851. (Uruguay). *See also* **Colorados**.

Bless. "To be blessed." A phrase used to say "good-bye." (Iceland).

Bless Bless. (Iceland). *See* **Bless**.

Blockos. A street dance. (Grenada).

Bloco. The Portuguese word for "group." (Brazil).

Bloemkoel. Cauliflower. (Netherlands).

Bloke. An Australian colloquialism meaning "guy." (Australia).

Blynai. Pancakes. (Lithuania).

Bo. A term Grand Comorians use when calling out to someone. It precedes the addressee's name. (Comoros).

Boa continuação. A Portuguese parting phrase meaning "Have a nice day." (Angola).

Boa noite. "Good evening." A Portuguese greeting. (Mozambique, Portugal).

Board bus. A truck-turned-bus with a canvas top and wood sides that can be chartered for special events. (Grenada).

Boa tarde. "Good afternoon." A Portuguese greeting. (Mozambique, Portugal).

Bocadillo. A sandwich. (Spain).

Bocce. An Italian game similar to lawn bowling. (Italy).

Bocci. A traditional form of outdoor bowling. (Malta).

Bochas. Lawn bowling. Often played by older men. (Argentina).

Boda boda. A "bicycle-taxi" with a padded passenger seat over the rear wheel, used to travel short distances. (Uganda).

Bodegas. Neighborhood grocery stores. (Cuba).

Bodhrán. A traditional Celtic drum. (Ireland).

Boerewors. Spiced sausage. (South Africa).

Boer(s). Dutch and Afrikaans word meaning "farmer." White colonists primarily of Dutch descent in southern Africa. (Botswana, South Africa).

Bøf. Hamburger steak with a brown sauce and fried onions. (Denmark).

Bogadi. The bride-price paid by the groom's family to the bride's family. (Botswana).

Bogobe. Porridge. Made from sorghum, maize, or millet. (Botswana).

Bogolan. "Mud cloth." Specially primed fabric painted with mud. (Mali).

Bohz ooi. Round tents. (Kyrgyzstan).

Boilin'. Fish boiled with green bananas and vegetables. (Saint Vincent and the Grenadines).

Bok. "Hi." A common Croatian greeting. (Croatia).

Bokshi. The Nepali word for "witch." The Nepalese believe *bokshi* can cause disease, crop failures, or accidents. (Nepal). *See also* **Bhoot, Graha dasha, Pret**.

Bolas criollas. A popular game in Venezuela, similar to lawn bowling. (Venezuela).

Bolero. A popular dance. (Cuba).

Bolimbisi. "Please" in Lingala. (Congo).

Bolívar. Venezuela's national currency. (Venezuela).

Boliviano. Bolivia's national currency. (Bolivia).

Bollo(s). Corn mush that has been boiled in the husk. (Panama).

Bolludagurinn. Cream Puffs Day, celebrated on the third Monday in February. (Iceland).

Bom apetite. "Enjoy." A Portuguese phrase that allows visitors to politely decline joining in a snack or a meal. (Brazil).

Bomba. A rhythmic dance with African influences. (Ecuador, Puerto Rico).

Bombachas. Loose-legged pants. A traditional piece of clothing worn by Argentine cowboys. (Argentina, Uruguay).

Bombilla. A metal straw that has a screen at the bottom. Used to drink **Mate** or other herbal teas. (Argentina, Paraguay, Uruguay).

Glossary of Cultural Terms

Bom dia. "Good day." A Portuguese greeting. (Angola, Mozambique, Portugal).

Bom dia mama fulana. "Good morning, dear Mother." A polite greeting used to respectfully greet one's female elders. (Mozambique).

Bom dia papa fulano. "Good morning, dear Father." A polite greeting used to respectfully greet one's male elders. (Mozambique).

Bon. A traditional belief that good and evil spirits animate nature. The beliefs include charms, astrology, offerings to spirits, and worship at small shrines. (Bhutan).

Bon appétit. A French saying that means "Good appetite." (Bolivia, Cameroon, Ecuador, Netherlands, Slovakia, Slovenia).

Bondo. A secret society for women where they dance, share lessons about womanhood, and initiate new members by circumcision and other rituals. (Sierra Leone).

Bonġu. "Good morning." A Maltese greeting. (Malta).

Boniatos. Sweet potatoes. (Cuba).

Bonjou kouman ou ye? "Good day, how are you?" The most common Haitian Creole greeting. (Haiti).

Bonjour. "Good day." A common greeting. Used in French-speaking countries..

Bonjour tout le monde. "Hello, everyone." A French greeting used at larger gatherings. (Gabon).

Bonnet. The hood of a car. (New Zealand). *See also* **Boot.**

Bonsoir. "Good evening." A common greeting. Used in French-speaking countries..

Bonswa. "Good evening." A common Maltese greeting. (Malta).

Booshiyya. A black veil that covers the face. Only the most conservative women wear these. (Bahrain). *See also* **Burqa.**

Boot. The trunk of a car. (New Zealand). *See also* **Bonnet.**

Bo pen nyang. "Never mind." A common expression that characterizes Lao feelings toward life. (Laos).

Bor. The Lao word for "not yet." (Laos).

Borsak. Fried dough. (Kyrgyzstan).

Borsch. [NOTE: Spelling varies because it is a transliteration of Russian.] Vegetable soup. (Belarus, Russia, Ukraine).

Borscht. (Israel, Latvia, Moldova). *See* **Borsch.**

Bosanski lonac. A stew with cabbage and meat. (Bosnia and Herzegovina).

Bosnjak. An old surname meaning "Bosnian." A nonreligious term referring to Muslims. (Bosnia and Herzegovina).

Botaki. A feast. Feasts are held at a **Maneaba(s)**. (Kiribati).

Botondi. "Thank you" in Lingala. (Congo).

Boubou(s). A long cotton robe or an outfit with trousers and a long, loose top. Worn in African countries..

Bouillie. A millet-and-peanut porridge flavored with lemon and sometimes sugar. (Chad).

Boule. A heavy porridge formed into a ball and dipped in sauce. Chad's national food. (Chad).

Boules. A form of lawn bowling. (Belgium).

Boul-joul. Salted codfish sautéed in olive oil with vegetables. (Saint Vincent and the Grenadines).

Boumba. A loose blouse worn by women with a **Pagne(s)**. (Benin).

Bounce. A colloquialism meaning "car accident." (Grenada).

Bouneschlupp. Bean soup. (Luxembourg).

Boutou. A word of West African origins meaning "insult." (Saint Vincent and the Grenadines).

Bowgee. Sister-in-law. (Trinidad and Tobago).

Box food. Food eaten out of a box when one is away from home. Generally consisting of fish, chicken, or goat served over rice and **Peas**. (Jamaica).

Boyo. A coconut flavored pastry. (Suriname).

Boza. A malt-based drink; a typical breakfast beverage. (Bulgaria).

Braai(s). Barbecue, a traditional way of cooking. (Namibia, South Africa). *See also* **Potjiekos.**

Bracelet fighting. A traditional Sudanese sport. (Sudan).

Brae. A hill. (Scotland).

Brahma. The creator. One of three supreme gods of Hinduism. (Nepal). *See also* **Shiva, Vishnu.**

Brahma Vihara. Buddhism's four pillars of virtue. (Laos). *See also* **Karunna, Metta, Mudhita, Uppekkha.**

Brahmin(s). The highest of the four Hindi castes. Composed of intellectuals and priests. Also used to refer to the people of the caste. (India, Nepal). *See also* **Chaturvarna Vyavasta, Kshatriya, Shudra(s), Vaishya.**

Brânza. Sheep cheese. (Moldova).

Brasa. (Suriname). *See* **Abrazo.**

Bratwurst. "Grilled sausage" in German. (Switzerland).

Brazilero. A language that is a mixture of Spanish and Portuguese. It is spoken in northern border towns. (Uruguay). *Also called* **Portuñol.**

Breek. A thin fried dough stuffed with an egg, cooked vegetables, and tuna. (Tunisia).

Briani. Rice and vegetables with a mixture of meat, chicken, or fish and a number of spices. (Mauritius).

Bringue. A weekend singing and drinking party that lasts until early morning. (French Polynesia).

Broadsheets. A type of newspaper that is more serious than a tabloid. (England).

Brochette. A type of food similar to a shish kebab. (Burkina Faso, Niger).

Broken English. An English-based creole. (Barbados, Grenada).

Brother. A term used to address males of the same age, regardless of relationship. (Ghana, Sierra Leone).

Brujería. Witchcraft. Practiced by small groups. (Cuba).

Bryndzové halušky. Small dumplings with processed sheep cheese. The Slovak national dish. (Slovakia).

Bsawao. A wraparound cloth worn by women. The term is used in the north. (Togo). *Also called* **Sata.** *See also* **Avo tata.**

Bua. "Hello." A common Mende greeting. (Sierra Leone).

Buai. Betel nut. (Papua New Guinea).

Bub. The Marshallese word for "pandanus." (Marshall Islands).

Bubu. A long, loose-fitting shirt with open collar, worn over pants. (Mozambique).

Bubuti. A verbal agreement or request that cannot be turned down. The word is never used lightly. (Kiribati).

Budoh mongoi. "Come and eat." A common greeting on the outer islands of Yap, Chuuk, and Pohnpei. (Micronesia).

¡Buenas! A common casual Spanish greeting. (Belize, Costa Rica, Guatemala, Panama).

¡Buenas noches! "Good evening." A common greeting. Used in Spanish-speaking countries..

¡Buenas tardes! "Good afternoon." A common greeting. Used in Spanish-speaking countries..

¡Buen día! "Good day." A popular Spanish greeting used in the morning. (Argentina, Uruguay).

Glossary of Cultural Terms

¡Buenos días! "Good day." A common greeting used in the morning. Used in Spanish-speaking countries..

Buen provecho. "Enjoy your meal." A Spanish phrase used to express appreciation or gratitude for the meal. Used in Latin American Spanish-speaking countries..

Buia. A raised platform with a thatched roof but no walls. Used to entertain visitors. (Kiribati).

Buibui. A large black shawl, worn by women on the island of Zanzibar. (Tanzania).

Buitenvrouw. "Outside woman." Surinamese men in common-law relationships often have a *buitenvrouw*, which may be a short-term mistress or a more formal partner (with children) over several years. (Suriname).

Bula! "Health." The most common way to say hello. Pronounced "MBOOLA." (Fiji).

Bumiputras. "Sons of the soil." A term to describe the Malays and indigenous groups together. (Malaysia).

Bună. "Good." A Romanian greeting used by women. (Romania).

Bunad. A traditional costume that is specific to each region. (Norway).

Bună dimineata. "Good morning." A common Romanian greeting. (Romania).

Bună seara. "Good evening." A common Romanian greeting. (Romania).

Bună ziua. "Good day." A common Romanian greeting. (Moldova, Romania).

Bundesrat. The Federal Council. The upper house in the legislature. (Austria, Germany).

Bundestag. The Federal Assembly. The lower house in the German legislature. (Germany). *See also* **Bundesrat**.

Bundesversammlung. The Austrian Parliament with two houses, the **Bundesrat** and the **Nationalrat**. (Austria).

Bunge. The National Assembly. (Kenya, Tanzania).

Bunraku. Japanese puppet theater. (Japan).

Buns. Cupcakes. (England).

Bun That Luang. A weeklong festival in November at a temple housing a relic of Buddha. (Laos).

Buonasera. "Good afternoon" or "Good evening." A common Italian greeting. (Italy).

Buongiorno. "Good morning." A common Italian greeting. (Italy).

Bure. The traditional Fijian home. It is usually built of local hardwood, a thatched roof, and woven floor covers. (Fiji).

Burek. (1) A meat pie. (Bosnia and Herzegovina). (2) A meat- or cheese-filled pie. (Macedonia).

Burékas. A pastry filled with cheese and spinach. (Israel).

Burkha. (Qatar). *See* **Burqa**.

Burns Suppers. Banquets that honor poet Robert Burns on his birthday, 25 January. (Scotland).

Burqa. [NOTE: Spelling varies because it is a transliteration of Arabic.] (1) A veil worn by conservative women that covers the bridge of the nose and cheeks. (Bahrain, Kuwait, Oman, Pakistan, United Arab Emirates). (2) A head-to-toe covering worn by women. (Afghanistan). *Also called* **Chadiri**.

Busetas. A Spanish term for minibuses used in rural areas of Ecuador. In urban areas they are called **Colectivos**. (Ecuador).

Bush gardens. A vegetable garden owned and worked by an entire family. (Niue).

Bushido. The Code of the Warrior, which stressed honor, courage, politeness, and reserve. (Japan).

Bush meat. Snake, monkey, porcupine, etc.; a delicacy in the south. (Cameroon).

Bush tea. An herbal tea. (Montserrat, Saint Kitts and Nevis, U.S. Virgin Islands).

Bush trucks. A colloquialism for "four-wheel-drive trucks." (Guyana).

Bush walking. A colloquialism for "hiking." (Australia).

Busi dresi. Forest medicines typically linked to traditional religious rituals. (Suriname). *See also* **Oso dresi**.

Buuz. A steamed dumpling stuffed with diced meat, onion, cabbage, garlic, salt, and pepper. (Mongolia).

Buzkashi. A game similar to polo. Played with a goat or headless calf. The teams try to carry the carcass from one spot to another and then back to the original spot. (Afghanistan, Tajikistan).

Bwana. "Boss." A term of address for persons in authority. (Malawi).

Byarozavik. Birch sap. A common drink. (Belarus).

Bye ch'nam, pram-bye kai, m'pai t'gnai. The three-year, eight-month, twenty-day rule of the **Khmer Rouge**. During this rule, nearly two million people were killed or died of starvation and disease. (Cambodia).

Byen mèsi, e ou? "Well, thank you, and you?" The proper creole response to the greeting **Bonjou kouman ou ye?** (Haiti).

Byolko. A dark, long loaf of bread. (Kyrgyzstan).

Byrek. A pastry with vegetables, cottage cheese, or minced meat. (Albania).

Bytromme. Town drum, a native musical instrument. (Denmark).

Byvai. "Bye." An informal Belarusian parting phrase. (Belarus).

Cabanes à sucre. Some Canadian maple-syrup farms are known by this name, which means "sugar cabins." (Canada).

Cabidela. Chicken with rice. (Portugal).

Cacana mboa. Pumpkin leaves. (Mozambique).

Cachupa. The Caboverdian national dish. A stew made of corn and meat or fish with manioc (cassava) that is cooked slowly in water. (Cape Verde).

Cadance. Lively dancing music from the French Antilles. (Saint Lucia).

Ca dao. Unaccompanied vocal Vietnamese music. (Vietnam).

Café com leite. Coffee with milk. (Brazil).

Cafézinho. Black coffee. (Brazil).

Cai luong. A type of musical comedy developed in the early 1900s. (Vietnam).

Cajón. An athletic dance performed in Lima by those of African descent. (Peru).

Caldeirada. Fish stew. (Portugal).

Caldo de bola. Plantain-based soup with meat and vegetables. (Ecuador).

Caldo verde. Soup made with potatoes, cabbage, and olive oil. (Portugal).

Caliente. The Spanish word for "hot." Refers to temperature rather than spiciness. (Mexico). *See also* **Picante**.

Callaloo. (1) A green, leafy plant similar to spinach. (Grenada). (2) A local plant that is cooked with coconut milk, pepper, and pumpkin. (Trinidad and Tobago).

Calling by. An Irish colloquialism for "visiting." (Ireland).

Call name. A colloquialism for "nickname." (Grenada).

Calulú A dish made of dried fish, vegetables, and palm oil. (Angola).

Glossary of Cultural Terms

Calypso. A form of social commentary invented in Trinidad and sung by performers called calypsonians. (Trinidad and Tobago).

Calypsonians. Performers of calypso music. (Trinidad and Tobago).

Cambute. A Costa Rican folk dance. (Costa Rica).

Cameros. The 15th-century Portuguese word for "prawns" and root of the word *Cameroon*. (Cameroon).

Camogie. The women's version of **Hurling**. A game played on a soccer-type field with wooden sticks and a small leather ball. (Ireland).

Campesino(s). A Spanish word meaning "farmers." Inhabitants of rural areas; often poor. (Bolivia, El Salvador, Panama, Paraguay, Peru).

Campo. The Spanish word for "countryside." (Dominican Republic).

Cana. Cane alcohol. (Guinea-Bissau).

Canadienses. A Spanish term for "Canadians." (Chile).

Cançoillotte. The French name for a type of soft cheese. The Luxembourgish term is **Kachkéis**. (Luxembourg).

Candombe. An African-influenced rhythm played with three drums. (Uruguay).

Canh ca. Fish and vegetable soup. (Vietnam).

Canteens. Cafés. (Ukraine).

Canton(s). (1) "County." Several villages led by a local traditional chief. (Chad). (2) A political region. (Luxembourg, Switzerland).

Capulana. A wraparound skirt worn by married women. It is a symbol of respect. (Mozambique).

Caribana. The local word for Carnival. (Antigua and Barbuda).

Carnaval. A three-to-five-day festival celebrated by parades, dances, and parties prior to Ash Wednesday. Celebrations are often marked by riotous excess in the days before Lent, a season of fasting and penitence. *Carnaval* is also spelled "carnival" in several countries. Celebrated in countries with high Roman Catholic populations..

Carnaval de Québec. A two-week period in February filled with activities. (Canada).

Carne guisado. A dish made of stewed meat with tomatoes and spices. (Panama).

Car park. A minibus station. (Guyana).

Carretas. Oxcarts. (Costa Rica).

Carry. A colloquialism for "bring." (U.S. Virgin Islands).

Căruța. Horse- or donkey-drawn carts. (Romania).

Casabe. Cassava baked into rounds of crisp cracker bread. (Dominican Republic).

Casă de piatră. "House of stone." A wish given to newlyweds, meaning a long and durable marriage. (Romania).

Casado. A meal of rice, beans, plantains, meat, and salad or eggs. (Costa Rica).

Casareep. A cassava extract. (Guyana).

Cassave. Bread made from manioc. (Haiti).

Castañuelas. Castanets. (Spain).

Castellano. Spanish. (Bolivia, Chile, El Salvador, Paraguay).

Catholicos. A supreme patriarch. The head of the Armenian Apostolic Church. (Armenia).

Čau. "Ciao." A common Czech parting phrase. (Czech Republic).

Causé! Literally, "speak." Mauritian Creole for "How are you?" (Mauritius).

Ça va? "How's it going?" or "Everything OK?" A common French greeting. (Canada, Central African Republic, France).

Ça va aller, Dieu est grand. French term meaning "Everything will be all right, God is great," it expresses the typically easy-going Ivorian attitude about life. (Ivory Coast).

Cavadee. A Hindu holiday that celebrates the feat of the god Idoumban, who carried two mountain peaks on his shoulders. (Mauritius).

Cavaquinho. The ukulele. (Cape Verde).

Cawl. A traditional Welsh soup. (Wales).

Cayes. Small islands. Pronounced "KEYS." (Belize).

Cazuela de ave. Chicken soup. (Chile).

Ceau. "Ciao." A Romanian greeting used among young people. (Romania).

Ceif. A common attitude. To act spontaneously for enjoyment and without regard for consequences like cost and time. (Bosnia and Herzegovina).

Ce mai facetz. "How do you do?" A Romanian greeting. (Moldova).

Cembalo. The Romanian term for "harpsichord." (Moldova).

Cena. The evening meal. Consists of a light snack. (Dominican Republic, Mexico).

Centres de santé. The French term for "health centers." (Guinea).

Cepelinai. Meat cooked inside a ball of potato dough, served with a special sauce. (Lithuania).

C'est doux. A French phrase meaning "It's sweet," some Ivorians might say this after a meal to compliment the cook and thank the host. (Ivory Coast).

Ćevapčići. Small elongated, minced meatballs eaten with chopped onions. (Serbia and Montenegro).

Ceviche. Raw fish seasoned with lemon and vinegar or lime. (Ecuador, Peru).

CFA franc. Communauté Financière Africaine franc (African Financial Community franc). The currency used in francophone African countries. (Benin, Burkina Faso, Cameroon, Central African Republic, Chad, Equatorial Guinea, Gabon, Guinea-Bissau, Ivory Coast, Mali, Niger, Senegal, Togo).

Chacabana. A white shirt, typically embroidered with four pockets. Worn over dark trousers. (Dominican Republic).

Chadiri. A head-to-toe covering worn by women. (Afghanistan). *Also called* **Burqa**.

Chador. A long dress worn over regular clothing by women in public. (Iran, Lebanon).

Chaebol. Huge conglomerates that dominate the South Korean economy. (South Korea).

Chai. Tea. (Afghanistan, Kyrgyzstan).

Chaihana. A building or tent used as a gathering place. (Azerbaijan).

Chakijane. A rabbit trickster who is the subject of children's stories. (Swaziland).

Chalga. A mix of Turkish, Romany, and Serbian music. (Bulgaria).

Ch'alla. Blessing of any material possession or event by offering symbolic articles and alcohol to **Pachamama** and **Achachila**. Part of indigenous beliefs. (Bolivia).

Chamorrita. An unaccompanied female chorus singing in harmony. (Guam).

Changua. Potato-and-egg soup. (Colombia).

Chao. "Hi." An informal French greeting. (Switzerland).

Glossary of Cultural Terms

Chao. (1) "Good-bye." A common Spanish parting phrase. (Chile, Colombia, El Salvador, Panama, Venezuela). (2) "Greetings." A common Vietnamese greeting. (Vietnam).

Chap. A Scottish term of address for males. (Scotland).

Chapan. A long coat worn by village men. Kept closed with a bandana-type tie around the waist. (Tajikistan). *Also called* **Joma.** *See also* **Chorsi.**

Chapati. Flat bread. (Kenya, Pakistan, Uganda).

Chapines. A colloquial term for Guatemalans as a group. (Guatemala).

Chaponlar. Long, open, quilted robes usually worn by older men. (Uzbekistan).

Charamuscas. Frozen fruit juice in plastic bags. (Honduras). *Also called* **Topogios.**

Charango. A musical instrument similiar to a guitar. (Bolivia, Peru).

Charreada. A Mexican form of rodeo. (Mexico).

Charshab. A long piece of cloth wrapped loosely around a skirt. A traditional piece of clothing worn by rural women. (Azerbaijan).

Chat. (Ethiopia). *See* **Khat.**

Chattel houses. Wooden homes set on coral stone 3 or 4 feet above ground for better air circulation. (Barbados).

Chaturvarna Vyavasta. The Brahmin classification philosophy. A four-class system. (India). *See also* **Brahmin(s), Kshatriya, Shudra(s), Vaishya.**

Chaty. The Czech term for "cottages." (Czech Republic).

¡Chau! "Good-bye." A common Spanish parting phrase. (Argentina, Bolivia, Uruguay).

Chau. "Nephew." A Vietnamese term used by a man to refer to himself when speaking to an older woman of his mother's generation. (Vietnam). *See also* **Co.**

Chau, chau. (Bolivia). *See* **¡Chau!**

Chaya. Traditional baggy drawstring pants with many extra folds between the legs that provide ventilation in the heat. Worn by Wolof and Fula men. (Gambia).

Check on. Dropping in at a friend's house to see how he or she is doing. (U.S. Virgin Islands).

Chee khel shoomo? "How are you?" A common Tajik greeting. (Tajikistan).

Cheers. A common parting phrase. (Scotland).

Chef. "Chief." A term of address for men, used to show respect. (Chad).

Chenchu'le. The Chamorro word for "support." People provide *chenchu'le* to family members in need. May take the form of money, time, or donations of food or drink. (Guam).

Cheongsam. (1) A traditional Chinese dress. (Singapore). (2) A traditional red and gold Chinese wedding dress. (Hong Kong).

Chereh. A form of millet **Couscous.** (Gambia).

Chévere. A Spanish colloquialism meaning "very well" or "cool." (Venezuela).

Chhetris. (India). *See* **Kshatriya.**

Chia. Baggy pants worn by men. (Mauritania).

Chibalo. A policy of forced labor. Workers were paid low wages and forced to work in fields to generate exports for the Portuguese. (Mozambique).

Chibuku. Bars that sell sorghum beer. (Botswana).

Chibwabwa. Finely cut and boiled pumpkin leaves cooked with salt and oil. (Zambia).

Chicha. (1) A fruit drink. (Chile, Panama). (2) A home-brewed alcoholic drink made from corn. (Bolivia).

Chicharias. Bars that serve **Chicha.** Indicated by a white flag hanging outside the establishment. (Bolivia).

Chicken cafriela. Chicken cooked in lemon, onions, and butter. (Guinea-Bissau).

Chicken souse. A spicy chicken stew. (Bahamas).

Chico. The Spanish word for "small." (Costa Rica, Mexico).

Chimurenga. Combines traditional Shona music with electric instruments. Draws from political and social themes. (Zimbabwe).

Chimwali. "Sister." A common Chichewa term of address among young adults and teens. (Malawi).

Chimwene. "Brother." A common Chichewa term of address among young adults and teens. (Malawi).

Chinellas. "Flip-flops." Worn by women and men, especially in rural areas. (Nicaragua).

Ching Ming. A festival that honors the dead. (Hong Kong, Mauritius).

Ching tzuo. "Please sit." A common Mandarin Chinese greeting. (Taiwan).

Chipa. Hard cheese bread. (Paraguay).

Chiperoni. A damp fog or heavy cloud cover. (Malawi).

Chips. French fries. (Australia, Montserrat).

Chirimía. The Spanish word for "oboe." (Costa Rica).

Chirmole. Soup. (Belize).

Chishlik. Skewered meat or fish. (Turkmenistan).

Chitenge. A colorful wraparound skirt. (Zambia).

Chitenje. A 7-foot-long African-print cotton fabric worn by women. Protects dresses from dust and dirt. Can also be used as a baby carrier or for a variety of other purposes. (Malawi).

Chivas. Minibuses. (Panama).

Chivito. Steak and egg with cheese and mayonnaise. (Uruguay).

Chocalat. A dark, gravy-like sauce made from **Odika.** Literally "chocolate" in French. (Gabon).

Choi. Tea. (Tajikistan, Uzbekistan).

Choihona. A tearoom or café. (Uzbekistan).

Choku. A religious ceremony. (Bhutan).

Choli. A tight blouse worn by Hindu women. (Mauritius).

Cholitas. Rural women. (Bolivia).

Cholo. A blouse worn by women. (Nepal).

Ch'ondogyo. An indigenous Korean religion. An eclectic combination of Buddhist, Confucian, and Christian beliefs. (North Korea). *Also called* **Tonghak.**

Choops. Sucking air through the teeth. Expresses irritation. (Antigua and Barbuda).

Choopsing. (Saint Lucia). *See* **Choops.**

Chops. Small engraved stamps. (Taiwan).

Chorba. A soup made with small pieces of meat and vermicelli. (Algeria).

Chorek. The traditional Turkmen bread, which is cooked in an outdoor clay oven. (Turkmenistan).

Chorsi. A bandana-type tie used as a belt. (Tajikistan). *Also called* **Meeyonband.** *See also* **Chapan.**

Chouriços. A salted or smoked sausage made from various meat pieces. (Portugal).

Chpabs. Moral proverbs that are passed down through oral recitations. (Cambodia).

Christian. A practicing member of a Protestant church. (Jamaica).

Christmas Second Day. Boxing Day. Celebrated on 26 December. (U.S. Virgin Islands).
Chronia polla. "May you live many years." A traditional Greek holiday greeting. (Greece).
Chuch'e. The idea of self-reliance. (North Korea).
Chun Ben. An important Buddhist festival, during the last week of September, is marked on behalf of the dead and one's own salvation. (Cambodia).
Chung Yeung. A festival that honors the dead. (Hong Kong).
Chu nôm. A unique writing system developed using Chinese characters to write Vietnamese words. (Vietnam).
Chuños. Freeze-dried potatoes used in soups or side dishes when rehydrated. (Bolivia).
Chups. (Antigua and Barbuda). *See* **Choops.**
Chupse. (Barbados). *See* **Choops.**
Churra gerte. Crushed peanuts and rice boiled together. (Gambia).
Churrasco. (1) A barbecue with a variety of meats. (Brazil). (2) A piece of grilled chicken. Cooked on a charcoal stove at food stands. (Angola).
Churros. A batter made of flour, salt, and water, deep-fried, and sprinkled with sugar. (Spain).
Ch'usŏk. Harvest Moon Festival, held in the fall. Family members visit ancestral tombs to offer food in honor of the dead. (South Korea).
Chuups. (U.S. Virgin Islands). *See* **Choops.**
Chyny. The Kyrgyz word for "bowls." (Kyrgyzstan).
Chyr bau le meiyou? "How are you?" A common Chinese greeting. (Taiwan).
Ciamar a tha thu. "How are you?" A Gaelic greeting. (Scotland).
Čiao. "Hello" or "good-bye." A common Slovak greeting. (Slovakia).
Ciao. "Good-bye." A common parting phrase. (Bosnia and Herzegovina, Bulgaria, Italy, Luxembourg).
Ciaw. "Bye." A common parting phrase. (Malta).
Cibaeños. Residents of the Cibao Valley. (Dominican Republic).
Çiftelia. A type of mandolin with two strings. A unique Albanian instrument. (Albania).
Čika. "Uncle." A term of address used for older men who are not relatives. (Serbia and Montenegro).
Cimbalino. A strong espresso-type coffee. (Portugal). *Also called* **Bica.**
Cinco de Mayo. Celebrates an 1862 victory over the French. Celebrated on 5 May. (Mexico).
Cirene. Bulgarian feta cheese. (Bulgaria).
Ç' kemi? "What's up?" A common Albanian greeting. (Albania).
Clarsach. A small harp. (Scotland).
Co. "Aunt." A Vietnamese term used to address an older woman of one's mother's generation. (Vietnam). *See also* **Chau.**
Coal pots. Clay ovens. (Antigua and Barbuda).
Cobo. A gesture involving clapping cupped hands three or more times. Practiced when accepting a gift and on other occasions. Pronounced "THOMBO." (Fiji).
Cobra-Grande. A huge snake in Brazilian folklore. It lives in the Amazon and frightens people by changing shape. (Brazil).
Cobza. A short-necked lute. A folk instrument. (Romania).
Cocido. (1) A hot drink consisting of **Mate**, cooked sugar, and milk. (Paraguay). (2) Castilian soup. (Spain).

Coco. (1) A common term of address used for grandmothers. (Comoros). (2) A musical instrument similar to a maraca. Accompanies the **Séga** dance. (Mauritius).
Cocoa tea. Hot chocolate. (Saint Kitts and Nevis, Saint Lucia).
Cofradías. Religious fraternities dedicated to a particular saint. (Guatemala).
Co khoe khong? "How are you doing?" A popular Vietnamese greeting. (Vietnam).
Colada morada. A thick drink made with berries, sweet spices, and purple flour. (Ecuador).
Coladeira. A music and dance style that is upbeat and joyful. (Cape Verde).
Colcannon. A cooked mixture of potatoes and cabbage. A local delicacy. (Ireland).
Colectivos. Minibuses. (Colombia, Ecuador).
Colegios. Private schools. (Dominican Republic).
Collège. Junior high. (Chad, Comoros).
College. High school. (New Zealand).
Collèges. Secondary education. (France).
Colmados. Neighborhood markets. (Dominican Republic).
Colón(es). Costa Rica's national currency and El Salvador's former currency before switching to the U.S. dollar. (Costa Rica, El Salvador).
Colorados. "Reds." The name given to the urban liberals during the civil war from 1839 to 1851. (Uruguay). *See also* **Blancos.**
Comadre. A Spanish term of address used for women in the countryside. Literally it means "friend." (Dominican Republic).
Combies. Minibuses. (Botswana, Namibia, South Africa).
Come around. A colloquialism for "come over." (New Zealand).
Comersants. Traveling merchants. (Uzbekistan).
Comfort room. A colloquialism for "bathroom." (Philippines).
Com hare. "Come here" in the accent of a St. Thomian. (U.S. Virgin Islands). *See also* **Com heh, Com yah.**
Com heh. "Come here" in the accent of a Cruzian. (U.S. Virgin Islands). *See also* **Com hare, Com yah.**
Comida. The main meal of the day. (Cuba, Dominican Republic).
Comment allez-vous? "How are you?" A standard French greeting phrase. (France). *See also* **Ça va?**
Commune. A political division of a **Canton(s).** (Luxembourg).
Como está? "How are you?" A Portuguese greeting. (Angola, Mozambique).
¿Cómo estai? "How are you?" An informal Spanish greeting used in Chile. (Chile).
¿Cómo estás? "How are you?" A common informal greeting. Used in Spanish-speaking countries..
Como estás? (Cape Verde). *See* **Como está?**
¿Cómo está (usted)? "How are you?" A common greeting. Used in Spanish-speaking countries..
¿Cómo has pasado? A los tiempos que nos vemos. "How have you been? It has been a long time." A Spanish greeting used after a long absence. (Ecuador).
¿Cómo le va? "How's it going?" A common Spanish greeting used among the youth. (Nicaragua).
Como vai? "How are you?" A common Portuguese greeting. (Brazil).
Compadre. A Spanish term of address used for men in the countryside. Literally it means "friend." (Dominican Republic).

Glossary of Cultural Terms

Compañero/Compañera. "Comrade." A Spanish term used to address strangers. Masculine *compañero,* feminine *compañera.* (Cuba).

Complet. Pants and a matching shirt jacket that buttons to the collar. (Central African Republic, Chad).

Complimento. A party that takes place at the bride's home after the wedding feast. (Guam).

Comptoirs Français du Pacifique franc. French Polynesia's national currency. (French Polynesia).

Com yah. "Come here" in the accent of a Cruzian. (U.S. Virgin Islands). *See also* **Com hare, Com heh.**

Confianza. The Spanish word for "trust." (Dominican Republic).

Congee. A porridge-like rice dish. (Hong Kong).

Congreso Nacional. The Honduran National Congress. (Honduras).

Conkies. Cornmeal, coconut, pumpkin, raisins, sweet potatoes, and spices steamed in a banana leaf. (Barbados).

Con permiso. A Spanish phrase meaning "with your permission," used to excuse oneself when passing between conversing individuals. (Argentina, Mexico, Venezuela).

Conquistadores. Spanish explorers who battled and conquered the indigenous people. (Honduras, Nicaragua).

Contribuição. A special celebratory meal at which guests are asked in advance to bring food or drinks (or money to pay for them). (Angola).

Cook-up rice. A dish with coconut milk, rice, meat or fish, and almost anything the cook has on hand. (Guyana).

Cook-ups. Informal get-togethers with friends. (Saint Vincent and the Grenadines).

Cool-drink. Any soft drink or juice. (Namibia, South Africa).

Coolin' out. Standing shoulder deep in the water and chatting with a group. (U.S. Virgin Islands).

Córdoba. The Nicaraguan currency. (Nicaragua).

Cornetto. A cream-filled croissant. (Italy).

Coro. A Luo term for a traditional strategy board game played with seeds or stones. (Uganda). *Also called* **Omweso.**

Corps de gars. An open-air structure where rural men socialize and work together. (Gabon).

Corrida de toros. A bull fight. (Spain).

Corridos. A traditional form of music in which the songs tell stories. (Mexico).

Corte. A wraparound skirt worn by rural Mayan women. (Guatemala).

Costa. The dry coastal plain. (Peru).

Costeños. Ecuadorian coastal inhabitants. Considered to be cosmopolitan, open, and liberal; generally are the businesspeople. (Ecuador). *See also* **Serranos.**

Cou cou. The Bajan national dish, made of cornmeal and okra. (Barbados).

Couscous. A pasta-like semolina often cooked with vegetables and meats. (Algeria, Burkina Faso, Mauritania, Morocco, Tunisia, West Bank and Gaza).

Couscousi. (Libya). *See* **Couscous.**

Couscousi bil-bosla. A dish consisting of pasta with sautéed onions. (Libya).

Cousin. A term of address used for relatives and friends. (Central African Republic, Guinea).

Cozido à Portuguesa. A mixture of meats with potatoes, rice, and vegetables. (Portugal).

Crab in a crab bucket. A phrase that compares a person to a crab trying to escape from a bucket but failing because other crabs keep pulling it down. The phrase relates to the tension between the desire to improve one's situation and the pressure from others not to act above one's station in life. (Bahamas).

Criollo. People who are of mixed indigenous and European heritage. (Bolivia).

Crook. A colloquialism used to describe a person who is unwell. (Australia).

Croque-monsieur. Toasted ham and cheese on bread. (France).

Crubeens. Pig feet; a local delicacy. (Ireland).

Crumbles. Fruit pies. (Scotland).

Csárdás. A courting dance that has two parts (slow then fast); the national dance. (Hungary).

Cuatro. A small guitar. (Venezuela).

Cueca. A traditional dance of courtship. It is the national dance of Chile. (Bolivia, Chile).

Cuisine. The French word for "kitchen." (Gabon).

Cumbia. A Latin dance. (Colombia, Costa Rica).

Cumpleaños de quince. A girl's 15th birthday. The most important birthday, celebrating the end of childhood. (Argentina).

Cum-rum. Small family-owned shops. (Grenada).

Curandeiros. Traditional healers. (Angola). *Also called* **Kimbondeiros.**

Curandero/a. (Peru). *See* **Curanderos.**

Curanderos. Native healers. The singular forms are masculine *curandero*, feminine *curandera*. (Dominican Republic).

Curta. Colorful traditional Tajik dresses. (Tajikistan).

Cusa. Squash filled with meat and rice. (Kuwait).

Cutarras. Leather sandals worn by men. (Panama).

Cutting down the tall poppies. A colloquialism for "bringing down people of power and influence to the common level." (Australia).

Cuy. Roast guinea pig. (Ecuador).

Cycles. Phases within primary and intermediate schools. (Bahrain).

Cymraeg. The Welsh language. (Wales).

Cześć. A common Polish greeting among friends. (Poland).

Da. An Ewe term children use to address their mothers. (Togo).

Dabkah. A traditional dance performed with handkerchiefs and accompanied by the pounding of feet. (Lebanon, West Bank and Gaza).

Dab Shiid. "Starting Fire." The ancient Persian New Year celebration. (Somalia).

Dacha(s). The Russian word for a "summer cottage." (Kazakstan, Kyrgyzstan, Russia, Ukraine).

Dada. (1) "Sister." A respectful term of address used to address an older female. (Benin). (2) A Mina term children use to address their mothers. (Togo). (3) A term Imazighen use to show respect to male elders, including siblings. (Algeria).

Daddy. A term of address a younger person will call an older man even if they are not related. (Saint Lucia).

Dagit. A skirt-and-blouse outfit worn by younger women. (Gambia).

Dahl. (1) Lentils. (Bhutan, Sri Lanka). (2) Curried chickpeas. (Grenada).

Dai. "Older brother." A term of address used instead of names or titles. (Nepal).

Dáil The Irish House of Representatives. (Ireland).

Dair. Somalia's season of short rains. Lasts from October to November. (Somalia).

Glossary of Cultural Terms

Dairies. Convenience stores. (New Zealand).

Daiza. "Aunt." A common term of respect added to a female formal acquaintance's name. (Turkmenistan). *See also* **Gelneje, Hanum.**

Daje. An Albanian term used for an uncle who is one's mother's brother. (Albania).

Daju. "Older brother." A Nepali term of address. (Bhutan).

D'akujem. A Slovak phrase used to express gratitude. (Slovakia).

Dal. A spicy soup. (Bangladesh).

Dalasi. The Gambia's national currency. (Gambia).

Dal bhaat. White rice and lentil soup. (Nepal).

Dalits. "Downtrodden." A collective group that is composed of two of India's classes, scheduled castes (SC) and scheduled tribes (ST). In the past, they were referred to as "untouchables." (India).

Damask. Woven textiles made in Damascus. (Syria).

Dame. A game similar to checkers, often played by Ivorian men and boys. (Ivory Coast).

Dan bau. A single-stringed instrument used to play traditional music. (Vietnam).

Dancehall. A popular form of Jamaican music that incorporates elements of reggae, disco, and rap. (Barbados, Jamaica, Saint Vincent and the Grenadines).

Danke, nein. "Thank you, no." A German phrase that allows a person to politely decline an offer. (Austria).

Dan tranh. A multiple-stringed instrument used to play traditional music. (Vietnam).

Dan vong co. A modified guitar used to play traditional music. (Vietnam).

Danwei. Mandarin Chinese for "work group." (China).

Danza puertorriqueña. A popular form of music for singing and dancing. (Puerto Rico).

Da pabachennya. "Good-bye." A formal Belarusian parting phrase. (Belarus).

Dara'a. (1) A long, draping robe in white or blue. (Mauritania). *Also called* **Boubou(s).** (2) A traditional dress. (Kuwait).

Dara surwal. Traditional Nepali attire worn by men. Includes tight, thin cotton pants and a flowing, knee-length cotton tunic. (Nepal).

Darbuka. An hourglass shaped drum. (Libya).

Dari mana? "Where are you coming from?" A phrase that usually follows an initial greeting. (Indonesia).

Dariy. "Nothing." A typical Yapese response to the greeting **Mogethin.** (Micronesia).

Dar vueltas. A Spanish phrase meaning "to take walks." Groups of youths in Bolivia walk around a central plaza while making eye contact and flirting as part of the initial dating process. (Bolivia).

Dasain. (Bhutan). *See* **Dashain.**

Dash. A common social gesture whereby people show their appreciation for kindnesses rendered them. For example, a market woman might add extra fruit to a purchase. (Ghana).

Dashain. [NOTE: Spelling varies because it is a transliteration of Nepali. Also, Hindu holidays are based on the phases of the moon.] A Hindu holiday that celebrates the inevitable triumph of virtue over evil. (Nepal).

Dashiti. A small top or short-sleeved shirt worn by rural men in casual settings. (Benin).

Dasho. A social rank comparable to that of a knight. (Bhutan).

Dastarkhan. "Spread." A table filled with food, candy, bread, drinks, and more. (Kazakstan).

Dav. A common Danish greeting. Pronounced "DOW." (Denmark).

Daw. "Aunt." A term used to address older women, regardless of relationship. (Myanmar).

Day does run 'til night catch it. A Bajan proverb meaning "Whatever you do will catch up with you in the end." (Barbados).

Dayi. "Uncle." A common Azeri term of address used after a man's given name. (Azerbaijan).

Ddok. Pounded rice cake. (South Korea).

Deara. A delicate cloth, worn by women at home, with holes for the arms and head, and a half-slip underneath. (Yemen).

Debka'. A group dance in which men hold hands in a circle and dance to the beat of a drummer and flute player. Traditionally performed at weddings. (Iraq). *See also* **Tabbal, Zummar.**

Debkah. Dances that are accompanied by a rhythmic stomping of feet. (Jordan).

Debs. An Irish graduation ball similar to the high school prom in the United States. (Ireland).

Dedo. Mush made of cornmeal, millet, or buckwheat. (Nepal).

Deel. A traditional Mongol gown or tunic worn by men and women. (Mongolia).

Deepavali. [NOTE: Spelling varies because it is a transliteration of Hindi. Also, Hindu holidays are set according to phases of the moon.] Festival of Lights, which celebrates the triumph of light over darkness. Celebrated in countries with Hindu populations. (Malaysia, Singapore).

Deepawali. (Sri Lanka). *See* **Deepavali.**

De facto marriage. A common-law marriage. (Australia).

Defunción. A three-day Fang celebration to honor the passing of the dead, which occurs four to six months after the death. (Equatorial Guinea).

Déjeuner. The French word for "lunch." (France).

Děkuji. The Czech phrase for "thank you." (Czech Republic).

Denar. Macedonian currency. (Macedonia).

Dendê. The Portuguese word for "palm oil." (Brazil).

Dendiko ba. Colorful traditional shirts worn by older women. (Gambia). *Also called* **Grandmbuba.**

Departamentos. Geographical and political regions similar to provinces or states. (Colombia, Honduras, Nicaragua, Paraguay, Peru, Uruguay).

Départements. Administrative divisions of France. Overseas divisions have representatives in the French government as well as some local autonomy. (France).

Derija. The Arabic word for "dialect." (Morocco, Tunisia).

Desayuno. The Spanish word for "breakfast." (Cuba, Dominican Republic).

Descanso. A midday break. (Bolivia).

Dessan. A mixture of poetry and singing that tells a story of a folk hero. (Turkmenistan).

Deus Volunte. "God willing." A parting phrase used by older or rural people. (Saint Kitts and Nevis).

Deutsche Mark. Germany's national currency prior to the euro. (Germany).

Devali. (Guyana). *See* **Deepavali.**

Dewan Negara. The Malay Senate. (Malaysia).

Dewan Perwakilan Daerah. The House of Regional Representatives. (Indonesia).

Glossary of Cultural Terms

Dewan Perwakilan Rakyat. The House of Representatives, Indonesia's unicameral parliament. (Indonesia).

Dewan Rakyat. The Malay House of Representatives. (Malaysia).

Dhal. Lentil soup with rice. (Fiji).

Dhananbaad. "Thank you." (Bangladesh, Fiji).

Dharma. (1) The Hindi word for "light." (Mauritius). (2) Buddhist doctrine. (Bhutan).

Dholak. A drum. (Pakistan).

Dhoti. A large piece of cloth wrapped around the waist. Traditional Indian attire worn by men. (India).

Dhow. Sailboat. (Bahrain, United Arab Emirates).

Dhuku. A headscarf worn by rural women. (Zimbabwe).

Dhul al-Hijjah. The month in the Islamic lunar calendar in which the **Hajj** to Makkah takes place. (United Arab Emirates).

Día de la Amistad. Friendship Day. Celebrated on 30 July. (Paraguay).

Día de la Raza. Day of the Race. Columbus Day. Celebrates the indigenous roots of Latin America. Celebrated on 12 October. (Chile, Colombia, Costa Rica, Guatemala).

Día del Mar. Sea Day. Celebrated on 23 March. (Bolivia).

Día de los Muertos. Day of the Dead. Celebrates life while honoring the dead. Celebrated 1 to 2 November. (Mexico).

Día de los Reyes. Day of Kings. Celebrated on 6 January. (Dominican Republic).

Dia Dhuit. "God to you." A typical Irish-language greeting. (Ireland).

Dia is Muire duit. "God and Mary to you." A typical Irish-language response to the greeting **Dia Dhuit**. (Ireland).

Di dau day? "Where are you going?" A common Vietnamese greeting used between friends. (Vietnam).

Didgeridoo. A 5-foot-long wooden Aboriginal instrument blown to produce a distinctive resonating sound. (Australia).

Didi. "Older sister." A term of address used instead of names or titles. (Nepal).

Did-o-bazdid. The Farsi term for "visiting." (Iran).

Diet. (1) The Japanese legislative power. (Japan). (2) The lower house of the Polish Parliament. (Poland). *Also called* **Sejm.**

Dimije. Long, wide, traditional Turkish pants. (Bosnia and Herzegovina).

Dim sum. Chinese dumplings. (Hong Kong, Malaysia, Singapore).

Dinar. The national currency of various countries. (Algeria, Bahrain, Jordan, Kuwait, Libya, Serbia and Montenegro, Sudan, Tunisia, West Bank and Gaza).

Dios le pague. "God will repay you." A common Spanish expression of thanks for an invitation or gift. (Ecuador).

Dios te bendiga. "May God bless you." A Spanish phrase. (Dominican Republic).

Director. A professional title, meaning "director," used to address strangers. Masculine *director*, feminine *directora*. (Chile).

Direh. A long, billowing dress worn over petticoats. (Somalia).

Dirham. Morocco and the United Arab Emirates's national currencies. (Morocco, United Arab Emirates).

Dirndl. A traditional dress with an apron. (Austria).

Dirndlkleider. Traditional dresses with gathered waists and full skirts, worn with an apron. (Germany).

Dishdasha. A long robe worn by men. (Iraq, Kuwait, Oman, United Arab Emirates). *Also called* **Kandurah.**

Divali. (Mauritius, Trinidad and Tobago). *See* **Deepavali.**

Dīvāns. A living room couch that folds out into a bed. (Latvia).

Diwali. (Bhutan, Fiji, India). *See* **Deepavali.**

Diwaniyah. A separate part of a house or compound where the male host and his male guests relax, converse, eat, drink tea or coffee, watch television, and listen to music. The term may also refer to a large gathering hosted by a political candidate at which he outlines his platform. (Kuwait).

Diyan lang. "There, only." A typical Tagalog response to the greetings **Saan ka pupunta?** and **Saan ka galing?** (Philippines).

Djambia. A curved dagger. (Yemen).

Djedje? "How? How?" A common informal greeting used on the island of Anjouan. (Comoros).

Djeli. Praise singers. (Burkina Faso). *Also called* **Griots.**

Djelleba. The national garment. A hooded caftan worn by men and urban women. (Morocco).

Djembe. A large goatskin-covered drum. (Gambia, Guinea).

Djerma. A textile art that has fabric strips sewn together forming geometric patterns. (Niger).

Doamna. "Mrs." A Romanian title used by adults for all but close friends and relatives. (Moldova).

Dobar dan. "Good day." A common Serbo-Croatian greeting. (Bosnia and Herzegovina, Serbia and Montenegro).

Dober dan. "Good day." A common Slovene greeting. (Slovenia).

Dober den. "Good day." A Bulgarian greeting. (Bulgaria).

Dober tek. "Good appetite." A Slovene wish made before eating. (Slovenia).

Dober večer. "Good evening." A common Slovene greeting. (Slovenia).

Dober vetcher. "Good evening." A Bulgarian greeting. (Bulgaria).

Dobra dan. "Good day." A common Croatian greeting. (Croatia).

Dobra vecer. Macedonian for "Good afternoon." (Macedonia).

Dobra večer. "Good evening." A common Croatian greeting. (Croatia).

Dobro jutro. "Good morning." A common Serbo-Croatian and Slovene greeting. (Bosnia and Herzegovina, Croatia, Slovenia).

Dobro utro. "Good morning." A common greeting. (Bulgaria, Macedonia).

Dobro vecer. "Good evening." A common Serbo-Croatian greeting. (Bosnia and Herzegovina).

Dobroye utro. "Good morning." A common Russian greeting. (Russia).

Dobrú chut. "Good appetite." A Slovak wish made before a meal. (Slovakia).

Dobrý deň. "Good day." A formal Slovak greeting. (Slovakia).

Dobry den. "Good day." A common Czech greeting. (Czech Republic).

Dobry dien. "Good day." A common Russian greeting. (Russia).

Dobry dzen'! Yak spravy? "Hello! How are you?" A common Belarusian greeting. (Belarus).

Dobryj den'. "Good day." A common Ukrainian greeting. (Ukraine).

Dobry vecher. "Good evening." A common Russian greeting. (Russia).

Glossary of Cultural Terms

Dobry wieczór. "Good evening." A common Polish greeting. (Poland).

Doce de coco. A snack made of coconut and sugar. (Cape Verde).

Doce de leite. A snack made of milk, sugar, and lemon. (Cape Verde).

Doganym. "Sibling." A term of address used with equals and younger acquaintances. (Turkmenistan). *See also* **Jigim.**

Dohl pouri. Thin bread with meat and curry sauce inside. (Mauritius).

Doi moi. The Vietnamese economic policy of "renovation." Characterized by economic restructuring, more private enterprise and other market-oriented policies, and more open international trade. (Vietnam).

Doira. A drum-like tambourine. A traditional Uzbek musical instrument. (Uzbekistan).

Dollard Des Ormeaux. Many French-speaking Canadians celebrate this holiday instead of Victoria Day on the third Monday in May. While Victoria Day honors England's Queen Victoria, *Dollard Des Ormeaux* celebrates a battle hero from Québec's early days. (Canada).

Dolma. Grapes or cabbage leaves stuffed with meat, cracked wheat, greens, and spices. (Armenia).

Dolmuşes. Shared taxis. (Turkey).

Dolo cabarets. Local beer stands where both men and women gather for drink, food, and conversation. (Burkina Faso).

Doma. Betel nut. (Bhutan).

Dombra. A two-stringed instrument similar to a mandolin. (Kazakstan).

Dominsoara. "Miss." A Romanian title used with the family name for all but close friends and relatives. (Moldova).

Dom kultury. "House of culture." A community recreation center. (Russia).

Domnul. "Mister." A Romanian title used with the family name for all but close friends and relatives. (Moldova).

Domoda. Peanut butter stew. (Gambia).

Don. (1) A Spanish title used with a male's first name to show respect. Used in Spanish-speaking countries.. (2) A robe. (Turkmenistan).

Doña. A Spanish title used with a female's first name to show respect. Used in Spanish-speaking countries..

Dona. "Lady." A term of address used as a sign of respect. (Cape Verde).

Dong. Vietnam's national currency. (Vietnam).

Doo doo. Someone who looks good. (Trinidad and Tobago).

Do parana. "Good afternoon." A common Bari greeting. (Sudan).

Do pure. "Good morning." A common Bari greeting. (Sudan).

Dorood. "Greetings." A typical Farsi greeting. (Iran).

Dorood-bar-to. "Greetings to you." The proper response to the Farsi greeting **Dorood**. (Iran).

Doručak. The Serbian word for "breakfast." (Serbia and Montenegro).

Dost. The Uzbek word for "friend." Specifically, a very close friend. (Uzbekistan).

Do svidaniya. "Good-bye." A formal Russian parting phrase. (Belarus).

Dot. Gifts that a groom must give to the bride's family when they get engaged and when they marry. (Gabon).

Do te shihemi. "See you later." A common Albanian parting phrase. (Albania).

Dóttir. The Icelandic word for "daughter." (Iceland).

Doubles. Popular fast-food Indian dish which consists of fried dough stuffed with chickpeas and hot sauce. (Trinidad and Tobago).

Doucana. A dish with coconut, sweet potatoes, flour, sugar, and spices, served with spicy **Saltfish**. (Antigua and Barbuda).

Dovga. Rice mixed with yogurt and herbs. (Azerbaijan).

Do videnia. "Good-bye." A formal Slovak parting pharse. (Slovakia).

Do vidjenja. "Good-bye." A Croatian parting phrase. (Bosnia and Herzegovina, Croatia).

Dovijdane. "Till I see you again." A common Bulgarian parting phrase. (Bulgaria).

Do widzenia. "Good-bye." A common Polish parting phrase. (Poland).

Drachma. Greece's national currency prior to the euro. (Greece).

Drago mi je. "I am pleased." A Serbian expression used upon introduction. (Serbia and Montenegro).

Dragstors. The Serbian word for "drugstores." (Serbia and Montenegro).

Dram. Armenia's national currency. (Armenia).

Dramnyen. A lute. (Bhutan).

Draughts. A game similiar to checkers. (Antigua and Barbuda, Barbados, Grenada).

Dreamtime. According to Aboriginal belief, the time when ancient ancestors created the land and living things. (Australia).

Dreich. A word for "dull." (Scotland).

Dressers. People who staff dispensaries and provide first aid. (Tuvalu).

Driglam namzha. A traditional code of etiquette. (Bhutan).

Droog. The Russian word for "friend." Specifically, a very close friend. (Uzbekistan).

Drug. "Comrade." A Serbo-Croatian term of address for men. (Bosnia and Herzegovina).

Drugarice. "Comrade." A Serbo-Croatian term of address for women. (Bosnia and Herzegovina). *See also* **Gospodijica, Gospodin, Gospodja.**

Du. The familiar "you" form of address in German. (Liechtenstein).

Dub. A style of music in which disc jockeys rap street poems. (Grenada, Montserrat, Saint Lucia).

Duduk. An oboe carved from apricot wood. The Armenian national instrument. (Armenia).

Duendes. According to legend, little elves that live in the jungle and play tricks on people. (Guam).

Duff. Pudding. (Bahamas).

Duglas. A group of people descended from East Indians and Africans. (Grenada).

Dugutigi. A village chief. (Mali).

Duka. An informal shop. (Tanzania).

Dulceață. Fruit preserves. (Romania).

Duma. A 450-seat house in the Federal Assembly. (Russia).

Dumela. Literally, "I see you." A Sotho greeting meaning "hello." (South Africa).

Dumela Rra/Mma, O tsogile jang? "Greetings, sir/madam, how did you wake?" A common adult Setswana greeting. (Botswana).

Dundun. The "talking drum." Its tones can be understood as words. (Nigeria).

Glossary of Cultural Terms

Dupalar. Squarish hats with a traditional design that identifies the wearer's home region. (Uzbekistan).

Dupatta. A scarf worn by women. (Pakistan).

Durbakkah. An earthenware drum. (Jordan).

Durchlaucht. "Your Serene Highness." A German phrase used to address the Liechtenstein prince. (Liechtenstein).

Dussehra. A Hindu holiday that celebrates the triumph of good over evil. (India).

Dvorets kultury. "Palace of Culture." A community recreation center. (Russia).

Dyed Morosz. The Russian name of Grandfather Frost. At the beginning of the year, he delivers gifts to children. (Kazakstan, Russia). *See also* **Ayaz Ata, Noviy Gohd, Zhanga Zhyl.**

Dyna. Minibus used in Ivory Coast. (Ivory Coast). *See also* **Badjan, Gbaka.**

Dzèkounmè. A cornmeal mixture stirred into boiling tomato sauce and eaten with fried meat, chicken, crab, or fish. (Togo).

Dzhorgosalysh. Horseback races characterized by the gait known as a pace. Popular for betting. (Kyrgyzstan).

Dziękuję. The Polish phrase for "thank you." (Poland).

Dzień dobry. "Good day." A common Polish greeting. (Poland).

Dzongda. A person who has broad authority to implement and enforce government programs at the district level. (Bhutan).

Dzongkhag. A district in the Bhutanese government. (Bhutan).

Dzongs. Monastic fortress complexes built in the 17th century. Today they serve as government centers. (Bhutan).

E aa koe na? "What are you doing?" or "How are you?" A casual Tuvaluan greeting. (Tuvalu).

Eba. Gari boiled in water and served as a side dish. (Benin).

Echar una zorrita. (1) A Spanish phrase meaning "to throw a little fox." (2) A Venezuelan colloquialism that means "to take a nap." (Venezuela).

École de Base. Basic Education, grades 1 to 6. (Tunisia).

École primaire. French for "primary school." (Comoros).

Ecuavolley. Ecuadorian volleyball. Played with a heavy ball and three players on each side. (Ecuador).

Edep. A quality referring to politeness, graciousness, modesty, hospitality, respect toward elders and guests, and responsibility toward family. (Turkmenistan).

Edje. "Hello." A Shingazidja greeting used between social equals. (Comoros).

Educación básica. "Basic education." A three-year program following elementary school for youth ages 12 to 15. (El Salvador).

Eduskunta. The Finnish Parliment. (Finland).

Eet smakelijk. "Eat deliciously." An expression used to begin a meal. (Netherlands).

E fano koe ki fea? "Where are you going?" A common Tuvaluan greeting. (Tuvalu).

Efes. The Turkish name for the city of Ephesus. (Turkey).

Eh. (1) A Canadian phrase used in similar ways to the phrases "Ya know" and "Isn't it?" (Canada). (2) Expresses disbelief when used with the gesture of tossing one's head to the side. (Rwanda).

Ei. "Hi." A Tahitian greeting used when passersby are not close enough for a handshake. (French Polynesia).

Eid al Adha. (Bahrain, Oman, Saudi Arabia, Somalia). *See* **Eid al-Adha.**

Eid al-Adha. [NOTE: Spelling varies because it is a transliteration of Arabic. Also, Muslim holidays are set according to the lunar calendar.] Feast of the Sacrifice. A Muslim holiday that commemorates Abraham's willingness to sacrifice his son. Celebrated in predominantly Muslim countries. (Iraq, Jordan, Kuwait, Libya, Qatar, Syria, United Arab Emirates, Yemen). *Also called* **Aid al Kebir, Eid Arafat.**

Eid al-Fitr. (Iraq, Ivory Coast, Jordan, Kuwait, Libya, Qatar, Syria, United Arab Emirates, Yemen). *See* **Aid al Fitr.**

Eid al Fitr. (Bahrain, Guinea, Oman, Saudi Arabia, Somalia). *See* **Aid al Fitr.**

Eid Arafat. Feast of the Sacrifice. A Muslim holiday that commemorates Abraham's willingness to sacrifice his son. (Yemen). *Also called* **Eid al-Adha.**

Eid el Adha. (Eritrea). *See* **Eid al-Adha.**

Eid el Fitr. (Eritrea). *See* **Aid al Fitr.**

Eid-el-Fitre. (Gambia). *See* **Aid al Fitr.**

Eid-el-kabir. (Gambia). *See* **Aid al Kebir.**

Eid-i-Milad-un-Nabi. (Pakistan). *See* **Mouloud.**

Eid Milad el-Nabi. (Eritrea). *See* **Mouloud.**

Eid-ul-Adha. (Mauritius). *See* **Eid al-Adha.**

Eid ul-Adha. (Ghana, Lebanon). *See* **Eid al-Adha.**

Eid-ul-Azha. (Bangladesh, Pakistan). *See* **Eid al-Adha.**

Eid-ul-Fitr. (Bangladesh, Mauritius, Pakistan, Trinidad and Tobago). *See* **Aid al Fitr.**

Eid ul-Fitr. (Ghana, Lebanon). *See* **Aid al Fitr.**

Ei Iaora. "Hi." A Tahitian greeting used when passersby are not close enough for a handshake. (French Polynesia).

Eingyi. A short-collared shirt worn by Burmese men. Accompanies a **Taikpon** and a **Longyi**. (Myanmar).

Eisteddfod. A national Welsh festival held the first week of August. It features competitions in music, drama, literature, and art. (Wales).

Ejay. "Older sister." A Kyrgyz title used to address a woman older than the speaker. (Kyrgyzstan).

Ekalesia Niue. A local denomination related to Congregationalism; an offspring of the London Missionary Society. (Niue).

Ekalesia Tuvalu. The Christian Church of Tuvalu. (Tuvalu).

E karo. "Good morning." A common Yoruba greeting. (Benin).

Ekushe. A political holiday on 21 February that honors six people killed in a 1952 political protest. (Bangladesh).

El Congreso Nacional. The Bolivian National Congress. (Bolivia).

El desayuno. Spanish for "breakfast." (Spain).

El Fitr. (Mauritania). *See* **Aid al Fitr.**

El gaucho Martín Fierro. Argentina's national epic poem. Describes the life of a cowboy. (Argentina). *See also* **Gaucho(s).**

El hadj. (Niger). *See* **Hadj.**

Elhamduli Allah. (Algeria). *See* **Al hamdu lillah.**

Elinize sağlik. "Bless your hand." A Turkish phrase used to compliment the cook. (Turkey).

El Intelaka. A Muslim holiday that celebrates the anniversary of the first day of Fatah resistance. (West Bank and Gaza).

El interior. "The interior." The area of land located outside the Panama Canal Zone. (Panama).

El Loco. "The Madman." A nickname for Abdalá Bucaram because of his flamboyant personality. He won the 1996 presidental elections. (Ecuador).

El Mouled. (Tunisia). *See* **Mouloud.**

El pato. A Spanish word meaning "the duck." Argentina's national sport is nicknamed el pato because the ball game used to be played with a leather stuffed duck. (Argentina).

El pesebre. The Spanish phrase for "the nativity." (Colombia).

Glossary of Cultural Terms

El Shabka. "Big Feast." A wedding celebration held at hotels or large homes. (West Bank and Gaza).

El trópico. Wet, hot, forested lowlands found in the east and northeast of Bolivia. (Bolivia). *Also called* **Llano(s).**

Ema datsi. A hot curry of red chilies and farmer's cheese. (Bhutan).

Emahiya. (Swaziland). *See* **Lihiya.**

EmaKhandza embili. Tribes present in the region now known as Swaziland when the Swazi people migrated there in the mid-1700s. (Swaziland).

EmaSwati. "People of Mswati." The Swazi people. (Swaziland).

Empanadas. Meat, vegetable, or cheese turnovers. (Argentina, Chile, Colombia, Costa Rica, Ecuador, Paraguay).

Empanadas de horno. Meat turnovers with beef, hard-boiled eggs, onions, olives, and raisins. (Chile).

Enah. "Yes." Meaning "hello." A Machushi response to the greeting **Morogeh koman honah**. (Guyana).

Enchiladas. Tortillas filled with meat and covered in a chile sauce. (Mexico).

Endemin neh? "How are you?" An Amharic phrase used to greet males among friends and peers. (Ethiopia).

Endemin nesch? "How are you?" An Amharic phrase used to greet females among friends and peers. (Ethiopia).

Endlini kaGogo. "Grandmother's hut." The best and most highly respected place on the homestead, usually offered to overnight guests. (Swaziland).

E noho ra. "Stay well." A Maori expression commonly used to reply to the phrase **Haere ra**. (New Zealand).

Ensalada chilena. Tomato-and-onion salad served chilled. (Chile).

Entrik. The Armenian word for "dinner." (Armenia).

Epos. Tajik historical or legendary poems. (Tajikistan).

Equib. A savings club. (Ethiopia).

Erythrea. The Greek word for "red" from which Eritrea derived its name. (Eritrea).

Escabeche. Onion soup. (Belize).

Escudo. Cape Verde's national currency. (Cape Verde).

Esh. Boiled millet flour. (Chad).

Esha. The Arabic word for "supper." (Bahrain).

Eshloanak. "How are you?" A common Arabic phrase used to greet men. (Bahrain, Kuwait).

Eshloanich. "How are you?" A common Arabic phrase used to greet women. (Bahrain, Kuwait).

Español. The Spanish word generally used for the Spanish language. In some countries, however, Spanish is called **Castellano**. (Paraguay).

Estadounidense. A Spanish word for U.S. citizens. (El Salvador).

Está en su casa. "You are in your house." A traditional Spanish greeting used to welcome visitors to one's home. (Peru).

Estar limpio. (1) To be clean. A Spanish phrase. (Venezuela). (2) To be out of money. A Venezuelan colloquialism. (Venezuela).

Estar pelado. (1) To be bald. A Spanish phrase. (Venezuela). (2) To be out of money. A Venezuelan colloquialism. (Venezuela).

Está servido? "Will you join me?" A Portuguese expression used to invite guests to join in a meal or a snack. (Brazil).

Estilo manabita. A Spanish phrase for "common-law marriages." (Ecuador).

Estou bem. "I am fine." A Portuguese response to the greeting **Como está?** (Cape Verde).

Estou bem, obrigado. "Fine, thank you." A Portuguese response to the formal greeting **Como está?** (Mozambique).

Estoy lleno. "I am full." A Spanish phrase. (El Salvador).

Etrennes. A New Year's gift. (France).

Evala. Traditional wrestling. (Togo).

Evangélicos. Evangelical protestants. (Bolivia, Guatemala, Honduras).

Ewegba. An Ewe term for a communal bowl that meals are served in. (Togo).

Fa'alupega. The official list of names and ranks of each village's chiefs and orators. (American Samoa). *See also* **Matai, Tulafale.**

Faamu. Adoptive parents. (French Polynesia).

Faano. Traditional skirts worn by older women. (Gambia).

Faapu. The family garden. (French Polynesia).

Fa'a Samoa. "The Samoan Way." A casual way of life that is careful to respect and preserve tradition. (American Samoa, Samoa).

Faatele. A traditional Tuvaluan dance. (Tuvalu).

Fado. A style of Portuguese folk singing that has influenced Guinea-Bissauan pop music. (Guinea-Bissau).

Fadys. The Malagasy word for "taboos." (Madagascar).

Fafa. A type of spinach. (French Polynesia).

Fafaru. "Smelly fish." Fish that is fermented in seawater for several days. (French Polynesia).

Fa fu den sama? "How is your family?" A Ndyuka greeting. (Suriname).

Fahu. The leader over the nuclear family in the highly organized extended family system; usually the father's eldest sister. (Tonga). *See also* **Mehikitanga.**

Fa'i. Green bananas. (Samoa).

Faikai. Chunks of fish marinated in coconut cream. (Niue).

Faikava. The dating practice of making **Kava**; a boy may ask a girl to have a *faikava* at her home. (Tonga).

Faja. A woven belt worn by men and women. (Guatemala).

Fakaala. The Tuvaluan word for "feast." (Tuvalu).

Fakaalofa atu. "Love be with you." A Niuean greeting. (Niue).

Faka Tonga. "The Tongan Way" of life. Characterized by being easygoing and relaxed. (Tonga).

Falafel. Pita bread filled with fried balls of crushed garbanzo beans. (Israel, West Bank and Gaza).

Falaninii. Sleeping mats. (Samoa).

Fale. A house or shelter. (Niue, Tonga, Tuvalu).

Fale Alea. The Tongan Legislative Assembly. (Tonga).

Fale fono. Village council house. (American Samoa).

Fale telefoni. Telephone house, where the telephone for the village or several villages is kept. (Tonga).

Famadihana. "Turning of the bones." An ancestor veneration ceremony in which a family exhumes an ancestor's body to wrap it in a new burial shroud. (Madagascar). *See also* **Lambamena.**

Fandango. A large party. (Guam).

Fanmi Lavalas. A political party in Haiti named after the Lavalas family. (Haiti).

Fanorona. A traditional game played by strategically placing small stones in hollows of a board or on the ground. (Madagascar).

Farakha. A wavy, knotted tassel worn at the neck by men. (Oman). *Also called* **Kashkusha.**

Glossary of Cultural Terms

Faranji. A head covering worn by rural women. (Tajikistan).
Farashiya. A garment worn by older, traditional women in Libya; it is a white, sheet-like cover that conceals the entire body, the head, and one eye. (Libya).
Faratas. A food similar to pancakes. (Mauritius).
Fårikål. Cabbage and mutton. (Norway).
Farmhouse restaurants. Irish restaurants that feature traditional recipes. (Ireland).
Fasching. A German word for Carnival. (Austria, Germany).
Fasika. Easter. (Eritrea).
Fasnacht. A German word for Carnival. (Liechtenstein).
Fastelavn. A Danish holiday marked by public celebration and games. (Denmark).
Fasule. Boiled dried beans. (Albania).
Fat cakes. Deep-fried dough. (Botswana).
Fatta. A dish made of bread, peas, tomatoes, cheese, lentils, and other ingredients. (Sudan).
Favelas. Shantytowns located on the outskirts of urban centers. (Brazil).
Fa waka? Literally, "How are you walking?" A Sranan Tongo greeting meaning "How are you?" (Suriname). *See also* **Fa'y go?, Fa'y tan?**
Fa'y go? Literally, "How are you going?" A Sranan Tongo greeting meaning "How are you?" (Suriname). *See also* **Fa waka?, Fa'y tan?**
Fa'y tan? Literally, "How are you staying?" A Sranan Tongo greeting meaning "How are you?" (Suriname). *See also* **Fa waka?, Fa'y go?**
Fedayeen. Palestinian resistance members. (Jordan).
Fedoras. Fur caps worn by men. (Lithuania).
Fefe hake? "How do you do?" A Tongan greeting used upon introduction. (Tonga).
Feijoada. Black beans with beef, pork, sausage, and sometimes a pig's ears, feet, and tail. (Brazil).
Feiticeiros. Witches. People believe that witches can free them from a problem or help them obtain wealth, usually at the expense of others. Deaths or accidents are often attributed to witchcraft. (Angola). *Also called* **Macumbeiros.**
Feliz Arabia. "Happy Arabia." The name the ancient Romans gave to Yemen because of its people's hospitality and strong society. (Yemen).
Feliz noite. A Portuguese parting phrase meaning "Good night." (Angola).
Fenkata. Stewed rabbit. (Malta).
Ferias. Traveling markets or fairs. (Chile, Venezuela).
Festa(s). Feast Day. A holiday that honors a local patron saint. (Malta).
Festival. Fried dough. (Jamaica).
Fête. A party. (Saint Lucia).
Fête de Mouton. [NOTE: Muslim holidays are set according to the lunar calendar.] A Muslim holiday that commemorates Abraham's willingness to sacrifice his son. (Cameroon, Gabon). *Also called* **Eid al-Adha.**
Fête de Notre Dame. A very large festival generally held in August. (Haiti).
Fête des Masques. The "Festival of Masks" is an event that takes place in the region around Man every November. During the festival, local people compete in dances and honor the spirits they believe live in large wooden masks. (Ivory Coast).
Fête des Mères. Mother's Day. Celebrated at the end of May. (Central African Republic).

Fête Dieu. A Haitian celebration held the first Thursday in June. The festivities mark the institution of the sacrament or communion. (Haiti).
Fête du 3 janvier. A holiday in commemoration of the 3 January 1966 uprising. (Burkina Faso).
Fête du Dipri. The "Festival of the Dipri" is an overnight exorcism event that takes place in Gomon during the spring. (Ivory Coast).
Fête du Ramadan. The feast celebrated at the end of the month of **Ramadan**. (Cameroon).
Fête du Travail. Labor Day or May Day. Celebrated on 1 May. (Central African Republic, Gabon).
Fête National. A holiday that commemorates independence. Celebrated on 17 August. (Gabon).
Fetes. (1) Fund-raising parties. (Montserrat). (2) Parties. (Barbados).
Fèt Gede. A holiday that honors the dead. (Haiti).
Fiafia. A party. (Niue, Samoa).
Field trip. Ships that transport passengers and supplies to and from outer islands. (Micronesia).
Fiereljeppen. Pole-vaulting for distance. (Netherlands).
Fiestas. The word for "parties." Used in Spanish-speaking countries..
Fietspaden. The Dutch word for "bike paths." (Netherlands).
Fihavanana. A well-maintained relationship. (Madagascar).
Fil. A kind of yogurt. (Sweden).
Finadene. A sauce made of soy sauce, lemon juice, hot peppers, and onions. (Guam).
Finants. The Estonian word for "finance." (Estonia).
Fincas. Agricultural plots in the forest. (Equatorial Guinea).
Fin du Ramadan. The feast celebrated at the end of the month of **Ramadan**. (Gabon). *Also called* **Aid al Fitr.**
Fine'eiki. "Mrs." A Tongan title. (Tonga).
Finmark. The name of the former Finnish national currency. (Finland). *Also called* **Markka.**
Fish-and-chips. Fish and french fries. (England).
Fish suppers. Fish and chips seasoned with salt and vinegar. (Scotland).
Fish water. Fish stew. (Antigua and Barbuda).
Fisting. Hitting fists together. Often replacing a handshake or embrace between friends when coming or going. (Saint Vincent and the Grenadines).
Fit fit. Bits of bread. (Eritrea).
Fit like. A Scottish colloquialism for "How are you?" (Scotland).
Flats. Apartments. (England, Ireland, Scotland, Singapore, Wales).
Fo. An Ewe term of address children use for their fathers. (Togo).
Fofo. (1) A Mina term of address children use for their fathers. (Togo). (2) "Brother." A respectful term of address used to address an older male. (Benin).
Föhn A warm southerly wind. (Liechtenstein).
Folkeshøjskole. The Danish word for "community college." (Denmark).
Folkeskole. Literally, "people's school," it is a primary school. (Denmark).
Folketing. The Danish Parliament. (Denmark).
Fondue. A traditional dish in which pieces of bread are dipped in melted cheese. (Switzerland).

Glossary of Cultural Terms

Fono. (1) Village council. (American Samoa, Samoa). (2) Legislative Assembly. (Samoa).

Fonopule. Island councils that manage local government. (Tuvalu).

Football. The game people in the United States call "soccer." A term used outside the United States..

Footy. An Australian colloquialism for Australian-rules football. (Australia).

Foreninger. Local community clubs. (Denmark).

Form. A grade in school. (England, Guyana, Lithuania, Malawi, Montserrat).

Fostering. The custom of loaning a child to a childless woman or a wealthy person. (Sierra Leone).

Fou. Flower garlands that are worn in the hair on festive occasions. (Tuvalu).

Foul. (Egypt). *See* **Ful.**

Foutour. The Arabic word for "breakfast." (Bahrain). *Also called* **Iftar.**

Franc. (1) The national currency of various countries. (Comoros, Congo, Guinea, Liechtenstein, Rwanda, Switzerland). (2) The former national currency. (France, Madagascar).

Frau. "Mrs." or "Miss." A German title used with the last name. (Austria, Germany).

Freetambos. Miniature deer. (Sierra Leone).

Frère. "Brother." A familial title used with strangers as well as family. (Guinea).

Frijoles. Red beans. (El Salvador).

Frijoles con chicharrón. Pork and beans. (Colombia).

Frikadeller. Danish meatballs. (Denmark).

Fritada. Fried pork. (Ecuador).

Frittatensuppe. Soup with shredded crêpes. (Austria).

Fritten, Ham an Zalot. French fries, ham, and salad. (Luxembourg).

Frituras. Foods fried in oil. (Puerto Rico).

Frokostbord. A cold buffet of many different foods. (Denmark).

Fuaga mei. Breadfruit. (Tuvalu).

Fualah. A ritual meal of sweets and fruits. Provided to first-time visitors. (United Arab Emirates).

Fufu. A stiff paste made by boiling flour. (Cameroon, Ghana, Togo).

Führer. The German word for "leader." (Germany).

Fuji. Nigerian music that has several drums but no guitars. Dancing will often accompany the music. (Nigeria).

Ful. Spicy beans. (Yemen).

Funáná. A lively and popular form of dance music with a strong beat. (Cape Verde).

Fundi. A title for a teacher or craftsman. (Comoros).

Funge. A paste of ground cornmeal, similar to thick porridge. A staple food at lunch and dinner. (Angola).

Fungee. A soft bread made with cornmeal and okra that is baked in a bowl. (Antigua and Barbuda).

Fungi. Cooked cornmeal with okra. (U.S. Virgin Islands).

Funkasunntig. Bonfire Sunday. A holiday with folk and pagan origins. (Liechtenstein).

Fürst. The ruling prince. (Liechtenstein).

Fusi. A co-op store that carries staple foods and sundry items. (Tuvalu).

Fußball. The German word for "soccer." (Germany).

Fustanelle. A full, colorful wool skirt, part of a traditional outfit. (Albania).

Futah. (1) A dark wraparound dress worn by older Amazigh women. (Tunisia). (2) A patterned cotton cloth wrapped around the lower part of the body. Worn by men. (Yemen).

Fútbol. The word for "soccer." Used in Spanish-speaking countries..

Futebol. The Portuguese word for "soccer." (Brazil, Cape Verde).

Futi. Plantains or cooking bananas. (Tuvalu).

Fu true. A common Montserratian phrase used to add emphasis. (Montserrat).

Futu. A heavy paste made of pounded yams, cassavas, and plantains; southern Ivorians make this dish, often dipping it in sauce. (Ivory Coast).

Futur. Breakfast. (Iraq). *Also called* **Riyuq.**

Fye. "Good evening." A Ewe greeting. (Togo).

Fylker. The Norwegian word meaning "province." (Norway).

Ga'at. A thick barley porridge. (Eritrea).

Gabay. Political poetry. (Somalia).

Gaboot. Raisin-filled dumplings in a meat stew. (Kuwait).

Gado-gado. A dish of vegetables and tofu topped with peanut sauce. (Indonesia).

Gaelic football. A sport played with a round ball. Combines elements of soccer and basketball. (Ireland, Northern Ireland).

Gagaku. Japanese music played with string and wind instruments and drums. (Japan).

Gagimarjos. "Hello." An informal Georgian response to the greeting **Gamarjoba.** (Georgia).

Gahwa. Coffee flavored with cardamom. (Kuwait).

Gaida. A bagpipe. A traditional musical instrument. (Bulgaria).

Gaines. A caste of professional singers that perform Hindu songs and tell stories. (Nepal).

Gaita. A type of accordion. (Cape Verde).

Gaitas. (1) Bagpipes. (Spain). (2) Traditional Christmas music. (Venezuela). *See also* **Aguinaldos.**

Gajda. A type of bagpipe. Used in the traditional music that accompanies folk dances. (Macedonia).

Gajde. A type of bagpipe. (Albania).

Gala. The Latvian word for "meat." (Latvia).

Gallebeyya. A long dress-like robe worn by rural men. (Egypt).

Gallo pinto. A dish of rice and beans fried together. (Costa Rica, Nicaragua).

Gallos. Tortillas with meat and vegetable fillings. (Costa Rica).

Galyn. Bride-price. (Turkmenistan).

Gaman. "Enduring patience," a respected Japanese trait. (Japan).

Gamarjoba. "Hello." A Georgian greeting. Literally, "Let you win." (Georgia).

Gamelan. A traditional music orchestra with gongs, xylophones, drums, and other percussion instruments. (Indonesia, Malaysia, Suriname).

Ganoon. A charcoal basket used for cooking. (Chad).

Gara. Dyed fabrics. Artists apply wax designs to the fabric, place it in a dye bath, and remove the wax to reveal the pattern. (Sierra Leone).

Garabouts. Boys who attend **Qur'anic** schools and must beg for food daily. (Mali).

Garamut. A traditional musical instrument. A log with a small hollowed-out portion where a stick is rhythmically beaten. (Papua New Guinea).

Garçom. Literally, "boy." A French term used to call a waiter. (Brazil).

Glossary of Cultural Terms

Garçon. A greeting used among male peers that is equivalent to "man" or "dude." (Saint Lucia).

Gari. A type of grits made from cassava. (Benin).

Garinagu. People of mixed Caribbean and African descent. (Belize).

Garnaches. Fried tortillas with beans, cheese, and sauce. (Belize).

Garri. Grated cassava that is dried over a fire until light and flaky. (Cameroon).

Garrison constituencies. Communities over which political parties strive to maintain control. Parties have joined with urban gangs to force citizens to vote in certain ways. (Jamaica).

Garrobo. Iguana soup. (Nicaragua).

Gasabah. Cane flute. (Jordan).

Gaspa. A long bamboo flute. (Algeria).

Gasthaus. A pub. (Austria).

Gate jo-ni mo? "Where are you going?" A common Dzongkha greeting to passersby. (Bhutan).

Gaucho(s). The Spanish word for "cowboy" or "herdsman." (Argentina, Uruguay).

Gaung-baung. A round cap of pink or yellow silk stretched over a rush frame. Worn by Burmese men on the most formal occasions. (Myanmar).

Gazpacho. Cold vegetable soup. (Spain).

Gbaka. Minibus used in Ivory Coast. (Ivory Coast). *See also* **Badjan, Dyna.**

Gebetta. A strategy game played with pebbles on a playing surface that is created by making depressions in the ground. (Eritrea).

Geduk. A short drum made from a hollow tree trunk. (Malaysia).

Gefilte. A dish of baked or stewed ground fish. (Israel).

Gekookte aardappelen. Boiled potatoes. (Netherlands).

Gelneje. "Sister-in-law." A common term of respect added to a female formal acquaintance's name. (Turkmenistan). *See also* **Daiza, Hanum.**

Gemütlichkeit. A relaxed and happy approach to life; an Austrian trait. (Austria).

Gena. A rural sport similar to field hockey. (Ethiopia).

Genji. A sleeveless vest worn by rural men. (Bangladesh). *See also* **Lungi.**

Genkan. A small hallway between the door and living area, where one stands to remove one's shoes. (Japan).

Genki? "How's it going?" A common casual greeting used among the youth. (Japan). *See also* **Ohayou.**

Gerobak jualan. A mobile eatery. The vendors are called **Kaki lima.** (Indonesia).

Ger(s). A wooden tent covered in sheep-wool felt and a white cloth. (Mongolia).

Getna. A holiday celebrated when the dates are ripe. (Mauritania).

Gezondheid. The Dutch equivalent of saying "Bless you." One can also say **Proost.** (Netherlands).

Gezuar. "Cheers." An Albanian phrase used by vistors before drinking. (Albania).

Ghada. The Arabic word for "lunch." (Bahrain).

Ghana. A type of Maltese music that incorporates both Arabic and Italian influences. Pronounced "ah-nah." Performed by **Ghannejja.** (Malta).

Ghannejja. Singers. (Malta). *See also* **Ghana.**

Gharara. A long blouse worn over a long skirt with a matching shawl. (Suriname).

Gharbata. Tea. (Belarus).

Ghatak. A matchmaker. (Bangladesh).

Ghee. Clarified butter. (Nepal, Somalia).

Ghidaa'. Lunch. (Iraq).

Ghishwa. A face veil worn by conservative Muslim women. (United Arab Emirates).

Gho. A long-sleeved, ankle-length robe that is hoisted to knee level and belted tightly so that it forms pleats in the back and a deep pocket at the belly. Traditional attire worn by men. (Bhutan).

Ghozi. A whole lamb or kid goat stuffed with seasoned rice. (Qatar). *Also called* **Kubsa.**

Ghutra. (Qatar, Saudi Arabia). *See* **Gutra.**

Gidday. A colloquialism for "Good day." An informal greeting. (New Zealand).

Gimnazija. General education high school that prepares students for university studies. (Macedonia).

Githeri. A dish of corn and beans. (Kenya).

Gjelle. A dish of boiled beans or vegetables with meat. (Albania).

Gjithe te mirat. "All the best." A typical Albanian parting phrase. (Albania).

Glamorgan sausages. A meatless dish made with cheese, bread crumbs, herbs, and leeks. (Wales).

Glasnost. The Russian policy of openness. (Latvia, Russia).

Glens. Valleys. (Scotland).

Goat water. A spicy stew made with goat meat. (Antigua and Barbuda, Montserrat, Saint Kitts and Nevis).

Goddag. "Good day." A Danish greeting. (Denmark).

God dag. "Good day." A Norwegian and Swedish formal greeting. (Norway, Sweden).

God morgon. "Good morning." A formal Swedish greeting. (Sweden).

Godo. "Other side." An Ewe term. Combined with **To,** "waters," it forms the name of the lakeside village of Togodo, for which Togo is named. (Togo).

Goedemorgen. "Good morning." A common Dutch greeting. (Suriname).

Goeiedag. "Good day." A Dutch greeting. (Belgium).

Goeie môre. "Good morning." An Afrikaans greeting. (South Africa).

Gogo. (1) A traditional music rhythm. (Benin). (2) The siSwati word for "grandmother." (Swaziland).

Goiabeira. A square-cut, embroidered shirt worn by government and office workers. (Mozambique).

Golubtsy. Stuffed cabbage leaves baked with tomato sauce and eaten with sour cream. (Russia).

Gombo. A sauce made with okra, small fish, and baobab leaves. (Togo).

Gomesi. A many-layered traditional dress. (Uganda).

Goombay. A type of island music created with goatskin drums, saws, and maracas. (Bahamas). *See also* **Rake n' scrape.**

Gordita. A Spanish word meaning "little fat one." In some places, it is not considered rude to comment on such physical attributes. (Argentina).

Goro. Kola nuts. (Niger).

Gospa. "Madam." A Slovene title used to show respect. (Slovenia).

Gospod. "Sir." A Slovene title used to show respect. (Slovenia).

Glossary of Cultural Terms

Gospodična. "Miss." A Slovene title used to show respect. (Slovenia).

Gospodijica. "Miss." A Serbo-Croatian title. (Bosnia and Herzegovina).

Gospodin. "Mister." A Slavic title. (Belarus, Bosnia and Herzegovina, Bulgaria, Macedonia, Russia, Serbia and Montenegro).

Gospodine. "Mister." A Croatian title. (Croatia).

Gospodja. "Mrs." A Serbian title. (Bosnia and Herzegovina, Serbia and Montenegro).

Gospodjice. "Miss." A Croatian title. (Croatia).

Gospodjo. "Mrs." A Croatian title. (Croatia).

Gospogja. "Mrs." (Macedonia).

Gospogjica. "Miss." (Macedonia).

Gospozh. (Belarus). *See* **Gospozha.**

Gospozha. "Mrs." A Bulgarian and Russian title. (Bulgaria, Russia).

Gospozhitsa. "Miss." A Bulgarian title. (Bulgaria).

Gostilne. Local inns. (Slovenia).

Góðan daginn. "Good day." An Icelandic greeting to a stranger. (Iceland).

Go to the loo. A colloquialism for "go to the bathroom." (New Zealand).

Gourde. Haiti's national currency. (Haiti).

Gozinaki. A honey-and-walnut confection. (Georgia).

Gozo. A thick paste made by soaking cassava root in water, drying it in the sun, grinding it into flour, and boiling it. (Central African Republic).

Grabar. The Armenian word for "standard." (Armenia).

Gracias. The Spanish word for "Thank you." (Bolivia, Mexico).

Graha dasha. A traditional Nepali belief in which a bad position of the planets can cause disease, crop failures, or accidents. (Nepal). *See also* **Bhoot, Bokshi, Pret.**

Gran Colombia. A federation, including parts or all of present-day Colombia, Panama, Venezuela, and Ecuador. Led by Simón Bolívar, it was later dissolved. (Colombia, Ecuador).

Grand boubou. A robe that reaches a man's knees or feet. (Central African Republic). *See also* **Boubou(s).**

Grandes Ecoles. French schools to study for careers in government, the military, education, and industry. (France).

Grande soeur. French term meaning "big sister." Ivorians may call each other by familial names to show respect and affection even if they are not related. (Ivory Coast).

Grand frère. French term meaning "big brother." Ivorians may call each other by familial names to show respect and affection even if they are not related. (Ivory Coast).

Grandma. A term of address used by children for any older women. (Ghana).

Grandmbuba. Colorful traditional shirts worn by older women. (Gambia). *Also called* **Dendiko ba.**

Grandpa. A term of address used by children to address older men. (Ghana, Guyana).

Grannie. A term of address used by children to address older women. (Guyana).

Gratin. Potatoes sliced and baked with white sauce and cream. (Switzerland).

Green Book. Book in which Libyan leader Muammar Qaddafi explains his concepts about creating a direct democracy and new economy; however, the book does not include plans for implementation. (Libya).

Greenies. Environmentalists. (Australia).

Griessnockerlsuppe. Soup with small semolina dumplings. (Austria).

Gri gri. Good-luck charms. (Guinea, Mali, Senegal).

Grillad lax med spenat, citron och potatis eller ris. A dish of grilled slices of salmon with spinach, slices of lemon, and potatoes or rice. (Sweden).

Griots. Orators. (Burkina Faso, Gambia, Guinea, Mali, Mauritania, Senegal, Togo).

Gris. Coconut water. (Papua New Guinea).

Gris-gris. Charms. (Burkina Faso, Chad, Comoros, Mauritania).

Grita. A personally styled yell used to express friendship, break the monotony of fieldwork, and show joy at **Fiestas**. (Panama).

Gritería Day A holiday that celebrates Christ's conception. The Virgrin Mary is especially celebrated at this time. (Nicaragua).

Groentesoep. Vegetable soup. (Netherlands).

Grogue. Strong rum made from sugarcane; the national drink. (Cape Verde).

Groundnuts. A term for peanuts. (Ivory Coast).

Ground provisions. Root crops such as sweet potatoes and yams. (Guyana, Montserrat, Saint Lucia).

Groupe de grain. Informal peer groups. (Mali).

Grüezi. "Greetings." A Swiss German phrase used to greet strangers. (Liechtenstein).

Grundtvigianism. "The happy Lutheranism." A Danish movement. (Denmark).

Grüß Dich. "Greetings to you." A casual German greeting. (Austria).

Grüss Gott. "Greetings." A German phrase used to greet strangers. (Liechtenstein).

Grüß Gott. (Austria, Germany). *See* **Grüss Gott.**

Grütsie. "Hi." A typical Swiss German greeting. (Switzerland).

Gu. Somalia's season of heavy rains. Lasts from March to June. (Somalia).

Guacho. Rice soup. (Panama).

Guagua. A van or bus used as a taxi that runs a long fixed route. (Dominican Republic).

Guai. A Mongol term of address used to show honor to an elder or someone of higher status. (Mongolia).

Guampa. A container, usually made of wood, cattle horns, or gourds, used to drink tea. (Paraguay).

Guanacasta. A large fast-growing tree found in Central America. (Belize).

Guanxi. A principle that commits friends and associates to do what they can for each other when called upon. (China).

Guaraní. Paraguay's national currency. (Paraguay).

Guava cheese. A chewy dessert made by boiling and puréeing guavas before mixing them with sugar. (Grenada, Saint Kitts and Nevis).

Guayabera(s). A traditional, embroidered dress shirt worn by men. (Belize, Cuba, Honduras, Nicaragua, Panama, U.S. Virgin Islands).

Guayano(s). A scraping percussion instrument. (Dominican Republic).

Gud aftanun. "Good afternoon." A common Solomon Island Pijin greeting. (Solomon Islands).

Gudden Owend. "Good evening." A common Luxembourgish greeting. (Luxembourg).

Gudey. "Good afternoon." An English greeting adapted by the Ewe. (Togo).

Glossary of Cultural Terms

Gudivin. "Good evening." An English greeting adapted by the Ewe. (Togo).

Gud mone. "Good morning." A common Solomon Island Pijin greeting. (Solomon Islands).

Gud naet. "Good night." A common Solomon Island Pijin greeting. (Solomon Islands).

Guilder. The former currency of the Netherlands, before the euro was adopted in 2002. This currency was also known as the *florin*. (Netherlands).

Guiso. A dish made of ground beef with rice, onion, egg, etc. (Uruguay).

Guitarra. A cittern-like instrument. (Cape Verde).

Guitarrón. A 25-string guitar. (Chile).

Güle güle. "Good-bye." The response to the phrase **Allahaısmarladık**. (Turkey).

Gule Wamkulu. "Great Dance." Incorporates symbolic masks to tell stories and teach traditions. (Malawi).

Gulyás. "Goulash." A soup of meat, potatoes, onions, and paprika. (Hungary).

Gumbe. A popular musical rhythm. (Guinea-Bissau).

Gumboot. A popular dance developed by Black African gold miners. (South Africa).

Günaydin. "Good morning." A Turkish greeting. (Turkey).

Guntino. A 4-yard cloth worn by women; tied over one shoulder and wrapped around the waist. (Somalia).

Gurban Bayramy. A one-day festival commemorating Abraham's willingness to sacrifice his son. (Turkmenistan). *See also* **Eid al-Adha**.

Guriltai shul. Mutton-and-noodle soup. (Mongolia).

Gusle. A single-stringed instrument. (Bosnia and Herzegovina, Serbia and Montenegro).

¡Gusto de verte! "Nice to see you." A traditional Spanish greeting. (Chile).

Guten Abend. "Good evening." A common German greeting. (Austria, Switzerland).

Guten Morgen. "Good morning." A common German greeting. (Austria, Switzerland).

Guten Tag. "Good day." A common German greeting. (Austria, Germany, Switzerland).

Gutnait. "Good evening." A common Melanesian Pidgin greeting for acquaintances. (Papua New Guinea).

Gutra. A light cloth headdress worn by men. (Bahrain, Kuwait).

Guugs. Horse racing. (Ethiopia).

Gwata. A musical instrument played by the Acholi to accompany dance performances. A half gourd struck with metal bicycle spokes. (Uganda).

Gwon ada? "How are you?" A common Bari greeting. (Sudan).

Gyalpo. The Bhutanese king. (Bhutan).

Gymnasia. High school. (Switzerland).

Gymnasio. The level of schooling after elementary school. (Greece).

Gymnasium. A high school that prepares students to attend a university. (Bosnia and Herzegovina, Germany, Slovenia).

Habari? "News?" A common Swahili greeting. (Comoros, Kenya).

Habari gani? "What is the news?" A common Swahili greeting. (Kenya).

Habari za nyumbani? "How are things at your home?" A common Swahili phrase used to inquire about family. (Tanzania).

Habichuelas. Beans. (Dominican Republic).

Habichuelas con dulce. A dessert similar to rice pudding but made from beans. (Dominican Republic).

Hackbrett. A hammered dulcimer. A common Austrian folk instrument. (Austria).

Hadith. The Islamic prophet Muhammad's compiled sayings. (Oman, Qatar).

Hadj. [NOTE: Spelling varies because it is a transliteration of Arabic.] An Arabic title for Muslim men who have completed the pilgrimage to Makkah, Saudi Arabia. (Morocco).

Hadji. (Sudan). *See* **Hadj**.

Hadjia. An Arabic title for Muslim women who have completed the pilgrimage to Makkah, Saudi Arabia. (Niger).

Hadjilidj. A type of nut offered to favored guests. (Chad).

Ha-dudu. A sport played by village boys where two teams try to eliminate all the other team's players. One player will enter the other team's zone while holding his breath. He will try and touch the other players and make it back to his own zone. If he makes it back to his side while still holding his breath, the players he touched will be out. Otherwise, he is out. (Bangladesh). *Also called* **Ka-baddi**.

Haere ra. "Farewell." A common Maori parting phrase. (New Zealand).

Hafa adai. "Hello." A common Chamorro greeting. (Guam).

Hafa tatatmanu hao? "How are you?" A common Chamorro greeting. (Guam).

Hagaa. Somalia's dry season. Lasts from June to August. (Somalia).

Hagelslag. Chocolate sprinkles. (Netherlands).

Haggis. Ground sheep entrails that are mixed with oats and spices, tied in a sheep's stomach, and cooked. (Scotland).

Hai hau ma? "Is everything okay?" A common Mandarin greeting. (Taiwan).

Hailing. (Belize). *See* **Hail(s)**.

Hail(s). To greet. (Belize).

Hairouna. "Home of the Blessed." The Carib name for Saint Vincent. (Saint Vincent and the Grenadines).

Haj. (Oman, Pakistan). *See* **Hajj**.

Haji. (Afghanistan). *See* **Hadj**.

Hajimemashite. "Nice to meet you." A Japanese greeting used in formal situations. (Japan).

Hajj. [NOTE: Spelling varies because it is a transliteration of Arabic.] One of the Five Pillars of Islam, the *Hajj* is a pilgrimage to Makkah, Saudi Arabia. A religious practice followed in Muslim-populated countries.. *See also* **Salat, Saum, Shahada, Zakat**.

Hajoghootiun. "Good luck." A common Armenian parting phrase. (Armenia).

Haka. A Maori war dance. (New Zealand).

Hakkebøf. A Danish hamburger. (Denmark).

Hala. "Aunt." A common Azeri term of address used after a woman's given name. (Azerbaijan).

Haladnik. Cold vegetable soup. (Belarus).

Halal. A Muslim requirement that meats should prepared according to Islamic law. This includes not eating pork and having the animals slaughtered humanely by a butcher who has first said a prayer. (Libya, Singapore).

Halászlé. Fish soup. (Hungary).

Halk Maslahaty. The People's Council. Members offer advise and recommendations to the national government. (Turkmenistan).

Glossary of Cultural Terms

Hallå. "Hello." A Swedish greeting used to answer the phone. (Sweden).

Hallacas. A thick, deep-fried pancake stuffed with stewed meat, potatoes, olives, raisins, and other spices. Similar to **Arepa(s)**. (Venezuela).

Halle. An Albanian word for "aunt," specifically the father's sister. (Albania). *Also called* **Teto**.

Halling. A well-known Norwegian folk dance in which male dancers perform challenging kicks and leaps. (Norway).

Hallo. "Hello." A common greeting. (Belgium, Germany).

Halló. "Hello." A casual Icelandic greeting. (Iceland).

Halo. "Hello." A casual greeting. (Malaysia, Solomon Islands).

Haló. "Hello." A common Hungarian phrase used for greeting and parting. (Hungary).

Halo-halo. A drink made from sweetened beans, milk, and fruits, served with crushed ice. (Philippines).

Halvo. A paste of sugar and oil. (Tajikistan).

Halwa. (Tunisia). *See* **Seqer**.

Halwa. A starch pudding mixed with crushed cardamom seeds, saffron, sugar, and fat. (Bahrain).

Hamdellah. (Eritrea). *See* **Al hamdu lillah**.

Hamdullah. (Tunisia). *See* **Al hamdu lillah**.

Hamjambo. A casual Swahili greeting used when addressing two or more people. (Tanzania).

Ha na? "How are you?" An informal Pidgin English greeting. (Cameroon).

Hanbok. Traditional attire that is reserved for special occasions. For women, this is a long two-piece dress that is often very colorful. For men, this includes trousers and a loose-fitting jacket or robe. (North Korea, South Korea).

Hangi. A dish composed of meat, seafood, potatoes, sweet potatoes, carrots, and other vegetables all cooked in wire racks lined with cabbage leaves. (New Zealand).

Hangikjöt. Smoked mutton. (Iceland).

Hanikotrana. Snacks such as cassava or sweet potatoes. (Madagascar).

Hanim. A Turkish title following a woman's given name. (Turkey).

Hanoot. A basic convenience store. (Morocco).

Hant. A rummy-like card game. (Macedonia).

Hanukkah. Festival of Lights, a Jewish holiday. (Israel).

Hanum. (1) "Miss" or "Mrs." An Azeri title used after a woman's given name. (Azerbaijan). (2) "Lady." A term of respect added to a female formal acquaintance's name. (Turkmenistan). *See also* **Daiza, Gelneje**.

Hao jiu bu jian le. "Long time no see." A Mandarin Chinese phrase used between acquaintances who have not seen each other in a long time. (China).

Haqibh. Chants and chorus accompanied by instruments such as the **Tabla** and the **Oud**. (Sudan). *See also* **Madeeh**.

Harees. A blend of wheat and meat cooked until mushy, with butter melted over the top. (Bahrain, Kuwait).

Harina de maíz. Cornmeal. (Cuba).

Harira. A tomato-based soup with beef or mutton, chickpeas, and lentils. (Morocco).

Hari Raya Haji. [NOTE: Muslim holidays are set according to the lunar calendar.] Feast of the Sacrifice. A Muslim holiday that celebrates Abraham's willingness to sacrifice his son. Celebrated at the end of the pilgrimage to Makkah, Saudi Arabia. (Malaysia, Singapore). *Also called* **Eid al-Adha**.

Hari Raya Puasa. [NOTE: Muslim holidays are set according to the lunar calendar.] A three-day feast celebrated at the end of the month of **Ramadan**. (Malaysia, Singapore). *Also called* **Aid al Fitr**.

Harisa. A dish of wheat and chicken cooked in large pots for several days. (Armenia).

Här Minister. "Mr. Minister." A Luxembourgish title. (Luxembourg).

Hashi. The Japanese word for "chopsticks." (Japan).

Hassa. Libyan gravy made of lamb, oil, crushed tomatoes, flour, and spices such as garlic, cilantro, and mint. (Libya).

Hasta luego. "Until later." A common parting phrase. Used in Spanish-speaking countries..

Hasta mañana. "Until tomorrow." A common Spanish parting phrase. (Bolivia).

Hat bo. Traditional Chinese opera. (Vietnam).

Hat boi. Traditional Chinese opera. (Vietnam).

Hat cheo. Vietnamese operettas. (Vietnam).

Hatte. A blouse that leaves the midriff bare. (Sri Lanka).

Hat tuong. Traditional Chinese opera. (Vietnam).

Hatujambo. "We're fine." A common Swahili response to the greeting **Hamjambo**. (Tanzania).

Hau. "Temporal Ruler," an office created by the Tongan monarchy in 1470. (Tonga).

Havli. Compounds of mud-brick structures of several rooms, surrounded by high mud walls that provide security, protect gardens, and keep animals inside. (Tajikistan).

Hawli. A long tunic worn by Libyan men and women during cooler weather. It is always white for men but may be any color for women. (Libya).

Hawn kif aħna. "Hi. How are you?" A Maltese greeting. (Malta).

Haya Kala? "How are you?" A common Arabic greeting. (Qatar).

Hayeren. The Armenian language. (Armenia).

Hœ. "Hi." A casual Icelandic greeting. (Iceland).

Head isu. "Good appetite." An Estonian phrase used at the beginning of a meal. (Estonia).

Headman. An elder appointed by the village chief. The plural form is *headmen*. (Botswana).

Headmen. (Botswana). *See* **Headman**.

He done reach. "He has arrived." An example of the Bahamas's unique idioms. (Bahamas).

Héé. A welcoming answer to visitors who call out the phrase **Odi! Odi!** (Mozambique).

Hegira. [NOTE: Spelling varies because it is a transliteration of Arabic.] The Islamic New Year. The migration of Muhammad from Makkah to Al Medina in the seventh century. (Saudi Arabia).

Hei. "Hi." A common greeting. (Finland, Norway).

Heilige Drei Könige. Holy Three Kings. Celebrated on 6 January. (Austria).

Heiliger Abend. Holy Evening. Christmas Eve. (Austria, Germany).

Heisei. "Achievement of universal peace." The Japanese name referring to the reign of Emperor Akihito. (Japan).

Heiva Taupiti. A season of celebrations that culminates with **Tiurai**. (French Polynesia).

Hej. "Hi." A common greeting. Pronounced "HEY." (Denmark, Sweden).

Glossary of Cultural Terms

Hej då. "Good-bye." A casual Swedish parting phrase. (Sweden). *See also* **Adjö**.

Heladería. An ice cream shop. (Argentina).

Here tilena wa? "Did you have a good day?" A greeting used between friends. (Mali).

Hermano/a. "Brother" or "sister." A Spanish term often used as a term of address. Masculine *hermano*, feminine *hermana*. (Panama).

Herr. "Mr." A German title used with the family name. (Austria, Germany).

Hetman. Military chieftain. (Ukraine).

Hexagone. Another name for France. (France).

Hey de mon, leh we go limin. A typical Creole invitation between male friends to go out on the town. (U.S. Virgin Islands).

Hey how? A common greeting between acquaintances. (Belize).

High. A type of island characterized by volcanic peaks, fertile valleys, lush tropical forests, rushing streams, waterfalls, and white-sand beaches. (French Polynesia). *See also* **Low**.

Highlife. Popular Ghanaian dance music. (Ghana, Nigeria, Togo).

Hijab. A scarf worn by Muslim women to cover their hair. (Bahrain, Iraq, Kuwait, Lebanon, Qatar, Sudan).

Hijra. (United Arab Emirates). *See* **Hegira**.

Hijri. The Islamic lunar calendar. (Bahrain).

Hike. (Namibia). *See* **Hiking**.

Hiking. Hitchhiking or traveling in crowded **Combies**. (Namibia).

Hin. A curry dish, usually of fish, chicken, or shrimp. Served with rice. (Myanmar).

Hindi. Cactus fruit. (Tunisia).

Hindi-pop. A blend of East Indian music, traditional Creole music, European pop, and Caribbean rhythms. (Suriname).

Hinna. A party held with family at the bride's home the night before her wedding. (West Bank and Gaza).

Hiragana. A Japanese phonetic alphabet. (Japan). *See also* **Kanji, Katakana, Romaji**.

Hiva kakala. Love songs accompanied by a guitar or ukulele. (Tonga).

Hneh. A type of oboe. (Myanmar).

Hochdeutsch. High German; it is the standard form of German used in written material in Switzerland. (Switzerland).

Hoe gaat het? "How are you?" A common Dutch greeting. (Netherlands, Suriname).

Hogmanay. New Year's Eve. (Scotland).

Hogy vagy? "How are you?" A Hungarian phrase that often follows the initial greeting. (Hungary).

Hoi. A casual greeting used among friends. (Liechtenstein).

Hojatolislam. A Muslim religious title. (Iran).

Hola. "Hi." A casual greeting. Used in Spanish-speaking countries..

¡Hola! ¿Cómo estás? "Hi. How are you?" An informal Spanish greeting. (Paraguay).

Holi. A holiday that is celebrated by people throwing colored water on passersby. (India, Mauritius, Nepal).

Holi Phagwah. (Suriname). *See* **Phagwah**.

Holodomor. The Ukrainian word for "famine." (Ukraine).

Holubtsi. Cabbage leaves stuffed with ground meat and rice. (Ukraine).

Hongi. A traditional Maori greeting where people press noses together with their eyes closed. (New Zealand).

Hopak. A showy Ukrainian folk dance in which men jump, twirl, and kick; the women perform simpler movements. (Ukraine).

Hosselen. The informal selling of goods and services. Many Surinamers maintain a formal job for its pension and health benefits, while relying on *hosselen* to earn extra money without the interference of a boss or the government. (Suriname).

Hotely. An inexpensive restaurant. (Madagascar).

Housecker. St. Nicholas's helper who brings birch twigs to bad children. (Luxembourg).

How! "But of course!" A phrase used in the Antiguan English dialect. (Antigua and Barbuda).

Howa, gowy Allaha shukur. "Yes, thank God." (Turkmenistan). *See also* **Howa, yakshi Hudaya shukur**.

Howa, yakshi Hudaya shukur. "Yes, thank God." (Turkmenistan). *See also* **Howa, gowy Allaha shukur**.

Hows tings? "How are things?" A casual Grenadian creole greeting. (Grenada).

How things? An informal greeting used between friends. (Saint Vincent and the Grenadines).

How ya gine? "How are you doing?" An informal Bajan greeting used between young people. (Barbados).

How you do? An informal greeting used between friends. (Saint Kitts and Nevis, Saint Vincent and the Grenadines).

Howzit. "How are you?" A slang expression used among young English speakers. (South Africa).

Høyesterett. The Norwegian Supreme Court. (Norway).

Hoyo-hoyo! A welcoming answer to visitors who call out the phrase **Odi! Odi!** (Mozambique).

Hryvnia. Ukraine's national currency. (Ukraine).

Hsien. The Taiwanese word for "counties." (Taiwan).

Htamin. Rice. Eaten with every lunch and dinner meal. Synonymous with the word for "food." (Myanmar).

Huan Ying. "Welcome." A Mandarin greeting used by shopkeepers to passersby. (China).

Huasos. Cowboys. (Chile).

Huayno. (1) A type of music from the mountains. (Peru). (2) A dance with many jumps. (Peru).

Hui. Important family meetings. (New Zealand).

Huipil. A Mayan blouse. Its design identifies a woman's social position and hometown. (Guatemala).

Huisarts. The family doctor. (Netherlands).

Hujambo. A casual Swahili greeting used when addressing one person. The plural form is **Hamjambo**. (Tanzania).

Hujra. A special room where male hosts receive male guests. (Afghanistan).

Hura. The Hausa term for a drink made of millet flour mixed with water and sometimes spices, milk, or sugar. (Niger).

Hurling. A sport played on a soccer-type field with wooden sticks and a small leather ball. (Ireland, Northern Ireland).

Hurtitruten. Coastal steamboats. (Norway).

Hush Kalipsis. "Welcome." An Uzbek greeting to visitors. (Uzbekistan).

Hussars. Fifteenth-century light cavalry who were famous for their horsemanship. (Hungary).

Huushur. A fried dumpling stuffed with diced meat, onion, cabbage, garlic, salt, and pepper. (Mongolia).

Hwan'gap. A celebration commemorating a family member's 60th birthday. (South Korea).

Hyvää huomenta. "Good morning." A Finnish greeting. (Finland).

Glossary of Cultural Terms

Hyvää päivää. "Good afternoon." A typical Finnish greeting. (Finland).

Ia orana. A polite and formal Tahitian greeting used by everyone. (French Polynesia).

I baii? "How are you?" A Sara greeting. (Chad).

Ibans. Sea Dayaks. An indigenous people that live in Malaysia. (Malaysia).

Ibbi jay. "They are fine; they are there." A customary response to the Mandinka greeting **Summo lay?** (Gambia).

Ibe. Mats made of pandanus leaves. (Fiji).

Ibn. "Son of." An Arabic title combined with the father's name. (Bahrain). *See also* **Bin.**

Ibtida'i. Primary school. (Saudi Arabia).

Ibu. "Mother." An Indonesian term of address used to show respect to older women. (Indonesia).

Ibuto aber? "How did you sleep?" A common Luo greeting. (Uganda).

Id al-Adha. (Afghanistan, Ethiopia, Sudan). *See* **Eid al-Adha.**

Id-al-Adha. (Comoros). *See* **Eid al-Adha.**

Id al-Fatar. (Ethiopia). *See* **Aid al Fitr.**

Id-al-Fitr. (Comoros). *See* **Aid al Fitr.**

Id al-Fitr. (Afghanistan, Sudan). *See* **Aid al Fitr.**

Idd Adha. (Uganda). *See* **Eid al-Adha.**

Idd Fitr. (Uganda). *See* **Aid al Fitr.**

Idhin. A kind of butter often poured on **Couscous.** (Mauritania).

Idil-Fitr. (Rwanda). *See* **Aid al Fitr.**

Id-i-Navruz. The Islamic New Year. (Tajikistan). *Also called* **Hegira.**

Id-i-Qurbon. Feast of Sacrifice. A Muslim holiday honoring Abraham's willingness to sacrifice his son. (Tajikistan). *Also called* **Eid al-Adha.**

Idir. Local burial society meetings. (Ethiopia).

Id-i-Ramazon. A feast at the end of **Ramazon,** the Muslim holy month. (Tajikistan). *Also called* **Aid al Fitr.**

Idul-Adha. (Indonesia). *See* **Eid al-Adha.**

Idul Adha. (Nigeria, Sri Lanka). *See* **Eid al-Adha.**

Id ul Azha. (Guyana). *See* **Eid al-Adha.**

Id-ul-Fitr. (India). *See* **Aid al Fitr.**

Idul-Fitr. (Kenya, Malawi). *See* **Aid al Fitr.**

Idul Fitr. (Nigeria, Sri Lanka). *See* **Aid al Fitr.**

Id ul Fitr. (Guyana, Suriname). *See* **Aid al Fitr.**

Idul-Fitri. (Indonesia). *See* **Aid al Fitr.**

Ietoga. Fine mats; offered by the bride's family to the groom's family after a wedding reception. (Samoa).

Ifil. A slow-growing tropical tree. Guam's official tree. (Guam).

Ifisashi. Any green vegetable boiled and mixed with pounded groundnuts. (Zambia).

Ifisela. Drama. (Zambia).

Iftar. (1) The Arabic word for "breakfast." (Bahrain). *Also called* **Foutour.** (2) Special snacks eaten at night to break the fast during **Ramadan,** the Muslim holy month. (Bangladesh).

Igal. A braided black cord that holds in place the **Ghutra.** (Saudi Arabia).

Ighyuwa. Performers that sing praises and recite oral histories and poetry. (Mauritania). *Also called* **Griots.**

Igisoro. A traditional game in which small black seeds are strategically placed in hollows of a wooden board. (Rwanda).

Igneri. A name that means "Ancient Ones." The Igneri were the first known inhabitants of what are now the U.S. Virgin Islands. (U.S. Virgin Islands).

Igra oro. Folk dances. (Macedonia).

Ihram. A white, two-piece, towel-like garment worn by men during the **Hajj.** (Saudi Arabia).

Iishana. Oshiwambo word for temporary water holes caused by flooding in the rainy season. The singular form is **Oshana.** (Namibia).

Ikat. A common handwoven textile involving an intricate dye process. (Laos).

Ikebana. Flower arranging. (Japan).

Iki. "Later." An informal Lithuanian parting phrase used between friends. (Lithuania).

Il humdu li'llah. (Mauritania). *See* **Al hamdu lillah.**

Ilienden. A holiday on 2 August that celebrates the uprising against the Ottoman Turks in 1903. (Macedonia).

Il-Maltija. The national dance. (Malta).

Imams. (1) Muslim religious leaders. (Oman). (2) Holy men revered by Shi'ite Muslims as the descendents of Fatima, the prophet Muhammad's daughter, and her husband, Ali. Shi'ites believe the *Imams* disappeared but will reappear in the future to guide Muslims to their destiny. (Azerbaijan, Iran).

Imenden. A person's name day. Commemorates the saint after whom a person is named. The person throws a party and receives gifts from friends and family. (Macedonia).

Imma. The traditional turban. (Sudan).

Immen den. Name days, which are celebrated with a family meal. (Bulgaria).

Imqaret. A pastry filled with dates. (Malta).

Ina ini? "How did you pass the day?" A Hausa greeting used in the afternoon. (Niger).

Ina kwana? "How did you sleep?" A Hausa greeting used in the morning. (Niger).

Inanga. Harps. (Rwanda).

Inchpes ek? "How are you?" A formal Armenian phrase used after an initial greeting. (Armenia).

Incwala. A celebration that includes feasting, singing, dancing, and the slaying of a bull. The highlight is the king tasting the new harvest's fruit. (Swaziland).

Indianista. An Indian novel genre that focuses on indignities suffered by native peoples. (Peru).

Indígenas. The Spanish word for "indigenous." A term collectively referring to indigenous peoples. (Guatemala).

Ingeniero/a. A Spanish title used to address a person with a bachelor of science degree. Masculine *ingeniero*, feminine *ingeniera*. (Panama).

Ingera. Sour bread made of **Teff,** millet, or corn flour fermented in water. (Eritrea). *Also called* **Taitah.**

Ingoma. (1) A dance that celebrates past victories of the Ngoni ethnic group. (Malawi). (2) Drums. (Rwanda).

Ingrato. "Ungrateful." A term used to describe those who fail to show respect for friends and acquaintances. (Cape Verde).

I ni ce. "Hello." A Bambara greeting. (Mali).

Injera. Bread made from a native grain known as **Teff.** (Ethiopia).

Inkhundla. A constituency or district. (Swaziland).

Inona no vaovao? "What is new?" A common Malagasy phrase asked after the initial greeting. (Madagascar).

Inset. A plant from which the stem is used to make **Koocho** bread. (Ethiopia).

Insha'Allah. [NOTE: Spelling varies because it is a transliteration of Arabic.] "God willing." An Arabic phrase used to acknowledge God's hand in a person's life. Used in Muslim-populated countries. (Comoros, Egypt, Morocco).

Glossary of Cultural Terms

Inshallah. (Mauritania, Niger, Pakistan, Tunisia). *See* **Insha'Allah.**

Insh'allah. (Qatar). *See* **Insha'Allah.**

In shallah. (United Arab Emirates). *See* **Insha'Allah.**

Inside. A word called out by visitors as they approach a person's gate. (Antigua and Barbuda).

Insulamnyambeti. A siSwati phrase meaning "wiper away of tears." This refers to one of two cows that a bride's mother receives as part of the bride-price. (Swaziland). *See also* **Lobola.**

Intifada. An uprising of Palestinian Arabs against the Israelis. Palestinians have waged two uprisings, the first breaking out in 1987, the second in 2000. (Israel, West Bank and Gaza).

Inti Raymi. Festival of the Sun. Celebrated at the Incan ruins near Cuenca. (Ecuador).

Intshwarele. "Excuse me." A Setswana phrase used when passing between two conversing individuals. (Botswana).

Ipelegeng. The Setswana word for "carry yourselves." Reflects the Batswana attitude toward community self-help. (Botswana).

¡Iporã! "Just fine." A Guaraní phrase used to respond to the greeting **¿Mba'eichapa?** (Paraguay).

Iran. Supernatural beings. (Guinea-Bissau).

Irasshaimase. "Welcome." A greeting used by a worker to a customer. (Japan).

Irie. "Everything is cool." (Grenada).

Irma. "Sister." A Kriolu term of address used between good friends. (Guinea-Bissau). *See also* **Irmon.**

Irmon. "Brother." A Kriolu term of address used between good friends. (Guinea-Bissau). *See also* **Irma.**

Irooj. Land-owning chiefs. A position in the traditional social system that is now incorporated into the formal government. (Marshall Islands). *See also* **Alaps, Rijerbal.**

Iroojlaplap. Paramount chief. (Marshall Islands).

Irxoxt. The Maltese word for "Risen Christ." (Malta).

'Isha'. Dinner. (Iraq).

Ishkhan. The Armenian word for "prince." (Armenia).

Ish mwe. "My child." A Saint Lucian creole phrase used by adults to address children. (Saint Lucia).

I siibi mooi? "Did you sleep well?" A Ndyuka greeting. (Suriname).

Iska warran? "What's the news?" A Somali phrase used to mean "How are you?" (Somalia).

Islam. A religious faith, *Islam* literally means "submission." A **Muslim** is one who submits to the will of **Allah**. (Bahrain, Mauritania).

Isombe. A favorite dish made from cassava leaves. (Rwanda).

I somogo be di? "How is your family?" A Bambara inquiry that follows an initial greeting. (Mali).

Ita. "Brother" or "sister." A Sango term of address used for a close friend. (Central African Republic).

Ita ti mbi. A Sango term that can mean "brother," "sister," "half brother," "cousin," or "close friend." (Central African Republic).

Itau. A traditional friendship. (Fiji).

-ito. A Spanish suffix that is used to form a diminutive. Masculine *-ito,* feminine *-ita.* (Chile).

Itok im moña. "Come and eat." A common Marshallese greeting. (Marshall Islands).

Iu bin stap long wea? "Where are you coming from?" A Solomon Island Pijin greeting. (Solomon Islands).

Iu go long wea? "Where are you going?" A Solomon Island Pijin greeting. (Solomon Islands).

Iwe. "You." A term of address for children. (Malawi).

Iyak labass. "On you no evil." A Hassaniya greeting used by Moors. (Mauritania). *See also* **Labass.**

Iyi günler. "Have a nice day." A Turkish greeting used when one enters a room. (Turkey).

Iyiyim, teshekur ederim. "Fine, thank you." A typical Turkish response to the greeting **Nasisliniz?** (Turkey).

Jaajmi. Raw fish. (Marshall Islands).

Jaanipäev. Midsummer's Day. Marks the beginning of the summer's "white nights," when the sun sets for only a few hours. (Estonia).

Jakaro. Coconut sap. (Marshall Islands).

Jaki. Mats woven from pandanus leaves. (Marshall Islands).

Jakshi baringiz. "Go well." A Kyrgyz parting phrase used by a host as guests depart. (Kyrgyzstan).

Jakshi kalingiz. "Stay well." A Kyrgyz response to the parting phrase **Jakshi baringiz.** (Kyrgyzstan).

Jalabas. [NOTE: Spelling varies because it is a transliteration of Arabic.] Long robes worn by men. (Syria).

Jalabia. (Sudan). *See* **Jalabas.**

Jalabiyas. (Eritrea). *See* **Jalabas.**

Jam. (1) "Fine." A Fulfulde response to the greeting **Jam na?** (Cameroon). (2) "No evil." A Soninke response to the greeting **An moho**. (Mauritania). (3) A greeting in which men lightly touch closed fists. (Saint Lucia).

Jamahiriya. The official term describing nature of the state of Libya, it means a nation governed by the masses. (Libya).

Jambo. (1) "Hello." A common Swahili greeting. (Congo, Kenya, Tanzania, Uganda). (2) The Marshallese practice of wandering around to visit and chat. (Marshall Islands).

Jameed. Yogurt sauce. (Jordan).

Jamhuri Day. Independence Day. Celebrated on 12 December. (Kenya).

Jam na? "How are you?" A Fulfulde greeting. (Cameroon).

Jam puffs. Jam-filled sourdough pastry. (Barbados).

Jam rekk. "No evil." A Wolof response to the greeting **Nanga def.** (Mauritania).

Jam sukaabe? "How are the kids?" A Fulfulde greeting. (Burkina Faso).

Jam tan. "No evil." A Pulaar response to the greeting **M'bda**. (Mauritania).

Jam waali. "Good morning." A Fulfulde greeting. (Burkina Faso).

-jan. "Dearest." An Armenian suffix added to a person's first name as a sign of affection between close friends.

Jandals. Rubber flip-flops. (Samoa).

Jāṇi. Midsummer's Day. Marks the beginning of the summer's "white nights," when the sun sets for only a few hours. (Latvia).

Jan mashtami. A Hindu festival celebrating the birth of Lord Krishna. (India).

Jarabe tapatio. The Mexican Hat Dance. (Mexico).

Jash. The Armenian word for "lunch." (Armenia).

Jatakas. Stories of the Buddha's previous lives. (Cambodia).

Jatiya Sangsad. Bangladesh's National Parliament. (Bangladesh).

Jaunkundze. "Miss." A Latvian title added after the surname. (Latvia).

Jause. Afternoon coffee. (Austria).

Glossary of Cultural Terms

Je demande la route. French phrase meaning "I ask for the road." Guests may say this to hosts after they accompany each other to the road at the end of a visit. (Ivory Coast).

Jeepney(s). A decorated minibus built on the frame of an old military jeep. (Philippines).

Je Khenpo. The Buddhist chief abbot. (Bhutan).

Jélé. A caste whose members are players of traditional music. (Mali).

Jerk. Spicy barbecued pork or chicken. (Jamaica).

Je te donne la moité de la route. French phrase meaning "I give you half the road (use the second half to come back)." Hosts may say this to guests after they symbolically accompany each other to the road at the end of a visit. (Ivory Coast).

-ji. A suffix used with the last name to show respect. (India).

Jiaozi. Chinese dumplings. (China).

Jigim. "Sibling." A term of address used with equals and younger acquaintances. (Turkmenistan). *See also* **Doganym**.

Jihad. A Muslim holy war. (Guinea, Niger).

Jikhalsi. Special cities. (South Korea).

Jilal. Somalia's harsh and dry season. Lasts from December to March. (Somalia).

Jimbôa. A cooked leafy vegetable similar to spinach. (Angola).

Jindungo. Small, hot peppers frequently added to meals. (Angola).

Jirga. The village council. (Afghanistan).

Jiti. A style of music in which **Mbira** music has been adapted to the electric guitar. (Zimbabwe).

Jitney. A small bus holding up to 25 passengers. (Bahamas).

Jitu ka ten. "There is nothing one can do." A common Kriolu phrase. (Guinea-Bissau).

Jitu ten ku ten. "There has to be a way." A new Kriolu slogan. (Guinea-Bissau).

Jó estét kívánok. "Good evening." A polite Hungarian greeting. (Hungary).

Jó étvágyat. "Good appetite." A Hungarian phrase used before eating or when entering a room where someone is eating. (Hungary).

Joget. A popular Malaysian dance. (Malaysia).

Jogorku Kenesh. The Kyrgyz Supreme Council. (Kyrgyzstan).

Johnnycakes. Sweet fried dumplings. (Antigua and Barbuda, Saint Kitts and Nevis, U.S. Virgin Islands).

Joie de vivre. A French phrase meaning "joy of living." (French Polynesia).

Jolok bod. "Excuse me." A Marshallese phrase used when passing between people who are conversing. (Marshall Islands).

Joma. A long coat worn by village men. Kept closed with a bandana-type tie around the waist. (Tajikistan). *Also called* **Chapan**. *See also* **Meeyonband**.

Jó napot kívánok. "Good day." A polite Hungarian greeting. (Hungary).

Jó reggelt kívánok. "Good morning." A polite Hungarian greeting. (Hungary).

Joropo. The traditional music of Venezuelan cowboys. (Venezuela). *See also* **Llaneros**.

Jota. A soup of kidney beans, sauerkraut, and bacon. (Slovenia).

Jounet Creole. Creole Day. A local festival celebrated on 31 October. (Saint Lucia).

Jour de l'An. New Year's Day. (Gabon).

Jour de l'an. A French phrase meaning "New Year's Day." (France).

Jouvert. A street parade during Carnival that begins at sunrise with bands and costumed marchers. (Saint Lucia).

Judd mat Gaardebounen. Smoked collar of pork with broad beans. (Luxembourg).

Jug-jug. Sorghum and green pigeon peas. (Barbados).

Juju. (1) Nigerian music that incorporates guitars with the **Dundun**. (Nigeria). (2) Supernatural phenomena. (Ghana).

Juku. Private, after-hours Japanese schools that help students "cram" for exams. Students attend these schools after a full-day spent at their regular private or public schools. (Japan).

Jul. The Swedish word for "Christmas." (Sweden).

Julenisse. Father Christmas. (Norway).

Jultomte. (1) The name of the Swedish Santa Claus. (Sweden). (2) A Christmas gnome who lives under the house. (Sweden).

Juma. The Arabic word for "Friday." (Niger).

Jum'a. (Egypt). *See* **Ju'mma**.

Jumbie. Unpleasant spirit or ghost. (Trinidad and Tobago).

Jumbos. Motorized tricycles. (Laos).

Ju'mma. [NOTE: Spelling varies because it is a transliteration of Arabic.] Muslim prayer services held midday on Fridays. (Bangladesh).

Jumpers. An Australian term for "sweaters." (Australia).

Jumpups. Block parties that involve street dancing. (Montserrat).

Junta local. A town council. (Panama).

Just cool. "Everything is fine." A typical Grenadian creole response to the questions **W'happen dey?** or **Hows tings?** (Grenada). *See also* **Ah dey**.

Jutho. The Hindu principle of ritual impurity. (Nepal).

-jye. A Nepali suffix used with the last name, to be polite. (Nepal).

-jyu. (Nepal). *See* **-jye**.

Ka. The Fang word for "no." (Equatorial Guinea).

Ka'abah. The cube-shaped stone building in Makkah, Saudi Arabia, that all Muslims in the world face during their daily prayers. (Saudi Arabia).

Kaatsen. A team sport similar to baseball in which players hit a small soft ball with the hand. (Netherlands).

Kabaddi. A type of wrestling. (Pakistan).

Ka-baddi. A sport played by village boys where two teams try to eliminate all the other team's players. One player will enter the other team's zone while holding his breath. He will try and touch the other players and make it back to his own zone. If he makes it back to his side before taking a breath, the players he touched will be out. Otherwise, he is out. (Bangladesh). *Also called* **Ha-dudu**.

Kabaka. The Luganda word for "king." (Uganda).

Kabary. Traditional Malagasy oratory. (Madagascar).

Ka'been. Marriage registry. (Bangladesh).

Kabne. A ceremonial shawl for men and a scarf for women. (Bhutan).

Kabsa. [NOTE: Spelling varies because it is a transliteration of Arabic.] Rice mixed with meat. (United Arab Emirates).

Kabsah. (Saudi Arabia). *See* **Kabsa**.

Kabuki. Highly stylized drama that blends dance, music, and acting. Known for its spectacular sets and costumes. (Japan).

Kachkéis. A soft cheese. (Luxembourg).

Kackavall. A type of cheese. (Albania).

Kadaif. A special dessert in syrup, eaten on New Year's Eve. (Albania).

Glossary of Cultural Terms

Kadaw. A gesture made by kneeling and touching the forehead and both palms to the floor three times. Customary when a person takes leave from a monk. Respect is paid to images of Buddha in the same way. (Myanmar).

Kadri. Celebrated on 25 October. A day for children to go to neighbors' houses, sing special national songs, dance, and ask to be let in out of the cold. The children are given candy and fruit. (Estonia).

Kafel. "It was good." A Yapese greeting or parting phrase. (Micronesia).

Kaffee-trinken. Afternoon coffee. (Germany).

Kaffiyah. A checkered headscarf worn by men. (Iraq). *See also* **Yashmagh.**

Kaftans. Long tailored robes worn by older men. (Gambia).

Kaganat. The Kyrgyz word for "kingdom." (Kyrgyzstan).

Kahve. A thick brew of coffee served in very small cups with nearly every meal. (Turkey).

Kaif al hal? (Chad). *See* **Kaif halak?**

Kaif halak? [NOTE: Spelling varies because it is a transliteration of Arabic.] "How are you?" A common Arabic greeting. (United Arab Emirates).

Kaiga i taeao, inuti. The Tuvaluan word for "breakfast." (Tuvalu).

Kaiga i tuutonu. The Tuvaluan midday meal. A major occasion on Sundays. (Tuvalu).

Kaimen Pugar. "Peace be with you." A Wapisiani greeting. (Guyana).

Kaimoana. The Maori word for "seafood." (New Zealand).

Kaisé ba? "How are you?" The standard Bhojpuri greeting. (Mauritius).

Kaiu. The Tuvaluan word for "stingy." (Tuvalu).

Kai yang. Barbecued chicken. (Laos).

Kajmak. A cheese that consists of the accumulated skim of boiled milk. (Serbia and Montenegro).

Kaka. Father. This term is added to an elder male relative's name to show respect. (Turkmenistan). *See also* **Aga.**

Kak dela? "How are you?" A common Russian greeting between friends. (Russia, Tajikistan).

Kaki lima. Street vendors selling food. Literally "five feet" in Indonesian, meaning two of a man and three of a cart. (Indonesia).

Ka kite ano. "See you later." A Maori parting phrase that is common and informal. (New Zealand).

Kako e semejstvoto? Macedonian for "How is your family?" (Macedonia).

Kako se imaš? "How are you?" An informal Slovene greeting. (Slovenia).

Kako se imate? "How are you?" A formal Slovene greeting. (Slovenia).

Kako si? An informal way of saying "How are you?" in Macedonian. (Macedonia).

Kako ste. A formal way of saying "How are you?" in Macedonian. (Macedonia).

Kak si? "How are you?" An informal Bulgarian greeting used between friends and family. (Bulgaria).

Kak ste? "How are you?" A standard Bulgarian greeting. (Bulgaria).

Kalbatono. "Madame." A Georgian term of address. (Georgia).

Kalbi. Marinated short ribs. (North Korea, South Korea).

Kalevala. Finland's national epic. A compilation of folk songs and stories. (Finland).

Kalevipoeg. "Son of Kalev." The Estonian national epic. (Estonia).

Kalimba. A traditional instrument played by plucking small metal strips with the thumbs. (Zambia).

Kaliméra sas. "Good morning." A Greek greeting. (Greece).

Kalindula. A popular dance music. (Zambia).

Kalispéra sas. "Good evening." A Greek greeting. (Greece).

Kallaloo. A stew traditionally made with pig tail, conch, blue fish, land crab, salt beef, or oxtail. (U.S. Virgin Islands).

Kalojam. Dough boiled in syrup; a popular sweet. (Bangladesh).

Kalondolondo. Hide-and-seek. (Malawi).

Kalym. A large sum of money given to the bride's parents to solidify the engagement. (Kyrgyzstan).

Kamaimai. Boiled toddy (coconut sap) that forms a thick, sweet molasses. (Kiribati). *See also* **Kaokioki.**

Kamanche. A spiked fiddle; a traditional Iranian instrument. (Iran).

Kamelaha? "How are you?" A Tigrinya greeting to a man. (Ethiopia).

Kamelehee? "How are you?" A Tigrinya greeting to a woman. (Ethiopia).

Kamisa. A cotton loincloth worn by Amerindian men. (Suriname).

Kamma. A round embroidered hat worn by men. (Oman).

Kamoolal. Thanksgiving Day. Celebrated the first Friday in December. (Marshall Islands).

Kanda. Meat, fish, fruit, or termites wrapped in a leaf and steamed. (Central African Republic).

Kandaisiz? "How are you?" A common Uzbek greeting. (Uzbekistan).

Kan dikdik kan in yokwe. "Little food with lots of love." A common Marshallese expression. (Marshall Islands).

Kandongas. Pickup trucks with seats and a roof for baggage. Used to travel between towns. (Guinea-Bissau).

Kandu. A traditional white robe worn by elders, rural men, and urban men going to a mosque. (Comoros).

Kandurah. A white robe worn by men. Worn with an **Agal** and **Kitra**. (United Arab Emirates). *Also called* **Dishdasha.**

Kang. The Thai word for "curry." (Thailand).

Kanga(s). Colorful cotton cloth worn by women. (Kenya, Tanzania).

Kanji. The Japanese writing system based on Chinese characters. (Japan). *See also* **Hiragana, Katakana, Romaji.**

Kannan. A wooden stringed instrument similar to the zither. The Estonian national instrument. (Estonia).

Kantele. A stringed instrument played with the fingers; it is also the Finnish national instrument. (Finland).

Kantsi. An embroidered deer, bull, or goat horn. (Georgia).

Kanza. An instrument similar to a three-stringed banjo. (Morocco). *Also called* **Lotar.**

Kanzu. A long, embroidered cotton gown worn by men. (Tanzania, Uganda).

Kao. The Thai word for "rice." Usually a long-grained jasmine rice. (Thailand).

Kaoha. "Hi." A common greeting used in the Marquesas Islands. (French Polynesia).

Kaokioki. Fermented toddy (coconut sap); an alcoholic drink. (Kiribati). *See also* **Kamaimai.**

Kapelica. Small shrines. (Slovenia).

Glossary of Cultural Terms

Kapiteins. Maroon and Amerindian chiefs who receive public salaries and have authority over some local matters. (Suriname).

Kāpostu zupa. Cabbage soup. (Latvia).

Karagöz. A shadow play created by casting shadows of puppets on a curtain. (Turkey).

Karai. A term of address for men that is followed by the first name. Used in rural areas. (Paraguay).

Karakul. Sheepskin. (Namibia).

Karakuli. A fez-type hat. (Pakistan).

Karamin sallah. "Little feast." A celebration at the end of the month of **Ramadan**. (Niger).

Karavay. A traditional wedding pie. Includes honey and vodka to make the future life of the couple sweet and merry. (Belarus).

Karbonade. Pork chop. (Netherlands).

Karbonāde. Pork steak. (Latvia).

Kare-kare. A stew of meats and vegetables served in a peanut sauce. (Philippines).

Kargad ikavit. "Bye, take care." A Georgian parting phrase. (Georgia).

Karibu. "Welcome." A Kiswahili response to visitors who announce their presence. (Rwanda, Tanzania).

Karibuni. "Welcome." A Kiswahili response to visitors who announce their presence. This term is used when responding to more than one person. When responding to an individual, the term **Karibu** is used. (Tanzania).

Karma. A force, generated by one's actions in the present life, that determines the nature of one's next life. A Buddhist and Hindu belief. (Bhutan, Mauritius, Myanmar, Nepal).

Kartor. The Lao national game in which players try to keep a rattan ball in the air without using their hands. (Laos).

Kartupeli. Potatoes. (Latvia).

Karunna. Compassion. One of Buddhism's pillar virtues. (Laos). *See also* **Brahma Vihara.**

Karutsa. Horse-drawn carts. (Moldova).

Kaseko. A musical style that combines traditional Creole music and Caribbean rhythms. Uses call-and-response singing and percussion instruments such as the **Skratsji.** (Suriname).

Kaselaleliah. "Hello." A Pohnpei greeting. (Micronesia).

Kasha. Cooked or baked cereal. (Belarus, Moldova, Ukraine).

Kashkaval. A yellow cheese. (Macedonia).

Kashkazi. The hot, humid rainy season. Runs from November to March. (Comoros). *See also* **Kusi.**

Kashkusha. A wavy, knotted tassel worn at the neck by men. (Oman). *Also called* **Farakha.**

Kashrut. Jewish dietary laws. (Israel).

Käsknöpfle. A pasta with sharp cheese. (Liechtenstein).

Katakana. A Japanese phonetic alphabet. (Japan). *See also* **Hiragana, Kanji, Romaji.**

Katei ni Kiribati. "The Gilbertese way." The attitude that the future will take care of itself. (Kiribati).

Kathakali. A mimed dance that traditionally lasts all night. (India).

Katta sambol. A spicy mixture of fried onions and chilies. (Sri Lanka).

Kaukau. Sweet potato. (Papua New Guinea).

Kava. (1) A mildly narcotic, nonalcoholic beverage made from the crushed *kava* root, a shrub in the pepper family. (American Samoa, Fiji, Samoa, Tonga). (2) Coffee. (Belarus).

Kaval. A type of flute; a traditional instrument. (Bulgaria).

Kawanatanga. Maori word for "governance." (New Zealand).

Kawiarnia. Polish word for "café." (Poland).

Kayfak? "How are you?" A common Arabic greeting. (Qatar).

Kayf haalak? (Sudan). *See* **Kaif halak?**

Kayf halak? (Libya, Oman, Qatar). *See* **Kaif halak?**

Kayf innakum? "How are you?" A common Arabic greeting. (Sudan).

Każini. Pubs. (Malta).

Kde Slovák tam spev. "Wherever there is a Slovak, there is a song." A Slovak saying. (Slovakia).

Kebab. Skewered meat. (Israel).

Kebaya. A traditional Malay dress. (Singapore).

Kebbeh. Spiced meatballs. (Syria).

Kebero. A drum. (Ethiopia).

Kecap manis. A sweet dark sauce. (Indonesia).

Keef haalak? (Syria). *See* **Kaif halak?**

Keef halak? (Lebanon). *See* **Kaif halak?**

Keef halik? "How are you?" A common Arabic greeting used when addressing women. (Lebanon).

Keep time. A colloquialism meaning "to visit." (Sierra Leone).

Kefelhal? (Eritrea). *See* **Kaif halak?**

Keffiyah. A head covering worn by Bedouin men. (Syria).

Kefir. Fermented cow's milk. (Belarus).

Kefta. Ground beef or mutton that is seasoned and cooked over charcoal. (Morocco).

Ke itumetse. "I am pleased." A Setswana phrase to thank the host after a meal is completed. (Botswana).

Kelaguen. Grilled chicken mixed with lemon juice, green onions, hot peppers, and grated coconut. (Guam).

Kemem. Marshallese word for "feasts." (Marshall Islands).

Kena. "Come in." The host's response to **Ko ko**, the visitor's announcement of his or her arrival. (Lesotho).

Kendo. The sport of fencing with bamboo poles. (Japan).

Kente. Colorful woven cloth; used for robes worn by men. (Ghana, Togo).

Kerekere. A custom that allows a relative or neighbor to ask for something that is needed. It must be given willingly, without expectation of repayment. (Fiji).

Ke teng. Literally, "I am here," meaning "fine." A Setswana reply to the greeting **O kae?** (Botswana).

Ke tsogile sentle. "I awoke well." A Setswana reply to the greeting **Dumela Rra/Mma, O tsogile jang?** (Botswana).

Kezét csókolom. "I kiss your hand." A formal Hungarian greeting used to address older women. (Hungary).

Kgotla. A meeting place where neighborhood and village decisions are made. (Botswana).

Khadag. A blue silk bag filled with **Airag** that can be presented to an elder or a person of higher social rank as a sign of deep respect and well-wishing. (Mongolia).

Khadi. A Muslim religious leader who performs weddings. (Israel).

Khaen. A type of bamboo flute used to play Lao folk music. (Laos).

Khair. "Good-bye." A common Tajik parting phrase. (Tajikistan).

Khalah. (Iraq). *See* **Khaleh.**

Khaleh. "Aunt." An Arabic term of address for an older woman. (Syria).

Khalo. The Arabic word for a maternal uncle. (West Bank and Gaza).

Glossary of Cultural Terms

Khalto. The Arabic word for a maternal aunt. (West Bank and Gaza).

Khamari. A dance performed at weddings and other social gatherings by women. (Kuwait).

Khamasiin. A hot, driving, dusty wind that blows in the spring. (Egypt).

Khamauk. A conical bamboo hat worn by farmers. (Myanmar).

Khamsa ou Khmis Aalik. A phrase used to express that a meal was satisfying. Roughly means "You've done an excellent job." (Tunisia).

Khan. "Sir." An Arabic title. (Afghanistan).

Khana khanu bajou. "Have you eaten your rice already?" A Nepali greeting used to mean "How are you?" (Nepal).

Khanjar. An ornamental dagger. (Iraq, Oman).

Khash. Cow's feet that are cooked all night and often served at sunrise on winter weekends. (Armenia).

Khat. A leafy plant that produces a mildly stimulating effect when chewed. (Somalia).

Khatchapuri. Cheese-filled cookies. (Georgia).

Khatchkars. Decorative stone monuments. (Armenia).

Kheer. A type of rice pudding. (Pakistan).

Khleb. Coarse, Russian-style bread. (Turkmenistan).

Khmer Rouge. "Red Khmer." This radical communist organization began a violent restructuring of the entire society that killed nearly two million people through violence, starvation, and disease. The educated and business classes were all but eliminated and the economy was completely destroyed. (Cambodia). *See also* **Bye ch'nam, pram-bye kai, m'pai t'gnai.**

Khoda hafiz. [NOTE: Spelling varies because it is a transliteration of Arabic.] "Good-bye" or "May God be with you." A common Arabic parting phrase. (Afghanistan, Bangladesh, Iran).

Khodha haafis. (Pakistan). *See* **Khoda hafiz.**

Khon. Masked plays that feature ornate costumes. (Thailand).

Khorovats. Marinated meat placed on sticks and cooked over coals by men. (Armenia). *Also called* **Kyabab.**

Khoskap. "Tying of Promise." An event at which the groom presents a ring to his intended bride as a promise to marry. (Armenia).

Khotso. "Peace be with you." A formal Sesotho greeting. (Lesotho).

Khubus ti? "How are you?" A common Dari greeting. (Afghanistan).

Khubz. Flat bread. (Iraq).

Khumiss. Fermented mare's milk. (Kazakstan).

Khun. A respectful Thai title used with the first name. (Thailand).

Khuru. A game similar to lawn darts. (Bhutan).

Kia ora. "Be well." A Maori phrase that can mean "hello" or "thank you." (New Zealand).

Kibare. "Hi." A common Mooré greeting. (Burkina Faso).

Kibba. A fried cracked wheat dough stuffed with meat or vegetables. (Iraq).

Kibbeh. A popular beef dish that can be baked, fried, or eaten raw. (Lebanon).

Kibbutz. A place where families live and share the land, work, food, and dining hall equally. They concentrate on agriculture and technology. (Israel). *See also* **Moshav.**

Kiekie. A traditional skirt made from pandanus leaves and woven into different designs that hang as strips from the waist. It is still sometimes worn over skirts, dresses, and **tupenus**. (Tonga).

Ki kati? "What's up?" A Luganda greeting used among young Baganda. (Uganda).

Kilshi. Spiced beef or sheep jerky. (Niger).

Ki manière? "How are you?" A common Mauritian Creole greeting. (Mauritius).

Kimbondeiros. Traditional healers. (Angola). *Also called* **Curandeiros.**

Kimch'i. A spicy pickled cabbage. (North Korea, South Korea).

Kimeshek. A Muslim-style head wrap worn by older Kazak women. (Kazakstan).

Kimono(s). A long traditional robe with long sleeves and tied closed with a special sash. (Japan). *Also called* **Wafuku.** *See also* **Obi.**

Kina Gecesi. "Henna evening." An event for women at which the hands and fingers of the bride are decorated with henna leaf dye. The beginning event of a traditional Turkish wedding. (Turkey).

Kindy. An Australian colloquialism for "kindergarten." (Australia).

Kinh. The Vietnamese ethnic group. (Vietnam).

Kin khow leo bor? "Have you eaten?" An informal Lao greeting. (Laos).

Kinte. Colorful, intricately patterned cotton fabric wrapped around the body as clothing; worn for special events in the southern Ivory Coast. (Ivory Coast). *Also called* **Kita.**

Kiondo. Kikuyu word for a woven bag used to bring gifts. (Kenya).

Kioskos. Small neighborhood shops. (Argentina). *See also* **Almacenes.**

Kiosks. Small newsstand shops that offer a variety of goods. (Poland).

Kip. Laos's national currency. (Laos).

Kippah. An embroidered cap worn by men. (Israel). *Also called* **Yarmulke.**

Kira. The traditional Bhutanese outfit for women. A large rectangular cloth wrapped from ankle to bodice and belted at the waist; it is fastened at the shoulders and worn under a jacket. (Bhutan).

Kirikiti. Samoan cricket. (American Samoa, Samoa).

Kisel. A fruit puree. (Belarus).

Kisra. Thinly layered food made from flour paste. (Sudan).

Kissar. A light sourdough crêpe. (Chad).

Kita. Colorful, intricately patterned cotton fabric wrapped around the body as clothing; worn for special events in the southern Ivory Coast. (Ivory Coast). *Also called* **Kinte.**

Kitandeiras. Women who sell fruit and other goods on street corners or by walking through the city carrying their products on their heads. (Angola). *Also called* **Zungueiras.**

K'itcha. Unleavened bread. (Eritrea).

Kitchen gardens. Small plots of land that produce various fruits, **Ground provisions**, and herbs for tea. (Montserrat).

Kitenge. Several pieces of colorful cotton wraparound fabric used as clothing. (Tanzania). *Also called* **Kanga(s).**

Kitfo. A finely chopped, raw red meat mixed with butter, cheese, and cabbage. Served with the bread **Koocho**. (Ethiopia).

Kitra. (United Arab Emirates). *See* **Gutra.**

Kitumbua. Fried bread. The plural form is *vitumbua*. (Tanzania).

Glossary of Cultural Terms

Kiunguju. The word for "Kiswahili" on the island of Zanzibar. (Tanzania).

Kiyit. A wedding custom in which relatives of the bride and groom exchange clothes. (Kyrgyzstan).

Kizomba. A popular musical style. (Angola).

Kkoktukaksi. Puppet theater. (South Korea).

Klambi koeroeng. A tight-fitting jacket worn with a **Sarong** and **Slendang**. (Suriname).

Kleeschen. The Luxembourgish name for "St. Nicholas." (Luxembourg).

Klibbere goen. An Easter tradition where young boys announce church services with rattles because, according to legend, all church bells leave and go to Rome, Italy, for confessional. When the bells return on the Saturday before Easter, the children collect money and Easter eggs from each home as their reward. (Luxembourg).

Klompen. Dutch wooden shoes or clogs. (Netherlands).

Klongs. Canals that are often used for transportation in rural and some urban areas. (Thailand).

Knäckebröd. Crisp bread. (Sweden).

Knedlo, vepřo, zelo. A meal of sauerkraut, pork roast, and dumplings. (Czech Republic).

Knesset. The Israeli Parliament. (Israel).

Knobkerrie. A traditional club. Part of male traditional dress. (Swaziland). *See also* **Lihiya, Lijobo.**

Knock-it. A greeting in which friends (particularly men) lightly touch closed fists. (Belize).

Knödel. Moist dumplings. (Austria).

Ko. "Big brother." A term used to address young men, regardless of relationship. (Myanmar).

Koba. The Marshallese equivalent to living in a common-law marriage. (Marshall Islands).

Kobouz. Unleavened bread. (Bahrain).

Kobuz. A stringed instrument that **Ashugs** use to accompany their performances. (Azerbaijan).

Koddeyo. "How are the home people?" A Lysonga greeting. (Uganda).

Koe kia. "Good-bye." A Niuean parting phrase. (Niue).

Kofia. An embroidered cap worn by men. (Comoros).

Koha. A gift of money one leaves when welcomed on a **Marae**. The *koha* is a donation toward the cost of hospitality. (New Zealand).

Koka'anga ngatu. Parties in which women make **Tapa**. (Tonga).

Ko ko. "Knock knock." A phrase used to announce one's presence when visiting a home. (Lesotho).

Kokoko. A phrase visitors use to announce their presence. (Gabon).

Kokoretsi. Liver, lungs, and spleen wrapped in intestines and roasted on a spit. (Greece).

Kokpar. A traditional horseback competition in which opposing teams try to move a goat's carcass to a central goal. (Kazakstan). *See also* **Baiga.**

Koláč. Nut or poppy seed rolls. (Slovakia).

Kolah. A turban cap. The color and design are distinctive to the wearer's ethnic background. (Afghanistan).

Kola nuts. Caffeine-containing tree nuts that have been traded in West Africa for centuries; these are sometimes exchanged as a sign of respect at formal ceremonies in the north. (Ivory Coast).

Kolatsche. A Bohemian pastry made out of yeast dough. (Austria).

Koliadki. Christmas carols. (Ukraine).

Koline. A seasonal holiday celebrating the new harvest. Farmers celebrate by sharing newly butchered pork and special sausages with neighbors. (Slovenia).

Kolo. A folk dance. Characteristics may vary depending on the country. (Bosnia and Herzegovina, Croatia, Serbia and Montenegro).

Kolokolo. Coconut fiber string. Made by elderly men for use around the home. (Tuvalu).

Kolpak. A traditional white wool pointed hat worn by men for protection against the elements and as a sign of patriotism. (Kyrgyzstan).

Kombis. Minivan taxis. (Zimbabwe).

Komšija. "Neighbor." A Serbian title used with the last name. (Serbia and Montenegro).

Komsija. Serbo-Croatian word for neighbor. (Bosnia and Herzegovina).

Komuz. A three-stringed instrument similar to the guitar. Used to play traditional music. (Kyrgyzstan).

Ko naera? "Where are you going?" An informal Kiribati greeting. (Kiribati).

Konjak. A strong alcoholic drink. (Albania).

Konnichiwa. "Hello." A standard Japanese greeting. (Japan).

Konpa. A style of music especially popular in urban areas. The music is related to big band music played in the United States during the 1940s. (Haiti).

Koocho. A bread prepared from the stem of a plant called **Inset**. Served with **Kitfo**. (Ethiopia).

Koofiyad. An embroidered cap. (Somalia).

Koopkari. A traditional polo-like sport in which participants on horseback attempt to carry a sheep carcass to a central goal without having it taken away by their competitors. (Uzbekistan).

Kop ango? "What issues?" A Luo greeting. (Uganda).

Kopjes. Huge granite rocks that often rest on smaller formations. (Zimbabwe).

Kop pe. "No issues." The Luo response to the greeting **Kop ango?** (Uganda).

Kora. A traditional stringed instrument made from a gourd. (Gambia, Guinea, Guinea-Bissau, Senegal).

Korfbal. A sport played on a grass field or indoors that combines elements of soccer and basketball. (Netherlands).

Korite. [NOTE: Spelling varies because it is a transliteration.] A feast that marks the end of the Muslim holiday **Ramadan**. (Senegal).

Koritee. (Gambia). *See* **Korite.**

Korjaals. Motorized river canoes used to access Suriname's interior villages. (Suriname).

Korpacha. Mats that are used for sitting. (Uzbekistan).

Koruna. The Czech Republic and Slovakia's national currencies. (Czech Republic, Slovakia).

Kosai. A deep-fried bean cake. (Niger).

Košava. Strong winds. (Serbia and Montenegro).

Kosh bogula. "Good-bye." A common Kyrgyz parting phrase. (Kyrgyzstan).

Kosilo. Slovene word for the main meal of the day. Eaten in the midafternoon or after work. (Slovenia).

Kosu. The Saramaccan term for a traditional wraparound dress. (Suriname). *Also called* **Pangi.**

Glossary of Cultural Terms

Kota. "Elder." A term used to address older men. (Angola).

Koto. A Creole dress consisting of many layers of colorful fabric; it is accompanied by a head scarf (**Angisa**). (Suriname).

Köttbullar med kokt potatis, brun sås och lingonsylt. Meatballs with brown sauce, boiled potatoes, and lingonberry jam. (Sweden).

Kozaks. Zaporozhian Cossacks. (Ukraine).

Kpessosso. The New Year celebration in Aného. Each resident enters blindfolded into the house of **Kpessou** (Aného's local god) to retrieve a colored stone. The color of the stone is a personal omen. (Togo).

Kpessou. Aného's local god. (Togo).

Kpu. A contraption similar to a mortar and pestle, used to grind leaves and prepare many other foods. (Central African Republic).

Kraal. An animal corral. (Lesotho, Swaziland).

Krama. A large scarf that may be used in a variety of ways, including a hat, small blanket, and baby carrier. (Cambodia).

Krapfen. A type of doughnut. (Austria).

Kravata. Croatian word for "tie." (Croatia).

Krentenbollen. Raisin rolls. (Netherlands).

Kresovanje. Midsummer's Night Eve. (Slovenia).

Kroket. A deep-fried sausage. (Netherlands).

Krona. Sweden's national currency. (Sweden).

Króna. Iceland's national currency. The plural form is *krónur*. (Iceland).

Krone. Denmark's national currency. (Denmark).

Kroner. Norway's national currency. (Norway).

Krónur. (Iceland). *See* **Króna.**

Kroon. Estonia's national currency. (Estonia).

Kshatriya. The Hindu caste composed of rulers and warriors. (Nepal). *See also* **Brahmin(s), Chaturvarna Vyavasta, Shudra(s), Vaishya.**

Kubsa. A whole lamb or kid goat stuffed with seasoned rice. (Qatar). *Also called* **Ghozi.**

Kučios. Christmas Eve. (Lithuania).

Kuduro. A popular musical style, heavily influenced by rap and rhythm and blues. (Angola).

Kuftal. Pounded, boiled meat. (Armenia).

Kufteta. A fried meat patty with bread crumbs. (Bulgaria).

Kugelis. Potato pudding with a sour cream sauce. (Lithuania).

Kuidas elate? "How's life?" An Estonian phrase used to begin a conversation. (Estonia).

Kuidas läheb? "How is it going?" An Estonian phrase used to begin a conversation. (Estonia).

Kūkas. Cakes. (Latvia).

Kuk Hoe. The South Korean National Assembly. (South Korea).

Kukri. A place where urban people can buy cooked rice. (Sierra Leone).

Kukurai. "Big man" or leader. There is one in each village. (Papua New Guinea). *Also called* **Bikman.**

Kuma? "How are you?" A typical Kriolu greeting. (Guinea-Bissau).

Kuma di kurpu? "How is your body?" A polite Kriolu inquiry. (Guinea-Bissau).

Kumara. Sweet potatoes. (New Zealand, Solomon Islands).

Kumari. A title used with the last name of an unmarried woman to show respect. (India).

Kumiss. Fermented mare's milk. (Kyrgyzstan).

Kumu. Greens of any kind. (Papua New Guinea).

Kumusta ka na? "How are you doing?" A formal Tagalog greeting. (Philippines).

Kuna. Croatia's national currency. (Croatia).

Kundu. A traditional drum that is hourglass-shaped and covered with lizard skin. (Papua New Guinea).

Kundze. "Mrs." A Latvian title added after the name when an introduction is made. (Latvia).

Kungs. "Mr." A Latvian title added after the name when an introduction is made. (Latvia).

Kunjani? "How are you?" A common Zulu and Swazi greeting. (South Africa, Swaziland).

Kunta. Fabric strips sewn together to form geometric patterns. Often woven into blankets given as wedding presents and kept as family heirlooms. (Niger).

Kurban Ait. [NOTE: Muslim holidays are set according to the lunar calendar.] Day of Remembrance; a Muslim holiday. (Kyrgyzstan).

Kurban Bairam. [NOTE: Spelling varies because it is a transliteration. Also, Muslim holidays are set according to the lunar calendar.] Feast of the Sacrifice. A Muslim holiday commemorating Abraham's willingness to sacrifice his son. (Albania, Bosnia and Herzegovina, Croatia). *Also called* **Eid al-Adha.**

Kurban Bairami. (Azerbaijan). *See* **Kurban Bairam.**

Kurban Bayramı. (Turkey). *See* **Kurban Bairam.**

Kurent. A demon figure who chases away the winter. (Slovenia). *See also* **Kurentovanje.**

Kurentovanje. The evening before **Pust** when **Kurent** chases away winter. (Slovenia).

Kures. The Kazak form of wrestling. (Kazakstan).

Kurja obara. Chicken stew with buckwheat groats. (Slovenia).

Kurova guva. A weeklong party held a year or two after a family member dies. At this time the departed spirit is united with the living. (Zimbabwe).

Kurpacha. Thick cushions that are spread on the floor and used for sitting. (Tajikistan).

Kurta surwal. Colorful pants, tight from the calves down, with a matching, knee-length tunic. Worn by unmarried girls and women in Terai. (Nepal). *Also called* **Punjabi.**

Kushe. "Hello." A common Krio greeting. (Sierra Leone).

Kusi. The pleasant season with warm, clear, breezy days and cool nights. Lasts from April to September. (Comoros). *See also* **Kashkazi.**

Kutyapi. A two-stringed lute. (Philippines).

Kuzuzangpo? "Is your body well?" A common Dzongkha greeting and parting phrase. (Bhutan).

Kuzuzangpo la dasho. A Dzongkha title used to address superiors. (Bhutan).

Kvass. A tangy Russian juice made from dried bread. (Kazakstan).

Kwacha. Malawi and Zambia's national currencies. (Malawi, Zambia).

Kwaito. A popular style of music that mixes African melodies and lyrics with hip-hop and reggae. (South Africa).

Kwanjin. Breadfruit baked on coals and then scraped. (Marshall Islands).

Kwanza. Angola's national currency. (Angola).

Kwasa kwasa. A Congolese style of dance music. (Botswana, Congo, Malawi, Namibia).

Kwela. (1) A style of music that incorporates the distinctive penny whistle. (South Africa). (2) The Kimbundu term for a

Glossary of Cultural Terms

strategy game played with beads or seeds placed in holes on a wooden board or in the ground. (Angola). *Also called* **Wela.**

Kwezi. Part of a child's greeting to an elder. A child will cup both hands and extend them while saying *Kwezi*. (Comoros).

Kwon kaal. Millet bread. (Uganda).

Kyabab. Marinated meat placed on sticks and cooked over coals by men. (Armenia). *Also called* **Khorovats.**

Kyat. Myanmar's national currency. (Myanmar).

Kyeshki as. Kazak word for a light evening meal. (Kazakstan).

Kygyzcha. A style of eating without utensils. (Kyrgyzstan).

Kýna. Papua New Guinea's national currency. (Papua New Guinea).

Kyrk. The Kyrgyz word for "forty." (Kyrgyzstan).

Kyz. The Kyrgyz word for "girls." (Kyrgyzstan).

Kyz Dzharysh. Girls' races on horseback. (Kyrgyzstan).

Kyz kuumai. Chasing the bride. A common village ritual in which the bride is provided with the fastest horse and must try to outrace the groom. If she outraces him, she can "choose" not to marry him. (Kyrgyzstan).

Kyzy. The Kyrgyz word for "daughter." In Kyrgyz, a girl is greeted by her father's first name, followed by *kyzy,* and then the girl's own given name. (Kyrgyzstan).

Kyzyl chai. "Red tea." A popular drink. (Kyrgyzstan).

La. A sound attached to words in Dzongkha or English to show respect. (Bhutan).

Laba diena. "Good day." A common Lithuanian greeting. (Lithuania).

Laban. A yogurt drink. (Oman).

Labas. "Hello." An informal Lithuanian greeting used among friends. (Lithuania).

Labas rytas. "Good morning." A common Lithuanian greeting. (Lithuania).

Labass. "No evil." A response to the Hassaniya greeting **Iyak labass.** (Mauritania).

Labas vakaras. "Good evening." A common Lithuanian greeting. (Lithuania).

Labess. A greeting that means "How are you?" and "Fine." (Morocco).

La cena. The Spanish word for "dinner." (Spain).

La comida. The Spanish word for "lunch." (Spain).

Laddie. A term people use to refer to males. (Scotland).

La dictadura. A period of time in which a military junta ruled for 12 years, beginning in 1968. (Peru).

Ladino. Descendants of the Spanish and Maya. They more closely identify with their Spanish heritage. (Guatemala).

La Fête Nationale. Bastille Day, celebrated 14 July. The holiday commemorates the storming of the Bastille prison in Paris during the French Revolution. (France).

Lafia ngai. "Much peace." A Sara greeting. (Chad).

Lagting. The upper chamber of the Norwegian Parliament. (Norway). *See also* **Storting.**

Lahaf. An embroidered headdress worn by women. (Oman).

Lahatra. Malagasy word for "fate." (Madagascar).

Lahiya lau. "In health." A Hausa response to the greetings **Ina kwana?** and **Ina ini?** (Niger).

Lahko noč. "Good night." A common Slovene greeting. (Slovenia).

La hora chapina. The Guatemalan hour. A term that refers to putting people before schedules in such a way that events rarely start on time. (Guatemala).

La hora Ecuatoriana. Ecuadorian time; referring to the Ecuadorian tendency to arrive late. (Ecuador).

La hora latina. "Latin time." The notion that individuals' needs are more important than schedules. Thus, being late is the norm. (Honduras).

Lahuta. A one-stringed instrument played with a bow. (Albania).

Lailat El-Dakhlah. An Arabic phrase meaning "wedding night." (Jordan).

La Isla de la Trinidad. Island of the Holy Trinity. (Trinidad and Tobago).

Lala salama. "Sleep peacefully." A common parting phrase used in the evening. (Kenya).

Lalé. A greeting used when joining a large group. Both palms are raised while greeting. (Chad).

Lali. Wooden drums. (Fiji).

La lucha. Professional wrestling. (Mexico).

Lamas. Buddhist monks who teach. They officiate at most events, from naming babies to village festivals to public ribbon cuttings. (Bhutan).

Lamba. Long white cotton wrap. Traditional attire for men and women in the highlands area. (Madagascar).

Lambamena. "Red cloth." A burial shroud. (Madagascar). *See also* **Famadihana.**

Lambaoany. A light, colorful wrap worn by men and women in coastal areas. (Madagascar).

Lambi. Conch. (Grenada).

Lam gi day? "What are you doing?" A common Vietnamese greeting. (Vietnam).

La multi ani. "Happy New Year." A Romanian greeting used at the beginning of the new year. (Moldova).

Lamvong. The Lao national folk dance, in which dancers form three rings and are encircled by the audience. (Laos).

Länder. German states that have their own legislatures and control over local issues. (Germany).

Landtag. The Liechtenstein Parliament. (Liechtenstein).

Lang Arm. Waltz music. Literally, "long arm." (Namibia).

Langouti. An ankle-length cotton garment tied at the waist. A traditional outfit worn by Hindu men. (Mauritius).

La novena. The nine days before Christmas that are marked by religious observances and parties. (Colombia).

Lao. "Old." A Mandarin Chinese term used with or instead of a title to show special respect to a friend. (China).

Lao Lum. "Lowland Lao." The largest ethnic group in Laos. The *Lao Lum* are culturally and linguistically related to the Isaan people of northeastern Thailand. (Laos).

Lao Sung. "Highland Lao." An ethnic group that includes the Hmong, Kor, and Yao peoples. Their origins are in southwestern China. (Laos).

Lao Theung. "Midland Lao." An ethnic group that includes the Khmu, Katang, Makong, and Xuay ethnic groups. (Laos).

Lap. Sautéed meat mixed with onions, lemongrass, and spices. Served with a rice-flour sauce. (Laos).

Laplap. A wraparound sarong worn by men and women. (Papua New Guinea).

Lappas. Two yards of ankle-length cloth worn by women; tied about the waist and topped with an African or Western blouse. Commonly made of brightly colored cotton. (Sierra Leone).

La punta. A popular style of music with a complex rhythm. It originated with traditional Garífuna music and dance. Played

Glossary of Cultural Terms

with instruments such as drums, conch shells, and maracas. (Honduras).

La revedere. "Good-bye." A Romanian parting phrase. (Moldova).

Lari. Georgia's national currency. (Georgia).

Larimar. A blue stone unique to the Dominican Republic. Used to make jewelry. (Dominican Republic).

Las Cortes Generales. Spain's bicameral legislature. (Spain).

Las murgas. Small groups of singers and actors who present parodies of the year's main events. (Uruguay).

Lassie. A term people use to refer to females. (Scotland).

Lat. Latvia's national currency. (Latvia).

Laulu. The Tuvaluan word for "spinach." (Tuvalu).

Lau Susuga. A general Samoan title suitable for chiefs and married or professional people. (American Samoa, Samoa).

Lavalava(s). Large rectangular pieces of cloth worn as clothing. (American Samoa, Micronesia, Samoa, Solomon Islands).

La Vanguardia. "The Vanguard." A literary movement that seeks to restore Nicaragua's cultural identity. (Nicaragua).

Lavash. Lightly browned flat bread, rolled out in large circles and baked in a **Tonir**. (Armenia).

Laver bread. A mixture of seaweed and oatmeal that is fried and served with bacon. (Wales). *Also called* **Bara lawr.**

La Vielle. French term meaning "elderly woman." If there is no male figurehead, families may be headed by the oldest woman in the family, who is called this name. (Ivory Coast).

La Violencia. Colombian civil war between conservatives and liberals from 1948 to 1957. (Colombia).

Lay. Condensed milk with sugar. (Gambia).

Leban. Diluted yogurt. (Kuwait).

Lebaran. A feast at the end of **Ramadan**. (Indonesia). *Also called* **Idul-Fitri.**

Leberknödelsuppe. A soup with liver dumplings. (Austria).

Lechon. A stuffed pig roasted over a charcoal fire. (Philippines).

Lechoza. Papaya. (Venezuela).

Lederhosen. Leather knee-length pants. Traditional clothing worn by men. (Austria, Germany).

Le Huit Mai. French Armistice Day. Celebrated on 8 May. (France).

Lek. Albania's national currency. (Albania).

Leka nosht. "Good night." A Bulgarian greeting. (Bulgaria).

Lempira. Honduras's national currency. (Honduras).

Lengua en salsa. "Tongue in sauce." A common Costa Rican dish. (Costa Rica).

Leone(s). Sierra Leone's national currency. (Sierra Leone).

Lesiba. A stringed reed. A popular traditional instrument often played by young men as a method of herding cattle. (Lesotho).

Leso. A printed shawl. (Comoros).

Le truck. A truck converted into a bus that is a popular form of local transportation. (French Polynesia).

Letterboxes. A colloquialism for mailboxes. (Wales).

Lettres. An education track that focuses on humanities and social sciences. (Tunisia).

Lëtzebuergesch. The Luxembourgish language. (Luxembourg).

Leu. Moldova and Romania's national currencies. (Moldova, Romania).

Lev. Bulgaria's national currency. (Bulgaria).

L'Exode. Young men that work for wages in neighboring countries and return to Niger during the rainy season. (Niger).

Liamuiga. The name, meaning "Fertile Island," given to Saint Kitts by the Caribs who lived on the island prior to its colonization by Europeans. (Saint Kitts and Nevis).

Licensiado. A professional title. (Peru).

Liceo. A government-subsidized secondary school. (Uruguay).

Lift. Elevator. (New Zealand).

Lihiya. A single length of printed cloth. The plural form is **Emahiya**. It forms the basis of traditional clothing for men and women. (Swaziland). *See also* **Knobkerrie, Lijobo.**

Lijobo. An animal skin worn at the waist. Part of male traditional dress. (Swaziland). *See also* **Knobkerrie, Lihiya.**

Likembe. A traditional instrument; a board with thin metal strips plucked with the thumbs. (Congo).

Lilangeni. Swaziland's national currency. (Swaziland).

Lim. A flute. (Bhutan).

Lime. A term that refers to the time people spend relaxing and socializing with each other. (Antigua and Barbuda, Trinidad and Tobago). *Also called* **Liming.**

Limey. A derogatory nickname for people from the United Kingdom. The source is believed to be the Montserratian lime juice used by the British navy to combat scurvy. (Montserrat).

Limin. A colloquialism for "hanging out with friends." (U.S. Virgin Islands). *Also called* **Out on a lime.**

Liming. A term that refers to the time people spend relaxing and socializing with each other. (Antigua and Barbuda, Barbados, Grenada). *See also* **Lime.**

Liming. Activities include listening to music, chatting, and relaxing. Dropping by a home unannounced is acceptable, but staying too long once doing so is rude. (Trinidad and Tobago).

Lingala. An upbeat Congolese dance music. (Congo, Kenya).

Liphalishi. A stiff porridge made from maize. (Swaziland).

Liputa. The Lingala word for **Pagne**. (Congo).

Liqoqo. A council of elders. (Swaziland).

Lira. The national currencies of various countries. (Italy, Malta, Turkey).

Litas. Lithuania's national currency. (Lithuania).

Llajua. A spicy salsa. (Bolivia).

Llamar. "To call." A Spanish verb. Typically pronounced "yah-MAHR." In parts of Argentina it is pronounced "shah-MAHR." (Argentina).

Llaneros. Venezuelan cowboys. (Venezuela).

Llano(s). (1) Spanish word for "plains." (Venezuela). (2) Wet, hot, forested lowlands found in the east and northeast of Bolivia. (Bolivia). *Also called* **El trópico.**

Llapingachos. Cheese and potato cakes. (Ecuador).

Loaka. A term that describes meat, fish, eggs, vegetables, or basic broth. (Madagascar).

Lobi. A Lingala word meaning both "yesterday" and "tomorrow." (Congo).

Lobola. The bride-price paid by the groom or his family to the bride's parents. Traditionally it included cattle, although cash is now accepted. (Malawi, Namibia, South Africa, Swaziland, Zambia, Zimbabwe).

Lobolo. The bride-price paid by the groom's family to the bride's parents in the form of cattle or cash. (Mozambique).

Lochs. Deep blue lakes. (Scotland).

Locro. Soup made with potatoes, meat, and vegetables. (Argentina, Ecuador). tea ceremony.

Loi. The Uzbek word for "mud." A term of special significance in the Uzbek (Uzbekistan).

Glossary of Cultural Terms

Lok Sabha. House of the People. The lower house in India's Parliament. (India). *See also* **Rajya Sabha.**

Lola. "Grandmother." A Tagalog word used as a term of address for elderly women. (Philippines).

Lolo. (1) Coconut milk. (Fiji, Tuvalu). (2) "Grandfather." A Tagalog word used as a term of address for elderly men. (Philippines).

Lonche. A light breakfast-type meal served around 6 p.m. (Peru).

Longyi. An ankle-length wraparound sarong worn by Burmese men and women. The male *longyi* is tied at the front, while the female *longyi* is tucked in at the side of the waist. Material patterns differ for men and women. Women wear the the *longyi* with a blouse. Men wear the *longyi* with an **Eingyi** and a **Taikpon**. (Myanmar).

Loonie. The Canadian dollar's nickname. Refers to the image of the loon minted on the gold-colored coin. (Canada).

Lorries. Small trucks. (Guyana).

Loshoto da ne chue. "Do not let evil hear." A Macedonian phrase said by older rural women to ward off bad luck. (Macedonia). *See also* **Skraja da e.**

Lotar. An instrument similar to a three-stringed banjo. (Morocco). *Also called* **Kanza.**

Loti. Lesotho's national currency. The plural form is *Maloti*. (Lesotho).

Lot song teow. Vehicles with two rows of seats; a form of public transportation. (Laos).

Louages. Group taxis that run on set routes between cities. (Tunisia).

Loubo. Yam flour, often used to make a stiff porridge. (Benin). *Also called* **Amala.**

Lovespoons. Intricately carved wooden spoons that people traditionally gave to their loved ones. (Wales).

Lovo. Ground oven. (Fiji).

Low. A type of island characterized by small sand-and-coral bars surrounding a lagoon, dotted with shrubs and coconut palms. (French Polynesia). *See also* **High.**

Loya Jirga. Grand Council. A body of locally elected and tribal officials that convenes to discuss special issues, such as constitutional amendments. (Afghanistan).

Loy Krathong. A Buddhist holiday that honors the water goddess for providing water throughout the year. People float small "boats" with candles, coins, or flowers on waterways. (Thailand).

Lucia. A festival coinciding with the longest night of the year (13 December). A girl assumes the role of St. Lucia and dresses in white with a crown of candles in her hair. She sings a special song and serves coffee and **Lussekatter**. This marks the beginning of the Christmas season. (Sweden). *See also* **Jul.**

Ludo. A board game. (Togo).

Luiet. A black or colorful cloth that Muslim women use to cover their dresses. The cloth can be loosely draped or sewn to be more tailored. (Eritrea).

Lukim iu. "See you later." A common Solomon Island Pijin parting phrase. (Solomon Islands).

Lumela. "Hello." A common Sesotho greeting. (Lesotho).

Lung. "Uncle." A term of address. (Laos, Thailand).

Lungi. (1) A circular piece of cloth, knotted at the waist, that extends to the ankles. Worn by rural men with a **Genji**. (Bangladesh). (2) The most common headwear for men. It is worn with a **Kolah**. (Afghanistan).

Lu pulu. Cooked taro leaves with coconut cream and corned beef. (Tonga).

Lusekwane. A traditional Swazi event and a type of tree used in the event. For the event, young men bring branches of the *lusekwane* tree to the royal residence to build a cattle byre. (Swaziland).

Lussekatter. "Lucia cats." A type of roll. (Sweden).

Luta livre. Traditional wrestling. (Guinea-Bissau).

Lutefisk. Cod or coalfish soaked in potash lye. (Norway).

Luumos. Weekly markets that sell livestock, household goods, fabric, and food. (Gambia).

Lycée(s). Secondary schools. (Comoros, France, Tunisia).

Lyceums. A three- or four-year course that prepares a student for higher education. (Greece).

Lyonpo. A Buddhist minister. (Bhutan).

Ma. (1) A term used to address older women, regardless of relationship. (Saint Lucia, Sierra Leone). (2) "Sister." A term used to address girls and young women, regardless of relationship. (Myanmar). (3) A Chinese word that has five different meanings, including "horse" and "mother." It can also function as a question marker, depending on the tone or voice inflection with which it is spoken. (Taiwan).

Ma'a el-salameh, deer balak. "Good-bye, take care." A common Arabic parting phrase. (West Bank and Gaza).

Ma'alesh. "Don't worry" or "Never mind." An Arabic term that is used to dismiss concerns or conflicts that are inevitable or not serious. Reflects the relaxed and patient Egyptian life. (Egypt).

Ma' al-salamah. An Arabic term meaning "go in safety." (Libya).

Maandazi. Small doughnuts. (Tanzania).

Ma'asina ruru. "Marching Rule." A nationalist movement of self-reliance opposed to British rule. *Ma'asina ruru* helped lay the groundwork for independence, even though it eventually failed in its own right. (Solomon Islands).

Ma'assalameh. "Good-bye." A common Arabic parting phrase. (Bahrain).

Ma'awiis. A Somali kilt. (Somalia).

Mabele. Sorghum. (Botswana).

Mabkhara. A special stand used to burn incense. (Bahrain). *See also* **Bakhour.**

Mabrouk. An Arabic phrase used to offer congratulations for weddings, graduations, new employment, etc. (Tunisia).

Macaroni pie. (1) A popular dish made with cheese or mincemeat. (Barbados). (2) Macaroni baked with cheese, butter, and milk. (Trinidad and Tobago).

Machbous. (1) A dish with rice, meat, tomatoes, and lentils. (Bahrain). (2) Rice flavored with saffron and served with a tomato sauce and lamb or chicken. (Kuwait).

Machetta. A headscarf worn by men on Fridays and religious holidays. Can also be used to protect one's face in sandstorms, mask foul odors, or be used as a towel. (Yemen).

Machismo. The male attitude of proving one's manliness or superiority. (Belize, Dominican Republic, Honduras, Mexico, Nicaragua, Panama, Philippines).

Macumbeiros. Witches. People believe that witches can free them from a problem or help them obtain wealth, usually at the expense of others. Deaths or accidents are often attributed to witchcraft. (Angola). *Also called* **Feiticeiros.**

Glossary of Cultural Terms

Mada'a. A water pipe filled with tobacco. (Yemen).

Madame. (1) "Mrs." A common title for married women. Used in French-speaking countries.. (2) A common title for female elders. (Namibia).

Madeeh. Islamic gospel music sung to commemorate the prophet Muhammad. It is also the foundation of **Haqibh**. (Sudan).

Mademoiselle. "Miss." A common title. Used in French-speaking countries..

Madrinha. Portuguese word for "godmother." (Portugal).

Mãe. "Mother." A term of address used as a sign of respect. (Angola, Cape Verde).

Maestro/a. A Spanish title used to address a teacher. Masculine *maestro*, feminine *maestra*. (Panama).

Mafola? "OK?" An informal Niuean greeting. (Niue).

Maftool. A dish of vegetables and meat served with **Couscous**. (West Bank and Gaza).

Magafaoa. Niuean word for "extended family." (Niue).

Magalimoto. Toy cars that are made out of scrap metal and bits of trash. (Malawi).

Mageu. A thick sorghum drink. (Botswana).

Maghlobah. Vegetables, meat, and rice served with salad and yogurt. (West Bank and Gaza).

Maghna-eh. A black traditional Iranian head covering worn by women. (Iran).

Magolli. An alcoholic drink most popular in rural areas. (South Korea).

Magrud. Semolina cookies stuffed with dates and dipped in syrup. (Libya).

Magtaal. Poetic songs of praise; the heart of much of Mongolian literature. (Mongolia).

Mahabharata. An epic Sanskrit poem that continues to influence national and regional literature. (India).

Ma Ha 'inyanim? "What's happening?" A Hebrew phrase that may follow the initial greeting **Shalom**. (Israel).

Maha la shegay? "What are people saying?" A Somali greeting used to ask "How are you?" (Somalia).

Mahangu. Millet. (Namibia).

Maharram. The Muslim New Year. (Indonesia).

Maha Shivaratree. A Hindu holiday in which it is popular to dress in white and pour sacred water on a representation of the god Shiva. The water is drawn from the Grand Bassin, a high-altitude lake that is located in a volcano crater. (Mauritius).

Mahjong. A Chinese table game played with tiles. A cross between dominoes and cards. (Hong Kong, Philippines).

Mahleb. A paste of crushed black seeds that women apply to their faces during a visit. (Oman).

Mahram. Arabic word for a male relative. (Qatar).

Mahshi. Stuffed vegetables. (Jordan).

Mahu. The Fon name of a supreme god of an indigenous belief system. (Benin).

Mai kana. "Come eat." A person is greeted with this phrase when passing a rural house. (Fiji).

Mai mota. "Person with the car." A name used to address taxi drivers. (Niger).

Main gasing. A traditional activity of spinning tops that weigh several pounds for long periods of time. (Malaysia).

Mai Pen Rai. "Never mind." A Thai expression that characterizes a general feeling that life is to be enjoyed for the moment; problems and setbacks should not be taken too seriously. (Thailand).

Maizītes. Small sandwiches. (Latvia).

Majbous. Rice cooked in a sauce until it is yellow and then served with chicken, fish, or meat. (United Arab Emirates).

Majelis Permusyawaratan Rakyat. The People's Consultative Assembly. (Indonesia).

Majiang. (China). *See* **Mahjong.**

Majilis. The Kazak Parliament. (Kazakstan).

Majlis. (1) Arabic word for "sitting room." Used to entertain guests. (Oman, Qatar, United Arab Emirates). (2) Parliament, the Islamic Consultative Assembly. (Iran). (3) A traditional Islamic administrative system that allows people to petition the **Emir** directly. (Bahrain). (4) The supreme legislative branch of government. (Turkmenistan).

Majlis al-Chaab. The People's Council, the legislative body. (Syria).

Majlis al-Dawla. Council of State. The upper body of the Omani Council. Consists of appointed senior dignitaries. (Oman).

Majlis al-Nuwaab. The Chamber of Deputies, the legislative body. (Tunisia).

Majlis al-Shura. Consultative Council in the national government. (Oman, Qatar, Saudi Arabia).

Majlis al-Shuyukh. The Mauritanian Senate. (Mauritania).

Majlis al-Umma. The National Assembly. (Kuwait).

Majlis al-Watani. The Mauritanian National Assembly. (Mauritania).

Majlisi Milliy. The upper chamber of the Tajik parliament, or **Majlisi Oli**. (Tajikistan).

Majlisi Namoyandogon. The lower chamber of the Tajik parliament, or **Majlisi Oli**. (Tajikistan).

Majlisi Oli. The Tajik parliament. (Tajikistan).

Makadii? "How are you?" A Shona phrase that follows an initial greeting such as **Mhoroi**. (Zimbabwe).

Makala. Fried dough. (Central African Republic).

Makaruna mbakbaka. Refers to any pasta simmered in tomato and lamb stock with a mixture of spices. (Libya).

Make. A social title added to an adult woman's name to show respect. Pronounced "MAH-gay." (Swaziland).

Makha Bucha. An important Buddhist holiday. Set according to the lunar calendar. (Thailand).

Making a turn. "I am leaving." A phrase used among friends and youth at parting. (Saint Vincent and the Grenadines).

Makkara. Sausage. (Finland).

Makossa. An indigenous style of Cameroonian music. (Cameroon, Equatorial Guinea).

Makrout. A semolina pastry with date filling. (Algeria).

Maktoub. "Fate." A concept used to explain difficult times. This attitude provides comfort and encourages perseverance. (Tunisia).

Makunji. Village chief. (Central African Republic).

Mak yong. A musical play. (Malaysia).

Malabar. A long-sleeved striped or plaid shirt reaching to the knees and worn over pants. Traditional attire for men in the highlands area. (Madagascar).

Malamba. Cane alcohol. (Equatorial Guinea).

Malekum Salaam. (Gambia). *See* **Waalaikum assalaam.**

Malica. Slovene word for a midmorning snack. (Slovenia).

Malo e lelei. "Hello." A common daytime greeting. (Tonga).

Malo e lelei ki he efiafi ni. "Good evening." A Tongan greeting. (Tonga).

Malo e lelei ki he pongipongi ni. "Good morning." A common Tongan greeting. (Tonga).

Glossary of Cultural Terms

Malo e tau mo eni. "Good morning." A common Tongan greeting. (Tonga).

Malo lava. "Hello." An informal Samoan greeting. (American Samoa, Samoa).

Malo soifua. A polite reference to good health and well-being. A common greeting. (American Samoa).

Maloti. (Lesotho). *See* **Loti.**

Malouf. A musical style played by small orchestras with instruments such as drums, lutes, sitars, and violins. (Tunisia).

Malu. A tatoo for women. It covers the top of the thigh to the knee. (American Samoa). *See also* **Pe'a.**

Mama. (1) "Mother." A term of address for older women. (Central African Republic, French Polynesia, Gabon, Papua New Guinea, Saint Kitts and Nevis, South Africa). (2) An expression of surprise or shock. One can also say **Aye.** (Central African Republic).

Mamá. "Mother." A term of address used as a sign of respect. (Angola, Cape Verde).

Mamaguy. (1) Grenadian patois for "flatter." (Grenada). (2) Trying to fool someone. (Trinidad and Tobago).

Mamaliga. Cornmeal mush. (Moldova, Romania).

Maman. French word for "mom." A term of address children use for adult women even if they are not related. (Ivory Coast, Togo).

Ma nabad baa? "Is there peace?" A Somali greeting used in the north. (Somalia).

Manao ahoana tompoko? "How are you, sir/madam?" A common Malagasy greeting. An informal greeting would omit the word *tompoko*. (Madagascar).

Manas. The longest and most significant Kyrgyz epic. *Manas* was an important folk hero who has come to represent the strength, independence, and unity of the Kyrgyz people. (Kyrgyzstan).

Manat. The national currency. (Azerbaijan, Turkmenistan).

Mandalas. A circular pattern fashioned out of different media, such as paint and sand. It is the creator's interpretation of religious concepts such as the universe or deity and is often used in meditation. (Bhutan).

Mandazi. A doughnutlike food. (Kenya).

Mandioca. Cassava. (Paraguay).

Mane. "To collect and/or bring together." (Kiribati). *See also* **Aba, Maneaba(s).**

Maneaba ni Maungatabu. The Kiribati House of Assembly. (Kiribati).

Maneaba(s). A meeting house used for formal entertaining. It is the center of community life. Strict traditions govern construction, seating arrangements, member duties, etc. (Kiribati). *See also* **Aba, Mane.**

Maneapa(s). A community hall used for feasts. (Tuvalu). *Also called* **Ahiga.** *See also* **Fakaala.**

Mang. A Pilipino title used before a male elder's last name. (Guam).

Mangbele. Cassava dough wrapped and boiled in leaves. (Central African Republic).

Ma ngi fi rek. "I am all right; I am here." A Wolof response to the greeting **Na ka nga def?** (Gambia).

Mangwanani. "Good morning." A common Shona greeting. (Zimbabwe).

Manheru. "Good evening." A common Shona greeting. (Zimbabwe).

Manicou. A type of opossum. (Grenada).

Manioc. Cassava. (Gabon).

Ma Nishma? "What's up?" A Hebrew phrase that may follow the initial greeting **Shalom.** (Israel).

Manjar. A bread spread and baking ingredient that is made by boiling an unopened can of sweetened condensed milk for hours. (Chile).

Mannginge'. A traditional custom in which a Chamorro greets an elder by kissing his or her hand. (Guam).

Mansaf. A large tray of rice covered with chunks of stewed lamb (including the head) and **Jameed.** The Jordanian national dish. (Jordan).

Mansef. Rice, lamb, yogurt, bread, and nuts. (West Bank and Gaza).

Manta. A shawl worn by rural women. (Bolivia).

Mante. Dumplings with meat or vegetables. (Uzbekistan).

Manti. Large steamed dumplings filled with chopped beef, pumpkin, and onions. (Kazakstan).

Mantin-Majel. The Marshallese manner. Generally, it means a casual or carefree way of life. (Marshall Islands).

Man tou. Steamed bread. (China).

Mantu. Pasta dishes. (Afghanistan, Tajikistan).

Manty. Steamed meat and onions sealed in dough patties. (Kyrgyzstan).

Manueline. A unique baroque style. (Portugal).

Manyattas. Walled communities in which Karamojong live to protect their livestock and families from raids by rival groups. (Uganda).

Man, yoh overtake meh. "Friend, you surprised me." A local English Creole phrase. (U.S. Virgin Islands).

Maoloeud. (Chad). *See* **Mouloud.**

Maqhas. Coffee shops. (Kuwait).

Maquiladoras. Border industries where U.S. investments employ Mexican labor. (Mexico).

Maquis. Small outdoor restaurants that sell alcohol and basic dishes to travelers and local men. People may gather there to eat fried plantains, drink beer, and chat. (Ivory Coast).

Marabout(s). Muslim teachers and leaders. (Libya, Mauritania, Senegal).

Maracas. Rattles made of gourds. (Venezuela).

Marae. The sacred space in front of a Maori **Wharenui.** (New Zealand).

Marag laham. A lamb and vegetable stew. (Kuwait).

Marama. A handkerchief worn on the head by older rural women to keep hair away from the face. (Macedonia).

Maravi. "The sun's rays." The origin of the word *Malawi*. (Malawi).

Mardi. Celebrated on 10 November, a day for children to go to neighbors' houses, sing special national songs, dance, and ask to be let in out of the cold. They are given candy and fruit. (Estonia).

Marenda. A light midmorning meal of fish, cheese, and bread. (Croatia).

Marhaba. (1) "Hello." A casual Arabic greeting. (Iraq, Jordan, Lebanon, Saudi Arabia, Syria). (2) "Fine." An Arabic response to the greeting **Kefelhal?** (Eritrea).

Marhabah keif halak? "Hello, how are you doing?" A common Arabic greeting. (West Bank and Gaza).

Marhaban bikoum. "Hello to you." A common Arabic greeting. (Algeria).

Glossary of Cultural Terms

Mariachi. A type of band music that originated in Mexico. Bands vary in size but generally consist of a singer, violins, trumpets, and guitars. (Mexico).

Marimba. An instrument similar to a xylophone. (Guatemala, Honduras, Nicaragua).

Marisa. A sorghum beer. (Sudan).

Marka. Bosnia and Herzegovina's national currency. (Bosnia and Herzegovina).

Markka. The name of the former Finnish national currency. (Finland). *Also called* **Finmark.**

Maroon. A cooperative effort in which people come together to finish a work project and share a meal or have a party. (Grenada).

Marquetry. The art of affixing wood patterns on boxes, trays, and furniture. (Syria).

Marraine. "Godmother" in French. (Belgium).

Married quarters. A married couple's own apartment. (Hong Kong).

Martenitza. A celebration of spring. On 1 March people exchange *martenitza,* a red-and-white yarn design that symbolizes health. They wear the design until they see a stork or a blossoming tree. Then they either put the *martenitza* on a tree branch to bring spring or hide it under a rock to represent the wish that evil spirits in nature and humankind will go to sleep. (Bulgaria).

Mărțisor. A holiday on 1 March in which men give women and girls small brooches. (Romania).

Mas. (1) A title used to address an older man or a superior. (Montserrat). (2) Short for masquerade. Also known as Carnival. (Trinidad and Tobago).

Masa al-khair. (Bahrain). *See* **Mesah al-Khair.**

Masa' al-khayr. (Libya). *See* **Masa' el-khair.**

Masa al-nur. The Arabic reply to the greeting **Masa al-khair**. (Bahrain).

Masa' el-khair. "Good afternoon." A common Arabic greeting. (West Bank and Gaza).

Masakhane. "Let us build together." A Nguni phrase that was the motto of Nelson Mandela's campaign in 1994. (South Africa).

Maseche. A Malawian rattle. (Malawi).

Mash. Green lentils cooked with rice in a stew. (Turkmenistan).

Ma' Sha' Allah. (Libya). *See* **Insha'Allah.**

Ma Shlomcha? "How are you?" Addressed to men, a Hebrew phrase that may follow the initial greeting **Shalom**. (Israel).

Ma Shlomech? "How are you?" Addressed to women, a Hebrew phrase that may follow the initial greeting **Shalom**. (Israel).

Mashramani. An Amerindian word for the celebration at the end of a cooperative project. The name is also used for Republic Day, celebrated on 23 February, which marks the date Guyana became the Cooperative Republic of Guyana. (Guyana).

Masi. Cloth produced from bark and decorated with stencils to create elaborate patterns. (Fiji).

Masikati. "Good afternoon." A common Shona greeting. (Zimbabwe).

Maslahat. Meeting. (Turkmenistan).

Ma soeur. "My sister." A French term of address used among people of the same age. (Gabon).

Massar. A turban worn by men. (Oman).

Massegohoun. A traditional music rhythm. (Benin).

Más tarde. "Later." A common Spanish parting phrase. (Guatemala).

Mata-bicho. The term for "breakfast" that literally means "kill the beast" (the one growling in an empty stomach). (Angola, Mozambique).

Matai. A male or female chief that holds authority in the extended family or kinship group. He or she is selected based on loyal service to family members and the village community. Traditional qualifications include oratory skills and a body tattoo. (American Samoa, Samoa).

Mataqali. Fijian landholding units composed of families living communally. (Fiji).

Matatus. Small pickup truck taxis with cabs on the back that run on regular routes but without schedules. (Kenya).

Mate. (1) An herb tea that is served hot. Pronounced "MAH-tey." (Argentina, Brazil, Paraguay, Uruguay). (2) A term of address used between male friends. (Australia).

Mate dulce. An herb tea made with sugar. Women traditionally drink *mate dulce*. (Uruguay). *See also* **Mate.**

Mathapa. Manioc leaves. (Mozambique).

Matisa. "How are you?" A Nama/Damara greeting. (Namibia).

Matooke. Mashed bananas. (Uganda).

Matryoshka. Nested dolls. A Russian folk craft. (Russia).

Matua. A Niuean term for "parent" that refers not only to the biological parent but also to the guardian of a child. Sometimes it is used to address elderly family members. (Niue).

Matura. An exam that is required to continue on to higher education. (Liechtenstein, Slovenia).

Maulid. (Comoros). *See* **Mouloud.**

Maulid an-Nabi. (Nigeria). *See* **Mouloud.**

Mauloud-el-Nabi. (Gambia). *See* **Mouloud.**

Maung. "Younger brother." A term used to address boys, regardless of relationship. (Myanmar).

Maur. An English variation of the spelling of the term **Moor**. (Mauritania).

Maure. French term for **Moor**. (Mauritania).

Mauri. "Blessings." A common Kiribati greeting. (Kiribati).

Maw lam. Lao folk theater. (Laos).

Mawliid. (Somalia). *See* **Mouloud.**

Mawloud. (Guinea, Senegal). *See* **Mouloud.**

Maxi-taxis. Mini-buses. (Trinidad and Tobago).

Maybahay. A Pilipino title for a married hostess. (Philippines).

¿Mba'eichapa? "How are you?" A common Guaraní greeting. Pronounced "m-buy-ay-SHA-pah." (Paraguay).

Mbalatsara? "Doing well?" A common greeting in the north. (Madagascar).

Mbalax. A style of music that incorporates tribal drumming and Afro-Caribbean pop. (Senegal).

Mbaqanga. A popular style of dance music that originated in apartheid-era townships. (South Africa).

Mbaxal-u-Saloum. A sauce of ground peanuts, dried fish, meat, tomatoes, and spices. It is a traditional Wolof dish served with rice. (Senegal).

M'bda. "On you no evil." A Pulaar greeting. The response is **Jam ṭan**. (Mauritania).

Mbewa. Roasted mice on a stick. (Malawi).

Mbira. An instrument with small metal strips that are plucked by the thumbs. (Zimbabwe). *See also* **Jiti.**

Mbo. Fang word for cassava. (Equatorial Guinea).

Mbolo. "Hello." A common Fang greeting. (Equatorial Guinea, Gabon).

Glossary of Cultural Terms

Mbona. An elder's response to the child's greeting **Kwezi**. The elder clasps the child's hands and says *Mbona*. (Comoros).

Mbote. "Hello." A common Lingala greeting. (Congo).

Mdraha. A pebble-and-board game. (Comoros).

Me. A Montserratian word that indicates first person singular and past tense. (Montserrat). *See also* **Me no me know.**

Mealie meal. Cornmeal porridge. (Lesotho, Namibia, South Africa).

Me dear. An informal term of address. (Saint Kitts and Nevis).

Medex. An individual trained in primary health care. (Guyana).

Meet-and-greet. Conversations that are held on the street. (Jamaica).

Me'etu'upaki. "Paddle dance." A dance performed by male groups in which they gracefully twist paddles to the rhythm of a chorus and hollow log gongs. (Tonga).

Meeyonband. A bandana-type tie used as a belt. (Tajikistan). *Also called* **Chorsi.** *See also* **Joma.**

Mehana. A Bulgarian eating establishment that features traditional food, folk music, and dancing. (Bulgaria).

Mehikitanga. The father's eldest sister. She is the leader over that nuclear family in the extended-family system. (Tonga). *See also* **Fahu.**

Meke. Dances that describe legends and historical events. (Fiji).

Mekhmonlar. Uzbek word for "guests." (Uzbekistan).

Melkooptoviye Rynki. Wholesale markets. (Russia).

Melodeon. An instrument similar to an accordion. (Dominican Republic).

Meme. A term of address for older Owambo women. (Namibia). *See also* **Tate.**

Me na able. "I can't cope." An example of the Saint Vincent dialect of English. (Saint Vincent and the Grenadines).

Me no me know. "I did not know." A Montserratian phrase showing the different uses of the word **Me**. (Montserrat).

Menudo. Spicy tripe soup. (Mexico).

Merak. A relaxed pace of life. A Bosnian general attitude. (Bosnia and Herzegovina).

Merengue. A ballroom dance of Caribbean origin and the rapid music that accompanies the dance. (Colombia, Costa Rica, Dominican Republic, Panama, Saint Kitts and Nevis, Venezuela). *See also* **Meringue.**

Merhaba. "Hello." A Turkish greeting. (Turkey).

Meri. Brightly colored blouses worn by women over a **Laplap**. (Papua New Guinea).

Merienda. A snack between meals. (Colombia, Guam, Mexico, Philippines, Spain).

Meringue. A music style and dance that is a mixture of African rhythms and European music. Haiti's national dance. (Bahamas, Haiti). *See also* **Merengue.**

Mesadoras. The Dominican word for "rocking chairs." (Dominican Republic).

Mesah al-kair. (Yemen). *See* **Mesah al-Khair.**

Mesah al-Khair. [NOTE: Spelling varies because it is a transliteration of Arabic.] "Good evening." A common Arabic greeting. (Saudi Arabia).

Meshrano Jirga. House of Elders. Part of Afghanistan's bicameral National Assembly. (Afghanistan).

Meshwi. Shish kebab. (Jordan).

Meskel. A holiday in late September that celebrates the finding of Jesus Christ's "true cross" in the fourth century. (Eritrea, Ethiopia).

Mestiços. People of mixed Portuguese and African origin. (Angola).

Mestiza. A skirt, camisole, and mesh top with puffy butterfly sleeves, worn by women. (Guam).

Metemgee. A dish made with coconut milk, **Ground provisions**, meat or fish, and other ingredients. Similar to **Cook-up rice.** (Guyana).

Meter. "Godmother" in Dutch. (Belgium).

Metical. Mozambique's national currency. (Mozambique).

Meto. An elaborate system of navigation using wave and current patterns represented in stick charts. (Marshall Islands).

Métro. The name for subways throughout France. (France).

Métro Léger. The light-rail system in Tunis. (Tunisia).

Metta. Loving-kindness and the practice of goodwill. A pillar virtue in Buddhism. (Laos). *See also* **Brahma Vihara.**

Meu camba, fixe? "Friend, are you okay?" An informal Portuguese greeting used among young men. (Angola).

Me vex fu true. "I was really angry." A Montserratian phrase. (Montserrat). *See also* **Fu true.**

Me we see you. "I'll see you later." A common Jamaican English parting phrase. (Jamaica).

Meza. A traditional four- to five-hour meal for special occasions. (Lebanon).

Meze. (1) An antipasto of various hors d'oeuvres. (Albania, Bosnia and Herzegovina, Serbia and Montenegro, Turkey). (2) A mixture of ham, cheese, vegetables, and eggs. (Macedonia).

Mezza. A table full of appetizers, which include pastes made from chickpeas and eggplant, meat dishes with spices and wheat, pickles, olives, and breads. (Syria).

Mhoroi. "Hello." A common Shona greeting. (Zimbabwe).

Mida. A low, round, wooden table. (Tunisia).

Middag. The main meal of the day. (Sweden).

Mi de. "I'm fine." A Sranan Tongo response to a greeting such as **Fa waka?**, **Fa'y tan?**, or **Fa'y go?** (Suriname).

Midori No hi. Greenery Day. A day to celebrate nature's beauty; 29 April. (Japan).

Midsommar. Summer solstice celebrations in late June. Festivities include dancing around the maypole and having picnics. (Sweden).

Miklavžovanje. The holiday of St. Nicholas Eve. (Slovenia).

Milanesa. Fried, breaded steak. (Uruguay).

Milk bar. A corner shop where people buy items such as bread and milk. (Australia).

Milk tart. A custard-like pie. (South Africa).

Milli Majlis. Azerbaijan's Parliament. (Azerbaijan).

Milonga. A traditional Uruguayan dance. (Uruguay).

Mince. Ground meat. (Scotland).

Minestra. Vegetable soup. (Malta).

Min-gala-ba. A formal "Hello" in Burmese.

Mingas. Community improvement projects. (Ecuador).

Mi orait. Na yu? "I'm fine. And you?" A Melanesian Pidgin response to the greeting **Yu orait?** (Papua New Guinea).

Miorita. A well-known ballad. (Moldova).

Mir dita. Albanian for "Good day." (Macedonia).

Miremengjes. "Good morning." An Albanian greeting. (Albania).

Mire se erdhet. (1) "Welcome." An Albanian greeting to welcome guests. (Albania). *See also* **Mire se vini.** (2) A host and hostess's reply to the phrase **Mire se ju gjeta** before drinking. (Albania).

Glossary of Cultural Terms

Mire se ju gjeta. "I am glad I find you well." An Albanian phrase guests say before drinking. (Albania).

Mire se vini. "Welcome." An Albanin greeting to welcome guests. (Albania). *See also* **Mire se erdhet.**

Mirmenjezi. Albanian for "Good morning." (Macedonia).

Mir u pafshim. "Good-bye." An Albanian parting phrase. (Albania).

Mir wëlle bleiwe wat mer sin! "We want to remain what we are!" Luxembourg's national motto. This reflects Luxembourgers independence and unique identity in Europe. (Luxembourg).

Mishlah. A cloak men wear over a **Thobe.** (Qatar, Saudi Arabia).

Misniar. Informal wives. (Qatar).

Miso. Bean paste. (Japan).

Mititei. Grilled meat sausages. (Moldova, Romania).

Mittagspause. A traditional midday break. (Austria).

Mi wokabaot nomoa. "I'm just walking around." A Solomon Island Pijin response to the greetings **Iu go long wea?** and **Iu bin stap long wea?** (Solomon Islands).

Mixed. People who are primarily descendants of Afro- and Indo-Guyanese. (Guyana).

Miyess. A honey mead. (Eritrea).

Mlada Bosna. "Young Bosnia." A multiethnic group responsible for the assassination of the heir to the Austro-Hungarian throne, the spark that initiated World War I. (Bosnia and Herzegovina).

Mme. "Mother." A Sesotho term of address used for older women. (South Africa).

Mo-. A prefix used when referring to one person. (Botswana). *See also* **Ba-, Batswana, Motswana.**

Mobylettes. Mopeds. (Burkina Faso).

Modi ki bu sta? "How are you?" A standard Crioulo greeting. (Cape Verde).

Mogethin. "What did you come here for?" A greeting used between friends. (Micronesia).

Mohinga. A fish and noodle soup often enjoyed for breakfast. (Myanmar).

Moi. (1) "Hi." An informal Finnish greeting. (Finland). (2) The Uzbek word for "butter." A term of special significance in the Uzbek tea ceremony. (Uzbekistan).

Moien. "Morning." A common Luxembourgish greeting. (Luxembourg).

Mok kai. Poultry cooked in a banana leaf. (Laos).

Moko. Traditional facial tattooing, featuring elaborate designs. (New Zealand).

Mokorotlo. A traditional straw hat, conical in shape, that has an intricately designed knob on top. (Lesotho). *Also called* **Molianyeoe.**

Mok paa. Fish cooked in a banana leaf. (Laos).

Mola(s). Appliqué for clothing or textiles. (Costa Rica, Panama).

Mole. A spicy sauce served with meat. (Mexico).

Molianyeoe. A traditional straw hat that is conical in shape with an intricately designed knob on top. (Lesotho). *Also called* **Mokorotlo.**

Molo. Literally, "I see you." A Xhosa greeting meaning "Hello." (South Africa).

Momo. Tibetan ravioli. (Bhutan).

Mondongo. (1) Tripe and beef knuckles. (Honduras, Nicaragua). (2) Intestine soup. (Costa Rica).

Mon frère. "My brother." A French term of address used among people of the same age. (Gabon).

Mon frère, même mère, même père. "My brother, same mother, same father." An introduction that one takes special pride in due to large families where the man may have more then one wife. (Central African Republic).

Moni. "Hello." A greeting used by northern men and women after they clap their hands three times. (Mozambique).

Moni bambo! "Hello, sir!" A Chichewa greeting. (Malawi).

Moni mayi! "Hello, madam!" A Chichewa greeting. (Malawi).

Moning. "Good morning." An adapted English greeting. (Papua New Guinea, Togo).

Moning kaikai. "Morning food." The Melanesian Pidgin word for breakfast. (Papua New Guinea).

Monire adada! "Hello, sir!" A Chitumbuka greeting. (Malawi).

Monire amama! "Hello, madam!" A Chitumbuka greeting. (Malawi).

Monno. Millet porridge. (Gambia).

Monsha. The Kazak word for "sauna." (Kazakstan).

Monsieur. "Mr." A common title. Used in French-speaking countries..

Montuno. Baggy shorts and matching embroidered top. A traditional costume worn by men with **Cutarras** and palm-fiber hats. (Panama).

Monuina [e fenoga]! "Blessings [on the voyage]!" A Niuean parting phrase used if an individual is leaving for a long time. (Niue).

Mophane. Trees in the northeast that are used to harvest the **Phane** worm. (Botswana).

Mora-mora. A relaxed pace of life. (Madagascar).

Môre. "Good morning." An Afrikaans greeting. (Namibia).

Moreneng. The chief compound; a place for socializing. (Lesotho).

More times. "Until we meet again." An informal parting phrase. (Saint Vincent and the Grenadines).

Morin-khuur. A bowed lute with a carved horse head at the neck. A symbol of Mongolian culture. (Mongolia).

Morn. "Morning." A Norwegian greeting used regardless of the time of day. (Norway).

Morna. A style of music with a slow rhythm and melancholy lyrics. (Cape Verde).

Moro. "Good morning." An Otjiherero greeting. (Namibia).

Morogeh koman honah. "I'm glad to see you." A Machushi greeting. (Guyana).

Moroho. Cooked vegetables. (Lesotho).

Mosakhan. Vegetables, meat, and rice served with salad and yogurt. (West Bank and Gaza).

Mos Craciun. The Romanian name for Santa Claus. (Moldova).

Moshav. A small village where families live separately but cooperate in providing community needs and in marketing the village's products. (Israel). *See also* **Kibbutz.**

Moso'oi. A fragrant plant. (American Samoa). *See also* **Moso'oi festival.**

Moso'oi festival. A week-long festival held in October. (American Samoa).

Mosquito coils. Mosquito repellent. (Sierra Leone).

Mother. (1) A term of address used for older women. (Saint Kitts and Nevis). (2) A term of address also used for aunts. (Sierra Leone).

Motorela. A three-wheeled motorized carriage. (Philippines).

Glossary of Cultural Terms

Motovilec. A salad green called "corn salad" or "mâche." (Slovenia).

Motswana. A Tswana person. (Botswana). *See also* **Ba-, Batswana, Mo-**.

Motta. "Friend." A general Marshallese term of address that follows the greeting **Yokwe**. (Marshall Islands).

Motu. Niuean word for "islanders." (Niue).

Motum. Stone/earth ovens. (Solomon Islands).

Mouharem. The Islamic New Year holiday according to the lunar calendar. (Algeria).

Moulah. Sauce. (Chad).

Moulid. (Ethiopia). *See* **Mouloud**.

Moulid al-Nabi. (Iraq). *See also* **Mouloud**.

Moulid al-Nebi. (Jordan). *See* **Mouloud**.

Mouloud. [NOTE: Spelling varies because it is a transliteration of Arabic; the name may vary from country to country. Also, Muslim holidays are set according to the lunar calendar.] A Muslim holiday celebrating the birth of Muhammad. Celebrated in predominantly Muslim countries. (Burkina Faso, Morocco, Niger).

Mountain chicken. Frog, a popular dish. (Montserrat).

Mourides. A large Muslim brotherhood and spiritual order. (Senegal).

Moussaka. A casserole made with pork or lamb, potatoes, tomatoes, and yogurt. (Bulgaria).

Moussems. Muslim religious festivals that are held throughout the year. (Morocco).

Mo yeke. "Are you okay?" Part of a common Sango greeting, it usually follows the phrase **Bara ala** or **Bala mo** (Greetings to you!). (Central African Republic).

Mpanandro. "Day maker." People consult with the *mpanandro* person for help in choosing the best day to get married, start construction, and so on. (Madagascar).

Mpihira gasy. Traditional performers who sing, dance, and play music in an open-air concert. (Madagascar).

Msa'a al khair. (Jordan). *See* **Mesah al-Khair**.

Msa al Kheir. (Morocco). *See* **Mesah al-Khair**.

Mshvidobit. "Peace be with you." A Georgian parting phrase used for an extensive parting. (Georgia).

M'to kari. "I'm fine." A Sara response to the greeting **I baii?** (Chad).

Mtsvadi. Marinated, skewered, grilled meat. (Georgia).

Mua kia! "Good-bye!" A Niuean parting phrase used when addressing two people. (Niue).

Mua roi nuoc. Water puppetry. (Vietnam).

Muchas gracias. "Many thanks." After finishing a meal, each person, including the cook, uses this phrase to thank everyone at the table. (Guatemala).

¡Mucho gusto! "Pleased to meet you." A common Spanish greeting used for strangers. (Guatemala, Paraguay).

Mucho gusto de conocerle. "Glad to meet you." A Spanish greeting used when meeting another person for the first time. (Nicaragua).

Muciro. Beauty cream that is made from grated plant stems mixed with water. Used by women to clean and beautify their faces. (Mozambique).

Múcua. The fruit of the baobab tree. The white-and-pink edible interior is a favorite treat. It is also made into ice cream. (Angola).

Mudhita. Sympathetic or altruistic joy. One of Buddhism's four pillar virtues. (Laos). *See also* **Brahma Vihara**.

Mufradsh. A room with cushions and pillows on the floor. Used for visiting and chewing **Qat**. (Yemen).

Mugam. Folk music derived from classical poetry. Based on improvisation. (Azerbaijan).

Muhallebi. Milk pudding. (Turkey).

Mujahideen. Holy Muslim warriors. (Afghanistan).

Muktaaq. A term meaning whale meat, used by indigenous tribes in Canada. (Canada).

Mukulukhana. Witch doctors. (Mozambique). *Also called* **Nhangas**.

Mulafa. A large piece of colored cloth worn by Moorish women that is wrapped around the body and draped over the head. (Mauritania).

Muli bwanji? "How are you?" A common greeting. (Malawi, Zambia).

Muli shani? "How are you?" A Bemba phrase used to greet a friend. (Zambia).

Muli uli? "How are you?" A Chitumbuka phrase that follows the greetings **Monire adada!** and **Monire amama!** (Malawi).

Mullah(s). "Giver of knowledge." A Muslim religious leader. (Afghanistan, Iran).

Mullo. (Tajikistan). *See* **Mullah(s)**.

Mulţumesc pentru masă. "Thank you for the meal." A Romanian phrase used to thank the cook. (Romania).

Mum. A synonym for "mom." (Scotland).

Mummy. A respectful term of address used to address older women, regardless of relationship. (Saint Lucia).

Mumu. A ground oven. (Papua New Guinea).

Muqmad. Dried beef in clarified butter. (Somalia).

Muraho. "Hello, it's been a while." A common Kinyarwanda greeting. (Rwanda).

Murawarawa. A strategy game played on a board with 18 to 32 holes. Each hole has two seeds in it. The object of the game is to collect the most seeds. (Mozambique).

Mürebbe. Preserves made of fruits or nuts. (Azerbaijan).

Musakhan. Chicken with onions, olive oil, pine seeds, and seasonings. (Jordan).

Musha'irahs. Poetry readings. (Pakistan).

Musibityendo ssebo/ngabo? "How are you, sir/madam?" A Luganda greeting. (Uganda).

Muslim. Literally, "one who has submitted." A follower of the religion **Islam**. (Mauritania).

Mutawassit. Intermediate school. (Saudi Arabia).

Muti. A curse. (Swaziland). *See also* **Batsakatsi**.

Mutolu kia! "Good-bye!" A Niuean parting phrase used when addressing three or more people. (Niue).

Muumuu. A long wraparound skirt worn by women. (Samoa).

Muwatiniin. Locals that are Arab descendants of great tribal confederations or long-time immigrants from Persia and Arabian Gulf countries. (United Arab Emirates).

Muyongo. Witchcraft. (Cameroon).

Mwabonwa. "Welcome." A common greeting used in the south. (Zambia).

Mwami. The Kinyarwanda word for "king." (Rwanda).

Mwana hangu. "My child/brother." A title used to address good friends. (Comoros).

Mwapoleni. "Welcome." A Bemba greeting used between friends. (Zambia).

Mwapolenipo mukwai. "Welcome, very respectfully." A Bemba greeting used to address elders. The *po-* suffix shows added respect. (Zambia).

Glossary of Cultural Terms

Mwaramutse. "Good morning." A common Kinyarwanda greeting. (Rwanda).

Mwiriwe. "Good afternoon" or "Good evening." A common Kinyarwanda greeting. (Rwanda).

Mzé. A title used to address an elder man. (Comoros).

Mzuri. "Good." A common Kiswahili response to the greetings **Habari?** and **Habari gani?** (Kenya).

Ña. A term of address for women, used with the first name. Commonly used in rural areas. (Paraguay).

Naa. "Aunt." A Lao term of address used when a person has no specific title. (Laos).

Naadam. Mongolian People's Revolution. A holiday celebrated on 11 to 13 July with horse races, wrestling, and other events. (Mongolia).

Naag Panchami. A summer festival in which snakes are venerated because of their association with Hindu gods. (India).

Nabad. "Peace." A common Somali greeting. (Somalia).

Nabad miya? "Is there peace?" A common Somali greeting used in the southern areas. (Somalia).

Nacatamales. (1) Pork tamales. (Honduras). (2) A dish of meat and vegetables, with spices. (Nicaragua).

Nadenitsa. Stuffed pork sausage. (Bulgaria).

Nadie es más que nadie. "No one is better than anyone else." A Spanish phrase that expresses a commonly held democratic viewpoint in Uruguay. (Uruguay).

Naengmyon. A cold noodle dish. (North Korea).

Na fo biah. "You must bear it." A common Krio response to the expressions **Na so God say** (It is God's will) and **Ow fo do?** (What can you do?). (Sierra Leone).

Na gosti. To go visiting. (Bulgaria, Macedonia).

Nagra. Flat shoes that curl upward in front. Part of a groom's wedding attire. (Bangladesh). *See also* **Pagri, Shirwani.**

Naguas. Colorful dresses worn by Ngöbe-Buglé women. (Panama).

Nahili sen? Gowy my? "How are you? Well?" (Turkmenistan).

Nai. Reed pipe or flute. (Lebanon, United Arab Emirates).

Nain dat. "That's all." A Krio parting phrase used to mean good-bye. (Sierra Leone).

Naira. Nigeria's national currency. (Nigeria).

Na ka nga def? "How are you?" A common Wolof greeting. (Gambia).

Nakfa. Eritrea's national currency. (Eritrea).

Nakhajash. The first meal of the day. It usually consists of coffee or tea and a pastry for adults and bread, butter, cheese, boiled eggs, honey or jam, and warm milk for children. (Armenia).

Nama. Meat. (Lesotho).

Nama ea khoho. Chicken. (Lesotho).

Nama ea khomo. Beef. (Lesotho).

Nama ea kolobe. Pork. (Lesotho).

Namaskar. A traditional greeting and parting gesture for superiors and elders. A person places the palms together with the fingers up in front of the chest or chin and says *Namaskar*. (Nepal). *See also* **Namaste.**

Namaskaram. A traditional southern Indian greeting in which one places the palms together with the fingers up below the chin and says *Namaskaram*. (India).

Namaste. A traditional greeting in which one places the palms together with the fingers up below the chin and says *Namaste*, sometimes bowing slightly. (Bhutan, Fiji, India, Mauritius, Nepal).

Nan. Unleavened bread. (Afghanistan, Uzbekistan).

Nana. A term Imazighen use to show respect to female elders, including siblings. (Algeria).

Ñandutí. Intricate and delicate lace. A craft introduced by the Spanish. (Paraguay).

Nane Nane. International Trade Day. Celebrated 8 August. (Tanzania).

Nang. "Ms." A Lao term of address used when a married woman has no specific title. (Laos).

N'anga. Witch doctors. (Zimbabwe).

Nanga def. "On you no evil." A common Wolof greeting. The response is **Jam rekk** (No evil). (Mauritania).

Nangi. "Younger sister." A term of address used among close friends and relatives. (Sri Lanka).

Nang sbek. Shadow plays in which the characters are black leather puppets. The plays often tell religious stories. (Cambodia).

Nao. "Man." A Kiribati word that is used to get someone's attention. (Kiribati).

Narcoterroristas. Drug traffickers. (Colombia).

Nareau. "The Creator." A supreme being the I-Kiribati worshiped before the introduction of Christianity. (Kiribati). *See also* **Te maaka.**

Narodna muzika. Folk music, which is especially favored in rural areas. (Serbia and Montenegro).

Narodni pesni. Folk songs that describe historical battles and life in Macedonia. (Macedonia).

Narodno Sobranyie. The Bulgarian National Assembly, which has 240 members. (Bulgaria).

Na schledanou. "Good-bye." A formal Czech parting phrase. (Czech Republic).

Nashif. Chopped beef with a spicy tomato sauce; traditionally eaten with **Kissar**. (Chad).

Nasi campur. Javanese vegetable dishes with white rice, noodles, and chicken. (Indonesia).

Nasi Lemak. Buttered rice with dried anchovies and peanuts. (Malaysia).

Nasisliniz? "How are you?" A common Turkish greeting. (Turkey).

Na so God say. "It is God's will." A common Krio expression. The response is **Na fo biah** (You must bear it). (Sierra Leone).

Nasvidenje. "Good-bye." A common Slovene phrase used when parting or exiting a room or an elevator, even if one does not know the others present. (Slovenia).

Nat. A spirit. Many of Myanmar's Buddhists practice *nat* worship; shrines to these spirits are common, especially in rural areas. (Myanmar).

Naten e mir. Albanian for "Good night." (Macedonia).

Nationalrat. National Council. The 183-seat lower house of the Austrian Parliament. (Austria). *See also* **Bundesversammlung.**

Natsionalnoye Sobranie. Belarus's National Assembly. (Belarus). *See also* **Palata Predstaviteley, Soviet Respubliki.**

Nau mai. "Welcome." A ceremonial Maori greeting. (New Zealand).

Nauriz. (Kazakstan). *See* **Naw Ruz.**

Navruz. (Uzbekistan). *See* **Naw Ruz.**

Navy biscuits. Crackers. (Solomon Islands).

Nawrooz. (Afghanistan). *See* **Naw Ruz.**

Glossary of Cultural Terms

Naw Ruz. The New Year. Celebrated in connection with the spring equinox. (Iran).

Nazdrave. Bulgarian word for "toasting." Done at the beginning and throughout a meal. (Bulgaria).

Na zdravie. "To your health." A Slovak phrase used to toast someone. (Slovakia).

Nbe sira dari. Dyula phrase that guests use to "ask for the road" from hosts after they accompany each other to the road at the end of a visit. (Ivory Coast).

Ndaga. A popular style of Senegalese music. (Gambia).

Ndaguta. "I am satisfied." A phrase used after a meal to show respect and indicate one has been well provided for. (Zimbabwe).

Ndalale. "I passed the night well, and you?" The response to the Umbundo greeting **Walale**. (Angola).

Ndi. "Good morning." A common Ewe greeting. (Togo).

Ndili bwino! "I am fine!" A Chichewa response to the greeting **Muli bwanji?** (How are you?). (Malawi).

Ndili makola! "I am fine!" A common Chitumbuka response to the greeting **Muli uli?** (How are you?). (Malawi).

Ndiwo. A sauce or condiment. Balled **Nsima** is often dipped in it. (Malawi).

Ndo. "Good afternoon." A common Ewe greeting. (Togo).

Ndombolo. An upbeat dance style performed in urban discos. (Congo).

Neeps. Boiled turnips. (Scotland).

Negrito. A Spanish word for "little dark one" or "little black one." In some places it is not considered rude to comment on such physical attributes. (Argentina).

Nei. "Miss" or "Mrs." A Kiribati title used in formal situations to show respect. (Kiribati).

Neih hau ma? (Hong Kong). See **Ni hao ma?**

Neih sihkjo faan meih a? "Have you eaten yet?" A common Cantonese greeting. (Singapore).

Neih sik msik a. "Have you eaten?" A typical Chinese greeting. (Hong Kong).

Neiko. "Woman." A Kiribati word that is used to get someone's attention. (Kiribati).

Nejasiniz? "How are you?" An Azeri phrase used after the initial greeting between acquaintances and friends. (Azerbaijan).

Ne-kaun-ba-deh. "I'm well." The response to the greeting **Ne-kaun-yeh-la?** (Myanmar).

Ne-kaun-yeh-la? "Are you well?" An informal Burmese greeting. The response is **Ne-kaun-ba-deh**. (Myanmar).

Nene. "Mother." An Albanian term used to address older women. (Albania).

New cedi. Ghana's national currency. (Ghana).

New Israeli shekel. Israel's national currency. (Israel, West Bank and Gaza).

New riel. Cambodia's national currency. (Cambodia).

Next time. A common parting phrase. (Jamaica).

Ne y yibeogo. "Good morning." A common Mooré greeting. (Burkina Faso).

Ne y zaabre. "Good afternoon." A common Mooré greeting. (Burkina Faso).

Ngalabi. A long drum played by the Baganda people. (Uganda).

Ngambe. Fortune-tellers. (Cameroon).

Ngapi. A fish or shrimp paste; added to a variety of dishes. (Myanmar).

Ngepi Nawa. "Good afternoon." An Oshiwambo greeting. (Namibia).

Ngola. The title of the king of the Ndongo; the word from which Angola derives its name. (Angola).

Ngoma. Popular traditional music. Dancers follow the rhythm of drums, accompanied by a chorus, xylophones, and whistles. (Tanzania).

Ngultrum. Bhutan's national currency. (Bhutan).

Ngunza. A thick sauce made from ground cassava leaves, tomato paste, and peanut butter. (Central African Republic).

Ngwenyama. The siSwati word for "lion." In 1921, King Sobhuza II was crowned *Ngwenyama* of the nation. His rule lasted until his death in 1982. (Swaziland).

Ngwetsa. A festival that celebrates the harvest. (Malawi).

Nhangana. Leaves of **Nhemba** beans. (Mozambique).

Nhangas. Traditional healers or witch doctors. (Mozambique).

Nhemba. A type of bean. (Mozambique).

Ni chi fan le ma? "Have you eaten yet?" A common Chinese greeting. The reply is "Yes," even if one has not eaten. (China).

Nien. The Vietnamese word for "years." (Vietnam).

Nieves. The Spanish word for "snows." (Saint Kitts and Nevis).

Nightcrawling. A method of dating in which a young man approaches a young woman's house at night and invites her to join him. (Marshall Islands, Micronesia).

Ni hao ma? "How are you?" A typical Chinese greeting. (China, Singapore).

Ni hau ma? (Malaysia, Taiwan). See **Ni hao ma?**

Nikoh. A blessing from a religious leader. The capstone of a three-day Tajik wedding. (Tajikistan).

Ni meza. "Fine." A typical response to the greetings **Amakuru?** (How's the news?) and **Bite se?** (How are things going?). (Rwanda).

Ni meza cyane. "Very fine." A typical response to the greetings **Amakuru?** (How's the news?) and **Bite se?** (How are things going?). (Rwanda).

Ni molo. Chilled coconut water. (Marshall Islands).

Niña. A less formal title used to address young women and girls. (El Salvador).

Ninde? "Who's there?" A response to a visitor's greeting announcing his or her presence. (Rwanda).

Ni Sa Bula! A formal Fijian greeting. (Fiji).

Nitijela. The national parliament. (Marshall Islands).

Njangis. Savings societies in which members pool their capital, provide loans to each other, and sponsor social activities. (Cameroon). *Also called* **Tontines**.

Njatjeta. "Hello." A common Albanian greeting. (Albania).

N Justa. "I've had enough." A Kriolu phrase used to decline a meal after having at least one bite. Pronounced "NG JUICE-ta." (Guinea-Bissau).

Nkhokwe. A structure for storing grain. (Malawi).

Nkhosi. The praise name for royalty. Can be used as a title when one is unsure of a person's title. (Swaziland).

Nliwalè. "Good morning." A common Kabyè greeting. (Togo).

N'na. Kabyè word for "mother." (Togo).

Nob. "Salute." A formal Lao greeting in which one places one's hands together in a prayer position at chest level but not touching the body. The higher the hands are held, the greater the sign of respect, although they should never be held above the level of the nose. Can also be used to express thanks or regret. (Laos).

Noche Buena. Christmas Eve. (Guatemala, Mexico).

Noël. The French word for "Christmas." (France, Gabon).

Glossary of Cultural Terms

Nofo a. Literally "You stay." A parting phrase said by the person leaving. The person staying responds with **'Alu a.** (Tonga).

No, gracias; estoy satisfecho. "No, thank you; I am satisfied." A host will continue to offer food until guests use this phrase. (El Salvador).

Noh. Highly stylized drama that blends together dance, music, and acting. (Japan).

Non. Unleavened bread. (Tajikistan).

Nong. "Little brother" or "little sister." A Thai title used to refer to younger or lower status people, regardless of relationship. (Thailand).

Nonishta. The Tajik word for "breakfast." (Tajikistan).

No no no. A phrase that expresses disagreement. Accompanies the gesture of raising the hand, palm out, and wagging an extended index finger from side to side. (Antigua and Barbuda).

Nonu. An apple-like fruit. (Samoa). *See also* **Vi.**

Nooruz. (Kyrgyzstan). *See* **Naw Ruz.**

No problem man. A good-natured answer to life's challenges even if there is no solution at hand; reflects Jamaicans flexible approach to life. (Jamaica).

Ñoquis. Gnocchi. (Uruguay).

Nori. Dried seaweed. (Japan). *See* **Norimaki.**

Norimaki. Sushi wrapped in dried seaweed. (Japan). *See* **Nori.**

Normal. "Fine." A Pidgin response to the greeting **Ha na?** (How are you?). (Cameroon).

Noroc. (1) "Cheers." A common Romanian greeting. (Moldova, Romania). (2) "Good luck." A Romanian phrase used after a close friend or family member sneezes. (Romania).

Norteamericanos. A Spanish term used to refer to people from the United States and North America. (Bolivia, Chile, Mexico, Paraguay).

Nosnja. A long white skirt and cotton blouse worn by Bosnian Serb women on special occasions. (Bosnia and Herzegovina).

Nošnja. Traditional attire that includes long skirts and cotton shirts for women and wide pants, vests over shirts, and **Opanke** for men. Worn by older people and varies depending on the region. (Serbia and Montenegro).

Nos vemos. A common Spanish parting phrase meaning "see you later." (Colombia, El Salvador, Guatemala, Venezuela).

Notables. A community's group of elders. (Comoros).

No tenga pena. "Don't worry." A phrase used to set others at ease in social interaction. (Guatemala).

No tro way you belly and tek trash tuff um. "Don't lose the substance for the shadow." A traditional saying. (Antigua and Barbuda).

Nouvelle cuisine. A style of cooking that emerged in the 1960s. The food is made of expensive ingredients, is light, has small portions, and is artistically presented. (France).

Novelas. (Angola). *See* **Telenovelas.**

Novenas. Nine days of prayer. The origin of the holiday Nine Mornings. (Saint Vincent and the Grenadines).

Noviy Gohd. The Russian term for the New Year celebration. (Kazakhstan).

Novrus Bairami. The New Year celebration that occurs at the beginning of spring. Families make food for the celebration. Young people make fires and jump over them, dance, and play games. (Azerbaijan).

Now for now. A Grenadian English idiom for "urgent." (Grenada).

Nshima. (Zambia). *See* **Nsima.**

Nsima. A thick porridge made from cornmeal. (Malawi, Zambia).

Nsomba. Dried fish. (Malawi).

N'sta bom. "I am fine." A Crioulo response to the greeting **Modi ki bu sta?** (Cape Verde).

N sta bon. "I am fine." A Kriolu response to the greeting **Kuma?** (How are you?). (Guinea-Bissau).

Ntate. "Father." A SeSotho term used to address older men. (South Africa).

Ntchuva. A strategy game played on a board with 18 to 32 holes. Each hole has two seeds in it. The object of the game is to collect the most seeds. (Mozambique).

Ntlo. A traditional circular home built of stone and sticks held together with cow dung, which dries hard and can be painted. It has a thatched roof and windows. The diameter of the main house reflects socioeconomic status. (Lesotho). *Also called* **Rondavel(s).**

Ntoma. A long colored cloth worn by men in the south that is wrapped around the body somewhat like a toga. (Ghana).

Nuestra Señora de la Alta Gracia. Our Lady of High Gratitude. A national holiday celebrated on 21 January. (Dominican Republic).

Nuestra Señora de las Mercedes. Our Lady of Mercies. A national holiday celebrated on 24 September. (Dominican Republic).

Nuevo sol. Peru's national currency. (Peru).

Nuoc mam. A fermented fish sauce that can be used as a dip or a seasoning. (Vietnam).

Nu'u. Village. (American Samoa).

Nvet. A traditional stringed rhythm instrument. (Equatorial Guinea).

Nyam. "To eat." A creole word with African origins. (Antigua and Barbuda, Saint Vincent and the Grenadines).

Nyama choma. Barbequed meat. (Tanzania).

Nya-na dhoo. "Good evening." A common Kabyè greeting. (Togo).

Nya-na wysy. "Good afternoon." A common Kabyè greeting. (Togo).

Nyatiti. An eight-string lyre played by the Luo to accompany lyrics about fables and legends. (Kenya).

Nyckelharpa. Key fiddle; a Swedish invention. (Sweden).

Nyepi. The Hindu New Year. (Indonesia).

O a mai oe? "How are you?" A common Samoan greeting. (Samoa).

O a mea sa fai? Roughly "What have you been up to?" (American Samoa).

Obi. A special sash worn with the traditional **Kimono(s).** (Japan).

Obid. The main meal, which is eaten midafternoon. It consists of two main courses, the first being soup and the second containing meat or fish. (Ukraine).

Oblast(s). Political region(s). (Kazakhstan, Kyrgyzstan, Russia).

Obrigada. (Mozambique). *See* **Obrigado.**

Obrigado. Portuguese word for "Thank you." Masculine *obrigado*, feminine *obrigada*. (Mozambique, Portugal).

Obyed. The Russian word for "lunch." (Kazakhstan).

Ocal. (Bahrain). *See* **Ogal.**

Occasion. A "bush taxi" used to travel long distances. (Gabon).

Ochi. Greek word for "no." *Ochi* Day commemorates the day when Joannis Metaxas, then prime minister, said no to Hitler.

Greece then entered World War II on the side of the Allies. (Greece).

Odelsting. The lower chamber of the Norwegian Parliament. (Norway). *See also* **Storting.**

Odika. A substance from wild mango pits used to make a gravy-like sauce called **Chocalat**. (Gabon).

Odini! A welcoming answer to visitors who call out the phrase **Odi! Odi!** (Malawi).

Odi! Odi! A phrase visitors use to announce their presence. (Malawi, Mozambique).

Odun Idi. A feast at the end of the Muslim holy month of **Ramadan**. The Arabic name is **Aid al Fitr**. (Benin).

Odun Lea. Muslim Feast of Sacrifice. The Arabic name is **Eid al-Adha**. (Benin).

Ogal. A weighted black cord worn by men to hold a headdress in place. (Kuwait).

Oghol. (Qatar). *See* **Ogal.**

Ohayou. "Good morning." An common casual greeting used among the youth. (Japan). *See also* **Genki?**

Ohayougozaimasu. "Good morning." A Japanese phrase used to greet a superior. (Japan).

Oi. "Hi." An informal Portuguese greeting. (Angola, Brazil, Mozambique).

Oilai kalon. Extended family. The center of Tajik society. (Tajikistan).

Oil down. A stew made of Callaloo, breadfruit, meat or salt fish, and coconut oil; the Grenadian national dish. (Grenada).

OK. "Hello, I'm OK, how are you?" A typical casual black Bahamian greeting. (Bahamas).

O kae? "How are you?" An informal Setswana greeting. (Botswana).

Okay, Okay. The response to the greeting **Alright**. (Antigua and Barbuda).

Okeme. The Luo word for the thumb piano. (Uganda).

Okoumé. A hardwood. (Gabon).

Olá. "Hello" or "Hi." A common Portuguese greeting. (Angola, Mozambique, Portugal).

Olá. Tudo bem? "Hello. Is everything fine?" A common Portuguese greeting. (Brazil).

Older father. A paternal uncle. Called *older father* or **Younger father** depending on the uncle's age in relation to the child's father. (Kenya).

Older mother. A maternal aunt. Called *older mother* or **Younger mother** depending on the aunt's age in relation to the child's mother. (Kenya).

Old Year's Night. New Year's Eve. Friends and relatives toast the coming year at each home they visit. (Saint Lucia).

Oling, oling. "Take, take." A phrase hosts use to encourage guests to eat more. (Uzbekistan).

Olla de carne. A beef stew with potatoes, onions, and vegetables. (Costa Rica).

Olodumare. The Yoruba name of the supreme God. (Benin). *Also called* **Olorun.**

Olorun. The Yoruba name of the supreme God. (Benin). *Also called* **Olodumare.**

O mais velho. A term meaning "the elder" used to refer to the eldest man (and head) of the extended family. (Angola).

Ombiasy. A person who heals or divines with charms and magic and can alter destiny. (Madagascar). *See also* **Vintana.**

Omeen. At the end of a meal, Muslims will say *Omeen* as they bring their hands together in a "prayer" position in front of the chest, raise them together to make an invisible circle, and return them to face level. (Kyrgyzstan).

Omurambas. Dry riverbeds that are a distinctive part of the Namibian landscape. (Namibia).

Omweso. A traditional strategy board game played with seeds or stones. (Uganda). *Also called* **Coro.**

Ona. "Grandmother." An Uzbek term used to address elderly women. (Uzbekistan).

Onces. Afternoon teatime when beverages, small sandwiches, and cookies or cakes are served. (Chile).

Ondol. Floor cushions for sitting that are heated from below. Used in traditional Korean homes. (South Korea).

One-pot. A common rural stew that may have different ingredients based on availability and is usually cooked on an outdoor coal pot. (Saint Lucia).

One time. A Grenadian idiom for "at the same time." (Grenada).

Oodarysh. The sport of wrestling on horseback. (Kyrgyzstan).

Oo la ndi? "Will you still sleep?" A Mungaka greeting used in the morning. The response is **Oo sat ni?** (Cameroon).

Oolesi. Papaya. (Tuvalu).

Oom. "Uncle." A term of respect used by Afrikaans-speaking people to address older males. (South Africa).

Oo sat ni? "Have you arisen?" The Mungaka response to the greeting **Oo la ndi?** (Cameroon).

Opa. "Big sister." An Uzbek term used to address female strangers. (Uzbekistan).

Opanke. Traditional shoes with upturned toes. (Bosnia and Herzegovina, Serbia and Montenegro).

Opintotuki. Finnish word for "stipend." (Finland).

Opko chaboo. A wedding custom in which a sheep is sacrificed for the meal. (Kyrgyzstan).

Oraet. "All right." A common Solomon Island Pijin parting phrase. (Solomon Islands).

Oraet, mi go nao. "All right, I'm leaving." A common Solomon Island Pijin parting phrase. (Solomon Islands).

Ordo. A game children play with sheep bones. (Kyrgyzstan).

Oreano. A unique Kiribati game in which two teams of 10 players throw a heavy, stone, soccer-sized ball wrapped in coconut husk fiber. A team scores if the opposing team drops the ball. The first team to earn 10 points wins. (Kiribati).

Oriort. A title of respect for single women; used with the last name. (Armenia).

Orisha. The Yoruba word for local divinities through which people worship the supreme God. (Benin). *See also* **Voodoos.**

Oro. A popular dance at wedding receptions and other celebrations. Consists of holding hands while dancing particular steps and constantly moving in a circle. (Macedonia).

Orozo Ait. [NOTE: Muslim holidays are set according to the lunar calendar.] A feast at the end of **Ramadan**. The Arabic name is **Aid al Fitr**. (Kyrgyzstan).

Or paa. A spicy fish soup. (Laos).

Orpack. A small piece of cloth worn by women. It is wrapped around the head and shoulders. (Azerbaijan).

Országgyulés. The Hungarian National Assembly; the 386-seat House of Parliament. (Hungary).

Orta oyunu. A type of comedy for the theater. (Turkey).

Os barbudos. A Portuguese term meaning "bearded ones." The origin of the name *Barbados* because of an abundance of bearded fig trees on the islands. (Barbados).

Oshana. (Namibia). *See* **Iishana.**

Glossary of Cultural Terms

Osnovna. The basic level of school, which is the first eight years. (Serbia and Montenegro).

Oso dresi. Home medicines typically linked to traditional religious rituals. (Suriname). *See also* **Busi dresi.**

Ota. "Grandfather." An Uzbek term used to address elderly men. (Uzbekistan).

Otai. A mixture of cut fruit. A refreshment often served to visitors. (Tonga).

Oud. A traditional type of lute. (Jordan, Kuwait, Lebanon, Libya, Sudan, Syria, Turkey, United Arab Emirates, Yemen).

Ouguiya. Mauritania's national currency. (Mauritania).

Oulaha. Advance notice. Given to hosts when someone visits from out of town, allowing the hosts time to prepare. (Comoros).

Out on a lime. A colloquialism for "hanging out with friends." (U.S. Virgin Islands). *Also called* **Limin.**

Outside children. Children born out of wedlock. No stigma is associated with the title. (Bahamas). *See also* **Sweethearting.**

-ovanje. A Slovene suffix that indicates the eve of a holiday. (Slovenia). *See also* **Miklavžovanje, Silvestrovanje.**

Over the road. A colloquialism for "across the street." (New Zealand).

-ovich. A Russian suffix meaning "son." Attached to the end of the father's first name to form a patronymic. (Kyrgyzstan, Uzbekistan).

-ovna. A Russian suffix meaning "daughter." Attached to the end of the father's first name to form a patronymic. (Kyrgyzstan, Uzbekistan).

Ow di bodi? "How are you?" A Krio greeting. A typical response is **A tel God tanki**. (Sierra Leone).

Ow fo do? "What can you do?" A common Krio expression. The response is **Na fo biah** (You must bear it). (Sierra Leone).

Oy gosh. A collection of household goods and clothes. (Turkmenistan).

Oz-komus. A mouth harp used to play traditional music. (Kyrgyzstan). *Also called* **Temir-komuz.**

Ozodii zanon. "Freedom for women." Because of this campaign, women are not required in Tajikistan to comply with certain traditional Islamic restrictions. (Tajikistan).

Pa. (1) A term used to address older men, regardless of relationship. (Sierra Leone). (2) "Aunt." An informal Thai title. (Thailand).

Paali. An ancient language from which Khmer is derived. *Paali* developed as a successor to Indian Sanskrit. (Cambodia).

Pa'anga. Tonga's national currency. (Tonga).

Pabellón criollo. A dish of black beans, rice, shredded meat, plantains, and **Arepa(s)**. (Venezuela).

Paçe. A traditional breakfast served at a restaurant. It consists of a creamy soup made with a cow or calf head, tomato sauce, garlic, flour, butter, and seasonings. (Albania).

Pachamama. Goddess Mother Earth. Part of an indigenous tradition that Altiplano Bolivians mix with Catholic beliefs. (Bolivia). *See also* **Achachila, Ch'alla.**

Padarias. Neighborhood shops that sell bread and basic food items. (Brazil).

Padi. "Friend." A term used to address both friends and strangers. (Sierra Leone).

Padrinho. Portuguese word for "godfather." (Portugal).

Pad Thai. Pan-fried noodles. (Thailand).

Paella. Rice with fish, seafood, and/or meat. (Spain).

Pagne. A wraparound skirt. Worn by women in Central and West African countries..

Pagnes. Ivorian women wear these long, colorful bolts of cloth wrapped around the waist, along with a blouse. (Ivory Coast).

Pagri. A traditional cap. Part of a groom's wedding attire. (Bangladesh). *See also* **Nagra, Shirwani.**

Pahela Baishak. The New Year according to the Bangla calendar. (Bangladesh).

Pahu. An indigenous drum. The *pahu*, the guitar, and the **Toere** provide accompaniment to singing performances. (French Polynesia).

Pai. "Father." A term of address used as a sign of respect. (Cape Verde).

Paillotte. A thatched hut. (Comoros).

Pai Sai Maa. "Where are you coming from?" An informal Lao greeting. (Laos).

Päivää. A general Finnish greeting. (Finland).

Pajama. White religious clothing worn by men that is similar to a Western pajama bottom. Worn with **Panjabi.** (Bangladesh).

Pajomah. Long pants worn by women under a traditional dress (**Curta**). (Tajikistan). *Also called* **Aezor.**

Pakeha. New Zealanders of European descent. (New Zealand).

Pakinou. The Baoulé term for Easter. (Ivory Coast).

Palamene. The unicameral Parliament. (Tuvalu).

Palata Predstaviteley. Chamber of Representatives. Part of the Belarus National Assembly. (Belarus). *See also* **Natsionalnoye Sobranie.**

Palav. A dish of rice mixed with meat and carrots. (Tajikistan).

Paleche. White maize. It is replacing sorghum as the primary grain, though vulnerable to drought. (Botswana).

Palolo(s). Coral worms. A delicacy that Samoans gather during Swarm of the *Palolo*, which occurs in late October and early November, when the worms come out to propagate their species. (American Samoa, Samoa).

Paloo. A dish of rice with lamb, carrots, onions, and garlic. (Kyrgyzstan).

Palov. The Uzbek national dish, generally made with rice, meat, and carrots. (Uzbekistan).

Palow. Turkenistan's national dish, a mixture of sticky rice and meat, eaten frequently at celebrations. (Turkmenistan).

Palusami. Coconut cream baked in taro leaves. (American Samoa, Samoa).

Pamanhikan. An engagement tradition wherein the suitor's family visits the prospective bride's family to propose marriage. (Philippines).

Pamplemousse. Grapefruit. (Haiti).

Pán. "Sir." A formal title that precedes a professional title and/or the last name. (Czech Republic, Slovakia).

Pan. (1) "Mr." A title used with the last name. (Poland, Ukraine). (2) Steel drums used in many Grenadian music styles. (Grenada).

Pana. A staple root crop. (Solomon Islands).

Panadería. A bread shop. (Spain).

Panades. Fried corn shells with beans or fish. (Belize).

Pancasila. Five principles: belief in one God, humanism, unity of the state, consensus, and social justice. A national philosophy first embraced by the government in the 1970s. (Indonesia).

Panchai baja. Five-instrument musical ensembles that accompany special activities and festivals. (Nepal).

Pancit. A noodle dish. (Guam).

Glossary of Cultural Terms

Panele. "Miss." A Lithuanian title used with the last name during an introduction. (Lithuania).

Pangi. The Ndyuka term for a traditional wraparound dress. (Suriname). *Also called* **Kosu.**

Panglamaran. A formal ritual among Javanese families in which the parents of a prospective groom go to the parents of the prospective bride to ask permission for the marriage. (Suriname).

Pan-hsai-myo. Myanmar's ten traditional plastic arts, which include painting, sculpture, metalwork, and wood carving. (Myanmar).

Paní. "Madam." A formal title that precedes a professional title and the last name. (Czech Republic).

Pani. "Mrs." A title used with the last name. (Poland, Slovakia, Ukraine).

Panjabi. White religious clothing worn by men that is similar to a knee-length Western pajama top. Worn with **Pajama.** (Bangladesh).

Panna. "Miss." A title used with the last name. (Ukraine).

Panove. "Sirs" or "Gentlemen." A term of address used in official situations. (Ukraine).

Pan sobao. Puerto Rican flat bread that is made with flour, shortening, and water. (Puerto Rico).

P'ansori. Musical drama performed by a soloist. (South Korea).

Papá. "Father." A term of address used as a sign of respect. (Cape Verde).

Papa. (1) A term used to address older men. (French Polynesia, Gabon, Papua New Guinea). (2) A French word for "father." Used by children to address adults. (Ivory Coast, Togo). (3) A stiff cornmeal porridge that is eaten with every meal. (Lesotho). (4) A pandanus mat on which people sit. (Tuvalu).

Papa a la Huancaina. A baked potato topped with sliced eggs and a sauce. (Peru).

Papa graun. The system of tribally owned land, which allows everyone to own land by birthright. (Papua New Guinea).

Papah. A traditional high, round, lambskin hat worn by older men. (Azerbaijan).

Papai Noel. Father Noel. Brings gifts on Christmas Eve that are opened on Christmas Day. (Brazil).

Papá Noel. Father Christmas or Santa Claus. Brings gifts on Christmas Eve. (Argentina, Bolivia).

Papiamento. Dutch Creole. A language spoken on Saint Croix. (U.S. Virgin Islands).

Pâques. Easter. (Gabon).

Parang. Spanish Christmas carols. (Trinidad and Tobago).

Paranging. An activity in which groups of friends go from house to house singing Spanish Christmas carols as well as dancing, eating, and playing homemade instruments. (Trinidad and Tobago).

Parata. A sword dance. An important event at the Carnival celebration in Valletta. (Malta).

Pareu. Wraparound cloth. Traditional clothing worn by men and women. (French Polynesia, Niue).

Parish. A Grenadian region. Each is named after a Catholic saint. A festival is held in honor of the *parish* saint. (Grenada).

Pari-vente. A fund-raising party with free food but expensive beer; organized by women. (Chad).

Paron. A title of respect for older men or officials; used with the last name. (Armenia).

Paros cívicos. Strikes. Occasionally interfere with business hours. (Bolivia).

Parrain. "Godfather" in French. (Belgium).

Parrandas. A Christmas celebration in which groups of friends go door-to-door and sing Christmas songs. The singers expect food and drinks in return. (Puerto Rico).

Pasacalle. Folk music. (Ecuador).

Pasalubong. A small, inexpensive gift that a guest will bring for the host family after being away a long time. (Philippines).

Pasho. Maize paste. (Uganda).

Pasillo. Folk music that has slow, waltz-like rhythms. (Ecuador).

Påsk. Easter. Children celebrate by dressing up as old witches with brooms and going door-to-door (among friends and neighbors) to collect candy. Colored Easter eggs are also common. (Sweden).

Paskha. Special cakes. Family and friends gather to make *paskha* at Easter. (Belarus, Ukraine).

Pass a friend straight. Grenadian creole for passing by someone on the street; considered rude to do so without at least nodding or saying hello. (Grenada).

Passementerie. Decorative trim for clothing or furniture. (Colombia).

Pastel de choclo. A baked dish of beef, chicken, onions, corn, eggs, and spices. (Chile).

Pasterma. Dried salt mutton. (Albania).

Pasties. Meat pies in the shape of burgers. (Northern Ireland).

Pastizzi. Cheesecake. (Malta).

Pasulj. Beans. (Serbia and Montenegro).

Pâte. A doughy corn flour porridge eaten with a spicy stew. (Benin).

Pâte. The French word for a stiff porridge made of cornmeal and water and served with a spicy sauce of okra, spinach, and fish or meat. (Togo). *Also called* **Akoumé.**

Pates. A dish similar to a fish turnover. (U.S. Virgin Islands).

Pa thung. A wraparound skirt worn by women with a simple blouse. (Thailand). *Also called* **Sarong.**

Pâtisseries. A pastry shop that sells cakes. Some may sell crêpes. (France).

Patois. A French-based *creole* language. (Jamaica, Saint Lucia, Trinidad and Tobago, U.S. Virgin Islands).

Patuiki. Head chief. (Niue).

Pavement. A term for "sidewalk." (South Africa).

Pawa. A long shawl worn over the shoulders by Burmese women. (Myanmar).

Paw paw. A race in which students run carrying smaller students on their backs. (Sierra Leone).

Pawpaws. Papaya. (Congo, Grenada, Solomon Islands, Zimbabwe).

Pazar. Open-air markets. (Macedonia).

Pchiwang. Violin. Often accompanies folk music. (Bhutan).

Pe'a. A traditional body tattoo for men. (American Samoa, Samoa).

Peanut cake. A form of peanut brittle. (Bahamas).

Pears. Smooth-skinned avocados. (U.S. Virgin Islands).

Peas. A variety of legumes, including lentils, red beans, pigeon peas, chickpeas, etc. (Antigua and Barbuda, Barbados, Grenada, Jamaica, Saint Lucia).

Peas n' rice. Rice combined with **pigeon peas**, a certain type of bean. (Bahamas).

Pee. "Older brother" or "older sister." A Thai title used to refer to slightly older or higher-status people. (Thailand).

Glossary of Cultural Terms

Pe'epe'e. Coconut cream made by straining a mixture of warm water and mature coconut meat gratings and adding salt or lemon juice. Popularly used as a sauce. (Samoa).

Pelau. (1) A dish made with rice, beans, and chicken. (Montserrat, Saint Kitts and Nevis, Saint Vincent and the Grenadines). (2) A rice dish prepared with chickpeas. (Trinidad and Tobago).

Pelmeni. A pasta dish. (Russia).

Pelotear. In Cuba, a Spanish verb that means "to pass the buck." (Cuba).

Penlop(s). A regional governor. (Bhutan).

Pentecôte. The Christian holiday of Pentecost. (Gabon).

Pepernoten. Gingerbread. Thrown by the servants of **Sinterklaas** during parades. (Netherlands).

Pepper pot. A meat stew flavored with **Casareep**. (Guyana).

Pepperpot. A spicy vegetable stew. (Antigua and Barbuda, Barbados).

Perahan. A knee-length shirt worn with a **Tunban**. Typical clothing for Afghan men. (Afghanistan).

Perahan tunban. A knee-length shirt (**Perahan**) worn over baggy trousers (**Tunban**) that are pulled tight with a drawstring. Typical clothing for Afghan men. (Afghanistan).

Père Noël. The French name for Santa Claus. (France).

Perestroika. Restructuring. A policy of reform introduced by Mikhail Gorbachev in the late 1980s. (Latvia, Russia).

Pesach. [NOTE: Jewish holidays are set according to the lunar calendar.] Passover. Takes place six lunar months and two weeks after New Year's. (Israel). *See also* **Rosh Hashanah**.

Pesäpallo. Finnish baseball. (Finland).

Peso. The national currencies of various countries. (Argentina, Chile, Colombia, Cuba, Dominican Republic, Honduras, Mexico, Philippines, Uruguay).

Pétanque. French lawn bowling. (Burkina Faso, France, Singapore).

Peter. "Godfather" in Dutch. (Belgium).

Petits boubous. Muslim-style robes with a matching **Pagne**; worn by women. (Guinea).

Pet name. A nickname. Often a shortened or slightly altered version of a person's given name. (Jamaica). *Also called* **Yard name**.

Petrol. Gasoline. (New Zealand).

Peul. The French name for Mbororo. The Mbororo are descendants of the Fulbé and are migratory herders. (Central African Republic).

Phaakhamaa. A traditional sarong worn by men. (Laos).

Phaasin. A calf-length, sarong-style skirt worn by Lao women. Made of locally handwoven materials in multicolor designs. Worn with a Western-style blouse and a silver link belt. (Laos).

Phagwah. A celebration to welcome spring. (Guyana).

Phane. A worm that is considered a delicacy. It is gathered from **Mophane** trees, dried in hot ashes, and eaten. (Botswana).

Pi. Coconuts. (Tuvalu).

Pibimbap. Rice mixed with bits of meat and seasoned vegetables. (South Korea).

Picante. A Spanish term used to describe spicy food. (Mexico). *See also* **Caliente**.

Pierogi. Stuffed dumplings. (Poland).

Pierozhki. Meat- or potato-filled pastries. (Kazakhstan).

Pigeon peas. A type of bean. (Bahamas). *See also* **Peas n' rice**.

Pigtails. A long, single plait at the back of the head; a hairstyle worn by men. (Saint Vincent and the Grenadines).

Pilau. Pilaf. (Afghanistan, Azerbaijan, Tanzania).

Pilav. Pilaf. (Turkey).

Pillau. Lightly fried rice with vegetables. (Pakistan).

Pi Mai. A three-day Lao New Year celebration in the spring. (Laos).

Piman zwazo. Small, hot pimentos that are often added to dishes. (Haiti).

Piment. Hot peppers. (Chad, Gabon).

Pinasse. Covered, motorized canoe. Commonly used on the Niger River year-round. (Mali).

Ping kai. Grilled poultry. (Laos).

Pinol. A natural beverage made of corn. (Nicaragua).

Pinyin. A romanized Chinese alphabet used for international communication and in schools to help teach Chinese. (China).

Pīrāgi. Meat-filled pastries. (Latvia).

Pirão. A paste of ground cassava, similar to thick porridge. A staple food at lunch and dinner. (Angola).

Pirogues. Traditional outrigger canoes. (French Polynesia).

Pirópos. Flattering personal comments made by Mexican men to women. The women generally do not respond. (Mexico).

Pirozhki. A stuffed pastry. (Moldova, Russia).

Pirukas. A pastry with meat and/or vegetables. (Estonia).

Pisco. Grape brandy. The Chilean national drink. (Chile).

Piti. A lamb broth with potatoes and peas cooked in clay pots in the oven. (Azerbaijan).

Pitso. A town meeting called by the local chief to share important news or discuss something. An impromptu party may follow good news. (Lesotho).

Pjazza. The village square; a popular location for socializing. (Malta).

Placinte. A flaky stuffed pastry. (Moldova).

Planting. Fancy embroidery in a contrasting color, placed around the shirt collar and pant cuffs. (Sierra Leone).

Plassas. "Sauce." Most commonly made from pounded cassava leaves, palm oil, and chili peppers. Eaten with rice. (Sierra Leone).

Plátanos. (1) Plantains. (Cuba, Dominican Republic, Nicaragua). (2) Bananas. (Guatemala).

Plaza Bolívar. A city park the size of a block that honors the Venezuelan hero Simon Bolívar; found in most cities near the city center. (Venezuela).

Plaza de armas. The town plaza. (Peru).

Plazas. Large parking areas that have supermarkets, banks, department stores, post offices, fast-food restaurants and other stores. (U.S. Virgin Islands).

Plena. A popular form of music for dancing and singing. A type of Puerto Rican folk music that deals with life's hardships. (Puerto Rico).

Plov. A popular Uzbek dish of rice, carrots, onions, and mutton. (Kazakhstan).

-po. A suffix added to a greeting to indicate respect. (Zambia).

Pocket sulu. A tailored **Sulu** worn with a short-sleeved shirt and sometimes a tie. Worn by businessmen, clergy, and civil servants (Fiji). *Also called* **Sulu vakataga**.

Poda-podas. Small pickup trucks fitted with seats and a roof. They carry people, goods, and animals. (Sierra Leone).

Poe'. Fruit puddings made with coconut milk; a popular dessert. (French Polynesia).

Poftă bună. "Enjoy the meal." A Romanian phrase used at the beginning of the meal. (Romania).

Glossary of Cultural Terms

Poh piah. Spring rolls filled with shredded turnip, bamboo shoots, bean curd, prawns, and pork. (Singapore).

Poisson cru. Raw fish marinated in lime juice. Eaten with breadfruit cooked in coconut milk. (French Polynesia).

Pojadok. The Macedonian word for "breakfast." (Macedonia).

Poka. "Bye." An informal Russian parting phrase. (Belarus).

Polders. Western areas of land that have been reclaimed from the sea. (Netherlands).

Polhovka. A traditional fur hat made from dormouse skins. Worn in southern regions of Slovenia. (Slovenia).

Politburo. Vietnam's 19-member Government Council. (Vietnam).

Polla. Market. (Sri Lanka).

Pollera. (1) A full, colorful skirt. (Bolivia). (2) A full-length dress with embroidery. (Panama).

Pol sambol. Scraped and spiced coconut. (Sri Lanka).

Polska. Polka. A common type of music. (Sweden).

Polyclinics. Clinics that provide free medical and dental care to all Barbadians. (Barbados).

Pom. A Creole dish named for the ingredient **Pomtayer**. (Suriname).

Pomodoro. Tomato sauce. (Italy).

Pomtayer. A local root used in the dish **Pom**. (Suriname).

Ponas. "Mr." A Lithuanian title used with the last name upon introduction. (Lithuania).

Poncho. A blanket-like cloak with a slit in the middle for the head. (Colombia).

Ponerse las pilas. (1) "To insert batteries." A Spanish phrase. (Venezuela). (2) "To be aware" or "to watch out." A Venezuelan colloquialism. (Venezuela).

Ponia. "Mrs." A Lithuanian title used with the last name upon introduction. (Lithuania).

Pop downtown. "Go downtown." A New Zealand colloquialism. (New Zealand).

Popol Vuh. A literary work that describes the Maya creation story. Written in the mid-1500s. (Guatemala).

Por favor. "Please." A common Portuguese phrase. (Portugal).

Por la ventana. "Through the window." Refers to common-law marriage. (Dominican Republic).

Pôro. Male initiation rites that take place in Senoufo communities, once every seven years. (Ivory Coast).

Por puesto. A popular form of transportation in which taxi-like automobiles travel a regular route throughout the city, picking up and letting off passengers at any point. (Venezuela).

Porteño. The Buenos Aires Spanish accent that has been influenced by the Italian language. (Argentina).

Porteños. Argentine coastal inhabitants in the early 1800s who favored a centrist government that would be based in Buenos Aires. (Argentina).

Portuñol. A mixture of the Spanish and Portuguese languages. Spoken in northern border towns. (Uruguay). *Also called* **Brazilero.**

Posadas. Nightly parties that take place during Christmas celebrations. (Mexico).

Postre. Spanish word for "dessert." (Mexico).

Potica. A traditional nut roll served during Christmas and Easter. (Slovenia).

Potjiekos. "Pot food." Any meal cooked in a three-legged cast-iron pot over a fire. (Namibia, South Africa). *See also* **Braai(s).**

Pour-out. A bag of small change scattered by the best man onto the pavement or road after the bride and groom have driven away. (Scotland). *Also called* **Scramble.**

Pousse-pousse. Pedicab. A common form of transportation. (Madagascar).

Poutine. Fries covered with spicy gravy and cheese curds. A favorite fast food. (Canada).

Poya. A holiday held every full moon. (Sri Lanka).

Pozole. Pork-and-hominy soup. (Mexico).

Praça. The town plaza. A popular location to socialize. (Cape Verde).

Prang. "Fender bender." An Australian English colloquialism. (Australia).

Prasad. Blessings from the gods in the form of saffron powder, holy water from the Ganges River, and food. Offered to visitors in Hindu temples. (India).

Presepju. The nativity. A traditional part of Christmas. (Malta).

Pret. "Evil spirits." The Nepalese believe *pret* can cause disease, crop failures, or accidents. (Nepal). *See also* **Bhoot, Bokshi, Graha dasha.**

Priedka tat-Tifel. The traditional Boy's Sermon that is included in Midnight Mass. (Malta).

Prima. "Cousin." A feminine term of address used between good friends. (Guinea-Bissau). *See also* **Primo.**

Primatywny. Polish word for "primitive." A label for people who do not observe public courtesies. (Poland).

Primo. "Cousin." A masculine term of address used between good friends. (Guinea-Bissau). *See also* **Prima.**

Privet. [NOTE: Spelling varies because it is a transliteration of Russian.] "Hello." An informal Russian greeting. (Belarus, Moldova, Russia).

Privyet. (Kazakstan, Kyrgyzstan). *See* **Privet.**

Prodavnici. Small, family-owned stores. (Macedonia).

Profesor/a. (Peru). *See* **Profesor(a).**

Profesor(a). A professional title. Masculine *profesor*, feminine *profesora*. (Chile).

Proost. The Dutch equivalent of saying "Bless you." One can also say **Gezondheid**. (Netherlands).

Prosím. The word for "Please." It is polite to use this word before making any requests and for saying, "You're welcome." (Czech Republic, Slovakia). *See also* **D'akujem, Děkuji.**

Provincien. Provinces. (Belgium).

Pryvit. "Hi." An informal Ukrainian greeting. (Ukraine).

Pryvitanne! "Hi!" A Belarusian greeting used between young friends. (Belarus).

Puan. "Madam." A Malay title. (Malaysia).

Public house. Called a "pub," these establishments serve alcohol and food. People often gather here to socialize. (England, Ireland).

Public motor vehicle. PMV. A bus or truck used for public transportation. (Papua New Guinea).

Públicos. (1) Informal taxis that follow certain routes. (Dominican Republic). (2) Large cars that fit as many as six passengers and travel from specified terminals to fixed destinations with no stops in between. (Puerto Rico).

Public schools. A British idiom for "private schools." (England). *See also* **State schools.**

Pudding(s). A term used to refer to dessert. (Scotland, Wales). *See also* **Sweet.**

Pueblo. A Spanish word for "village." (Bolivia).

Glossary of Cultural Terms

Pugua. Betel nut mixed with powdered lime and wrapped in a pepper leaf. Chamorros often chew *pugua* after a meal. (Guam).

Pula. (1) "Rain." The name of the Batswana national currency. (Botswana). (2) "Good wishes." A Setswana phrase used as a greeting or at the end of speeches. (Botswana).

Pulaka. Swamp taro. (Tuvalu).

Puletasi. A fitted two-piece dress. (American Samoa, Samoa).

Pulkogi. Marinated beef. A Korean delicacy. (North Korea, South Korea).

Pulla. A sweetbread often flavored with cardamom. Comes in a variety of forms. (Finland).

Pulperias. Small shops that are run out of people's homes. *Pulperias* sell food, medicine, and cleaning and school supplies. (Honduras).

Pumari. Head dresses made of toucan and parrot feathers. Worn by Trio and Wayana Amerindians. (Suriname).

Punjabi. Colorful pants, tight from the calves down, with a matching knee-length tunic. Worn by unmarried girls and women in the Terai. (Nepal). *Also called* **Kurta surwal.**

Punjene paprike. Stuffed peppers. (Serbia and Montenegro).

Punt. Ireland's old currency, before the euro came into use. (Ireland).

Punta-rock. A favorite style of music and dance that has its roots in the Garífuna culture. (Belize).

Puntatrasera. A tender steak. (Venezuela).

Punto Guanacaste. A folk dance. The Costa Rican national dance. (Costa Rica).

Pupusas. Thick tortillas stuffed with meat, beans, or cheese. (El Salvador).

Pura vida. "Pure life." A common Costa Rican response to the greeting ¿*Cómo estás?* (Costa Rica).

Purdah. A state of living in which women are not seen by males, unless they are close family members. (Afghanistan).

Puri puri. Black magic. A belief that coexists with Christianity on both the community and individual level. (Papua New Guinea).

Purotu. "Missionary dresses." *Purotu* cover more of the body than traditional clothing. Worn by women performing slow hula dances. Literally, "Good in appearance." (French Polynesia).

Pushing. The action of a host accompanying a guest to the road. (Ivory Coast).

Pushtunwali. Code of the Pashtuns. A local behavioral code. (Afghanistan).

Pust. The Slovene equivalent of Mardi Gras. (Slovenia).

Puszi. A greeting in which Hungarians hug and kiss each other lightly on each cheek. (Hungary).

Putonghua. Mandarin Chinese. (China, Hong Kong, Singapore).

Putu. A hot pepper sauce Comorians use to season all types of food. (Comoros).

Pwe. A live show incorporating acting, singing, music, dancing, and sometimes clowns or puppets. (Myanmar).

Pyelmeni. Small boiled dumplings. A Russian dish. (Kazakstan).

Pyithu Hluttaw. People's Assembly. A 485-seat unicameral parliament elected in 1990 but never allowed to convene. (Myanmar).

Pysanka. Easter-egg painting. A Ukrainian art form. (Ukraine).

Pytt i Panna. A dish of potatoes, leftover meats, and onions, fried with an egg on top and served with pickled beets. (Sweden).

Qahwa. (Bahrain). *See* **Qahwah.**

Qahwah. [NOTE: Spelling varies because it is a transliteration of Arabic.] Coffee. (Qatar).

Qahwah Saadah. Bedouin coffee that is bitter and drunk quickly from small cups. (Jordan).

Qameez. A long tunic. (Pakistan). *See also* **Shalwar qameez.**

Qarakuli. A cap worn by men in the winter; made from the skin of a karakul sheep. (Afghanistan).

Qassatat. A pastry filled with either cheese or peas, and occasionally anchovies or spinach. (Malta).

Qat. An addictive stimulant leaf that grows on a bush. Chewed during afternoon visits, holidays, wedding celebrations, and so on. (Yemen).

Qawwali. An Islamic song of worship performed by Sufi mystics. Accompanied by instruments such as the **Dholak** and the **Rabab.** (Pakistan).

Qazi. A Muslim holy man who completes the marriage contract between the families of the bride and groom. (Pakistan).

Qedra. A spicy rice dish. (West Bank and Gaza).

Qeleshe. A traditional white cap worn by men. (Albania).

Qobqob. A gold headpiece worn by the bride during her wedding celebration. (Bahrain).

Qorma. A vegetable sauce. (Afghanistan).

Quadrille. A style of dance similar to square dancing, but with an island beat. (U.S. Virgin Islands).

Qubbajt. A pastry filled with nougat. (Malta).

¡Que aproveche! "Enjoy your meal." A Spanish phrase often used to politely refuse an invitation to join a meal. (Spain).

Québeckers. Canadians from Québec. (Canada). *Also called* **Québécois.**

Québécois. Canadians from Québec. (Canada). *Also called* **Québeckers.**

¿Qué hay de bueno? "What's good?" A common Spanish greeting. (Panama).

Que le vaya bien. "May it go well with you." A common Spanish parting phrase. (Guatemala, Honduras, Panama).

Quelle sont les nouvelles? French phrase meaning "What is the news?" After initial questions, Ivorians eventually ask each other this question, which opens the conversation to deeper discussion. (Ivory Coast).

Quena. An instrument similar to a recorder. Used to play traditional music. (Peru). *See also* **Antara, Charango.**

Quenelles. Small dumplings made with meat or fish and served with a sauce. (Luxembourg).

Quesadillas. Tortillas baked or fried with cheese. (Mexico).

Que sea lo que Dios quiera. "Whatever God wills." A Spanish expression Colombians use to express their faith. (Colombia).

¿Qué tal? "How are you?" or "What's up?" A common Spanish greeting. (Cuba, Guatemala, Panama, Puerto Rico).

Quetschentaart. Plum tart. (Luxembourg).

Quetzal. Guatemala's national currency. (Guatemala).

Quijongo. A traditional stringed instrument. (Costa Rica).

Quinceañera. A girl's 15th birthday party, which marks her entrance into the social world. (Ecuador, El Salvador).

Quinoa. A protein-rich grain often included in soup. (Bolivia).

Quisaca. Dried and ground cassava leaves cooked in water. (Angola).

Quoc-Hoi. The Vietnamese National Assembly. (Vietnam).

Glossary of Cultural Terms

Qur'an. The Koran; contains the word of **Allah** as revealed to the prophet Muhammad through the angel Gabriel. The scriptures of Islam. Used in Muslim-populated countries..

Qur'anic. (Cameroon, Chad, Comoros, Kuwait, Mauritania, Qatar, Senegal, Sudan, United Arab Emirates). *See* **Qur'an.**

Qurban khait. Day of Sacrifice. A Muslim holiday that honors Abraham's willingness to sacrifice his son. (Uzbekistan). *Also called* **Eid al-Adha.**

Rabab. A stringed instrument. Accompanies the **Qawwali.** (Pakistan).

Rababa. One- or two-stringed fiddle used to accompany singing. (United Arab Emirates).

Rabel. An instrument similar to a fiddle. (Chile).

Raclette. Melted cheese on a piece of potato. (Switzerland).

Radio trottoir. Pavement radio. A system of verbal relays that pass news and information with great speed. (Cameroon).

Radunitsa. A holiday to remember the dead. (Belarus).

Ragamuffin. A style of music that mixes rock and reggae. Also, the untucked fashion that these musicians wear. (Grenada).

Ragù. Sauce with meat. (Italy).

Raï. A style of music popular among young people. (Algeria, Morocco).

Rajya Sabha. Council of States. The upper house in India's Parliament. (India). *See also* **Lok Sabha.**

Rake n' scrape. A type of island music created with goatskin drums, saws, and maracas. (Bahamas). *See also* **Goombay.**

Rakhmat. "Thank you." A phrase used when departing after visiting friends or family. (Kyrgyzstan).

Raki. A strong alcoholic drink. (Albania).

Rakija. (1) An alcoholic drink. (Bosnia and Herzegovina, Serbia and Montenegro). (2) A brandy made of apples, grapes, or plums. (Macedonia).

Ramadan. [NOTE: Spelling varies because it is a transliteration of Arabic. Also, Muslim holidays are set according to the lunar calendar.] The month in which **Allah** revealed the **Qur'an** to the prophet Muhammad. During this month, Muslims fast from sunrise to sunset. Observed in Muslim-populated countries..

Ramadhan. (Oman). *See* **Ramadan.**

Ramakian. An important traditional literary work containing stories of the Hindu god Rama. Based on the epic Sanskrit poem the **Ramayana.** (Thailand).

Ramasan Bairam. A feast at the end of **Ramadan.** Celebrated by Muslims. (Albania, Bosnia and Herzegovina, Croatia).

Ramayana. An epic Sanskrit poem. Continues to influence national and regional literature. (Cambodia, India, Thailand).

Ramazan. (Uzbekistan). *See* **Ramadan.**

Ramazan Bairami. A feast at the end of **Ramadan.** Celebrated by Muslims. (Azerbaijan).

Ramazon. (Tajikistan). *See* **Ramadan.**

Ramen. A type of noodles. (Japan).

Ramzaan. (India). *See* **Ramadan.**

Ramzan. (Bangladesh). *See* **Ramadan.**

Ran annim. "Good morning." A greeting used by the Chuukese. (Micronesia).

Ranchera. A traditional form of music. (Mexico).

Rand. South Africa's national currency. (South Africa).

Ranovola. Golden water. A drink made from water boiled in the browned rice that remains stuck to the bottom of the pan after cooking. (Madagascar).

Rapa. A cloth women wear wrapped around the waist. (Cameroon). *Also called* **Pagne.**

Rappée. A pie made with grated potato and ground meat. (Canada).

Raqaq. A very thin bread served with a sauce. (United Arab Emirates).

Rara. (1) A more traditional version of **Carnaval.** Celebrated mainly in urban areas. (Haiti). (2) Local bands that perform in the streets from mid-January to Easter. (Haiti).

Ras El Am El Hejri. The Islamic New Year. (Tunisia).

Ras El Sans El Hejria. The Islamic New Year. (West Bank and Gaza).

Rashogolla. Dough boiled in syrup; a popular sweet. (Bangladesh).

Raspaitos. Shaved ice; a popular treat. (Venezuela).

Ratu. A title used with the first name when addressing a chief. (Fiji).

Rau luoc. Boiled vegetables. (Vietnam).

Ravane. A tambourine-like drum often ringed with bells. Accompanies the **Séga** dance. (Mauritius).

Ravitoto sy henakisoa. Ground manioc leaves with pork. A popular form of **Loaka.** (Madagascar).

Rayons. Districts within Azerbaijan. (Azerbaijan).

Razana. Ancestors. Intermediaries between the gods and the living. People report their activities and needs to the *razana*, who provide directives and taboos. (Madagascar). *See also* **Fadys.**

Razha. A dance involving sword throwing and an exchange of poetry. The Omani national dance. (Oman).

Real. Brazil's national currency. (Brazil).

Reamker. The Cambodian version of the Hindu **Ramayana.** An important literary work; stories from the epic are carved on the walls of the temple **Angkor Wat.** They are also acted out in shadow plays. (Cambodia). *See also* **Nang sbek.**

Rebab. A bowed instrument. Used in **Gamelan** ensembles. (Indonesia).

Rebaba. A one-stringed instrument. (Saudi Arabia).

Rebambaramba. "A free-for-all." A Spanish idiom unique to Cuban society. (Cuba).

Rebana. A single-headed drum. (Malaysia).

Rebetiko. A type of folk music with themes of poverty and suffering. (Greece).

Rebozo. A shawl used by women for a variety of purposes, including carrying a child or covering the head or arms. (Mexico).

Recuerdos. Tokens of affection or remembrance. (Ecuador).

Redda. A woman's wraparound skirt that is tucked in at the waist. Worn with a **Hatte.** (Sri Lanka).

Refresquerias. Fruit-and-drink stands that sell **Batidos de fruta.** (Venezuela).

Regalo. Spanish word for "gift." (Venezuela).

Regierungschef. The Liechtenstein prime minister; serves as head of government. (Liechtenstein).

Regressados. Refugees who have returned to their home regions. (Angola).

Regulos. Traditional chiefs, who have great influence over local matters. (Mozambique).

Rendang Padang. A spicy meat dish cooked in garlic, shallots, ginger, chilies, lemongrass, and coconut milk. (Indonesia).

Renminbi. China's national currency. (China). *See also* **Yuan.**

Glossary of Cultural Terms

Respect. "I respect you" or "It's nice to meet you." An informal greeting used among friends and youth. (Saint Vincent and the Grenadines).

Responsables populares de salud. Community health-care workers that are trained in basic skills by local nurses and doctors. They serve the rural population. (Bolivia).

Retablos. Wooden boxes that feature three-dimensional religious or everyday scenes; a form of folk art. (Peru).

Revista. A popular theater where politics and social issues are satirized. (Portugal).

Rezen. Breaded steak. (Slovakia).

Rhamadan. (Yemen). *See* **Ramadan.**

Rial. The name of the Iranian and Yemeni national currencies. (Iran, Yemen).

Rial Omani. The name of the Omani national currency. (Oman).

Ribab. A single-stringed instrument often used to accompany poetry. (Morocco). *Also called* **Amzhad.**

Rice pudding. Blood sausage. (Antigua and Barbuda). *Also called* **Black pudding.**

Riebel. Cornmeal stirred in a frying pan with milk, water, and salt. The Liechtenstein national dish. (Liechtenstein).

Riigikogu. The Estonian Parliament. (Estonia).

Rijerbal. Workers. A position in the traditional social system that is now incorporated into the formal government. (Marshall Islands). *See also* **Alaps, Irooj.**

Riksdag. The Swedish Parliament. (Sweden).

Ring. A colloquialism for "call on the telephone." (Australia).

Ringgit. Malaysia's national currency. (Malaysia).

Rinok. An open-air market where meat, cheese, fruits, vegetables, and spices are sold. (Kazakstan).

Risorgimento. The Italian unification movement that began in the 1800s. (Italy).

Riyal. The name of the Qatari and Saudi national currencies. (Qatar, Saudi Arabia).

Riyuq. Breakfast. (Iraq). *Also called* **Futur.**

Rogora khar? "How are you?" An informal way to begin a conversation. (Georgia).

Rogor brdzandebit? "How are you?" A more formal way to begin a conversation. (Georgia).

Romaji. A Japanese phonetic alphabet that uses Roman letters. (Japan). *See also* **Hiragana, Kanji, Katakana.**

Ro mazava. A stew made with **Zebus** and green leafy vegetables. (Madagascar).

Rondadors. Panpipes. (Ecuador).

Rondavel(s). (1) A traditional circular home built of stone and sticks held together with cow dung, which dries hard and can be painted. It has a thatched roof and a few windows. The diameter of the main house reflects socioeconomic status. (Lesotho). *Also called* **Ntlo.** (2) Round, thatched dwellings that are located within a family compound. (Botswana).

Roora. The bride-price paid by the groom's family to the bride's parents. Traditionally it included cattle, although cash is accepted. (Zimbabwe). *Also called* **Lobola.**

Rosh Hashanah. The Jewish New Year. (Bosnia and Herzegovina, Croatia, Israel).

Rosolje. A pink potato salad made with beets and herring. A Russian dish. (Estonia).

Roštilj. Grilled meats. (Serbia and Montenegro).

Rösti(s). Grated and fried potatoes. (Liechtenstein, Switzerland).

Roti. (1) Flat bread. (Fiji, India, Mauritius, Nepal, Pakistan, Trinidad and Tobago). (2) Flat bread wrapped around meat and vegetables. (Grenada, Guyana, Suriname).

Roti chanai. Bite-sized balls of cooked wheat dipped in lentil curry. (Malaysia).

Roti prata. An Indian dough-bread; a popular breakfast item. (Singapore).

Rottab. Fresh dates. (Bahrain). *See also* **Tamr.**

Route taxis. A form of transportation that follows set routes and has set fares. (Jamaica).

Roze-Maulud. A Muslim holiday celebrating the birth of the prophet Muhammad. (Afghanistan).

Rtveli. A rural harvest holiday in midautumn that celebrates variety and abundance. (Georgia).

Ruanas. Woven wool shawls. (Colombia).

Rubab. A traditional two-string guitar. (Uzbekistan).

Ruble. (1) Russia's national currency. (Russia). (2) Tajikistan's former national currency. (Tajikistan). *See also* **Somoni.**

Ručak. The main meal of the day. Eaten after work around 4 p.m. Includes soup and a meat dish. (Serbia and Montenegro).

Rucek. The Macedonian word for "lunch." (Macedonia).

Rüfen. Debris slides. Previously a natural threat, they are now enclosed and rendered harmless. (Liechtenstein).

Rugbrød. Pumpernickel bread or rye bread traditionally used for sandwiches. (Denmark).

Ruhname. President Saparmyrat Niyazov's thoughts on philosophy and Turkmen identity. (Turkmenistan).

Rui. Millet porridge. (Gambia).

Rumbero. A Spanish adjective that describes the Colombian ability to both work and play hard. (Colombia).

Rum shop(s). Small bars where men socialize, drink, and play dominoes and cards. (Grenada, Montserrat).

Rupee. The national currency of various countries. (India, Mauritius, Nepal, Pakistan, Sri Lanka).

Rupiah. Indonesia's national currency. (Indonesia).

Rupmaize. Rye bread. (Latvia).

Saaang, I gridi! "You are greedy!" A phrase people call out when a child does not share, or when someone finishes a plate of food without offering some to others. (Suriname).

Saan ka galing? "Where have you been?" A common, informal Pilipino greeting. (Philippines).

Saan ka pupunta? "Where are you going?" A common, informal Pilipino greeting. (Philippines).

Saba al-khair. (Bahrain). *See* **Sabah al-Khair.**

Saba al-nur. The proper reply to the Arabic greeting **Saba al-khair.** (Bahrain).

Sabah al-kair. (Yemen). *See* **Sabah al-Khair.**

Sabah al khair. (Jordan). *See* **Sabah al-Khair.**

Sabah al-Khair. "Good morning." A common Arabic greeting. (Saudi Arabia).

Sabah al-khayr. (Libya). *See* **Sabah al-Khair.**

Sabah el-khair. (West Bank and Gaza). *See* **Sabah al-Khair.**

Sabah El-Kheer. (Tunisia). *See* **Sabah al-Khair.**

Sabaidii. "May you have happy health." The most common Lao greeting. (Laos).

Sabar. A set of five to seven tuned drums. Played by the Wolof people to accompany dancing. (Senegal).

Saba Saba. Farmer's Day. Observed on 7 July. (Tanzania).

Sabji bazaar. A weekend open-air market. (Bhutan).

Sabkha. Salt flats. (United Arab Emirates).

Sabor. Croatia's parliament. (Croatia).

Glossary of Cultural Terms

Sachak. Cloth. (Turkmenistan).

Sachertorte. A rich chocolate cake with apricot jam and chocolate icing. (Austria).

Sadiq. "Friend." An Arabic term of address used for strangers. (Qatar).

Sadjèn. Food sacrifices made to the world of spirits. A central feature of **Agama Djawa**. (Suriname). *See also* **Slametan.**

Sadu. The traditional Bedouin handicraft of weaving rugs and tents using sheep, goat, or camel wool. (Kuwait).

Sadza. A stiff porridge made from white cornmeal. *Sadza* is rolled into a ball and dipped in a sauce. (Zimbabwe).

Saeima. The Latvian Parliament. (Latvia).

Safsari. A rectangular piece of cloth worn by older women that completely covers the clothing. Worn for protection from rain and dust. (Tunisia).

Sagas. Medieval Icelandic stories from A.D. 1200 to 1400. The *sagas* cover centuries of Scandinavian and British history. (Iceland).

Sagh ol. "Be well." An Azeri parting phrase. (Azerbaijan).

Sah. "Hello." A greeting used between rural Fang women. (Equatorial Guinea).

Saħħa. "Health to you." A Maltese parting phrase. (Malta).

Sai hankuri. "Have patience." A Hausa phrase. (Niger).

Saing-waing.

Sain uu. "Hello." A casual Mongol greeting. (Mongolia).

Sai pe, Malo. "Fine, thank you." A polite response to the Tongan greeting **Fefe hake?** (How do you do?). (Tonga).

Sa ka fet? "What's happening?" A common patois greeting. (Saint Lucia).

Sakau. An alcoholic beverage. (Micronesia).

Sakay. A side dish of jalapeños, ginger, and garlic. (Madagascar).

Saksak. A starchy extract from the sago palm. A staple food on the coast and in the lowlands. (Papua New Guinea).

Salaam. (1) "Peace." A common greeting. (Eritrea, Mauritius, Uzbekistan). (2) A gesture with the right hand used as an informal greeting. (Nepal, Singapore).

Salaam Alaikum. (Guinea). *See* **Assalaam alaikum.**

Salaam alaykum. (Mauritania). *See* **Assalaam alaikum.**

Salaam' alaykum. (Sudan). *See* **Assalaam alaikum.**

Salaam Aleikum. (Kyrgyzstan, Niger). *See* **Assalaam alaikum.**

Salaam alek(i). (Chad). *See* **Assalaam alaikum.**

Salaam ale kum. (Burkina Faso). *See* **Assalaam alaikum.**

Salaam Malekum. (Gambia). *See* **Assalaam alaikum.**

Sala gashi. "Go well in peace." A Sesotho parting phrase. (South Africa).

Sala hantle. "Stay well." A Sesotho parting phrase used by the person leaving. The person staying says **Tsamaea hantle**. (Lesotho).

Salam. (Azerbaijan, Iran, Sudan, Turkmenistan). *See* **Salaam.**

Salama. "Peace" (a common greeting) or "Peaceful" (a common response to a greeting). (Kenya, Madagascar, Tanzania).

Salamalek. (Turkmenistan). *See* **Assalaam alaikum.**

Salamaleykum. (Turkmenistan). *See* **Assalaam alaikum.**

Salamatsyzby. "Hello." The standard Kyrgyz greeting. (Kyrgyzstan).

Sala sentle. "Stay well." A parting phrase said to a person who is staying. (Botswana).

Salat. Praying five times daily facing Makkah, Saudi Arabia. One of the Five Pillars of Islam. (Iran, Malaysia). *See also* **Hajj, Saum, Shahada, Zakat.**

Salawar kameez. A traditional Punjabi pajama-like outfit. (Singapore).

Saldais ēdiens. Dessert; the third course of the main meal. (Latvia).

Salegy. Popular dance music that combines East African guitar rhythms with local beats. (Madagascar).

Salem. "Hi." A common Kazak greeting. (Kazakstan).

Salemetsis-ba? "How do you do?" A common Kazak greeting. (Kazakstan).

Salom. "Peace." A Tajik greeting used between friends. (Tajikistan).

Salomka. Straw plaiting used to create dolls, animals, baskets, and other decorative items. (Belarus).

Salon. (1) The living quarters, which consist of the living room and the bedrooms. (Gabon). (2) The sitting room. (Madagascar).

Saloneh. Mixed vegetables. (Bahrain).

Salteñas. Meat or chicken pies with potatoes, olives, and raisins. (Bolivia).

Saltfish. (1) Usually means cod that has been dried and salted. (Antigua and Barbuda, Jamaica, Montserrat). (2) Fish cured in salt. (Trinidad and Tobago).

¡Salud! "Health." A saying used if someone sneezes. (Mexico).

¡Saludos! "Hi." An informal Spanish greeting. (Dominican Republic).

Salut. (1) "Hello." A French greeting common among friends and youth. (Belgium, Canada, Central African Republic, France, French Polynesia, Lebanon, Romania, Switzerland). (2) A common parting phrase used among young people. (Luxembourg).

Salut, comment ça va? "Hi, how are you?" An informal French greeting. (Burkina Faso).

Salvator Mundi. The name of the sculpture of Christ in San Salvador's cathedral. One of the few major works of art in El Salvador left after natural disasters ruined older works. (El Salvador).

Salwaar kameez. A type of pantsuit with a long shirt. (Fiji).

Salwaar-kameez. (Mauritius). *See* **Salwaar kameez.**

Salwar. A long blouse worn over long pants with a matching shawl. (Suriname).

Salwar khamis. (Malaysia). *See* **Salwaar kameez.**

Sambal. Any foods fried with chilies. (Indonesia).

Samlor. A three-wheeled motorized taxi. (Thailand).

Samoon. An oval-shaped bread loaf. (Iraq).

Sampot. Worn by women, a large rectangular piece of colored cloth that is wrapped around the hips like a skirt down to the ankles. (Cambodia).

Samri. A dance performed at weddings and other social gatherings by women. (Kuwait).

-san. A suffix used with the family name. (Japan).

Sanatate. "Good health." A Romanian phrase used after a close friend or family member sneezes. (Romania).

Sancocho. (1) Vegetable-and-meat stew. (Colombia, Dominican Republic). (2) Chicken soup. (Panama).

Sandae. Masked theater. Performed at festivals and for entertainment. (South Korea).

Glossary of Cultural Terms

Sandinistas. A Marxist-oriented revolutionary group that gained control of the Nicaraguan government in July 1979 after a prolonged civil war. (Nicaragua).

Sanga ye? "How are you?" A common Pashto greeting. (Afghanistan).

Sangoma. A person consulted for divination. A traditional practice. (Swaziland). *See also* **Batsakatsi, Tinyanga.**

Sango nini? "What's new?" A Lingala phrase that follows the greeting **Mbote** (Hello). (Congo).

Sangría. A popular drink made with wine, fruit, and soft drinks. (Spain).

Sanibonani. "I see you." A siSwati greeting used to address two or more people. (Swaziland). *See also* **Sawubona.**

Santa Cruz. Words that mean "holy cross" in Spanish. Christopher Columbus gave this name to the island that is now St. Croix. (U.S. Virgin Islands).

Santería. Religious beliefs that combine Catholicism and ideas of African origin. (Cuba).

Santos. Carved religious figurines found in almost every home. A common folk art. (Puerto Rico).

Santur. A traditional stringed instrument. (Iran).

Sanusis. An Islamic religious and political group that fought Ottoman and Italian invasions into Libya and North Africa. (Libya).

Sanza. A thumb piano; a traditional instrument. (Central African Republic).

Sa-pi-bi-la? "Have you eaten?" A common Burmese greeting. (Myanmar).

Sarangi. A traditional four-stringed instrument used to accompany singing and dancing. (Nepal).

Sarape. A wool poncho that a man may wear over his shirt and pants when it is cold. (Mexico).

Saree(s). (Bangladesh, India, Mauritius, Sri Lanka). *See* **Sari.**

Sari. A long piece of cloth that is wrapped around the body in a special way. Worn by women. (Fiji, Nepal, Singapore, South Africa, Suriname).

Sari-saris. Small convenience stores run out of homes. (Philippines).

Sarma. Cabbage leaves stuffed with minced meat and rice. (Macedonia, Serbia and Montenegro).

Sarmale. Minced meat with rice, rolled in pickled cabbage or grapevine leaves. (Romania).

Sarmi. A pepper or cabbage stuffed with pork and rice. (Bulgaria).

Sarod. A traditional northern Indian instrument. (India).

Saron demung. A traditional Indonesian instrument similar to a xylophone. (Indonesia).

Sarong. A long cloth wrapped around the waist. Worn by both men and women, depending on the country. (Cambodia, Indonesia, Senegal, Sri Lanka, Suriname, Thailand).

Sarong soet. A large rectangular piece of colored cloth worn by men that is wrapped around the hips like a kilt down to the ankles. (Cambodia).

Sarung. A long piece of cloth worn about the waist by Muslim men when they attend mosque on Fridays. (Malaysia).

Sărut mâna. "Kiss your hand." A Romanian phrase men use to greet women as a sign of respect. (Romania).

Sarut mâna. "I kiss your hand." A Romanian phrase men use to greet women. (Moldova).

Sărut mâna pentru masă. "Kiss your hand for the meal." A Romanian phrase used to thank the person who cooked and served the meal. (Romania).

Sasa. A group dance involving slapping, clapping, and stylized hand, arm, and leg movements. (American Samoa).

Sashimi. Raw fish; a popular dish. (Japan, Micronesia).

Sat. "Chastity." The most important virtue a woman can bring to marriage. (Nepal).

Sata. A wraparound cloth worn by women. The term is used in the north. (Togo). *Also called* **Bsawao.** *See also* **Avo tata.**

Satay. Barbecued pork or chicken on a stick with peanut sauce. (Malaysia, Thailand).

Satsivi. Fried chicken or turkey soaked in walnut sauce and spices. (Georgia).

Satversme. The Latvian constitution. (Latvia).

Saucisse. French term for "grilled sausage." (Switzerland).

Saum. Fasting during **Ramadan**. One of the Five Pillars of Islam. (Iran, Malaysia). *See also* **Hajj, Salat, Shahada, Zakat.**

Sausage roll. A sausage wrapped in pastry. (New Zealand).

Sawasdee ka. "Hello" or "Good-bye." A greeting used by women in conjunction with the **Wai**. (Thailand).

Sawasdee kraab. "Hello" or "Good-bye." A greeting used by men in conjunction with the **Wai**. (Thailand).

Sawubona. "I see you." A common greeting. (South Africa, Swaziland).

Saya. A traditional Bolivian dance. (Bolivia).

Sayazhai. Kazak word for a "summer cottage." (Kazakstan).

Sayedaty. "Mrs." An Arabic title used with the last name. (Syria).

Sayedy. "Mr." An Arabic title used with the last name. (Syria).

Sayyed. "Mr." An Arabic title used with the last name. (West Bank and Gaza).

Sayyedeh. "Mrs." An Arabic title used with the last name. (West Bank and Gaza).

Saz. A type of long-necked lute. A common folk instrument. (Turkey).

Sbah al Kheir. (Morocco). *See* **Sabah al-Khair.**

S Bohom. "God be with you." A traditional Slovak greeting. (Slovakia).

School-leaving. Graduation. (Montserrat).

Schrebergarten. Small garden plots located in or near the city. Urban dwellers own or rent them. (Germany).

Schweizerdeutsch. Swiss German; it is the dialect used for everyday conversation in Switzerland. It can be hard for other German speakers to understand. (Switzerland).

Schwiizertütsch. The Swiss German dialect that is similar to the Alemannic dialect spoken in Liechtenstein. (Liechtenstein).

Schwinger. Traditional wrestling that is similar to Graeco-Roman wrestling but does not have weight classifications. (Switzerland).

Sciences. An education track that focuses on math and sciences. (Tunisia).

Scramble. A bag of small change that is scattered by the best man onto the pavement or road after the bride and groom have driven away. (Scotland). *Also called* **Pour-out.**

Sea bathe. Playing in shallow water. (Antigua and Barbuda).

Seanad. The Irish Senate. (Ireland).

Secretos en reunión es mala educación. "It is bad manners to tell secrets in gatherings." A common Spanish expression used if not everyone is included in mealtime conversation. (Peru).

Glossary of Cultural Terms

Séga. A Mauritian dance that integrates Creole texts and modern percussion instruments with the rhythm of African, Caribbean, and Latin American pop music. Traditional accompanying instruments are the triangle, the **Coco**, and the **Ravane**. (Mauritius).

Seghanapet. Toastmaster. Proposes toasts when guests are present. (Armenia). *Also called* **Tamada.**

Seimas. The Lithuanian Parliament. (Lithuania).

Sejm. The lower house of the Polish parliament. (Poland). *Also called* **Diet.**

Seke. "Hello." A common Temne greeting. (Sierra Leone).

Seker Bayramı. "Sugar holiday." A three-day holiday in which people eat sweets to celebrate the end of **Ramazan**. (Turkey).

Seke-seke. A percussion instrument used in Amerindian music. Consists of a closed piece of metal pipe with seeds or gravel, shaken to the rhythm. (Suriname).

Sekona singabusalina. "I am fine." A typical Ndebele response to **Siyabonga linjani?** (Hello, how are you?). (Zimbabwe).

Sœl. (Iceland). *See* **Sœll.**

Selam. "Salute." A Turkish greeting used by youth. (Turkey).

Selamat malam. "Good evening." A Malay greeting. (Singapore).

Selamat pagi. "Good morning." A typical Malay greeting. (Malaysia, Singapore).

Selamat petang. "Good afternoon." A Malay greeting. (Singapore).

Selamat sejahtera ke atas anda. "I wish you peace and tranquility." A formal Malay greeting. (Singapore).

Seljanka. A meat soup with pickles, onions, and olives. (Estonia).

Sœll. "Happy" or "glad." An Icelandic greeting. Masculine *Sœll*, feminine *Sœl*. (Iceland).

Selsko meso. A meat and mushroom dish. (Macedonia).

Selteh. Spicy stew made with fenugreek. (Yemen).

Semana de Turismo. Tourism Week. The week preceding Easter when people travel throughout the country and participate in a variety of local festivals. (Uruguay).

Semana Santa. Holy Week. Celebrated the week before Easter, an important time for family gatherings. (Costa Rica, Dominican Republic, El Salvador, Honduras, Mexico, Paraguay, Venezuela).

Semba. A popular musical style. (Angola).

Senat. The upper house of the Polish legislature. (Poland).

Sendero Luminoso. "Shining Path." A violent Maoist group that used guerrilla warfare to try to overthrow the government during the 1980s and 1990s. As many as 70,000 Peruvians have died in the battles between the government and the rebels. (Peru).

Senedd. The 60-member Welsh Assembly. (Wales).

Senhor. "Mr." A Portuguese title used with the surname. (Angola, Brazil, Cape Verde, Mozambique).

Senhora. "Mrs." A Portuguese title used with the surname. (Angola, Brazil, Cape Verde, Mozambique).

Señor. "Mr." A title used with the last name. Used in Spanish-speaking countries..

Señora. "Mrs." A title used with the last name. Used in Spanish-speaking countries..

Señorita. "Miss" or "young woman." A title used with the last name. Used in Spanish-speaking countries..

Sepaktakraw. A traditional competitive team sport played with a rattan ball. (Malaysia).

Sepo. The wedding custom of a dowry for the bride. (Kyrgyzstan).

Seqer. A women's party before a wedding. The bride's body hair is "waxed" off with a sugar, water, and lemon paste prior to applying designs of henna dye. (Tunisia).

Serranos. People from highland areas, said to be more formal, conservative, and reserved. (Ecuador). *See also* **Costeños.**

Servus. (1) "Hello." A casual greeting. (Austria, Romania, Slovakia). (2) "I am here to serve you." Latin word that is the root of the Hungarian terms **Szervusz** and **Szia**. (Hungary).

Sette Giugno. A public holiday commemorating an uprising against the British. Observed 7 June. (Malta).

Seu. A Portuguese title for men used with the first name in less formal situations. (Brazil).

Sevdalinka. Love songs. (Bosnia and Herzegovina).

Sevdidzan. Soft cake. A Bosniac dessert. (Bosnia and Herzegovina).

Seytesootiun. "See you later." A common Armenian parting phrase between friends. (Armenia).

Shaabi. A working-class, socially-minded form of urban Egyptian pop music with roots in folk music and dance. (Egypt). *See also* **Al-jil.**

Shabbat. Hebrew word for "Sabbath." (Israel).

Shabeen. An informal neighborhood bar. (Namibia).

Shab-i-Barat. A Muslim holiday. A special night to ask for blessings. (Bangladesh).

Shahada. The act of professing that there is no god but **Allah**. One of the Five Pillars of Islam. (Iran, Malaysia, Saudi Arabia). *See also* **Hajj, Salat, Saum, Zakat.**

Shah Namah. "Book of the Kings." The first great literary work in Dari; completed in A.D. 1010 by Firdausi. (Afghanistan).

Shaikh. An Arabic title used to greet men that are clergy or members of the royal family. (Bahrain, United Arab Emirates).

Shaikha. [NOTE: Spelling varies because it is a transliteration of Arabic.] A title used to greet women who are members of the royal family. (Bahrain).

Shaikhah. (United Arab Emirates). *See* **Shaikha.**

Shailah. A rectangular scarf that covers the head. Worn by women. (Qatar, United Arab Emirates).

Shak Barak? "How are you?" A common Arabic greeting. (Qatar).

Shalom. "Peace." A common Hebrew greeting and parting phrase. (Israel).

Shalwar. A pair of loose-fitting pants. (Pakistan). *See also* **Shalwar qameez.**

Shalwar qameez. An outfit, typically made of cotton, that consists of the **Shalwar** (a pair of loose-fitting pants) and the **Qameez** (a long tunic). Styles differ for men and women. (Pakistan).

Shamagh. A scarf worn by men. (Oman).

Sham el-Nasseem. A holiday celebrated at the beginning of spring. (Egypt).

Shamija. A scarf-like head covering. (Macedonia).

Shapka. A Russian fur hat worn in winter. (Kyrgyzstan, Russia). *See also* **Tumak, Ushanka.**

Sharba libiya. Meaning "Libyan soup," it is a dish made of lamb and tomato stock, orzo pasta, chickpeas, cilantro, lemon, mint, and curry. (Libya).

Shared accommodations. Nursing homes. (Northern Ireland).

Glossary of Cultural Terms

Shari'a. Islamic law. (Afghanistan, Bahrain, Kuwait, Nigeria, Pakistan, Qatar, Saudi Arabia, Somalia, Sudan, Syria, United Arab Emirates, Yemen).

Sharshaf. A black cloak worn by women over their clothes to hide their body and hair. (Yemen).

Shashlik. Skewered meat. (Tajikistan).

Shavu'ot. Pentecost. A Jewish holiday. (Israel).

Shawarma. Pita bread filled with spit-roasted meat and salad. (Israel).

Shawarma(s). A sandwich made with marinated chicken or beef with dressing and salad and wrapped in a thin dough wafer. The sandwich is wrapped in paper and peeled like a banana. (Kuwait, Qatar).

Shea butter. A fruit extract used in beauty products and foods. (Togo).

Shebka. Wedding jewels presented by the groom to the bride. They usually include gold and diamond earrings, a bracelet, and necklace. (Kuwait).

Sheik. [NOTE: Spelling varies because it is a transliteration of Arabic.] A tribal leader. (Yemen).

Sheikh. (Oman). *See* **Sheik.**

Shendet! "Stay healthy!" A common Albanian parting phrase. (Albania).

Sherut. Taxis that operate on fixed routes. (Israel).

Shetha tongni. Sharing jokes, stories, and local gossip. (Bhutan).

Sh'hili. South wind. (Tunisia). *Also called* **Sirocco.**

Shi. Soup with sour cabbage. (Russia).

Shi'a. (Pakistan, Syria). *See* **Shi'i.**

Shih. Municipalities. (Taiwan).

Shi'i. Shi'ite Muslims. Shi'ism reveres Muhammad's daughter, Fatima, her husband, Ali, their sons, Hassan and Hussein, and their descendants, called **Imams**. (Afghanistan, Azerbaijan, Bahrain, Iran, Iraq, Kuwait, Lebanon, Oman, Qatar, United Arab Emirates).

Shikamoo. "Is anyone there?" A typical Kiswahili greeting when approaching someone's home. The response is **Karibu**. (Tanzania).

Shinkansen. Bullet trains that provide rapid transportation between major Japanese cities. (Japan).

Shinty. A Celtic sport similar to hockey. (Scotland).

Shi-par-say-taw. "Let it be." A saying that characterizes people's laid-back approach to problems. (Myanmar).

Shir. An open deliberation forum of extended families or clan groups. Decisions are made by consensus. A *shir* can declare war or peace, settle family disputes, and so on. (Somalia).

Shirdeg. Richly ornamented felt carpets. (Mongolia).

Shiromani. Traditional cloth worn by Anjouan women over clothes and pulled up over their heads. (Comoros).

Shirt-jacket. (Antigua and Barbuda, Montserrat). *See* **Shirt-jac(s).**

Shirt-jac(s). A square-cut cotton shirt. (Barbados, Grenada, Guyana, Saint Kitts and Nevis, Saint Lucia).

Shirwani. A knee-length coat. Part of a groom's wedding attire. (Bangladesh). *See also* **Nagra, Pagri.**

Shishcheta. A pork shish kebab. (Bulgaria).

Shiva. The destroyer. One of three supreme gods of Hinduism. (Nepal). *See also* **Brahma, Vishnu.**

Shkubbah. A traditional card game. (Tunisia).

Shlonach. "How are you?" An Arabic greeting used to address women. (Qatar).

Shlonak. "How are you?" An Arabic greeting used to address men. (Qatar).

Shodo. Calligraphy. (Japan).

Shoguns. Japanese feudal lords who held political control from the 12th century until the late 19th century. (Japan).

Shok. "Comrade." A title used before 1990 with the last name in introductions. (Albania).

Shopska salata. A salad made with cucumbers, tomatoes, and **Cirene**. (Bulgaria).

Showa. "Enlightened peace." The name of Emperor Hirohito's reign, which was from 1926 to 1989. (Japan).

Show days. Festivals featuring athletics and handicraft displays. (Niue).

Shqip. The Albanian language, which is an Indo-European language directly descended from Illyrian. (Albania).

Shreemati. A title used with the last name for married women to show respect. (India).

Shudra(s). The lowest class in the Brahmin classification philosophy (not to be confused with the caste system). Composed of workers. Also used to refer to the people of the class. (India, Nepal). *See also* **Brahmin(s), Chaturvarna Vyavasta, Kshatriya, Vaishya.**

Shu'ra. A sauce made from chopped onions and spices marinated in warm cooking oil. (Bangladesh).

Shura. A governing council. (Afghanistan, Bahrain, Egypt).

Shuro. A typical meal of garbanzo bean flour and spices. (Eritrea).

Siapo. Traditional fabric made from bark that has been repeatedly pounded with a mallet. The fabric is printed with geometric patterns in dye made from clay and plants. (American Samoa, Samoa).

Sibhaca. A dance performed by young men in which they stamp their feet to the rhythm of music and chants. (Swaziland).

Si Dios quiere. "God willing." A Spanish phrase that expresses one's faith. (Colombia, Dominican Republic, Honduras, Nicaragua).

Siesta(s). Afternoon rest. Some businesses close for 1 to 3 hours; workers often go home to eat their lunch and relax. (Chile, Honduras, Mexico, Nicaragua, Paraguay, Peru, Spain, Uruguay).

Sièste. An afternoon break. Government offices and private stores close to escape from the afternoon heat. (Niger).

Sigheh. A temporary marriage that can last between a few days and 99 years. A woman marrying in this arrangement and any children born in the marriage do not have the same rights and privileges as conventional wives and children, although they are legitimate. (Iran).

Sijambo. "I'm fine." A common Swahili response to the greeting **Hujambo**. (Tanzania).

Si jeni? "How are you?" A common Albanian greeting. (Albania).

Sijo. An ancient poetic form. Themes include Confucian principles, love, nature, and politics. (South Korea).

Si keni kaluar? "How are you doing?" A common Albanian greeting. (Albania).

Silat. A style of martial arts. (Malaysia).

Silor. Mini-cab. A form of local transportation. (Thailand).

Silvestrovanje. New Year's Eve. (Slovenia).

S'il vous plaît. "Please." A valued French phrase. (France).

Sim. The Dzongkha word for "younger sister." (Bhutan).

Glossary of Cultural Terms

Sina. The informal pronoun "you." It is used with friends and relatives. (Estonia). *See also* **Teie.**

Sinappi. Mustard. (Finland).

Sing'anga. Traditional healers. (Malawi).

Singlish. A colloquial dialect that combines a modified English with elements of Chinese, Malay, and Tamil. (Singapore).

Sing-Sing. An intervillage ceremony of the highlands that involves thousands of costumed dancers. (Papua New Guinea).

Sinterklaas. St. Nicholas. He dresses like a Catholic bishop, rides a white horse, and leaves gifts in children's shoes. (Netherlands).

Sira beyi. Dyula phrase that hosts use to "give the road" to guests after they accompany each other to the road at the end of a visit. (Ivory Coast).

Sirenje. Feta cheese. (Macedonia).

Sirnica. Cheese pie. (Bosnia and Herzegovina).

Sirocco. A hot, sandy, south wind. (Algeria). *Also called* **Sh'hili.**

Sisi. A social title added to a girl's name to show respect. (Swaziland).

Sister. A term used to address females of the same age, regardless of relationship. (Ghana, Sierra Leone).

Sitar. A traditional stringed instrument. (India, Sri Lanka, Suriname, Tunisia).

Siva. A modern dance in which young women dance and sing as young men play the guitar and sing. (Tuvalu).

Siyabonga linjani? "Hello, how are you?" A Ndebele greeting. (Zimbabwe).

Sjenički sir. A soft and fatty cheese often crumbled on **Sopska**. (Serbia and Montenegro).

Sjómannadagurinn. Fisherman's Day. A holiday observed on the first Sunday in June. (Iceland).

Skål. A toast. (Sweden).

Skalmeje. The folk clarinet; a native instrument. (Denmark).

Skara. Grilled meat. (Bulgaria).

Skir ai. Rolling and blinking the eyes. A gesture that expresses disapproval. (Suriname).

Skraja da e. "Do not let evil hear." A Turkish phrase said by older rural women to ward off bad luck. (Macedonia). *See also* **Loshoto da ne chue.**

Skratsji. A percussion instrument consisting of a low wooden bench played with sticks. (Suriname).

Skupstina. The Parliamentary Assembly. (Bosnia and Herzegovina).

Skyr. A popular dish similar to yogurt. (Iceland).

Slametan. A ritual feast, typically held for births, circumcisions, marriages, and funerals. A component of **Agama Djawa**, the feast strengthens or repairs harmony between the spirits and the living. (Suriname). *See also* **Sadjèn.**

Slan. Literally, "safe." An Irish term used for "good-bye." (Ireland).

Slan agus Beannacht. A formal Irish parting phrase meaning "safe and blessed." (Ireland).

Slanina. Home-smoked bacon. (Slovakia).

Slendang. A shoulder drape worn with a **Sarong** and **Klambi koeroeng**. (Suriname).

Slivovica. Plum liquor. (Slovakia).

Smalahode. Sheep's head; a Norwegian specialty. (Norway).

Smock. A long tunic worn by men in northern Ghana. Made of wide strips of rough cotton cloth that are sewn together. (Ghana).

Smörgåsar. Open-faced sandwiches. (Sweden).

Smörgåsbord. A lavish buffet eaten on holidays or for special occasions. (Finland, Sweden).

Smørrebrød. Traditional open-faced sandwiches. (Denmark).

Snackette(s). A stand that sells finger food and drinks. (Guyana).

Snags. Sausages. (Australia).

Snedanne. Belarusian word for "breakfast." (Belarus).

Snidanok. The Ukrainian word for "breakfast." (Ukraine).

Snooker. A billiards game. (England).

Soba. (1) A type of noodles. (Japan). (2) A village chief. (Angola).

Sobranie. A term that may refer to Macedonia's national parliament or a municipality parliament. (Macedonia).

Soca. A mixture of soul music from the United States and calypso music. (Antigua and Barbuda, Bahamas, Barbados, Belize, Costa Rica, Grenada, Jamaica, Montserrat, Saint Kitts and Nevis, Saint Lucia, Saint Vincent and the Grenadines, U.S. Virgin Islands).

Sofra. A low table. Traditionally, people sit around the table on the floor. (Albania).

Sogetrag. An intercity bus service. (Guinea).

Sogi. A gesture used for greeting in which relatives press their faces to the other's cheek and sniff deeply. (Tuvalu).

Soju. A common alcoholic drink served with meals. (South Korea).

Sok sebai. A common Khmer greeting. (Cambodia).

Solevu. A great feast that accompanies wedding ceremonies. (Fiji).

Solitaire. A game and a decoration that consist of a polished round wooden support laden with semiprecious stones in carved holes. (Madagascar).

Soljanka. Russian soup. (Latvia).

Som. Kyrgyzstan and Uzbekistan's national currencies. (Kyrgyzstan, Uzbekistan).

Somogo do? "How is your family?" A common Dioula greeting. (Burkina Faso).

Somoni. Tajikistan's national currency. (Tajikistan).

Somsa. Fried dough pockets stuffed with meat and onions. (Turkmenistan).

Son. A genre of music that combines the sound of maracas, guitars, bongos, trumpets, and the **Tres**. (Cuba).

Songkhran. The Thai New Year. People throw buckets of water on each other and hold other festivities to celebrate. (Thailand).

Songkok. A black velvet cap worn by Muslim men on Fridays. (Malaysia).

Songlines. Aboriginal musical stories that focus on creation legends of the **Dream time**. (Australia).

Songo. A traditional strategy game played on a wooden board with pebbles or seeds. (Gabon).

Sonin yu baina? "What's new?" A casual Mongol greeting. (Mongolia).

Soon come. A common phrase that expresses a casual approach to life and a relaxed view of time. (Antigua and Barbuda, Jamaica).

Sopa de Maní. Peanut soup. (Bolivia).

Glossary of Cultural Terms

Sopaipillas. Deep-fried pumpkin dough sprinkled with sugar. (Chile).

Sopa Paraguaya. Cornbread baked with cheese, onions, and sometimes meat. (Paraguay).

Sop bening. Vegetable soup. (Indonesia).

Sopilka. A flute. (Ukraine).

Soppa ta' l-armla. "Widow's broth"; a common soup. (Malta).

Sopropo. Bitter melon. A popular tropical vegetable. (Suriname).

Sopska. A Greek-like salad. (Serbia and Montenegro).

Sorabe. A Malagasy script with Arabic origins used prior to introduction of the Latin alphabet. (Madagascar).

Sore. The time period just before evening when temperatures cool and work is finished. People bathe and dress in traditional attire to relax or visit. (Indonesia).

Sorpa. A broth used to make **Besbarmak**. (Kazakstan).

Sorpresas. Small egg-shaped cases that display miniature scenes and figures of everyday life. Literally, "surprises." (El Salvador).

Sorrel. A tart, acidic drink made from the petals of the sorrel plant. (Grenada, Saint Kitts and Nevis).

Sorullos. A locally prepared variety of **Frituras** made of corn flour. (Puerto Rico).

Soukous. A style of music that combines African and Caribbean influences. Played with a high-pitched guitar. (Congo, Equatorial Guinea, Togo).

Souk(s). An open-air market. (Egypt, Kuwait, Morocco, Oman, Saudi Arabia, Tunisia).

Souq. (Chad). *See* **Souk(s)**.

Souse. Pickled pigs' feet. (Antigua and Barbuda, Montserrat, Saint Kitts and Nevis).

Souses. Boiled meat in a seasoned broth. (Grenada).

Souvlaki. A shish kebab with meat (pork or lamb), mushrooms, and vegetables. (Greece).

Soviet Respubliki. Council of the Republic. Part of the Belarus National Assembly. (Belarus). *See also* **Natsionalnoye Sobranie**.

Spadar. "Mr." A formal Belarusian title used with the last name. (Belarus).

Spadarynya. "Mrs." A formal Belarusian title used with the last name. (Belarus).

Spanglish. An informal dialect in which English words are mixed with spoken Spanish. (Puerto Rico).

Spanish rice. A rice dish cooked with vegetables. (Trinidad and Tobago).

Sparks. Intelligent and knowledgeable; may be a nickname for a highly educated man. (Saint Lucia).

Spaza. Small retail businesses run from suburban homes. *Spaza* shops sell a variety of items to neighborhood residents. (South Africa).

Spaziergang. Taking a walk; a popular Austrian pastime. (Austria).

Speaking Bajan. An English-based creole. (Barbados). *Also called* **Broken English**.

Speaking dialect. (Montserrat). *See* **Speaking Montserratian**.

Speaking Montserratian. A form of English mixed with elements of Irish brogue and various African tongues. (Montserrat).

Spektakel. Dutch creole word meaning "noise" or "din." (U.S. Virgin Islands). *See also* **What a pistarkel**.

Spetakel. Danish word meaning "noise" or "din." (U.S. Virgin Islands). *See also* **What a pistarkel**.

Spicy curry. A favorite dinner. (Guyana).

Spot on. "Right on." (Australia).

Sranan bubbling. A variant of reggae music. (Suriname).

Srange. A wedding custom in which the bride is detained by young men in her village until the groom ransoms her. (Slovenia).

Srednja škola. Optional middle school that includes grades 9 to 12. (Serbia and Montenegro).

Sredno uciliste. Vocational high school. (Macedonia).

Ssali kaleve. Warm, freshly cut toddy; often served with breakfast. (Tuvalu).

Ssrom. A unique form of wrestling in which contestants hold on to pieces of cloth tied around their opponent's legs during their match. (South Korea).

Sta ima? "What's up?" An informal Serbo-Croatian phrase that follows the greeting **Zdravo** (Hello). (Bosnia and Herzegovina).

Stalls. Booths. Vendors sell items from outdoor *stalls* during market days. (Wales).

Stamping drum(s). A bamboo tube covered on one end with cloth. It produces a tone when beat rhythmically on the ground. (Solomon Islands).

Standard(s). School levels or grades. (Lesotho).

Stara Nova Godina. Literally means "Old New Year's." Celebrated on 14 January, marked according to the Julian calendar still used by the Macedonian Orthodox Church. (Macedonia).

State schools. A British idiom for "public schools." (England). *See also* **Public schools**.

Steel drums. Lids of oil drums that have been hammered into the shape of an inverted turtle shell. (Trinidad and Tobago).

Stekt falukorv med senap och potatis. Fried slices of thick German sausage with mustard and boiled or fried potatoes. (Sweden).

Steupsing. A tooth-sucking noise used to display disgust, frustration, or disapproval. (Trinidad and Tobago).

Stewed chicken. Chicken simmered in carmelized sugar and oil. (Trinidad and Tobago).

Stewps. To suck air through the teeth. Expresses exasperation. (Saint Vincent and the Grenadines).

Stick fighting. A traditional Sudanese sport. (Sudan).

Stolovii. Workplace canteens. (Turkmenistan).

Stori. To talk. (Papua New Guinea, Solomon Islands).

Storting. The Norwegian Parliament. (Norway). *See also* **Lagting, Odelsting**.

Stovies. A dish of roast beef, onions, and potatoes. (Scotland).

Street blockoramas. Open-air parties. (Montserrat).

Street food. Snacks such as bread and margarine, fried potatoes, fried plantains, fruit, etc. (Sierra Leone).

Strina. An aunt who is the father's brother's wife. (Croatia). *See also* **Tetka, Ujna**.

Strippenkaart. A universal ticket for public transportation. (Netherlands).

Stroop. A sweet drink available in many flavors. (Suriname).

Stroopwafels. Syrup waffles; a favorite snack. (Netherlands).

Strukli. A salt or sweet-cheese dumpling. (Croatia).

Stupa. A Buddhist shrine. (Nepal).

Sua/Dona. A Portuguese title for women. Used with the first name in less formal situations. (Brazil).

Glossary of Cultural Terms

Sua phrara-chathan. A high-necked jacket worn by a groom. (Thailand).

Succot. [NOTE: The Jewish calendar is based on the lunar standard.] "Tabernacles." A weeklong festival that begins on the 15th of the month **Tishrei**. (Israel).

Sucking the teeth. A gesture in which individuals purse their lips and make a sound by sucking air through their teeth. Expresses disgust or anger. (Saint Kitts and Nevis).

Suck teeth. (Bahamas). *See* **Sucking the teeth**.

Sucre. Ecuador's former national currency. (Ecuador).

Su Diev. "Go with God." A common Lithuanian greeting. (Lithuania).

Sudzuka. A sausage. (Bosnia and Herzegovina).

Sujukh. Minced beef with greens and spices. (Armenia).

Sukuma wiki. Collard greens. (Kenya).

Sukupira. The main open-air market; located in Praia. (Cape Verde).

Sula. Juice. (Latvia).

Sült. Head cheese. (Estonia).

Sulu. An article of clothing consisting of colorful, medium-to-long wraparound cloth. (Fiji, Tuvalu).

Sulu vakataga. A tailored **Sulu** worn with a short-sleeved shirt and sometimes a tie. Worn by businessmen, clergy, and civil servants. (Fiji). *Also called* **Pocket sulu.**

Sulu vaka toga. (Fiji). *See* **Sulu**.

Summo lay? "How are your people?" A common Mandinka greeting. (Gambia).

Supakanja. Okra soup. (Gambia).

Supermercado. The Spanish word for "supermarket." (El Salvador).

Supper. A snack before bedtime. (Australia).

Suq. (Yemen). *See* **Souk(s)**.

Surnai. A traditional Afghan instrument similar to a clarinet. (Afghanistan).

Suru. A raised platform with a table in the center and mats for sitting. (Uzbekistan).

Suruhana(s). Old women who provide folk medicine. *Suruhanas* mix local leaves, roots, and bark to prepare medicines. (Guam).

Surular. Platforms located in the courtyard of family compounds that are used to sleep and eat on during the summer. (Uzbekistan).

Survachka. A small decorated stick. On New Year's Day, children go door-to-door carrying the *survachka*, with which they tap people on the back in exchange for candy and money. (Bulgaria).

Susu mai. "Welcome" or "Come in." A respectful Samoan greeting. (American Samoa, Samoa).

Suwa. A beer. (Eritrea).

Svadva. A wedding reception. Involves food, music, and dancing. (Macedonia).

Sveika. "How are you?" A friendly Lithuanian greeting used when addressing a woman. (Lithuania).

Sveikas. "How are you?" A friendly Lithuanian greeting used when addressing a man. (Lithuania).

Sveiki. "How are you?" A friendly Lithuanian greeting used when addressing a group or in a formal situation. (Lithuania).

Sweet. A term used to refer to dessert. (Wales). *Also called* **Pudding(s).**

Sweethearting. A practice in which a man fathers children with multiple women. (Bahamas). *See also* **Outside children**.

Sylvester. Marks the beginning of the New Year's celebrations on 31 December with midnight fireworks and parties, followed by a public holiday on 1 January. (Germany).

Szervusz. "Hello." An informal Hungarian greeting. (Hungary). *See also* **Servus**.

Szia. "Hello." An informal Hungarian greeting. Also, a parting phrase. (Hungary). *See also* **Servus**.

Ta'ahine. "Miss." A Tongan title. (Tonga).

Taalofa! "Greetings!" A Tuvaluan greeting. (Tuvalu).

Ta'amu. A large, coarse root. (Samoa).

Taaniko. The Maori folk art of weaving flax to produce clothing with colorful geometric patterns. (New Zealand).

Taara. The name of a god Estonians worshiped prior to Christianity. (Estonia).

Tabang. Teahouses. (South Korea).

Tabaski. Feast of the Sacrifice. A Muslim holiday honoring Abraham's willingness to sacrifice his son. Celebrated in predominantly Muslim countries.. *Also called* **Eid al-Adha.**

Tabasky. (Mauritania). *See* **Tabaski**.

Tabbal. Drummer. (Iraq).

Tabboule. A popular salad made with parsley, minced onions, diced tomatoes, and other vegetables. (Lebanon).

Tabla. (1) Small different-sized hand drums. (India, Sudan). (2) Both a strategic board game and a card game. (Macedonia).

Tablados. Stages; used to perform Carnival theater productions. (Uruguay).

Tablah. A traditional drum. (Lebanon).

Tabots. Arks of the covenant. Many are found in Ethiopia's churches. (Ethiopia).

Tabouleh. (Syria). *See* **Tabboule**.

Tabuna. A round bread. *Tabuna* is also the name of the cylindrical clay oven in which the bread is baked. (Tunisia).

Tacos. Folded tortillas with meat or other filling. (Mexico).

Taekwondo. A martial art. (South Korea).

Tafadal. "Please come in." An expression of goodwill and welcome. (West Bank and Gaza).

Tafadhali. Swahili word for "please." (Congo, Tanzania).

Tafiti. A term describing traders who settled on Niue a century ago. (Niue).

Tagalog. A Pilipino dialect from Luzon. (Philippines).

Tahina. A sesame-seed paste. (Egypt).

Tahngdyr nahn. Flat bread. (Kyrgyzstan).

Tahteh. "Older sister." A Kazak term added to the end of a name to show respect to an older woman. (Kazakstan).

Tahyar. Embroidered skullcap. (Turkmenistan).

Tai chi. A martial art used for relaxation. (Vietnam).

Taijiquan. A traditional form of shadowboxing that provides exercise and therapy. (China, Singapore).

Taikpon. A round-necked jacket worn by Burmese men. Accompanies an **Eingyi** and a **Longyi**. (Myanmar).

Tai'mamahlao. "Having no shame." An ill-mannered person will be referred to as *tai'mamahlao*. This is a severe criticism. (Guam).

Taitah. Sour bread made of **Teff**, millet, or corn flour fermented in water. (Eritrea). *Also called* **Ingera.**

Taituuj. Fried banana pancakes. (Marshall Islands).

Tajine. A meat-and-vegetable stew. (Algeria, Morocco, Tunisia).

Tajub. A dance party at which Javanese families celebrate a marriage. (Suriname).

Tak. Danish word for "Thank you." (Denmark).

Glossary of Cultural Terms

Taka. Bangladesh's national currency. (Bangladesh).

Tak bhat. "To scoop rice." Because Buddhist monks cannot own anything, they receive their food from villagers who line up daily to *tak bhat*. (Thailand).

Take-away. Take-out. (Australia, England, Jamaica, Namibia, Scotland, Swaziland).

Tak for mad! "Thanks for the meal!" A Danish expression used to thank the hostess. (Denmark).

Takihi. Slices of taro and papaya wrapped in leaves and baked. (Niue).

Takk for maten. "Thank you for the food." A Norwegian phrase said before leaving the table at mealtime. (Norway).

Takk for sist! "Thanks for the last time!" A Norwegian greeting used when people have not seen each other for a while. (Norway).

Takro. A traditional sport in which players try to keep a wicker ball in the air without using their hands. (Thailand).

Tala. Samoa's national currency. (Samoa).

Talib. Arabic word for "student." (Afghanistan).

Taliban. "Seekers of knowledge." A group that gained control of Afghanistan in 1996 but were ousted during the U.S. war in Afghanistan (2001–2). (Afghanistan).

Talitali fiefia. "Welcome." A Tongan phrase used to greet visitors. (Tonga).

T'all. "Not at all." A phrase used in the Antiguan English dialect. (Antigua and Barbuda).

Tallarines. A pasta similar to spaghetti. (Uruguay).

Talofa lava. "Hello." A formal Samoan greeting. (American Samoa, Samoa).

Tamaaraa. A traditional feast common at holidays and other special occasions. (French Polynesia).

Tamada. Toastmaster. Proposes toasts when guests are present. (Armenia, Georgia).

Tamales. A cornmeal dough stuffed with a filling, wrapped in banana or plantain leaves, and then steamed. (Belize, Costa Rica, Mexico).

Tamalitos. Cornmeal dough wrapped in corn husks and steamed. (Guatemala).

Tambal. A stringed folk instrument played with small mallets. (Romania).

Tambora. A small drum. (Dominican Republic).

Tambores. Drums. (Uruguay).

Tamborito. Panama's national dance. (Panama).

Tamboura. An instrument similar to a harp, used to accompany singing. (United Arab Emirates).

Tambura. A stringed instrument. Used in the traditional music that accompanies folk dances. (Macedonia).

Tamburitza. A traditional instrument used to accompany the **Kolo**. (Croatia).

Tamil Eelam. An independent Tamil state. (Sri Lanka).

Ta'miyya. A traditional food prepared from fava beans. (Egypt).

Tamkharit. [NOTE: Muslim holidays are set according to the lunar calendar.] The Islamic New Year. Also, the day on which **Allah** determines people's destinies. (Senegal).

Tamr. Half-dried dates. (Bahrain). *See also* **Rottab**.

Tam-tam. Traditional dancing in which drummers play so that young women can dance in the moonlight. (Niger).

Tamure. A traditional style of dance that incorporates rapid hip and leg movements. (French Polynesia).

Tanboura. A dance performed at weddings and other social gatherings by women. (Kuwait).

Tandor. A clay oven. Used to prepare **non**. (Tajikistan).

Tanga. A small covered horse-drawn cart. (India).

Tangata'eiki. "Mr." A Tongan title. (Tonga).

Tangyertengi as. The Kazak word for "breakfast." (Kazakstan).

Tan kul. A sauce that is mixed with fish, meat, or beans for special occasions. (Chad).

Tannia. A type of root crop. (Montserrat).

Tannie. "Auntie." A term of respect used by Afrikaans-speaking people to address older females. (South Africa).

Tanoa. A special wooden bowl used to prepare **Yaqona**. (Fiji). *See also* **Bilo**.

Tante. "Aunt." A familial title used with strangers as well as family. (Guinea, Ivory Coast).

Tantie. A term children use to address adult women even if they are not related. Derived from the German word for "aunt." (Togo).

Taotaomo'na. Ghosts of Guam's ancient people. Chamorros believe they are revered protectors of the land and will cause near or actual harm to those who do not respect the land. (Guam).

Ta'ovala. A piece of fine material made from the leaves of the pandanus tree. Wrapped around the waist and tied with a coconut-fiber rope. Worn by men. (Tonga). *See also* **Kiekie, Tupenus**.

Tapa. Bark cloth. (Papua New Guinea, Tonga).

Tapado. A stew of beef, vegetables, and coconut milk. (Honduras).

Tapan. A type of drum. Used in the traditional music that accompanies folk dances. (Macedonia).

Tapas. An informal meal where guests take small bites from shared dishes. (Spain).

Tapochki. Slippers. (Kyrgyzstan).

Tap-tap(s). Brightly painted pickup trucks fitted with benches and covered tops. Travel fixed routes but not on a fixed schedule. (Haiti).

Tapu. Niuean word for "taboo." (Niue).

Taqya. Small, decoratively embroidered caps worn by older Kazak men and young boys. (Kazakstan).

Tar. A traditional stringed instrument. An ancestor to the guitar. (Azerbaijan, Iran).

Taraab. Music with Arab influence. (Kenya, Tanzania).

Tarator. A cold soup made of cucumbers, yogurt, garlic, dill, walnuts, and oil. (Bulgaria).

Tarawih. An evening prayer. (Algeria).

Tarha. A veil worn by women. (Sudan).

Tarranga. Hosting international guests. (Gambia).

Ta sain baina uu? "How do you do?" A standard Mongol greeting. (Mongolia).

Tasbe. Worry beads. (Afghanistan).

Tassa drums. Cone-shaped drums made of clay and goat skins. (Trinidad and Tobago).

Tass'bah Ala Kheer. "Good night." A standard Arabic greeting. (Tunisia).

Tata. "Father." A Xhosa term of address used for older men. (South Africa).

Tatami. Straw-mat floors. (Japan).

Tate. A term of address for older Owambo men. (Namibia). *See also* **Meme**.

Tatties. Potatoes. (Scotland).

Taualuga. A traditional dance performed by women. (American Samoa, Samoa).

Glossary of Cultural Terms

Taupou. The daughter of the village high chief. (Samoa).

Tautua. Loyal service. (American Samoa, Samoa). *See also* **Matai.**

Tavale. "Cousin." A term of address that may be used between male cousins. (Fiji).

Tave kosi. Meat or liver baked in yogurt. (Albania).

Tawiz. An amulet worn to protect against evil. (Afghanistan).

Tawjihi. An exam students must pass to attend a university. (Jordan, West Bank and Gaza).

Taxi brousse. A bush-taxi. (Central African Republic, Chad, Madagascar).

Taxi moto. A motorcycle taxi. (Rwanda).

Taxis de brousse. Bush-taxis. (Niger). *See also* **Autogare.**

Taxi velo. A bicycle taxi. (Rwanda).

Tchaa. A Kabyè term children use to address their fathers. (Togo).

Tcháu. "Good-bye." A common Portuguese parting word. (Angola, Brazil).

Tchisangua. A breakfast drink made of water, ground cornmeal, and sugar. (Angola).

Tchouk. Millet beer. (Togo).

Tea. (1) The evening meal. (Belize, Niue, Northern Ireland, Wales). (2) A term that refers to both the evening meal and afternoon refreshments. (Australia, England, New Zealand). (3) Any breakfast drink, such as tea, Milo, or Ovaltine. (Barbados). (4) Any hot drink. (Jamaica).

Tea kitchens. A type of restaurant that serves hot drinks, homemade cakes, and pastries in the afternoon. (Ireland).

Te ano. A traditional game similar to volleyball but with a heavier ball. (Tuvalu).

Teatime. Dinnertime. (Ireland).

Te bee. (Kiribati). *See* **Lavalava(s).**

Tebetei. A fur hat decorated with a foxtail. (Kyrgyzstan).

Teff. A native grain. (Eritrea, Ethiopia). *See also* **Ingera, Injera.**

Teie. The formal pronoun "you." It is used when meeting someone for the first time, with older people, and with those in authority. (Estonia). *See also* **Sina.**

Te ka. "The car." An English word that has been adapted to the Kiribati alphabet and pronunciation. (Kiribati).

Tekemets. Woven rugs made of felt or wool. (Kazakstan).

Télécarte. Phone cards. Used to operate pay phones. (France).

Telenovelas. Television soap operas. (Brazil, Mexico, Venezuela).

Televiisor. Estonian word for "television." (Estonia).

Telly. A television. (Australia).

Telpek. Hat made of sheep fur. (Turkmenistan).

Te maaka. Power or magic. A prevalent traditional belief prior to the introduction of Christianity. (Kiribati). *See also* **Nareau.**

Temir-komuz. A mouth harp. (Kyrgyzstan). *Also called* **Oz-komus.**

Tempos. Motorized three-wheel vehicles. (Nepal).

Ten. "Mr." A Kiribati title used in formal situations to show respect. (Kiribati).

Tena koe. A polite Maori way to say "Hello" to one person. (New Zealand).

Tena korua. A polite Maori way to say "Hello" to two people. (New Zealand).

Tena koutou. A polite Maori way to say "Hello" to many people. (New Zealand).

Tena Yistilin. "God give you health." A formal Amharic greeting. (Ethiopia).

Tenge. Kazakstan's national currency. (Kazakstan).

Tenor banjo. A ukulele. (Grenada).

Tenue de fonctionnaire. A civil servant suit, with shirt and pants made of the same cloth. (Burkina Faso).

Tere. "Hello." A common Estonian greeting. (Estonia).

Tere hommikust. "Good morning." A common Estonian greeting. (Estonia).

Tere Õhtust. "Good evening." A common Estonian greeting. (Estonia).

Tere päevast. "Good day." A common Estonian greeting. (Estonia).

Tereré. A mildly stimulating tea served cold. In Argentina it is often mixed with lemonade. (Argentina, Paraguay). *See also* **Mate.**

Terno. Worn by women, a full-length dress with a scoop neckline and butterfly sleeves. (Philippines).

Terra. Portuguese word for "homeland." (Portugal).

Tertulias. Social clubs that meet regularly in cafés to discuss ideas, events, and politics. (Spain).

Teshkoto Oro. A folk dance in which a series of steps depicts the fate of Macedonian fighters struggling against the Ottoman Turks. Females participate in some parts of this dance by portraying those who assisted the rebels in their battle. Dancers wear colorful embroidered costumes reflective of the clothing of past generations. (Macedonia).

Teši ma. "Pleased to meet you." A formal Slovak greeting. (Slovakia).

Těší mne. "Pleased to meet you." A Czech greeting. (Czech Republic).

Test match. An international cricket competition. (Montserrat).

Tet. The Vietnamese word for "holiday." (Vietnam).

Tetka. (1) An aunt that is a mother's or father's sister. (Croatia). *See also* **Strina, Ujna.** (2) "Auntie." An informal term of address used for older people who are not family. (Serbia and Montenegro).

Tet nguyen dan. [NOTE: Vietnamese holidays are set according to the lunar calendar.] The Lunar New Year. Celebrated in late January or early February. (Vietnam).

Teto. An Albanian word for "aunt," specifically the father's sister. (Albania). *Also called* **Halle.**

Tet thuong nguyen. [NOTE: Vietnamese holidays are set according to the lunar calendar.] A holiday celebrated on the first full moon of the new year. (Vietnam). *See also* **Tet trung nguyen.**

Tet trung nguyen. [NOTE: Vietnamese holidays are set according to the lunar calendar.] A day to pardon the sins of the dead by reading the **Vu lan.** Celebrated on the full moon of the seventh month. (Vietnam). *See also* **Tet thuong nguyen.**

Teuila Week. Tourism Week. Celebrated in September with a parade; sports competitions; music, dance, and cultural demonstrations; and other activities. Named after the national flower. (Samoa).

Teyze. "Aunt." A Turkish term of address for an older woman. (Turkey).

Teze. An Albanian word for "aunt," specifically the mother's sister. (Albania).

Thaan. A title added to the name of a person of high status. (Laos).

Glossary of Cultural Terms

Thadingyut. A light festival in September or October (determined according to the lunar calendar) at which people offer a candle or electric light to Buddha. (Myanmar).

Thai-Pongal. A Tamil holiday that marks the "return" of the sun after a month of evil days; the sun brings a new period of goodwill. (Sri Lanka).

Thanawi. Secondary school. (Saudi Arabia).

Thangka. Iconographic pictures painted on scrolls to depict Buddha, other great religious masters, and **Mandalas**. (Bhutan).

Thanh. The Vietnamese word for "fresh." (Vietnam).

Thanh nien. The Vietnamese word for "youth." A combination of the words **Thanh** "fresh" and **Nien** "years." (Vietnam).

The Festas Juninas. The June Festivals, which coincide with the feasts of St. John and St. Peter and are celebrated with local fair-type activities. (Brazil).

The food. A phrase that refers to lunch. (Saint Lucia).

The mainland. A phrase that refers to the island of Saint Vincent. (Saint Vincent and the Grenadines).

Thiebou dien. A meal of fish and rice. Popular at lunch. (Senegal).

Thingyan. A water festival marking the Buddhist New Year in April or May (determined according to the lunar calendar); Myanmar throw water on each other to clean away the dirt and sins of the previous year. (Myanmar).

Thit kho. Pork cooked in fish broth. (Vietnam).

Thobe. A long, light robe that reaches the ankles. Worn by men. (Bahrain, Qatar, Saudi Arabia).

Thu. A piece of cloth wrapped around the waist. Worn by men. (Micronesia).

Thukpa. Noodle soup. (Bhutan).

Ti. "You." An informal pronoun. (Bosnia and Herzegovina, Serbia and Montenegro, Slovenia).

Tia. "Aunt." A Portuguese term used to address older people. (Angola, Cape Verde, Guinea-Bissau, Mozambique).

Tiar. A title of respect for older men or officials; used with the last name. (Armenia).

Tiares. Leis made of white flowers. Worn by the bride and groom on their wedding day. (French Polynesia).

Ti boy. "Little boy." A creole phrase used by adults to address male children. (Saint Lucia).

Tibuta. A loose-fitting blouse gathered at the neck. Worn by women. (Kiribati).

Ticas. (Costa Rica). See **Ticos**.

-tico. A suffix used in Costa Rica to form a diminutive. (Costa Rica).

Ticos. A term used throughout Central America to refer to Costa Ricans. Comes from the habit of ending words and phrases with the suffix **-tico**. Masculine *ticos*, feminine *ticas*. The mixed company reference is *ticos*. (Costa Rica).

Tidak. The Indonesian word for "no." (Indonesia).

Tidnit. A four-stringed lute. (Mauritania).

Tienda. A small store. (El Salvador).

Tifaifai. A two-layer patchwork quilt. (French Polynesia).

Ti fi. "Little girl." A creole phrase used by adults to address female children. (Saint Lucia).

Tiga diga na. Peanut butter and tomato sauce. (Mali).

Tihar. [NOTE: Hindu holidays are based on the phases of the moon.] A holiday to worship the Goddess of Wealth. Celebrated for three days in October and/or November. Rows of light are displayed on every building. Married women go home to their parents, receive special treatment, ritually purify themselves, and pray for sons. (Nepal).

Tika. (1) A red dot made from vermilion powder. Worn by women on their foreheads to signify their husbands are alive. (Mauritius, Nepal). (2) Coconut oil often used on the hair and body. (Micronesia).

Tikin. A title of respect for married women; used with the last name. (Armenia).

Tikling. Herons. (Philippines). See also **Tinikling**.

Ti ma mai. "My little one." A creole phrase used by adults to address children. (Saint Lucia).

Timket. A holiday celebrating the baptism of Jesus. Celebrated in January. (Eritrea).

Timpana. Baked macaroni pastry. (Malta).

Tingatinga. A style of painting in which artists paint animals and natural scenes using tiny brightly colored dots. (Tanzania).

Tinikling. The Filipino national dance in which performers mimic the actions of the **Tikling** while dancing between bamboo poles. (Philippines).

Tinku. A traditional Bolivian dance. (Bolivia).

Tinyanga. A person who heals by faith or with traditional medicines. (Swaziland). See also **Batsakatsi, Sangoma**.

Tio. "Uncle." A Portuguese term used to address older people. (Angola, Cape Verde, Guinea-Bissau, Mozambique).

Tío/a. "Uncle" or "aunt." A Spanish term often used as a term of address. Masculine *tío*, feminine *tía*. (Panama).

Típico. Traditional Panamanian music. Played by a band composed of a singer and players with an accordion, a guitar, and percussion. Lyrics usually pertain to love and life. (Panama).

Tirgi. Open-air markets. (Latvia).

Tiripo kana makadiiwo. "We are fine if you are fine." A Shona response to the question **Makadii?** (How are you?). (Zimbabwe).

Tishrei. [NOTE: The Jewish year is based on a lunar calendar.] A Jewish month that corresponds to September/October. Begins with **Rosh Hashanah**. (Israel).

Tita. "Auntie." A Tagalog term used by young adults to address older adult female strangers. (Philippines).

-tito. A Spanish suffix used to form a diminutive. (Costa Rica). See also **-tico**.

Tito. "Uncle." A Tagalog term used by young adults to address older adult male strangers. (Philippines).

Tiurai. "July." *Tiurai* festivities begin with a cultural parade on 29 June. (French Polynesia).

Tjuri. A gesture that expresses dissatisfaction or annoyance; one points the lips and sucks in air between the teeth and lips while looking away. (Suriname).

Tô. A hard porridge made from sorghum, millet, or corn. (Burkina Faso, Ivory Coast, Mali).

To. Ewe word for "waters." Combined with **Godo**, meaning "other side," it forms the name of the lakeside village of Togodo, for which Togo is named. (Togo).

Tobaski. Feast of the Sacrifice. A Muslim holiday. (Gambia). See also **Eid-el-kabir**.

To didana! "See you later!" A Tajik parting phrase. (Tajikistan).

Todu maolek. "Everything is good." A Chamorro response to the greeting **Hafa tatatmanu hao?** (How are you?). (Guam).

Toere. An indigenous wooden drum often played together with the guitar and the **Pahu**. (French Polynesia).

Tofa soifua. "Good-bye." A Samoan parting phrase. (American Samoa, Samoa).

Glossary of Cultural Terms

Toi. The Kyrgyz word for "party." (Kyrgyzstan).

Tojiki. The Tajik language. (Tajikistan).

Tok Pisin. Melanesian Pidgin. (Papua New Guinea).

Tok Ples. "Talk place." A term that refers to local languages. (Papua New Guinea).

Tol. A child's first birthday. (South Korea).

Tolar. Slovenia's national currency. (Slovenia).

Tomorrow then. A common parting phrase. (Jamaica).

Tom yam. Lemon-flavored soup. Usually includes shrimp. (Thailand).

Tonadas. Chilean folk music that has been influential in political and social reform. (Chile).

Tonga na nyen? "How's it going?" Part of a common Sango greeting, it usually follows the phrase **Bara ala** or **Bala mo** (Greetings to you!). (Central African Republic).

Tonghak. An indigenous Korean religion. An eclectic combination of Buddhist, Confucian, and Christian beliefs. (North Korea). *Also called* **Ch'ondogyo.**

Tonir. A special oven dug in the ground. (Armenia).

Tontines. Savings societies in which members pool their capital, provide loans to each other, and sponsor social activities. (Cameroon). *Also called* **Njangis.**

Tonton. French term meaning "uncle." Ivorians may call each other by familial names to show respect and affection even if they are not related. (Ivory Coast).

Tontons macoutes. The secret police. Used by former Haitian president François Duvalier to kill his opponents and maintain rule from 1957 to 1971. (Haiti).

Too. A porridge made from cassava or rice powder. Eaten by the Malinké. Pronounced "TOE." (Guinea).

Toonai. Samoan word for "Sunday meal." (American Samoa, Samoa).

Tope. Palm wine. (Equatorial Guinea).

Topogios. Frozen fruit juice in plastic bags. (Honduras). *Also called* **Charamuscas.**

Toqi. A four-cornered or round hat. Worn by men. (Tajikistan). *Also called* **Tupi.**

Torge shygynyz. "Have the seat of honor." A Kazak phrase used to welcome guests in the home. (Kazakstan).

Torrejas. A type of food similar to French toast; served at Christmas. (Honduras).

Torta. Slovak word for "cake." (Slovakia).

Tortas. Hollow rolls stuffed with meat, cheese, or beans. (Mexico).

Tortilla. An omelette. (Cuba).

Tortilla española. An omelette with potatoes and onions. (Spain).

Tot siens. "Till we see each other again." An Afrikaans parting phrase. (South Africa).

Tour de France. An annual bicycle race. (France).

Toussaint. All Saints' Day. A holiday observed on 1 November. (French Polynesia, Gabon).

Tout va bien. French term meaning "All is well." It is a proper response to questions about one's general wellbeing. (Ivory Coast).

Tovarishch. "Friend" or "comrade." A Soviet-era title still used by some today. (Russia).

Town. An urban, commercial area. (Barbados).

Toy. A large wedding celebration with dancing and food. (Turkmenistan).

Tracht. A traditional costume. A woman's *tracht* includes a dress with a full skirt, an apron, and a headdress. Men's attire includes knee breeches, a straight loden jacket, and a flat black hat. The plural form is **Trachten**. (Liechtenstein).

Trachten. Traditional costumes. (Austria, Liechtenstein).

Trachtenanzug. A traditional suit worn by men. (Austria).

Trachtenjacken. A traditional woolen jacket worn by men. (Austria).

Trachtenkostüm. A traditional suit worn by women. (Austria).

Trade fair. A fair that sells a variety of goods and foods. Prices are lower than in stores and bargaining is acceptable. (Georgia).

Train à grande vitesse. The TGV. One of the world's fastest passenger trains. (France).

Träipen. Black pudding commonly eaten on Christmas Eve. (Luxembourg).

Tram. A streetcar. (Australia).

Tramping. Hiking. (New Zealand).

Tranquilidad. "Tranquility," an ultimate desire of Paraguayans. (Paraguay).

Transport. Private minivans that run regular routes. They leave from a central location when full and pick up or drop off passengers along the way. (Saint Lucia).

Tres. A small three-paired stringed instrument. (Cuba).

Trini. A language that uses English with French, Spanish, Hindi, and African influences and is often difficult for visitors to understand. (Trinidad and Tobago).

Trinkgeld. An extra tip. (Germany, Liechtenstein).

Tro-tro. A minibus used for short-distance travel. (Ghana).

Tsagaan Sar. "White Month" or "White Moon." The name of the Lunar New Year. Celebrated with family gatherings. (Mongolia).

Tsamaea hantle. "Go well." A parting phrase used by the person staying. The person leaving will say **Sala hantle**. (Lesotho).

Tsamaya sentle. "Go well." A phrase said to a person who is departing. (Botswana). *See also* **Sala sentle.**

Tsechhu. A three-day festival at which local monks perform legends from Buddhist scripture. (Bhutan).

Tsenatsil. A type of musical rattle. (Ethiopia).

Tshogdu. The Bhutanese National Assembly. (Bhutan).

Tshulnt. Traditional bean stew. (Israel).

Tsoho. "Old man." A term of address used for elderly men. (Niger).

Tsohoa. "Old woman." A term of address used for elderly women. (Niger).

Tsymbaly. A dulcimer. A traditional instrument. (Belarus).

Tsy misy. "Nothing." A Malagasy response to the question **Inona no vaovao?** (What is new?). (Madagascar).

Tú. "You." The informal singular Spanish pronoun. (Argentina, Chile, Dominican Republic, Paraguay).

Tuba. A type of fermented coconut juice. (Guam).

Tube. The London subway. (England).

Tudo bem? "How's it going?" A common Portuguese greeting used between urban youth. (Mozambique).

Tufahija. Boiled apple stuffed with nuts and sweet cream. (Bosnia and Herzegovina).

Tughrik. Mongolia's national currency. (Mongolia).

Tuisi. "Twist." *Tuisi* dances are popular fund-raising events enjoyed by young people. (Tuvalu).

Glossary of Cultural Terms

Tulafale. An orator. Speaks for a village chief during formal ceremonies and serves as the spokesperson for the entire village during inter-village disputes. (American Samoa).

Tulou. "Excuse me." A phrase used after a variety of offenses such as touching someone's head, walking between people having a conversation, reaching for something above someone's head, and so on. (Fiji, Tuvalu).

Tumak. A Russian fur hat worn in winter. (Kyrgyzstan). *See also* **Shapka.**

Tumba. Flies that lay eggs on wet clothing; if the eggs hatch, the flies can burrow into the skin. (Zimbabwe).

Tunban. Baggy trousers that are pulled tight with a drawstring. Worn with a **Perahan**. Typical clothing for Afghan men. (Afghanistan).

Tung. Albanian for "Hello" and "Good-bye." (Macedonia).

Tungjat jeta. "Have a long life." An Albanian greeting used by males from northern villages. (Albania).

Tuo zaafi. A thick porridge made of corn or millet. (Ghana).

Tupenus. Calf-length pieces of material wrapped around the waist. (Tonga). *See also* **Kiekie, Ta'ovala.**

Tupi. A four-cornered or round hat. Worn by men. (Tajikistan). *Also called* **Toqi.**

Tupuna. Respect for ancestors and their culture. (French Polynesia).

Turbofolk. Dance music popular among young people and prevalent in larger cities; a combination of folk tunes and rock instruments. (Serbia and Montenegro).

Turn the crack. A Scottish English idiom meaning "change the subject." (Scotland).

Turn their pots down. "To cook less." Typically during mango season, people cook less and eat large amounts of mangoes. (Antigua and Barbuda).

Turshi. Vegetables preserved in salt water. (Albania).

Turshija. Pickled vegetables. (Macedonia).

Tushuk. A velvet floor mat; used for sitting during meals. (Kyrgyzstan).

Tutaonana. "We will see each other." A common parting phrase. (Kenya).

Tuwo. The Hausa term for a thick, gelatinous millet paste. Usually eaten with a tomato or okra sauce. (Niger).

Twisting. Recreational dancing. (Kiribati).

Twoonie. A nickname for the Canadian two-dollar coin. (Canada).

Tyin Enmei. Falconry on horseback; a traditional equestrian sport. (Kyrgyzstan).

Tyski as. The Kazak word for the "midday meal." (Kazakstan).

Tze pau le ma. "Have you eaten?" A Chinese greeting. (Malaysia).

Tzuica. Plum brandy. (Romania).

U. "Uncle." A term used to address older men, regardless of relationship. (Myanmar).

Ubugali. A thick, doughy paste made from corn, sorghum, or cassava flour. (Rwanda).

Udon. A type of noodles. (Japan).

Ufi. Yams. (Samoa).

Uga. Coconut crab. (Niue).

Ugali. A stiff dough made from cassava, corn, millet, or sorghum. (Kenya, Tanzania).

Uha. Fish soup. (Belarus).

Uhn-uhn. Said while one nods to indicate "yes." (Madagascar). *See also* **Ahn-ahn-ahn.**

Ujamaa. "Familyhood." A principle emphasized in Tanzanian society. (Tanzania).

Uji. Porridge made from cornmeal, millet, or sorghum. (Kenya).

Ujna. An aunt that is a person's mother's brother's wife. (Croatia).

Ulak. A type of polo played with a goat carcass. (Kyrgyzstan).

Uli. Ornamental body paint that decorates ritual participants in religious ceremonies. (Nigeria).

Ulpan. Government-sponsored classes to learn Hebrew. (Israel). *See also* **Ulpanim.**

Ulpanim. An educational system that offers immigrants a chance to learn Hebrew. (Israel). *See also* **Ulpan.**

Ulster. A region comprised of the six counties in Northern Ireland and three counties in Ireland. (Northern Ireland).

Ulu. Breadfruit. (Samoa).

Ulumoeaga. Mats the bride's family offers to the groom's family after the wedding. (American Samoa, Samoa). *See also* **Falaninii, Ietoga.**

Um. (1) "Mother." An Arabic term of address used by children. (Qatar). (2) "Mother of." An Arabic title combined with a child's name to show respect. (Iraq, Jordan, United Arab Emirates).

Um ghayib. "Awaiting mother." A respectful term used to address a woman without children. (Iraq). *See also* **Abu ghayib.**

Umhlanga. The Reed Dance. A traditional Swazi event that honors the Queen Mother. Traditionally has served as a display of marriageable girls. Takes place in late August or early September. (Swaziland).

Umm. (Afghanistan). *See* **Um.**

Umu. (1) A traditional ground oven. (American Samoa, French Polynesia, New Zealand, Niue, Samoa, Tonga). (2) Cooking house; a separate structure that contains an open fire. (Tuvalu).

Umukechuru. "Old woman." An affectionate name for an elderly woman. (Rwanda).

Umusaza. "Old man." An affectionate name for an elderly man. (Rwanda).

Un cafecito. A thick black coffee served in a small cup; a symbol of hospitality and a way of extending friendship to visitors. (Venezuela).

Un chin. "A little bit." A Spanish phrase used in the Caribbean. (Dominican Republic). *See also* **Un poquito.**

Uncle. A term a younger person uses to address an older man, even if they are not related. (Barbados, Gambia, Ghana, Guam, Guyana, Saint Kitts and Nevis, Saint Lucia, Sierra Leone, Uganda). *See also* **Aunt(ie).**

Un cousin. "A cousin" or a very distant relative. (Central African Republic).

Underground. The London subway. (England). *Also called* **Tube.**

Un frère. A half brother or another family relation. (Central African Republic).

Uni. An Australian colloquialism for "university." (Australia).

Unimane. "Old men" that comprise the **Maneaba(s)** council. (Kiribati).

Un poquito. "A little bit." A Spanish phrase. (Dominican Republic). *See also* **Un chin.**

U phela joang? "How are you?" A Sesotho phrase that follows the initial greetings **Khotso** or **Lumela**. (Lesotho).

Uphumaphi? "Where have you come from?" A common siSwati question. (Swaziland).

Uppekkha. Equanimity. A Buddhist pillar virtue. (Laos). *See also* **Brahma Vihara.**

Upsa. A paste made from sun-dried cereals, usually cornmeal. (Mozambique). *Also called* **Xima.**

Ushanka. A Russian fur hat worn in winter. (Russia). *Also called* **Shapka.**

Ustashe. Fascist Croats. Collaborated with the Nazis during World War II and caused the deaths of thousands of civilian Jews, Serbs, and Gypsies. (Bosnia and Herzegovina, Croatia).

Usted. "You." A formal Spanish term of address. (Argentina, Chile, Dominican Republic, Honduras, Uruguay).

Uszka. A type of ravioli. (Poland).

U tsamaea kae? "Where are you going?" A common Sesotho question that follows the initial greeting. (Lesotho).

U tsoa kae? "Where have you been?" A Sesotho question that commonly follows the initial greeting. (Lesotho).

Uulu. "Son." A term used after a person's father's first name in a greeting. (Kyrgyzstan).

U-weekíi. Literally, "You have awaken." A Ndyuka greeting meaning "Good morning." (Suriname).

Uyaphi? "Where are you going?" A common siSwati question. (Swaziland).

Užgavinės. A pre-Lent holiday in which people dress in costumes and children go door-to-door asking for treats. (Lithuania).

Uzhyen. Russian word for a light evening meal. (Kazakstan).

Vaalaikum assalaam. (Uzbekistan). *See* **Waalaikum assalaam.**

Vaishya. The third class in the Brahmin classification philosophy, composed of merchants and farmers. (India). *See also* **Brahmin(s), Chaturvarna Vyavasta, Kshatriya, Shudra(s).**

Vaisyas. (Nepal). *See* **Vaishya.**

Vajrayana. Tibetan Buddhism. Shares the common Buddhist goals of reincarnation and individual release from suffering. (Mongolia).

Vaka. An outrigger canoe; commonly used for fishing. (Niue).

Vaka Atua. Powerful priests, prior to the introduction of Christianity, who acted as intermediaries between the people and the gods; they presided over special ceremonies. (Tuvalu).

Valiha. A cylindrical harp-like instrument. (Madagascar).

Valle. A folk dance. (Albania).

Vallenato. A tropical Colombian style of music. (Colombia).

Valli-e-faghih. The supreme leader of Iran. (Iran).

Vals. Swedish word for "waltz." (Sweden).

Valtioneuvosto. The Finnish cabinet. (Finland).

Vanakkam. "Hello." A Tamil greeting. (Singapore).

Vannakkam. (Sri Lanka). *See* **Vanakkam.**

Vanneyen. Chopped fish meatballs in a fish broth. (Mauritius).

Vánočka. A fruit bread; eaten during the days leading to Christmas and during Lent. (Czech Republic).

Vappu. May Day. Celebrated 1 May in honor of springtime and laborers. (Finland).

Varaynya. Preserves. (Kyrgyzstan).

Varenyky. Dumplings. (Ukraine).

Vary mitsangana. An outdoor vendor who sells hot food to be eaten while standing. (Madagascar).

Vasilopitta. A special cake with a coin in it. At midnight on New Year's Eve, the cake is cut into various pieces; whoever gets the coin is supposed to have good luck during the new year. (Greece).

Vastlapäev. A holiday on 15 February during which people go sledding and eat special foods. A long sled ride indicates good luck with the fall harvest. (Estonia).

Vau o kai! "Stop and eat with us!" A greeting to passersby who are friends or family members. A person will usually stop and chat briefly but does not normally stay to eat. (Tuvalu).

Vecera. The Macedonian word for "dinner." (Macedonia).

Večerja. Light supper. (Slovenia).

Vecheria. Dinner; eaten around 6 or 7 p.m. (Ukraine).

Vedarai. Cooked potatoes and sausage stuffed into pig intestines. (Lithuania).

Vedejparis. "Matchmaking couple." Traditionally, the *vedejparis* introduced the bride and groom. Today, it is an honorary position for admired friends. The *vedejparis* helps with wedding arrangements and serves as the ceremony's witnesses. (Latvia).

Vegemite. Yeast extract; used as a bread spread. (New Zealand).

Vegeta. A mixture of seasoning salt and dried vegetables. (Macedonia).

Veicaqe moli. "Kick the orange." A traditional Fijian game played by village women during January to celebrate the New Year. The winning team presents the losers with clothes; the losing team will mix and serve **Yaqona** to the winners that night. (Fiji).

Vejigantes. "Monsters." During various festivities, the *vejigantes* wear bells and elaborate papier-mâché masks with multiple horns. They roam the streets, threatening to "hit" people on the head with a dried pig's bladder. Children try to gather bells from *vejigantes'* costumes. (Puerto Rico).

Vencavka vo crkva. The religious ceremony that takes place on a couple's wedding day. The ceremony takes place in a church in the presence of family and friends. It is here the bride and groom exchange rings and vows. (Macedonia).

Venchaniye. An elaborate and traditional wedding ceremony. Literally, "coronation." (Russia).

Verabredung. German word for "appointment." (Germany).

Vereine. German word for "associations." (Liechtenstein).

Verivörst. Blood sausage. (Estonia).

Verkhovna Rada. The Ukrainian Parliament. (Ukraine).

Vœr så god. A Danish phrase used when passing and receiving food. It means "Please, eat well." (Denmark).

Vesak. A holiday that celebrates the birth, enlightenment, and nirvana of Buddha. Held during the fifth lunar month. (Singapore).

Veselica. A summer picnic. (Slovenia).

Vi. (1) "You." A formal pronoun. (Serbia and Montenegro, Slovenia). (2) An apple-like fruit. (Samoa). *See also* **Nonu.**

Viadu. A sweet raison-almond bread. (Suriname).

Vidalita. A traditional Uruguayan dance. (Uruguay).

Vidimo se. "See you." An informal Serbo-Croatian greeting. (Bosnia and Herzegovina).

Vidovdan. A holiday on 28 June that commemorates the Battle of Kosovo. (Serbia and Montenegro).

Vigorón. A dish of vegetables and pork skins. (Nicaragua).

Vinaka. The phrase "Thank you" in Fijian. (Fiji).

Vintana. "Destiny," which brings good or bad luck based on the time and date of a person's birth. A Malagasy belief. (Madagascar). *See also* **Ombiasy.**

Viola. A kind of guitar. (Cape Verde).

Glossary of Cultural Terms

Virgen de la Caridad del Cobre. A holiday on 8 September that honors the patron saint of Cuba and African goddess Ochún. (Cuba).

Visakha Bucha. An important Buddhist holiday. Set according to the lunar calendar. (Thailand).

Viša škola. "Higher school." A two-year technical college. (Serbia and Montenegro).

Vishnu. The preserver. One of three supreme gods of Hinduism. (Nepal). *See also* **Brahma, Shiva.**

Viso. "Bye." An informal Lithuanian parting phrase. (Lithuania).

Viso gero. "Good-bye." A Lithuanian parting phrase. (Lithuania).

Viszlát. A Hungarian parting phrase. (Hungary).

Viszontlátásra. "See you again." A Hungarian parting phrase. (Hungary).

Vitumbua. (Tanzania). *See* **Kitumbua.**

Vivaha. The Hindu marriage ceremony. (Mauritius).

Vlaggetjesdag. Little Flag Day. Celebrated in May in coastal areas. Marks the beginning of the herring season. Ships leave the harbor, decorated with little flags. (Netherlands).

Voan-dalana. "Gifts from the journey." People returning from a trip or visiting from out of town will give *voan-dalana* to their extended family. (Madagascar).

Vodiondry. The bride-price. Literally, "lamb's rump." (Madagascar).

Volynka. A hornpipe. (Ukraine).

Vonts es? "How are you?" An Armenian question that usually follows an initial greeting. (Armenia).

Voodoos. The Fon word for local divinities through which people worship the supreme God. (Benin). *See also* **Orisha.**

Vos. "You." An informal singular Spanish pronoun. (Argentina, Paraguay).

Vouli. The informal name of the Greek Chamber of Deputies. (Greece). *See also* **Vouli ton Ellinon.**

Vouli ton Ellinon. The Greek Chamber of Deputies. (Greece).

Voy a pasear. "I am going visiting." A Spanish phrase. Visiting is a common weekend pastime. (Equatorial Guinea).

Vsichko hubavo. "All the best." A common Bulgarian parting phrase used between friends. (Bulgaria).

Vu lan. The Buddhist prayer book. (Vietnam).

Vyachera. Belarusian word for "supper." (Belarus).

Vyshyvanka. A traditional shirt or blouse embroidered in a regional pattern. The patterns have not changed for centuries. (Ukraine).

Waalaikum assalaam. [NOTE: Spelling varies because it is a transliteration of Arabic.] "And peace be upon you." A response to the greeting **Assalaam alaikum**. Used in countries with large or predominantly Muslim populations..

Wa'alaikum salaam. (Indonesia). *See* **Waalaikum assalaam.**

Wa alaykum Asalaam. (Syria). *See* **Waalaikum assalaam.**

Wa alaykum As-salaam. (Kuwait, Qatar). *See* **Waalaikum assalaam.**

Wa'alaykum assalaamu. (Yemen). *See* **Waalaikum assalaam.**

Wa alaykum salaam. (Mauritania). *See* **Waalaikum assalaam.**

Wa alek asalaam. (Chad). *See* **Waalaikum assalaam.**

Wa alikum assalaam. (United Arab Emirates). *See* **Waalaikum assalaam.**

Wa Alikum Assalam. Arabic phrase meaning "I offer you peace, too"; it is the proper response to the greeting **Assalamu alikum**. (Libya).

Wa di gwan? "What's happening?" A Creole greeting. (Belize).

Wadis. Dry riverbeds. (Libya, Oman).

Wafidiin. A person who has left his or her own country to live in another. (United Arab Emirates).

Wafuku. A long traditional robe with long sleeves, tied closed with a special sash. (Japan). *See also* **Kimono(s), Obi.**

Wah eye no see heart no grieve. "What you don't know won't hurt you." A traditional saying. (Antigua and Barbuda).

Wai. A Thai greeting in which one places the palms of the hands together at chest level with fingers extended. Men bow slightly; women curtsy. (Thailand).

Waisak. A Buddhist holiday. (Indonesia).

Walalapo Nawa. "Good morning." An Oshiwambo greeting. (Namibia).

Walale. A common Umbundo greeting meaning "Good morning," but literally "How did you pass the night?". The reply is **Ndalale**. (Angola).

Wali. Arabic word for "governor." (Oman).

Walk with. "Carry." A phrase used in the Antiguan English dialect. (Antigua and Barbuda).

Wa-lo hla-lo. "You are looking more plump and more beautiful." A common Burmese greeting. Plumpness (to a certain extent) is regarded as a sign of beauty and health. (Myanmar).

Wa muka? "Are you well?" A greeting from an elder to a child. (Botswana).

Wan. "Afternoon." A common Mandarin Chinese greeting. (China).

Wanan. "Evening." An informal Chinese greeting. (China).

Wantok. "One talk." A system in which individuals help and share possessions with relatives or others in their language group or village. Reciprocation is expected. Participants in the system are called *wantoks*. (Papua New Guinea, Solomon Islands).

Warambas. Flowing robes worn by men. (Gambia).

Waraq dawalee. Stuffed grape leaves. (West Bank and Gaza).

Ward(s). A neighborhood. A village is divided into *wards*, each of which is led by a **Headman**. (Botswana).

Warri. A strategy game in which one tries to capture the opponent's 24 seeds. (Antigua and Barbuda).

Wasabi. A hot, green Japanese paste containing horseradish. (Micronesia).

Waso. A full moon holiday in June or July. Begins the three-month period of the Buddhist Rains Retreat. (Myanmar).

Water closet. A toilet. (Slovakia).

Wat(s). (1) A Buddhist temple. (Laos, Thailand). (2) A stew made from chicken, beef, or vegetables. (Ethiopia).

Wayang. Chinese mobile street theaters. A popular event during holiday festivities. (Singapore).

Wayang kulit. Shadow puppet theater. (Indonesia, Malaysia).

Wayang topeng. Masked dances in which performers act out legends and stories. (Indonesia).

We go see. "See you later." A casual Grenadian creole farewell. (Grenada).

Wéi geet et? "How are you?" A common greeting. (Luxembourg).

Wei qi. A strategy game played in more educated circles. (China).

Wela. The Umbundo term for a strategy game played with beads or seeds placed in holes on a wooden board or in the ground. (Angola). *Also called* **Kwela.**

Welsh cakes. Similar to small pancakes, these can be served hot or cold. (Wales).

Wesak Day. A holiday in May that commemorates the birth of Buddha. (Malaysia).

Wesak Poya. A day in May that celebrates Buddha's birth, enlightenment, and death. (Sri Lanka).

Whaaa? A phrase that indicates surprise or disbelief. (U.S. Virgin Islands).

Whaapun? "What's happening?" A common patois greeting. (Jamaica).

Wha' it saying? A Creolese greeting. (Guyana).

W'happen dey? "What's happening?" A casual Grenadian creole greeting. (Grenada).

Wharenui. A Maori "great house," or meeting place. (New Zealand).

What a pistarkel. "What a spectacle." A Creole phrase. (U.S. Virgin Islands). *See also* **Spektakel, Spetakel.**

Whei. "Hello." A Mandarin Chinese greeting. (Singapore).

Whitmonday A religious holiday around the time of Pentecost. (Montserrat).

Whuh wunna doin' tonight? "What are you all doing tonight?" A Bajan phrase. (Barbados).

Wie geht es Ihnen? "How are you?" A German phrase. (Austria).

Wiener schnitzel. Breaded veal cutlets. (Austria).

Wifey. A term used to refer to females. (Scotland).

Wilayaat. A district or region. (Algeria).

Wilayat. (Oman). *See* **Wilayaat.**

Wilayet. Region. (Turkmenistan).

Wind and grind. Dancing. (Grenada).

Wo. Corn flour. Used to make a stiff porridge. (Benin). *Also called* **Amiwo.**

Województwa. Polish word for "provinces." (Poland).

Wolesi Jirga. House of People. Part of Afghanistan's bicameral National Assembly. (Afghanistan).

Wôn. South Korea's national currency. (South Korea).

Wooshay! Wooshay! "Hello! Hello!" A common greeting used by the Kanouris. (Niger).

Workbook. A document received after completing eighth grade and passing a matriculation exam; necessary to get a job. (Bosnia and Herzegovina).

Wôro-wôro. Taxis that rent seats on fixed routes; they are available in Abidjan. (Ivory Coast).

Wuh you sayin'? "How are things?" An informal Bajan greeting used between young people. (Barbados).

Wuh yuh sayin'? How are you? (Trinidad and Tobago).

Wukking up. A uniquely Bajan dance style, usually performed to calypso music, that features rhythmic waist-winding movements. (Barbados).

Wurst. Sausage. (Germany).

Xhamadan. A wool vest worn by men. (Albania).

Xhaxha. An Albanian term used for an uncle on the father's side. (Albania).

Xiao. "Young." A Mandarin Chinese term used with or instead of a title to show special respect to a friend. (China).

Xima. A paste made from sun-dried cereals, usually cornmeal. (Mozambique). *Also called* **Upsa.**

Xin chao. A formal Vietnamese greeting used between strangers. (Vietnam).

Yaa "Hi." A casual greeting generally used among men. (Japan).

Yaka. Long, loose-fitting dresses with hand-embroidered collars. (Turkmenistan).

Yakhshi me seez? (Tajikistan). *See* **Yakshimisiz?**

Yakshimisiz? "Are you well?" A common greeting. (Uzbekistan).

Yang di-Pertuan Agong. The Supreme Head of State. Refers to the Malaysian king. (Malaysia).

Yaqona. A mildly stimulating drink made from the root and lower stem of a shrub in the pepper family; Fiji's national drink. Pronounced "YANGGONA." (Fiji). *Also called* **Kava.**

Yard name. A nickname. Often a shortened or slightly altered version of a person's given name. (Jamaica). *Also called* **Pet name.**

Yarmulke. An embroidered cap worn by men. (Israel). *Also called* **Kippah.**

Yashmagh. A checkered headscarf worn by men. (Iraq). *See also* **Kaffiyah.**

Yassa. Rice and chicken covered with a sauce made of sliced onions and spices. (Senegal).

Yaum an Nibi. A Muslim holiday commemorating the prophet Muhammad's birthday. (Guyana).

Yavusa. A chiefly system that ordered society for centuries. Established by early settlers. (Fiji).

Yayechnya. Scrambled or fried eggs. (Belarus).

Yeah, Gidday. A common greeting. (New Zealand). *See also* **Gidday.**

Yebo. "Yes." A Zulu and Swazi response to the greetings **Sawubona** (I see you) and **Kunjani?** (How are you?). (South Africa).

Yela. A musical style reserved for women. (Senegal).

Yen. Japan's national currency. (Japan).

Yerba. The Spanish word for "herb." (Paraguay).

Yerba mate. An herbal tea. (Bolivia).

Ye yapvo? "What's up?" A Shingazidja question that follows the initial greeting **Edje** (Hello). Used between social equals. (Comoros).

Yo. The Spanish word for "I." Usually pronounced "YOH," in Uruguayan Spanish it is pronounced "SHOW." (Uruguay).

Yoghurtvla. Yogurt pudding. (Netherlands).

Yokwe. A Marshallese greeting appropriate in almost any situation. It can mean "Hello," "Good-bye," "love," and more. Meaning is based on inflection. Pronounced "YAH-quay." (Marshall Islands).

Yom Kippur. Day of Atonement. A Jewish holiday. (Bosnia and Herzegovina, Croatia, Israel).

Yondo. A secret ritual of initiation into adulthood. (Chad).

Yorkshire pudding. A baked batter usually served in muffin form. (England).

You alright? "How are you?" A casual Montserratian greeting. (Montserrat).

You lie. A phrase that can mean "You are kidding." (Antigua and Barbuda).

Younger father. A paternal uncle. Called *younger father* or **Older father** depending on the uncle's age in relation to the child's father. (Kenya).

Younger mother. A maternal aunt. Called *younger mother* or **Older mother** depending on the aunt's age in relation to the child's mother. (Kenya).

Glossary of Cultural Terms

Yuan. The standard unit of China's national currency. (China). *See also* **Renminbi.**

Yuca. Cassava. (Cuba, Dominican Republic, Equatorial Guinea).

Yue. The Cantonese language. (China, Hong Kong).

Yuh stickin'. You are moving too slowly. (Trinidad and Tobago).

Yumbo. Ecuadorian folk music. (Ecuador).

Yu orait? "How are you?" A common Melanesian Pidgin greeting. (Papua New Guinea).

Yurta. A tent used by nomads. (Kazakstan).

Zadušnice. A day for Orthodox Serbs to honor the dead; occurs four times a year. (Serbia and Montenegro).

Zain, al-Humdulillah "Good, thanks be to **Allah**." A response to the Arabic greetings **Eshloanak** and **Eshloanich**. (Bahrain, Kuwait).

Zajal. A form of poetry in which improvised dialogue is sung between several poets. (Lebanon).

Zajjaleen. Singers who lead celebrations. (West Bank and Gaza).

Zajtrk. Slovene word meaning "breakfast." (Slovenia).

Zakat. Giving alms to the poor. One of the Five Pillars of Islam. (Iran, Kuwait, Malaysia, Saudi Arabia, Sudan). *See also* **Hajj, Salat, Saum, Shahada.**

Zakuski. Russian word meaning "appetizers." (Russia).

Zampoña. Panpipes. (Bolivia).

Zam-rock. A form of rock music with lyrics in local languages. (Zambia).

Zanahary. A supreme being of Malagasy indigenous beliefs. (Madagascar). *Also called* **Andriamanitra.**

Zang zho. Bowl of warm water used to wash one's hands before eating. (Bhutan).

Zanna. A long white dress worn by Muslim men on Fridays and religious holidays. Worn with a **Machetta**. (Yemen).

Zao. "Morning." An informal Chinese greeting. (China).

Zaouia. Small mausoleums built in memory of especially holy men. (Tunisia).

Zatar. Thyme. (West Bank and Gaza).

Zavtrak. The Russian word meaning "breakfast." (Kazakstan).

Zbogom. "Farewell" or "With God." A common parting phrase. (Bosnia and Herzegovina, Croatia).

Zdrasti. "Hello." An informal Bulgarian greeting. (Bulgaria).

Zdrave. "Hello." An informal Bulgarian greeting. (Bulgaria).

Zdraveite. "Hello." A formal Bulgarian greeting. (Bulgaria).

Zdravo. "Hello." A casual greeting. (Bosnia and Herzegovina, Croatia, Macedonia, Serbia and Montenegro, Slovenia).

Zdravstvuite. (Moldova). *See* **Zdravstvuyte.**

Zdravstvuite. Kak pozhivaete? "Hello. How are you?" A Russian greeting. (Belarus).

Zdravstvuy. "Hello." An informal Russian greeting. (Russia).

Zdravstvuyte. "Hello." A formal Russian greeting. (Kazakstan, Kyrgyzstan, Russia).

Zebus. Oxen-like cattle. (Madagascar).

Zed. The Canadian pronunciation of the letter *z*. (Canada).

Zeljanica. Spinach-and-cheese pie. (Bosnia and Herzegovina).

Zemidjan(s). Motorcycle taxis. (Benin, Togo).

Zenmoyang? "How's it going?" An informal Chinese greeting. (China).

Zeze. A one-string violin. (Malawi).

Zhanga Zhyl. The Kazak term for the New Year celebration. (Kazakstan).

Zhug. A relish in which bread is dipped. (Yemen).

Zikak. A type of fruit. (Haiti).

Zito. A mush made of wheat, sugar, and nuts. (Serbia and Montenegro).

Živijo. "Long live." A Slovene greeting or toast. (Slovenia).

Zloty. Poland's national currency. (Poland).

Zmittag. The main meal of the day. (Liechtenstein).

Zmorga. Breakfast. (Liechtenstein).

Znacht. Dinner. (Liechtenstein).

Zogbedji. An Ewe word meaning "inhospitable land." A burial site for people who died violently (accident, suicide, murder) or badly (illness, childbirth). (Togo).

Zokela. A style of music that blends traditional and Western music. (Central African Republic).

Zokra. A North African instrument similar to the bagpipes. (Libya).

Zolgah. A gesture used when meeting for the first time after the New Year. The younger person holds the elbows of the older person, whose forearms rest on the younger person's forearms; the older person lightly touches his or her lips to the younger person's forehead. (Mongolia).

Zongo. Separate sections of town in which nonindigenous people live. (Ghana).

Zonja. "Mrs." An Albanian title used with the first or last name. (Albania).

Zonjushe. "Miss." An Albanian title used with the first or last name. (Albania).

Zorries. Rubber or plastic flip-flops; the common footwear. (Micronesia).

Zoteri. "Mr." An Albanian title used with the first or last name. (Albania).

Zouglou. A style of music that originated in Ivory Coast; it features a fast beat and humorous lyrics. (Ivory Coast).

Zouk. A Caribbean style of music. (Burkina Faso, Suriname).

Zow. A puffed rice snack. (Bhutan).

Zrig. A whipped drink made of milk, water, and sugar. (Mauritania).

Zud. A type of weather in which blizzards send enough snow to cover the grass; livestock cannot graze and therefore die. (Mongolia).

Zui jin mang ma. "Have you been busy lately?" A Chinese greeting used between people who have not seen each other in a long time. (China).

Zuls. Traditional flutes. (Nicaragua).

Zummar. Flute player. (Iraq).

Zungueiras. Women who sell fruit and other goods on street corners or by walking through the city carrying their products on their heads. (Angola). *Also called* **Kitandeiras.**

Zupa. The Latvian word for "soup." (Latvia).

Zwarte Piet. "Black Peter." According to tradition in the Netherlands, he is the servant of St. Nicholas. (Netherlands).

WITHDRAWN